Europe from War to War, 1̲ ̲ ̲ ̲ ̲

Europe from War to War, 1914–1945 explores this age of metamorphosis within European history, an age that played a crucial role in shaping the Europe of today. Covering a wide range of topics such as religion, arts and literature, humanitarian relief during the wars, transnational feminism, and efforts to create a unified Europe, it examines the social and cultural history of this period as well as political, economic, military, and diplomatic perspectives.

Thematically organized within a chronological framework, this book takes a fully comparative approach to the era, allowing the reader to follow the evolution of key trends and ideas across these 31 turbulent years. Each period is analyzed from both an international and a domestic perspective, expanding the traditional narrative to include the role and impact of European colonies around the world while retaining a close focus on national affairs, everyday existence within Europe itself, and the impact of the wars on people's lives. Chapters include discussion of regions such as Scandinavia, the Balkans, and the Iberian peninsula that are less frequently covered, emphasizing the network of connections between events and places across the continent.

Global in scope, accessibly written, and illustrated throughout with photographs and maps, this is the perfect introductory textbook for all students of early twentieth-century European history.

Alice-Catherine Carls is Tom Elam Distinguished Professor of History at the University of Tennessee at Martin, U.S. Her publications include *La Ville Libre de Dantzig en Crise Ouverte, 1938–1939* (1982) as well as numerous book chapters and journal articles.

Stephen D. Carls is University Professor of History at Union University, U.S. His publications include *Louis Loucheur and the Shaping of Modern France, 1916–1931* (1993, also published in France in revised form in 2000).

Europe from War to War, 1914–1945

Alice-Catherine Carls and
Stephen D. Carls

Routledge
Taylor & Francis Group

LONDON AND NEW YORK

First published 2018
by Routledge
2 Park Square, Milton Park, Abingdon, Oxon OX14 4RN

and by Routledge
711 Third Avenue, New York, NY 10017

Routledge is an imprint of the Taylor & Francis Group, an informa business

British Library Cataloguing in Publication Data
A catalogue record for this book is available from the British Library

Library of Congress Cataloging in Publication Data
Names: Carls, Alice-Catherine, author. | Carls, Stephen Douglas,
    author.
Title: Europe from war to war, 1914-1945 / Alice-Catherine Carls
    and Stephen D. Carls.
Description: Abingdon, Oxon : Routledge, 2017.
    | Includes bibliographical references and index.
Identifiers: LCCN 2017018357| ISBN 9781138999145 (hardback :
    alk. paper) | ISBN 9781138999152 (pbk. : alk. paper)
    | ISBN 9781315159454 (ebook)
Subjects: LCSH: Europe—History—1918-1945.
Classification: LCC D424 .C29 2017 | DDC 940.5—dc23
LC record available at https://lccn.loc.gov/2017018357

ISBN: 978-1-138-99914-5 (hbk)
ISBN: 978-1-138-99915-2 (pbk)
ISBN: 978-1-315-15945-4 (ebk)

Typeset in Garamond 3 LT Std
by Swales & Willis Ltd, Exeter, Devon, UK

Visit the companion website: www.routledge.com/cw/carls

Printed and bound by CPI Group (UK) Ltd, Croydon, CR0 4YY

To our children – Philip, Elizabeth, and Paul

Contents

Figures

Maps

Preface

Europe is a geographically ill-defined, uneasy continent divided between rival peripheries that have shifted many times since its birth in the Middle Ages: northern, eastern, central, southern, and western. In the nineteenth century, Western Europe, with its global ambitions, was at its height in cultural, economic, military, and political power, creating important rivalries. Significant differences also appeared between the different parts of Europe. While Western Europe consolidated ethnicities into nation-states, including the newly unified states of Germany and Italy, most of Central and Eastern Europe – including Russia – remained dominated by multinational empires. While Western Europe thrived on industrialization, Eastern Europe and Scandinavia remained predominantly agricultural. As the pace of change accelerated towards the end of the nineteenth century, political and social reforms were enacted and expectations for democracy clashed with the fear of anarchy, often leading to conservative or reactionary governments, as in Russia under Tsar Nicholas II, Austria-Hungary under Emperor Franz-Joseph I, and Germany under Wilhelm II.

If Europe's internal situation was not as stable or powerful as it appeared, the one-sidedness of European colonial powers' application of equality, justice, and rights in their colonies made Europe's external situation potentially vulnerable, as demonstrated by the independence movements that started in many of the European powers' colonies after World War I. The days of Europe's political and cultural dominance were numbered, even if this was not yet visible. The increased European rivalries that erupted in the Near East and Central Asia in the early years of the twentieth century became an important factor in driving Europe to war in 1914. World War I seemed to demonstrate clearly to many in Europe that European power and influence was beginning to wane, while European colonial powers became increasingly dependent on their colonies. In that sense, World War I was much more than a war only for the control of Europe: it was a contest for global power, something that was confirmed by the war aims and the nature of World War II. Thus, the issue of a new world order dominated the years 1914–1945.

Just as important in Europe's history during the first half of the twentieth century were demographic changes. Births, deaths, and migrations complicated the ethnic fabric of Europe significantly. Before World War I broke out, significant transnational migrations taking place in East Central Europe and at the border of Russia began to unravel the multinational empires in the region. Continued population displacements during the war and the inability of political leaders at the Paris Peace Conference to make geographic and ethnic borders coincide showed the precariousness of national states and the difficulty in implementing the policy of self-determination of peoples. Although these population displacements were more pronounced in East Central Europe, they spread across Europe throughout the interwar years, primarily as a result of the flood of refugees from the Spanish Civil War and the Nazis' persecution of Jews in Germany. Also, the existence of German minorities living outside of Germany gave Hitler a pretext for going to war in 1939. The unprecedented number of deaths and involuntary population movements that occurred during World War II made this conflict unparalleled in world history.

Europe's cultural identity also changed significantly during the first half of the twentieth century. By 1900, Enlightenment values that had served as a universalizing force in European civilization were questioned. By 1914, a quest for new paradigms had begun in biology, physics, psychology, sociology, philosophy, art, literature, and music. The work of Albert Einstein and Fredrich Nietzsche questioned Newtonian and Cartesian definitions of reality, while painters such as Pablo Picasso and Georges Braque fundamentally altered aesthetic values that had long dominated Europe. The years 1914–1945, through the trauma of war and genocide, accentuated these developments and heightened the search for a new social ethos in the wake of mass society while increasing a loss of purpose and ushering in the absurd. Framed by two world wars, however, mass civilization continued to promote a series of firsts. The modern age was coming in the form of sewers, universal education, factories, political rallies, and sports stadiums. The first truly global cross-cultural exchanges took place, women worked outside the home, and fashion and transportation were revolutionized. The social upheavals and transformations taking place, already introduced in European culture before 1914, caused numerous values and traditions to be revisited.

The first half of the twentieth century transformed Europe politically as well. Up to the outbreak of World War I, Communist revolutionaries, monarchist reactionaries, and other extremists attacked the Enlightenment principles that marked European society. The interwar period and World War II saw the Enlightenment ideas of democracy and humanism severely challenged, this time in the form of fascism and established state Communism. Nevertheless, Enlightenment values made steady gains, and once World War II was over, they were accepted across large parts of the globe and served as the foundation for an emerging unified Europe. Indeed, the tumult of the first half of the twentieth century advanced the thinking about European renewal, making the years 1914–1945 the matrix of a post-World War II unified Europe. Europe's collective embrace of universal human rights and interstate cooperation served as a definitive rebuke of the violence and trauma of World Wars I and II, and sought to ensure that such calamities would never again happen in Europe. Hence, one could argue that the precariousness of borders, the loss of human life, and the unprecedented violence seen in the first half of the twentieth century had at least one positive consequence.

Methodology and organization of the book

To examine such a complex period in European history, a comparative method is in order. Comparison allows one to think of European trends rather than of unique situations. Comparison also allows the student to look at longer periods of time and to follow trends and themes throughout the entire period of 1914–1945. To make this method more effective, the structure of the first eight chapters is parallel. Each of the four time periods identified (1914–1923, 1919–1929, 1929–1939, 1939–1945) is comprised of two chapters, one devoted to international developments, and the other to domestic developments. The chapter structures are also parallel, with similar sub-headings. The international chapters covering the two world wars discuss military and diplomatic questions, including the participation of the colonies. The domestic chapters concerned with those wars focus on economics and politics on the home front, as well as everyday life during the conflicts. The international chapters dealing with the interwar years explore European security, European reconstruction, colonial developments, and colonial conflicts. The chapters examining interwar domestic history center on five factors that are indicative of modernization: political systems, demographic changes, economic developments, social transitions, and urbanism/ transportation. This approach is designed to encourage students to make connections between events in different countries, and to show them a complete thematic coverage that includes Europe's geographic periphery (Scandinavia, Mediterranean/Iberian realm, Eastern Europe) as well as often neglected topics such as humanitarian relief in World Wars I and II, religion, urban and human destruction, the devaluing of life, transnational feminism, efforts to create a unified Europe, and the role of the colonies during both world wars.

The last two chapters, dedicated to culture and identity, cover the entire period 1914–1945. Chapter 9 deals with culture in the broad sense of the term: literature, art, science, religion, fashion, entertainment, propaganda, and education. Its periodization mirrors that of the preceding chapters. This chapter provides a coda, a space for thinking about Europe from one war to the other through the prism of culture with its intimate portrait of individuals and societies. Indeed, the creations of artists, thinkers, and scholars reflect the important dilemmas and dynamics of their times and for that reason they give an accurate measure of their times in ways that no institutional, political, or economic analysis can give. Chapter 10 concludes with Europeans' thoughts and discussions about the future of their continent. Hopefully this will further students' understanding and interest in European culture and its relationship to social, political, military, and economic developments. It is also meant to encourage them to see European developments from one war to the other. It is our hope that this approach will help students understand the roots of contemporary Europe's accomplishments and challenges.

Acknowledgments

We owe a debt of gratitude to the University of Tennessee at Martin, Union University, and a number of individuals. Both of us received a semester-long leave, a summer research grant, and other forms of encouragement from our respective universities to advance our textbook project. Jefferson Rogers of the University of Tennessee at Martin graciously designed one of the maps in the printed text and drew several more for the textbook's website. Gerhard Weinberg, Professor Emeritus of the University of North Carolina, Nancy Rupprecht, of Middle Tennessee State University, and John Morrow, of the University of Georgia, gave generously of their time to comment on parts of the manuscript in its early stages. Our son Paul, a doctoral candidate at the University of Montreal, made important recommendations toward the end of our project to strengthen the text in two of the chapters. We are also grateful to John McCole, of the University of Oregon, who carefully read the manuscript and made valuable suggestions for improvement. In addition, we benefited greatly from the helpful support and professional expertise of Eve Setch and her editorial team at Routledge and Megan Symons at Swales & Willis. We want to add, however, that any factual errors or instances of historical misinterpretation in the book are ours alone, and we accept full responsibility for them.

Part 1

World War I and after, 1914–1923

1 The war's international dimensions and aftermath

Introduction

World War I, also referred to as the Great War, was the first truly global conflict in history. There were several major fronts in Europe: the Western Front in northeastern France and across Belgium; the Eastern Front located along a 2,000-mile long line stretching from the Baltic Sea to the Black Sea; the Italian Front that affected northeastern Italy and the western frontier of Austria–Hungary (the Dual Monarchy) beginning in the spring of 1915; and the Balkans Front that touched several countries in Southeastern Europe. Military operations also took place in Africa, the Middle East, East Asia, and at sea. The campaigns beyond Europe, though of less overall importance, often included important military commitments and fierce fighting. Indeed, the extensive combat that occurred outside Europe testifies to the new dimension that the conflagration represented.

Domestic and diplomatic policies were tightly woven into military strategy. When the war did not end quickly, both sets of belligerents began to mobilize their countries' economies and societies. The global nature of the fighting and the sudden expectation of a long conflict required large amounts of human and material resources, courting new allies, securing alliance reversals, advancing peace proposals, and supporting massive military operations. The monumental scale of economic mobilization necessitated not only unprecedented government controls at home, but also increasing cooperation among allies, thus creating another level of diplomatic activity. To win the war required the coordination of efforts at many levels.

Military operations

As Europe hovered on the edge of war in the summer of 1914, the continent's Great Powers were split into two rival alliance systems. On one side was the Triple Alliance of Germany, Austria–Hungary, and Italy, and on the other the Triple Entente of France, Russia, and Great Britain. Because of the entangling nature of the alliances, it appeared likely that if a member of one alliance fell into war with a party from the other, the remaining alliance members would follow suit. The possibility of keeping any conflict localized seemed remote.

The turmoil of nationalities in Austria–Hungary and the Balkans was decisive in the tensions that erupted into war in 1914. Inside Austria–Hungary were several ethnic groups with nationalist aspirations that threatened the well-being of the empire. The presence of ambitious states in southeastern Europe and the impact this had on the Great Powers also contributed greatly to the war's outbreak. Thus, while the assassination of Austrian Archduke Franz Ferdinand, the heir to the Austro-Hungarian throne, and his wife Sophie (Duchess of Hohenberg) by a Bosnian Serb student named Gavrilo Princip in the Bosnian

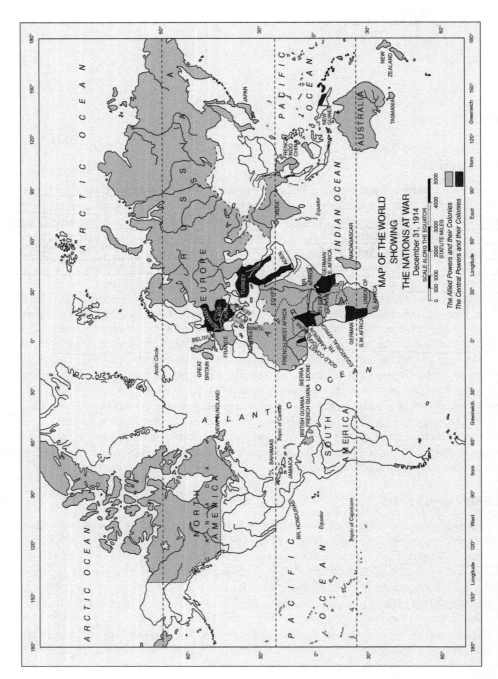

Map 1.1 World nations at war, 1914

city of Sarajevo on June 28, 1914, precipitated the final steps to war, there were deeper causes to the crisis. Among them were two Balkan wars in 1912–1913. The Treaty of London that ended the First Balkan War in 1913 resulted in the partition of Ottoman lands among members of a Balkan League consisting of Serbia, Greece, Montenegro, and Bulgaria, and the creation – at the behest of Austria–Hungary – of an independent Albanian state on the Adriatic Sea. Signed by the Great Powers, the treaty nevertheless failed to resolve all boundary issues satisfactorily, and a Second Balkan War quickly ensued. In this war, Serbia and Greece, joined by Romania and the Ottoman Empire, defeated Bulgaria, which had started the conflict to obtain better territorial provisions than it had gained in the London treaty. Serbia emerged from the conflicts stronger, but bitter that Austria–Hungary had prevented it from expanding through Albania to the Adriatic Sea.

In the Near East, the Ottoman Empire was subject to Great Power ambitions. By 1913, Germany, France, and Britain had entrenched themselves in Ottoman territories. Germany was expanding its investment in Anatolia, particularly on the construction of a railroad from Berlin to Baghdad. Britain was developing its oil interests in northern and southern Iraq and securing its presence in the Persian Gulf. France showed interest in Syria. Russia had long sought control of the Black Sea and the Dardanelles. Added to this volatile situation were wider tensions among European nations, including commercial competition, colonial conflicts, intense nationalist feelings, Russian expansionism, and an Anglo-German naval arms race. These created wars of words where chauvinists became shrill, and the press and public strident.

The tragedy in Sarajevo ignited a global war that, because of its complexities, was not completely settled at the peace table in 1919. Conflicts continued on the periphery of Europe and elsewhere until 1923, ranging from border hostilities to colonial struggles to internationalized civil wars. The belligerents' aims were still largely traditional: more land, more status, and more power.

The outbreak of war in Europe

On July 23, the Austro-Hungarians, long fearful of Serbia's intentions in the Balkans and convinced of its complicity in the assassination of Franz Ferdinand, sent their Balkan neighbor an unconditional ultimatum containing demands that would have compromised Serbian sovereignty. Serbia's response was conciliatory, but it failed to comply fully with the Dual Monarchy's demands. The Austrian government, armed with the knowledge of German support in the matter, declared war on Serbia on July 28. Viewing his country as the protector of Serbian interests, Russian Tsar Nicholas II (r. 1894–1917) initially reacted by ordering a partial mobilization along Russia's border with the Austro-Hungarian province of Galicia, but he ordered full mobilization the next day after his top generals warned him that partial mobilization was technically impossible. Germany responded with full mobilization and a declaration of war on Russia on August 1. Germany also mobilized against France and delivered an ultimatum to neutral Belgium demanding free passage across that country. When the Belgian government rejected the ultimatum, the Germans invaded. The German actions against Belgium shifted British public opinion from being quite opposed to the war to being enthusiastically in favor of it. Great Britain on August 4 declared war against Germany. With Britain's action, all of the European Great Powers were now locked in a war that had the Central Powers of Germany and Austria-Hungary fighting against the Allied (Entente) forces of France, Great Britain, and Russia. Britain's entry also arrayed her empire against the Central Powers.

When war came, there was general excitement and jubilation in the European countries that found themselves engaged in the enterprise. Elated crowds poured onto the streets in St. Petersburg and Berlin. Joyous Frenchmen went to the Paris train stations to cheer for mobilized soldiers as they boarded trains. In non-conscript Britain, volunteer enlistments surged. Not everyone approached the war with a deep sense of celebration, however. There were anti-conscription riots in Russia and talks of an international general strike among the members of several countries' socialist parties, even though workers ultimately allowed a nationalist sense of duty to prevail over international working class solidarity, and they joined their respective nations' war efforts.

The consensus among European economists, political leaders, and military planners was that the conflict would be short – no more than a few weeks or a couple of months. Military plans on both sides called for offensive actions. France's Plan XVII involved a massive attack along the border with Germany, but was short on details. The Germans' blueprint for the war, known as the Schlieffen Plan, consisted of an initial holding action against the Russians, while launching a major offensive in the West with a large wheeling movement through Belgium, across France to the west of Paris, and then back to eastern France to defeat the French army trapped by a massive encirclement. The Germans would then shift their forces to the Eastern Front to defeat the isolated Russians in a quick campaign. Austria's plans were limited to war against Serbia. Russia, aware that its army would be slow to mobilize, planned an initial holding action against German attacks, followed by an offensive plan when its army was fully deployed. The British had extensive defensive plans to protect their imperial trade routes.

The Germans' offensive across Belgium and into France soon revealed shortcomings in the Schlieffen Plan. For one thing, the Belgians unexpectedly slowed down the German advance through their tenacious resistance. Also, a British Expeditionary Force (BEF) of 100,000 men, whose participation the Germans had not even considered in their planning, arrived in France quickly enough to retard the German advance in the latter part of August. Meanwhile, German General Alexander von Kluck's First Army, whose position on the extreme right wing of the German invasion force required travel across considerable territory very quickly, began to suffer from fatigue, low provisions, and difficult communications. Kluck, eager to close a gap between his soldiers and the Second Army to their left, obtained the approval of Helmuth von Moltke, the indecisive and overly reflective chief of the German General Staff, to wheel his army to the east of Paris instead of enveloping the city from the west. That decision, which exposed the right flank of the First Army, proved fateful. Opposing him was Joseph Joffre, the imperturbable French commander-in-chief, who had watched France's Plan XVII in eastern France turn into a debacle. Joffre remained confident in spite of the adversity his forces had endured militarily.

What ensued was the decisive First Battle of the Marne, which began on September 5. The French threw every available soldier into the battle; to supplement rail transport, they had to commandeer some 1,200 Parisian taxicabs to transport 6,000 troops to the battlefront. At the end of an intense week of fighting, the French, along with the BEF, prevailed. The Allies had shattered what was left of the Schlieffen Plan and ended German hopes for a quick resolution of the war in the West. German Emperor Wilhelm II (r. 1888–1918) relieved a physically and emotionally broken Moltke of his command on September 14 and appointed Erich von Falkenhayn as his successor. Joffre emerged from the battle as a hero, and the French soon referred to their victory as the "Miracle of the Marne." In the weeks that followed, both sides, in a series of attacks and counterattacks, tried to outflank each other in a northward race to the sea. In the last of these actions, fought in the mud around the Belgian town of Ypres from mid-October to November, the British stopped the Germans from reaching the French Channel ports.

The overall casualties on the Western Front in 1914 were staggering. The Germans lost 667,000 men and the French 995,000, British totals reached 96,000, and those of Belgians were close to 50,000. The human carnage in the west was an indication of what the cost of the war would be for the belligerents in forthcoming campaigns. The war of maneuver turned into a war of stalemate and attrition, since both camps lacked the ability to dislodge the other and there was no more space for either side to outflank the other. The rival armies dug into their positions with trenches, creating two thin lines along a battle-front that extended from the English Channel to the border of Switzerland.

In the East, the Russians launched an offensive faster than German planners had calculated and actually got troops into German East Prussia. Moltke, unhappy with the German commander on the Eastern Front, replaced him in late August 1914 with General Paul von Hindenburg, a 67-year-old Prussian aristocrat who came out of retire-ment to do his duty. Moltke assigned Erich Ludendorff, a hard-working, determined officer who proved to be a brilliant military strategist, to serve as Hindenburg's chief of staff. A lack of coordination among the two Russian armies moving into Prussia from the east and the south helped the Germans defeat each Russian force separately. The Germans first mauled the army of Aleksandr Samsonov in what was subsequently named the Battle of Tannenberg on August 26–30, and then defeated the second Russian army on September 8 in the First Battle of the Masurian Lakes. The completeness of his army's loss caused Samsonov to commit suicide. By September 13, all remaining Russian forces had abandoned Germany. The defeats set back the Russians' ability to fight on this front indefinitely. On the other hand, the German victories made Hindenburg and Ludendorff instant national heroes.

Meanwhile, the Austro-Hungarians, under the guidance of the surprisingly self-confident and energetic Chief of the General Staff Franz Conrad von Hötzendorf, struggled in their two-front war against the Russians and the Serbians. Russia sent four armies to challenge the Austro-Hungarian Empire along the frontier of Galicia, where the combined armies totaled approximately 2.2 million men. Despite some early successes along the northern section of the front in late August, Austrian forces were routed and fell back over 100 miles to the passes of the Carpathian Mountains. Along the way, they strengthened the defense of their military fortress of Przemysl, which was pivotal to the protection of Hungary. The Russians trapped some 120,000 Austrian soldiers at the fortress in late September, though the besieged fort did not surrender until March 1915. The impact of the Galician fighting in the war's first weeks was devastating for the Austrians, since they suffered losses of more than 350,000 men and much of Galicia fell under Russian occupation. Moreover, the Russians were in a position to launch attacks against Hungary and the German state of Silesia. The Central Powers ultimately succeeded in preventing the Russians from attacking either of those places in 1914.

Austria-Hungary also faced difficulties against Serbia on the Balkan front. In the first important encounter of the two armies in August 1914, Serbian troops defeated the Austrians at the Battle of the Tser Mountains. In the months that followed, the Austrians advanced against the Serbs, capturing Belgrade on December 2. Within days, however, the Serbs pushed the Austrians out of the city, and the Austrian retreat quickly became a rout. Soon there were no Austro-Hungarian troops left on Serbian soil.

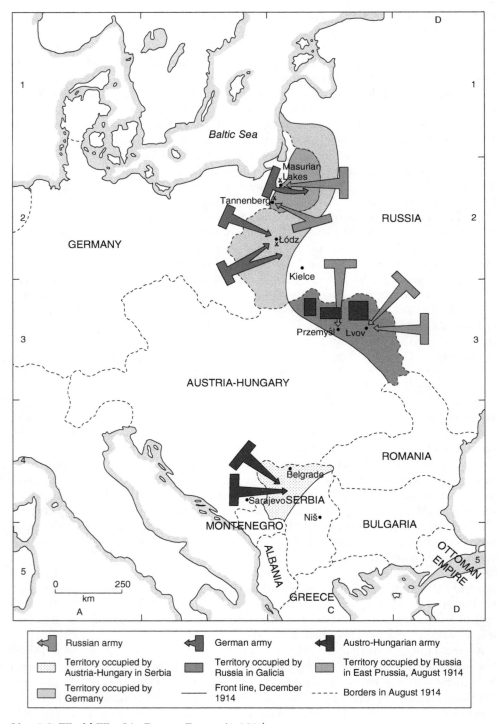

Map 1.2 World War I in Eastern Europe in 1914.

In late October, the Ottoman Empire entered the war on the side of the Central Powers, when ships flying the Turkish flag bombarded the Russian Black Sea port of Odessa, and the Ottomans closed the Dardanelles, thereby cutting off an important supply route for Russia through the Black Sea. The intervention of the Ottoman Empire was a sign of a spreading war, since the conflict now reached the Middle East. Another sign was Japan's entry into the conflict in 1914 on the side of the Allies, as the Japanese were eager to take control of German colonial possessions and spheres of influence in the Far East. Indeed, the war that began as a European conflict had reached global proportions by year's end.

The technology of mass death

A major reason for the enormous casualty figures in the fighting was that war planners applied nineteenth-century principles to a conflict transformed by new and improved technology. One of these changes was the development of smokeless gunpowder. It made for a clearer battlefield, and it reduced bore fouling (deposits that form in the rifle bore from firing), thus allowing for the emergence of increased firepower. There was also a major transformation in small arms going back to the 1880s with the development of clip-fed breech-loading rifles that had a longer range and greater velocity than their predecessors. In addition, manufacturers produced newly shaped bullets that were smaller, more stable, and had a longer range. The result of these innovations was an advantage for the defense over the offense.

The weapon most frequently mentioned when referring to the killing fields of World War I is the machine gun. The first modern model came in the 1880s. Improved versions followed, and by 1914, the machine gun's firepower had increased to between 450 and 600 rounds per minute. When the fighting began, the Germans had 12,000 machine guns at their disposal, while the British and French had only a few hundred. Machine guns quickly became prevalent in the arsenals of all the major warring nations.

Artillery saw significant changes. The introduction of recoil systems enabled the artillery tube to move back to its original position after recoiling against springs in its carriage upon firing. The result was an increased firing rate and improved accuracy. New steel alloys allowed for the manufacture of more durable artillery weapons with greater firing ranges. Many European armies developed and standardized the procedures for using indirect artillery fire, which involved targeting a remote site and massing one's artillery fire on it. As for types of artillery in hand when the war broke out, the French relied heavily on their 75 mm field gun, a highly effective offensive weapon that was light, mobile, rapid, and had an impressive firing range of 6,000 yards. On the other hand, the shells of this French artillery piece could not penetrate enemy embankments or entrenchments. When the war started in 1914, the French had 3,840 75mm field guns and only about 300 heavy artillery pieces (howitzers). The Germans had a heavy artillery force of 2,000 guns that represented one-third of all their artillery weapons in 1914. The howitzers had much greater destructive power than light field guns, more accuracy in hitting enemy targets, and a much longer firing range. The popularity of heavy artillery increased on both sides during the conflict, and even in France, heavy guns constituted close to half of its artillery strength by war's end. Estimates indicate that artillery was responsible for as many as 70 percent of all soldiers' deaths at the battlefront.

Airplanes, an invention of the Wright brothers in America in 1903, were a minor factor in the war in 1914, but their importance grew significantly as the fighting progressed.

Their potential was evident in the conflict's initial weeks, when French reconnaissance planes discovered and confirmed that the German First Army had shifted its line of movement to the east of Paris, helping Joffre decide to launch a counterattack near the Marne in September. At the Battle of Verdun in 1916, the Germans concentrated air-craft in a manner not seen before, consequently ridding the sky of French fighter planes and chasing off French observation aircraft trying to track German troop movements; at the same time, the Germans used their own observation planes to assist their artillery units in pinpointing enemy targets. Before 1918, the military use of planes was confined primarily to artillery observation, dogfights among individual fighter pilots, and the destruction of enemy observation balloons. Yet in August 1916, the British at the Battle of the Somme used close to 400 aircraft to bomb and strafe German lines, bleeding the enemy soldiers "like lemons in a press." During an American offensive in the fall of 1918, the Allies sent upwards of 1,500 planes into the air to attack the Germans. The importance of aviation in the plans of wartime leaders was also evident in: the Germans' use of strategic bombing raids, albeit small in number and minimally damaging in their results, against British cities in 1917 and 1918; a British decision to create a Royal Air Force (RAF) in the spring of 1918; and an intensive French manufacturing effort that had more than 3,200 military planes in place at war's end.

As both sides settled into trench warfare in the West in 1914, barbed wired began to appear in large quantities. Wiring teams, doing one of the least desirable jobs on the front because of the dangers involved, set up barbed wire entanglements at night to protect their side of the trenches. By the spring of 1915, the Germans had an elaborate trench network in the West shielded by a double belt of barbed wire, each 30 meters deep and 5 feet high. Later in 1915, Falkenhayn had a second line of trenches con-structed that also included two belts of barbed wire. The result was the creation of two killing zones to stop any Allied frontal assaults on the German lines.

The Germans introduced the use of poison gas into the war in the spring of 1915 in their only offensive on the Western Front that year. Launched in the vicinity of Ypres in April against an Allied salient, chlorine gas, propelled by the wind, caught French-Algerian and Canadian soldiers by surprise and opened up a 4-mile wide gap in the Allied lines. Because of Falkenhayn's skepticism about the effectiveness of the new weapon, the Germans had insufficient reserves to exploit the situation and they failed to score a breakthrough. The Germans tried a mass poison attack again in May, but the element of surprise was gone and the Allies held firm. The Allies resorted to this form of warfare as well, with the British first using it at Loos in Belgium in September 1915. By 1916, both sides were loading poison gas in artillery shells and firing them at enemy lines during artillery bombardments.

Other wartime technological changes included the introduction of flamethrowers and tanks. The Germans were the first to employ flamethrowers, directing them against the British at the Battle of Hooge in Flanders in the summer of 1915. The British intro-duced tanks, which were tracked, armored vehicles equipped with large caliber guns, during their Somme offensive of 1916. France eventually developed a light tank that French and American forces employed in large numbers in 1918.

The war of attrition, 1915

The Dual Monarchy appeared on the verge of collapse in the early spring of 1915, fol-lowing a bloody struggle against Russia in the Carpathian Mountains during the winter and the March 15 surrender of the fortress of Przemysl to the Russians. To avert disaster, Falkenhayn planned and supervised a major campaign involving German and Austrian troops against the Russians in Galicia. Beginning their offensive on May 2, the Central Powers recaptured the fortress of Przemysl on June 3; by the end of June, they had retaken Galicia from Russia. Farther north, German forces drove eastward across Poland during the summer, took Warsaw in early August, and reached Latvia at the end of September. Logistical problems and adverse weather conditions brought an end to the offensive, but not before the Russians had retreated 300 miles at the deepest point and lost close to 2 million men, half of them as prisoners. Russia's disastrous summer militarily resulted in Nicholas II's decision to take personal control of the Russian army in August, even though he lacked military experience and the ability to command.

While Austria–Hungary gained some breathing space in the war against Russia in 1915, it faced a new enemy that year when Italy, after having been heavily courted by the Allies, declared war on it in May. The Italians focused their attention along the Isonzo River that separated the northeastern corner of Italy from the Dual Monarchy. Chief of the Italian General Staff Luigi Cadorna, known for his penetrating military mind and his willingness to push his soldiers unrelentingly with little concern for their well-being, considered that area to be Italy's best point of entry into Austria. The Italians launched four attacks on the Isonzo Front in 1915, and none of them succeeded. The bloodletting on both sides was chilling: the Italians had 250,000 casualties while the Austrians lost 165,000. Only the arrival of winter stemmed the carnage.

In Britain, a group of government officials, led by First Lord of the Admiralty Winston Churchill, contended at the beginning of 1915 that the Allies should send a powerful fleet of ships against the Turks and use it to breach the Dardanelles, take

Figure 1.1 Habsburg soldiers move forward in the Carpathian Mountains during the winter of 1914–1915.

control of Constantinople, and force the Ottoman Empire out of the war. Known as Easterners, they believed that by moving through this "back door" to get at the Central Powers, Britain and France would show good faith to the beleaguered Russians who were seeking relief from a Turkish assault in the Caucasus. To this end, the British and the French put together the most powerful flotilla ever seen in the Mediterranean, but the fleet encountered greater resistance from the Turks in the Dardanelles than anticipated. Furthermore, the Allies had made no provision for a land army to take control of one or both shores of the Straits to allow the task force to move forward. A purely naval presence might still have prevailed had the British admiral in charge been courageous enough to stay the course in a large Allied assault that began on March 18, but he called off the operation after the loss of three capital ships.

British officials then turned to land operations on the Gallipoli Peninsula and limited naval activities to bombardments and supplies. Allied troop landings at Gallipoli took place in late April, but fierce opposition from the Turks prevented them from doing much more than to establish beachheads. Fighting on the peninsula continued for some time thereafter, yet it was evident by October that the Gallipoli campaign had utterly failed. An Allied withdrawal was completed in early January 1916. The casualties in the campaign were enormous, with each side losing more than 250,000 men, many of them through disease and exposure. Turkey remained a major player in the war.

In the West in 1915, the French were still in the driver's seat in Allied strategic decision making, with the British serving as a junior partner. Since Joffre was convinced that the war would be won or lost on the Western Front, he was eager to get back to a war of maneuver and drive the Germans out of France. Consequently, the Allies conducted several offensives in 1915 that Joffre referred to as "nibbling tactics." They began the assaults with large-scale preparatory bombardments intended to "soften up" the enemy for ensuing infantry attacks. But the bombardments, which became larger and larger in scope during the year, also had the effect of telling the enemy where the attacks were coming. Once the opening artillery barrages were over, waves of infantry soldiers went "over the top" to advance on the enemy trenches, where the Germans were waiting for them. The attacks achieved minimal territorial gains, caused frightening numbers of casualties, and managed no permanent breakthroughs. This happened in the spring of 1915, for example, in the Franco-British Artois offensive (May 9–June 18) where the French lost 102,000 men compared to 73,000 German soldiers. In this war of attrition, Joffre believed that the use of greater manpower and firepower against the enemy would enable the Allies to wear down the Germans and ultimately achieve victory. The problem was that the casualty toll was higher on the attacker than on the attacked, and France, with a much smaller population than Germany, was in a difficult position to make such a strategy work.

More Allied offensives against the Germans took place in the fall, in part to provide relief for the desperate Russians on the Eastern Front. One of these was a British offensive at Loos. The British preceded their infantry attack against the entrenched Germans with their first use of chlorine gas in the conflict. After getting through the Germans' initial defense line on the first day of the drive, the British on the next day came out of hastily dug trenches and started marching toward the Germans' second line of defense. The event turned into a slaughter as the well-entrenched German machine-gunners cut down wave after wave of British soldiers. The British forces finally broke and began to flee to the rear. The German gunners, having seen enough bloodletting, just quit shooting and let the remaining British soldiers reach safety. It was one of the few times during the war that the Germans did this.

The "corpsefield of Loos" symbolized the butchery of the 1915 Allied campaigns generally on the Western Front, a year in which the British suffered close to 279,000 casualties, the Germans more than 600,000, and the French a startling 1.292 million.

In the war against Serbia, the Central Powers pressed toward complete victory in 1915. A key step was the creation of an alliance between the Central Powers and Bulgaria in early September, following the Germans' military gains against Russia in the summer and the fading chances of the Allies at Gallipoli. Not long thereafter, the Germans and Austro-Hungarians pushed into Serbia from the north, and Bulgaria followed suit from the east. By early November the invaders controlled half of Serbia, and the Serbian army was rapidly collapsing. What was left of the Serbian army retreated into Albania in early December. The Central Powers controlled all of Serbia, Montenegro, and most of Albania by year's end. Their success against Serbia meant that they now had a land route for supplies to the Ottoman Empire.

As 1915 concluded, the Allies had little to cheer about. Outside of Italy's entry into the war on their side, they had experienced a number of wartime setbacks. The Central Powers, on the other hand, had enjoyed an impressive string of successes. Yet victory in the war continued to elude them, not only because their military triumphs in 1915 were essentially local in nature, but also because the stalemate on the Western Front continued unabated. Moreover, ethnic tensions were rising in the Austro-Hungarian Imperial Army and its military dependence on Germany was increasing. Nevertheless, both sides optimistically planned for the 1916 campaign, confident that victory in the war would finally be theirs.

Stalemate, 1916

As 1916 approached, Falkenhayn, arguing that time was against Germany, concluded that the way to achieve full victory was to defeat Britain, and that the best way to do that was to knock Britain's "best sword" – the French army – out of the war by attacking a vital location on the French front. Falkenhayn selected the fortress city of Verdun, a salient with poor communications links and three vulnerable sides. Historically, Verdun had great significance for the French as a fortification site going back to the ancient Romans; its loss would severely damage French morale and the massive losses of French soldiers would force France to make peace. Falkenhayn obtained Wilhelm II's approval for his plan in December 1915, and quickly put his assault force into place. It included 1,100 artillery pieces in the vicinity of Verdun, 541 of which were heavies.

The German attack began at dawn on February 21, with a deafening artillery barrage that went on with chilling intensity for nine hours. German infantry soldiers then moved out and quickly conquered France's outer defense zone, using flamethrowers in large numbers for the first time in the war. On February 25, the Germans took Fort Douaumont, considered the lynchpin in the French system of defense at Verdun. The French rushed in reinforcements and put Philippe Pétain in command. A master of defensive warfare, the taciturn and austere Pétain was known as someone who refused to give up. To maintain morale, he rotated in fresh troops on a regular basis. As a result of this furlough system, 70 percent of the French army saw service at Verdun in 1916. By February 27, the German offensive had essentially ground to a halt. Meanwhile, French leaders quickly concluded that the Battle of Verdun was a question of national honor and must be defended at all costs. But German national pride was involved as well, so Falkenhayn had to continue his attacks.

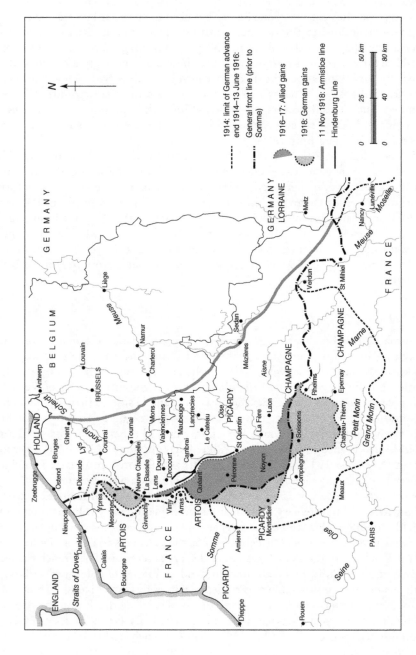

Map 1.3 The Western Front in World War I.

The battle lasted ten months, the longest of the war. The Germans continued to apply pressure on the French in the spring, but the French held on to their pulverized lines. In mid-July German soldiers came within 2.5 miles of the city of Verdun – the closest they were ever to get. In the fall, the French went on the offensive, retaking Fort Douaumont on October 24. By the third week of December, when the attacks finally ceased, the French were once again securely in control of the fortress area. Verdun made Pétain a French national hero, but the French paid a heavy price for their victory, losing 540,000 men. Joffre was held accountable for the carnage which, combined with sharp criticism of his failed strategy of 1915, led to his ouster as French commander-in-chief in December 1916. Falkenhayn, although successful in making Verdun a battle of attrition, did not anticipate that the Germans would bleed almost as badly as the French. In the end, Germany lost 430,000 men. He was relieved of his command at the end of August and replaced by Hindenburg, who brought Ludendorff with him.

While the French and Germans were bitterly fighting at Verdun, Joffre put pressure on Sir Douglas Haig, commander of the BEF, to execute a planned offensive on the Somme River to force the Germans to divert troops away from Verdun. Self-confident, self-righteous, stubborn, and well-connected, Haig was convinced that the war would be won on the Western Front; he believed in massive frontal assaults and a strategy of attrition. Haig opened the Battle of the Somme with a seven-day artillery bombardment that used more than 1,500 artillery guns and consumed 1.5 million shells. The bombardment inflicted heavy damage on the Germans' front trench line while the bulk of the German forces sat in the protection of the deep bunkers they had constructed since claiming the area in 1914.

On July 1, over 100,000 British soldiers advanced toward the enemy's trenches. They marched forward in straight rows, as if in parade formation, with 50- to 100-yard intervals between them. They were confident that the British artillery barrage had

Figure 1.2 British machine-gun crew members wear gas masks as they fire their weapon during the Battle of the Somme on the Western Front in July 1916.

largely wiped out the German defenders. What they walked into was a meat grinder. German machine-gun crews unleashed a torrent of fire that was so long and so intense that the water completely evaporated in some of the guns' water-cooling mechanisms. The almost 60,000 casualties that the British endured on July 1 was the single worst day for dead and wounded in Britain's military history. German losses that day were 6,000.

Despite the heavy British losses, Haig refused to abandon the battle. The fighting in the Somme sector quickly deteriorated into a deadly stalemate. In September, Haig surprised the Germans with a newly developed tracked, armored vehicle called the tank, but the number successfully deployed were too few to alter the course of the battle, which ended with the onset of winter weather in November. In the five-month encounter, the Allies managed to make a dent in the German front that was at its deepest penetration only 7 miles forward from the point of the British attack on July 1. For such small gains, the loss of lives was staggering. The British had nearly 420,000 casualties and the French close to 200,000. German losses approached 450,000.

In spite of the carnage on the Western Front in 1916, government and military leaders on both sides were not ready to abandon the idea of defeating the enemy. They began to plan for yet another campaign season in 1917, even though morale among their soldiers showed signs of cracking.

In the East, the Russians, under pressure from the French to divert enemy attention away from Verdun, prepared an offensive against a weakened Austro-Hungarian army in Galicia. The commander of the Russian forces in Galicia was Alexei Brusilov, one of Russia's most talented World War I generals, who contended that victory was possible through the use of innovative ideas. One of these was to attack the enemy simultaneously at several points over a broad front rather than to concentrate forces at one place for a massive assault; such an approach would prevent the enemy from sending reinforcements to the main attack point, because none existed. Another called for brief artillery barrages before sending infantrymen over the top, since such bombardments would enhance the element of surprise and minimize the enemy's response time. The Brusilov offensive began in early June and continued into September, when it collapsed. It was Russia's most impressive military operation during the war, and in terms of territory gained it was a success. But it came at a very heavy price: the Russians suffered a loss of 1.412 million men, though they inflicted heavy casualties on the Austro-Hungarians as well. Among the Russians, discontent on both the military and home fronts increased, as many saw Brusilov's offensive as one more example of Russian military failure.

Brusilov's success against the Dual Monarchy in mid-1916 convinced Romania, whose leaders were eager to obtain the Hungarian province of Transylvania, to enter the war on the side of the Allies in late August. Romania's badly trained and poorly led army, after quickly taking over a quarter of Transylvania, ran into a German–Austro-Hungarian counterattack that by mid-November had pushed through the Transylvanian Alps onto the Romanian central plain. Another force made up of Bulgarians, Germans, and Turks drove Romania out of Bulgaria in September. Both armies converged on the Romanian capital of Bucharest which fell on December 5. By the end of the year, the Central Powers controlled most of Romania. The occupation of the country gave them access to Romanian oil and grain, which proved vital at a time when a British naval blockade was causing shortages of many kinds. Success in Romania was a bright spot for the Central Powers in a year that tested their tenacity and resilience.

War at sea

As soon as Britain entered the war, it used its dominance on the high seas to impose a naval blockade against Germany. It issued a large list of contraband items that even included foodstuffs affecting noncombatants. The effects of the blockade were quickly felt, with German imports dropping 55 percent from prewar levels by 1915. Those in charge of Britain's main naval arm, the Grand Fleet, and Germany's primary naval force, the High Seas Fleet, kept their two fleets largely inactive on opposite sides of the North Sea in 1914. The Grand Fleet waited for the High Seas Fleet to venture out from the safety of its harbors in northern Germany in order to engage it, but the latter refused to do so because of the numerical advantage in ships that the British enjoyed. Consequently, the fighting in the North Sea was limited, consisting primarily of mine laying, skirmishes, and submarine attacks.

Elsewhere, the British attempted to hunt down German naval ships scattered across the globe, although not always successfully. In the Mediterranean, two German warships eluded British efforts to trap them and took refuge in Constantinople, where the Germans transferred the vessels to the Turkish navy. The German gift played an important role in the Ottomans' decision to enter the war on the side of the Central Powers at the end of October 1914. In another episode, a German naval squadron commanded by Maximilian Graf von Spee sailed from a German base in China across the Pacific Ocean to the waters of South America where Spee hoped to disrupt Allied merchant shipping. Spee's ships engaged a British naval squadron in the Battle of Coronel off the coast of Chile on November 1, 1914, and Britain experienced its first naval defeat in a century. The British reversed their fortunes in December 1914, when British warships destroyed most of Spee's squadron at the Battle of the Falkland Islands; Spee was among the 2,200 German sailors who drowned. The Germans also suffered maritime setbacks in the Indian Ocean in late 1914 and off the coast of Chile in early 1915, and the British trapped another enemy warship in German East Africa. As a result of the losses to Germany's overseas fleet, the world's high seas were largely free of the menace of German surface warships by the spring of 1915.

By early 1915, many German leaders believed that the one effective weapon their country had left on the high seas was the submarine. In October 1914, the commander of the German U-boat fleet recommended a policy of using submarines to sink Allied merchant ships. Support for the idea intensified after Great Britain in November 1914 declared the North Sea to be a war zone. The debate culminated in a German declaration in February 1915 that the waters around the British Isles were now a war zone and that merchant ships, even neutral ones, would be open to submarine attacks without warning. Germany's policy of unrestricted submarine warfare quickly ran into problems with the United States after 124 Americans died in the sinking in May 1915 of the British ocean liner *Lusitania*, and the torpedoing of another ship in August, in which three Americans drowned. Following these events, the Germans dropped their unrestricted submarine warfare campaign by promising that they would not sink unresisting passenger-carrying ships without warning and would make efforts to provide for the safety of passengers on board. In March 1916, the Germans, in violation of their pledge, sank the French cross-Channel steamer *Sussex* with some Americans aboard, and the American government threatened to sever diplomatic relations with Germany. The German government, wishing to smooth out relations with Washington, reaffirmed its abandonment of unrestricted submarine warfare. At the same time, Germany more than doubled its submarine fleet by adding 78 U-boats. At the end of 1916, the Germans, looking for courses of action to break the military stalemate on land and avoid collapse at home once again considered the possibility of unrestricted submarine warfare to force Britain to its knees.

Meanwhile, the war's only major surface naval battle took place in 1916 near Jutland in the North Sea. Admiral Reinhard Scheer, who took command of the German High Seas Fleet in early 1916, was eager to take an aggressive approach against the British on the high seas, but not to the point of a full-fledged encounter against the Grand Fleet. On the British side, Sir John Jellicoe, the Grand Fleet's commander, was also anxious for battle, although the stakes were higher for him, since a loss for the Grand Fleet would jeopardize the security of Great Britain. In the Germans' case, a defeat would merely oblige them to revert to the defensive posture they had had in place since 1914. In late May, the British intercepted German messages indicating that Scheer was planning a major operation on May 31. Armed with this knowledge, Jellicoe set sail with the Grand Fleet to engage the Germans off the coast of Denmark. What occurred on May 31–June 1 was the Battle of Jutland. During the two days of maneuvering that occupied the opposing fleets, there were several intensive exchanges of fire. In the end, Scheer's High Seas Fleet successfully retreated to its bases under cover of darkness. Although the Germans claimed victory in the battle, their assertion was debatable. The Germans based their contention on the fact that they suffered fewer losses of ships, tonnage, and men than the British. But they had failed to deal a crippling blow to the Grand Fleet or to weaken the British blockade of Germany. Furthermore, the German fleet remained bottled up in harbor for the rest of the war. When seen in that light, the battle was a strategic victory for the British.

The winter of 1916–1917

In spite of costly attempts, neither side could break the military stalemate in 1916. Consequently, dramatic changes took place on both sides in the fall and winter of 1916–1917. On the side of the Central Powers, Hindenburg and Ludendorff emerged as the de facto military rulers of Germany. Wilhelm II endorsed the generals' commitment to fight the war to the bitter end, which included the renewal of unrestricted submarine warfare. In Austria–Hungary, Karl I (r. 1848–1918), who succeeded to the Habsburg throne after the death of Franz Joseph I (r. 1916–1918) in November 1916, dismissed Conrad as the Austrian chief of staff in February 1917; he also looked for ways to achieve peace, although his efforts were unsuccessful.

On the Allied side, French Premier Aristide Briand in December replaced Joffre as commander-in-chief with a dashing, smooth-talking general named Robert Nivelle, and established a separate armaments ministry under Socialist Party leader Albert Thomas. In Great Britain, the dynamic David Lloyd George became prime minister in December 1916, and he quickly reinvigorated British morale. But he also infuriated BEF Commander Haig and Chief of the Imperial General Staff Sir William Robertson in February 1917 with a surprise announcement to put the British army under the control of Nivelle for an upcoming spring offensive. Their threats to resign finally forced him to back off, but the distrust they developed toward him in the episode remained.

In Russia, conditions steadily deteriorated. Tsar Nicholas II, as supreme commander of the Russian army, was on the military front, and he was increasingly held

Figure 1.3 German Field Marshal Paul von Hindenburg (left) and General Erich Ludendorff stand together following a celebration of Hindenburg's 70th birthday on October 2, 1917.

responsible for Russian military setbacks. A general war weariness swept across the Russian army and the home front. People in Petrograd took to the streets in early March 1917, initially to protest food shortages, but the demonstrations quickly became generalized and political in nature. Nicholas II abdicated as emperor on March 15, ending the tsarist system in Russia. The ensuing provisional government promised the Western Allies that it would honor its commitments to the war. The moderate socialist Aleksandr Kerensky became the war minister in May, and he joined with Brusilov, the new army chief of staff, in planning a massive July offensive. They did this in spite of strong opposition to the war among the Russian people. They also acted in the face of a powerful rival government in Petrograd – a socialist-sponsored workers' soviet – that had in mid-March announced in Order No. 1 that the army's common soldiers should elect soldiers' committees to control their units. The order caused a deterioration of army discipline and the summary execution of numerous officers. In light of these conditions, it was questionable whether any Russian offensive could succeed in 1917.

A year of momentous change, 1917

When the Germans announced a resumption of unrestricted submarine warfare at the end of January 1917, they believed that this measure would quickly force Britain out of the conflict. But the policy carried with it the risk of war with the United States. After fighting broke out in 1914, America adopted a policy of neutrality. President Woodrow Wilson implored Americans to be neutral in both their thoughts and actions. In reality, however, the U.S. showed a certain level of sympathy for the Allied powers, partly because of the extensive trade and financial links it cultivated with them during the conflict, but also because of propaganda that abounded in the U.S. about German war atrocities. Tensions likewise existed between the United States and Britain during the war owing to the latter's seizure, in violation of the rights of neutrals on the high seas, of American merchant ships carrying cargoes intended for Germany. Wilson even received authorization from Congress to impose an embargo on Great Britain if necessary, but none was ever implemented. After Germany launched unrestricted submarine warfare on February 1, 1917, the United States immediately severed diplomatic relations with that country. Adding to tensions between the two nations was the publication on March 1 of the Zimmerman Telegram; in it German Foreign Minister Arthur Zimmerman promised Mexico assistance, should America join the war with the Allies and Mexico ally with Germany, in the recovery of territories lost to the U.S. in the Mexican War of 1846–1848. The telegram caused outrage across America and created a pro-interventionist sentiment in many parts of the country. Following the German sinking of four American merchant ships in March, the United States declared war on Germany on April 6, 1917. The news of its entry raised spirits in both France and Britain.

As for the U-boat campaign, the Germans achieved impressive numbers for sunken tonnage in the early months of 1917. The campaign climaxed in April, when German submarines sank 881,000 tons of Allied shipping. Over the summer Allied tonnage losses continued at about 500,000 tons a month, and then descended to about 350,000 tons in September, when the Allies adopted a convoy system to protect their merchant ships. While the submarine campaign created hardships and shortages for the Allies, it was a German gamble that failed. It did not drive the Allies out of the war, and it brought the tremendous economic and military potential of the United States into play against the Central Powers.

The early months of 1917 included a hope among the Allies that they could win the war on the Western Front after France's new Commander-in-Chief Nivelle presented French leaders with plans for a major spring offensive that he claimed would win the war quickly and without great cost. At its heart were an intense preliminary artillery bombardment with large numbers of heavy guns and a massive infantry attack moving behind the protection of a precisely timed "creeping barrage" of artillery fire. Success would come within 24 to 48 hours of the infantry attack and send the enemy on the run. Nivelle, whose mother was of British origin, used his ability to speak fluent English to win over Lloyd George to his ideas in early 1917, and he instilled enthusiasm in his soldiers by assuring them that the upcoming attack would not be another attrition-based operation. But not everyone shared his enthusiasm. Haig, recently promoted to field marshal, was unconvinced and feared that his own plans for an offensive in Flanders would be jeopardized. Several leading French generals and politicians were also pessimistic about the plan's chances for success. French War Minister Paul Painlevé hoped that Nivelle would call off his offensive after they learned that Ludendorff had undertaken a strategic withdrawal of German forces on the Western Front in the latter half of March, thereby removing the French offensive's main target, but that did not happen.

The much-anticipated Nivelle offensive went into action on April 16. A 14-day artillery bombardment that included more than 5,500 guns firing millions of shells at the enemy preceded the attack, but its effect proved to be far less than intended. The infantry assault threw 1.2 million men into action along a 40-mile front. The morale of the men was sky-high on the morning of the attack. Some troops had refused to go on leave, so as not to miss the great offensive. But the Germans were waiting. Rain, sleet, snow, and mist impeded the infantry's advance, and German machine guns inflicted a frightful toll of losses as the soldiers climbed the slopes of a large ridge called the Chemin des Dames. The French artillery's "creeping barrage" proved useless, because the French soldiers moved too slowly to keep up with its forward progress. By the end of the second day, the French had advanced far less than expected, absorbed heavy casualties, and failed to rupture the German lines. Nivelle pushed on until May 9 without breaking through. Although the French had secured more territory than during any operations in 1915–1916, their success was disappointingly short of what was supposed to have occurred, and they suffered dreadful losses.

When it became evident that the Nivelle offensive would fall short of its goals, disillusionment set in among the French troops. Reinforcement troops, while passing in front of their commanding officers, baaed like sheep headed to slaughter. Mutinies that had first broken on April 17 quickly spread in the weeks thereafter, eventually touching half the French army divisions. The mutinies were a spontaneous reaction to despair, fatigue, a sense of neglect, a feeling of betrayal, and a sense of being used as cannon fodder in senseless offensives. On May 15, Pétain took over for Nivelle as the French commander-in-chief, and he soon restored discipline through a combination of restrained repression and steps to improve the conditions of the soldiers. He also put the French army into a purely defensive mode pending the arrival of soldiers from the United States. Fortunately for the French, the Germans did not learn about the mutinies until it was too late. Consequently, the mutinies did not significantly alter the general strategic situation of the war in 1917.

After the failure of the Nivelle offensive, the initiative on the Western Front passed to the British. Haig put together plans for a Flanders offensive that he hoped would allow British forces to break out of their Ypres salient, take control of Belgium, and then outflank the Germans' defensive position to the south. Unfortunately for the British soldiers, the sector of the front that Haig chose as his embarkation point for what became known as the Third Battle of Ypres, also known as the Battle of Passchendaele, was an area composed of finely grained clay that inhibited water from soaking into the ground. When it rained, the land became a massive quagmire. British forces began their push on July 31, following a 14-day preparatory artillery barrage that inadvertently included the destruction of dikes keeping out water. It rained nearly every day in August, turning the battlefield into a muddy morass that impeded the British attack. Soldiers slipped off paths, fell into water-filled artillery craters, and drowned. The weather turned dry in September, allowing the British to make shallow infantry advances accompanied by powerful creeping artillery barrages. The rains returned in October, but Haig insisted on continuing the offensive. Dominion troops played a key role in the final push that began in mud and slime in late October, and the Flanders offensive concluded in November with the capture of the village of Passchendaele by Canadian troops on November 6 and a final push to consolidate Allied lines. The Third Battle of Ypres symbolized the futility of the fighting on the Western Front. Fighting in hideous, surreal conditions, the British advanced less than 5 miles at a cost of 245,000 casualties (including 14,000 prisoners of war). Many of the soldiers were never found – they had been swallowed up by the mud. The Germans suffered at least 200,000 dead and wounded, and perhaps considerably more. Haig came under severe criticism for the heavy losses that Britain experienced in the campaign for so little territorial gain, but he kept his job.

On the Italian Front, following a long period of indecisive campaigning by both sides in 1916 and 1917, a critical showdown in the fighting took place in the fall of 1917 at Caporetto. The Austro-Hungarian forces, under Italian attack along the Isonzo River, called on the Germans for assistance. Ludendorff organized a new German–Austro-Hungarian army and launched an attack at the Isonzo on October 24. His troops achieved complete surprise and by the end of the first day the German-led forces had captured the Italian town of Caporetto, torn through the Italian lines, and pushed ahead over 10 miles. The Italian army was routed and lost massive amounts of military hardware to the attacking forces. The Italian battlefront stabilized in mid-November behind the Piave River, 20 miles from Venice. The arrival of French and British reinforcements helped bolster the Italians' position, but the Italian losses were heavy: more than 275,000 prisoners of war, 350,000 deserters, and 40,000 casualties. The Italian debacle also cost Italian Commander-in-Chief Cadorna his job. With foreign troops now occupying the northeastern corner of their country, the Italian people prepared to fight the war to the bitter end as they rallied around new Prime Minister Vittorio Orlando's call to resist at any cost.

In the East, the Russians attempted to carry out a successful summer offensive in 1917, while the Germans, with Austro-Hungarian cooperation, worked to inflict a fatal blow on the Russian war effort as a part of their Eastern Front strategy. Hindenburg and Ludendorff, long convinced that the war could only be won by defeating Russia, were its chief proponents. In Russia, the key man was the moderate socialist Kerensky, who had become war minister in May. Committed to keeping Russia in the war, Kerensky named Brusilov as commander-in-chief of the Russian army at the end of May. Brusilov put together a plan that directed the bulk of Russia's remaining resources against the Austro-Hungarian forces in Galicia. As he put his operation into place, Brusilov was aware that there was widespread discontent within the Russian army toward the war. There were numerous mutinies and large-scale desertions among the Russian forces during the two-day artillery bombardment prior to the offensive's launch on July 1. After the offensive began, some Russian units refused to storm the enemy when ordered, and reserves ignored commands to exploit infantry successes. Nevertheless, the Russians initially made impressive gains, especially since many Austrian troops had also lost interest in fighting. But the Germans launched a carefully planned counteroffensive on July 19, and the Russian army rapidly disintegrated. By the end of the month, the Russian army as an effective fighting force was largely non-existent. The Germans followed up their July success by capturing the fortress city of Riga on the Baltic in two days, opening the way to Petrograd. Political turmoil engulfed the Russian provisional government at that point, with various political groups and factions vying for influence and power. Kerensky, who became prime minister in July, insisted on keeping Russia in the war, with disastrous results. The Bolshevik revolution of early November 1917 (see pp. 62–64) brought to power Vladimir Lenin who quickly signed an armistice with the Germans. With no enemy left to contend with in the East, Ludendorff began to transfer troops to the Western Front in preparation for a final showdown against the Western Allies, hopefully before the resources of the United States could have much effect. The German–Russian negotiations for peace reached an impasse in January 1918. The Germans responded by resuming military operations in mid-February in what one German general called "the most comical war I have ever experienced."[1] Most Bolshevik leaders wanted to fight back but there was no army left. At Lenin's urging, the two sides met again at the beginning of March for peace negotiations, and the Soviet delegation signed the German-dictated terms at Brest–Litovsk on March 3.

The psychological aspect of the conflict heated up on Russia's western border as well. Minorities in the western parts of the Russian Empire wished for their independence. The populations of the Caucasus hoped to strengthen their ties with the Near East and to check Slavic dominance. Germany created the League of the Foreign Peoples of Russia in April 1916, fueling revolutionary and separatist claims among ethnic groups living on Russia's western borderlands, including Muslims. To further weaken Russia, Germany was instrumental in the transport of Lenin from Switzerland to Russia following the toppling of the tsarist regime in March 1917, in the hope that he would add to Russia's unstable political situation. The military disintegration of the Russian front in 1917 did much to advance the German cause as, one by one, Russia's western minorities fell under German control and influence. The Bolsheviks counterattacked by creating Soviet republics in Estonia, Latvia, Lithuania, Belarus, and Ukraine in early 1918. This resulted in more misery for the people, as these territories became extensions of a Russian civil war.

War in the colonies

Shortly after World War I began, British Dominion troops seized Germany's Pacific island possessions of Rabaul and Samoa. After China declared war on Germany in 1917, the German concessions at Tsingtao, Tientsin, and Wuhan in China were immediately occupied. But it was Germany's African colonies that saw most of the fighting. Boer troops took Germany's second largest colony, Southwest Africa, in the spring of 1915. Allied forces moved in August 1914 against German Central Africa, and used guerrilla warfare there to win in early 1916. In German East Africa, Colonel Paul Emil von Lettow-Vorbeck commanded a German-dominated army that never exceeded 14,000 soldiers in an unwavering four-year guerrilla campaign against a considerably larger British-led force that included South African and Indian troops. His success earned him a promotion to general in late 1917, and though his army was still undefeated when news of Germany's surrender to the Allies reached him, Lettow-Vorbeck and his remaining force of 3,000 men nevertheless capitulated to the British on November 25, 1918.

Meanwhile, the Ottomans sent agitators to India and Mesopotamia to create trouble against Britain's imperial presence there, supported independence sentiments in Egypt where the British had a protectorate, encouraged local Berber revolts in Morocco and Algeria against their French colonial rulers, and stirred up resentment in Russia's Muslim regions against Russian domination; the northwest region of India was particularly vulnerable. The level of distraction that French and British troops experienced in their colonies was substantial and is illustrated by an invasion that a Muslim fundamentalist group called the Senussi, based in eastern Libya, made into Egypt in 1915; it compelled Britain to deploy a force of almost 40,000 men, backed by armored vehicles and planes, to push the invader out by early 1917.

One cannot discuss the colonial fighting without stressing the importance of colonial manpower contributions generally. Over 3.5 million colonial soldiers participated in World War I, and several hundred thousand of them fought on European battlefields. Africa and the British Dominions (Canada, Newfoundland, South Africa, Australia, and New Zealand) contributed some 1.4 million men, while India added another 1.4 million. Many of them served on the French front as shock troops where they suffered heavy casualties during the first winter of the war. The French already had some 122,000 indigenous soldiers in their colonial forces in 1914, and they recruited significantly more men from their empire during the war. The French integrated their black and North African troops and used them on the Western Front. The French soon found out, however, how strong the taboo was against using black men to fight alongside of or against white men. They could not prevent a public outcry, for example, when French West African soldiers used machetes in combat. Up to 72,000 French colonial combatants died serving in the war. The British kept their African troops in Africa, and segregated them. Other British colonial troops were often used in India, Africa, or the Near East, to suppress mutinies and colonial unrest.

Another essential colonial contribution was the labor corps needed to perform noncombat auxiliary tasks such as digging trenches and defense lines, maintaining railways, repairing trucks, burying the dead, and transporting supplies and food to the front. At the start of the war, the existing white labor corps was poorly organized, as there was no precedent for military operations that required large reserves of common laborers ready to move quickly. Plans to increase these auxiliaries were only made after trench warfare began. The French and British relied on colonial porters – human carriers of goods and materials – and laborers, and their dependence on colonial manpower only increased as the war progressed. By the end of the war, the colonial non-combat labor corps numbered in the hundreds of thousands.

War in the Ottoman Empire

Both sets of belligerents had deep interests in the Near East. Prewar oil discoveries in Mesopotamia had made the Ottoman Empire's Arab lands very desirable in the West. The British, for example, wanted to establish a land bridge from Cairo to India to ensure the future of the Anglo-Persian Oil Company. On the other side, the Ottomans nursed a pan-Turkish project to unite all Turkish peoples from East Thrace in Europe to India in Asia. The delicate balance of power that had been achieved in the Near East with the signing of an Anglo-Russian treaty in 1907 was threatened when the Ottoman Empire joined the war in Europe in late October 1914. Two months later, with German help, the Ottomans launched an offensive against the Russians that carried them into the Caucasus Mountains, and then toward northern Persia.

In 1916, the British participated in a series of secret agreements with France, Italy, and Russia to divide Ottoman lands among themselves once the war was won. The most important of the accords was the Sykes-Picot Agreement that the British and French reached in May 1916, with Russia's assent. In this treaty, the two countries agreed

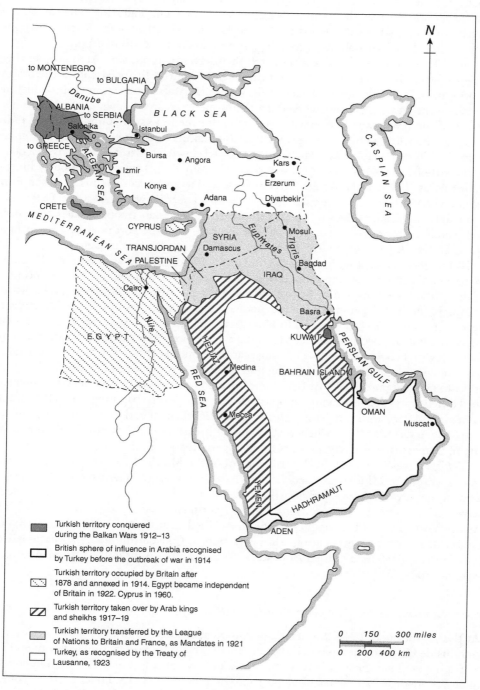

Map 1.4 The Mesopotamian Front in World War I.

that after the war the French would obtain modern-day Syria, Lebanon, and southern Turkey, while the British would gain Iraq, Transjordan, and Palestine. The parties also agreed to support Russia's claims to the Dardanelles in exchange for Russian recognition of French and British interests in the Arab parts of the Ottoman Empire.

Soon thereafter, the British contradicted themselves by promising Arab peoples their independence from the Ottomans and making substantial financial commitments for Arab wars of independence to achieve this. One such Arab insurrection erupted in June 1916, on the western side of the Arabian Peninsula in an area known as the Hejaz. The leader of the revolt was Hussein ibn Ali, who dreamed of establishing a single, independent Arab kingdom made up of all Arab-speaking territories that the Ottomans controlled in the Middle East. The revolt advanced slowly at first, but it received a boost in the fall of 1916 with the arrival of British Captain T. E. Lawrence, famously known in history as "Lawrence of Arabia." Lawrence served as an advisor to Hussein's son Emir Faisal, who led a group of irregular Arab forces in a guerrilla war against the Turks. The Arab fighters pinned down important numbers of Ottoman troops needed elsewhere, and scored an impressive victory in 1917 when they took the port of Aqaba at the head of the Gulf of Aqaba, which divides Arabia from Egypt's Sinai Peninsula.

Britain focused on other issues pertaining to the Middle East as well. By early 1917, the Mesopotamian Front was important enough that the British War Cabinet took over control of its military operations from British officials in India. After revolution engulfed Russia in March, the British promised the Italians and Greeks territories in southern Anatolia to keep them committed to the war. In November 1917, Foreign Secretary Arthur Balfour issued the Balfour Declaration that supported the creation "in Palestine of a national home for the Jewish People" while also claiming that "nothing shall be done which may prejudice the civil and religious rights of existing non-Jewish communities in Palestine."[2] It was an effort to rally support for the British war effort among the Jews in Austria, Germany, and the United States. To seal Zionist support, Britain used Jewish battalions in its Palestinian campaign. After capturing Jerusalem in early 1918, British and French troops marched into Syria in October 1918, where they, along with Arab forces, drove the Turks out of the city of Damascus, effectively ending Ottoman participation in the war.

The road was now open for British control of the Middle East. They deployed their troops across the Middle East and Central Asia as soon as the Germans sued for peace, gaining an advantage over other Allied troops in the region, and positioning themselves to supervise Allied operations. Under British supervision, the Allies moved into Anatolia, opened the Dardanelles to the first Allied fleet on November 12, 1918, and established a military occupation administration in Constantinople. Arab nationalists' hopes in late 1918 for a unified Arab state rising from the ruins of the Ottoman Empire were not to be fulfilled.

Last offensives on the European Fronts, 1918

At the beginning of 1918, the arrival of American troops in Europe and rising disaffection inside Germany necessitated that Germany's military leaders find a way to end the war quickly. Their answer was to unleash a massive attack, known as the Ludendorff offensive, against British defensive positions on March 21, 1918. Ludendorff, the offensive's architect, was convinced that if he could force the British to surrender, the French would soon follow suit. His main target was the southern sector of the British lines – in the old battle area of the Somme. A short but highly intensive artillery barrage preceded the Germans' infantry attack. The Germans drove the surprised British back 7 miles on the first day, but the British lines did not break. By March 26, the Germans had created a wedge in the British positions that was 30 miles deep. Movement like this on the Western Front had not happened since the first weeks of the war. A lack of close cooperation between Haig and Pétain threatened to create a serious gap between the two Allied armies. The crisis prompted British and French leaders to meet on March 26 at the French town of Doullens where they agreed to a Unified High Command for the Western Front under the control of French General Ferdinand Foch. The United States joined this arrangement in April, so that Foch became the head of all Allied forces in the West with the title of supreme allied commander. Foch was known for his optimism, tenacity, and commitment to an offensive strategy. As the German offensive continued in late March, Ludendorff dispersed his troops into three separate actions, dissipating the strength of his forces enough to make a breakthrough impossible. Despite calling off the offensive on April 5, Ludendorff accomplished a brilliant tactical success that won large tracts of land reaching 40 miles deep. Yet he achieved nothing strategically, at a cost of about 250,000 men for each side.

The Germans launched more offensives in the weeks that followed, each less powerful than the March attack. In one of the German assaults (April 9–29), which focused on Flanders and is known as Operation Georgette, German and British tanks engaged in the first tank-to-tank battle in military history. During the Germans' offensive codenamed Operation Blücher (May 27–June 6), American forces launched their first wartime offensive, quickly taking the village of Cantigny, and then fought hard at Chateau-Thierry to help force an official halt to a German advance. The last German strike came in mid-July in what became known as the Second Battle of the Marne; Ludendorff was forced to suspend his offensive on July 18, three days after it began, when Foch unleashed a strong Allied counterattack. The Allies took the momentum away from the Germans on July 18, and they never lost it in the war's final months.

Germany increasingly suffered from morale problems. Prior to the Germans' mid-July offensive, there was a small but steady flow of German deserters who provided their Allied captors with details about the Germans' forthcoming attack. The increasing presence of American troops on the front lines deepened feelings among German troops that victory was no longer achievable. Moreover, while an influenza pandemic struck both sides in the summer, it was especially deadly for the Germans who physically were more vulnerable because of wartime deprivations. Approximately 400,000 German soldiers contracted the flu, and 186,000 of them died from it.

Foch on August 8 launched an offensive along all sectors of the Western Front. By the time the offense ended in early September, the Allies had retaken most of the territory they had lost in the Germans' spring offensives. The next phase of the Allied attacks was a general push all along the front from Ypres to Verdun. The French and Americans began the effort on September 26 with the launching of the Meuse–Argonne offensive. The British followed suit with attacks at other points along the front. The Allied forces kept up relentless pressure on the Germans who retreated grudgingly and slowly, in spite of the surrender of large numbers from their ranks.

Adding to Germany's problems was the defeat of its wartime partners. The Allies attacked the Bulgarians on September 15 and the latter's army collapsed several days later. Bulgaria signed an armistice that took effect on September 30, 1918. The Italian army, reinforced with soldiers from several Allied countries, inflicted a decisive defeat on the Austro-Hungarians at the Battle of Vittorio-Veneto in late October–early November.

The Austro-Hungarian High Command followed by agreeing to an armistice that took effect on November 4. On October 30, the Ottoman Turks signed an armistice that the British dictated to them without consulting their allies.

As Germany's allies collapsed during the fall, the Germans' own military situation became more vulnerable. By the beginning of November, the Allies had cleared most of France of German forces and about one-fifth of Belgium. It was in a charged atmosphere of unrest among German sailors, soldiers, and workers that Germany entered into armistice discussions with Allied military leaders. On September 29, Ludendorff and Hindenburg told Wilhelm II to seek an armistice and to put a new government in place. The new chancellor, the politically moderate Prince Max von Baden, quickly sent Wilson a request for an armistice. He accepted as the basis for the peace negotiations the American president's Fourteen Points, an idealistic set of principles for a peaceful postwar world formulated in January 1918. After lengthy negotiations, Foch at Compiègne on November 8 bluntly presented the German delegation with a set of armistice provisions, and told it that Germany had 72 hours in which to accept them. German and Allied representatives met at Compiègne at 5:00 a.m. on November 11 to sign the armistice that took effect at 11:00 a.m. the same day. More than four years of nightmarish battles and terrifying bloodletting came to an end. The Great War was over.

Conclusion

The human impact of the war from military operations was tremendous. Almost 74 million men were mobilized during the fighting, and 9.4 million of these died or disappeared. Among the dead were 1.376 million Frenchmen, 1.8 million Russians, 908,000 British (including empire and Dominion soldiers), 2.034 million Germans, and 1.1 million Austro-Hungarians. Another 21.2 million soldiers were wounded, with as many as 7 million of the wounded suffering permanent disabilities. The war's unceasing appetite for soldiers made the supply of adequate manpower an urgent priority; for the Allies, this meant that their dependence on colonial troops, laborers, and porters increased throughout the war. For many, the repeated use of soldiers as cannon fodder during the conflict, with the violence that this entailed, eroded the value of human life. War also showed the dependence of the colonial powers on colonial manpower to win the war. While military campaigns were concentrated in Europe, the war had other noteworthy theaters of operations. The fighting in the Middle East, Africa, and elsewhere was an extension of the European fronts, making the war truly global. In military terms alone, World War I was one of the great watershed events of modern European history.

Diplomatic interactions

Europe not only had the military blocs of the Triple Alliance and Triple Entente in the summer of 1914, but also a significant number of neutral states that included Norway, Sweden, Spain, Portugal, the Netherlands, Belgium, Switzerland, and countries situated on the Balkan Peninsula. Once war came, this alignment underwent rapid changes through determined and time-consuming diplomatic negotiations. The Ottoman Empire, whose Arab lands were of interest to several European powers, was the object of intense lobbying well before the war. Despite strenuous Franco-British pressure, the Ottomans sided with the

Central Powers by signing a secret alliance with Germany on August 2, 1914, and engaging Russian troops in combat in October of that year. This reversal forced the Entente Powers (Allies) to open up a Middle Eastern theater of operations that historians now believe prolonged the war by two years.

Jockeying for allies

The two sets of belligerents worked hard to enlist other Balkan countries to their side. The Allies viewed neutral Bulgaria, with its formidable army, as the key to the formation of a Russian-led Balkan League that would also include Serbia and Montenegro. But the Allies failed to persuade the Bulgarians to join their side. Bulgaria remained neutral during the war's first year and then joined the Central Powers when the Allies experienced setbacks fighting the Ottomans at Gallipoli in 1915. The Bulgarians, whose closest trading partners were Austria–Hungary and Turkey, concluded that they would gain more territorially by joining the Central Powers than the Allies. Romania entered the war on the side of the Allies in August 1916, after being promised Austro-Hungarian-controlled Transylvania. A Romanian offensive against Transylvania quickly collapsed, however, when the Germans sent in reinforcements, despite facing major enemy offensives on both the Western and Eastern fronts. Romania's collapse at the end of 1916 forced the British to destroy oil fields in anticipation of their transfer to the Central Powers.

The neutrality of Greece, another Balkan state, was more vexing. The country was divided into two large political factions. Prime Minister Eleftherios Venizelos, a Greek nationalist who favored territorial expansion and supported the Allies, led one faction. On the other side was King Constantine I (r. 1913–1917, 1920–1922) who, as German Emperor Wilhelm II's brother-in-law, harbored pro-German feelings and sought to keep Greece neutral. The King prevented Greece from aiding the Allies in their failed Gallipoli campaign in 1915, and his decision may have cost the Allies a victory there. The Allies forced Constantine's abdication in mid-1917, and Greece, which Venizelos now completely controlled, immediately declared war on the Central Powers.

Another country of considerable interest to both sides was Italy. Technically a member of the Triple Alliance, Italy elected to remain neutral when fighting broke out in 1914. In early 1915, the Italians gave serious attention to joining the Allies when a Russian victory in the Carpathian Winter War seemed imminent. The Allies were eager for Italy's services in the war against Austria–Hungary. Rumors of possible Italian participation in the conflict started a bidding war between the Central Powers and the Allies. On April 26, 1915, France, Britain, Russia, and Italy signed the secret Treaty of London guaranteeing to Italy important territorial gains at the expense of Austria–Hungary along or near the Adriatic Sea once the Allies had secured victory. The Allied powers also promised Italy a protectorate over Albania, parts of Germany's colonial possessions in Africa and Asia, and a portion of the Anatolian peninsula should a partition of Turkey proper eventually occur. Italy declared war on Austria–Hungary shortly thereafter.

Among other uncommitted states, the kingdoms of Norway and Sweden remained steadfast in their neutrality, although Sweden showed sympathy toward Germany and Norway toward Britain. When the Germans increased their submarine warfare in 1917, Sweden and Norway strengthened a policy of cooperation between them that had begun early in the conflict, since Germany's maritime actions created serious problems for both states. The two countries also intensified their work for peace, and they were important in swaying the Allies to establish the League of Nations after the war. Their work on behalf of international peace and disarmament became a landmark policy during the interwar years and assured Scandinavian countries a key role as international peace negotiators.

Early peace proposals

Both the Central Powers and the Allies made efforts to end the war via diplomacy starting in 1915. Whether genuine or not, these undertakings reveal a general weariness with the human and economic costs of the war. After the Belgians valiantly resisted the German invasion of 1914, Germany offered them a separate peace in 1915, trying to enlist President Wilson as an intermediary in the discussions. But the Belgian King refused what amounted to a victor's peace that would have given Germany access to the resources of the Belgian Congo, blamed Britain as the aggressor, and strengthened the Germans' position on the Western Front. Belgium paid a heavy price for its courage, as the Germans exploited its resources and its population starved. In November 1915, the German emperor made an overture to Tsar Nicholas in an effort to bring him to his side, also to no avail. After Austrian Emperor Franz Joseph died in late 1916, his successor, Karl I, appealed to Britain for peace through Wilson. The Allies rejected the proposal because it named Britain as the aggressor. Austria–Hungary's mounting minorities' agitation and demands caused the government to make further overtures for a separate peace, causing increased friction between the Dual Monarchy and Germany. A follow-up diplomatic mission entrusted to Karl's brother-in-law, Prince Sixtus of Bourbon-Parma, offered to create an independent Kingdom of Poland and a Southern Slavic state composed of Serbia, Montenegro, Albania, Bosnia, and Herzegovina. In May 1917, Wilson asked the belligerents to state their war aims as a preliminary to peace negotiations. His mediation efforts were followed by the passage of a peace resolution in the German Reichstag in July and the issuance of a seven-point papal peace plan in August. Even though none of these overtures succeeded, they show that the war was not conducted solely by military means.

German–Russian relations

When the Bolsheviks took power in Russia in early November 1917, Lenin was determined to fulfill a pledge to the Russian people to make peace. He immediately issued a Decree on Peace that called on all belligerent states to end the world war at once. When the Western Allies balked at the idea, Lenin unilaterally signed an armistice with the Germans on December 15, 1917, that went into effect two days later. The Germans and Russians began peace negotiations in the Polish city of Brest-Litovsk on December 22. Leading the Russian delegation was Leon Trotsky, who naively believed that the two sides could reach a peace agreement without annexations or indemnities. The Germans had compiled a list of harsh demands that the stunned Russians refused to accept. Trotsky, in an act of defiance, announced to the Germans in January that the Russians had adopted the formula of "no war, no peace." In other words, the Russians proclaimed that the war was over and that no peace agreement with the Germans would be signed to prove it. Eventually, the Russians, incapable of resuming hostilities, went back to the bargaining table. The Treaty of Brest-Litovsk, signed on March 3, 1918, forced Russia to make significant territorial concessions in the west and to cede Transcaucasia to the Ottoman Empire.

The treaty even gave Romania, then suing the Central Powers for peace, the Russian territories of Bessarabia and northern Bukovina. Russia lost more than 300,000 square miles of territory and 5 million people, one-third of its agricultural production, and 70 percent of its coal and iron ore production. Germany's military success had pried the long stretch from the Baltic Sea to the Black Sea from Russian control, checked Pan-Slavism, and become energy-secure by extorting from Romania in May 1918 a 90-year lease on the Romanian oil fields. The situation changed in the summer of 1918, when Germany, desperate for foodstuffs and war materiel, signed agreements with Russia involving these items. The arrangements exemplify the pragmatic nature of German–Russian relations both then and during the interwar years. It was a case where the two governments set aside ideological differences to advance the national interests of their respective states. Even after the end of the war in November 1918, German armies continued to occupy Russia's ceded lands in the west, in part because Germany could not feed its returning soldiers, but also because the Allies needed the Germans to provide transitional order in Eastern Europe.

Creating an independent Polish state

When World War I began, Poland did not exist as a national state, since Russia, the German Kingdom of Prussia, and Austria had partitioned it out of existence in the late eighteenth century. Since the Russian, German, and Austro-Hungarian empires needed Polish soldiers for their armies in 1914 and beyond, however, the conflict put Poland in a privileged position. To bolster their war effort, Austria–Hungary and Germany in 1916 created an autonomous Kingdom of Poland from territories that the Russians and Austrians had controlled since the late 1700s. The Dual Monarchy also permitted Polish patriot Józef Piłsudski to create a force called the Polish Legions for the war against Russia, and the Germans allowed Polish institutions to reopen, including the University of Warsaw. But there were also Poles who believed that an independent Poland could only be achieved through cooperation with the Allies. Roman Dmowski, a Polish nationalist in exile who had initially backed Russia in the war, looked to the West for support beginning in the summer of 1915. He set up a National Polish Committee in August 1917, and it was this organization that the Allies recognized as the legitimate representative of the Polish people late in the war.

The disintegration of Austria–Hungary

The demands of Austria–Hungary's minorities for self-determination were pivotal in the unraveling of the Dual Monarchy. After Austria–Hungary ceded eastern Galicia to the autonomous Polish state in 1916, the empire slowly disintegrated. Following Franz Joseph's death in December 1916, war weariness took the form of ethnic polarization; the minorities worked through lobbies, governments-in-exile, and immigrant societies to advance their nationalist causes. When the Austrian Parliament met on May 20, 1917, its Czech and South Slav delegates called for a federal state granting equal rights to each of its national groups. By 1918, secessionist feelings were high, and as World War I came to an end, Austria–Hungary broke up into several new or parts of new states: Austria, Hungary, Czechoslovakia, Poland, and the Kingdom of Yugoslavia (Kingdom of Serbs, Croats, and Slovenes).

Conclusion

Wartime diplomatic activities were a complex ballet that became an increasingly flawed and inadequate performance, as seen in the continuation of secret diplomacy. By the fall of 1918, the main phases of the war were over, and the guns fell silent. The war left behind stateless zones on the Eastern Front, demands of Eastern European minorities for statehood, and the collapse of four major empires. A return to the political stability and balance of power of the prewar years was impossible. More importantly, diplomacy as an instrument of peacemaking was challenged since the defeated powers' armies were not demobilized. The Russian Civil War, the presence of many groups waiting for an opportunity to use force to stake their claims in the existing power vacuum, and the volatile state of the Ottoman Empire raised fears of continued fighting. The war, indeed, was far from over in Eastern Europe, the Balkans, and the Near East. It was in this volatile setting that the Allies decided to convene a peace conference. Allied leaders, in recognition of France's sacrifices during the war, agreed on Paris as the site for negotiating a peace settlement. Nevertheless, many felt that the choice of Paris was unwise, because the city was too emotionally charged from its wartime experiences to serve as the proper site for the peace conference.

The Paris Peace Conference and the peace treaties

By the end of the hostilities, the European balance of power had shifted. Gone were the four continental empires that had towered over Europe in the nineteenth century. The peace settlements were dominated by three Western powers: France, Britain, and the United States. It was the first contest of wills of postwar diplomacy.

A charged setting

The Paris Peace Conference convened on January 18, 1919. Nearly 30 countries sent representatives. Lobbyists of all kinds and from all corners of the world came, and a vast array of experts gathered to participate in the birth of a new world order. Freedom, democracy, and peace were on the agenda. It looked as though the wish of American leaders that the conference be an event with universal appeal would be fulfilled.

Woodrow Wilson, David Lloyd George, and Georges Clemenceau – known as the Big Three – dominated the conference negotiations, which soon became a test of wills among them. Wilson approached the negotiations with a moralism and idealism that bordered on the naïve. French Premier Clemenceau brought a healthy dose of realism to the conference table, and he fought first and foremost for French security against future German aggression. Lloyd George, the consummate politician, often served as a mediator between his two quarreling colleagues, although his country was not always flexible on issues either. Unforeseen events cast a pall over the proceedings. A French anarchist shot at Clemenceau's car in February, seriously wounding the French leader, but Clemenceau was once again negotiating just days thereafter. In March, Wilson came down with the Spanish flu and remained in poor health during the remainder of the conference; his weakened health adversely affected his conference leadership.

Wilson expected his Fourteen Points to serve as a guide for the conference negotiations. The first five points expressed general principles that included: open covenants openly arrived at; reductions in national armaments; freedom of the seas in war and peace; the elimination of economic barriers; and an impartial adjustment of colonial claims. Other points dealt with territorial changes following the war, such as the return

Figure 1.4 Allied leaders Vittorio Orlando, David Lloyd George, Georges Clemenceau, and
Woodrow Wilson (left to right) sit together at the Paris Peace Conference in 1919.

of Alsace-Lorraine to France and the creation of an independent Polish state. The principle of self-determination for various ethnic groups permeated several of his points. The last and most important point for Wilson was the creation of an international association of nations to keep the peace.

Wilson's hopes for the application of his idealistic principles ran up against powerful obstacles, however. One was the existence of Allied wartime treaties and agreements that contained promises to aspiring nationalist groups and that involved the parceling out of lands irrespective of the people living on them. Second, European leaders had economic and national security priorities that ran afoul of Wilson's abstractions. The British, for example, scuttled Wilson's point on freedom of the seas well before the conference began. Finally, revolutionary events in Central and Eastern Europe in the spring of 1919 influenced Allied leaders' willingness to compromise the principle of national self-determination to enlarge countries that they saw as barriers to the spread of Russian Communism. For instance, they stretched the frontier of the newly created state of Czechoslovakia eastward to include Ruthenians, who were related ethnically to the Ukrainians to their east.

One of the first issues needing attention was how many treaties to draft for the four defeated powers of Germany, Austria–Hungary, Bulgaria, and the Ottoman Empire. Using national self-determination as its guiding principle, the conference wrote five separate treaties, having divided the old Habsburg Empire into the independent states of Austria and Hungary. Collective security was chosen to safeguard the principle of self-determination, and its enforcement was entrusted to an international body, the League of Nations. The first draft of the Covenant of the League of Nations was ready by mid-February and became Part I of the Treaty of Versailles. It established a permanent consultative system to prevent war, and Article X obligated the signatories to "respect and preserve" the territorial integrity and political independence of all League members.

Heir to the nineteenth-century ideals of arbitration and economic and social justice, the Covenant was a shining example of a humanitarian spirit that stressed pacifism and the welfare of people. Wilson hoped that it would be adopted as the first section of all the peace treaties signed with the defeated countries.

Serious disagreements occurred among the negotiators, reaching the point where there was talk of the conference's imminent demise in April. One major storm erupted over the status of the German Rhineland. Clemenceau insisted on the creation of an independent Rhineland state under French domination. Wilson, on the other hand, saw this as a violation of the conference principle of national self-determination and vehemently opposed Clemenceau's idea. Wilson, Clemenceau, and Lloyd George finally reached a compromise on the issue. The Rhineland would remain a part of Germany, but it would become a demilitarized zone in which the Germans would have no military presence whatsoever. The Allies would maintain an occupation force in the region for 15 years, gradually withdrawing in five-year stages. In addition, the United States and Great Britain promised France treaties of guarantee against future German aggression. The compromise provided the French with a military buffer zone on its eastern frontier without violating Wilson's principle of self-determination.

Another major point of contention among the Allied negotiators was reparations. The British and French initially sought huge reparations sums from Germany to cover their war costs, both military and civilian. The British even insisted on including military pensions in the total. The Americans argued for a much more modest reparations bill. The French eventually moderated their bottom line to the point where they came very close to the American position. The British, however, continued to put forward demands for large reparations amounts even though their country had experienced virtually no physical damage during the war. Two of their key reparations negotiators were nicknamed the "heavenly twins" because of the sky-high sums they sought. In the end, British resistance prevented the Allies from putting a firm reparations total in the peace treaty with Germany. Instead, the Allies set up a Reparation Commission in the German peace treaty to study the question and come up with a final reparations bill by the spring of 1921. The Allies justified their demand for German reparations in Article 231 of the German treaty; known as the "war guilt" clause, the article declared "the responsibility of Germany and her allies for all the loss and damage caused to the Allied countries as a consequence of the war imposed on them by the aggression of Germany and her allies."[3]

A number of powers found themselves on the outs. Smaller states as well as Asian and African peoples had only indirect access to and influence at the conference. In April, the Italian delegation stormed out of the Conference when Italy failed to obtain the fulfilment of promises made in secret wartime treaties. There was no Russian government representation at the conference, and the Allies invited a German delegation to attend only after their own protracted negotiations had essentially ended.

While the conference sat, armed conflicts flared up or resumed from Finland to the Ottoman Empire. Borders changed on an almost daily basis. The situation was particularly dire in East Central Europe where fledgling countries faced refugees, famine, epidemics, environmental desolation, and political and social unrest. This situation put enormous pressure on the peacemakers who scurried to meet emergencies, alleviate frustrations, avoid territorial fragmentation, and blunt the Bolshevik contagion. It was nigh impossible in these conditions to determine fairly how the vanquished should be punished and the victors rewarded, and to sort out the unholy financial trinity of war debts, war loans, and reparations. Virtually every clause of every peace treaty was rife with conflict. Nevertheless, the negotiators remained committed to fashioning a peace that would prevent future wars and make the world safe for democracy.

Disposing of the defeated powers' colonies

Every political group had its own vision of the postwar colonial order, ranging from Wilson and Lenin's advocacy of the abolition of colonialism to imperialist powers' insistence on maintaining and expanding their colonial empires. Wilson wanted a general discussion of the Arab case for independence at the Paris Peace Conference, but it never took place. The British and French, who were determined to expand their rule in the Middle East, found justification for their imperialist aims in what was called the "colonial conscience." Article 22 of the Covenant of the League of Nations discussed territories "inhabited by peoples not yet able to stand by themselves" and the "sacred trust of civilisation" incumbent on advanced societies to help them develop.[4] Article 22 became the basis for a new form of colonialism called the mandate system. The League set up a Permanent Mandates Commission comprised of European states with colonies to oversee the system, but the commission let the developed nations themselves decide how to guide their mandates toward the goal of eventual self-government. In the Middle East, the British gained mandates over Iraq, Transjordan, and Palestine, while the French acquired them for Syria and Lebanon. Japan received mandates for several German-controlled island groups in the Pacific and German holdings in China. Countries that benefited from mandates in Africa included the Union of South Africa, Britain, France, Portugal, Belgium, and Italy. The mandate system bitterly disappointed Arab peoples and caused a deep sense of distrust among them toward Western nations. When an Arab congress declared an independent Syria in 1920 and another did so in Iraq the same year, the French and British governments reacted by sending in soldiers to quash the movements. Arab nationalism did not go away, however, and the British and French either had to use force or play on religious and ethnic divisions to maintain their imperial authority in the region.

The Treaty of Versailles

The Treaty of Versailles was the peace settlement that the Allies arranged for Germany. The German delegation arrived in Versailles on April 29 and was housed in barrack-style quarters surrounded by barbed wire. The Germans received the text of the treaty on May 7 without any prior negotiations. Any exchange of information between the two sides was limited to written notes. When the Germans balked at accepting the treaty, the Allies on June 16 threatened to resume hostilities if they did not agree to its terms within a week. Following a cabinet crisis over the issue, Germany caved in on June 23. News of Germany's acceptance reached Allied leaders at 5:40 p.m., less than 90 minutes before the 7:00 p.m. deadline the Allies had set for compliance. Allied leaders quickly issued orders to Allied Supreme Commander Foch to halt a planned military advance on Germany.

According to the territorial provisions of the treaty, Germany lost 13 percent of its prewar land and 10 percent of its population. The relinquished lands in the west included Alsace-Lorraine to France, the districts of Eupen and Malmedy to Belgium, and northern Schleswig to Denmark. The treaty also granted France the right to use the Saar's coal mines under Allied supervision for 15 years. A Polish Corridor was carved out of German territory in the east to allow Poland access to the Baltic Sea, and the Baltic seaport of Danzig, with its roughly equal mix of Poles and Germans, was designated as a Free City under the supervision of the League of Nations. A plebiscite under League supervision was to determine how to divide Silesia, the industrial German basin of the east, between the Poles and Germans. In addition, Poland received the Posen area that had been in Prussian hands since 1772. The Sudetenland, predominantly German in its population, was granted to Czechoslovakia. The treaty also forbade Germany from forming a political union, or *Anschluss*, with German-speaking Austria; this meant that the two German-speaking nations could not exercise the principle of self-determination. Globally, Germany lost all of its colonies.

The military clauses of the treaty placed strict limits on Germany's armed forces. The army was limited to 100,000 soldiers with conscription prohibited, the navy was reduced to a skeletal force containing no submarines, and no air force was allowed at all. Moreover, there was the demilitarized zone in the Rhineland that prevented Germany from building fortifications or stationing military personnel along its western border with France. Finally, the reparations provisions proved especially vexing to the Germans. Article 231, with its strong moral condemnation of Germany and its allies as the parties responsible for the outbreak of the war, was anathema to the Germans. Since there was no total reparations sum included in the treaty, the Germans were placed at the mercy of the Allies on how much they would ultimately have to pay.

The treaty signing ceremony took place on June 28, 1919, in the Hall of Mirrors at the Palace of Versailles, the same room where the German Second Empire had been proclaimed in 1871. For all its incomplete provisions and flaws – a compromise viewed by some as too harsh to reconcile the Germans to its terms and by others as too lenient to remove the German danger – the Treaty of Versailles was finally an officially signed document. But resentment toward the treaty in Germany was deep and pervasive. Many felt that Wilson, who had promised them peace based on his Fourteen Points, had betrayed them. When he died in 1924, Germany's embassy was alone among the foreign embassies in Washington in refusing to fly its flag at half-staff. Germans referred to the treaty as a "Diktat" or "dictated peace." Right-wing nationalists used the treaty as evidence for their "stab in the back" theory, which was an unfounded claim that Germany had lost the war on the home front through the treacherous actions of republicans who had toppled the monarchy. Germany became a revisionist power, eager to rectify the wrongs that it saw in the treaty's provisions.

There were also expressions of discontent with the peace agreement on the Allied side. China refused to sign the Treaty of Versailles because of the Allies' decision to award the Shantung Peninsula in China to Japan as a mandate. The Chinese signed a separate treaty with Germany in 1921. While America participated in the signing ceremony in June, the United States Senate rejected the treaty in the fall of 1919, arguing that it tied American diplomacy to future European conflicts. The United States eventually signed separate peace treaties with Germany, Austria, and Hungary in August 1921. Wilson's promised treaty of guarantee to the French against German aggression also died in the Senate in late 1919. Using the U.S. rejection of the security treaty as an excuse, the British reneged on their own military vow to the French shortly thereafter. Not surprisingly, the French felt a deep sense of betrayal over the American and British failures to fulfill their security pledges.

The "Little Versailles" treaty

The contradictions between the ideals and realities of national self-determination were revealed when it became clear that mixed populations made clean ethnic borders impossible. To solve the minorities problem, the conference leaders appointed a Committee on

New States to draft a model treaty guaranteeing all peoples total protection of life and freedom regardless of birth, nationality, language, race, or religion under the supervision of the League of Nations. Unable to ready a comprehensive, universal set of provisions, the committee produced a template treaty applicable to Polish and German minorities living in Poland and Germany, and made the document a prerequisite for Poland's territorial settlement and independence. Officials from Germany, Poland, and Allied countries initialed the agreement at Versailles right after the signing ceremony for the Treaty of Versailles.

The treaties with Austria and Bulgaria

Allied peace treaties with other defeated members of the Central Powers undermined the principle of national self-determination in the Balkans, where the Allies helped in the creation of new nations with little understanding of ethnicity or country size. In the Treaty of St. Germain that the shrunken state of Austria signed on September 10, 1919, the Austrians recognized the independence of Hungary, and ceded territories to Czechoslovakia, Poland, Yugoslavia, Romania, and Italy. Austria was formally forbidden to enter into a political union with Germany, and its army was limited to 30,000 soldiers. Bulgaria signed the Treaty of Neuilly-sur-Seine on November 27, 1919. By its terms, the Bulgarians ceded territory to Greece and Yugoslavia and accepted a limit of 20,000 soldiers in their army.

Peace in Hungary

Military actions continued in various parts of the Balkans, as newly created countries moved to define their borders by taking advantage of the breakup of the Austro-Hungarian Empire. Yugoslavia feasted on the defunct empire by sending Serbian forces into lands to the north, northwest, and southwest of Serbia; many of these had been a part of Hungary. In the winter of 1918–1919, Czechoslovakia ordered soldiers along a broad front to advance 50 kilometers into former Hungarian territories, and Romania used soldiers to occupy a substantial portion of the prewar Hungarian region of Transylvania. Almost all the actions of these three states had the support of the French government whose forces comprised most of the Allied presence in Central Europe. The Allies' unsympathetic attitude toward the Hungarians' territorial plight contributed to the fall of a fledgling democratic government in Hungary in March 1919, and the creation of a Communist-led regime under Béla Kun. Kun declared Hungary a soviet republic and began to reorganize the country's army. He temporarily rallied Hungary's military forces against the Czechoslovakians and Romanians during the spring. But the Allies pressured Hungary into withdrawing from territories gained at Czechoslovakia's expense, and Romania launched a major counterattack against the Hungarians in late July. With Romanian soldiers rapidly closing in on Budapest, Kun fled Hungary and eventually reached Russia. On August 3, Romanian forces entered Budapest, where they remained until early 1920.

On the day that Hungary finally signed the Treaty of Trianon with the Allies in June 1920, officially ending its role in World War I, the Hungarian government flew flags at half-mast on public buildings back home. Hungary lost almost three-quarters of its prewar territory and two-thirds of its population; moreover, almost 30 percent of ethnic Hungarians now lived under the rule of Hungary's neighbors.

Romania gained Transylvania, while Czechoslovakia received Slovakia and Ruthenia. Yugoslavia was awarded Croatia and Slavonia. Hungary's army was reduced to 35,000 men. For Hungarians, "Trianon" became a byword for Allied harshness, and the treaty made Hungary a revisionist power in the interwar years.

The Italian–Yugoslav quarrel over Austro-Hungarian lands

There was also a dispute between Italy and the newly created Kingdom of Yugoslavia after the war, as they tried to settle differences over former Austro-Hungarian territories near or along the Adriatic Sea. A part of the problem was that the Allies had promised Austro-Hungarian lands where a majority of people were of Slavic origin, to Italy in the secret Treaty of London of 1915. Consequently, Wilson insisted at the Paris Peace Conference in 1919 that the London treaty be set aside because it violated the principle of national self-determination. This development caused the Italian delegation to make an exit from the Peace Conference in April. The Italians returned several days later to accept what they viewed as an unfair compromise in the Adriatic. Rival territorial claims between Italy and Yugoslavia remained, with the city of Fiume at their center. While the two countries negotiated, an Italian ultra-nationalist poet named Gabriele D'Annunzio led a volunteer force into Fiume in September 1919 and began a 15-month occupation that Italy seemed incapable of shutting down. After Italy and Yugoslavia finally settled their dispute by creating an independent Free State of Fiume in late 1920, the Italian navy drove d'Annunzio out of the city, ending an embarrassing episode for the Italians. But Italy still hoped to rectify what it viewed as the injustices dealt to it during the peace settlement.

Russia estranged

The armistice that the Allies signed with Germany in November 1918 cancelled the Treaty of Brest-Litovsk and other peace agreements that Germany and its allies had signed with countries they had defeated in the war. Yet Russia was denied access to the Paris Peace Conference or to any of the spoils of war; therefore, its borders remained unsettled. In the south, Russia refused to surrender Bessarabia to Romania, causing the Romanians to declare war in November 1918. Ukraine and Belorussia remained caught in the Russian Civil War that erupted in 1918. To relieve some of the pressure from its ongoing civil war, Bolshevik Russia made peace with the Baltic countries of Estonia, Lithuania, Latvia, and Finland by recognizing their independence in 1920.

In newly independent Poland, Piłsudski took a leading role and dreamed of expanding the frontiers and influence of the recently created independent Polish state to include non-Polish ethnic groups in areas of Lithuania and Ukraine that had once been a part of a large eighteenth-century Polish kingdom. In the world of ill-defined frontiers there, Poland declared war on the newly created West Ukrainian People's Republic on November 1, 1918, with the province of Galicia as the center of attention. The Polish–Ukrainian War dragged on well into 1919; the Poles ultimately bested the Ukrainian army and achieved their territorial goal of incorporating most of Galicia into the Polish Republic. The defeated Ukrainian government went into exile at the end of the fighting.

Territorial disputes also led to the outbreak of war between Poland and Soviet Russia. Tensions between them mounted after February 1919. The Poles took control of Vilna in Lithuania in April 1919, and Minsk in Belorussia in August. To settle a territorial dispute between Poland and Russia in the east, the Allied Supreme Council – the key decision-making body in the Paris peace process – in December 1919 drew up a demarcation line between them that largely corresponded with the geographic division of ethnic Poles to the west of the line and Russians to the east. Both sides rejected the proposal and what became known as the Polish–Soviet War broke out in the spring of 1920 when Polish soldiers attacked the Red Army. Piłsudski's forces moved into Kiev, the Ukrainian capital, in May, but a powerful counterattack led by Soviet Western Front Commander Mikhail Tukhachevsky stunned a Polish force in the south and drove it into a major retreat. Farther north, another Russian army pushed from the east and threw the Polish army into a disorderly withdrawal.

In July 1920, with the Soviets in a commanding position militarily, the British government carried the Supreme Council's proposed demarcation line to the Soviets and threatened them with trade sanctions in case of a refusal. The Soviets, believing victory to be at hand, rejected what became known as the Curzon Line, since it was British Foreign Secretary George Curzon who presented the proposal. By the beginning of August, the Russian army in the north approached Warsaw while that in the south threatened the Polish city of Lvov. With defeat imminent, Piłsudski launched a bold, daring counterattack in what became known as the Battle of Warsaw, and the Poles routed the Russians. The battle, called the "Miracle at the Vistula" in Poland, was the decisive event of the war. With their forces in full retreat, the Soviets soon sued for peace. In the Treaty of Riga of March 1921, which officially ended the war, Poland made sizable territorial gains, as its eastern frontier was set at about 155 miles (250 kilometers) to the east of the Curzon line.

A transformed Turkish state

As for the Ottoman Empire, it had to cope with the imperialist claims that several Allies had on its lands as well as an Allied military occupation. The Allies' efforts to achieve their territorial ambitions culminated in the Treaty of Sèvres that the impotent Ottoman government signed in August 1920 to end its role in World War I. It was the harshest of all the peace agreements that the defeated Central Powers signed. The document demilitarized and internationalized the Dardanelles Straits, limited the size of the Turkish army to 50,000 men, allowed no air force, and sanctioned only a minimal naval fleet. Territorially, the treaty's provisions reduced Turkey's borders essentially to the Anatolian peninsula, and even there the Turks lost territory to the newly created state of Armenia in the east. The treaty's provisions also carved large parts of the peninsula into foreign spheres of influence and called for the transfer of important parts of the Ottoman Empire to France, Britain, Italy, and Greece. There was serious fallout from the actions of the British and French in the Middle East. The inclusion of the Balfour Declaration's (see p. 26) promise of a Jewish homeland in Palestine in the Treaty of Sèvres raised anger throughout the Arab world, caused riots in Palestine, and contributed to Turkey's refusal to ratify it.

In the case of the Greeks, they had already taken steps in 1919 to realize their dreams of a new Hellenic Empire in Asia Minor. They occupied the western Anatolian seaport town of Smyrna and the surrounding area in May 1919, and immediately began a military buildup in the region in anticipation of staying there and even sending Greek troops inland. At Sèvres, the Greeks' control over Smyrna was confirmed. Greece also received Eastern Thrace in Europe, and two Aegean islands that commanded the Dardanelles.

The heavy-handed actions of the Allies against the Ottoman Empire after 1918 sparked a wave of Turkish nationalism that found its champion in Mustafa Kemal, surnamed Atatürk, who was a Turkish war hero and fervent nationalist. Kemal, viewed as the father of modern Turkey, launched a reorganization of the Turkish army and set up an alternate Turkish government to that of the sultan in April 1920; its capital was the central Anatolian city of Ankara. Kemal denounced the Sèvres treaty and launched a military campaign against its implementation. Among those his forces moved against were the Greeks. In June 1920, Greek troops began pushing into the Turkish interior. By mid-1921, a Greek force of 200,000 men had reached a point 400 miles from Smyrna, and they were zeroing in on Ankara. The Turks stopped them short of the capital, however, and the Greeks retreated back to positions they had held earlier in the summer. After a military stalemate of several months, the Turks in August 1922 launched a massive offensive, the climax of which was the recapture of the city of Smyrna on September 9. The Turkish success was so complete that the Greeks no longer had any forces in Anatolia by mid-September. In light of the new situation in Turkey, the Allies convened a new peace conference in Lausanne, Switzerland, in November 1922, and the Turks participated as equals. It was during these peace talks that Greece and Turkey independently reached a population exchange agreement in January 1923. By its terms, 1.5 million Greeks were uprooted from Turkey for resettlement in Greece, and 500,000 Turks were expelled from Greece. The conference negotiations led to the Treaty of Lausanne that the participants signed in July 1923. The treaty established the boundaries of the modern, secular republic of Turkey, which regained all European and Anatolian territory lost to the Greeks in the Treaty of Sèvres and territory once designated for the short-lived Republic of Armenia that collapsed in late 1920 after failed wars against the Turks and Russians. The success of the Turks in challenging an imperialist peace settlement by force of arms inspired peoples living under colonial or semi-colonial rule elsewhere. Even if they lost their Arab lands in the Middle East, however, the Turks checked British ambitions in the eastern Mediterranean Sea during the remainder of the 1920s.

Inter-Allied debts and reparations

The issue of reparations was inseparable from Allied war debts and Allied loans, although few saw or even accepted this at the Paris Peace Conference. To finance the war, Russia and smaller European powers had borrowed extensively from the French and British, who in turn had borrowed from the United States. At war's end, the international financial and trade systems as well as many national economies were in shambles. National debts skyrocketed. Rolling stock and merchant fleets were destroyed. Wartime controls had replaced free trade. Allied countries big and small owed the United States a gigantic $10 billion. Loans cascaded from the United States to France and Britain, then to the smaller Allied powers, creating a maze of interconnected obligations. Russia owed debts from the tsarist era to the French, British, Belgians, and Germans, and every major European nation was cash-strapped. Besides the Treaty of Versailles, the Allies incorporated an obligation to pay reparations into the peace treaties signed with Austria, Hungary, the Ottoman Empire, and Bulgaria; outside of Bulgaria, however, no specific amount was established. Austria and Hungary's postwar economies were so weak that neither country ever paid any reparations. In the case of Turkey, reparations were waived in the Treaty of Lausanne in 1923. John Maynard Keynes, a British economist who represented the British Treasury at the Paris Peace Conference, argued that the reparations portion of the Treaty of Versailles was impractical and immoral, and that reparations, war debts, and Allied loans should be forgiven so that the financial system could start afresh. But the Allies were intractable: the British and French would not make major concessions on German reparations; the United States was unwilling to forgive Allied war debts; and the French and British were unwilling to forgive tsarist and provisional government debts in Russia, even while the Bolsheviks refused to acknowledge any responsibility for paying them. Financial hardship would impose financial inflexibility as long as the arrears were not cleared. After leaving the conference in frustration, Keynes correctly warned in *The Economic Consequences of the Peace* (1919) that a combination of punitive reparations and the territorial fragmentation would lead Europe to the abyss.

Conclusion

Overcome by the magnitude of the peace settlements, the Allied diplomats left several issues unfinished, relying heavily on the League of Nations to tidy up borders, finances, and disarmament. One such key issue was the unrequited French request of an Anglo-American guarantee of its borders in exchange for relinquishing France's hopes of a French-dominated independent Rhineland state. To make newly established governments abide by their wishes, the Allies interfered in their internal affairs. Thus, they forbade the Hungarian monarch from returning to power and prohibited Austria from uniting with Germany in order to limit German-Habsburg influence in the Danube River basin and Balkans. Yet these prohibitions had mixed effects. Former Habsburg Emperor Karl tried to claim the throne of Hungary in March 1921, and only a vote of the National Assembly forced him back into exile. Austria and Germany, meanwhile, flirted with a customs union throughout the interwar years. Moreover, the military limitations on Germany, Hungary, Austria, and Bulgaria left dangerous weaknesses in the heart of Europe. The Allied peacemakers also established two sets of powers in East Central Europe. Among the winners were Yugoslavia, Romania, and Poland. They, along with Finland, Latvia, Estonia, Lithuania, and Czechoslovakia, formed a cordon sanitaire of Allied-friendly states to protect the West from Communist/Bolshevik Russia. Among the revisionist states were Germany, Austria, Hungary, and Bulgaria. Eastern Europe was fragmented. Indeed the Versailles settlement created an incomplete peace.

Overall conclusion

World War I mobilized close to 74 million soldiers, and resulted in the deaths or disappearance of some 9.4 million men. Eight million horses perished in the conflict, as did millions of mules, donkeys, and dogs. As a result of the war, the borders of Europe changed considerably. Europe's center of gravity shifted eastwards, but the attitudes of many Europeans did not follow suit: large numbers of Western Europeans still considered Eastern Europe as unequal, the region's main value being that of a buffer against Communist/Bolshevik Russia. The difficulties of the new political geography that the Versailles settlement created bore the seeds of future conflicts. Borders were moved to fit local populations, creating chaos and unrest for several years. The West's treatment of the Ottoman Empire, from the conflict's Mesopotamian Front to the wartime secret treaties to the postwar dismemberment of its lands, revealed the large scale of French and British neocolonial ambitions. The peace was imperfect at best. There was no family of nations, and no completely satisfactory postwar international system either, in part because the United States, Russia, and Germany were absent from the League of Nations when it began its operations.

While the battlefronts were decisive to the war's outcome, the Great War showed the importance of other dimensions to the conflict such as diplomatic warfare and economic mobilization. Because of its global dimension, the conflagration blurred the distinction between the battlefield and the home front by inextricably linking military, diplomatic, and economic victory to psychological warfare, terror against civilians, and civil war. The unprecedented global movement of persons, animals, and goods during the war changed nations' ways of doing business, and had a profound impact on postwar Europe. These developments earned the Great War the name of "total war," and caused it to be remembered as a watershed event that dramatically transformed warfare in modern times.

Notes

1 Eric Born Brose, *A History of the Great War: World War One and the International Crisis of the Early Twentieth Century* (New York: Oxford University Press, 2010), 313.
2 This Day in History, "The Balfour Declaration, 1917," www.history.com/this-day-in-history/the-balfour-declaration (accessed July 15, 2015).
3 Philip Mason Burnett, ed., *Reparation at the Paris Peace Conference from the Standpoint of the American Delegation* (1940; repr., New York: Octagon Press, 1965), 1:142.
4 Martin Housden, *The League of Nations and the Organization of Peace* (Harlow: Pearson, 2012), 119.

Suggestions for further reading

Brose, Eric Dorn. *A History of the Great War: World War One and the International Crisis of the Early Twentieth Century.* New York: Oxford University Press. 2010.
Clark, Christopher. *The Sleepwalkers: How Europe Went to War in 1914.* New York: HarperCollins. 2012.
Ferguson, Niall. *The Pity of War: Explaining World War I.* New York: Basic Books. 1999.
Fischer, Fritz. *Germany's Aims in the First World War.* Trans. C. A. Macartney. New York: W. W. Norton. 1967.
Herwig, Holger. *The Marne, 1914: The Opening of World War I and the Battle That Changed the World.* New York: Random House. 2009.
Jankowski, Paul. *Verdun: The Longest Battle of the Great War.* New York: Oxford University Press. 2014.
Lincoln, W. Bruce. *Passage through Armageddon: The Russians in War and Revolution, 1914–1918.* New York: Simon & Schuster. 1986.
MacMillan, Margaret. *Paris 1919: Six Months That Changed the World.* New York: Random House. 2003.
McMeekin, Sean. *The Ottoman Endgame: War, Revolution, and the Making of the Modern Middle East, 1908–1923.* New York: Penguin Books. 2015.
Morrow, John. *The Great War: An Imperial History.* London: Routledge. 2004.
Prior, Robin and Trevor Wilson. *The Somme.* New Haven, CT: Yale University Press. 2005.
Strahan, Hew, ed. *The Oxford Illustrated History of the First World War.* New edn. Oxford: Oxford University Press. 2014.

2 The home fronts, 1914–1918

Introduction

The emergence of total war fundamentally altered economies, politics, ideologies, and the lives of the people on the home front. Diplomatic and military developments echoed at home, not just in the way of military bulletins and casualty lists, but in countless new rules affecting the distribution of food and fuel, industrial output, patriotic songs, propaganda, charitable work in support of the soldiers, rents, schooling, and labor relations, to mention just a few. Individuals who followed politics closely could infer much from the news about the enlargement of national wartime systems: the centralization of economic life, increased government intervention in people's lives, the introduction of modern industrial techniques, participation in new mechanisms for international cooperation, and the suspension of normal political procedures. The war transformed numerous areas of life among the civilian populations of Europe.

War needs dictated and changed domestic policies, because the home front was essential to the success of military operations in the new age of total war. Similar conditions and developments occurred across the belligerent countries, occupied territories, and colonies, where the retooling of the economies to support the war effort resulted in profound social and labor changes. Countless numbers of people went hungry and suffered from the cold, work patterns changed, families became separated, women went to work, cultural patterns were modified, and the schooling of children was transformed. Under such conditions, socialist thought began to challenge the dominant ideologies of nationalism and patriotism. By 1917, labor unrest and soldiers' mutinies constituted enough of a threat to political stability and the pursuit of the war to warrant varying degrees of political change from relaxed labor contracts to war cabinets and revolution.

Wartime economies

When World War I erupted in the summer of 1914, the consensus among leaders of all belligerent countries was that the conflict would be short. Millions of men left their everyday occupations to march off to battle, and economic activity in the warring states largely stopped. The expectation was that once the brief interruption of the war had ended, normal economic routines would quickly resume without peril to the general welfare of the country. Following the First Battle of the Marne in September 1914 and the ensuing "race to the sea," however, both the German-dominated Central Powers and the Allies (Entente Powers) concluded that the conflict would not end anytime soon. Suddenly, the home front became a major focal point, especially since the war effort had already consumed the bulk of the participants' munitions. During the fall of 1914, government leaders in both alliance systems began to organize their countries for the production of war materiel. Their decisions launched economic mobilization efforts across Europe. As the conflict dragged on, state intervention intensified, and by war's end, governments were involved in virtually all aspects of their countries' economies.

The economic policy of the Central Powers

In Germany, Walther Rathenau, a highly successful entrepreneur in the electrical industry and a first-generation technocrat, took the lead in organizing the home front for war. In response to an Allied naval blockade of Germany, Rathenau used political connections in the first days of the war to gain access to War Minister Erich von Falkenhayn with whom he discussed a centralized system for the allocation of raw materials. Thus, it was in the German private sector that the idea of government controls over raw materials originated. On August 13, Rathenau established a government-run Department of War Raw Materials that exercised supervisory and administrative responsibilities in close collaboration with the private sector. His department oversaw the establishment of 25 private procurement agencies, each of which handled a specific commodity. The agencies were known as War Raw Materials Corporations, and each one had the responsibility of purchasing raw materials and allocating them to war manufacturers on the basis of efficiency of production and needed products. But Germany's initial superiority over the Allies in armaments production gradually slipped away in 1915, even though its own output continued to improve.

It was only in the late summer of 1916, in the wake of Germany's huge outlays of materials during its offensive actions at Verdun and defensive measures along the Somme, that Germany woke up to the need for a major shift in its armaments program. At the end of August, the new military leadership of Hindenburg and Ludendorff introduced a proposal that called for dramatic increases in the production of arms and munitions in a very brief time span. A key feature of what became known as the Hindenburg Program was the creation in November 1916 of a new War Bureau at the Ministry of War to coordinate the activities of relevant ministerial departments – such as the War Raw Materials Department – with greater efficiency as the expected outcome. Another part of the program called for the full mobilization of labor in the country. To realize this, the government in December 1916, enacted the Patriotic Auxiliary Service Law that made all German men between the ages of 17 and 60 not serving in the armed forces subject to compulsory civilian service. The responsibility for implementing the Hindenburg Program was given to General Wilhelm Groener, a technocratic-minded officer who was viewed as one of the most talented members of the German General Staff. He worked tirelessly to mobilize his country's economic resources to tip the balance of the war in Germany's favor.

The Germans faced critical problems as they moved forward with the Hindenburg Program. The transportation system, already strained before the program's implementation, buckled under the weight of the plan's new demands. The transportation crisis contributed to a coal shortage that caused production interruptions at factories. A scarcity of metals compelled the government to call for a "mobilization of metal"; this led to the meltdown of numerous items, including church bells, door handles, statues, and copper brewery and distillery equipment. The unavailability of labor on the home front, in spite of the Auxiliary Service Law of December 1916, resulted in factory employees working longer hours and the Supreme Army Command recalling large numbers of workers from military duty. Serious food shortages during the harsh winter of 1916–1917 contributed to a wave of strikes in the first months of 1917. In July 1917, Groener tried to rein in excessive heavy industry profits by recommending government restrictions on them. This action angered industrial leaders, and their opposition to Groener, along with his inability to fulfill some of the ambitious demands of the Hindenburg Program, led to his dismissal in August 1917. The Supreme Army Command introduced another set of proposals for total economic mobilization in June 1918, in an effort to redress the situation in the war. But military and civil officials overseeing the war economy were quick to point out that everything possible was already being done at home to support the war economically and that any further reorganization was pointless. In spite of such realistic assessments, the Supreme Army Command and leading heavy industrialists continued to pursue utopian plans right up to November 1918.

The only other Central Power that had a domestic armaments industry was Austria–Hungary. Once the war began, military officials, as laid out in the War Production Law of 1912, assumed control over areas of the economy considered essential to the war effort, including the commandeering of munitions production. In December 1914, the Austro-Hungarian government also adopted a system of raw materials distribution similar to that of Germany. The Dual Monarchy had a state-owned arsenal in Vienna and a well-established private armaments industry; one of the main private firms was the Skoda Works that in 1917 had some 35,000 employees at its central facility in Bohemia. Armaments production in the empire peaked in 1917; monthly shell production in the first half of that year, for example, hit 1.476 million as compared to 375,000 in 1914. But the Austro-Hungarians encountered serious general shortages in the latter stages of the conflict, and these took precedence over other considerations. As a result, the Austro-Hungarian average monthly output of munitions and weapons was less in 1918 than in 1914, and the monarchy's soldiers were ill-equipped, ill-clothed, and ill-fed.

The economic policy of the Allies

On the Allied side, the French began to mobilize economically in September 1914, after the French High Command – the GQG – submitted requests for artillery shells that far outstripped the ability of the state-operated munitions plants to produce them. France was particularly challenged because it lost a vital segment of its heavy industry and coal mines when the Germans occupied the northeastern corner of France during the execution of the Schlieffen Plan. At a meeting held on September 20, French War Minister Alexandre Millerand and leading industrialists laid the foundations for French munitions production during the war. They divided private munitions factories into regions, each of which had an industrial "group chief" who was responsible for assigning received munitions orders among production plants in his geographical area. This decision enabled the private sector to develop its own munitions manufacturing network that functioned apart from the government. Millerand held weekly meetings with industrial representatives to discuss the progress of their munitions efforts.

A key player in the war ministry's work to advance industrial mobilization in France was Socialist Party member Albert Thomas, a one-time history teacher and pre-war pacifist. Brought into the war ministry in 1914, Thomas initially sought workers and workshops for munitions manufacture. As war production expanded, Thomas's responsibilities increased to the point where his department was transformed into an Undersecretariat of State for Artillery and Munitions within the war ministry in the late spring of 1915. Thomas' undersecretariat found itself under pressure in 1916 after the Germans demonstrated the superior quality and greater numbers of heavy artillery that they had vis-à-vis the French at the Battle of Verdun. The French adoption of an ambitious program for the fabrication of heavy artillery guns paved the way for a highly successful private munitions manufacturer and first-generation technocrat named Louis Loucheur to become an undersecretary at Thomas' newly created Ministry of Armaments in December 1916. Loucheur's chief initial task was to oversee the development of France's heavy artillery production. The creation of the armaments ministry marked a new stage in the rapid growth of French munitions output and reflected the expanding role of the government in the country's economy.

The pattern of increasing French government intervention in the economy continued in 1917 and 1918. In March 1917, in reaction to the German campaign of unrestricted submarine warfare, the government prohibited imports except with their approval. It also commandeered the French merchant fleet and imposed controls on foreign exchange. The French Ministry of Commerce, taking advantage of the import prohibition, established consortiums – or single purchasing agents – for key raw materials and bound relevant manufacturers and importers together for each item. By the beginning of 1918, the government had set up consortiums for virtually all critical raw materials and numerous manufactured items. After Loucheur's appointment as armaments minister in September 1917, his ministry, which already had numerous responsibilities in the areas of manufacture, supply, and manpower, saw its activities expand to include the administration of an ambitious aviation program. In 1918, his ministry presided over a production network of more than 1.5 million people. By war's end, the French government was engaged in the country's economic life on a massive scale.

The British, like the French, found themselves unprepared for a war of long duration in the fall of 1914. As Britain's army grew and its consumption of munitions far exceeded supply, the country scrambled to increase output. The government's initial response was to hand out munitions and arms contracts to private manufacturers with reckless abandon, but British munitions makers, having just experienced a long period of government parsimony, were in no position to increase production levels swiftly. Even though the government by the end of 1914 had given out contracts to domestic and foreign producers totaling about 10 million artillery shells, only a half million had actually been produced. A similar pattern existed for other military supplies and hardware.

The creation of a Ministry of Munitions in May 1915, with the energetic David Lloyd George at the helm, represented the beginning of close collaboration between the government and private industry. In contrast to other government departments, Lloyd George made the ministry into what he called a "businessman's organization" by filling key administrative positions with captains of industry. When it came to determining production targets, Lloyd George violated normal procedures by going around the War Office and directly asking commanders in the field about their projected requirements. As a result, his ministry handed out orders for substantially larger quantities of war materials than what the War Office had in place. The ministry also expanded significantly the number of state munitions factories and embraced the establishment of many new private munitions plants. The growth efforts allowed the government to rein in costs and even to impose fixed prices. During Lloyd George's time at the Ministry of Munitions (May 1915–June 1916), armaments production experienced an enormous increase. Lloyd George's initiatives marked the end of business as usual in the government's approach to armaments production.

Figure 2.1 Female workers in a munitions factory in Nottingham, England, move 6-inch howitzer shells in 1917.

By late 1916, it was apparent that Britain would need to intensify government controls over the economy, since serious strains were emerging in a number of areas such as skilled labor, steel, coal, and foodstuffs. The Germans compounded the problem in early 1917 by greatly enlarging their economic war against the Allies with the inauguration of unrestricted submarine warfare. An expansion of state controls had taken place under the wartime coalition government of Herbert Asquith, but these had occurred in a piecemeal fashion, with no real plan or strategy in place to guide decision making. The feeling of governmental drift ended when Lloyd George became prime minister in early December 1916. He immediately began a series of dramatic and decisive actions to reinvigorate the war effort. He created four new ministerial posts, including one for shipping and another for food, and, just as he had done at the munitions ministry, he brought in industrial leaders to assist him.

A key component in Lloyd George's efforts was a considerable expansion of Britain's economic mobilization, with an emphasis on results. To head the new Ministry of Shipping, he chose a highly successful shipbuilder from Glasgow. Lloyd George was confident that this choice, combined with patriotic exhortations and cost-plus contracts for shipbuilders, would lead to a boost in ship production. The 1917 shipbuilding results demonstrated the success of his approach as British shipyards churned out more than 1 million tons of new shipping for the merchant fleet. In February 1917, the government assumed control of all British coal mines, and to help end a miners' strike in the fall of that year, Lloyd George – at least in theory – even nationalized the industry. He also used patriotic appeals to get miners to extract ever greater amounts of coal.

Overall, Lloyd George demonstrated a remarkable gift for wartime leadership and a tremendous ability to organize the home front for total war.

With regard to Russia, the outbreak of the war caught the empire with its industrial base still in an early stage of development. The Russians quickly proved to have an inefficient wartime economy. Before the war, the government, fearful of the emergence of private munitions monopolies that would force up prices, had a state-run armaments enterprise that it gave preference to over private manufacturers. Only in 1913 did the Russian attitude toward the formation of private industrial groupings begin to soften. During the war's first year, government policy was essentially non-existent in the area of armaments output. In the absence of government controls, exorbitant prices and corruptly gained contracts among private producers were the order of the day. Bureaucratic rivalries created ordering problems for munitions once the war started, and lingering distrust between tsarist officials and private munitions makers prevented a close partnership between the two entities. The bulk of munitions and arms production remained concentrated in St. Petersburg (Petrograd). In addition, Russia's inadequate railroad system was incapable of meeting the demands of industrial mobilization. Since the government did little to promote increases in arms production and the armaments manufacturing sector was small, the Russian military soon faced weapons and munitions shortages of all kinds.

Following battlefield setbacks in the spring of 1915, efforts to alter Russia's war production arrangement emerged. One was a private sector initiative that in June led to the creation of private, regional War Industries Committees to mobilize unused production capacity. A central War Industries Committee was set up in Petrograd to coordinate private-sector production in cooperation with the regional committees. On June 26, 1915, the Tsar appointed General Alexei A. Polivanov, an able administrator, as minister of war. Polivanov shifted course from his predecessor by insisting that the needs at the front had to determine supply and by cultivating better relations with the armaments industry. Under Polivanov's direction, Russia experienced a revitalization of its armaments effort during the winter of 1915–1916. The production of 3-inch shells, for example, went from a monthly total of 852,000 in July 1915, to 1.512 million in November 1915, where it roughly remained until May 1916, when it again shot up dramatically. On the other hand, the Russians continued to lag in the manufacture of rifles and heavy artillery. In early 1917, they still had only half as many heavy guns deployed on the Eastern Front as the Central Powers. Some areas of armaments manufacture – machine guns being one – continued to grow in the revolutionary year of 1917, but munitions production in general declined.

Colonial riches

In 1914, large parts of the world felt the presence of Europe. The British Empire extended over 12 million square miles, 24 percent of the world's land mass, and included: the Dominions of Newfoundland, Canada, Australia, New Zealand, and the Union of South Africa; the Indian sub-continent; and large stretches of southeast Asia, Africa, and the West Indies. Russia, with her immense possessions in Poland, the Caucasus, Central Asia, and Siberia ranked second. France, with the third largest empire, oversaw close to 5 million square miles – 9 percent of the world's land mass – consisting of Indochina, and much of North, Central, and West Africa. Germany, albeit a latecomer, had possessions in Africa and the South Pacific as well as interests in China. Italy, another late entry into imperialistic ventures, by 1914 controlled Eritrea and Somaliland in East Africa, Libya in North Africa, and the Dodecanese Islands off the coast of Turkey. Belgium, the Netherlands, and Portugal were small nations with big overseas empires in Africa and Southeast Asia. Spain had possessions in Morocco and the Caribbean, as well as Africa's smallest country, Spanish Equatorial Guinea. The Danes managed Greenland and Iceland. Across the globe, Western culture, language, and technology were dominant.

Colonial domination in the pre-1914 era had become burdensome, however. The increasingly visible devaluation of non-white cultures and the inhumanity of imperial rule caused nationalist unrest and forced modest political concessions from Nigeria to India. Forced taxation, cultivation, and labor were the norm; individuals lived in appalling conditions, often in camps. British and French rule fell short of their ideals and reinforced inequalities between the colonies and the home country, and within the colonies themselves. By 1914, the destinies of Europe and the world had become fused by large population migrations, global economic exchanges, and geopolitical rivalries. Increasingly the European core merged with its periphery. Europe stretched to the Balkans, Suez, Istanbul, and North Africa. Farther away, Europe's inroads into the Ottoman and Chinese empires unleashed a contest for the riches of Eurasia that spread to the Balkans in 1911, as the European powers encouraged destabilization in the Ottomans' European possessions. The storm that the Europeans unleashed then made the colonies indispensable to their masters.

Colonial contributions

Once war came in the summer of 1914, the empires of the European belligerents became important sources of manpower and economic support. The British Dominions were legally bound to enter the war on the side of Britain, and the leaders of Newfoundland, Canada, Australia, and New Zealand took their countries into the conflict without hesitation. In the case of the Dominion of South Africa, the government's decision to support Britain by launching an invasion of the neighboring German colony of Southwest Africa triggered a rebellion in the Dutch-descended white Afrikaner community against the regime, beginning in October 1914. The rebels were defeated by January 1915, but the revolt delayed South Africa's invasion of its neighboring German-controlled colony.

The recruitment of colonial soldiers relied on the enlistment of volunteers and the use of conscription systems. The French accepted coercion as a necessary component in their recruiting methods, with colonial officials even using imprisonment, fines, hostage-taking, and other forms of intimidation to force compliance with their recruitment demands. The French and the British recruited among mostly non-educated rural populations that were believed to be the most loyal to the colonial authorities, and the least open to independence ideas. One of France's most successful colonial recruitment efforts occurred in 1918, when Premier Georges Clemenceau sent Blaise Diagne, a black African French parliamentary deputy from Senegal, to lead a campaign to sign up volunteers across French West Africa. Biagne's effort brought in 63,000 recruits by the time it ended in August, far more than the government had ordered. Many of the enlistees signed up because they saw Biagne as one of their own, and because he promised that in return for military service, France would eventually grant them expanded rights, even the possibility of French citizenship for distinguished military service.

Initially, the sacrifices made by the colonies disrupted their economies and led to unrest. Conscription, heavy taxes, and food and cattle requisitions caused considerable suffering among rural populations in Africa, India, and Palestine. Farms were left untended; with the countryside disordered, famine, disease, and destruction spread. The departure of European administrators, merchants, and soldiers created opportunities for sporadic outbreaks of violence that could escalate into full scale revolts, creating significant distractions for the French and the British. One major armed disruption was the Volta-Bani War in French West Africa. Reacting against a French campaign to recruit colonial soldiers in the region, tribesmen fought an anti-colonial war against the French in 1915–1916. At the peak of the fighting, the rebels had 15,000–20,000 men in their ranks. The French ultimately prevailed, but only after putting a colonial force of 5,000 men into the fray.

The Allied colonial powers relied heavily during the war on their empires' vast economic resources, from raw materials and food to war bonds and loans. India made a substantial financial contribution, and provided minerals, cotton, jute, military hardware, and animals for the war. Canada became an important source for munitions, raw materials, and foodstuffs, with grain and meat being its largest export commodities. The riches of the Belgian Congo, which produced 10 percent of the world's rubber in 1914, helped relieve the wartime sufferings of Belgium's civilian population. For some colonies, the war created an economic boom because of an increased global demand for their foodstuffs and raw materials. Infrastructure building, industrialization, and urbanization developed rapidly in places such as India and Nigeria, resulting in a large new urban working class whose living conditions were generally dismal. As the war progressed, these conditions, along with continued conscription and various forms of oppression, led to demands for systemic change. Colonial wartime contributions encouraged varying levels of indigenous nationalism. Colonial workers educated in class struggle as well as Western-educated students, lawyers, and journalists contemplated independence. The age of urban politics had arrived, and the war brought about the first sense of national awareness in many colonies in a "bloody baptism under fire." Imbued with a new sense of confidence and world awareness, colonial soldiers fought on Europe's battlefields while condemning atrocities at home. By the war's end, the prestige of the colonial rulers had considerably diminished, and the expectations of colonial populations for greater self-rule had risen, leading to postwar unrest in several places, most notably in India.

Economic impact of the war: mobilization, inter-Allied cooperation, and dislocation

World War I had a profound effect on the economies of countries throughout the world. The unprecedented demands from the war front compelled belligerent states to begin organizing their economies almost immediately, slowly at first, but at an ever increasing tempo as the struggle stalemated, intensified, and broadened. The strength of a country's industrial base and the effectiveness of that state's mobilization of economic resources became critical factors both to sustaining the conflict and determining its outcome. The depth of many states' management of their economies had no historical parallel, and some leaders saw in state economic intervention the dawn of a new era that would carry forward during peacetime. A new level of economic cooperation among the Allied powers was reached with the formation and development of the Allied Maritime Transport Council, which coordinated the pooled merchant fleets of the French, British, Italians, and Americans in the shipment of agreed-upon priority items.

Some hoped to strengthen the spirit of international cooperation after the war through the Maritime Transport Council's successor, the Supreme Economic Council.

On the other hand, the demands of the war put tremendous stress on European countries' means of production at home and disrupted traditional trade patterns. In the area of coal production, for instance, the British had worn-out, outmoded equipment by the war's end, and the resulting inefficiency caused high extraction costs and a lack of competitiveness on international markets. The French faced a special problem in that the Germans, albeit aware of their imminent defeat in 1918, engaged in the intentional destruction of French coal mines as they retreated in the conflict's final weeks from areas of northeastern France that they had occupied since 1914. The fighting on the Western Front also laid waste to large swaths of French farmland, and restoring these lands to productivity would involve considerable financial, human, and industrial resources. Because major belligerent powers in Europe emphasized armaments manufacture during the war, they largely neglected peacetime products. Partly owing to this, but also owing to their need for goods from abroad to support the war effort, Britain, France, Italy, and Germany imported far more than they exported, turning their traditional trade patterns topsy-turvy. In Russia's case, the war contributed not only to economic disorder, but also to its 1917 revolution and ensuing civil war. Neutral countries helped fill the void.

The cost of the war

At another level, the European powers spent enormous sums to finance the war. The chief beneficiary of this was the United States, which moved from the status of a debtor nation when the war broke out in 1914 to that of a powerful creditor nation by the time it entered the conflict in 1917. Even Britain, long viewed as the banker for its wartime partners, resorted to borrowing from the United States. By the end of the war, the British owed the U.S. close to $3.7 billion. As for the total cost of the war, a study done by the Carnegie Endowment for International Peace, published in 1920, pegged the direct cost at $186 billion. The same study claimed that the war's indirect expenses – including international trade lost, peacetime profits never made, the value placed on people killed, and other factors – added $151 billion to the bill. At the time, the total of almost $337 billion as the cost for the war was astronomical. Such a total was at best imprecise, in part because it incorporated intangibles that necessitated value judgments in its calculations. It was therefore subject to criticism and challenges. Nevertheless, it did give some quantitative perspective to the enormity of the financial burden that Europe incurred as a result of World War I.

Conclusion

The financial burdens of the conflict set many European economies back at war's end. Economically speaking, World War I created a major challenge for all European combatants that was exacerbated by the collapse of four major empires: Germany, Austria–Hungary, Russia, and the Ottoman Empire. More importantly, the war created a double economic dependency for the European Allies, namely on their colonies and on inter-Allied cooperation and American loans. The growth of transnational trade mechanisms also altered the mechanisms of international exchanges as well as the domestic organization of economies. Political life during the war reflected these pressures.

Wartime politics

Democracy, introduced in Europe in the late eighteenth century, represented political modernization; its institutions were meant to keep up with technological and economic innovations and respond to the needs of the people. Furthermore, it not only allowed for broader citizen participation in politics, but it embraced the principle of merit for political leadership rather than just birth. By 1914, several leading European countries had democratic institutions built into governments that had monarchical or republican frameworks. These included the French Third Republic, Great Britain, and the Kingdom of Italy. Other European states still had autocratic monarchies, whether they had constitutions and parliamentary representation in the nineteenth century or not. The most powerful were the Austro-Hungarian Empire (the Dual Monarchy), the Second German Empire, and the Russian Empire. But political groups and economic shifts in these autocracies were pushing them toward more representative political systems, if not the outright adoption of democratic principles. In the years before 1914, then, democracy was expanding, but it was put to the test in World War I. Could democratic governments survive a war of unparalleled proportions and function well enough to secure a military victory? Would democracy continue to expand in Europe or would the war blunt its momentum? What would happen to Europe's major autocracies in the face of the war's demands? Would the war revitalize them or lead to their demise? If the autocratic regimes survived the war, would they incorporate democratic ideas into their political structures? The political stakes were high in 1914 as Europe's major powers, divided into two rival alliances, confronted each other in the Great War.

Politics on hold

The governments of the major states that committed to war in the summer of 1914 enjoyed widespread support among their populations when the conflict began. Political parties muted their differences, made demonstrations of patriotic loyalty, and voted the funds needed to finance the war. After the war degenerated into a struggle with no end in sight, fissures began to appear in the united fronts, and government leaders faced intensified political challenges. Confidence and enthusiasm gave way to grim determination, political back-biting, self-doubt, war weariness, and open dissent. The magnitude of the war imposed unprecedented demands on the machinery of government, as the belligerent powers pushed their way through uncharted waters. Midway through the war, many governments experienced change and reshuffling, as they tried to develop the means to secure an elusive victory.

Patriotic fervor and political unity

Socialist parties in Europe found themselves in a serious dilemma in the summer of 1914. They were torn between their loyalty to the Second International – a global association of socialist parties – and its desire for peace, and their loyalty to their countries. In principle, if war broke out in Europe, socialists were, in accordance with Marxist thought, to view it as an inevitable imperialist conflict. European socialists had for years worked on plans to respond to such a war with a general strike, since they were confident that international worker solidarity would prevail over national loyalty. In July 1914, French socialist leader Jean Jaurès obtained a vote from the French Socialist Party that called for a general strike so long as the German socialists followed suit. But German socialists started to rally around their government once Russia ordered the mobilization of its forces against Germany at the end of July. Once a German declaration of war against France was issued on August 3, the German Reichstag (parliament), including representatives of the socialists' Social Democratic Party, voted unanimously in favor of the war credits requested by Chancellor Theobald von Bethmann-Hollweg. A political truce suddenly prevailed in German politics. On the French side, the trade unions had already agreed on July 31 not to resort to a general work stoppage as the prospect of a victory by Germany held out far greater risks for their cause than whatever might come from their own government. Socialist efforts for peace suffered another setback when an unstable right-wing fanatic shot Jaurès to death on July 31. French socialist and labor union leaders enthusiastically embraced President Raymond Poincaré's call for a "sacred union" or political truce involving all Frenchmen in defense of the republic, and two socialists accepted ministerial posts in the government of national unity formed in August. In Britain, Germany's violation of Belgian neutrality in early August was the decisive factor in producing a political truce. All parties quickly voted to approve the government's request for war appropriations. As for Russia, a general sense of harmony emerged as labor strikes stopped at the outset of August and Russian men overwhelmingly obeyed the order when the government called them to arms. This harmony was underscored when the Russian Duma (parliament) voted unanimously on August 8 to support war credits for the government. When it became obvious that the war would last longer than originally thought, governments took measures to insure political stability. Thus, the French Parliament in December 1914 passed legislation suspending national elections for the remainder of the conflict and announced that it would remain in permanent session. Likewise, parliamentary leaders from the three major British political parties (the Conservative, Liberal, and Labour parties) reached an agreement to refrain from political polemics for the duration of the war.

Leadership changes in the Allied camp, 1916–1917

By 1916, the relentless demands of war caused political dissatisfaction. Weariness with a seemingly unwinnable war brought about efforts to seek a compromise peace. In late 1916, the military situation was grim, political scandals and instability plagued governments, and a strong current of defeatism filled the air, influencing the troops' morale. The result was often the appointment of a strong leader and the waning of parliamentary and civilian influence.

In Britain, Liberal Prime Minister Asquith's cabinet adopted a "business as usual" attitude on the home front in the early stages of the war. Two events in the spring of 1915 forced the government to abandon that approach. One was a report in May in two British newspapers that a severe shell shortage had compelled the British to cut short an attack against the Germans at the Battle of Neuve Chapelle in France. The second was the resignation of Lord John Fisher as first sea lord; he had come under parliamentary attack for refusing to send ships with reinforcements for the Gallipoli campaign. As a result, Asquith was compelled to form a broad-based cabinet that included Liberals, Conservatives, and the leader of the socialist Labour Party. Lloyd George of the Liberal Party assumed the newly created position of munitions minister to handle the problem of ammunition shortages, and he quickly emerged as the dominant, dynamic force in transforming the war effort on the home front. He was also decisive in the government's introduction in January 1916 of compulsory military service. In June 1916, Lloyd George assumed the powerful post of secretary of state for war. As criticism against Asquith mounted because of his lackluster leadership and haphazard approach to war-related problems, Lloyd George on December 1 called for the establishment of a three-person council to direct the war effort, with him in charge and Asquith, though remaining prime minister, left out. While Asquith initially agreed to the new arrangement, he abruptly changed his mind and announced that he wanted to retain "effective control" of war policy. His decision caused the Conservative Party to withdraw its support for the government, forcing Asquith to resign. Lloyd George put together a new coalition government on December 7, but most Liberals joined Asquith in refusing to support it. Lloyd George's takeover marked the start of a bitter rift within the Liberal Party and a decline in the party's political importance.

Lloyd George immediately brought new energy to the war endeavor. He bolstered Britain's war effort by setting up a small, efficient five-man war cabinet that met almost daily and by establishing new ministries to handle war-related issues such as food, shipping, and labor. For new ministerial posts, he appointed self-made men, mostly businessmen, for whom he had great admiration. Tending to bypass parliament and normal party procedures, he ruled through direct appeals to the British populace. Because of Lloyd George's success in guiding Britain to final victory in November 1918, his national popularity was at its peak when the conflict ended.

In republican France, both the Chamber of Deputies and Senate formed secret committees to investigate the progress of the war, and the committees brought instances of military incompetence to light. In June 1916, charges were directed against the French High Command for failing to provide sufficient protection at Verdun against Germany's offensive that year. Finally caving in to criticism of Commander-in-Chief Joffre's military leadership, Premier Aristide Briand gently removed him from his post in December 1916 with a promotion to the honorific title of Marshal of France. The government then basically ignored him. To increase armaments output, Briand in that same month named Thomas the head of a new Ministry of Armaments and brought in businessman Louis Loucheur to work as an undersecretary in Thomas' department. Meanwhile, Briand secretly worked through intermediaries to make contact with Germany concerning peace. His peace efforts came up empty, and he left office in March 1917. The wartime sacred union unraveled in September 1917 when the Socialist Party abandoned the government after its refusal to let French socialists attend an international socialist congress on war and peace.

In November 1917, President Poincaré appointed 76-year-old Georges Clemenceau, a political centrist, as premier. Clemenceau, a caustic, stubborn, and combative politician, quickly established a form of civilian dictatorship, reserving most decision making for himself in consultation with a handful of close associates, although he always acted with parliamentary backing. In his first speech to parliament as premier, he declared his firm commitment to "the war. Nothing but the war."[1] Clemenceau regularly traveled to the battlefront to visit not just French military commanders but also common French soldiers in an effort to raise their spirits. He muzzled those who talked about a compromise peace, and the government arrested outright traitors who were then tried and executed. On the day the war ended in November 1918, members of the Chamber of Deputies roared their approval for Clemenceau when he entered their assembly hall. For Frenchmen everywhere, he became known as the "Father of Victory."

As for Russia, Tsar Nicholas II firmly believed in 1914 in the principles of autocracy, Orthodoxy, and nationalism as the foundation stones of his state. He viewed Russia's limited constitutional regime as an evil force and did not trust the Duma. His ineffective leadership became increasingly apparent as the war progressed. Costly Russian military setbacks in the Carpathian Mountains of Galicia in the spring of 1915 forced him to appoint a war cabinet that proved to be one of the most talented ministries that tsarist rulers ever had. Cabinet members were eager to improve the soldiers' treatment behind the front lines, and they recommended cooperation with the Duma, where a broad-based group of deputies asked for a wide range of reforms that included ending the arbitrary rule that the military exercised behind the battle lines, showing greater respect for workers' unions, and improving the rights of the empire's non-Orthodox religions and numerous ethnic groups. Nicholas II simply ignored the Duma and took personal command of the army in September 1915, leaving the responsibility for governance at home to Tsarina Alexandra and Grigori Rasputin, her spiritual guide and confidant. Rasputin was a corrupt, debauched, and lecherous Russian mystic who had gained the confidence and support of the Tsarina years earlier largely because of his ability to relieve the hemophilia that afflicted the imperial couple's oldest son. When the more liberal, capable government ministers criticized the Tsar's decision to assume the post of army commander-in-chief, Alexandra dismissed them from office. In January 1916, the Tsarina and Rasputin began a rapid series of appointments and firings at the highest level of government that made the regime more unpopular. Finally, two grand dukes and a right-wing politician took matters into their own hands and murdered Rasputin in late December 1916. Tsar Nicholas left the military front to attend Rasputin's funeral and remained at the Winter Palace near Petrograd for several weeks before returning in early March to his military headquarters where he slipped into a state of apathy. By early 1917, members of the court were searching for a strategy to avoid revolution.

Italy in 1914 had a constitutional monarchy with deep roots. While Italy was initially neutral in the conflict, King Victor Emmanuel III (r. 1900–1946), conservative Prime Minister Antonio Salandra, and Foreign Minister Sidney Sonnino irresponsibly committed their country to the struggle in 1915 on the side of the Allied powers, believing that Italy's participation would bring a quick end to the war and result in significant territorial gains for their country. Two powerful groups in Italy opposed this decision: the Catholic Church and the Socialist Party. Italy was ill-prepared for war and faced multiple problems on the home front. Wartime prime ministers were weak, imposed few controls on war manufacturers, failed to keep inflation in check, and did little to strengthen support for the war. In June 1916, a broad-based coalition government was formed in an attempt to create a greater sense of unity in the country, but the cabinet was plagued by bickering and divisions throughout its 16-month life and by a refusal of the Socialist Party to join it. Frustration with the war and domestic discontent intensified, as demonstrated by the Socialist Party's presentation in parliament of a peace resolution in December 1916, disorders in Milan against the war in May 1917, and bread riots in Turin in August 1917. Rumors of war profiteers hurt the morale of Italian soldiers. On the other hand, pro-war enthusiasts encouraged Army Chief of Staff Luigi Cadorna to establish a military dictatorship.

In late October 1917, as the Central Powers were unleashing their offensive strength against the Italians at Caporetto, Vittorio Orlando became prime minister of Italy. He was a long-time politician who had supported Italy's entry into the war. One of his first actions as government leader was to replace Cadorna as commander-in-chief with General Armando Diaz, who had far more concern for Italy's soldiers than his predecessor. The shock of Italy's disaster at the Battle of Caporetto and the presence of enemy forces in the country's northeastern provinces triggered a determination among the Italians to fight the war to the bitter end. As the Allies approached victory in late 1918, Orlando ordered hesitant Italian army leaders to launch an offensive against Austria–Hungary in northeastern Italy. The Italians' military success was instrumental in causing the dissolution of the Austro-Hungarian Empire at the end of October and an armistice in early November. While on the winning side, Italy was nevertheless an impoverished and exhausted country at the end of the war.

The Central Powers, 1916–1917

Germany, like other belligerents, initially enjoyed a time of strong domestic support for the war, followed by war-induced challenges that eventually caused strains. The home front generally held up well during the first two years of the war. Subject to a British naval blockade, the Germans resorted to food substitutes, such as meatless sausages and "war bread" during the winter of 1914–1915. The blockade also reduced supplies for the manufacture of war materiel, which caused the Germans to implement a national system of economic organization. The institution that emerged as dominant in Germany's wartime government was the Supreme Army Command. The popular Paul von Hindenburg and Erich Ludendorff, after being appointed as the country's military leaders in August 1916, proceeded to establish a form of military dictatorship over the country. When rumors emerged in the spring of 1917 that Germany's unrestricted submarine warfare, launched on February 1 of that year, was not working, a wave of strikes broke out. The strikes also came on the heels of the "turnip winter" of 1916–1917 during which the population experienced severe food shortages and endured cruel conditions. Unwilling to face a fourth harsh winter, Reichstag members in July 1917 prepared a peace resolution based on no annexations. When Bethmann-Hollweg, who had angered Hindenburg and Ludendorff earlier in the year by promising electoral reforms in the German state of Prussia, failed to head off a parliamentary debate on the resolution, the two military leaders threatened to resign their commands unless the emperor dismissed the chancellor. They obtained the forced resignation of Bethmann-Hollweg on July 14. The generals' success underscored their powerful position in government decision making. The Reichstag passed the peace resolution on July 19 with a strong majority, but the new government, which was completely dominated by the annexationist military leaders, ignored the result.

The firm grip of the Supreme Army Command on power in Germany continued into 1918. Ludendorff remained committed to an annexationist peace as the war in the West raged on, increasingly to the detriment of Germany after its 1918 spring offensives failed to score a major breakthrough. When Foreign Minister Richard von Kühlmann, hoping to launch negotiations with the Allies, suggested to the Reichstag in late June that the government's position on peace was moving toward the Reichstag's peace resolution of July 1917, he angered Ludendorff and Hindenburg and not long thereafter was replaced. Nevertheless, increasing numbers of Germans questioned whether the generals' insistence on a victor's peace was not a serious hindrance to shortening the war. At the same time, soldiers on furlough brought home discouraging news from the battlefront, and home-front morale was rapidly eroding from the effects of ongoing food shortages and inflation.

In the wake of bad news coming from all battlefronts, especially Bulgaria's demand for an armistice in late September 1918, Ludendorff shocked the German government on September 29 by admitting that the war was lost. He recommended that the government reach out to Wilson to seek an armistice on the basis of the President's peace plan known as the Fourteen Points. He also insisted that Germany set up a parliamentary system of government. Ludendorff was apparently ready to turn over the disagreeable business of negotiating a peace with the Allies to Germany's civilian authorities. Reichstag leaders, who had been kept in the dark about the battlefield situation for several weeks, were stunned when they heard on October 2 that Germany's military situation was futile.

Dramatic, decisive events took place in Germany between early October and November 11 as the country moved toward democracy and peace. Prince Max von Baden assumed the chancellor's office on October 3. Not necessarily an advocate of parliamentary democracy, he nevertheless oversaw the creation of a national political system in which the government was responsible to parliament and not the emperor. More importantly, his government on the night of October 3–4 composed a note to Wilson requesting the opening of peace talks and the preparation of an armistice document. During the ensuing exchanges of notes, Ludendorff, feeling that Wilson's demands amounted to an unconditional surrender, urged that Germany continue the war vigorously. When Prince Max's government, infuriated by Ludendorff's intervention, threatened to resign, Ludendorff was forced to step down from the Supreme Army Command on October 26.

As the imminence of a German defeat in the war became clear, events unfolded that pushed Germany to the brink of revolution. On October 29, a naval mutiny erupted among a number of battleship crews, after their commanders ordered the German High Seas Fleet to set sail in the North Sea for one last battle against the British. Many of the sailors believed the move was a way of scuttling the peace negotiations. The mutinies reached the port of Kiel on November 4, when sailors' demands for the release of some 600 mutineers imprisoned there resulted in a general uprising. Protesting sailors and striking dockworkers took control of the city and elected revolutionary councils. From Kiel, the unrest spread to all other naval bases as well as to several inland German cities where soldiers challenged the military's authority. In each instance, the main goal of the participants was to assure a quick end to the war. A wish for peace also lay behind revolutionary activity in the southern German Kingdom of Bavaria, where on November 7 antiwar leader and Independent Socialist politician Kurt Eisner, after overthrowing the Bavarian monarchy, proclaimed a revolutionary Bavarian government called the "Council of Workers and Soldiers"; it immediately began negotiations with the Allies for a separate peace. At that point, a breakup of the German Empire, of which Bavaria was a part, seemed within the realm of possibility.

In Berlin, large numbers of workers took to the streets on the morning of November 9 to demand peace. Troops that were expected to maintain order began to fraternize with the protesters. At noon, Prince Max announced the abdication of Wilhelm II as German Emperor and King of Prussia, and he turned over the chancellorship to Social Democratic leader Friedrich Ebert. Ebert and fellow Social Democrat Philipp Scheidemann proclaimed a German republic in front of a large, enthusiastic crowd assembled near the Reichstag. On November 11, Germany signed the armistice that terminated wartime hostilities in Europe. Even though the war had ended, the political situation in Germany remained fluid and uncertain.

In Austria–Hungary, any public enthusiasm for the war in 1914 faded quickly as hopes of a short, limited Balkan conflict evolved into a general European engagement in which Austria–Hungary faced off against Russia. In the Austrian half of the Dual Monarchy, the government in 1914 failed to recall the Reichsrat (national representative assembly), thus missing an opportunity to obtain the official backing of Austria's political parties for the war. This oversight meant that there was no pressure on the Austrian political parties to pledge themselves officially to the empire's defense. To meet the demands of the war at home, the regime imposed tight press censorship, restricted civil rights, and banned political meetings.

One major problem was the empire's dual system of government. The division of the nineteenth-century Austrian Empire into two sovereign regions – the Austrian Empire and the Kingdom of Hungary – took place in 1867 in what is known as the *Ausgleich* or Compromise of 1867. Each half had its own prime minister and parliament. Unity came through a common ruler, Emperor-King Franz Joseph I of the House of Habsburg, and certain common ministries – including war, foreign affairs, and finance. During World War I, the two entities of Austria and Hungary failed to create unified agencies to achieve greater efficiency. Administrative confusion, bottlenecks, and suspicions negatively affected their wartime relations. Hungarians complained of being disproportionately drafted, since Hungary's share of soldiers was more than 3.5 percent greater than its total percentage of the empire's population. Austrians countered that a portion of Austria's peacetime lands were at the time under Russian occupation which reduced the number of draft-eligible Austrian men. Such wrangling lowered morale in both halves of the realm. As for food, the Magyars, who enjoyed a much richer agricultural base than the Austrians, selfishly designated only a small fraction of their 1915 grain output for Austria. From the very outset of the war, the Austrians, who had a poor harvest in 1914, experienced serious food shortages, and the food crisis intensified as the war continued, creating tensions between the working class and the aristocratic system of government. Emperor Franz Joseph, after 68 years on the throne, died on November 21, 1916. His successor, the young Karl I, wished to end the war as soon as possible to secure the survival of the empire. Without informing his German ally, he put out feelers to the French in the spring of 1917, and indicated his willingness to support France in its claims to Alsace-Lorraine and to sign a separate peace. His peace efforts came to naught, but when the affair became public a year later owing to Clemenceau's publication of the correspondence related thereto, it caused a rift with Germany as Austria-Hungary's ally.

There was dissension among ethnic minorities too. In Bohemia, many Czechs were quietly sympathetic toward the Russians. In December 1914, Czech political leader Tomáš Masaryk went into exile to garner support among the Allies for an independent Czechoslovakian state, and he played a crucial role in the formation in 1917 of military units in Russia known as the Czechoslovak Legion to fight for the Allies. As the war moved forward with no end in sight, various minority groups, such as the Czechs, Slovaks, Poles, Croats, Slovenes, Romanians, Serbs, and Italians, increasingly spoke out against the regime, and defections in the army, first appearing in the ranks of the Czechs, became more and more common. The Austrian Reichsrat finally reconvened in May 1917, but its sessions quickly turned stormy when Czech and South Slav deputies declared for regional self-governance within a federal union, and Polish delegates demanded total independence. Government officials in both Austria and Hungary refused to make concessions, and domestic divisions deepened. When the imperial government further reduced the flour ration in January 1918, major strikes erupted in Vienna and other urban centers; the number of strikers rose to 600,000 in just a few days. It was only after the government annulled a bread decree, made promises of political reforms and larger amounts of food, and sent in army units to apprehend strike leaders that the strike movement abated. In the same month, all the Czech Reichsrat deputies joined together in Prague to issue a statement, known as the "Twelfth Night Manifesto," in which they insisted on the right of the Czechoslovak people to self-determination. The prime minister of Hungary, Sándor Wekerle, renewed an old demand that the Magyars be allowed to establish a separate army. The regime was forced to assign even more soldiers to the home front to assure order.

With his world rapidly unraveling around him, Karl, on October 16, 1918, tried to redeem the situation by announcing the creation of a federal state in the Austrian half of the empire that granted autonomy to its ethnic groups; he also promised to turn over Austria's Polish lands to a newly created independent Polish state. His actions were too little too late. The Allies had already recognized the Czechoslovak National Council, Masaryk's provisional government-in-exile headquartered in Paris, as the government of a future independent Czechoslovakia. On October 18, the Council issued Czechoslovakia's Declaration of Independence from Paris. The South Slavs in Austria also took steps to organize a new state and were joined by Hungarian Croats in declaring on October 29 the independence of a newly created State of Slovenes, Croats, and Serbs, which then united with Serbia to form the Kingdom of Yugoslavia on December 1. The Poles in the empire seceded on October 28 to join a Polish state that had already been declared in Warsaw. Hungary terminated its union with Austria on October 31, and proclaimed a Hungarian republic. The Austro-Hungarian High Command signed an armistice with Italy on behalf of the now defunct empire on November 3 to bring an official end to Austria–Hungary's role in the war. Finally, on November 11, Karl renounced his government functions, although he refused to abdicate. Austria declared itself a republic the next day, and Karl ended up in Switzerland in early 1919. His relinquishment of power ended some 650 years of Habsburg rule in Central Europe. The collapse of the Austro-Hungarian Empire in late 1918 set the stage for major political, economic, and social challenges for the successor states.

Conclusion

The demands of war halted politics as usual in all belligerent countries, albeit in different ways. The domestic political unity that carried them during the first months of the conflict disintegrated. Midway through the war, a general wish for peace, followed by the cruel disappointment of continued conflict, forced political leaders to act increasingly outside parliamentary bounds. Some states created military-dominated governments while others looked to strong civilian leaders. All created assertive executive branches that were able to carry the war forward. The popular will, increasingly perturbed by a horrible war that accentuated socio-economic divisions, moved toward direct action as the conflict dragged on. After 1917, the stage was set for popular protests and varying degrees of revolutionary activity that would strengthen in the immediate post-armistice months. But the desire for a return to normality was also evident when the Great War ended on November 11, 1918. The armistice was greeted with joyous celebrations in all the Allied states of Europe and beyond. By the time the guns had fallen silent, however, three major empires – Austria–Hungary, Germany, and Russia – had fallen, never to return to a monarchical regime, and the Ottoman Empire followed soon thereafter.

Wartime ideologies and activism

By 1914, modernization, industrialization, militarization, nationalism, and the birth of mass consumer-driven societies had created large urban populations and new social classes that were politically and socially conscious. As a response to the new demographic and socio-economic conditions, political ideals and programs emerged to explain, organize, and help lead the new societies. While governmental ideologies such as republicanism and nationalism endeavored to rationalize and bring about orderly national development within the framework of existing political regimes, oppositional ideologies such as socialism advocated radical change that often resulted in strikes and revolutions. In 1914, these ideologies were about to be tested by unprecedentedly brutal war conditions that would stretch governments and societies to the brink of crisis. While the questions regarding the distribution of wealth, access to political participation, and the balance between a country's agricultural and industrial sectors became more urgent, peace was the overwhelming concern. The miseries of the war polarized ideologies. Pacifist movements advocating a renunciation of violence coexisted with revolutionary movements advocating forceful change. Most democratic states in Europe successfully navigated domestic protests and the numerous pressures associated with waging total war, so their regimes were still intact at the end of the struggle. The autocratic regimes of Germany and Austria–Hungary, both autocracies, made it to the last days of the war before their systems completely collapsed. Russia's authoritarian government, however, fell victim to revolutionary change in 1917, in part because of the Russian people's desire for the war to end.

European pacifism: a broad spectrum

Pacifism grew in popularity as the war dragged on with no end in sight. In 1915, as the conflict turned into a war of attrition, pacifists from neutral countries organized into an international, anti-militarist effort known as the Zimmerwald Movement. Pacifism, which had existed as an important prewar movement with a strong bond to European socialism, experienced a rebirth. An international group of women held a peace conference at The Hague in 1915; so threatening was it to several governments on both sides of the conflict that they took measures to prevent their countries' delegates from attending. Plans for the unification of Europe were part of the pacifists' agendas. The British Quakers, an important group involved in relief operations in Europe, advocated pacifism; in their eyes, the best deterrent to war was a union of European countries. All these movements echoed deeply at governmental levels, where peace proposals were made by various belligerents in 1916.

European socialism in 1914

One of the significant political events in the decades before World War I was the emergence in virtually all European countries of socialist or social democratic parties that based their major tenets on the views of Karl Marx, a nineteenth-century economic and political theorist. They believed that class struggle based on economic interests was fundamental to society, and that in the current industrial age, the struggle was between an exploitative bourgeoisie (middle class) and an exploited proletariat (working class). Over time the ranks of the bourgeoisie would diminish as the means of production (capital, industrial equipment, and raw materials) became concentrated in ever fewer hands, while the proletariat would steadily grow poorer and larger in number. The situation of the working class would not improve until they overthrew the ruling middle class and its economic system of capitalism through a violent political revolution. Once the proletariat had replaced capitalism with socialism, the resulting society would include workers' control of the means of production, the abolition of private property, the distribution of goods and services according to need, and the elimination of class distinctions.

Marxian socialists split into two basic camps at the end of the century. One group, while remaining true to the spirit of Marxism, rejected Marx's theoretical rigidity and insistence on violent revolution in favor of a gradualist approach to the inevitable triumph of socialism. They argued that in the meantime socialist parties should work to improve the general condition of workers within the political frameworks that then existed. Opposed to the socialist revisionists were the doctrinaire Marxists who remained committed to revolutionary socialism. In spite of their differences, the two factions worked together in a global organization of socialist and labor parties known as the Second Workers' International.

Civilian unrest

The war created volatile situations in which riots had the potential to turn into full-fledged revolts. War-induced sufferings, such as food and fuel shortages, rationing, food price increases, failed harvests, and requisitions of basic life staples strained tempers. Millions of refugees were homeless, further fraying local communities. Heavily taxed workers saw their salaries frozen. In Germany, Austria–Hungary, and Russia, minorities chafed under foreign imperial rule. Civilians complained from Petrograd to Budapest to Vienna to Berlin to Paris. Bread riots occurred in 1915, especially in East Central European and Russian capitals where the suffering was greatest. During the winter of 1916–1917, the mid-point of the war, exhaustion and demoralization set in. Workers' protests became more widespread, owing to increased workloads in munitions factories. Bad news from the front, news of soldiers' mutinies and desertions, and food shortages triggered a wave of strikes in Italy during the first months of 1917, and the Russian revolution of 1917. In 1918, serious labor unrest took place in Paris when as many as 200,000 munitions workers went on strike and demanded that the government make known its conditions for peace. In response, Armaments Minister Loucheur used a combination of firmness and flexibility to end the shutdown that came on the eve of an anticipated German offensive. Civilian protests were a threat not just to national morale but to the war itself.

Russia's March revolution and after

In Russia, revolution was in the air long before World War I. Russia had already experienced a revolution in 1905, after suffering military defeat at the hands of Japan in the Russo-Japanese War. On that occasion, the Tsar introduced some reform measures, including a popularly elected Duma, but, once the revolutionary tide subsided, Nicholas II quickly reduced the Duma to a consultative body. Russia in 1914 still had a repressive regime, large numbers of landless and debt-ridden peasants, impoverished workers, and anarchists plotting terrorist schemes. Russian society was rife with class conflicts and sporadic strikes hindered its economy. The three-hundredth anniversary of Romanov rule, celebrated amidst great pomp in 1913, encountered hostile crowds.

One of the political organizations opposed to the tsarist regime was the Russian Social Democratic Workers' Party, a Marxist revolutionary group founded in 1898. The party broke into two factions at its 1903 congress. On one side were the Bolsheviks (the majority party), whose leader Vladimir Lenin argued that the party should be comprised of a small group of highly disciplined, professional revolutionaries. Julius Martov, who headed the Menshevik faction (the minority party), defended the idea of a more inclusive party that would include, besides a revolutionary elite, workers and intellectuals who supported the goals of the movement. Lenin's faction managed to keep the name Bolshevik even though his group represented a minority of the Russian Social-Democratic Party's membership. The differences between the two factions widened in the years after the congress.

Lenin, whose birth name was Vladimir Ilyich Ulyanov, became an implacable opponent of the tsarist regime in 1887, after his older brother was executed for participating in an assassination plot against the Tsar. Following law studies, Lenin immersed himself in the study of Marxism and became a propagator of socialist ideas in St. Petersburg. Arrested for sedition in late 1895, he was condemned to three years of exile in Siberia. Once released, he moved to Western Europe, where he largely remained for the next 17 years. During this time he established himself as one of Russia's foremost Marxist theoreticians. He also continued to guide the activities of the Bolsheviks in Russia.

As the war unfolded, its hardships and enormous human losses dispelled the country's August 1914 patriotic fervor. By the late fall of 1916, the Russian forces had sustained military losses approaching 5 million men. The Pyrrhic victory achieved in the Brusilov offensive that year demoralized Russian troops and resulted in a frightening increase in desertion rates. A widespread revolt occurred in Russia's Central Asian lands in 1916 after the government introduced conscription there; Russian forces brutally suppressed it. During the winter of 1916–1917, extraordinarily cold weather prevailed, inflation approached 400 percent, and urban food shortages grew worse, prompting strikes and food riots in Petrograd. By early 1917, members of the court were searching for a stronger monarch to avert a revolution. Russia's cities grew increasingly restless, and the number of striking workers reached 600,000. Government officials in Petrograd, concerned about the deteriorating situation, drew up a plan for putting down any revolt there.

A strike at the Putilov armaments factory in Petrograd on March 7, 1917, followed by spontaneous demonstrations of women protesting against bread shortages and strikers demanding wage increases on March 8, marked the start of the revolution. These manifestations quickly spread and resulted in the toppling of the tsarist regime in a matter of days. On March 9, police fraternized with demonstrators. On March 10, all factories and industrial establishments in the city closed down. The government finally responded by dissolving the Duma on March 10 and calling on troops to disperse the crowds. The soldiers, however, joined the revolutionary crowds, and the armed insurrection continued to spread in the streets. The Duma elected a provisional government on March 12. The Tsar, who had been visiting the troops at the front, returned to Petrograd too late. He abdicated on March 15 in his railroad car, 175 miles away from the capital. Russians across the land cheerfully accepted the new political order.

The provisional government, representing Russia's middle and aristocratic classes, quickly passed a classical liberal agenda that included equality before the law and freedom of assembly, speech, religion, and press. The new regime also promised to organize democratic national elections for a constituent assembly. Yet the new government's liberal and moderate socialist leaders stopped short of social revolution. The key figure in a new government that formed in May was Aleksandr Kerensky, a moderate socialist who became the country's prime minister in July. Its popularity eroded during the summer and fall of 1917. While most Russians wanted an end to the war, the patriotic Kerensky remained firm in his commitment to the conflict; he believed that the future of a free Russia was inextricably linked to the West, and he aimed for a peace that would include Russia's wartime territorial expansion. The provisional government lost peasant support when it failed to expropriate the lands of large landholders for redistribution among the peasants. It was also slow to organize elections for a national constituent assembly, leading to charges that the government intended to sabotage them.

The provisional government shared authority with a powerful counter-government known as the Petrograd Soviet, or Council of Workers' and Soldiers' Deputies, that took control of the capital city during the March Revolution. Comprised of 2,000 to 3,000 workers and ordinary soldiers, the Petrograd Soviet soon became the coordinating center for other soviets that sprouted up across Russia. Dominated by moderate socialists, it endorsed the provisional government's early domestic measures, but differences quickly developed between them on issues related to the army and foreign policy. On March 14, the Petrograd Soviet issued Order No. 1 that transferred power in the country's army units from officers to elected committees of ordinary soldiers. The common soldiers were to obey officers only when their orders were in harmony with the Soviet. Order No. 1 weakened the provisional government's ability to wage war by challenging its authority over the army and undermining military discipline. Many peasants simply abandoned their units and returned home to partake in unauthorized seizures of lands from great landowners. In the area of foreign policy, the Petrograd Soviet called for a peace without territorial annexations or compensations. The "dual power" rivalry between the two governments intensified during the spring and summer months, as did their quest for popular support. Adding to Russia's political confusion in the spring of 1917 was the arrival of Lenin in Petrograd on April 16 with 32 of his followers from Switzerland. He received travel help from the Germans, who sent the group across Germany in a sealed train lest the revolutionary contagion spread to their own country. The Germans' hope was that Lenin would help undermine the provisional government's flagging war effort.

Shortly after his arrival at Petrograd's Finland Station, Lenin laid out a radical program known as the April Theses to the Petrograd Bolshevik Committee. Denouncing the provisional government for backing an "imperialist" war and representing the "bourgeoisie," he called on the soviets to end their cooperation with it. He also contended that Russia was ready to move immediately from the bourgeois revolution achieved in March toward the socialist phase. To help with the process, Lenin demanded that the Bolshevik Party do its utmost to prepare the Soviets for an eventual takeover of power from the provisional regime. Other parts of the plan included the confiscation and distribution of landed estates among the peasants, the nationalization of Russia's banks, and the establishment of workers' control over factories. Lenin used his charisma to persuade the party to approve his program, which they initially found too radical. Leon Trotsky, another key Marxist revolutionary leader, returned to Russia from exile in New York in May 1917 to join the Bolsheviks. The leadership combination of Trotsky, who had great oratorical skills, and Lenin, who was an organizer and a strategist, gave the Bolsheviks a distinct advantage over their rivals.

Lenin coined the slogan "Peace, land, bread" which was widely reproduced on posters. The Bolsheviks also displayed a poster with white letters on a red background banner saying "All Power to the Soviets!" to appeal to the masses.

In July, the provisional government experienced a serious challenge to its authority. A major Russian military offensive in Galicia collapsed just a few days after its launch on July 1; large numbers of demoralized troops deserted in the aftermath. The military failure, combined with persistent economic problems, triggered demonstrations in Petrograd in mid-July, where protesters demanded that the Petrograd Soviet assume complete government authority. With their popularity growing, the Bolsheviks quickly assumed control of the uprising even though party leaders, including Lenin, feared that the revolt was premature. But troops loyal to the provisional government quickly crushed it, stormed the Bolshevik party headquarters, arrested Trotsky, and accused Lenin of being a German agent. Lenin fled to Finland. This failure of the Bolsheviks to overthrow the government was a severe setback for the party.

A turning point in the Bolshevik Party's fortunes came in September 1917, during a right-wing attempt to overthrow the government. General Lavr Kornilov, the recently appointed army commander-in-chief, refused to step down when Kerensky suddenly dismissed him, and the general ordered his soldiers to march on Petrograd. Kerensky turned to the Bolsheviks for support, allowed them to mobilize their workers' militia called the Red Guards, and freed Bolshevik political prisoners. Even though Kornilov's operation failed, the episode showed just how weak Kerensky's government had become; popular support for it shrank to virtually nothing shortly thereafter. The Bolsheviks came out of the affair with their prestige enhanced, and countless numbers of ordinary soldiers and workers flocked to their cause. They soon won majorities in both the Petrograd and Moscow Soviet elections and surged in strength in provincial elections.

Russia's November revolution and after

In the countryside, unrest was growing worse. In May, the peasants had spontaneously convened the first National Peasant Congress in Petrograd and called for the abolition of landed property and the banning of hired labor. Tired of waiting for a constituent assembly to convene and act on their program, peasants began to seize land by force and murder landowners during the summer. The peasant unrest grew worse in October and their leaders rallied to the Bolsheviks. Inflation was rampant, and food riots plagued the cities. Faced with strikes and industrial sabotage, factories shut down. Both Lenin and Trotsky concluded that the time had arrived to seize power. Lenin slipped back into Russia from Finland and convinced Bolshevik Party leaders at an all-night meeting on October 23–24 in Petrograd to accept the idea of an armed insurrection. Its planning was entrusted to Trotsky, who scheduled it to coincide with the upcoming Second All-Russian Congress of Soviets in early November. The Bolshevik coup, brilliantly executed by Trotsky, occurred during the night of November 6–7. The Petrograd Soviet's Red Guards, with the support of regular army troops, seized key points in the capital, stormed the headquarters of the provisional government, and arrested several government ministers. Kerensky managed to escape, and not long thereafter, he fled Russia. The provisional government fell with virtually no resistance. Petrograd awoke on November 7 to a Bolshevik (Communist)-controlled government. The Second All-Russian Congress of Soviets convened the same evening and legitimized the revolutionary regime with Lenin at the helm. Moscow fell to the Bolsheviks after a week's fighting against soldiers faithful to the provisional government.

Figure 2.2 Vladimir Lenin speaks to a crowd on Red Square in Moscow on November 7, 1918, the first anniversary of the Bolshevik revolution in Russia.

Lenin moved rapidly in November to implement the promises the Bolsheviks had made during 1917. He issued a Decree on Peace that called on warring states to begin immediate negotiations toward a peace without annexations and indemnities. After this initiative failed to evoke a response from the Allies, Lenin opted in late 1917 for a separate treaty with Germany, largely because he realized that the Russian army was now a largely ineffective fighting force. The Germans presented draconian terms that Russian negotiators initially refused. In the end, Lenin used his formidable powers of persuasion, as he did on other occasions, to convince his Bolshevik colleagues to accept the Germans' offer. The Russians reluctantly signed the Peace of Brest-Litovsk on March 3, 1918. His Decree on Land announced the confiscation of the estates of landlords and the church without compensation, and he allowed the peasants to continue seizing landowners' estates and splitting up the lands among themselves. Lenin also authorized local worker committees to take control of their factories.

Other important reforms took place over the next several months as the Bolsheviks worked to create a modern socialist society. Russia shifted from the Julian calendar to the Western world's Gregorian calendar in early 1918; this meant that the day following the Julian calendar's January 31 officially became February 14. The calendar change put Russia in line with virtually all of the rest of Europe. The Russian alphabet was simplified. Estate distinctions that classified Russians into groups such as peasants, gentry, and townspeople were eliminated, as were civil ranks. Past military titles and ranks were abolished, and soldiers were called upon to elect their officers. The new government provided for equality of all citizens before the law, including women. The church's jurisdiction was limited by the separation of church and state and the government's recognition of civil marriages only. Obtaining a divorce was simplified. Adult literacy campaigns and free medical care were also instituted. For many in Russia and elsewhere, the Bolsheviks' policies represented the wave of the future and the fulfillment of Marxist principles. On the other hand, Lenin also created a state security police organization called the Cheka in December 1917 to ferret out counter-revolutionaries and saboteurs.

One major hurdle Lenin faced early on was what to do with the Russians' demand for a democratically elected constituent assembly. The Bolsheviks had repeatedly pledged in 1917 to convene such an assembly, so Lenin felt compelled to do so even though he had misgivings about the outcome for his party. Free elections for the constitutional assembly were held on November 25 and it convened on January 18, 1918. Just as Lenin feared, the Bolsheviks did not win the election: they only obtained some 25 percent of the vote, while the rival Socialist Revolutionary Party, which represented the interests of Russian peasants, secured an absolute majority of 58 percent. When the assembly began taking steps contrary to Lenin's wishes, he closed it down by force after one day. His action represented an end to Russian parliamentary democracy and a confirmation that a Bolshevik dictatorship was in control. Further evidence of this fact came when Lenin, immediately after dismissing the constituent assembly, declared the Third All-Russian Congress of Soviets to be the supreme authority of the land and had it write a constitution for the country. The result – the Constitution of 1918 – created a highly centralized political structure that concentrated full power in the top state and party organs of government.

While the Bolsheviks had ended Russia's war with the Central Powers, their prospects for survival were still grim in the spring of 1918. A part of their challenge lay in the vast size and composition of the country. Russia comprised one-sixth of the earth's land mass, and it had a population of some 125 million people of diverse nationalities, ethnic groups, religious faiths, political beliefs, and aspirations. War-related problems such as feeding the cities and rebuilding Russia's army lingered. There was considerable dissension among Russia's socialists about the country's political future. The Bolsheviks' economic decisions were creating considerable economic dislocation. The greatest threat to the Bolsheviks, however, was the emerging power of counter-revolutionary forces in several regions of Russia. By the summer of 1918, Russia found itself locked in a bitter civil war between pro- and anti-Bolshevik forces.

The Russian Civil War

Domestic opposition to the Bolshevik government was initially disorganized, and many Russians believed that the Bolsheviks' time in power would be short. The counter-revolutionary effort began to take military form under General Mikhail Alekseev in late 1917, but divisions among its leaders compromised it. International developments began to create an entanglement of troubles that would prolong the fighting for three years. Following Russia's exit from World War I with the signing of the Treaty of Brest-Litovsk in March 1918, the Allies sent forces into Russia to prevent supplies they had provided the Russians from slipping into Germany's possession and to keep the Eastern Front alive. Some 24,000 British and French soldiers landed at Murmansk and Archangel in the spring of 1918. It was also in the spring that the Czechoslovak Legion, a military unit of 50,000 Czech and Slovak volunteers who had joined the Russian army as part of an effort to obtain an independent Czechoslovakian state, revolted against the Bolshevik authorities. Stranded in Russia following the Peace of Brest-Litovsk, the Czechoslovak soldiers were eager to reach Vladivostok in the Far East for redeployment to the Western Front. Traveling along the Trans-Siberian Railroad, a trainload of the Czechoslovak

Legion clashed with pro-Bolshevik forces in May. The Czechoslovaks moved eastward from the Urals and by July had seized control of most of the Trans-Siberian Railroad between there and Vladivostok. In fact, the Legion talked about a permanent presence there, proclaiming the autonomy of Siberia in June and gaining widespread peasant support. The actions of the Czechoslovak Legion encouraged Wilson to drop his reticence about American intervention, and he made an arrangement with the Japanese for a joint landing in Vladivostok. The Japanese quickly sent in more than 70,000 troops and the U.S. landed 7,000 in August 1918. Vladivostok was placed under Allied administration. Aided by Chinese forces, the Allies advanced in Siberia, reaching the city of Irkutsk in October 1918, where they made contact with the Legion.

In addition to the presence of foreign troops on the periphery of Russia, the counterrevolutionary forces, called the Whites, strengthened their effort and had soldiers in southern, northern, and eastern Russia under former tsarist generals. By the summer of 1918, the country was locked in a full-scale civil war. The Bolshevik army, known as the Red Army, was led by War Commissar Trotsky, who transformed an undisciplined volunteer body into a highly effective regular army led by former imperial officers. Trotsky often traveled in a special armored train to military flash points to badger, incite, and rally the Red forces, and over time the Red Army through its triumphs developed an *esprit de corps* that the Whites could not equal.

The winter of 1918–1919 was a precarious time for the Bolsheviks. Shortly into the winter, the French sent forces into southern Ukraine and the British put soldiers into the Caucasus region between the city of Batum on the eastern Black Sea and the port of Baku on the western Caspian Sea. Although they did not intervene militarily, the Allies provided moral support and equipment to the Whites. During these same months, the first serious threat to the Bolsheviks from the armies of the Whites occurred, when Admiral Alexander Kolchak, headquartered in Siberia and backed by the Czechoslovak Legion, marched his White forces westward to the point where they were in a position to launch an attack on Moscow in early 1919. There was also continued conflict in the Baltic States, where the November 1918 Armistice canceled Russia's peace treaties with the Central Powers. The Allies allowed Germany to keep order there after the armistice, which meant that German and Bolshevik troops were vying for control of former Russian lands. On November 22, the Bolsheviks invaded Latvia and Estonia, and set up a Soviet regime there; then they attacked Lithuania in December. In Latvia, the fighting dragged on for months thereafter. In Estonia, the Reds encountered stiff resistance from Estonian nationals who successfully drove the invaders out by the end of February 1919. Also in early 1919, Lithuanian volunteers received assistance from occupying German troops in stopping a Soviet military advance inside their country. The situation of the Bolsheviks became precarious enough in early 1919 that Lenin was ready to negotiate a deal with the Whites when leaders at the Paris Peace Conference, at the urging of Lloyd George and Wilson, called on the Russian factions to meet on Turkey's Prinkipo Island for talks. The Whites said no.

The tide in the Russian Civil War slowly turned in favor of the Bolsheviks as 1919 advanced. The Red Army drove Kolchak's forces back in the spring and inflicted a decisive defeat on them late in the year. A White army under the command of General Anton Denikin moved northward from the Black Sea and occupied all of Ukraine in mid-1919, but was decisively defeated in the fall. The Whites' last stand against the Reds took place in 1920 under Baron Pyotr Wrangel who took over the southern front. A massive Bolshevik army crushed Wrangel's army late in the year, and anti-Bolshevik refugees were evacuated via the Black Sea to Constantinople. One by one, the Allies also abandoned their positions on Russian soil. They first left Murmansk and Archangel in October 1919. The Czechoslovak Legion withdrew from Siberia in early 1920. American troops left Vladivostok in June 1920, although Japanese soldiers remained in the region until October 1922. In the south, the French withdrew from their positions in Ukraine in 1919 and the British followed suit in the Caucasus.

While the Bolsheviks gradually restored their control over a number of former tsarist borderland areas, they still suffered important territorial losses in the west during the years 1917–1920. Russia lost Finland when that country successfully declared its independence in December 1917, and ended its own civil war in May 1918, after being torn between factions of Bolshevik-backed Reds and German-backed Whites. The Russians also were forced to recognize the independence of Estonia at the end of 1919, and Lithuania and Latvia in 1920. The Poles not only established their own independent state partly at Russia's expense in 1918, but they also succeeded in obtaining territory well beyond their ethnic border with Russia in the east in the Polish-Soviet War of 1920–1921. These losses incited Lenin to strengthen his control of Russia's western borders. He had preached self-determination for ethnic minorities within the frontiers of tsarist Russia when he thought they would result in revolutionary states tied to an imminent workers' world revolution, but he abandoned the idea when he realized that his revolutionary Russia could end up alone. Thus, there was no longer any Bolshevik tolerance of self-determination when Russia regained control of Ukraine and Belorussia in 1919–1920.

The Bolsheviks's victory over the Whites can be attributed to several factors. White leaders were politically disunited and militarily uncoordinated, so that the Bolsheviks were able to defeat them one by one. Russian peasants did not wholly support the Whites, fearing that a White victory would result in their eviction from lands they had seized from landlords. The Bolsheviks benefited from the exceptional leadership of Trotsky, superior numbers, interior lines, slick propaganda, and a unified party. The Bolsheviks, however, did not achieve all their goals in the civil war, and they kept bitter memories of the Allies' actions toward them during the conflict. Their distrust and hatred of the West intensified as a result.

War Communism and terror

As the Bolshevik government slipped into civil war in the spring of 1918, it adopted an emergency program known as War Communism. Prompted by flight from cities due to shortages of consumer goods and food, high unemployment, runaway inflation, and food hoarding by the peasants, War Communism decreed grain requisitioning, nationalization, and labor mobilization. In May, Lenin inaugurated a "crusade for bread," and shortly thereafter the government's Food Supply Commissariat joined with the Cheka to establish a governmental "food dictatorship." In June, the government nationalized all large-scale industries and launched universal labor conscription. Amidst these developments, the government signed two decrees in September 1918 that signaled the beginning of a government campaign of violence known as the "Red Terror." An assassination attempt on Lenin's life the preceding month provided an excuse for the Cheka to arrest anyone suspected of counter-revolutionary activities. The campaign targeted the Russian middle class; the resulting summary executions punished political opponents and innocent citizens alike as the regime used intimidation to blunt resistance to its will.

Among the campaign's first victims were a number of officials associated with the tsarist regime, as well as members of the Menshevik and Socialist Revolutionary parties, whose numbers dropped by two-thirds over the next several months. While the official Red Terror ended in October 1918, the Bolsheviks continued to use terror until the end of the civil war. Although the exact number of Russians killed is unknown, evidence points to tens of thousands, if not more.

War Communism proved disastrous for the country. Attempts to centralize economic decision making resulted in nearly one Petrograd adult resident in four being named to government-run administrative production boards whose incompetence and overlapping responsibilities resulted in considerable confusion, mismanagement, and inefficiency. In the area of industry, government officials in Petrograd also suddenly comprised some 25 percent of the city's adult population and probably exceeded the number of factory workers there. Large numbers of workers continued to flee to rural villages where they were better paid and better fed, and where they worked as small repair men and artisans. Many workers responded to labor conscription by staying at home or by refusing to work when they did show up. By early 1920, industrial production had fallen to one-fifth its 1913 levels. The Russian currency had become virtually worthless and was replaced by a system of bartering, free goods, and free services.

In the countryside, War Communism was even more disastrous. In an attempt to find surplus grain, the government initially created Committees of the Poor, comprised primarily of armed city workers, to enlist poor peasants to rise up against the village kulaks, or well-to-do farmers. But most peasants refused to cooperate, and they passionately resisted the outsiders, who frequently used brutality in their desperation. Lenin abandoned the committees at the end of 1918 and replaced them with a hierarchical system of provincial food committees that had to meet a set of grain requisition targets in their regions. If the peasants revolted somewhere, armed food supply detachments were sent in to quell the uprising. Eventually, all agricultural products were requisitioned. The system amounted to outright confiscation, since the government paid the peasants with worthless paper money; the peasants responded by curtailing their sowings, and hiding or destroying their crops. During the winter of 1920–1921, peasant uprisings became widespread and there were numerous attacks on food requisition detachments. Agricultural output dropped during War Communism to about half of what it had been before its onset, and by early 1921 Russia was on the verge of mass starvation.

A climax to the domestic discontent came in the Kronstadt Revolt of March 1921, when sailors at the Kronstadt naval base not far from Petrograd revolted against the Bolshevik government. The Kronstadt sailors had been among the most ardent supporters of the Bolshevik revolution in 1917. Yet in February 1921, when workers in Petrograd went on strike to protest a one-third cut in food rations, the sailors were stirred to mutiny. They drew up a list of demands that included elections to the soviets by secret ballot, basic civil rights, egalitarian measures such as equal rations for all workers, the dismantlement of the harsh economic measures of War Communism, and an end to the Bolsheviks' dictatorship. Trotsky, in charge of the government's response, made no concessions and insisted that the "counter-revolutionary mutineers" surrender at once. It took a force of 50,000 Red Army soldiers to crush the revolt. Though the rebellion failed, it struck home with Lenin who shortly thereafter abandoned War Communism in favor of new economic policies.

Albeit an economic disaster, War Communism did help the Bolsheviks' consolidate their position politically. It reinforced authoritarianism through extreme centralization, the confiscation of surpluses, state ownership of the means of production, compulsory work, the extensive use of violence and intimidation, and the evisceration of competing political groups. Though the Bolsheviks represented a minority view in Russia, they transformed Russia into a repressive tyrannical state where brute force was routinely used to reinforce official positions. War Communism was a decisive stage in the establishment of a Communist totalitarianism state in Russia.

Conclusion

Leftist ideological radicalization occurred in varying degrees during the war. Socialism, born from the pressures of industrialization and workers' demands for improved working conditions, now mobilized large numbers of civilians, earning socialists the status of credible political partners. In the Western democracies, where socialism had gained slow acceptance before the war, socialists advanced their agendas by joining other political parties in broad-based coalition cabinets. In Eastern Europe, socialism contributed integrally to the political debate about the nature and identity of newly created states, particularly in Poland. It was in Russia that the socialist ideologies brought about the most radical transformations. The Bolsheviks, having adopted Marxist creeds, completely transformed civil society by challenging the fundamental principles of individualism and private property. For those, they substituted collective rights, privileges, and duties. Eventually, however, all European leftist ideologies and political parties translated workers' demands, which were limited in nature, into ambitious agendas of social reform. Their efforts tended to transcend national borders, just as the military operations and the economic and diplomatic developments had done.

Life during the war

World War I brought untold miseries to soldiers and civilians alike. In addition to the fighting, there were military occupations. In addition to the front-line fighting, there were military occupations, shortages of necessities, and numerous instances of civil unrest. Russian and East Central European civilian populations were particularly beset by interruptions to their daily lives. Soldiers also experienced difficult conditions. Italian troops, for example, faced serious food shortages during the harsh winter of 1916–1917, and Russian soldiers routinely lacked adequate food and shelter at the front. People in Western Europe were spared the most extreme hardships, though generally they still encountered hunger and cold, hard labor, exile, and death as part of daily life. Where there was a home front, life went on as normally as it could, but the lifestyle changes were momentous and the social fabric was often severely disrupted.

Refugees

As armies marched across Europe in the first days of August 1914, an unprecedented civilian exodus began. Refugees jammed roadways and stormed railroad stations. Urbanized Belgium was the first to experience the ravages of an invader in Western Europe. The Belgian city of Liège in Belgium was bombed by a German zeppelin aircraft on the night of August 5. On August 25, the Germans burned the town of Louvain, also in Belgium. Within just a few weeks, 200,000 Belgian refugees fled to France, 450,000 Frenchmen were displaced, and 870,000 Prussian civilians found themselves dislocated in the east.

Austria–Hungary also experienced population shifts. By the end of 1915, almost 90,000 Austrian Italians had fled to Italy, while another 290,000 remained internal refugees. Russia counted 7 million displaced people by the fall of 1917. Italy's disastrous defeat at Caporetto in October–November 1917 created a massive refugee crisis for the Italian government, when 400,0000 civilians fled the area that the Austro-Hungarian forces overran. By July 1918, 1 million Frenchmen had fled the German offensives in northern France that year. Along the 2,000-mile Eastern Front, millions, following the destruction of their villages and farms, survived in primitive conditions. All across Europe, multitudes of homeless and uprooted people faced temporary to long exiles.

Exile and persecution

Three groups of civilians became particularly vulnerable during the war: foreign workers, civilians in battle zones and occupied countries, and minorities living near national borders. The accelerating pace of economic migration in the decades preceding World War I had created large groups of foreign workers across Europe: Germans settled in western Russia, Britain, and France, while seasonal workers from the Netherlands, Italy, Russia, and Polish-inhabited areas of the Austrian Empire worked in Germany. They were soon viewed as enemy aliens. The plight of civilians in occupied areas near the battlefronts was dire; they were in constant danger, and food and shelter became increasingly scarce as the war progressed. The worst fate, however, awaited civilians in at least two Allied countries that the Central Powers occupied. In Belgium, the Germans quickly seized all available resources for their own war effort, ending the normality of life for the peaceful and defenseless country. In Serbia, which was under Austro-German occupation, more civilians than soldiers died when the occupying powers executed thousands and sent many others to concentration camps. In both occupied countries, the populations experienced starvation.

Minorities became suspect overnight. In Eastern Europe and Russia, they numbered in the millions. When war came, governments improvised internment camps where they relocated minorities living in frontier zones. They also confined entire populations and in some cases revoked their citizenship. Overnight, individuals were viewed as enemies of the state or potential traitors, as old ethnic hatreds were rekindled. Extreme cases of violence against minorities occurred in the Balkans and on the troubled Eastern Front. In the Ottoman Empire, the regime targeted the Armenians, a minority group that had long been subject to periodic government persecution. Numbering between 1.7 and 2.3 million people in northern Anatolia, the Armenians were resented in Muslim-dominated Turkey because of their Christian heritage and their disproportionate success economically and educationally in the realm. After hostilities broke out in 1914, Turkish military leaders viewed the Armenians as traitors, and the government introduced measures against them. What became known as the Armenian Genocide began on April 24, 1915, when Turkish authorities arrested some 250 Armenian intellectuals and political leaders in Istanbul, tortured and then killed them. In the months that followed, the government turned huge numbers of ordinary Armenians out of their homes and marched them across eastern Anatolia to concentration camps in the deserts of Syria. Turkish irregular forces systematically massacred multitudes of them along the way, and many of those who made it to Syria subsequently died of starvation or exposure. Hundreds of thousands of Armenians perished as a result of the events of 1915–1916, and by the end of the conflict, over 90 percent of the Armenian population in the Ottoman Empire had been removed. While the peace treaty that the Allies concluded with Turkey at Sèvres in 1919 called for an independent Armenia in northeastern Anatolia, an ensuing Turkish regime under Mustafa Kemal refused to accept that agreement. In the 1923 Treaty of Lausanne that his government and the Allies signed to replace the earlier accord, there were no references to the Armenian question whatsoever.

Epidemics

The magnitude of the dislocations in cities and villages created abnormal living conditions that, compounded by food shortages, made individuals across Europe vulnerable to disease. Large numbers of refugees lived in crowded and unsanitary shelters. In addition, the massive numbers of prisoners of war that the Central Powers captured on the Eastern Front in 1914 – the Russians alone numbered 1.4 million – created deplorable detention conditions. In these circumstances, contagious diseases such as smallpox, venereal disease, and tuberculosis were on the rise everywhere, adding to the misery of civilians and soldiers alike. Two epidemics, however, stand out. The first was a typhus epidemic that spread through lice. That epidemic originated on the Eastern Front where sanitary conditions among soldiers were less than ideal and quickly spread to the general population. In 1915, typhus killed 150,000 people in Serbia, and in 1917–1918, it claimed several hundred thousand in Romania. By contrast, in the West, where army sanitation was generally satisfactory, epidemics did not spread from the front to the population. The second epidemic was the 1918 influenza pandemic. Known as the "Spanish Flu," the pandemic spread from Portugal to Scandinavia and deeply touched various belligerents' armies. The pandemic knew no border and became an urgent international problem. The toll it took on soldiers was partly responsible for the cessation of hostilities in the fall of 1918, as a second and deadlier wave of the illness began in September 1918 and lasted until March 1919, when Europe was most vulnerable. By the time the pandemic had run its course, 2 million Europeans were dead.

Food and famine

War and food shortages often go hand in hand in modern times. When the Great War broke out, agriculture and food supply had become secondary to the needs of the military front, in part because the war was expected to be short. By 1915, however, diets had declined considerably across Europe as countries faced food shortages. Belgium found itself malnourished under the German occupation, for example, and Serbia was brought to the brink of starvation, because its foodstuffs were requisitioned by the occupying powers.

As the war turned into a conflict of attrition, securing foodstuffs became a serious concern for all European governments. In Germany, the government initially relegated agriculture to a secondary role. Since the country only produced 80 percent of its food needs before the war, it soon found itself facing a particularly acute wartime problem when shortages of manpower, fertilizers, and draft animals caused a drop in domestic food production. The British naval blockade intensified the Germans' alarm. The government introduced price controls in October 1914, beginning with bread grains and expanding to a wide range of other foodstuffs over the next year. Growers frequently reacted by moving their products to the black market or shifting to commodities that had no price controls. Rationing, initially for flour and bread, began in early 1915. Finally, owing to public pressure and crumbling conditions for food supplies, the German government established a War Food Administration in May 1916. Its creation consolidated under one roof the activities of a number of overlapping agencies, and it had the responsibilities of improving the food supply situation and overseeing general rationing. Its efforts failed to overcome many of the problems that plagued food supplies, however. A climax to the food crisis came during the winter of 1916–1917, following a poor harvest and an intensification of the country's transportation crisis: the result was a major disruption in the supply of foodstuffs to larger cities. In what became known as the "turnip winter," poor people were forced to substitute turnips for potatoes in their diets, and the average daily food intake for Germans plummeted to about 1,000 calories. Ultimately, some 750,000 Germans starved to death during the war as a result of the extremely low amounts of food available. The food crisis intensified the urban/rural divide among Germans and underscored the inequality that existed on the home front in the sharing of the country's wartime hardships.

In Britain, the government were slow to adopt a policy of strict import controls, increased domestic output, and rationing, since food did not become a major problem there until the end of 1916. In January 1917, landowners were placed in charge of local agricultural committees. The government emphasized the cultivation of cereals rather than the current specialization of animal husbandry, with the result that the production of grain and potatoes rose dramatically by 1918. The Ministry of Food put food retailers in charge of the rationing program that initially involved customers registering with a single retailer as their sole source for food purchases. To eliminate the problem of long lines – sometimes as many as 3,000 people outside a single London shop – the

Figure 2.3 Women and children stand in line in Berlin, Germany, in 1917 to obtain food rations.

government in 1918 introduced a scheme of consumer ration cards and retailer counterfoils; the rationing system had the intended result, as lines basically disappeared.

Russia experienced a fall in agricultural production with the onset of hostilities, but since it had exported significant amounts of food before the war and its export activity virtually stopped once the fighting began, the initial impact of the domestic drop in production was negligible. The chief problem the Russians faced was an inability to get suitable quantities of food to the cities, many of which were dealing with the added problem of large influxes of refugees. One reason for the urban food shortages was the peasants' increasing refusal to take their products to market, in part because they saw the prices of industrial goods they purchased rise much more rapidly than the prices they received for their agricultural items. Consequently, they consumed more of the grain they produced and stored the rest. A second cause of food shortages in urban areas was Russia's disorganized and inadequate transportation system, which impeded deliveries to large cities such as Petrograd and Moscow. When the authorities announced rationing in Russian cities during the winter of 1916–1917, people panicked, hoarded, and stood in line for hours to obtain bread and groceries. In March 1917, demonstrations over bread shortages in the streets of Petrograd helped lead to the collapse of the tsarist regime.

Relief operations

In every European country, private civic groups, charitable associations, citizens, and churches quickly came to the aid of beleaguered civilian populations, refugees, and orphans. From soup kitchens to medical dispensaries and orphanages, relief was organized on a massive scale. While France and Britain functioned mostly with the assistance of private relief operations, governments began to step in. In Italy, the Ministry of the Interior took charge of the administration of relief. Relief in Vienna was entrusted to the municipal administration with the help of the American Jewish Joint Distribution Committee. Soon, relief became an international effort. The British Red Cross and Scottish Women's Hospitals facilitated medical assistance and created the Serbian Relief Fund, which also operated in the United States. The distress in East Central Europe, Russia, the Ottoman Empire, occupied Belgium, and occupied Serbia prompted two massive relief efforts. One was the joint effort of the Near East Relief organization, established by U.S. Ambassador to the Ottoman Empire Henry Morgenthau, and Quaker humanitarian groups to help the persecuted Armenian minority in the Ottoman Empire. The Germans failed to pressure the Ottomans into stopping the massacre, but they sent medical personnel to help the deportees. A young German army medic, Armin Wegner, photographed at great risk the first genocide of the twentieth century and enabled the world to remember it. The second relief effort involved the American engineer Herbert Hoover, who, in 1914, organized and headed the Commission for Relief in Belgium. Working with the Belgian National Committee for Relief and Food, and braving British and German threats to shut him down, his operation was at first destined to feed children. By 1917, Hoover was feeding 7 million Belgians and 2 million war-zoned Frenchmen daily. After the United States entered the war on April 17, 1917, Congress named Hoover head of the U.S. Food Administration, and then, in February 1919, head of the newly created American Relief Administration that extended relief in the postwar era. Hoover's undertaking is to this day the largest humanitarian effort in history and represents the birth of humanitarianism.

The changing face of labor

When the war broke out, the general mobilization caused labor shortages among all the belligerents. As the conflagration dragged on, labor became a major issue for all countries involved. The changes most discussed by historians involve the replacement of male workers by women, and yet there were three other important aspects to this issue: forced labor, which the Central Powers used; colonial labor, which the Allies employed; and prisoners of war labor, which all the European belligerents relied upon.

The war sent women into the fields and factories, sometimes in leadership positions. From Britain to Russia, women volunteered for every position that was available and went where they were needed. They raised monies, helped manufacture medical supplies and clothing, and provided surveillance and hospitality. They manned soup kitchens and prepared packages for soldiers. They worked as nurses, clerks, and munitions workers. Other jobs open to women included streetcar conductors, ambulance drivers, and postal employees. British women were brought into the country's industries early in the war, while German women moved into them in 1916. To help married women with infants and young children, governments created nursery facilities. If this new situation placed stress on mothers, it gave a new independence to single women. Fashions changed, with women began wearing shorter skirts and clothes more befitting to their active lifestyle. Gender relationships shifted, as women began to go out in public by themselves. Women performed heroically on the home front and, when allowed, joined the war effort as army auxiliaries and civil guard personnel. In Russia, where they were accepted as soldiers, they distinguished themselves in the Brusilov offensive in 1916 and, in the summer of 1917, the 6,000-strong all-female Battalion of Death fought valiantly after barely a month of training.

Forced labor was a widespread practice in Europe between 1914 and 1918. Hundreds of thousands, if not millions, of civilians were deported from war zones or occupied territories. Labor-starved Germany made perhaps the widest use of forced labor during the war. It extended and adapted its prewar foreign seasonal agricultural workforce, most of them men from Poland. In 1915, Germany transported workers from Belgium and northern France to Germany for farm work, claiming that they were voluntary labor. The Germans abandoned all pretenses in August 1916, when they enrolled 62,000 Belgians in forced labor battalions to do local work in Belgium, and shortly thereafter deported 61,500 of them to Germany for agricultural and industrial work. In an ironic twist, the German authorities allowed some Polish workers to return home after Germany and Austria–Hungary proclaimed a new Polish state in November 1916, but western Poles began again to volunteer for work in Germany, and in 1918, they numbered between 500,000 and 600,000. As for forced labor, the foreign civilian workforce in Germany was an estimated 716,000 men and women. These alien civilians were treated slightly better than deportees from war zones and occupied territories in Austria-Hungary and Russia who were transported in cattle cars, used as unpaid labor, and housed in primitive, often unsanitary conditions. These East Central European peoples, often Jews or other minorities, totaled several hundred thousand.

The Allies solved their labor problem partly by conscripting colonial labor. The immense relocation of colonial workers represented a significant population migration. India provided 500,000 laborers and porters, while South Africa, the West Indies, Mauritius, the Fiji Islands, and Egypt provided another 215,000. French officials procured in excess of half a million workers from its colonies in Africa and Asia; these workers represented half of its foreign workforce. Hosting colonials was taxing on the local populations and required constant monitoring. The colonial workers were often segregated, and their living conditions rudimentary. In France, they were generally well received at first, but as the ills of war dragged on, the French became more hostile towards them. The British differentiated between skilled laborers to whom they often offered further education, and common laborers who were treated poorly, subjected to long work hours, poorly fed, and in constant danger of death from enemy action as they were often deployed near the front lines. The colonial workers show the dependence of Europe upon its colonies, and the demand for ever more logistical support.

The use of prisoners of war for labor changed the home front as well. Between 1914 and 1918, an estimated 8 to 9 million men were taken prisoner, half of them by the Germans and Austrians combined, and most of them taken on the Eastern Front. Germany captured 2.1 million Russian soldiers. The French and the British together took less than 800,000 German prisoners. The huge numbers of prisoners taken by the end of 1914, however, forced the belligerents to improvise places of detention on ships, in old fortresses and military barracks, and in hastily constructed detention camps with primitive living quarters. Prisoners in Germany suffered malnourishment, since the Germans were unwilling to waste precious food resources on them at the expense of the civilian population. In time, prisoners of war were used as forced labor, which increased dramatically as the war progressed. In 1915, the Central Powers transferred over half their prisoners to work task forces in agriculture or industry. The French also used German prisoners extensively as forced labor, often keeping them close to the war front and assigning them to tasks related to the war effort. Overall, forced labor gave governments across Europe experience in handling mass internment camps. Furthermore, prisoner transports in cattle cars and reduced food rations, to name but these two, made acceptable the suppression of human rights. Prisoners from Eastern Europe received the worst treatment and died in greater numbers than prisoners from Western Europe.

Conclusion

Life during the war changed dramatically for European civilians. The most significant feature was perhaps that of the displacement of millions of human beings across Europe and around the globe. It represented one of the largest and most concentrated population migrations in history. On the home fronts, families were broken, economies retooled, and societies' identities changed with the arrival of colonial labor. Sacrifices in the name of patriotism erased gender, class, and color lines for the duration of the war. At the end of the war, the arrival back home was problematic for millions of individuals who discovered their cities destroyed or found themselves in another country because of border changes. The colonial soldiers, porters, and laborers, whether they returned home or stayed in Europe, were proof that the war had modified the relationship between the European imperial powers and their colonies.

Overall conclusion

The war contributed to the collapse of dynastic empires in Russia, Austria–Hungary, Germany, and Ottoman Turkey. It was also a factor in the emergence of a Communist regime in Russia in 1917 and in the appeal of Communism to workers in many parts of Europe at the war's end. World War I halted the course of normal politics, tested new ideologies, and redefined political boundaries between governments and citizens. Numerous prewar demands for change were honored at the end of the war: they included democracy, increased popular representation, and female suffrage. By 1918, political systems appeared to favor democracy, largely under Wilson's influence, and yet a return to normalcy remained problematic, as countries were vulnerable to the rise of extremist utopias/dystopias that often follow war and revolution. Financially, the costs of the war were staggering: the direct war costs are estimated to have been $180 billion and the indirect war costs an additional $150 billion. Economically, the conflict weakened Europe: prewar trading ties with other countries had often been disrupted; war-incurred debts demanded attention; manpower shortages existed; key industries were in need of modernization; and in the case of war-damaged countries, major reconstruction was imperative. As a result, economic mechanisms were fundamentally altered by the increased role of governments in the economic and industrial life of the country. Socially, women took on a much more visible role in all warring countries by leaving the home and going to work in munitions factories, transportation systems, and government services; their wartime contributions earned them the right to vote in several European states right after the war. The struggle also created greater equality among social classes as demonstrated in the common experiences of food and heating fuel shortages, death, and other miseries that virtually everyone endured. Furthermore, World War I was a new kind of war. Genocide, the occupation of enemy territory, and the exploitation of its human and economic capital not only devalued life, but created a dangerous precedent. War brutalized relationships and traumatized civilians. Most important perhaps, for four long years, Europeans were subjected to a growing number of transnational processes ranging from international cooperation to epidemics and large-scale human displacement. These developments made a return to prewar normalcy impossible and shook national identities to their foundations.

Note

1 Stephen D. Carls, *Louis Loucheur and the Shaping of Modern France, 1916–1931* (Baton Rouge, LA: Louisiana State University Press, 1993), 57.

Suggestions for further reading

Adams, R. J. Q. *Arms and the Wizard: Lloyd George and the Ministry of Munitions, 1915–1916.* College Station, TX: Texas A & M University Press. 1986.

Becker, Jean-Jacques. *The Great War and the French People.* Trans. Arnold Pomerans. Providence, RI: Berg. 1993.

Broadberry, Stephen and Mark Harrison, eds. *The Economics of World War I.* New York: Cambridge University Press. 2005.

Carls, Stephen D. *Louis Loucheur and Shaping of Modern France, 1916–1931.* Baton Rouge, LA: Louisiana State University Press. 1993.

Feldman, Gerald D. *Army, Industry and Labor in Germany, 1914–1918.* Princeton, NJ: Princeton University Press. 1966.

Gatrell, Peter. *Russia's First World War: A Social and Economic History.* Harlow, UK: Pearson. 2005.

Grayzel, Susan. *Women and the First World War.* Harlow, UK: Pearson. 2002.

Kitchen, Martin. *The Silent Dictatorship: The Politics of the German High Command Under Hindenburg and Ludendorff, 1916–1918.* London: Croom Helm. 1976.

McMeekin, Sean. *The Russian Revolution: A New History.* New York: Basic Books. 2017.

Proctor, Tammy M. *Civilians in a World at War, 1914–1918.* New York: New York University Press. 2010.

Winter, Jay and Jean-Louis Robert, eds. *Capital Cities at War: Paris, London, Berlin, 1914–1919.* Cambridge: Cambridge University Press. 1997.

Zeman, Z. A. B. *The Break-Up of the Habsburg Empire, 1916–1918.* London: Oxford University Press. 1961.

Part 2

Brave new world, 1919–1929

3   In search of collective security

Introduction

The first postwar decade ushered in a time of experimentation in European diplomacy. After the failure in 1914 of Europe's Old Diplomacy involving alliances and secret treaties and the advent of the New Diplomacy at the Great War's end, European powers were searching for stability. Chief among their concerns was collective security. This goal proved elusive partly because of the changed situation in East Central Europe, an area consisting of the Baltic countries, Poland, Austria, Czechoslovakia, Hungary, and the Balkan states. National rivalries quickly developed within the region, and the major European powers faced the difficult task of incorporating the East Central European states into the postwar balance of power. In addition, diplomacy faced systemic pressures. The major Western powers still dominated diplomacy between 1919 and 1929, and men trained in traditional diplomatic practice conducted it, but the New Diplomacy set up the League of Nations to encourage open covenants and the peaceful resolution of disputes. This dual track between great power and open diplomacy, while potentially beneficial, put pressure on international relations. Another concern was peace. Pressures to establish a lasting peace came from the traditionally neutral European countries that insisted on disarmament, and from businessmen and entrepreneurs who dreamed of a united Europe. Attempts to create a European federation dominated the decade. Last but not least, diplomats faced challenges concerning German reparations, Inter-Allied war debts, German and Soviet hostility to the postwar order, the military occupation of the defeated powers, conflicts in the Middle East, and colonial demands for independence. Overall, the decade was one of innovation and diplomats often operated in uncharted waters.

The Versailles decade

Prewar European diplomacy had been based on a system of entangling alliances, one of which consisted of Britain, France, and Russia to guard against attack. Based on bilateral treaties, this Old Diplomacy favored power politics, advocated the use of force to settle conflicts, and often included secret agreements disposing of territories without the knowledge of the affected peoples or governments. President Wilson introduced the New Diplomacy at the Paris Peace Conference in 1919. Based on the idea that peace was best kept through open covenants, it relied on adherence to the principles of international law. It allowed some 50 countries to participate in open and egalitarian debates at an international assembly of states known as the League of Nations, where disputes would be discussed and mediated. Not only was the New Diplomacy based on a philosophy of openness and active engagement, but it reflected the growth of transnational issues and activities, and it testified to the great postwar aim of avoiding another major international conflict. At a practical level, the Allied control mechanisms that the peace treaties set in motion, including the military occupation of the Central Powers from Germany to the Ottoman Empire, required collective action, thus providing added support to the apparatus for the New Diplomacy. Soon, scores of experts and bureaucrats dealt with transnational, technical issues, while career diplomats kept practicing traditional, great power diplomacy, namely, bilateral representation and the negotiation of treaties. The transition between the Old and the New Diplomacy was not smooth; jurisdictions were often blurred, and dual track diplomacy resulted in some frictions and duplications.

The League of Nations

When the Paris Peace Conference formally adjourned on January 21, 1920, the League of Nations' Council – the international organization's small executive body – had already held its first meeting in Paris. The idea of a League of Nations had gained momentum among the belligerent powers during the First World War as the human, economic, and environmental costs of the struggle grew. As laid out in its Covenant, the League embodied the principles of peace through a voluntary association of nations, cooperative security, and equality. It became a must-join institution for all newly independent countries after an initial 44 nations signed the Covenant in June 1919 at Versailles. The League's headquarters, at first in London, moved in the fall of 1920 to Geneva, Switzerland, where it began operations in a converted luxury hotel overlooking Lake Geneva. In 1936, the League's headquarters, while remaining in Geneva, moved into a stately new building called the Palace of Nations.

The League was charged with a wide array of responsibilities ranging from the enforcement of the World War I peace treaties and the supervision of the defeated powers in areas of finance and disarmament, to the arbitration of territorial disputes, the allocation of territories through plebiscites, the creation of collective security mechanisms, and the development of international humanitarian organizations. This meant not only following the existing rules of international law, but creating new legal and administrative dispositions. Finally, the League was expected to act as a diplomatic clearing house, attracting and cleansing the diplomats' messes. Its members, meanwhile, had limited responsibilities: they pledged to respect the territorial integrity and political independence of fellow member states, and any state resorting to war faced the threat of diplomatic isolation and economic and financial sanctions.

The three bodies that constituted the League were the Council, the Assembly, and the Secretariat. The Council, as the organization's executive branch, initially consisted of four permanent members, i.e., France, Great Britain, Italy, and Japan, and four non-permanent members. It had important responsibilities, such as issuing arbitration decisions when states locked in international disagreements appealed to it, and overseeing the application of the League Covenant. The Assembly was the League's legislative wing which, though it met but once a year, was nevertheless influential, in part because debates about pressing global issues took place there and received widespread press coverage. It had the responsibility of electing the non-permanent members of the Council, controlling the budget, and accepting new members. Attached to it were numerous experts' commissions dealing with a multitude of issues such as international justice and social questions. Major decisions in both the Council and the Assembly had to be passed by unanimous vote. Finally, the Secretariat was a group of some 700 civil servants drawn from all over the world who worked year-round in Geneva to facilitate the labors of the Council, Assembly, and technical committees. The Secretariat represented the first time in history where a group of individuals were expected to demonstrate their first loyalty to a global governmental body rather than to any one state.

As Commissions and experts multiplied, so did conflicting jurisdictions and duplications of effort. The executive work of traditional diplomacy was still conducted at summit meetings where the foreign ministers and heads of government of the "Big Three," i.e., France, Britain, and Italy, were in attendance. Set in posh resort towns in Switzerland and northern Italy, these meetings and conferences often paralleled or superseded the League's work. In essence, international law and sovereign power often clashed, showing the difficult birth of the new world order. Strategic and security priorities frequently divided the countries that the League was attempting to bring together.

Settlements in disputed areas

The complexities of the new European states' borders due to the presence of mixed minorities consumed much of the League's time until 1923. Just as any problem was aggravated by the imperfect Versailles order, any solution appeared to challenge it; minuscule territories fueled disproportionate passions. From east to west, from north to south, the map of Europe was redrawn by plebiscites or lingering conflict: Finland received the Aaland islands over Sweden's objections, while plebiscites divided Schleswig-Holstein between Denmark and Germany, and left Germany with the Allenstein and Marienwerder districts along the German–Polish border in East Prussia. Klagenfurt (Carinthia) remained a part of Austria following a 1920 plebiscite that also ended an unauthorized Yugoslav military occupation. Most of German West Hungary, known as Burgenland after World War I, became a part of Austria in 1921, following the signing of an agreement that included the withdrawal of Hungarian troops from the area. Meanwhile, Yugoslavia's borders with neighboring Romania and Austria remained unsettled.

The Treaty of Versailles mandated a plebiscite in Upper Silesia, an ethnically mixed area of Germans and Poles along Germany's disputed postwar border with Poland. The territory, under the political control of an Inter-Allied Control Commission, held a plebiscite in March 1921 in which 60 percent of the voters favored Germany and 40 percent supported Poland. Silesian Poles reacted by launching an insurrection in May that continued until the Council of the League of Nations in October 1921 granted the area of Upper Silesia that contained a Polish majority – about 40 percent of the province – to Poland. The League's decision caused considerable anger in Germany, not only because it tore apart Upper Silesia, but also because it gave Poland the bulk of Silesia's coal mines and large industries.

Another point of contention was the city of Vilnius, over which the newly created states of Poland and Lithuania fought after the Great War. Although a Lithuanian government set up operations in Vilnius in late 1918, control of the city changed hands several times among the Lithuanians, Poles, and Soviet Russians in the years immediately thereafter. Poland formally annexed Vilnius in 1922, although Lithuania refused to accept the Polish action, and the two countries remained locked in a form of frozen conflict until World War II.

In general, the ethnic group with the largest population in multi-ethnic states exercised political control in the new countries of East Central Europe: Germans prevailed in Austria, Czechs in Czechoslovakia, Serbs in Yugoslavia, and Poles in Poland. This meant that the potential for discrimination against other national groups was present, although the Allies, to counter that, launched an international system of protection for national and religious minorities at Versailles in 1919 based on minority treaties, and they placed the arrangement under the auspices of the League of Nations. In the end, however, the system failed to protect minorities in Central and Eastern Europe in the way the Allies had intended.

Free cities

Port cities with mixed populations and important strategic and economic assets received special compromise solutions, while issues of jurisdiction and minority rights in those areas required near constant attention from the League. Memel, a German–Lithuanian port city on the Baltic Sea, formerly belonging to East Prussia, became an autonomous unit within Lithuania in 1923 after several years of direct Allied control. The Treaty of Versailles provided for the creation of the Free City of Danzig that included the Baltic port and surrounding territory. The semi-autonomous city-state, officially established in November 1920, was under the protection of the League of Nations through a high commissioner, but it was also locked into a customs union with Poland. The special arrangement for Danzig gave Poland access to the sea, while it also recognized that the city had a largely German population. Tensions between Poles and Germans were a constant, as the city's majority Germans discriminated against the Polish minority and challenged the Polish government's attempts to strengthen its presence there. In the 1930s, Danzig would become a significant element in Hitler's foreign policy ambitions.

The port city of Fiume, located along the upper Adriatic Sea, was also a postwar point of contention. It was a mainly Italian-inhabited port surrounded by a Slavic population. Fiume became a hotbed of hostility between Italy and Yugoslavia, and its status changed several times in the early postwar years. The two countries feuded for months over the city following the war, with the result that an Italian nationalist named Gabriele D'Annunzio took advantage of the situation to proclaim himself the dictator of an independent Fiume in September 1919. The Italians and Yugoslavs set aside their differences in November 1920 by signing a treaty that declared Fiume a Free State. Once the Italians had driven D'Annunzio from power through a show of force in December 1920, the Free State became a reality, but it experienced frequent political disorders during its brief existence. The Free State came to an end in early 1924, when Italy and Yugoslavia signed a treaty that allowed the former to annex Fiume and turned over the Free State suburb of Susak to the Yugoslavs.

Along the eastern shores of the Adriatic Sea, other postwar boundary disputes emerged, with Albania in the middle of them. One disagreement focused on Albania's frontier with Greece. To solve the problem, an Allied Boundary Commission was created to draw the frontier. In August 1923, unknown assailants assassinated members of the commission's Italian delegation. The Italian government accused Greek nationalists of carrying out the deed and ordered the bombing and occupation of the Greek island of Corfu. The Corfu incident was the first serious test between the rule of law as represented by the League of Nations and brute force under Italy's Fascist dictator Benito Mussolini. The Corfu episode showed that a powerful country could act with impunity against a weaker neighbor without concern for League interference. In the end, Italy lifted its occupation of Corfu, but only after it obtained League-approved reparations from the Greeks. Albania also experienced border harassment at the hands of Yugoslavia, which pursued an aggressive policy that culminated in a Yugoslav military thrust into

Albania in November 1921, beyond Albanian areas Yugoslavia already occupied. After an outraged League of Nations confirmed Albania's 1913 frontiers, a bitter Yugoslavia withdrew its troops from the contested areas. Looking for protection, Albania turned to Italy which, through a series of agreements with the Albanians beginning in 1925, increasingly involved itself in Albania's national life. Mussolini saw Albania as a door to the Balkans.

Allied military occupation of the defeated powers

Allied military occupations of the defeated powers were written into the peace treaties with Germany, Hungary, Austria, Bulgaria, and Turkey. Troops from Britain, France, Belgium, and the United States comprised the initial occupation force in Germany. The French occupation forces there triggered considerable anger among residents in the occupied lands. Local populations resented perceived French high-handedness in the Rhineland, Westphalia, and the Saar. The German right-wing press, for example, sharply criticized the presence of black colonial troops in the French army of occupation in the Rhineland, claiming that the inclusion of black soldiers in the occupation force was a French attempt to humiliate the German people. An Allied Saar Commission started administering that region's coal mines in February 1920 and its 15-year presence there also fueled hostility among the local population. Occupied areas became a seedbed of leftist unrest that soon divided the French and the British over occupation policies. The United States was the first to recall its troops from the Rhineland, doing so in January 1923. Soon thereafter, other occupying forces began to withdraw from the region. In September 1924, the Allies ended their naval control of Germany. In 1925, France left Westphalia. In the latter 1920s, German Foreign Minister Gustav Stresemann wrested important concessions from the Allies. The Inter-Allied Military Commission of Control, whose chief responsibility was to ensure that the defeated powers fulfilled the military clauses of the peace treaties, ended its duties in early 1927. All future armament questions were transferred to the League. The Allied military occupation forces in the Rhineland were substantially reduced later in the year and the French ended their military presence in the Saar altogether. The military occupation of Hungary and Bulgaria ceased in 1927 and 1928, respectively. The last French troops in the Rhineland were withdrawn in late 1930. The departure of Allied military forces from the defeated countries coincided with a rise in demands for treaty revisions from Germany and Italy.

Financing the new countries

In the adjustment to peace after the Great War, Austria was a pitiful poster child for the Paris peace settlement. Ruined and isolated, with almost one-third of its population living in the oversized European capital of Vienna, Austria was the smallest and weakest of the postwar Central European powers. Known as "Europe's beggar," Austria was choked by high tariff walls in neighboring countries, and its economy faced collapse. To aid its recovery, the Allies did not assign it a reparations amount, and Czechoslovakia in 1921 extended a helping hand by lowering trade barriers and issuing a loan. In addition, a substantial reconstruction loan from Britain, France, and Italy followed Austrian promises of reforms in 1922, by which time the Austrian currency had sunk to less than 1 percent of one American cent. The loan agreement was a mixture of enticement and punishment. In exchange for its continued existence, Austria renounced a political union with Germany, and its finances were placed under the League of Nations' Economic and Financial Section. By 1924, owing to the efforts of a young assistant secretary general of the League named Jean Monnet, Austria's revival was largely successful. Hungary and Bulgaria were not allowed such a clean break from reparations obligations, although the Allies showed some leniency towards them by rescheduling their reparation payments in 1923. In December 1923, the Allies also provided Hungary with a financial reconstruction package similar to that of Austria, with the League serving as the financial overseer.

German reparations

The European Allied powers met several times in 1920 to set German reparations percentages for each of them and deal with the issue of German reparations payments. According to the percentages that they agreed upon at the Spa Conference in July 1920, France was to receive 52 percent of the reparations payments, while 22 percent would go to Britain, 10 percent to Italy, and 8 percent to Belgium; the rest would go to smaller powers. In regard to reparations, the Allies, while waiting for an Allied Reparations Commission to determine Germany's total reparations bill, insisted that the Germans turn over $5 billion in gold and pay for Allied military occupation costs. The Germans dragged their feet and made only token payments in kind, including deliveries of coal, cattle, colorants, and ships. The Allies soon declared Germany to be in default and insisted that it explain why. At the Spa Conference of 1920, the Germans once again proved less than eager to cooperate on reparations, insisting that they had already exceeded their initial payment of $5 billion when the French demanded an increase in monthly coal deliveries; it was only after the Allies threatened to use military sanctions that the Germans agreed to raise monthly coal deliveries immediately to the level that the Allies demanded. In April 1921, the Allied Reparations Commission set the final reparations bill at 132 billion gold marks ($33 billion at the time; more than $400 billion in today's money), payable over 42 years. In May 1921, a newly formed German government accepted the Allies' demands and obtained a loan abroad to meet the first payment deadline.

War debts, reparations, and U.S. loans

The Allies spent considerable time between 1920 and 1924 discussing interrelated economic and financial issues of reconstruction, inter-Allied war debts, and prewar debts that included Russian tsarist obligations now repudiated by the Soviet government. In April 1922, Lloyd George convened representatives from 30 countries, including Great Britain, France, Italy, and the two postwar pariah states of Germany and Soviet Russia, in Genoa, Italy, to discuss European reconstruction as well as world economic and monetary problems. The Genoa Conference was the largest international meeting since the end of the world war. The most important event during the gathering occurred not at the conference, however, but in the neighboring resort town of Rapallo where Germany and Russia ended their postwar isolation by signing an agreement that established diplomatic relations, cancelled mutual war debts and obligations, and pledged economic cooperation. The Treaty of Rapallo caught the Allies off guard and caused the Genoa Conference to collapse without any European-wide economic agreement being reached. That the conference failed was a personal setback for Lloyd George, who had tried to use ad hoc conferences since the Versailles treaty to achieve conciliation with Germany within the larger framework of European reconstruction.

Figure 3.1 German and Soviet leaders meet in 1922 at the Italian resort town of Rapallo where they signed an agreement to establish diplomatic relations between their countries. In the photo are: German Chancellor Joseph Wirth (second from left, then continuing left to right), Soviet Trade Commissar Leonid Krassin, Soviet Foreign Commissar Georgi Chicherin, and Soviet diplomat Adolf Joffe.

The Rapallo treaty affected British and French policy makers differently regarding German reparations. Britain, fearful that without the Allies offering concessions, the Germans might drift fully into the Soviet orbit, sought relief in Germany's obligations. In August 1922, the British proposed a "great transaction" that called for the cancellation of all inter-Allied war debts, which in turn would have allowed for the liquidation of reparations. Opposition to a generalized debt cancellation came both from the French, who advocated for continued reparation payments to finance their postwar reconstruction, and from the United States, which insisted on debt payments from the Allies. United States President Calvin Coolidge represented American opinion when he commented "They hired the money, didn't they?"[1] The U.S. Congress earlier that year had established a United States War Debt Commission to negotiate revised and final loan settlements with individual debtor countries based on capacity to pay. Settlements were reached with most of the debtor nations by 1926 on more generous terms than previously, but even those arrangements failed to end the problem. By the end of the decade, little had been paid for Allied war debts, although considerable time had been spent negotiating and wrangling over the issue.

France, meanwhile, became more distrustful of the Germans and more determined to hold them in strict compliance with scheduled reparation payments. In late December 1922, French Premier Raymond Poincaré, over British objections but with Belgian and Italian support, succeeded in having the Reparations Commission declare Germany in default on its timber payments in kind. Using this as an excuse, France and Belgium sent troops to occupy the German Ruhr on January 11, 1923. The German government responded by financing a campaign of passive resistance at the cost of 40 million gold marks daily that quickly sent the value of the already weak German mark plummeting to catastrophic levels. Between June and September the value of Germany's currency fell from 100,000 marks to one U.S. dollar, to 100 million marks to one U.S. dollar. Hyperinflation in Germany reached its peak in November when the mark's value fell to more than 4 trillion to the dollar. While the economic and financial situation of Germany rapidly deteriorated, Britain and France continued to drift apart. On September 26, 1923, newly appointed German Chancellor Stresemann called an end to Germany's passive resistance, and the government took emergency steps that stabilized the German currency in November 1923. As for France's policy of aggressive action to force German reparations payments, it backfired since it pushed an already weak German economy into collapse, preventing the French from collecting any reparations at all.

One consequence of the Ruhr crisis was the return of the United States to the European scene for the first time since its official withdrawal at the end of 1919. U.S. banker and politician Charles G. Dawes led a team of international economic experts that worked out a plan involving the reorganization of Germany's finances. Two key components were a new schedule of reduced reparations payments and American loans to Germany. The plan intentionally refrained from indicating Germany's overall financial obligation. A trial period of five years was set up in which the Germans were to make a first year payment of $250 million and work up to $625 million in the fifth year at which rate they would continue for an undetermined time. The annual amount paid was subject to upward or downward change, contingent on the strength of Germany's economy. The Dawes Plan also insisted on the withdrawal of French and Belgian troops from the Ruhr, a procedure that began immediately after all parties had agreed to the plan in August 1924, and that was completed three months later. It was the last time that France attempted to force compliance with the Versailles settlement through military intervention.

By softening the reparations burden, the Dawes Plan, which was considered a temporary measure, proved critical to the revival of the German economy and the renewal of regular reparations payments, but the added international aid flowing into Germany also increased the country's dependence on foreign capital. The payment plan worked well for several years, as Germany paid its annuities on schedule. By 1930, the reparations paid came close to 2 billion dollars (some 7.6 billion marks). During that same period, Germany received 25 billion marks in foreign loans – mostly from the United States – that contributed to the prosperity it experienced until the loans sharply dropped off in 1929.

In the midst of Germany's economic upturn in the latter 1920s, Stresemann sought above all the withdrawal of all Allied occupation troops from the Rhineland, the sole region in Germany where they still remained. But Poincaré, once again the French premier (1926–1929), had no interest in evacuating French troops until a final reparations arrangement had been signed. Stresemann was also eager to win further Allied concessions on Germany's reparations obligations, so the German government called for a replacement of the Dawes Plan with a final fixed debt agreement in 1928. In February 1929, a committee of financial experts led by U.S. General Electric head and former Dawes Committee member Owen D. Young began deliberations on a final settlement. German reparations were lowered to $8 billion payable over 59 years. The amount was considerably less than the $33 billion that the Reparations Commission had imposed in 1921, and for the first time the Germans had a fixed date for the last reparations payment – 1988. The Young Plan fulfilled one of Stresemann's goals, but he made Germany's acceptance of it contingent on a complete Allied military withdrawal from the Rhineland. By the time of his death in October 1929, Stresemann knew that the Allies had agreed to that. The Allied occupation ended in 1930, five years earlier than scheduled. There were no more foreign soldiers on German soil. As for the Young Plan, it went into effect in 1930, but did not last long owing to the Great Depression. In 1931, an agreement was reached to suspend Germany's reparations obligations for one year, and at the Lausanne Conference of 1932, the Allied powers of Britain, France, Belgium, and Italy cancelled Germany's reparations altogether.

Conclusion

Reactive and burdened with unfinished business, the new political order created at the Paris Peace Conference was challenged from the very beginning. The states of Austria and Lithuania nearly disappeared. Albania, born in 1913, struggled to survive. Germany called Poland a "seasonal state." Revisionism was palpable in Italy, Hungary, and Germany. The authority of the League of Nations was severely challenged in the 1923 crises involving the Ruhr and Corfu. The reparations system was deeply flawed. Settlements reached with most of the debtor nations by 1926 failed to work. By the end of the decade, little had been paid on Allied war debts, although considerable time had been spent negotiating over them. One-third of Europe's minorities were not located in their home countries. League-directed compromise solutions in disputed areas such as Danzig and Silesia failed to resolve deep-seated ethnic tensions. Military and financial controls over the defeated powers insured peace, but were cumbersome and time-consuming. The new world order was fragile at best.

In search of collective security

The search for a new European balance of power began in 1920. Responsibility for European security rested squarely on the shoulders of the Allied Big Three in Europe, namely, France, Britain, and Italy. The League of Nations served as a reassuring umbrella, providing a legal backdrop to diplomatic summit conferences. From their background positions, Germany, Russia, and the United States forced the Big Three to tiptoe around each other on key issues. Moreover, each of the European Big Three had its own agenda. The British were distracted by Ireland and the empire, the French concentrated on continental matters and insisted on the continuation of wartime security alliances, and the Italians harbored revisionist ambitions – born of Italy's frustrated territorial claims at the Paris Peace Conference – in the Balkans and Near East. The United States, when present, worked on decoupling political from economic/financial matters, in part to avoid any entanglement in European conflicts. The British thought the French were "foolishly" obsessed with security matters, while the French believed the British were irresponsibly aloof from such issues. The Italians resented both for being dismissive of Italian aspirations. Diplomacy hobbled along until summit conferences and League diplomacy merged between 1924 and 1929, creating the golden years of Europeanism.

Western and East Central European security

Once the United States bowed out of the Versailles settlement, insuring European security became a challenge. The Americans abandoned their guarantee to France against future German aggression with the U.S. Senate's rejection of the Treaty of Versailles in late 1919, and the British quickly followed suit. France looked elsewhere to fill the void, and in 1920 it signed a military alliance with Belgium in which both countries pledged close cooperation against any German mobilization. For the French, the alliance meant that Belgium would serve as a battleground for a German offensive or as the launch pad for a French attack into the Rhineland. The treaty provoked an intense debate in Belgium over whether the alliance would provide the country with the security it sought or trigger an invasion that the alliance was supposed to forestall. As a result, the alliance with France had the potential for discord.

As for East Central Europe, Britain had no real interest in committing itself militarily to the region; Foreign Secretary Austen Chamberlain stated in 1925, for example, that "no British Government ever will or ever can risk the bones of a British grenadier" for the Polish Corridor.[2] France was the only Western country to extend a defensive, mutual aid treaty to Poland; it did so in February 1921, at the conclusion of the Polish-Soviet War. Motivated by the fear of Hungarian revisionism and Russian or German aggression, the Czechs, Yugoslavs, and Romanians signed a series of treaties in 1920 and 1921, forming a system known as the Little Entente. France supported the Little Entente by signing alliances with all of them. The crowning piece was the Franco-Czech Mutual Aid Treaty of January 1924. The Baltic countries of Estonia, Latvia, and Lithuania, meanwhile, formed a defensive league with Finland and Poland in 1922.

There could be no security in Europe generally, however, without the inclusion of Germany in the new European construct. Integrating Germany into the European mainstream achieved a major breakthrough in October 1925, when the foreign ministers of several European countries, including Germany, convened in the southern Swiss resort city of Locarno and reached agreement on a set of treaties of guarantee and arbitration, collectively known as the Locarno Pact. The most important accord, which Germany, Belgium, France, Britain, and Italy signed, guaranteed the French and Belgian borders against future German aggression and the demilitarization of the Rhineland. On the other hand, Germany refused to sign accords guaranteeing its borders with Poland and Czechoslovakia. The Germans only consented to arbitration treaties, which meant that they would settle any boundary revisions with these two countries peacefully. In other words, there was no "eastern Locarno." To counter the unwillingness of the Germans to guarantee their borders in the east, France reaffirmed its treaties of alliance with Poland and Czechoslovakia.

The Locarno Conference also paved the way for Germany to join the League of Nations in 1926, although the Germans conditioned their country's entry on an exemption from participating in League sanctions implemented in accordance with Article 16 of that body's Covenant. Germany's insistence was based on its desire to remain outside any League confrontation with the Soviet Union (Russia); Germany wanted to protect the friendly relationship established with the Soviets at Rapallo in 1922. The negotiators at Locarno hammered out a compromise that basically freed the Germans from any sanctions obligations.

The German and French architects of the Locarno Pact, Stresemann and Briand, received the Nobel Peace Prize for Peace in 1926, while Chamberlain viewed the accord as one of his noblest achievements. An era of "good feelings" known as the "Locarno spirit" began. For Poland and Czechoslovakia, the Locarno Treaty confirmed the divide between East and West, telling them that they were largely on their own. It was then that Józef Piłsudski formulated a balance of power strategy between Germany

Figure 3.2 Foreign Ministers Gustav Stresemann, Austen Chamberlain, and Aristide Briand (left to right) meet at the League of Nations in Geneva, Switzerland, following Germany's formal admission to the organization in September 1926.

and the Soviet Union as head of the Polish state in 1926, a strategy that Poland would pursue until 1939. Locarno lulled the Western European powers into a false sense of security.

A checkered Soviet foreign policy

The Soviet insistence on conducting an ideological war against anarchist, labor, and socialist parties from Norway to Spain triggered anti-Communist fears and rhetoric in the West. The call from the Comintern, the international Communist organization directed from Moscow, for the collapse of Western capitalist democracies contributed to continued Soviet isolation and proved counterproductive. It indirectly contributed to Mussolini's success in 1922, a Bulgarian right-wing coup in 1923, and Piłsudski's access to power in 1926. It was unable to inspire lasting revolutions elsewhere, and its zeal interfered with Soviet treaty obligations in Eastern Europe and Scandinavia, and with Soviet attempts to reestablish trade and settle debts with the West. Following the Locarno treaties, the Soviets offered separate non-aggression and commercial pacts to Finland, Estonia, Latvia, and Poland, in an attempt to dissolve a nascent anti-Soviet front.

With the West, true relations never developed. Leftist parties and governments in France and Britain were not durable enough to create lasting partnerships. In Britain, for example, the Labour government's extension of official diplomatic recognition to the Soviet Union on February 1, 1924, proved temporary. The publication in late 1924 of the Zinoviev letter, a forgery that caused a Red Scare in Britain owing to its call for Communist agitation on British soil, lay in the background of a break in diplomatic relations between the two countries in 1927, when the Conservatives held power. The issue of tsarist debts also continued to poison the air. Soviet negotiations for a final settlement of the tsarist debt to Britain resumed once diplomatic relations were restored under a new Labour government in 1929, but to no avail. The French government rejected a Soviet offer to repay 60 million gold francs in exchange for a $120 million loan.

Disarmament and collective security

Collective security and disarmament were high priority issues at the League of Nations in the 1920s. Indeed, the League represented the first large-scale attempt historically at collective security, and it had two options it could use in deterring aggression, namely, arbitration by the League Council and economic sanctions. The League's architects also believed that a reduction in global weaponry would lessen the chances of war. Already in 1918, Wilson had made arms reduction a part of his Fourteen Points, and this principle was incorporated into Article 8 of the League Covenant with the statement that "the maintenance of peace requires the reduction of national armaments to the lowest point consistent with national safety and the enforcement by common action of international agreements."[3]

The first major postwar attempt at disarmament occurred outside the structure of the League, when, at the invitation of American President Warren G. Harding, nine countries convened in Washington D.C. from November 1921 to February 1922 for what was the first truly international postwar conference. The Washington Conference settled a host of high seas and Asia-Pacific issues. In the area of disarmament, the world's five major naval powers – the United States, Great Britain, Japan, France, and Italy – agreed to respective ratios of 5:5:3:1.67:1.67 for capital ships and to a 10-year suspension of existing capital shipbuilding programs. On the other hand, they failed to settle on limits for cruisers and submarines. The nine nations at the conference – the five naval powers plus the Netherlands, Portugal, Belgium, and China – also signed a Nine-Power Pact that guaranteed the territorial integrity and independence of China as well as equal rights for all nations in business dealings with the Chinese. The Washington Conference was an example of Wilson's vision of open, multilateral diplomacy.

Disarmament talks took place in other forums during the 1920s. In June 1925, nations attending a conference in Geneva under the auspices of the League signed a Geneva Protocol that prohibited asphyxiating gases and bacteriological weapons in war. The world had already banned the wartime use of poison gas in The Hague Conventions of 1899 and 1907 but without effect after World War I began. In contrast to the prewar conventions, the Geneva Protocol largely succeeded: apart from Mussolini's violation of it in the Abyssinian war of 1935–1936, poison gas was not used in combat during the interwar years or World War II. In Scandinavia, Denmark adopted a policy of complete disarmament in March 1926 which it carried out immediately thereafter. The promise of collective security as a deterrent to war received a boost in the fall of 1926, when Germany formally entered the League of Nations in 1926 with a permanent seat on the Council.

While efforts toward disarmament moved ahead, there were those who believed that disarmament could not succeed without providing a collective security mechanism to fill the void. In 1924, left-of-center governments in Britain and France jointly sponsored the Geneva Protocol for the Pacific Settlement of International Disputes at the League of Nations. It called for the mandatory arbitration of all international disputes either before the World Court or the League Council and committed all signatories to a limitation on their sovereignty in favor of the League of Nations. Should a state refuse to submit, it would be labeled an aggressor and League members would be obligated to respond militarily to the extent that their geography and armaments situation allowed. The League member states gave their preliminary approval to the document at the 1924 General Assembly, but the Geneva Protocol of 1924 remained a dead letter when a recently elected Conservative government in Britain refused to ratify it in 1925. Ultimately, the British resisted the idea of compulsory intervention in disputes in East Central Europe or other regions where they believed their vital interests were not involved.

Another major peace initiative in international relations occurred in 1928, when U.S. Secretary of State Frank B. Kellogg and Briand introduced a multilateral treaty to outlaw war "as an instrument of national policy" and to settle disputes peacefully. The Kellogg–Briand Pact proved totally ineffective, however, since it contained no means for enforcement, and the signatories allowed themselves considerable latitude in how they interpreted it; wars of self-defense, for example, were deemed beyond the scope of the treaty. More than 60 nations signed the agreement which was negotiated independently of the League of Nations.

While the international negotiations and agreements of the 1920s did not achieve all their goals, the hopeful atmosphere that came from agreements such as the Locarno treaties and the Kellogg–Briand Pact gave heart to those who had disarmament as a goal. The League of Nations capitalized on the "Locarno spirit" by establishing in December 1925 a Preparatory Disarmament Commission that then engaged in several years of sometimes contentious discussions to lay the groundwork for a disarmament conference. When the World Disarmament Conference – with 59 countries present – convened in Geneva in 1932, it quickly fell into confusion as disagreements arose over what constituted offensive as opposed to defensive weapons and Germany demanded military rights equal to those countries whose forces were not restricted by peace treaties. After Adolf Hitler took power in Germany in early 1933, he persisted in arguing Germany's case for military equality. When France, fearful of Nazi intentions in Europe and aware of steps that Germany had already taken to rearm, refused Hitler's demand, he withdrew Germany from the conference and the League in October 1933. The conference ended in 1934 with nothing accomplished.

Conclusion

For all of the negotiations, conferences, and treaty signings that took place during the 1920s and early 1930s, very little was accomplished in the area of disarmament apart from the restrictions imposed on capital ships at the Washington Conference in 1921–1922. By the end of the 1920s, all powers not limited militarily by postwar peace treaties were spending on weaponry at levels beyond the prewar years. Even Germany, whose military apparatus was limited by the Treaty of Versailles, signed secret treaties with Soviet Russia in the 1920s to improve its military position in Europe. Collective security also suffered a decisive setback in 1931–1932, when the League of Nations failed to apply sanctions or any other strong measures to force a Japanese withdrawal from Manchuria following Japan's illegal occupation of the Chinese province in spite of pleas from China for League intervention.

Dreaming the United States of Europe

By 1914, it had become obvious to European rulers that change was imperative not just to protect the peace but, more importantly, to guarantee European hegemony at a time when the pressures of the larger world were being felt. Not only were minorities becoming restless within empires, but overseas countries such as the United States and Japan had become powerful economic rivals. Europe felt besieged from within and without, increasingly threatened in a globalizing world. Idealists and pragmatists began to rethink and redesign a unified Europe, addressing issues of borders, economic power, national identity, geographic integrity, and cultural heritage. World War I forced the debate into the open and gave it immediacy.

Federalist versus functionalist model

One of the most salient issues was that of a federalist versus a functionalist model. Federalists envisioned: a federal structure transcending nationalism; a teleological perspective; economic liberalism; economic and industrial modernization; pacifism; and a new international humanism. They advocated political integration with supranational institutions providing a new constitutional framework; new integrated legislation would eventually fill in the details. Functionalists advocated the creation of interstate boards and committees integrating industrial and economic sectors through cartels and ententes that would serve as administrative and organizational springboards towards broader economic integration; full financial, political, and cultural integration would follow. While most functionalists were businessmen who anchored their efforts in business and industrial ventures, the federalist movement had its supporters among conservative politicians and Christian thinkers and promoted the idea of professional and regional communities with a gradual renunciation of sovereignty.

European visions during the Great War

The Great War introduced new elements into the old debate about European unification. When hostilities broke out, a broad range of individuals responded to the challenge, from military leaders to trade unionists, philosophers, and theologians. They produced a remarkable diversity of proposals. The enormity of the task soon became apparent. East Central Europeans, for whom the problem of minorities was greatest, thought of intrastate or interstate federations. A wide range of individuals belonging to the Marxist or socialist family spoke in favor of a restored Poland made up of a federation of Poles, Lithuanians, Belorussians, and Ukrainians. Likewise, a Yugoslav federation of Croats, Slovenes, and Serbs had numerous supporters. Some of these plans were based on past solutions. Minorities, however, who had suffered under the repressive federal systems of the empires in which they lived, were often opposed to federalist plans and instead strengthened their demands for independence.

Western industrialists and businessmen believed that a form of European Union was desirable in the interest of continental power. Peace, for them, was a way to enhance their industrialized, modern potential; hence they sought some form of economic unification among themselves. Interestingly, pre-revolutionary Bolsheviks also advocated the economic unification of Europe, except not in a capitalist system. Lenin envisioned a brotherly association of liberated peoples modeled on the plans of late eighteenth-century French revolutionaries. The most concrete and comprehensive union proposal was the German-dominated union of Central European lands or *Mitteleuropa* (Middle Europe). One variation was a functionalist approach that advocated interstate sector by sector economic integration. Friedrich Naumann, in his work *Mitteleuropa* (1915), advocated a German-ruled Central Europe based on a gradualist series of steps that would give nations time to acquire habits of cooperation through a growing network of interstate economic and political boards and committees. German Chancellor Bethmann-Hollweg also gave primacy to economic unification under German domination. Feeling threatened by the rise of American economic power and by Slavic expansion, which he compared to a new "great migration," Bethmann-Hollweg initially saw an Anglo-German axis as the center of a Western and Central European federation. As the war progressed, his ideas adapted to Germany's war aims. In 1916, he advocated a United States of Europe that would bring under German leadership the economies of France, Belgium, Luxembourg, the Netherlands, Denmark, Poland, Austria–Hungary, Italy, Sweden, and Norway. France would be weakened, Britain thrown out of Belgium, and Russia stymied to insure the cohesion of Central Europe. Germany's defeat prevented the realization of the *Mitteleuropa* plan, but not the impact of the concept. *Mitteleuropa* became a point of reference at many interwar discussions of Europe, alternatively feared or emulated. These plans, however, took a backstage to more radical movements.

Early postwar European designs

After 1918, the federalist movement had a chance to be applied in the new countries of East Central Europe, where national identity and national institutions needed to be built from scratch. With the destruction of four large European empires, minorities with claims to independence proliferated. Not all could form viable states. Thus, federated states with multi-ethnic populations were created in places such as Poland, Czechoslovakia, and Yugoslavia. Proposals for the regional integration of the new small states were made to increase their security: Croat leader Stjepan Radić proposed a Balkan federation, and Czech leader Tomáš Masaryk offered a plan for a Mid-European Union of the small states of Central Europe. In the end, there arose a loosely built alliance: the Little Entente. Made up of Czechoslovakia, Yugoslavia, and Romania, it was designed primarily to prevent German or Hungarian ascendancy in the Danube Basin.

By 1919, Europe was in a state of despondency, with its weakened national institutions, blurred and confused borders, and destroyed industrial plants. Individuals and institutions from all walks of life saw in this despondency the opportunity to create a new Europe; these included Protestant and Catholic church leaders, Christian social movements, intellectuals, politicians, socialists, trade unionists, businessmen, bankers, and political parties. The phrase "United States of Europe" struck a chord in many influential circles. As the economic, financial, and diplomatic power of the United States captivated European nations, including the Soviet Union, a number of people concluded that only a modernized, united Europe could keep the continent globally relevant. Calls for "a crusade for Europe" were issued, followed by calls to surpass American economic power. What, however, were the possibilities? Britain lived for its colonial empire, and large parts of Russia and the Ottoman Empire were non-European. If these powers were out, continental Europe was left. But it was a two-speed machine, with an industrialized, wealthy, liberal-democratic

Map 3.1 Europe's borders in 1919.

northern and western region that controlled colonies, and an impoverished, authoritarian-prone, traditional, and agricultural eastern and southern belt. Could they be harmonized? Which country, if any, would take the lead? Also, what would one do with Germany? Various entities contributed to a new spirit of European cooperation that developed after the war. They included the small countries of East Central Europe that advanced regional federation plans, and Western and Northern Europe business communities that joined together to advance functionalist associations.

International associations

The League of Nations became a natural magnet for European projects, since it brought authority, visibility, a cooperative spirit, and an impressive organizational apparatus to any such negotiations. Its wide jurisdiction was defined in Article 23 of the League's Covenant which stated that League members would take necessary dispositions to insure freedom of communications and transit, and an equitable commerce among member states. As a result, four major areas came under the purview of the League: commerce, monetary stabilization, social issues, and customs unions. The League had a vast array of committees, such as Communication and Transit, Economy and Finances, and Opium and Drug Trafficking, to deal with issues related to those four areas. It also had mechanisms for peaceful arbitration in the form of the League Council and the Permanent Court of International Justice in The Hague, Netherlands. In addition, a number of outside institutions worked closely with it, such as the Universal Postal Union and the International Labor Organization. In the area of transit, the League held several conferences that had positive outcomes, such as the 1921 Barcelona Convention on Freedom of Transit and International Waterways (ports, roads, railways) that guaranteed the freedom of movement of commercial products by rail or boat across national frontiers.

European-wide technological projects

Additional impetus for a more unified Europe came from the world of technology, especially from the growing community of engineers. The world of engineering grew in importance after the war, supporting a techno-political revolution and creating an *esprit de corps* among engineers from Britain to the Urals. One area where this clearly emerged in the 1920s was electricity. Electrification predated the war, when some thought that an interstate energy grid would create political consensus, and that energy interdependency would help prevent war. Following World War I, Daniel Nicol Dunlop, a key player in developing the British electrical industry, laid the preparations for a World Power Conference that met in 1924. It was an example of the new internationalism that emerged after the war. Seventeen hundred delegates from 40 countries attended the conference, where they discussed the future of electrical energy. The meeting's success was demonstrated in 1925 with the founding of a permanent World Power Conference. When the Second World Power Conference convened in Berlin in 1930, German President Paul von Hindenburg told the delegates at its opening session that:

> on its foundation the World Power Conference was called the 'Technical League of Nations' and nothing is indeed better calculated to league together the nations of the earth than a mutual endeavor of this kind to further the common weal.[4]

It was there that German electricity executive Oskar Oliven, moving beyond the local and national electrification schemes that most engineers embraced, presented a visionary proposal for a European-wide supply network. The League of Nations Organization for Communications and Transit and the International Labor Organization under Thomas advanced the idea in the 1930s by studying the prospects of a European electricity network. Other international electro-technical organizations also emerged in the 1920s, including the International Council on Large Electric Systems and the International Union of Producers and Distributors of Electrical Energy (UNIPEDE), a worldwide electrical clearinghouse for technical, administrative, commercial, and financial issues. These efforts advanced until the early 1930s, when the Great Depression and the emergence of unstable international relations thwarted them.

The International Labor Organization

The breadth of the attempts at economic unification is reflected in the work that the International Labor Organization (ILO) did in standardizing international labor laws and practices. The ILO was an agency – albeit completely autonomous – of the League of Nations and overseen by former French socialist politician Albert Thomas, the indefatigable ILO director-general. Thomas sought to protect the rights of workers, standardize labor practices, and with the assistance of several Western European labor ministers, draft new labor laws. Trade unions had been among the first international organizations before the war, and as the workforce became more internationalized after 1919, the need to regulate labor competition and labor migration increased, particularly in regard to establishing equal treatment for immigrant workers. Until 1935, the ILO focused on European workers, partly because industrial Europe was still at the center of international economic and political life, but also because the Soviet Union and United States were not League members. In spite of its Eurocentric focus, the ILO also strove to abolish forced labor in colonial lands. The ILO expressed considerable frustration in 1928, when the world learned about Soviet forced labor practices. Two years later the ILO adopted a Forced Labor Convention that ten countries, mostly European, ratified by the end of 1932. The ILO had an important ally in the International Federation of Trade Unions, a primarily European body that lobbied governments and the League of Nations in support of ILO measures.

Thomas also used the ILO as a platform for another ambitious project: that of an organized, coordinated industrial Europe. His plan included the building of highways and canals, common customs duties, a European labor bank, the organization of a European-wide labor market, and the creation of a Pan-European bank. He believed that the confluence of international transportation, labor, transit of persons and goods, and financial services would in the end create a large market. At the League of Nations, Sir Arthur Salter, a British civil servant then serving as the director of the economic and financial section of the League, gave his full support to Thomas' scheme. Both Thomas and Salter stressed the need to organize Europe along industrial and agricultural lines, and both advocated a common market enhanced by technological progress in the areas of transportation and communication. The International Chamber of Commerce endorsed their ideas which became an integral part of Briand's United States of Europe proposal in 1930.

A Pan-Europeanist movement

The first popular European movement was Count Richard Coudenhove-Kalergi's Pan-European project. The heir to a distinguished noble family that had long served the Habsburg monarchy, Coudenhove-Kalergi was not only an internationalist by descent, but also a dedicated federalist. His immediate interest was to prevent the fragmentation of the Danube River basin and to serve the needs of the recently divided Balkans, but he soon broadened his regional plan to become the champion of Europe. He was one of the first individuals to talk about "regionalizing" the League of Nations into five areas, namely, Pan-America, the British Empire, Russia, Pan-Asia, and Pan-Europe. His continental federation scheme was based on Franco-German reconciliation and a customs union that would blossom into economic integration. Mandatory arbitration treaties would insure Europe's defense. Coudenhove-Kalergi created the Pan-European Union in Vienna in 1922, published his seminal work, *Pan-Europa*, in 1923, and launched a journal by the same title. With Pan-European committees in the major European countries, and 6,000–9,000 members, the Pan-European Union was well connected. It garnered its greatest support among French politicians, notably Briand, who actively promoted the European idea at the League of Nations after accepting the position of Honorary President of the Pan-European Union. But many saw Coudenhove-Kalergi's efforts as idealistic, and his Second Pan-European Congress of 1930 was derisively dubbed "the children's crusade."

Private Europeanist societies

By the mid-1920s, Europeanism had the backing of key players of the Versailles settlement of 1919 and several individuals who would become planners of the post-World War II order. A flurry of activities took place with the goal of enacting a pragmatic vision that involved a customs union, followed by financial integration and a common market. Two generations of leaders representing the worlds of banking, industry, commerce, and politics in Western and Central Europe formed several private organizations calling for economic cooperation. The European Customs Union, created in 1925, counted British economist and Versailles delegate John Maynard Keynes as a supporter, and its members came from 18 nations by 1930. One of them, French economist Francis Delaisi, wanted a monetary union, followed by a central bank with a common currency, while another, Belgian law professor and economist Paul van Zeeland, favored regional unions among states with similar economic profiles as the first step towards a common market. The European Federation, another influential group, was created in 1926 to advance the cause of political integration, and by 1930 it had members from 20 countries. Comprised mostly of committees made up of national parliamentarians, it worked closely with the League of Nations. In France, where the European movement was very strong, an Economic and Customs Action Committee was created in 1925 to promote a free market. The father of future French President Valéry Giscard d'Estaing was a member, and so was the future economic planner Jean Monnet, who presented a memorandum to the French foreign ministry in 1930 about it.

International economic and business initiatives

Businessmen and financiers seized the opportunities offered by the post-World War I relaxation of wartime economic *dirigisme* to promote associations that could link supply and demand and open new markets. One of them was the International Chamber of Commerce, established in 1920. Two of its main goals were to promote lower tariffs and encourage industrial ententes. Many European industrialists and key political leaders favored producers' ententes, although their efforts did not always generate the outcomes they sought. Emile Mayrisch, a Luxembourgian businessman, was pivotal in the creation in 1926 of the International Steel Cartel consisting of France, Germany, Belgium, Luxembourg, and the Saar. He served as its president until his death in an automobile accident in 1928. German Foreign Minister Stresemann, a convinced Europeanist, called the accord creating the steel cartel a "landmark of international economic policy, the importance of which cannot be overestimated."[5] The cartel began to come apart shortly after its creation, however, when German producers began exceeding their quotas, and it was dissolved in 1931. A reorganized steel cartel, formed in 1933 with a greater number of states as members, worked more effectively but it also collapsed with the onset of World War II in 1939. French politician Louis Loucheur was decisive in organizing a World Economic Conference, which brought 194 delegates from 50 countries to Geneva in 1927, though it failed to endorse Loucheur's call for arranging Europe's or even the world's principal industries into cartels, also known as horizontal producers' ententes. Undismayed, Loucheur continued to lobby for producers' ententes, seeing them as the first priority in organizing Europe economically.

Federation projects in agricultural Europe

In East Central European countries, whose economies were agriculturally based, federation projects centered on trade agreements and agricultural ententes as the foundation for economic integration. The Balkan Federation, heir to a nineteenth-century project, asked for land redistribution and agrarian ententes with the support of Communist and peasant parties. Another organization that encouraged agricultural cooperation, this time among agrarian political parties, was the International Agrarian Bureau that was created in 1921, with agrarian parties from Czechoslovakia, Poland, Bulgaria, and Yugoslavia giving it a definite Pan-Slav orientation. It served as a place to exchange information and to create an *esprit de corps* among agrarian parties. The Bureau's orientation expanded in the latter 1920s so that by 1929 it had 17 member parties. At the 1927 World Economic Conference, East Central European countries promoted the integration of the agricultural sector, an area where they suffered from overproduction, and their delegates were among the most supportive of the idea of an economic union in the name of European solidarity. Briand later talked about organizing Europe not just industrially but also agriculturally, and in a rare show of a Western commitment to strengthening ties with East Central Europe, Loucheur in 1930 traveled to several East Central European countries to garner support for the principle of economic cooperation.

The Briand era, 1925–1932

From 1925 to 1932, the spirit of Locarno, Germany's presence in the League of Nations, and a benign leadership at the League created the right conditions for the European project to blossom. During these six years, the League was the center of Europeanist efforts. Briand, the chief French delegate at the League of Nations since 1923, became the most visible spokesperson for Europe. At Locarno in 1925, he talked about "realizing the European destiny," and shortly thereafter he started working on his European idea. Aware that his ideas were "generous," he sought a middle way, reconciling functionalist and federalist ideas, avoiding an alienation of the United States, and preventing a duplication of the League of Nations' committee work, in particular its Conference on Tariffs. He postponed his proposals on Europe to take care of another important issue, namely disarmament, so it was not until after the Briand–Kellogg Peace Pact had been signed that he turned his attention back to European unity with a sense of urgency caused by continuing minorities problems, war debts rescheduling, and the end of the Allied military occupation of the defeated powers.

Filled with the sense that the Versailles era was closing, Briand was convinced that only unity could ensure the survival of Europe. Trying to expand the spirit of Locarno, he linked security, economic, and civilizational issues in a plan that he presented at the opening session of the League of Nations in September 1929. In it, he called for the creation of a federal Europe that, without affecting the sovereignty of its participating states, would be built on an "economic solidarity pact" leading to a common market. The response to his proposal from the 27 assembled nations' representatives was tepid, for the memorandum was perceived as a French power play. Briand allowed one year for foreign governments to formulate a response. There ensued in the next twelve months a flurry of governmental and non-governmental activities followed by several proposals. Among the most significant was Albert Thomas' ILO proposal for the development of an industrial Europe that would serve as the first step toward building Europe "sector by sector." East Central European agrarian parties proposed various plans for an agriculture-based Danubian economic entente.

In May 1930, Briand circulated among League members an ambitious memorandum that represented the official position of the French government. Calling for broad cooperation at all levels while guaranteeing state sovereignty, the document proposed the creation of a European Federal Union with complete free trade and a political structure capable of resolving economic disputes, an issue that had sunk earlier customs unions. A representative assembly and an executive body would insure the political cooperation of all participants. A gradualist, Briand recommended that Europe be organized industrially first, then agriculturally, with the two units eventually joined in a common market. While not new, his proposal synthesized ideas that had circulated since 1919 and had the merit of uniting the agricultural countries of East Central Europe with the industrialized states of Western Europe.

Responses were discussed at the League in September 1930. Most countries affirmed the need for European integration under the leadership of the League, but disagreed on other issues. Luxembourg stressed arbitration and Denmark arms reductions. Some members wanted the inclusion of non-League countries such as Turkey and the Soviet Union. Britain, the Netherlands, and Norway wanted colonies included. Most countries still objected to the creation of a supranational political authority. Germany, meanwhile, called for something entirely different, namely, a revision of the 1919 treaties.

Realizing the importance of promoting a united Europe, the League created a Commission of Enquiry for European Union to oversee all European-wide projects. Chaired by Briand, the commission met between 1930 and 1932. At the same time, Briand vigorously pursued the agricultural component of his union plan, sending emissaries to Prague, Budapest, Vienna, and Berlin, where they recommended an East–West agricultural production and credit agreement. With the worsening commercial climate, however, the Central and Eastern European states were more interested in bilateral or multilateral regional agreements, trying to repair their economies and to build blocs that would enable them to negotiate on equal terms with Western European countries. When the Germans and Austrians in March 1931 announced an Austro-German customs union project (see p. 165), partly as a countermove to France's goal of an agrarian bloc in Eastern and Central Europe, it sparked immediate opposition from the French. The proposal came before the League's enquiry commission in May 1931, where Briand personally condemned it, and the commission expressed its strong disapproval. Under pressure from several sources, Germany and Austria abandoned the plan in September. The French, meanwhile, continued to push the Briand plan by proposing broader East–West agricultural–industrial cooperation. In the end, no grand European design could be agreed upon by the time the League's opening meeting took place in September 1931. The enquiry commission was dissolved in late 1932.

Conclusion

The federalist model of European integration was not popular among many European leaders fearful of encroachment on national sovereignty, especially in Britain and the newly created East Central European countries. Functionalism contained elements that could address major roadblocks, but it did not fulfill its potential, mainly because its advocates failed to look beyond a common market. Another difficulty that proved insurmountable was the division between industrial Western Europe and agricultural Eastern Europe. For all these reasons, Briand's proposal was both too late and too early. It was too late, because it was unable to counter the rising tide of nationalism, and it was too early, because Europe was not ready for his blend of federalism and functionalism, or for uniting Eastern and Western Europe. Still, his vision of Europe would inspire the building of European institutions after 1945. Even though the 1920s ended without a consensus, the decade did much to promote peace and security in Europe and to advance the thinking about European integration. As the 1930s began, the only feasible governance models were nineteenth-century types of customs unions, commercial treaties, and the nation-state.

Colonial developments

In 1919, the colonial powers were still at their zenith, especially the British Empire which consisted of more than one-quarter of the world's land area and population. The British Empire featured more Muslim subjects than any native Muslim ruler could boast. But the British and French overextended themselves when they acquired some of the defeated powers' colonies after World War I; they found it difficult to control their new possessions in the Middle East and their new ones in North Africa. Besides, the continuation of colonialism caused disputes between the French and the British, and fueled new imperialist visions in countries as diverse as Italy, Germany, Poland, and Spain.

The British Dominions

Following World War I, the six white British Dominions (Canada, Newfoundland, South Africa, Australia, New Zealand, and the Irish Free State), which were self-governing entities, distanced themselves from Britain's European policies. Recognizing the collapse of its dream of an imperial federation, Britain in 1926 convened an Imperial Conference. The conference adopted the Balfour Report that defined the status of Great Britain and the Dominions as a free association of autonomous communities, equal in status, united by a common allegiance to the Crown, with freedom of conduct in domestic and foreign policy. This report, which launched the British Commonwealth of Nations, represented an end to any British legislative authority over the Dominions. The Statute of Westminster that the British Parliament passed in 1931 constitutionally confirmed the change.

Colonial leaders

The color line returned even before the ink had dried on the armistice documents in November 1918. Demobilized colonial soldiers were often exposed to humiliating treatment. Independence leaders who brought their demands to the Paris Peace

Conference were unable to make headway. Vietnamese leader Ho Chi Minh's petition for independence in Vietnam went unheard as did the Algerian veterans' pleas for self-determination. The British temporarily exiled the leaders of Egypt's nationalist liberal political party who pled for an end to Britain's occupation of their country. But demands for independence grew in spite of the repression.

The real spark for nationalism in black Africa originated in the Western Hemisphere. The protest of 15,000 West Indies men at the Taranto base in Italy in December 1918 started the unraveling of British colonial rule in the Caribbean. The founding of the Caribbean League in July 1919, which spread strikes across Trinidad, and the subsequent forced emigration of Belize soldiers to South America and Cuba internationalized the movement. One of the first black nationalist leaders was W. E. B. DuBois, an American historian and writer who was the first black to earn a Ph.D. at Harvard University. In 1919, he organized a Pan-African Congress in Paris to coincide with the Paris Peace Conference. Pan-Africanists were advocates of black solidarity and, ultimately, a large self-ruling state encompassing all African peoples. Peace conference leaders reluctantly endorsed the gathering, but none of them attended. The congress called on the peace conference negotiators to place Germany's colonies under the direct authority of the League of Nations, but that did not happen. Three more Pan-African congresses followed during the 1920s where the theme of African self-government was prominent. Using a more forceful tone, Dubois also condemned the British and Americans for oppressing Africans and looting African resources. Very few Africans participated in the last of these congresses, owing to strictures that the British and French authorities placed on those interested in attending as a way of discouraging future Pan-African assemblies. The movement then faded until 1945. Another leader of black nationalism was Marcus Garvey, a Jamaica-born Pan-Africanist who promoted African independence and the ouster of Europeans from Africa. He became the most powerful spokesman of Pan-Africanism in the first years after World War I.

Future African leaders of independence movements also began to emerge in various European colonies in the interwar years. One of those influenced by Garvey's ideas was Jomo Kenyatta, who entered politics full-time in the British colony of Kenya in the late 1920s in defense of the Kikuyu people, the colony's largest ethnic group. He traveled to London in 1929 to protest British plans for a closer union of Uganda, Tanganyika, and Kenya, since he believed that such a scheme would open the door to self-rule for white settlers while ignoring the rights of his people. During the 1930s, he briefly studied at the University of Moscow, became acquainted with other black African nationalists, earned a degree in anthropology at the London School of Economics, and led protests against Italy's war in Abyssinia. He became the first head of an independent Kenya in 1963. In French West Africa in the 1930s, Senegalese leader and poet Léopold Sédar Senghor fostered *négritude*, i.e., a feeling of pride in African cultures, arts, and traditions. His relation with France was not adversarial, despite the fact that the French Parliament rejected a Senegalese petition for independence.

These early demands for change were backed by organized movements that drew from broad segments of society: local leaders, European-educated bourgeois elites, demobilized soldiers, and vast numbers of postwar migrant workers. The continued rise of an urban workforce through postwar worker migrations created an ideal training ground for independence leaders. Political associations, newspapers, alumni groups, ethnic clubs, dance societies, and sports clubs nurtured the new political ideas and ushered in the age of urban riots. These movements, which matured in the 1930s, saw the creation of African women's and students' groups, the latter forming branches in Europe as well. Interwar political activism heightened demands for independence, and saw a consolidation of several small groups such as trade unions, small parties, and ethnic organizations into larger groupings. Islamic religious associations triggered the rise of the Khalifat movement that encouraged an Islamic resurgence from Morocco to the Dutch East Indies.

The more developed colonies had internationally educated leaders. In Vietnam, Ho Chi Minh learned Marxist socialism in France and spent time during World War I in the United States where he made friends in Harlem. Indian leader Mohandas Gandhi was a British-educated lawyer whose advocacy of a return to a simple life, home industries, and militant pacifism followed in the Hindu tradition and borrowed from English art critic John Ruskin and Russian novelist Leo Tolstoy. After organizing Indian workers in South Africa for 20 years, Gandhi returned to India in 1916 where he laid the groundwork for non-violent resistance to British authority.

The developed British colonies of India and Egypt illustrate how precarious colonial positions had become. The Indian nationalist movement reached a new level of strength in 1916, when the country's two leading political groups, one Hindu and the other Muslim, forged an alliance in 1916 demanding self-government for their country. The British responded with a reform measure that instituted a dual system of government – a diarchy – in the land. Enacted in 1919, the Government of India Act introduced locally elected provincial assemblies and endorsed gradual self-government, but it also maintained a level of British authoritarianism by keeping key matters such as taxes and justice under strict British control. For many in India, the legislation was a disappointment. Meanwhile, the British-dominated government of India in early 1919 passed a set of acts that indefinitely continued oppressive wartime emergency measures, sparking riots across the land. One result was the Amritsar Massacre in April 1919, when British-led Indian troops killed at least 379 and wounded 1,200 unarmed Indians protesting against the acts in the city of Amritsar. Gandhi reacted by launching a national campaign of civil disobedience that lasted from 1920 to 1922, when he was imprisoned. After his release in 1924, Gandhi spent several years trying to reunite what had become a fractured nationalist movement. It was a time when animosity in India toward British rule was considerable and intensifying.

In Egypt, the British faced a national insurrection in 1919, forcing them to occupy the country militarily and open independence talks, the bulk of which revolved around the Suez Canal. Egypt was granted complete independence in 1922, but the British made it into a de facto protectorate under the 1923 Lausanne treaty with Turkey, keeping control over vital communications, defense, foreign interests, and the Sudan. Especially important to the British was their control over the Suez Canal. During World War I, Egypt had become Britain's major base for Middle Eastern operations because of the canal, and it remained vital for postwar imperial defense.

The large Muslim communities in Africa and Asia witnessed a rapid growth of nationalist movements. Keeping these communities peaceful was considered essential to maintaining effective colonial control, and development aid was deemed vital to stemming nationalism. Development credits, more autonomy, a sense of privilege, humanitarian concerns about welfare, health, and education, and even self-government were aimed at cultivating local elites. Thus, social engineering was used as a panacea for social problems. One advocate for increased development aid was French Minister of Colonies

Albert Sarraut. In 1921, he introduced, as a deterrent to nationalism, an economic development and modernization plan for Africa that included long-term investment funding and close economic and financial partnerships. To gain support for his plan, he crafted a "red scare" climate, equating colonial nationalism with Communism. After using this approach in Sub-Saharan Africa, North Africa, and Syria, he applied it to Vietnam in the mid-1920s, where he assumed there was a vast conspiracy involving Dutch East Indies Communists, Soviet advisors in China, strike organizers, nationalist groups, and even pro-Communist sympathizers among the French troops deployed in Asia. By the time that serious anti-colonial protests occurred in French Indochina in 1930–1931, he believed that Pan-Islamism, Pan-Africanism, and Asian groups were conspiring to destroy European imperial power.

Political and administrative change in Africa

For the most part, change was reactionary, cosmetic, and self-serving, especially in Africa. In an effort to avoid a repetition of wartime unrest, administrative districts were redrawn and territories were renamed in the Sudan and Kenya. The British Crown colonies remained locked under autocratic white control. British West Africa, which had fewer European settlers than other African colonies, moved slightly away from direct rule when in 1922 Nigeria received a constitution that provided for elected councils. This model of British-supervised local councils left local people with little power, however, and in British minds, the strengthening of local self-government served as an antidote to nationalist movements or undesired behavior. In eastern and southern Africa, where the number of British settlers was greater, the human rights situation was slightly better for the indigenous populations. In the former German African colonies, which were under League scrutiny, the colonial authorities had to provide a modicum of human rights to the local populations.

In French West Africa, the French continued their longstanding "civilizing mission" and policy of assimilation, which involved integrating indigenous populations into France's cultural and administrative networks. For instance, the coastal inhabitants of Senegal, who were unique among French West Africans in holding the status of French citizenship regardless of ethnicity and having a representative in France's parliament, elected their first black representative – Blaise Diagne – to the French Chamber of Deputies in 1914. A product of French assimilation, he obtained parliamentary passage in 1916 of legislation formally acknowledging the French citizenship rights of Senegal's coastal residents. He remained in the French Chamber of Deputies until his death in 1934, advocating for equal rights for all Senegalese Africans within a French framework. Diagne served in the Ministry of Colonies from 1918 to 1920, and eventually reached the position of undersecretary of state for the colonies in the early 1930s. With the passage of time, he increasingly became an apologist for French colonialism and its assimilationist doctrine. As for France, its policies represented an attempt to stem the tide of change and to prevent independence movements from growing.

Reverse migration

The number of colonial peoples in Europe continued to grow, coming mostly as soldiers and students. Conscription in French Africa alone brought approximately 8,000 African soldiers into Europe each year. After World War I, troops from Senegal remained in

Europe, where they were sent as a part of France's occupation force to the Rhineland in 1919. The presence of black African troops in Germany added to the hostility that many locals felt toward the occupying army. Senegal also contributed large numbers of infantrymen, reservists, and men in labor brigades to participate in France's interwar colonial conflicts. The Algerian population of France increased several-fold in 1919, mostly from demobilized soldiers. Although their total number of 30,000 was small, frictions occurred with the local population. Unrest in the colonies often led to hostile demonstrations at home, such as the anti-North African protests in France in 1924. Immigrants lived in separate urban areas: Algerians were concentrated in the fifteenth *arrondissement* (an administrative district) in Paris and black Africans on Drury Lane in London. The result was de facto segregation.

The League of Nations, colonies, and health issues

Through League of Nations-sponsored international conferences, Europeans addressed the growing global issues of drugs and health after the war. The first conference on global health took place in 1922 to deal with epidemics that plagued postwar Europe. Later conferences dealt with tropical diseases that had ravaged Allied troops during the war and that remained a major issue in Africa. Efforts to improve health in Africa and India increased in the 1930s; the British, for example, created their Colonial Medical Service in 1934. The deadly disease tuberculosis had been contained by 1900, but during World War I cases of it again appeared. The Paris-based Louis Pasteur Institute developed a vaccine for it. Called BCG (Bacillus Calmette-Guérin), it had several trials in the 1920s, none convincing. By 1930, Albert Calmette, a Pasteur Institute researcher, chose a new venue for testing: the colonial city of Algiers, where the incidence of tuberculosis was devastating, and where the French kept population records that made it easy to control the experiments. Enlisting the help of the League of Nations' Health Organization and the Rockefeller Foundation, Calmette introduced an international dimension to his trials, justifying them on the basis of humanitarian concern and the need to create international standards for biological products. Once again, the colonies, where tuberculosis cases were four or five times higher than in Europe, became a laboratory of modernity. The clinical trial that Calmette started – he died in 1933 – became the largest of its kind in the world, involving 40,000 subjects over a period of 26 years. Only the onset of the Algerian War in the mid-1950s brought it to an end. Calmette's team obtained results much faster than it could have done in Europe, but at the same time, it blurred the border between medical trial and medical care by withholding treatment from the control population. Although Calmette's protocol obtained mixed results, it served as a model for future vaccination policies, especially for the World Health Organization after 1945.

Colonial labor

Labor issues were also considered global during the interwar years. The International Labor Organization addressed issues related to labor migration, and created support programs for relocating workers. These programs laid the groundwork for dispositions regarding income security, medical care of veterans and war workers, minimum standards of social policy in dependent territories, employment organization in transition from war to peace, and national planning of public works. But these policies generally failed to reach colonial populations. African workers were sometimes treated little better than slaves, as Europeans continued labor conscription practices after the war. While forced labor generally diminished after 1920, the system, which originated in South Africa, actually expanded in Britain's African colonies. South Africa even segregated workers in mines and kept land ownership in white settlers' hands, a practice that formed the basis for the 1948 South African policy of apartheid. The South African practice of racial segregation led to the creation of a powerful mass-based black Industrial and Commercial Workers Union (ICU) in 1919 and to demonstrations in Johannesburg in 1920.

Throughout Africa, levying high taxes on black African farmers often cost them their farms and forced them to seek work in mines and on plantations. This led to an increase in all-male migrant labor. Traditional systems of community life disintegrated, and native handicrafts – especially local metal and textile industries – were wiped out. The constant stream of mostly male emigration caused family separations and demographic stagnation, which in turn negatively affected the colonial economies. Migrant workers were housed in male-only compounds where their freedom was limited. Lowly paid laborers worked in Rhodesia's lucrative copper mines and Nigeria's tin mines. In the French and Belgian colonies, the situation was not much better. The French were intent on building the best road system in Africa to attract more settlers and create new economic opportunities. In the 1920s, 20,000 Africans lost their lives building a French railway to the ocean in the Congo. In the 1930s, forced cotton cultivation in the Belgian Congo was widely practiced; the Belgians also employed 500,000 workers in the Congolese mines before 1930, the highest total in tropical Africa. South Africa in the 1920s produced half of the world's gold, and significant amounts of manganese, platinum, and other precious metals. American businesses benefited as well: in Liberia, the Firestone Tire and Rubber Company created the largest rubber plantation in the world. Tea, another lucrative British export, was produced on Indian plantations where South American plantation charters were applied, which meant indentured labor.

Colonial economic development

During World War I, the French and British began to pay greater attention to their colonies and decided to shift from requiring colonial financial self-sufficiency to providing development aid. One step was the British decision in 1917 to create an Imperial Development Board. After the war, British Colonial Secretary Leo Amery and French Minister of the Colonies Albert Sarraut conceived of a rationalized, comprehensive framework for the development of their countries' colonies. A number of colonial research institutes were created to increase scientific and rational planning. These steps, to which were added the new ideal of development aid for the colonies, led to the expansion of colonial economies and to a rise in their exports in the 1920s. But problems remained. Aid was slow to come, owing in part to the colonial powers' war debt and reconstruction burdens. The modest French and British colonial budgets of the 1920s were spent primarily on the military, law and order, administration, and transportation. When output from mines and agricultural yields thrived, they were produced for large export companies that sent virtually all the profits abroad. Besides, cash crop monocultures such as cocoa and cotton did little to help local development. Even colonies with flourishing economies, such as British-controlled Nigeria, were vulnerable. The Portuguese colonies of Mozambique and Angola were disease-ridden and poor; their high commissioners were so corrupt and brutal that a scandal over slavery there contributed to a 1926 military coup in Portugal. Economic dependency, vulnerability to fluctuating market prices, and scandalous working conditions were the norm. The newly urbanized and unionized workers lived in segregated housing. Workers in the Congo's new mining towns lived in a semi-apartheid system of forced labor. This represented the "development of under-development."

The British African colony of the Gold Coast stands out as an exception, owing to the leadership of Sir Frederick Gordon Guggisberg, the Gold Coast's colonial governor in the 1920s. Improved transportation, better water supply and drainage, hydroelectric projects, the construction of public buildings, urban development, new schools, and expanded communication lines were among the results. The colony's first artificial deep-water port in the capital, Takoradi, was also built. In response to pressures from the educated indigenous elite, Guggisberg in 1925 promulgated the Guggisberg Constitution that provided for elections to a legislative council, although real lawmaking authority remained in the hands of the governor. The native elite, whose numbers on the legislative council were sparse, felt marginalized by the constitution, and they dreamed of eventual independence for their colony.

Africa was by and large left out of private investment, and public subsidies for health and welfare went to the richer and more developed colonies, most notably to the mandates of the Middle East. African public health, social needs, and education remained primarily the responsibility of missionaries. Most colonies had a two-tier educational system that amounted to educational apartheid, in which the elites and the poor received vastly different educations. Belgium, with the help of the Roman Catholic Church, the King, and white-owned companies, was the exception: it created the best vocational and elementary schooling for the indigenous population in Africa.

Transportation was given priority, because railroads were seen as the key to economic development. The French, British, and Belgians gave priority to infrastructure: port extension, railroads, railroad to port connections, and roads. Sarraut estimated in 1922 that the development of adequate transportation would triple the economic output of the colonies. Everywhere, massive railway construction programs occurred; based on the model of the Trans-Siberian railroad, the Trans-Ethiopian, Trans-Indochinese, Trans-Australian, and Trans-Sudanese railroads were built. In India, the British constructed an impressive 5,360 miles of railroad between 1925 and 1932, although this fell short of the projected 1,000 miles a year planned by the Indian Railway Board. Airplane routes were also created. The first lines were reserved for mail communication, and the pioneering feats of the French writer and pilot Antoine de Saint-Exupéry over the Sahara desert, narrated in his journal *Pilote de ligne*, were soon followed by others. In 1924, the Dutch airline company KLM launched the first passenger flight from Amsterdam to Jakarta, covering 9,600 miles. The first flight took 55 days, but by 1929, the length of the trip was reduced to 12 days. Roads were also given priority: 29,000 miles of paved roads were built in India between 1920 and 1929, and half of the 25,000 kilometers of roads constructed in Africa by Sarraut were stone-paved. Progress in the Dutch East Indies and Belgian Congo was also impressive.

The colonial city

Before World War I, the imperial city was the locus of colonial power, and plans were underway to underline this symbol. Impressive government buildings were erected; the Viceroy House in New Delhi, for example, which was begun in 1911, was more spacious than Versailles and its 2-mile long boulevard wider than the Champs Elysées in Paris. The French resident general's residence in Rabat, Morocco, was a grand affair located on the highest spot in the hills overlooking the old city. But these symbols were only part of the new colonial urbanism. A new movement, architectural preservation, was born under the leadership of Sarraut, who served as governor-general of Indochina in 1911–1914 and 1917–1919, and General Hubert Lyautey, a colonial administrator and Morocco's first resident general from 1912 to 1925. An admirer of Islamic culture, Lyautey blended "indigenous streets" and modern urbanism in a form of architectural syncretism. In 1914, he established a Central Service for City Planning in Morocco. It would become a model for other colonies, and it led to the first town planning laws.

Spectacular urban growth in the North African cities of Cairo, Tunis, Casablanca, and even Kano in northern Nigeria spurred innovation. There, the battles of modern architecture were fought; the nineteenth-century practice of razing entire sections of cities to make way for broad boulevards and grand mansions was abandoned. Iron began to replace wood, stone, and stucco. British architects were the most innovative. Henry Vaughan Lanchester promoted the "garden city," a suburb bridging city and country, in Madras, India, as early as 1916. This concept, first advocated by Ebenezer Howard in 1899, meant taking the city to the country. Posh, segregated suburbs for Europeans were created in a number of colonial cities in the 1920s. These suburbs featured bungalows with small parks, surrounded by pristine green belts. This segregated space was justified by a triple fear – of fire, epidemics, and native peoples. In Southeast Asia, towns spread rapidly because of the improvements in public transportation that made suburbs easily accessible. The colonial city was the living place for a majority of European settlers. Whereas before 1919 they had been mostly single men, after the war settlers began to reside permanently with their families in modern homes.

After 1919, construction moved ahead in the building of the new colonial capital cities of Rabat, New Delhi, Lusaka, and Nairobi, as well as in the development of the ports of Casablanca, Abidjan, and Singapore, where the Raffles Hotel already provided the model of colonial grandeur. The European urban model was often replicated there – a city center cut off from its surrounding countryside, with transportation and communication bypassing the countryside to serve as inter-city modes. The city cut off the natives, who lived in peripheral slums or shantytowns, creating de facto segregation across the colonial world.

Another design that was used in the 1920s to house urban workers was working-class tenements. A French law allowing the planning of and credits for inexpensive housing for workers – the *loi* Loucheur – was extended to North Africa and French West Africa at the end of the 1920s. Despite various efforts, slums multiplied in the neglected quarters of cities. Often epidemics provided an incentive for urban renovation. Cape Town redeveloped its urban landscape on the garden city model after the Spanish influenza epidemic of 1918–1920. But in Morocco, where high rural migration packed cities, a typhus epidemic in 1937–1938 led to the destruction of the slums, without any sound urban planning ensuing thereafter.

Shifting diplomatic tides in the Far East

Establishing a new balance of power in Asia was a priority in 1919, as the European withdrawal from Asia in 1914 weakened China's position and strengthened Japan's. When the Anglo-Japanese alliance, first signed in 1902, came up for renewal in 1921, a British-sponsored Imperial Conference of Britain and its Dominions reached no decision to support its renewal, owing to Canadian objections, and the treaty was allowed to lapse; the Canadian prime minister feared that Canada's security, which depended on the United States, could be adversely affected by a renewal of the treaty. American President Harding seized the opportunity to convene the Washington Naval Conference of 1921–1922, the first of the new world order. For the first time, the British Dominions attended as full diplomatic partners, and the leading diplomatic power was no longer Britain. The United States was ready to take charge in the Far East and to rein in Japanese expansionism. The conference settled several questions of international and regional importance related to arms limitations and control of the high seas. China's territorial integrity was guaranteed, along with the Open Door policy that guaranteed to all countries equal access to trade with the Chinese. Japan returned Kiaochow and Shantung to China. The United States, Great Britain, Japan, France, and Italy agreed to a formula for the capital ships in their navies (see p. 92). A Four-Power Treaty between the United States, Britain, France, and Japan initiated cooperation and mutual consultation mechanisms in case of a threat against their insular possessions in the Pacific. Thus was created the first "Washington system" in East Asia. The Washington Conference confirmed Europe's retrenchment from Asia.

German and Polish colonial ambitions

Germany, meanwhile, argued in 1919 that, since its former African colonies had made social and economic progress superior to that of other European colonizers in Africa before World War I, it should be granted trade and administrative benefits with its ex-colonies in the new spirit of cooperation that the League of Nations represented. Theoretically, German entrepreneurs were still free to conduct their activities in the former German colonies, but their share of contracts and markets in those areas plummeted once British administrators took control. In the 1930s, Hitler's Economics Minister Hjalmar Schacht again brought up the issue of Germany's former colonies by demanding that Germany be given the right to administer and economically develop them. In 1937–1938, negotiations took place between the Germans and British about Germany getting back its former African possessions, but nothing came of the talks.

Almost a footnote in history was the interest that existed in Poland concerning colonies. A Polish Maritime and Colonial League, a conservative association that had 1 million members at its peak, argued for a Polish claim to former German colonies proportionate to the amount of German land in Europe that Poland received at the end of World War I, should Germany regain its former colonies. In the mid-1930s, the Colonial League devised land schemes involving Polish settlers in Mozambique that came to naught, and it also organized a series of experimental farms in Liberia and Brazil that ended in failure. In 1937, the Polish Ministry of Foreign Affairs produced a document entitled "Colonial Theses of Poland" in which the Poles argued that Poland must possess colonial territories commensurate to those of the great powers of Europe. In the fall of the same year, the Poles argued before the League of Nations that Poland should obtain some say in the administration of the League-sponsored mandates and receive economic privileges in various colonies. But other countries ignored the claims that the Poles put forward.

Conclusion

The official policy of the colonial powers changed only incrementally in the first postwar decade. The colonial system was placed between two divergent forces and subjected to contradictory pressures. On the one hand, colonial powers desired to strengthen their bonds with the colonies; on the other, League of Nations' oversight forced them to modernize and develop their colonies. The colonial system was also in transition because the creation of Middle Eastern mandates in 1919 gave justification to Italy's search for empire, and for other neocolonial ventures. Overall, the economic importance of the colonies to help European industries rebuild and European colonial powers regain their economic prominence underscored the increasing dependence of Europe on its colonies.

Conflicts in the broader Middle East

The Middle East was never at peace in the interwar years and experienced a wide assortment of disruptions ranging from border disputes and anti-colonial revolts to large-scale wars. European powers were either fighting one another or joining forces against rebel armies in a wide arc that stretched from Morocco in Northwest Africa through Egypt, Syria, and Iraq in the Middle East to Iran and Afghanistan in Central Asia, and India in South Asia; it also included Abyssinia in the Horn of Africa. This vast region was a mixture of colonies and mandates. In the nineteenth century, the Arabs had fought Ottoman rule in the Near East, while Central Asia had been the focus of the Great Game that pitted Russia against Great Britain for economic and political domination there. After 1918, both areas turned against the West. In North Africa, nationalist movements became radicalized through the creation in 1931 of the League of the Ulemas that worked to establish a Pan-Arab movement. Likewise, Syrians and Lebanese formed a front against the French. Arab nationalism was tinged with anti-Semitism because of its proto-fascist orientations that included shirts of various colors: blue and green in Egypt, gray and white in Syria, and khaki in Iraq. Even though these groups had limited followings, they gave German Nazis and Italian Fascists a foothold in the Middle East.

Flare-ups in Afghanistan and the Maghreb

The first conflict in Central Asia was for control of the Silk Road. The Third Anglo-Afghan War of 1919 was a short-lived affair that resulted in the loss of British influence and the emergence of a "special relationship" between Afghanistan and Soviet Russia. In the west, Italy and Spain resumed prewar rivalries in Morocco. Spain, having lost the last remnants of its colonial empire in 1898, considered Morocco its natural hinterland, and had begun its conquest in 1912 with British support. Contesting France's presence in northern Morocco, Spain won concessions there in 1919, but the disputed city of Tangier was placed under international administration in 1923. When Berber rebels from the Rif Mountains of Morocco launched the Rif War in 1921 and defeated Spanish

Figure 3.3 An observation plane in 1925 brings back information to a French artillery battery, so it can adjust its firing range against nearby Moroccan Berber insurgents in the Rif War.

forces, the French moved in a force that eventually totaled some 150,000 troops and used their air force for the first time in a colonial conflict. The Rif War ended in the defeat of the rebels in 1926. Tangier in 1928 was placed under the authority of Spain, France, Britain, and Italy. In the mid-1930s, a nationalist political party in France's Moroccan protectorate sought radical reforms, but the French suppressed the group in 1937. The situation remained unstable in Spanish Morocco because the Spanish Civil War of the late 1930s split the colony's allegiances and complicated the status of Tangier.

Palestine

Palestine was the most volatile and vexing Middle Eastern problem. Jewish immigration in Palestine caused violent Jewish–Palestinian Arab clashes at the end of the 1920s. A British report affirmed Jewish rights but not the creation of the state of Israel. The year 1930 severely tested the British art of compromise: to alleviate Arab fears, the British halted Jewish immigration to Palestine until Palestinian unemployment ceased. This action unleashed strong criticism in the League of Nations and protests from London Zionist groups, i.e., Jewish nationalists in support of a Jewish homeland in Palestine; even the British Parliament erupted in acrimonious debate. Zionist and Arab nationalists became more intransigent in the 1930s. When Jewish immigration resumed after 1933, Germany and Italy supported an Arab Palestinian boycott of British goods. An unhealthy cycle of Arab insurrection, British repression, and British investigation began. By June 1938, an undeclared war existed between Palestinian Arabs and Jews, whose terrorist attacks the British had to subdue by military force. By May 1939, an impasse had been reached, and not even a new British White Paper promising an independent

Palestinian state, a joint Arab-Israeli government, the prohibition of land transfers, and a Jewish immigration ceiling could restore peace.

Egypt and Sudan

In Sudan and the Horn of Africa, conflict simmered throughout the interwar years. The British, who theoretically exercised joint authority over Sudan with Egypt, actually controlled the area and, owing to British cotton plantations there, they competed with the Egyptians for the Nile River waters. When the British governor-general of Anglo-Egyptian Sudan was assassinated in Cairo in late 1924, the British cut Egypt out of Sudan and dammed the Nile. At the same time, the British conducted intermittent negotiations with successive Egyptian governments toward the granting of true independence to Egypt. Sensing the slow erosion of British influence, Egyptian nationalists launched a violent uprising in the fall of 1935, and forced the conclusion of a treaty in 1936. The agreement ended Britain's protectorate over Egypt, established a military alliance between the two countries, and allowed the British to maintain a force of 10,000 men to protect the Suez Canal zone and keep a naval base at the Egyptian city of Alexandria.

Mussolini's backyard imperialism

In the years after World War I, the continuation of British, French, American, and Soviet colonialism, a general disinterest in the West toward the countries of Southeastern Europe, the continued use of colonial and migrant labor in Europe, and the blurring of boundaries between the primary and peripheral areas of ethnic groups contributed to the Italian dream of conquest in the eastern Mediterranean and beyond. Italy pieced together its Mediterranean empire almost imperceptibly with the help of the British, who were still trying to make good on wartime promises. In 1919, Italy's ventures against the Ottoman Empire were frustrated when President Wilson denied the Italians an Albanian mandate. After coming to power in 1922, Mussolini planned for an imperial Italy that included the creation of an Italian *mare nostrum* in the Mediterranean Sea and the takeover of Yugoslavia's Adriatic coast, Albania, Abyssinia, Somaliland, Eritrea, Libya, and Tunisia. When an Italian general and several of his aides who were part of a Greco-Albanian–Yugoslav border surveying team were murdered by a Greek insurgent in the summer of 1923, Mussolini bombed and occupied the Greek island of Corfu at the southern end of the Adriatic Sea. The Corfu Incident shook up Europe and brought back fears of another Sarajevo. Italy eventually backed down, but still came out of the episode with full control of the northern Adriatic Sea. Penetrating deeper into the Balkans, Mussolini signed a pact with Hungary, offered diplomatic and economic and diplomatic support to Bulgaria, and established a de facto protectorate over Albania. Between 1923 and 1928, he prodded the British in Egypt, made modest gains in Libya, Somaliland, and Abyssinia, and strengthened Italy's hand in the Red Sea by enticing Yemen to create a mini-front against the French, British, and Saudis on the Arabian Peninsula.

The Arab mandates

After the Allies signed the Treaty of Lausanne with Turkey in 1923, there were still two border areas involving the Turks that caused continued friction: one was Kurdistan, an area inhabited by Kurdish people along Turkey's border with northern Iraq, and the other was the Alexandretta province situated on the Mediterranean Sea at the Turkish–Syrian border. Both places became production and delivery points for the northern Iraqi Mosul oil fields starting in the late 1920s. The Mosul region was occupied by British forces from 1918 to 1926, when Iraq's possession of it was confirmed by a League of Nations-brokered treaty. In the midst of these postwar events, a series of Kurdish independence revolts began against both Iraq and Turkey. One of the rebellions erupted in 1931 in reaction to an Anglo-Iraqi treaty that provided for Iraq's independence by 1932. British military forces quelled the revolt, although the Kurds did gain a few minor concessions in a last-minute amendment that the British added to the independence treaty. In the end, Britain retained considerable influence with Iraqi leaders and received three new British air bases that were crucial to relieving pressure on the hotly contested Suez Canal. Iraq's subsequent admission to the League of Nations was considered a fitting conclusion to Britain's mandate in Iraq; indeed, Iraq was the only mandate to be emancipated during the interwar years. Ironically, emancipation provided the British with important leverage in Iraq by removing the League of Nations' control over their new ally. One could even argue that it introduced neo-imperialism because independence reinforced the prerogatives of the mandatory state – such as the power of the British ambassador and British participation in building the Iraqi defense forces and repressing minorities. As for Alexandretta, it had been assigned to France's Syrian mandate, and Turkey wanted it. Although the territory received autonomy in 1925, tensions continued for years among the Syrians, Turks, and French. The French and Turks agreed in 1938 to the transformation of Alexandretta into the Republic of Hatay that, over strong Syrian objections, became a Turkish province in June 1939.

Resentment in Syria against France's Syrian mandate boiled over in a major way in 1925, when Druze tribesmen, angry over French reforms that challenged traditional practices and eager for self-rule, launched a full-fledged rebellion that expanded into Lebanon to the south. In a dramatic display of military power, the French used modern weaponry, including heavy artillery bombardments and aerial bombings against rebel-held areas of the Syrian capital of Damascus in the fall of 1925 and again – with more effect – in 1926. After the French finally suppressed the Great Syrian Revolt in 1927, they adopted a softer tone in their rule over Syria. The French began to take steps toward granting Syria its independence, although not without disruptions along the way. In 1936, Syrian and French leaders signed a treaty that provided for an end to France's mandate within three years, but the French government never ratified the document. France's presence in Syria continued until 1946, when the Republic of Syria at last gained its full independence following the departure of all remaining French soldiers in April.

Conclusion

The conflicts in the Middle East were symptomatic of an unease that had its roots in the conflicting aims of the French and British on one hand, and the League of Nations on the other. They exemplify the persistence of colonial power-building by the Western European powers, even if it meant using violence, and their resistance to fulfilling their promises of treating Arab peoples as equals. These conflicts, however, diverted resources away from the domestic needs of the French and the British, and indigenous resistance to their rule created new vulnerabilities.

Overall conclusion

The 1920s were an in-between time, a decade of transition from an old to a new world order. This time of reprieve was based on a false sense of security that had inter-Allied occupation forces in Germany as the only guarantee against a revision of the Versailles treaty that several European countries considered unfair. The overarching concern of the 1920s was how to avoid war and secure a long-lasting peace. This was tried through different channels, from bilateral treaties achieved through regular diplomatic channels, to international initiatives under the auspices of the League of Nations. As if trying to keep Europe in balance was not enough, the continent's leading states had to contend with an ideologically hostile regional power, the Soviet Union, and a benevolent, yet largely absent world power, the United States. Finally, while this was not yet very visible, the victorious Western European colonial powers were growing increasingly dependent upon their colonies. For many, integration appeared the best option for the long-term health of a continent that was fragmented and vulnerable after the Great War. The men and women who saw the need for union floundered in the face of unfavorable political and economic circumstances that made most nations fearful of losing their sovereignty. Still, the decade of the 1920s had a list of achievements that included the outlawing of war, keeping the dialogue open among former enemies, supporting the ideals of national self-determination, and establishing a vision for a future united Europe without which the post-1945 European Union would have found it much more difficult to emerge.

Notes

1 Ronald E. Powaski, *Toward an Entangling Alliance: American Isolationism, Internationalism and Europe, 1901–1950* (New York: Greenwood Press, 1991), 39.
2 A. J. P. Taylor, *The Origins of the Second World War*, 2nd edn (New York: Fawcett World Library, 1960), 57.
3 The Avalon Project: Documents in Law, History and Diplomacy, "The Covenant of the League of Nations," http://avalon.law.yale.edu/20th_century/leagcov.asp (accessed November 23, 2015).
4 Rebecca Wright, Hiroki Shin, and Frank Trentmann, *From World Power to World Energy Council: 90 Years of Energy Cooperation, 1923–2013* (London: World Energy Council, 2013), 10, www.worldenergy.org/wp-content/uploads/2014/02/A-Brief-History-of-the-World-Energy-Council.pdf (accessed December 1, 2015).
5 Stephen D. Carls, *Louis Loucheur and the Shaping of Modern France, 1916–1931* (Baton Rouge, LA: Louisiana State University Press, 1993), 266.

Suggestions for further reading

Betts, Raymond F. *Uncertain Dimensions: Western Overseas Empires in the Twentieth Century.* Minneapolis, MN: University of Minnesota Press. 1985.
Callahan, Michael D. *Mandates and Empire: The League of Nations and Africa, 1914–1931.* Sussex, UK: Sussex Academic Press. 2008.
Clavin, Patricia. *Securing the World Economy: The Reinvention of the League of Nations, 1920–1946.* Oxford: Oxford University Press. 2013.
Fink, Carol. *The Genoa Conference: European Diplomacy, 1921–1922.* Chapel Hill, NC: University of North Carolina Press. 1984.

Hewitson, Mark and Matthew D'Auria, eds. *Europe in Crisis: Intellectuals and the European Idea, 1917–1957*. New York: Berghahn. 2012.

Housden, Martyn. *The League of Nations and the Organization of Peace*. Harlow, UK: Pearson. 2012.

Jacobson, Jon. *Locarno Diplomacy: Germany and the West, 1925–1929*. Princeton, NJ: Princeton University Press. 1972.

Marks, Sally. *The Illusion of Peace: International Relations in Europe, 1918–1933*. 2nd edn. London: Palgrave. 2003.

Neilson, Keith. *Britain, Soviet Russia and the Collapse of the Versailles Order, 1919–1939*. New York: Cambridge University Press. 2006.

Schuker, Stephen. *The End of French Predominance in Europe: The Financial Crisis of 1924 and the Adoption of the Dawes Plan*. Chapel Hill, NC: University of North Carolina Press. 1976.

4   Modernity's promises

Introduction

By the time the guns fell silent in 1918, European countries involved in World War I had suffered tremendous destruction. From the French front to the western Russian lands, cities and villages had been bombed, fields ruined by the battlefields, and the environment compromised by ammunition and other contaminants. Millions were homeless, especially in East Central Europe, and many of them had nowhere to go. Millions of children were orphaned. The human losses were staggering as well; a whole generation of men was missing. Civilian deaths from military action and crimes against humanity totaled over 2.2 million, and another 4.6 to 5.3 million died of malnutrition and disease (excluding the influenza epidemic). Between 22 and 23.6 million returning soldiers were wounded physically or psychologically. Demobilized soldiers and refugees returned to countries whose borders had changed and whose economies had endured several grueling years. The war had changed much, from the fabric of everyday life to the organization of civil society and community life. The physical devastation was widespread, so reconstruction was imperative in a number of countries. European nations' financial situations looked bleak. An immense task of reorganization lay ahead of the men and women who survived the war. In this dire situation, the neutral countries, especially the Scandinavian states, offered a picture of stability and hope. While exempt from the toils of reconstruction, they nonetheless dealt with many of the same issues that belligerent countries experienced: industrial and agricultural modernization, increased social mobility, the emancipation of women, the building of new urban environments fit for modern life, and the expansion of public welfare. These tasks required more government intervention than had previously been the case, and generated lively debates about the role of the state in the economy. These problems not only challenged politicians, but also the systems they operated under. Liberalism was under attack and democracy, lacking the mechanisms and processes that were required to solve questions quickly, found itself threatened by authoritarianism. Reconstruction meant experimentation to a large degree.

Modernization may be measured by five factors: political changes (democracy, human rights, political participation, liberal measures); demographic changes (refugees, resettlements, migrations, and growth); economic progress (industrial modernization, agricultural reforms, labor legislation); social policies (welfare, professional mobility, public health, and women's advancement); and urban development (urban planning, transportation). Each factor influenced the development of the others.

Political reconstruction

The world at the end of 1918 was considerably different than that of early 1914. The reestablishment of a European political, economic, and social equilibrium proved challenging. President Wilson mandated democracy in the newly formed countries of East Central Europe, where emperors had ruled before the war. Monarchies, where they remained, operated according to constitutions based on democratic principles. But everywhere political modernization gave countries new directions. Popular sentiment tested governments in all countries, and some countries experienced violent change. European countries generally were eager to return to or to achieve a peacetime stability quickly: free elections, sound finances, and economic liberalism were of high importance. Election outcomes were not always predictable, as new political parties and the emergence of female suffrage in many countries changed electoral campaigns and government priorities.

Britain between coalition and single-party governments

Having sustained minimal physical damage during the war, Britain was ready in 1918 to return to peace as quickly as possible. Prime Minister David Lloyd George's first major decision after the war was to hold national elections on December 14, 1918. It became known as the "coupon" election because the governing Liberal/Conservative coalition issued letters of endorsement, or what Lloyd George's Liberal Party rival Herbert Asquith called "coupons," to candidates that supported it in the campaign. Women voted for the first time in British history. The election was a resounding victory for Lloyd George and his Liberal/Conservative coalition forces and a major setback for the Asquith Liberals who won only 27 seats. Significantly, the socialist Labour Party, with 59 parliamentary members, emerged as the chief opposition group. The election outcome provided Lloyd George with a strong mandate to take a firm line against Germany at the Paris Peace Conference in 1919.

While triumphant at the polls, Lloyd George faced criticism as the country adapted to peacetime conditions. He promised demobilized soldiers in late 1918 of his intention to make Britain fit for heroes to live in, but the government's social legislation fell short of workers' expectations. He angered many Conservatives by granting Ireland its independence in 1921, following a bloody war between Irish nationalists and British forces. He lost credibility when he presided over an economic depression that began in 1920. In 1922, when the Conservative (Tory) Party, which actually held a majority of the parliamentary seats, wanted a protective tariff for Britain, he refused to endorse it, for fear of alienating his Liberal supporters. Not long thereafter, the Conservatives concluded that it was time to end the coalition, lest Lloyd George ruin the Tory Party just as they thought he had undermined the Liberals. Lloyd George resigned on October 19, 1922.

Conservative Party leader Bonar Law assumed the position of prime minister and led his party to victory in national elections in November 1922, but he died in early 1923. He was succeeded by fellow Conservative Stanley Baldwin, an affluent businessman and clever political tactician. Baldwin argued for a protective tariff in October 1923, claiming that it would help fight Britain's nagging unemployment. The issue united the Conservative Party, but Baldwin's tariff position was so dramatically opposed to Britain's longstanding policy of free trade that he felt compelled to hold new national elections in December, 1923. His party lost its majority in the House of Commons, and the Labour Party, now the second largest in parliament behind the Tories, formed a coalition government with the Liberals.

The prime minister of the Labour-led cabinet was Ramsay MacDonald, who had an aristocratic air about him even though he had humble family origins. Determined to prove that the Labour Party could govern the country prudently and careful not to offend his Liberal Party partners, MacDonald refrained from advancing anything approaching a socialist agenda. The government's budget was rigidly orthodox and contained no extra funds for public works projects to alleviate unemployment. On the other hand, the cabinet improved unemployment benefits, enhanced educational opportunities for working-class children, and enacted a comprehensive housing program. Internationally, the MacDonald government played an important role in planning the implementation of the 1924 Dawes Plan that eased Germany's reparations payments schedule and ended a French and Belgian military occupation of Germany's Ruhr region begun in early 1923. But MacDonald ran into trouble over Britain's relations with the Soviet Union. His Labour-led government had extended official diplomatic recognition to the Soviets, signed a commercial agreement with them, and negotiated a sizable British loan to them. Members of the Conservative Party vehemently opposed these moves and eventually the Liberals joined in opposing what they viewed as MacDonald's accommodation of Communism. This forced MacDonald to dissolve parliament in the fall of 1924 and call for new elections. During the campaign, the Tory press, capitalizing on a strong anti-Bolshevik sentiment among the British public, published a secret letter purportedly written by Grigory Zinoviev, secretary of the Communist International (Comintern), to British Communists urging them to revolution. While the letter was most likely a forgery, it nevertheless intensified the "red scare" that permeated the 1924 election campaign, and it sealed a sweeping Conservative victory at the polls. Tory leader Baldwin had previously gained favor among the electorate by expressly dropping trade protectionism from the Conservative Party platform.

Baldwin, once again prime minister, focused on domestic policy. He faced serious challenges, including uncompetitive industries and a stubbornly high unemployment rate that stood at more than 10 percent. One depressed area was the coal-mining industry which had been limping along since 1918. In 1925, the government ordered a study of the industry, but could not avert a general strike in May 1926. It was the most serious domestic crisis Baldwin faced in the 1920s. While the government's success in dealing with the general strike was a personal triumph for Baldwin, he failed to solve Britain's lingering economic problems. Unemployment continued to hover around 10 percent in 1929. Baldwin was still confident of a Conservative victory when he announced a general election for May 26, 1929. When the votes were counted, however, Labour became the single largest party in the House of Commons, although it failed to win a parliamentary majority. Consequently, MacDonald had to form another coalition government with the Liberals.

In many ways, the British muddled through the 1920s. No dramatic measures were passed to deal with the problem of high unemployment, and a return to the gold standard in 1925 actually damaged the country's competitive position in international markets as Britain tried to return to its former central position in global finances. Britain faced urgent domestic and international problems in mid-1929, but the new government approached them with confidence, since many of its cabinet members had already served in the Labour–Liberal government of 1924. Just a few months later, however, the government's problems reached unprecedented levels when the Great Depression struck.

France's coalition governments

In France too, political leaders were eager to return their country to normalcy, and to resume the economic growth that the country had experienced prior to World War I. The policy makers saw no need to make any serious foundational changes, since France's political and economic systems had successfully survived the test of the Great War. Premier Georges Clemenceau continued to enjoy almost dictatorial powers while overseeing France's transition from war to peace in 1919. Clemenceau focused the bulk of his energies during the first half of the year on the Paris peace negotiations. He left the formulation of France's postwar economic policies largely to others who devoted considerable energy to rebuilding the war-devastated regions of France and putting the country's financial house in order.

Politically, the country largely returned to a prewar dynamic that alternated power between center-right and center-left coalitions; this began in the fall of 1919, when the country at last held war-delayed parliamentary elections. Conservative right-wing parties and centrists joined together in a *Bloc national* to take advantage of a new election law that gave additional parliamentary seats to parties that established large electoral alliances. Capitalizing on an outpouring of postwar nationalist feeling, the conservative *Bloc national* won a decisive victory, though no drastic shift in policies or attitude from the prewar years occurred.

One casualty of the 1919 elections was the Unified Socialist Party (SFIO), which suffered not only from internal divisions between its revolutionary (radical) and evolutionary (moderate) factions, but also from its refusal to enter into an electoral agreement with any of country's "bourgeois" parties. Its representation dropped to 68 deputies from 102 in the last prewar elections. A climax to the party's internal dispute came at its Congress of Tours in December 1920, when the party split. The revolutionary socialists secured a majority of votes at the congress in favor of joining the Russian-controlled Communist International (Comintern) and adopted the name Communist Party. The moderates, led by Léon Blum, walked out of the congress with a minority of the Socialist Party members. Blum showed diligence and determination in rebuilding the SFIO over the next several years, and in the 1932 national elections, the Socialists won 131 seats in the Chamber of Deputies as opposed to ten for the Communists.

One of the dominant politicians in the 1920s was Aristide Briand. Beginning his career on the political Left, he gravitated rightward until he was associated with the nationalist Right in parliament. During the war, he began a slow shift back to the Left so that by 1925 he had the support of the center-left Radical Party and Socialists when he formed a new government. Although he seemed to have few serious convictions, he did have a successful politician's ability to adapt to new circumstances as needed. He served as premier in five governments during the 1920s, four of which – between 1925 and 1929 – were of very short duration. His real base of power in the latter 1920s was his position as foreign minister, a post he held continuously from 1925 to early 1932.

Raymond Poincaré was Briand's chief rival politically in the 1920s. In contrast to the more pliable Briand, Poincaré had a reputation for inflexibility. Lacking in personal warmth, he had few friends among his political colleagues, although he was generally respected for his unwavering honesty. Because of his standing as a fiscal expert and French patriot, he emerged as a major player during France's postwar financial crisis and the enforcement of the Treaty of Versailles. Poincaré served as premier in two lengthy postwar governments, from early 1922 to mid-1924 and from mid-1926 to mid-1929.

One challenging task the French had after 1918 was rebuilding those areas of the country devastated during the Great War. Most of the damage took place in northeastern France where major wartime battle lines had been located. The government committed itself financially to a rapid and total restoration of France's devastated areas, using the way things were in 1913 as its guide. In addition to the rebuilding of infrastructure, the government provided full indemnities for the reconstruction of factories, small businesses, homes, and farm buildings. The government borrowed heavily to finance reconstruction in anticipation of repayment through German reparations. Reconstruction in northeastern France was largely finished by 1926. One historian called France's rapid rebuilding of its devastated areas "the greatest economic achievement of post-war Europe."[1]

Public finance also consumed the energies of French leaders. The exchange value of the French franc, a rock-solid currency before World War I, came under heavy pressure in the immediate postwar years because of France's massive war-incurred deficit and postwar reconstruction costs. Governments resisted levying new taxes, and instead improved the tax collection system. After the Franco-Belgian occupation of the Ruhr in 1923 failed and serious questions arose about Germany's ability to pay for French war damages any time soon, a run on the franc began in 1924. A left-wing political alliance known as the Left Cartel and dominated by the center-left Radical Party won the 1924 French elections, but it failed to bring the country's finances under control. Serious cabinet instability emerged in 1925: in the nine months from late October 1925 to late July 1926, France had five different governments and six finance ministers in "the waltz of the portfolios." By the summer of 1926, the franc had dropped in value to two American cents from 20 cents before the war, and was on the verge of complete collapse.

The fiscally conservative Poincaré was then called upon to form a new government in order to save the franc. His mere presence at the head of the government halted the slide towards bankruptcy. Parliament granted him decree powers that it had denied to his predecessors, and he used his special powers to increase taxes and cut government spending dramatically. By the end of 1926, the value of the franc had stabilized at four American cents, and in 1928 Poincaré not only established that as its official value, but he also made the franc convertible to gold. Even though large numbers of Frenchmen, both bondholders and savers, had absorbed the lion's share of France's war costs owing to the currency's 80 percent drop in value from 1913, Poincaré and his conservative coalition were popular enough to win a firm endorsement from the electorate in the 1928 national elections.

By the end of the 1920s, France once more appeared to be on a solid footing politically and economically; normalcy had returned to French life. The country's democratic foundations seemed firmly in place. The franc was stable, the economy was expanding, and the country exuded a new sense of self-confidence. The French had finished with the reconstruction of northeastern France, and German reparations were arriving on time. Even when a sharp economic downturn began in other countries at the end of the decade, France continued for a time to experience an economic boom.

The healthy northern periphery

The northern periphery of Europe was made up of small, generally stable, and, for the most part, neutral countries. It consisted of the Low Countries (Belgium and the Netherlands), Scandinavia (Sweden, Norway, and Denmark), and Finland.

Both Belgium and the Netherlands had constitutional monarchies, with democratically elected legislative bodies running their countries' day-to-day affairs. In spite of a large number of political parties in the two countries, political stability prevailed during the 1920s. This can be in part attributed to the presence of religious parties in each country that cooperated with other leading political groups to make their respective parliamentary regimes function successfully. While the two political systems extended important prerogatives to their monarchs, such as the right to name new governments following national elections, the royal system in Belgium enabled the ruler to exercise even greater individual influence than his Dutch counterpart because he was the commander-in-chief of the country's armed forces. The popularity of the Belgian monarchy after World War I was assured in the person of King Albert I (r. 1909–1934), who had steadfastly led the country's army in fighting the Germans throughout the conflict. Belgium was not immune from ethnic and national divisions that were exacerbated by the scope of war-related reconstruction and that revealed a deep rift between the Flemings, who spoke a form of Dutch, and the Walloons, whose language was French. To deal with Flemish discontent, the government in 1921 separated the country into two parts administratively using language for the divide, and instituted other reforms thereafter – most significantly in the area of education – to provide the Flemings, long overshadowed by their French-speaking countrymen, with a greater sense of equality.

Finland and Scandinavia, likewise, proved resilient politically throughout the interwar years. Finland adopted a constitution that established a democratic parliamentary republic at the end of a brief civil war in 1918 in which conservative paramilitary forces – the White Guards – defeated socialist-inspired units known as the Red Guards. Beginning in 1922, Finland instituted major agrarian reforms that involved a very successful program of land redistribution, resulting in a greater incorporation of Finland's peasant families into the mainstream of Finnish society and in their support for the republic. The interwar governments also faced political challenges from the Far Left and Far Right. On at least two occasions in the 1920s the Finnish Communist Party, which was illegal in Finland until 1944, worked through front organizations with different party labels to participate in the national elections of 1922 and 1929. Though the Communists made respectable showings at the polls, garnering 14.8 percent of the vote in 1922 and 13.5 percent in 1929, their front organizations were banned shortly after each election. There was also a right-wing, anti-Communist, nationalist political strand in Finland that resulted in the creation of the proto-fascist Lapua movement in 1929. Lapua activists used violence to intimidate political leftists and labor groups. A climax to their extremism came in February 1932, when Lapua leaders participated in a failed attempt to overthrow the government. The abortive coup was the last major incident involving radical right-wing groups, and Lapua was banned thereafter.

In Sweden, which had a constitutional monarchy at its base, the Social Democratic Party became the single largest group in parliament after the war. Nevertheless, no party came close to winning a majority of parliamentary seats in the 1920s and early 1930s, so coalition governments or one-party governments dependent on short-term political support were the norm. Politically speaking, some have used the expression "minority parliamentarism" to characterize the period from 1917 to 1932. The average term of a government during these years was approximately 16 months. In spite of the political bickering and frequency of new cabinets, reform measures did pass, such as a compromise education law in 1927 that increased the number of years of compulsory education and made secondary schools open to women.

Denmark, like Sweden, had a parliamentary monarchy that relied principally on political coalitions to govern between the wars. The Social Democratic Party, under the leadership of Thorvald Stauning, became the largest single party in the Danish Parliament following the 1924 elections and the first to constitute a totally Social Democratic cabinet anywhere when Stauning formed a minority government that ruled from 1924 to 1926. In 1929, the Social Democrats and the moderately conservative Liberal Party formed a coalition government that remained in power until 1942.

Norway, after gaining its independence from Sweden in 1905, created a constitutional monarchy and placed power in the hands of a national parliament. The country experienced a procession of coalition and minority governments in the 1920s, with an average life span of about one year. Outside of the shipping and whaling industries, the country had a less robust economy than many other Western nations, in part because it pursued a deflationary monetary policy. A climax to this process came in 1928, when Norway returned to the prewar gold standard. The Labor Party (Norway's version of a Social Democratic Party), whose left wing bolted in 1921 to establish a Communist Party, became the country's largest party in parliament following the 1927 elections. It formed its first cabinet in 1928, and at once introduced a socialistic program that frightened the parliamentary defenders of capitalism, who overturned the government after less than two weeks in power. In the years immediately thereafter, no single party dominated nor did a stable coalition emerge.

Overall, the countries of the northern periphery spent the first postwar decade implementing or solidifying democratic political systems. Universal male suffrage had become law in Belgium, Norway, and Sweden before the war, and Denmark and the Netherlands granted all men voting rights during the conflict. Finland, which had granted both men and women the right to vote in 1906 as an autonomous Grand Duchy in the Russian Empire, incorporated that right into its Constitution Act of 1919. In fact, all the northern peripheral states had granted women the right to vote by 1919 except Belgium, which finally did so in 1948. As for political groups, the Social Democratic parties in Scandinavia saw their influence grow during the 1920s, in part because of strife inside their opponents' parties. In Belgium, the socialist Belgian Workers' Party, known for its flexibility, participated in several coalition governments in the 1920s. The Finnish Social Democratic Party used the decade to rebuild its strength after the country's bloody civil war of 1918; it adopted a more patriotic stance to improve its appeal to voters, and actually headed a short-lived minority government in the mid-1920s. The Dutch Socialists, meanwhile, saw their vote totals increase in the 1920s, but, because of their doctrinal rigidity, they were excluded from all Dutch cabinets. While all of the northern periphery countries confronted serious political tests during the 1920s, their parliamentary systems functioned well enough to deepen the support of the general citizenry for democracy as the decade drew to a close. The key to their success was the ability of political parties with sometimes sharp ideological differences to reach compromises that included benefits for their constituent groups.

From birth to the twilight of democracy in Germany

As World War I came to an end, Germany had the daunting task of constructing a viable democracy for the first time in its history. There was strong domestic hostility toward the new regime on both the political Left and Right. Germany's democracy became associated with the country's military defeat in the Great War and the unpopular Treaty of Versailles. There was economic uncertainty, made more troublesome by the Allied imposition of reparations. Economic and social tensions were reflected in labor unrest. Yet those charged with overseeing the new democracy moved ahead courageously, determined to make democracy in Germany workable and permanent.

Germany's Second Empire collapsed in November 1918. Emperor Wilhelm II abdicated on November 9, and Social Democratic Party leader Friedrich Ebert became chancellor. Fellow Social Democrat Philipp Scheidemann declared Germany a parliamentary republic the same day, and Ebert named a provisional government on November 11. Both Ebert and Scheidemann represented the views of the majority Socialists who were committed to a revisionist form of Marxism that included class struggle but also a willingness to work within the new parliamentary system to enact labor reforms. Opposed to them within the socialist movement were antiparliamentary Marxist revolutionaries known as Spartacists who, inspired by the Bolsheviks' success in Russia, sought an immediate social revolution that would put workers in control of the country. Ebert quickly accepted an offer of support from the Supreme Army Command to preserve domestic tranquility. The provisional government also organized battle-hardened former soldiers with anti-republican views into paramilitary organizations known as *Freikorps* to provide protection against internal threats. The government used *Freikorps* units in January 1919 to crush the Spartacist revolt against the regime. Germany experienced a political revolution in 1918, but it was limited in scope: the old empire's military leadership, the state bureaucracy, and the existing social order remained largely untouched by the shift from a monarchy to a republic.

Elections for a National Assembly to draft a new constitution were held in January 1919. The Social Democrats won the most seats, though not an absolute majority, followed by the Catholic Center Party and the Democratic Party. These three moderate parties, known as the Weimar Coalition, were a powerful force in German politics throughout the 1920s. The assembly, which met in the quiet city of Weimar as a way of disassociating the new regime from the old imperial system tied to Berlin, had as its first task the creation of a legal government to replace the provisional regime. It immediately elected provisional government leader Ebert president of the Reich; he in turn called upon Scheidemann to form the first cabinet of the Weimar Republic.

The assembly wrote a constitution for a parliamentary democracy that established an all-powerful Reichstag or Lower House, where the deputies were elected by universal suffrage and secret ballot. A Reichsrat or Upper House, comprised of delegates of the various German states, could delay legislation but not veto it. The executive branch consisted in part of a chancellor and his cabinet who needed majority support in the Reichstag to govern. There was also a president who was popularly elected to a seven-year term and granted important prerogatives, including the right to appoint the chancellor subject to parliamentary consent. The constitution drafters, in their efforts to give weight to all political points of view, created two potentially serious weaknesses in the new system. One was Article 48 that allowed the president to declare national emergencies and then rule by decree. The provision opened up the possibility of the president arbitrarily bypassing the parliamentary system, especially since no law was ever passed defining what constituted a national emergency. The other problem lay in the constitution's electoral system of proportional representation that granted political parties representation in the Reichstag in direct proportion to the number of votes they received in national elections. Fringe parties, some of which were anti-republican, could thus secure Reichstag representation, making it virtually impossible to form governments other than coalitions. The constitution became the law of the land in August 1919.

One of the early major assignments of the new republic was to make a permanent peace agreement with the Allies in regard to World War I. The Allied peace terms, which arrived in Berlin in early May 1919, stunned German government officials. Chancellor Scheidemann insisted that Germany would never accept the treaty unless dramatic revisions were made through negotiations. Since Germany was in no position to organize a serious military challenge, however, it had to accept the Allied proposal. As a result, many Germans associated the new republic with the German defeat, because its leaders had accepted what they argued was a vengeful and humiliating peace settlement; they called it the *Diktat*, or dictated peace. Nationalist circles quickly circulated the myth that leftist elements and Jews on the home front, including the founders of the republic, had "stabbed in the back" an unbeaten German army during the war.

The government's efforts to live up to the terms of the Versailles treaty triggered a major attempt from the Right to topple the republic in March 1920. The immediate cause of the Kapp Putsch was the republic's decision, under Allied pressure, to begin dismantling *Freikorps* units. One of the targeted units, the well-equipped and highly trained Marine Brigade of Captain Hermann Ehrhardt, marched on Berlin during the night of March 12. General Ludendorff and an obscure right-wing Prussian bureaucrat/politician named Dr. Wolfgang Kapp met the troops the next morning in the heart of the city. The Weimar government fled, and Kapp declared himself the chancellor of Germany. Kapp had no serious program to offer the people and faced opposition from the government bureaucracy and most people in Berlin. The Social Democratic Party quickly called for a general strike. Unable to establish control over Berlin, Kapp fled to Sweden after four days and the Ehrhardt Brigade withdrew from the city. The *Freikorps* units did not disappear, however. They often hid behind new identities and remained a threat to the republic right up to its collapse in the early 1930s. Some of them participated in a large assassination campaign in the early 1920s against people they referred to as "November criminals." The two most famous victims were: Matthias Erzberger, a Center Party leader remembered for signing the Armistice with the Allies in November 1918, who was murdered in August 1921; and Foreign Minister Walther Rathenau, who was assassinated in August 1922. By the end of the murder campaign, hundreds of civilians had lost their lives.

In the republic's first parliamentary elections in June 1920, the parties of the Weimar Coalition lost ground. To rule, the coalition had to rely on groups that were unenthusiastic about or hostile toward the Weimar Constitution. Even the Social Democrats, who saw their vote total drop significantly, decided to let others handle the responsibility of decision making. While party members held cabinet posts on a couple of occasions in the early 1920s, the Social Democrats did not reassume the role of leader in the national government until the late 1920s. Germany had six different chancellors during the next eight years, and there was a tendency to rely on presidential power and technical experts to make up for the lack of a clear parliamentary majority. In November 1922, for example, President Ebert used his decree power to appoint Wilhelm Cuno, a politically unaligned shipping magnate who was not even a Reichstag deputy, as chancellor.

Cuno put together a cabinet of nonparty economists who were soon grappling with a major inflationary crisis that created untold miseries for the German people. Inflation spiraled out of control when Cuno answered the Franco-Belgian occupation of the Ruhr in January 1923 by ordering factory workers and public employees to engage in passive resistance. The Cuno government agreed to pay the salaries of factory workers and public employees in the Ruhr region, which it did by printing more money. The German mark plummeted in value, going from 7,000 marks for one U.S. dollar in January 1923 to 4.2 trillion marks for one U.S. dollar in November of the same year. In August, Gustav Stresemann, the head of the German People's Party, formed a "Great Coalition" government made up of the main pro-democratic parties to deal with the crisis. With the republic seemingly on the brink of collapse, Stresemann ended Germany's policy of passive resistance in September. His action ignited sharp criticism at home, because it represented a capitulation to France. On the other hand, the decision put pressure on the French to adopt a more lenient policy toward Germany. The Stresemann government's actions regarding Germany's hyper-inflation culminated in November 1923 with the introduction of a temporary currency to replace the old mark. In August 1924, the Germans issued a new permanent currency, the Reichsmark, that was based on gold. Currency stabilization, combined with reduced reparations payments and a major infusion of foreign loans, paved the way for several years of German economic prosperity.

Meanwhile, separatist movements developed in several regions of Germany. Rhenish separatists took steps in the fall of 1923 to establish a "Republic of the Rhineland," but their movement foundered because it had French backing. When coalitions of the Communist and Social Democratic parties took power in the states of Thuringia and Saxony in October 1923, Stresemann ordered the army to oust the leftist regimes and imposed martial law. Separatist sentiment inspired by the political Right reached serious levels in Bavaria during the fall. Since the separatists had the support of the army commander in Bavaria, Stresemann's government was hesitant to intervene militarily. A few weeks later, on November 8 and 9, a far-right politician named Adolf Hitler and his National Socialist German Worker's Party (NSDAP) led an amateurish coup in Munich known as the "Beer Hall Putsch." Hitler was quickly arrested and order returned when the separatists desisted.

The country experienced a period of domestic calm after the stormy events of the early 1920s. Stresemann's brief government of 1923 did much to lay the groundwork for several years of political peace and economic growth. The 1924 Reichstag elections of May and December showed a shift to the right politically. The momentum for the political Right continued in 1925, following the death of Friedrich Ebert, the Weimar Republic's president, on February 18. He was followed by 78-year-old Field Marshal Hindenburg who agreed to run in the presidential election only after obtaining the approval of former German Emperor William II whom he still viewed as his "Imperial lord." Many who voted for him undoubtedly hoped that he would move the country in the direction of monarchy, but Hindenburg committed himself to republican institutions and conducted himself with dignity in the office of president, an attitude that gained him the respect of the country's republicans. He contributed to the stability of the republic in the mid- and late 1920s through his cautious approval of the government's actions.

The 1928 national elections brought to power a new Great Coalition government consisting of the same moderate parties that had joined together under Stresemann in 1923 to combat hyperinflation. Hermann Müller, a longtime leader in the Social Democratic Party, was chancellor. Unfortunately, there was considerable dissonance between two key groups in the coalition, namely, the Social Democratic Party and the German People's Party. The latter was dominated by propertied interests, many of whom were tied to industry and reluctant to cooperate with the Social Democrats. Many of the Social Democrats were trade union leaders determined to defend workers' rights. Such divisions did not bode well for the government should it face a major domestic crisis, which came with the Great Depression in 1929.

The new states

With the collapse of the Russian, German, and Austro-Hungarian empires, and a gravely weakened Ottoman domain at war's end, considerable political change took place in East Central Europe. New governments, most often in the form of parliamentary republics, emerged to fill the vacuum. The new parliamentary regimes faced major obstacles hindering political stability, including a lack of democratic traditions, extremist political groups trending toward authoritarianism, long-standing ethnic rivalries, and complex minorities issues. Furthermore, their economies had to be built anew, adding economic hardships to systems where agriculture dominated.

In Austria, which was barred from uniting with Germany by the treaties of Versailles and Saint Germain, a parliamentary republic was established in 1920. The country was deeply divided between Vienna with its population of 2 million, its cosmopolitanism, and its industrialism, and Social Democratic leanings, and the old empire's largely rural Alpine and Danubian provinces with their population of 4.5 million, their conservativism, their provincialism, and their heavily Catholic influence. Consequently, parliamentary politics was compromised right from the beginning. Under the country's decentralized federal system, the doctrinaire and inflexible Social Democrats, who controlled Vienna, were able to implement an extensive social-welfare program in the city, including massive public housing projects. A party-operated paramilitary organization (*Schutzbund*) reinforced its will in the city. The major political force in the rest of the country was the anti-Marxist, Catholic-dominated Christian Social Party, led by a cold-hearted priest named Father Ignaz Seipel. Seipel, who served as the Austrian chancellor for several years in the 1920s, cultivated a close relationship between his party and right-wing paramilitary groups collectively known as the *Heimwehr* that he used as a counterweight to the Socialists' *Schutzbund*. The hostilities between the two political groups spilled out into the open when massive left-wing protests in Vienna in July 1927 became unruly. Protestors burned down the justice ministry and the police retaliated by killing 89 people. Another major confrontation occurred in 1929, when the country's constitution was amended to increase the power of the president – in the eyes of the Socialists, toward a more authoritarian system.

To the east of Germany was the newly reconstituted state of Poland, which the Allies had treated favorably at the Paris Peace Conference. In a country of over 25 million, one-third of the population was composed of ethnic/religious minorities. The Poles were overwhelmingly Catholic, while the Ukrainians and Belorussians in Poland were mostly Russian Orthodox, and the newly incorporated Germans were chiefly Protestant. Poland's Jewish population, which totaled 3 million, was larger than in any other European state.

Politically, Poland operated under a constitution that went into effect in early 1921. The document concentrated power in the legislative branch of government that consisted of a Sejm (lower house) and a senate. A prime minister, who needed a parliamentary majority, oversaw the daily operations of government. The document also provided that the two houses of parliament elect a president whose prerogatives were strictly limited: he did not even have the power of a veto. The presence of some 59 political parties in the Sejm, many of which represented ethnic minorities, made it virtually impossible to achieve any kind of workable parliamentary majority at the national level. Coalition cabinets and ministerial instability became the norm, as Poland averaged close to two governments per year between the end of World War I and 1926. The parliamentary regime's inability to provide effective national leadership made it very unpopular.

By the mid-1920s many Poles placed their political hopes in Marshal Józef Piłsudski, a World War I hero whose Polish army had defeated a Russian force near Warsaw in August 1920 to preserve Poland's independence. He had refused to run for president in 1922 because of the inadequate powers that the constitution granted to the office. A critic of the parliamentary system, he wanted to see a "moral regeneration" of Poland. With the backing of the army and frustrated Socialists, he came out of retirement and toppled the parliamentary government in May 1926. While parliament contin-ued to exist and the press still operated with a degree of freedom, Pilsudski set up a semi-authoritarian regime with himself at the helm, although he refused to accept the presidency. His government instituted financial reforms, but these proved insufficient to protect Poland from the withering effects of the Great Depression.

The Republic of Czechoslovakia, which formally declared its independence in October 1918, was largely the creation of two men: a Slovak philosopher/politician named Tomáš Masaryk, who became its first president, and Edvard Beneš, a Czech sociology professor/diplomat, who served as foreign minister from the country's incep-tion to 1935. Czechoslovakia adopted a democratic parliamentary system that drew strength from a large middle class steeped in liberal traditions. A coalition consisting of the country's five main political parties, including the Social Democratic Party, provided stability for the regime in the early 1920s. Antonín Švehla, the leader of the centrist Agrarian Party, served as prime minister of the five-party coalition that ruled from 1922 to 1926 – longer than any other Czech interwar government. Following the general elections of 1925, in which the Agrarian Party won the most parliamentary seats, Švehla formed a coalition with conservative parties, since the number of Social Democratic seats in the legislature plummeted. Though the new coalition, by making concessions to the Catholic Church, was less anticlerical than its predecessor, there was still resentment among Catholics when the government made divorce legal, reduced the number of religious holidays, and declared the birthdate of Jan Hus, an early fif-teenth-century Czech church reformer whom the Catholics had burned at the stake as a heretic, to be a national holiday. One important goal that the Agrarians realized was the passage of protectionist legislation on farm produce; the Socialists opposed this, fearing higher food prices. Švehla, known for his skills in reaching compromise deals with other political groups throughout the decade of the 1920s, was forced to resign from office in 1929 because of illness.

The country had potentially serious ethnic problems, since its population not only consisted of Czechs (7.25 million) and Slovaks (5 million), but also of more than 3.25 million Germans in a western border area called the Sudetenland, and smaller numbers of Magyars (750,000), Ruthenians (500,000), and Poles (90,000). Separatist

Figure 4.1 Czechoslovakian President Tomáš Masaryk (left) and Prime Minister Antonín Švehla enjoy a horse-drawn carriage ride following Masaryk's re-election as president in 1927.

feelings among the Magyars and Sudeten Germans were never far from the surface; there were signs of ethnic discontent among the Slovaks as well. Nevertheless, Czechoslovakia enjoyed political stability in the decade following its founding, in part because of its tolerant policy toward ethnic minorities, who were allowed to administer their own schools and to conduct official business in the locally dominant language.

The interwar trend toward dictatorship was evident in Hungary and the Balkan states, and was buoyed in some of them by the example of Fascist Italy. In Hungary, after the Soviet Republic of Béla Kun fell in the summer of 1919, an authoritarian regime emerged under Admiral Miklós Horthy, who took the title of regent in a country that in early 1920 organized itself as a kingdom without a king. A brutal "white terror" soon targeted Communists, socialists, Jews, and city workers; it executed upwards of 5,000 people and imprisoned as many as 75,000 before ending in late 1921. Horthy appointed Count István Bethlen, a Hungarian aristocrat, as prime minister in 1921. For more than a decade, the two men used the conservative Party of National Unity that Bethlen founded to dominate Hungarian politics and to work for the traditional Hungarian ruling classes. Bethlen stabilized the country's currency in the mid-1920s and restored prosperity through efficient agricultural management practices.

To the south of Hungary, the newly created Kingdom of Yugoslavia experienced bitter quarrels in the 1920s between the Catholic Croats, who defended a federalist form of government, and the Orthodox Christian Serbs, who advocated for a strong central-ized political system and Serbian domination in a "Greater Serb" Yugoslavia. The Croats refused to attend the constitutional assembly elected in November 1919, and were imme-diately sidelined when the new constitution reaffirmed the predominance of Serbia. The ethnic tensions were quite evident in the country's parliament, where the Serbs held power and the Croats proved feisty opponents; a climax to the political feuding came in the summer of 1928, when a Serbian member of parliament shot several Croatian politicians on the floor of the legislative assembly hall – three of them died, including Stjepan Radić, the leader of Croatia's most powerful political party.

Romania and Bulgaria remained monarchies after the war. Romania maintained the semblance of a parliamentary regime during the 1920s, in the form of a liberal constitutional monarchy. The National Liberal Party (a center-right group) and the National Peasants Party (a mildly conservative party) alternated in power, and both succeeded in obtaining passage of some agrarian reform measures that broke up most of the country's large estates. When the Great Depression struck in 1929, the country's agriculturally based economy proved quite vulnerable. Bulgaria, after a period of unrest, in late 1918 chose a new king, Boris III (r. 1918–1943), though he was a mere figurehead. The real ruler was Aleksandar Stamboliyski, the head of the Agrarian Union Party, who came to power through democratic elections in 1919 under the country's liberal constitution and established an agrarian dictatorship in 1920. Although Bulgaria's large agricultural sector was already defined by small family farms at war's end, Stamboliyski instituted new land reforms to expand the smallholders' base even more. While his land reforms were successful, he alienated the urban middle class through his hostile rhetoric and unfriendly tax policies. He offended nationalists by signing what they saw as the harsh Treaty of Neuilly with the Allies to end World War I and cooperating with the Allies on international questions after that. An extreme right-wing government took power in June 1923, in a military coup that resulted shortly thereafter in Stamboliyski's murder at the hands of Macedonian nationalists over his establishment of cordial relations with neighboring Yugoslavia. A "white terror" ensued in which the government banned the influential Agrarian Union and Communist parties and killed thousands of people associated with them. The King installed a more moderate government in 1926, and the Agrarian Union Party – unlike that of the Communists – was allowed to resume its place in Bulgarian politics.

Greece started the interwar period with a constitutional monarchy, but the country was polarized between monarchists and republicans resulting from a bitter wartime rift between Greece's pro-German King and Eleftherios Venizelos, a pro-Allied politician who had taken complete control of Greece in 1917, after the Allies forced the King to flee the country. While one of the exiled king's sons assumed the throne, real power rested with Venizelos until his party suffered a devastating defeat at the polls in late 1920. Although the pro-royalists who took power had promised to end a war that Greece was waging against Turkey, they actually intensified the country's war effort in Anatolia. Yet they weakened Greece's position by dismissing a number of experienced Venizelist officers from the army, and they underestimated the determination of the Turks. Many Greeks blamed the royalist government for their country's humiliating defeat in the Greco-Turkish War of 1919–1922. Embittered Venizelos military officers in late 1922 staged a successful uprising against the royalist cabinet. Their military government paved the way for the creation in 1924 of the Second Hellenic Republic. Bitter divisions in Greek society remained, however, and political instability defined Greek politics during the decade that the republic lasted.

Albania was unsure that it would even emerge as an independent state after the war, since neighboring countries were determined to partition it. Only the intervention of Woodrow Wilson in 1920 saved the country from being divided among Greece, Italy, and Yugoslavia. Like so many other countries in Europe, Albania experimented with democracy in the early 1920s under a monarchy, but the democracy ended in 1924 with a military coup that set up Ahmet Zogu as a dictator in a short-lived republic. In 1928, Zogu transformed the government once again into a monarchy, assumed the title of king, and kept his dictatorial powers.

The Baltic states of Lithuania, Latvia, and Estonia declared their independence from Russia in 1918 only to find themselves dealing with the Russians again when the Bolsheviks tried to re-annex them during the Russian Civil War. The newly independent states adopted constitutions that instituted republican regimes with weak executive branches, powerful single-house legislatures, universal suffrage, and proportional representation. Political shortcomings began to call the Baltic countries' democratic regimes into question not too long after they were implemented. Politics in all three countries were marked by multiple political parties, democratic immaturity, and frequent ministerial changes. The end result was the establishment of authoritarian rule, first in Lithuania and later in Estonia and Latvia. In Lithuania, a military-led coup took place in December 1926, supposedly to prevent a Bolshevik takeover. Antanas Smetona, leader of the right-wing political party known as the Lithuanian Nationalist Union, became president, and he quickly established a one-party dictatorship that he dominated until 1940.

The end of democracy in Italy

Postwar Italy found itself weighed down by serious political, economic, and social divisions. Deep political rifts developed as the wartime coalition government of Vittorio Orlando limped along through the Paris peace talks before its lackluster performance there caused its downfall. Italy's war debt was two times greater than all governmental spending from 1861 to 1913 combined. Without Allied credit, the country quickly found itself immersed in inflation and a horrific international trade imbalance. In the elections of late 1919, three groups rose to prominence: the Socialists, the recently created Catholic Popular Party, and the Liberals. The Socialists had serious internal divisions, and their left wing abandoned the party in 1920 to form the Italian Communist Party. The Catholic Popular Party was united in its fight against anticlericalism in Italy, and refused to cooperate with either the Socialists or Liberals. The Liberals subscribed to a laissez-faire policy economically and practiced a hands-off approach to problems. This state of affairs did not bode well for Italy which had five governments from the end of the war to October 1922, and none of them lasted long enough to put together a constructive recovery plan for the country. When Italy's high hopes regarding territorial acquisitions faded at the conclusion of the Paris Peace Conference, a sense of disillusionment about the settlement set in at home where people dubbed it the "mutilated peace." The nationalists' anger was reflected in the seizure of the Adriatic port city of Fiume by the far-right poet Gabriele D'Annunzio in September 1919. After months of vacillation, the government finally ousted D'Annunzio in late 1920. His stand exposed the weakness of the regime.

Adding to the government's problems was social and labor unrest from both peasants and workers. Labor unrest grew in 1920–1921, and the government's indecisiveness in turn encouraged strikes and acts of labor insubordination. Property owners began to fear for their economic interests. Industrialists and wealthy landowners joined nationalist groups in looking for a more responsive political force. They ended up embracing an extreme right-wing political movement known as Fascism led by a one-time socialist become ardent nationalist named Benito Mussolini. He was a former teacher turned journalist who, as editor of the socialist newspaper *Avanti*, was briefly jailed in 1911 for his editorial attacks on Italy's colonial war in North Africa. During World War I, Mussolini shifted from favoring Italian neutrality, to supporting Italy's participation in the struggle in 1915, to championing the nationalists' demands that Italy obtain an annexationist peace settlement in 1918. In March 1919, he set up the National Fascist Party. Members wore black shirts and attempted to rally the workers with a poorly defined program.

Based in Milan, the Fascists ran a slate of candidates in the 1919 national elections, but failed to gain representation in parliament. In the aftermath of the election debacle, Mussolini began to appeal to the middle class, which feared for its economic and social standing, and gained the support of most of the ultra-nationalists' military adventurers following the collapse of D'Annunzio's scheme in Fiume. The Fascists made inroads with powerful industrialists, wealthy landowners, and the middle class during the workers' strikes and land crises in 1920–1921, and money started pouring into their coffers, allowing them to send out their black-shirted paramilitary units to challenge and intimidate Communists, Socialists, and agricultural laborers' unions. In spite of these gains, the Fascist Party might never have taken power by itself. The government of Giovanni Giolitti, a savvy long-time parliamentarian who was a left-leaning political moderate, invited them to be electoral allies in national elections held in the spring of 1921, in hopes of taming Fascist vehemence. The Fascist Party, by securing 35 seats in the Italian Parliament, obtained a new, prosecution-free forum for Mussolini's bombastic speeches. Giolitti's government fell in June 1921.

By August 1922, the unsolved domestic issues had reached a crisis point. The combination of a caretaker cabinet, continued street violence, and complicit government officials enabled the Fascists to expel Socialist- or Communist-dominated town councils and to claim control of northern Italy by the fall. Mussolini emerged as the self-proclaimed upholder of law and order, topping his power moves on October 22 with a "March on Rome" that involved 50,000 Fascists organized into three columns descending on the city from different directions. At the last minute, the Prime Minister requested the imposition of martial law in Rome to stop their advance, but King Victor Emmanuel III refused to sign the order. The government fell and the King invited Mussolini to form a national government. At the age of 39, Mussolini became the youngest prime minister in Italian history.

Having reached power through a combination of intimidation and legal means, Mussolini quickly moved to consolidate his power. He secured the key cabinet posts of justice and finance for the Fascists, added the titles of foreign minister and interior minister to his position, and gained parliamentary approval to govern by decree for 12 months. The Acerbo Election Law of June 1923 reinforced the Fascist Party's power by stating that whatever party received the most votes in a national election and obtained a minimum 25 percent of the election vote total would automatically get two-thirds of the seats in Italy's Chamber of Deputies. The vote indicated that many centrist and rightist deputies viewed national stability and order as more important at that point than true parliamentary government. National elections were held in April 1924. The Fascist coalition candidates garnered 65 percent of the votes and thereby claimed 374 of the Chamber's 535 seats. The Fascists' success was partially attributable to their control of the election machinery and their intimidation and violent actions against opposition groups and voters, but the outcome also reflected Mussolini's real popularity among a broad range of Italians, from the industrial conservatives in the north to the poorer rural regions of central and southern Italy. The April vote was Italy's last quasi-legitimate election for two decades.

Filled with a new sense of confidence, Mussolini increased the pressure on his political opponents. A number of Fascist assaults on opposition deputies took place, the most vicious of which was the murder of the socialist moderate Giacomo Matteotti on June 10, 1924, after he accused the Fascists of electoral fraud and brutality. Outrage across Italy forced Mussolini to beat a retreat. He removed his Fascist chief of police, reshuffled his cabinet to include liberals, and made conciliatory speeches. The King failed to ask for his resignation, fearing that such a decision would result in a Socialist takeover. By the end of 1924, the storm of criticism had died down, and Mussolini began to reassert his authority. He ousted the liberal members from his cabinet and tightened press censorship. In December, 1925, Mussolini received the title of Duce (leader). In 1926, he obtained unrestricted power to govern by decree and abolished all political parties except his own. By the end of that year, Mussolini presided over a powerful one-party dictatorship in Italy.

One of Mussolini's top priorities in the late 1920s was to improve the government's position with the Catholic Church which had earlier condemned the Fascist government for the destruction of Catholic workers' cooperatives. To do so, Mussolini in 1929 signed the Lateran Pact with the Vatican, ending decades of division between the Catholic Church and the Italian state. For the first time the Church officially recognized the modern state of Italy in return for Italy's recognition of the sovereignty of the pope's small state of Vatican City in Rome. Mussolini also won favor with many Catholics for his stand against Communism. By 1929, Mussolini's popularity had reached new heights, as he enjoyed the oft passive support of most Italians.

Fascism in Italy was the most powerful and dramatic form of authoritarianism that emerged in the hard times following World War I. As a doctrine, Fascism was conceptslim, and can be defined as much by what it opposed (liberal democracy, socialism, Communism, and perpetual peace) as by what it advocated (aggressive nationalism, a one-party dictatorship, a glorification of violence, a worship of the state, and the cult of the leader). Italian Fascism was primarily a pragmatic way of doing politics, and is best characterized by the corporatist state, which redrew the lines between private initiative and government intervention. A corporatist state involved the management of economic sectors by labor, management, and politicians under the leadership of the state, in order to promote harmony among the different interests and social classes they represented. The totalitarian tendencies in Fascism were evident in the affirmation that the individual had no meaning without the state, and that the state represented the synthesis of every value and had the responsibility to develop and strengthen the people.

Fascism's emphasis on the importance of outward appearances was reflected in Mussolini's relentless efforts to present himself to Italy and the world as a virile, dynamic ruler. Ever the showman, he delivered awe-inspiring speeches full of exaggeration, bombast, and flare. In his most striking moments, he could be seen jutting out his jaw and glaring fiercely. He gave considerable attention to what did or did not appear in the press: he would not allow journalists to make any mention that he was a grandfather, for example, and there could be no mention of his birthday or of his dancing, since he wanted the accent to be on youthfulness and seriousness. He leaped through fiery hoops to demonstrate his manliness, and he compelled close associates to do the same. By the early 1930s he insisted that journalists, when making references to him, capitalize the words He, His, and Him, just as people did when dealing with Jesus Christ or God. Early on, the French press referred to Mussolini as a "Carnival Caesar"; it was a moniker that not only stuck, but that aptly described the theatrics and publicity gimmicks he used to portray himself as a strongman ruler. Italian Fascism served as a model for extreme right-wing political groups in countries across Europe, many of which had been forced to adopt democracy as a result of the Paris Peace Conference and where monarchist traditions were still strong. Mussolini reined in political and social unrest, made Italy an imperial power, and dictated many diplomatic moves in Europe well into the 1930s, but he did so at a high cost. He silenced his political opponents, suppressed elections, stifled the press, and persecuted artists and free thinkers.

Spain between dictatorship and revolution

In 1918, Spain's parliamentary monarchy was in disarray, and King Alphonso XIII (r. 1886–1931) spent the next several years naming political leaders to nonaligned coalitions in an attempt to repair it. One key issue that his governments faced was rebellion in Morocco, and a major setback to their efforts took place in 1921 when the Spanish experienced a disastrous military defeat at the Battle of Anual, where countless numbers of young conscripts died. Mutinies followed at Spain's Malaga base when reinforcements were ordered to embark. An official investigation into the catastrophe risked touching the king himself, so Alphonso participated in a 1923 army coup that established a military dictatorship led by General Miguel Primo de Rivera. The regime change saved the king from political embarrassment, but in the long run, his complicity in the governmental shift compromised his authority. Primo de Rivera's most revered accomplishment was the success of a joint Spanish–French force in pacifying Morocco in 1925–1926. When the military directory was abolished in 1925, Primo de Rivera stayed on as the one-man ruler of a new civilian government. By no means a reactionary, he attempted to modernize the economy by bringing technical experts on board and to reduce unemployment through spending on public works programs, but his economic policies led to rapid inflation and widespread discontent. His failures led the king and army to withdraw their support for him in early 1930, and he resigned from office.

Autocracy in Portugal

In the aftermath of a revolution, Portugal emerged with a parliamentary republic in 1911. In late 1917, Sidonio Pais led a military coup against the republican government and established an authoritarian regime that lasted until his assassination at the end of 1918. Pais's dictatorship is generally considered the first in Europe, and it involved the restoration of traditional values, the cult of the homeland, and rule by a charismatic leader. Political instability plagued Portugal for several years after Pais's death. Amidst political corruption and ineptitude, General Antonio Carmona staged a successful military coup in 1926. Carmona, as Portugal's new president, quickly established a dictatorship. To assist him in bailing the country out of a financial crisis, Carmona in 1928 brought in Antonio de Oliveira Salazar, a devout Catholic and ex-seminarian who taught economics at the University of Coimbra at the time of his appointment. Owing to his administrative and fiscal talents, Salazar saw his power in the government steadily increase to the point where, after he was named prime minister in 1932, he became the governmental strongman. Salazar oversaw the introduction of a new constitution in 1933 that created an authoritarian system. The document incorporated the concept of a corporate state into its provisions by establishing a Corporative Chamber that represented interest groups as a part of a bicameral legislature. The constitution also provided for a National Assembly, but only the government-supported National Union Party was permitted to exist; the National Union movement won all the parliamentary seats in Portuguese elections between 1934 and 1973. Salazar's regime was conservative and nationalist in character, and in many ways modeled on Fascist Italy.

The Soviet economic debate and succession struggle

After the Bolsheviks (Communists) defeated the Whites in Russia's civil war, the country was on the brink of disaster, as it was threatened by widespread peasant protests, a major famine, and severe outbreaks of typhus and cholera. A climax to the domestic turbulence came in the Kronstadt revolt of early 1921, which the government quickly crushed. Lenin responded to the crisis by introducing the New Economic Policy (NEP) in March 1921. This represented a partial restoration of capitalism under strict government control. Peasants, after paying a tax in kind to the government, were allowed to sell their surpluses freely, and small enterprises, which had been nationalized in November 1920, were re-privatized. Heavy industries, transport, and banks, however, remained in the hands of the government. The economy under NEP revived in 1922, and agricultural and industrial production approached prewar levels by the mid-1920s. Lenin viewed NEP as a temporary tactical retreat from socialist ideology, contending that he needed to adjust socialism to the reality of the moment in order to preserve political power and prepare the way for a future surge to a utopian socialist state.

Lenin's policy changes spurred one of the most important economic debates of the twentieth century about the management of a mixed, public–private economy. In 1921, Russia needed investment capital to industrialize and modernize. Although Bolshevik Russia had no colonies, refused foreign credit for ideological reasons, and had already seized most of the country's private assets, it had a vast, albeit underdeveloped, supply of agricultural and natural resources. Should agriculture be given time – a decade or two – to flourish and help capital to accumulate? Or should industrialization be given priority and all investment capital earmarked for industry? Trotsky, second in importance to Lenin within the Bolshevik Party, emphasized the need to build a triple infrastructure of industry, transportation, and housing as quickly as possible. He believed that only a "dictatorship of industry" could realize socialism. Development capital, he argued, would come primarily from the collectivization of agriculture. Opposing him was economist Nikolai Bukharin, a small, zestful, boyish man with a sense of humor, and the darling of the Bolshevik revolution. He defended Lenin's ideas about creating a gradual "agrarian cooperative socialism." Experience had moderated Lenin's emphasis on central planning, investment in heavy industry, and collective farming. In adopting NEP, Lenin appeared committed to a mixed economy until Russia grew into socialism. For Bukharin, this meant cutting industrial prices, encouraging peasants to produce and save in order to generate capital, developing an internal market, and imposing progressive income taxes. Trotsky's position was ideologically motivated, whereas Bukharin's was economically driven and therefore more pragmatic and realistic. Bukharin acknowledged the backwardness of the Russian economy. He wanted Soviet industrialization to remain humane and to preserve the alliance between peasants and workers, but it would involve slow growth. Trotsky felt that Russia, officially constituted as the Union of Soviet Socialist Republics (Soviet Union) in late 1922, had little time to catch up with the rest of Europe.

The NEP was Lenin's last major policy decision, since he suffered a debilitating stroke in May 1922, followed by two others in the ensuing months. He died in January 1924. Trotsky seemed to have the inside track to succeed Lenin, but he had a major rival in the person of Joseph Stalin. Born Jozif Dzhugashvili in 1879, Stalin was the son of a cobbler in the province of Georgia. As a young man he briefly attended the Orthodox Theological Seminary in Tiflis before being expelled for socialist views. In 1903, Stalin joined the Bolshevik faction of the Russian Social Democratic Party. In and out of jail – including exile to Siberia – over the next several years for revolutionary activities, he was a member of the inner circle of Bolshevik leaders by 1917. During the Russian Civil War, he developed an intense dislike of Trotsky, when the two men clashed over strategy. Stalin's election to the post of general secretary of the Communist Party's Central Committee in 1922 proved pivotal in his rise to power, since it allowed him to dominate the party apparatus through his power of appointment and promotion. Stalin also benefited from the emergence of a new generation of party officials, many of them semi-educated workers or peasants, whose bureaucratic posts depended on him and who wished for a single forceful leader to move the party forward.

Trotsky's economic policy position was to the left of the expanding bureaucracy of party officials as was his advocacy of the theory of "permanent revolution." In this doctrine, Trotsky argued that it was incumbent on Russia to export Communism abroad through the promotion of revolutions; only through the triumph of world revolution could one guarantee the success of the Russian revolution. Trotsky had few friends and he alienated colleagues with his intellectual arrogance. These factors, and his lack of skill when it came to political infighting, worked against him when a succession struggle developed following Lenin's death. In contrast to Trotsky, Stalin used cunning, ruthlessness, and chicanery to outmaneuver his opponents in his drive for absolute power. He attacked Trotsky's theory of permanent revolution by offering up the doctrine of "socialism in one country." Stalin wanted to create a strong socialist state in Soviet Russia before promoting socialist insurrections abroad. In a show of strength, he obtained official approval for his policy at the Fourteenth Communist Party Congress in early 1925. Stalin also sided with Bukharin's moderate, gradualist approach against Trotsky's ideologically motivated plan in the debate over NEP: the government expanded its concessions to Russian peasants with a resultant increase in agricultural output. Trotsky steadily lost ground politically: he was ousted in 1925 from his post as war commissar and in 1926 from his seat on the Politburo, the chief policy-making body for both the party and the state. The following year saw Trotsky expelled from the party's Central Committee and finally from the party itself. In 1929 Trotsky went into forced exile abroad. Once Trotsky and his allies were gone, only the Bukharinists, who had sided with Stalin since 1925, stood between Stalin and total power.

Conclusion

Democracy between 1918 and 1929 encountered enormous difficulties. After leaders at the Paris Peace Conference insisted upon its introduction across the continent, many states that started with democracies drifted towards authoritarian regimes. Even where democracy survived during these years, its track record was often compromised, since most countries had to rely on coalitions to govern and these were inherently unstable. In spite of the political uncertainties that came with coalitions, a number of them succeeded in passing legislation concerning employment, housing, welfare, medical care, and education. Thus, pragmatic solutions, for which a consensus was easier to find, often trumped ideology, especially in Northern and Western Europe. Countries often succumbed to authoritarianism due to the lack of democratic traditions, the gravity of domestic problems, the absence of a large middle class, and deep ideological and political divisions. The example of Germany, which struggled to make its democratic institutions work smoothly, exemplified many of the political hazards that European governments experienced in the 1920s.

Demographic transitions

While the peace treaties of the Versailles settlement managed to solve many contentious population resettlements in the first years of peace, the effects of the Great War and attendant conflicts continued to create population problems. During the Russian Civil War, between 30,000 and 70,000 Jews died in Ukraine and some 500,000 were left homeless. Warfare that lasted into the 1920s in the East added to the misery of millions of civilians who fled from battle areas, revolution, or persecution. One million Russians escaped from the Russian Civil War, while two million Turks, Greeks, and Bulgarians fled from the Greco-Turkish War. In 1921, there were still hundreds of thousands of refugees across Europe. Among the most affected and most vulnerable groups in Europe were the displaced persons, namely, refugees, resettled individuals, and orphans. They not only posed serious social challenges, but required international humanitarian action and increased domestic welfare measures. Minorities also often suffered human rights and economic deprivations. Migrations thus continued well into the 1920s.

Repatriations

When the armistice was signed on November 11, 1918, the number of refugees and displaced persons in Europe was in the millions, although it is impossible to establish an exact figure. Many of them yearned to return home, although not all were able, and others were not willing to do so. Demobilized soldiers returned home quickly, except for the German soldiers on the Eastern Front. In the immediate postwar years, the League of Nations helped repatriate 400,000 prisoners of war in 26 countries, but hundreds of thousands more were still awaiting repatriation in 1921. As for civilians, repatriation was handled through diplomatic agreements. While such agreements existed for the Western Front areas, none existed in East Central Europe, where the new republic of Austria became a refugee haven. With its resources stretched thin, Austria limited its support to Christian and German-speaking refugees. Large numbers of Jewish, Polish, and Ukrainian refugees were placed in a difficult position, either because they refused to leave or because they could not, as was the case when Poland refused to allow Galician Jews to return.

The League of Nations stepped up to the challenge in 1921 by appointing a high commissioner for refugees. The League was also instrumental in the Greco-Turkish population exchange agreed upon in the 1923 Treaty of Lausanne. Greece absorbed 1.5 million Greeks from Turkey, while Turkey received 500,000 nationals from Greece – the largest single population resettlement of the postwar era. By 1930, some two million ethnic Europeans – Christian Armenians, Bulgarians, and Greeks – had been relocated from Turkey. Other resettlements took place in the Balkans where millions of individuals were dispersed among the old and new states and their centuries-old communities destroyed. Thus, significant population exchanges took place in the 1920s in a giant game of musical chairs.

The new minorities

Despite the goal of creating ethnically viable states, all the new East Central European states contained minority populations of 10 to 37 percent. Poland and Romania had the highest percentages. Yugoslavia gathered a dozen minorities that spoke different languages. Millions of Germans remained in Poland and Czechoslovakia, with many more in other European countries. Three million ethnic Hungarians lived outside the country of Hungary. To remedy the problem, the League of Nations organized plebiscites in several areas, but these did not guarantee permanent solutions.

The new regimes were not always kind to minorities. Lenin moved quickly to reintegrate Belorussia and Ukraine, which had seceded from Russia in 1917–1918, into his Soviet state. He expelled several million Poles from both territories, and encouraged Russian Jews living there to move to Crimea with the promise of a future Jewish state. Poland was home to several minorities, including 3 million Jews. The majority lived in the former Pale of Settlement (Galicia, Belorussia, and western Ukraine), and a smaller group from former German territories lived in the Posen area in western Poland. In 1919 and 1920, the two groups independently took up arms to win their independence, but the Polish army crushed both insurrections swiftly. The French expelled 150,000 Germans from Alsace-Lorraine. Human tragedies, lingering hatreds, and resentments festered throughout the interwar years. These feelings were strongest in East Central Europe where anti-Slavic, anti-Semitic, and anti-Communist sentiments remained high and caused significant economic and ethnic emigration.

Population movements left no European country untouched. European countries, both old and new, were increasingly ethnically diverse. Adding to the transnational dislocations of war and revolution, substantial internal and colonial migrations reshaped European demographics. The peasantry, especially in East Central Europe, was often affected by the double tragedy of civil war and land redistribution that forced many from their ancestral farms. Rural migration was common as well in Western European countries where industrial jobs became more attractive.

Orphanages and youth

Millions of European families remained separated at war's end, especially so in East Central Europe. After hostilities ended, not all could be reunited. There were millions of orphans after 1918. For the first time in history, all European states, following the example of religious institutions and Friends of Children societies, created orphanages and introduced innovative pedagogical methods to educate and rehabilitate the youth in their facilities.

Russia (which had lost several million men in World War I, the revolutionary terror, the Russian Civil War, and the famine of 1921–1923) had a major orphan problem. During the famine, the number young people living in orphanages swelled to between 4 and 7.5 million. Famished, orphaned, abandoned, or abused "wolf-children" begged and thieved for a living, becoming asocial elements addicted to alcohol, cocaine, and gambling. In the early 1920s, large numbers of juveniles flocked to Moscow, disrupting train stations, markets, and other public places. A generation grew up without the necessary labor and social skills to be successfully integrated into society. Stalin's renewed war on kulaks in 1928 created more broken families and homeless youth who were seen as socially dangerous elements. In 1919, the Bolsheviks created the Council for the Defense of Children. In 1921, Feliks Dzerzhinsky, who headed Russia's ruthless secret police force (Cheka) and who organized Russia's first concentration camps, launched a huge orphanage construction project. Dzerzhinsky created night shelters, a foster homes placement service, and labor communes for difficult youth. His activities involving orphaned young people must be put in context, however, since many children became orphans as a result of his murderous actions against their parents during periods of terror.

The American Relief Administration (ARA)

The United States, already involved in relief efforts during the Great War, expanded its operations by extending aid to East Central Europe once the war had ended in a push to alleviate further deterioration of the region's appalling conditions. President Wilson, with the support of Allied nations and the U.S. Congress, approved in early 1919 the creation of the American Relief Administration (ARA) under the leadership of Herbert Hoover. With a $100 million budget from Congress and another $100 million from private donations, Hoover fed people in 23 European states. His operation included foodstuffs, medical supplies, and relocation services. His actions were particularly instrumental in helping Poland and Serbia, which had suffered greatly. Yet relief for him knew no enemy. Despite Allied objections, Hoover insisted on including Germany as a food recipient. His relief operations also fed 400,000 Austrian children, which was two-thirds of their entire child population. Only after Communist leader Béla Kun started committing atrocities in Hungary in the spring of 1919 did Hoover withhold food from that country.

One special case was Russia, where a far-reaching famine gripped the country in 1921 owing to the effects of the Russian Civil War and a drought. At the end of the fall, 100,000 Russians were dying every week. Maxim Gorky, one of Russia's prominent writers, issued a plea to the West in July 1921 for food and medicine, and Soviet leaders, initially suspicious, finally consented to accept assistance. Hoover quickly launched a program of famine relief, with the first ARA shipment of food arriving in Petrograd in September 1921. By August 1922, the ARA was feeding 11 million people in 19,000 kitchens. Hoover added sanitizing stations and medical equipment to deal with a lingering epidemic of typhus and cholera. It was the largest relief effort to date, and was instrumental in saving the lives of large numbers of Russian people. Nevertheless, the famine had still taken the lives of more than 5 million people by the time it ended in 1923. Overall, Hoover did much to assist Europe in a humanitarian way: he fed 80 million people between 1914 and 1923, saving more lives than anyone else in history.

Demographic trends

With the loss of millions of young men in the war, there were not enough men to keep the marriage statistics at prewar levels. The first consequence was a drop in the number of live births. An asymmetry is visible in the live births between Western and East Central Europe (see p. 81). In the West, birth rates fell below 1 percent, whereas East Central Europe experienced a demographic transition that assured it of a rapid population growth. The largest drop in birth rates was among Western European urban workers and professionals who no longer produced enough offspring to replace themselves, partly because of their reluctance to bring up children in an unsafe, unsettled world. Another reason was the drop in the number of marriages in Western Europe after a brief upsurge in 1920–1921. Women opted to remain single or not remarry. Shattering the image of the spinster, they became financially self-sufficient salaried workers who lived by themselves. Young people postponed marriage and child birth. The number of same-sex couples increased. Economic and social policies had to take the new demographic factors into consideration in order to serve the people better, while optimizing their contributions to economic development.

Conclusion

Demographics were far from settled in the 1920s. While the pace of resettlements and repatriations slowed down in the late 1920s, it nonetheless altered Europe's social fabric and accelerated socio-economic and cultural changes.

Economic transitions

The priorities of reconstruction and the existing wartime controls gave governments an opportunity to embrace modernizing economic policies, yet in 1919 the general goal for most was a return to the economic environment of the prewar years. A number of countries also faced the challenge of reconstruction, a task made more difficult by war debts, economic dislocation, and, in some cases, reparations. Industrialization and mass consumerism changed societies across Europe, while standards of living fluctuated and economic development seesawed. Agriculture faced an unpredictable future as the sector confronted competition from abroad and demands for land redistribution. It was a time of uncertainty and experimentation.

Returning to peacetime economies

European governments attempted to return their economies to a normal peacetime footing as quickly as possible after World War I, but they had to deal with formidable obstacles as they did so. One of their greatest challenges was paying for the war, since they had borrowed heavily to help finance it. Allied states had obtained large loans in America, and were thus financially dependent on the United States after the war. Another challenge was the postwar instability of the international financial system that made stabilizing currencies and rebuilding foreign trade networks difficult. Old and new states grappled with conflicting priorities as they sought to modernize, urbanize, and industrialize while maintaining their agricultural sectors; war debt payments slowed economic development that was needed for military strength, national power, and consumers' happiness.

In rebuilding their economies, European governments often found their postwar means of production handicapped as a result of the war. British coal mining equipment, for instance, was outworn and outdated by the end of the conflict, causing a drop in Britain's production and competitiveness on international markets. Changes in trade patterns during the war also adversely affected Britain's position as a coal exporter. In France, the Germans intentionally destroyed coal mines in the northeast as they retreated in the conflict's final weeks, adding to France's postwar difficulties. The troubles over coal were but one aspect of the economic dislocation that Allied countries experienced following the Great War. In Poland, Czechoslovakia, and Hungary, the rebuilding process depended on the creation of new governmental systems and economic institutions. In many parts of Europe, the war had caused considerable devastation to agricultural lands, causing a reduction of agricultural products. Europe had to confront the challenge of land redistribution. Finally, the new countries from the Balkans to the Baltic States and Soviet Russia lacked the technology and skilled labor to industrialize.

Faced with these enormous problems in the immediate postwar years, countries fared unevenly. Southern Europe lost to Northern Europe; Eastern Europe to Western Europe. Poland, Czechoslovakia, Hungary, and the Baltic states quickly moved ahead because they were the most industrialized of the East Central European countries. Still, with high military, administrative, and debt service expenses, they remained heavily dependent on foreign capital in crucial sectors throughout the interwar years. The development of these peripheral states remained unbalanced and varied. The Danubian region for example, benefited partly from oil and electrical power plants that Western businesses financed and designed primarily for Western markets.

Poland was a special case. Even though Polish activists had been preparing since 1907 for the country's rebirth, the realities of mid-1918 caught them by surprise; 90 percent of Poland's territories had suffered considerable devastation in the area of agriculture and infrastructure, not to mention the economic exploitation of the land by Russian and German armies, and the sabotage that accompanied both armies' retreats during the war. Money was needed quickly to stabilize the new state, but no international credit was available at this time. The country had no clear borders, five prewar and war-time currencies, two railway gauges, no markets, and plenty of unscrupulous speculators. It was fighting high unemployment and considerable poverty. The country swiftly followed its political rebirth with efforts to integrate its economy. Tariffs, regulations, transportation, and language were harmonized. A new property tax system, a common currency, and a unified fiscal administration were created in 1919, followed by a unified income tax in 1920, and the removal of external and internal tariffs. Military costs, however, ate most of the state budget and caused serious inflation in the early 1920s. Prime Minister Władysław Grabski dealt with the country's hyperinflation in 1924 by introducing a new currency, the zloty, which he stabilized by tying it to the gold standard. An agrarian reform redistributing large estates and modernizing agricultural methods followed. By 1926, a national railway network was completed, adopting the European railway gauge. Whatever progress was achieved, however, was slowed down by parliamentary opposition and the Great Depression.

Other countries besides Poland experienced severe inflation in the 1920s. Germany's runaway inflation in 1923 was the most serious example. The origins of the crisis went back to the Great War, when the country relied heavily on credit to finance the conflict – selling war bonds and printing paper money. In 1919, Germany found itself deeply in debt, its gold reserves depleted, and its investments abroad in a shambles. Its territorial losses – the mines and industries of Alsace-Lorraine and Silesia, the Polish breadbasket lands, and the overseas colonies – were keenly felt. Germany also faced a reparations bill total of 132 billion gold marks or approximately 33 billion dollars. Since a part of the reparations were to be paid in kind, Germany had to hand over huge quantities of industrial machinery, merchant shipping, and rolling stock. To pay for reparations, Germany's postwar governments continued to borrow and print new money. As the value of the German currency – the mark – dropped, inflation intensified. The mark, whose value was at 4.2 marks to one U.S. dollar on the eve of the war, had dropped to 4,500 marks to the dollar by October 1922. The inflationary crisis was exacerbated in January 1923, when the French and Belgian governments sent troops into the Ruhr district to force the Germans to meet their reparation obligations. The government adopted a policy of passive resistance to the occupiers and printed more and more money to sustain the unemployed. The mark plummeted in value. A loaf of bread that had cost 3,465 marks in July 1923 cost 201 billion marks in November of the same year. Members of the German middle class who lived on fixed incomes saw their life savings evaporate overnight. In late 1923, Hjalmar Schacht, a banker and economist, was assigned the task of returning Germany to financial stability. As the country's currency commissioner, he introduced a new temporary currency – the *Rentenmark* – that gained the trust of the German people and provided monetary stability. Schacht followed that up in 1924 with the creation of a new permanent currency – the *Reichsmark* – that he tied to gold at its prewar parity. Currency stability and foreign loans that primarily came from the United States contributed to a German economic revival in the latter 1920s.

Key elements to Germany's improved industrial output in the 1920s were the adoption of largely American production methods and the introduction of the most modern machines and equipment. Large firms benefited from the German Central Bank's deflationary policies that drove weaker, smaller, and more marginal firms out of business. Large combines were formed such as the United Steel Trust that brought together a large number of iron, steel, and coal producers to account for close to 50 percent of the country's steel production. In 1927, Germany's national production finally equaled that of 1913, and in 1928 the country's national income was 50 percent higher than on the eve of World War I. The overall results were impressive, even if Germany's overdependence on foreign money continued.

Economically, Austria found its prewar system – centered on the largely self-sufficient Austro-Hungarian Empire – torn asunder. Owing to the loss of territory, the country had virtually no coal whatsoever, meeting only 8 percent of its needs in 1920 via domestic mining. Certain areas of industry, such as iron production and the fabrication of locomotive engines, were suddenly excessive for the size of the domestic market. The lack of a strong agricultural sector caused serious trade deficits throughout the 1920s. In 1922, a bout of hyperinflation ended with the receipt of a large international loan through the League of Nations (650 million gold Crowns) and the implementation of government austerity measures that included a balanced budget at low spending levels. In the ensuing period of readjustment, unemployment jumped from slightly more than 100,000 people in 1922 to 244,000 by 1926. While the economy improved in the latter 1920s to the point where industrial production in 1929 stood at 98 percent of that achieved in 1913, unemployment still averaged 9.6 percent during these years and the number of unemployed never dropped much below 200,000. Furthermore, the major political parties' use of armed brigades to support their positions in the streets frightened away foreign investors who believed the country to be on the threshold of civil war. In many ways, Austria was still an economically vulnerable country at the end of the 1920s.

Figure 4.2 Children play with bundles of essentially worthless paper currency during Germany's bout with hyperinflation in 1923.

The Scandinavian economies generally prospered in the interwar years, although they, like other countries, experienced a slowdown during the Great Depression. Finland, for example, had a predominantly agricultural economy and thriving paper and lumber industries. To modernize its agrarian sector, it expanded the cooperative movement that allowed farmers to obtain credit and marketing services at reasonable rates. When the Great Depression struck, the government imposed tariffs on agricultural imports to protect domestic production. The amount of land under cultivation increased thereafter, and farm incomes in Finland, though they dropped in the 1930s, still fared better than most elsewhere.

The Italian economy

Mussolini's Fascist government adopted an approach by the mid-1920s that had national self-sufficiency or autarky as its goal. In 1925, he launched the "Battle for Wheat," which consisted of high tariffs on imported grain, state subsidies, and an intense propaganda campaign. Mussolini even granted medals to the farmers deemed the most successful. While wheat production increased by 50 percent by 1930, it came at the expense of economic efficiency and a drop in the production of other agricultural products that had more value for the country's national income. The "Battle of the Lira" was Mussolini's rallying cry for the revaluation of the currency in 1926, a decision made partly for reasons of prestige. The result was a heavily overvalued currency that adversely affected trade and tourism. The "Battle for Land" described Mussolini's policy of draining marshlands for agricultural uses. It played a support role in Mussolini's effort to increase grain production and improve public health. The fact that Italy began experiencing an economic slump before the Wall Street Crash of 1929 may be ascribed to Mussolini's revaluation and autarky initiatives. In the end, the living standards of the Italian people during the 1920s failed to improve, and the country's real wages were below all other Western European states in 1930.

Industrial modernization

Industrial modernization was a major factor in European economic growth in the 1920s. Some of the fastest-growing industries were tied to recent innovations or inventions in transportation, communication, and chemical engineering. Innovative European industrialists implemented the American-conceived Taylorist methods that involved time and motion studies, productivity bonuses, and job simplification. Many also adopted the Ford assembly-line system in their factories. In the midst of these changes, however, the divide between the fast-growing Western European industries and the more slowly developing East Central European industries was highly visible.

In the West, France enjoyed steady economic growth during the 1920s. By 1929, the industrial production index stood at 140 as compared with 100 in 1913. Contributing to France's economic expansion were technologically advanced segments of the economy and a devalued franc that made French products less expensive in international markets and enabled investors to pay back loans with cheaper money. A modernized and enlarged iron and steel industry improved production enough to rival Great Britain for second place in output among European states. France emerged as a leader in the automobile industry, second worldwide only to the United States, owing to the inventive mind of André Citroën who used assembly-line methods to manufacture cars and creatively advertised his automobile brand through such devices as skywriting and bold neon-lit lettering on the Eiffel Tower. Other expanding French industries included coal mining, electricity, chemicals, petroleum, construction, and rubber. Nevertheless, France also had a large number of small firms that survived through high profit margins and market sharing arrangements, but that failed to generate enough income to undertake expansion or significant modernization. While the French enjoyed economic prosperity in the initial postwar decade, it was less than it might have been had there been more concern for economic modernization and less for preserving the status quo. This was reflected in the fact that France's economic growth fell well below the world average during that time.

On the Iberian Peninsula, Spain missed a golden opportunity to capitalize on its neutrality during World War I to plan for the future, as government leaders used wartime surpluses to pay off foreign debts rather than update the country's infrastructure, and members of the business community often failed to invest lucrative wartime profits to modernize their industrial plants. Nevertheless, some modernization took place in the latter 1920s, as Spain embarked on the construction of a modern highway system and the electrification of its rail lines, many of which had recently been brought into a single network under state control. In spite of increasing prosperity in the late 1920s, the country still lagged far behind the countries of Northern Europe in terms of wealth.

Among the new countries in East Central Europe, Czechoslovakia was the most industrialized, yet it was in a strange predicament at the end of World War I. The Czechs faced uncertain frontiers, their agricultural and livestock production had fallen to half its prewar levels, and their industrial productivity was reduced as well. When their ties with the old Austro-Hungarian economic system were severed, they had to change industrial locations and markets, import significant quantities of raw materials, and redirect their exports. Still employing almost half of the total labor force of the former Habsburg Empire, Czechoslovakia remained heavily dependent on trade with other East Central European states and Germany. The Czechs had a well-developed metallurgical industry with modern plant and machinery; metallurgy was also organized into a tightly controlled and highly effective cartel to improve industrial efficiency and production. The country's largest industrial firm was the Skoda Works, which expanded its manufacturing base from just weapons production to include locomotives, aircraft, ships, machine tools, and passenger cars; it held the dominant place in the mechanical engineering industry not just in Czechoslovakia but in East Central Europe generally. Overall, the expansion of industrial production in the 1920s brought general prosperity to Czechoslovakia, although it remained a middle-ranking industrial nation.

The slow development of industry in Eastern Europe was evident in the Balkans, where countries manufactured goods primarily to meet domestic needs and had no significant heavy industries. Bulgaria was a case in point. Even its small textile industry depended on significant tariff protection for survival. The government in 1920 embarked upon a modernization program that included the abolition of grain monopolies, land reform, labor laws, a progressive income tax, and compulsory secondary schooling. The redistribution of the national wealth raised the living standards of the lower classes somewhat, but failed to lift Bulgaria away from its agricultural base.

Land reform and agricultural modernization

Land redistribution became an acute problem during World War I in numerous European countries, since most of them, especially on the northern, eastern, and southern peripheries, had relied heavily on agriculture before the war to provide their economic well-being. As many governments made promises of land to the peasants in exchange for military service, land reform became a priority in the immediate postwar years. In Russia, for example, land reform was a cause of the Russian Revolution of 1917, and it was a major point in Lenin's political platform after his return to Russia in April 1917. In Britain, the Labour Party had plans to nationalize great estates in 1920 to break down the power of the landed gentry, but this program was never implemented. In addition to land reform, governments had to confront a need to modernize agriculture, which was still a major component in European economies. One nagging issue was that industrial prices rose much faster than those of agriculture, locking many peasants into poverty and creating a real social gap between rural and urban areas.

After the Bolshevik takeover of Russia, Lenin quickly issued a Decree on Land that legitimized the peasants' often violent seizures of landed estates in the preceding months. Peasant resistance to the government's policy of forced requisitioning during the period of War Communism, however, contributed to Lenin's decision to introduce the New Economic Policy in 1921. The NEP, which revived certain capitalist practices, allowed peasants to sell their surpluses freely once they had paid a tax in kind. Under certain conditions, they were also allowed to lease extra land and hire help. The reforms provided the incentives needed for small private farms to boost production rapidly. The most enterprising of the peasants were the kulaks, middle-class farmers who enjoyed a comfortable prosperity relative to the peasantry as a whole. Compromising 4 percent of the peasantry, the kulaks produced 15 percent of the country's grain. But in many ways, Soviet agriculture was still backward. Half the country's 1928 grain production was harvested with sickles and scythes. Millions of farmers still used wooden plows, and many had no plows at all. There was also a shortage of draft animals, as more than 28 percent of peasant households had none. The agricultural sector met the growing urban demand for grain through 1926, but the peasants began to sell less grain to the state thereafter because of the artificially low prices they were paid for it. One consequence was the introduction of bread rationing in cities across the country in 1929.

The successor states of East Central Europe had a huge, indebted, land-hungry, and revolutionary peasantry. The Baltic countries' economies, which relied heavily on agriculture, launched massive land redistribution programs and managed to rein in peasant unrest. A new group of small landowning farmers emerged in each country, but the immediate impact of the land shift was a drop in agricultural income. Building the new nations was exciting and land reform was seen as a national act because the landlords were foreign, mostly Germans, Russians, and Poles. Large landowners were expropriated, small farms were created, and agricultural production increased to the point of domestic self-sufficiency. The Baltic governments thus gained the support of small farmers who formed important agrarian parties with socialist tendencies. Estonia and Latvia also developed their industrial sectors and improved trade with the West during the 1920s, but agricultural output, which enjoyed a steady improvement in income levels owing to world markets, suffered from the dramatic drop in commodity prices during the Great Depression that undercut the Baltic economies and caused considerable stress and high unemployment in all of them.

Arguably the most successful former Russian province in redistributing land was the Nordic state of Finland where, beginning in 1922, a major and very successful shift of land from large landowners to landless peasants took place. As a result of these actions, close to 90 percent of Finland's farmers owned their own land by 1937. In East Central Europe, too, there were important shifts in land ownership after the Great War. In 1923, Poland introduced an agrarian reform to redistribute large estates and modernize agricultural methods. Opposition within parliament, however, partially derailed the reforms, because large landowners dominated its ranks, and the Great Depression occurred before any real progress had been made. Through the use of efficient agricultural methods Hungary, though greatly reduced in size after World War I, had more wheat exports than any other country in Europe during the 1920s. Hungary's economic prosperity collapsed when the bottom fell out of the world wheat market with the onset of the Great

Depression. Czechoslovakia, although it had a much better balance between agriculture and industry than its neighbors, undertook land reform by breaking up the country's crown lands and large, privately held landed estates and redistributing them among peasant farmers with smallholdings. Agricultural production grew and Czechoslovakia gradually achieved almost complete self-sufficiency in basic food items.

In the Balkans, too, agrarian issues were high on the agenda of governments after the Great War. In Bulgaria, the key person in postwar agricultural reform was Aleksandar Stamboliyski, a peasant leader who became the country's prime minister in 1919. Even though Bulgaria already had the most equitable system of land ownership in the Balkans, Stamboliyski instituted land reforms that broke up Bulgaria's few remaining large estates and limited land ownership to a maximum of 74 acres. Stamboliyski had no time for urban life and took no interest in industrial development. His goal was to make Bulgaria a "model agricultural state." Stamboliyksi's successors kept his land reforms in place following his removal in a bloody reactionary coup in 1923, and by 1934, some 94 percent of Bulgaria's agricultural sector consisted of rural farms under the prescribed limit. While formerly landless and poor peasants saw improvements in their lives in the 1920s, the standards of living for most were still very low. Bulgaria's agricultural sphere remained technologically backward. Yugoslavia's agricultural sector also dominated that country's economy. Reform measures in the 1920s and 1930s resulted in the transfer of some 2.5 million hectares of farmland to more than 600,000 peasants out of the country's 2 million. The landholdings that resulted from the reforms were mostly quite small, and they failed to generate prosperity for the peasants. Romania, meanwhile, began land reform during the Great War and continued it into the postwar era. The most radical land redistributions took place in 1920 in Bessarabia, a province recently acquired from Russia, to prevent peasants from turning to Bolshevism. Romania's land reforms resulted in the transfer of land from large landowners to 1.4 million peasants. Nevertheless, inheritance laws that called for the division of each of several, often widely dispersed plots of a father's small landholdings among all surviving sons equally continued to plague the country, as did a general failure to invest in new machinery and modern farming techniques. Thus, Romania's agricultural yields in the interwar years, when compared to Western European standards, were poor.

Austria and Germany had special problems. In Austria, where land available for cultivation was limited, and where Vienna contained nearly one-third of the country's population, tensions arose. The government tried to ease a serious famine right after the war through barter agreements with former Austro-Hungarian states. Austria's continued dependence on food imports from the Danube basin perpetuated a state of economic instability that in the 1930s contributed to Austria's vulnerability in the face of Hitler. In Germany, agriculture at the end of the war was in a shambles. As in the Soviet Union, agricultural prices remained low compared to fast-rising industrial prices, causing wealth gaps. When Germany experienced an economic resurgence in the latter 1920s, agriculture remained a troubled area. Farm debt increased four-fold between 1923 and 1930, and prices for farm products, after peaking in 1926, began tumbling again in 1927 from overproduction and foreign competition. To offset lost income, farmers purchased costly new equipment to boost production. The result was increased personal debt and a further lowering of farm prices. Already the beneficiaries of tariff protection, German farmers demanded even more protection at the end of the decade, which they obtained.

European countries also faced agricultural competition from abroad, as less expensive grains and other food products from places such as Australia, the United States,

Canada, and Argentina forced down the prices of European agricultural products. French agriculture, a major component in France's economy, lagged in the adoption of new farming techniques and investment in modern machinery, although there was an overall improvement in efficiency in the 1920s. Because agriculture was so critical to the economies of East Central Europe, governments there used protectionism, including tariffs, to undergird their agrarian sectors. Overall, the agricultural sector experienced depression, especially in East Central Europe, well before 1929.

Labor troubles

The end of the Great War presented governments with new challenges on the labor front. Unemployment loomed large as millions of soldiers returned from the battle front, and munitions workers were suddenly laid off. Labor issues, largely papered over during the war, reappeared as workers sought higher wages, shorter hours, more job protections, and greater say in their countries' production systems. In 1919, worker discontent was a real threat to domestic peace in many countries, and it remained one of the salient features of European economic policies in the 1920s.

Unemployment returned to Europe with the arrival of peace, and it remained troublesome during the 1920s in all countries except France and Russia. In Britain, unemployment during the interwar years never fell below 1 million people, and a showdown between the British government and its coal miners reflects the problems that marked the times. A postwar economic depression that struck Britain in 1920 threatened to force down wages. Coal miners asked for the nationalization of the coal mining industry, which was plagued by outdated technology and small, inefficient mining operations, in hopes of stabilizing their pay and modernizing the industry. Instead, the government ended its wartime control over the industry on April 1, 1921, and returned it to the private sector where owners immediately announced wage reductions. Britain's three biggest labor unions – the miners, railroad workers, and transport workers – tried to organize a general strike in mid-April 1921, but the workers' representatives failed to reach an agreement for action, and in the end the miners had to accept the owners' terms. The industry experienced new difficulties when coal output increased on the European continent following France's withdrawal from the coal-producing Ruhr region of Germany in 1924 and Britain reintroduced the prewar gold standard in 1925. Coal operators announced in June 1925, that miners would have to accept either a wage reduction or an extension of the workday. The mine workers rallied round the cry "Not a penny off the pay, not a minute on the day," and they gained the support of the Trades Union Congress (TUC), a general federation of British trade unions. To avert a strike, the government appointed a commission to study the industry.

Neither the mine operators nor the miners accepted the commission's report after its publication in March 1926, however, and on May 1, 1926, mine owners implemented a lockout against the miners. Three days later, the miners and workers from other front-line industries, under the guidance of the TUC, joined in the General Strike of 1926. Some 3 million workers participated in what was a sympathy strike in support of the coal miners. The government, well prepared for the strike, used military personnel and multitudes of volunteers from the general population to provide vital services. Baldwin stood firm against the strikers, claiming that the strike was unconstitutional. The TUC's governing board, fearing that the strike might spin out of control, jumped on an unofficial compromise proposal and the strike ended after nine days. But the government never endorsed the compromise, so it never took effect. The TUC's decision amounted to surrender, and the miners eventually went back to work with longer hours at lower wages. Union membership dropped by a half million after the strike, and parliament barred sympathy strikes in the Trade Disputes Act of 1927.

In France, a wave of strikes that included revolutionary militants and a strong anti-war sentiment occurred in the spring of 1918. In an effort to defuse tensions, Clemenceau enacted an eight-hour workday in April 1919. Worker protests nevertheless continued during the spring of 1919. Leftist extremists believed that France was on the verge of a revolution similar to that of the Bolsheviks in Russia in 1917. Railroad workers started another round of strikes in the early months of 1920, climaxing in May with a massive work stoppage that involved workers from several major industrial and transportation unions. It was an attempt at a general strike, but it was poorly planned and it provoked a strong response from the recently elected right-wing majority in the Chamber of Deputies. Government officials arrested strike leaders, used military personnel and volunteers to keep public transportation services in operation, and dismissed several thousand striking railway workers. The strikes ended in late May, and by the end of the year, union membership had dropped by more than half. For the rest of the 1920s, some 90 percent of France's workers stayed away from organized labor. Those who remained union members were divided among themselves, owing to the existence of three rival union organizations. Unable to exert much pressure on business or the government, workers in France got less than their full share of the country's prosperity during the 1920s.

Figure 4.3 A military armored car leads a food convoy into London during the General Strike of 1926.

In Italy, the government, in a wartime effort to maintain morale, had promised improvements in benefits for labor once the war had ended. Impatient to obtain their promised gains, workers resorted to violent strikes in 1919 and 1920. Labor unrest peaked in the fall of 1920, when metallurgical workers in northern Italy occupied several factories after a breakdown in wage negotiations with owners. The movement waned thereafter as an industrial crisis set in that caused massive job losses. After Mussolini took power in 1922, his Fascist government took steps to curb the power of the country's labor movement, climaxing in the banning of independent labor unions in 1925 and labor strikes in 1926.

Conclusion

The first postwar decade showed important signs of recovery in Western Europe, and the implementation of significant agricultural reforms in East Central Europe. The large disparity between the agricultural economies of Eastern Europe and the industrialized economies of the West could not be bridged. Overall, European countries recovered either up to or beyond their prewar economic levels. This was no small feat, as governments were trying new paths. Still, at the global level, the industrial predominance of Europe declined owing to competition from the Americas and Japan. Labor troubles characterized the return to peacetime economies in many Western European countries. To maintain morale during the war, governments had promised improvements in benefits for labor once the war had ended. The inability of governments to fulfill their promises after 1918 created serious tensions. Workers emerged from the 1920s with mixed gains. Finally, while prosperity was evident across much of Europe in the latter 1920s, the international economic system upon which it rested proved to be superficial and vulnerable at decade's end.

Social policies and transformations

Class and gender were two important issues that were redefined in the crucible of total war. As World War I unfolded, it required total mobilization, including the home front. Domestically, talent, skill, character, and determination were critical in deciding victory or defeat. After the war, the magnitude and scope of the tasks confronting European men and women continued to transform the social scene, even though traditional values often contradicted them. Governments, meanwhile, responded to rising pressures from the political Left and labor with new social welfare programs.

Public welfare

The transition from war to peace, with its accompanying economic distress, placed a heavy burden on multitudes of families and individuals. One of the first postwar actions of many governments was to freeze rents and food prices. Many countries also pushed for a comprehensive network of social protection. In fact, Germany was ahead of other countries, having been the first to legislate welfare in the 1880s for urban workers; the Austro-Hungarian Empire had followed suit in 1892. In countries that received former German and Austrian lands after World War I, such as France, Poland, Hungary, and Czechoslovakia, the prewar welfare provisions carried over.

Most Western European countries introduced industrial accident, sickness, and old age insurance over the next decade. Britain, in the midst of a postwar depression in 1920, extended unemployment insurance to the entire industrial workforce of about 12 million workers; the prior law had only covered some 4 million. The British Labour government of the late 1920s also started an attractive program to relieve unemployment and improve the economy, but this undertaking faded with the onset of the Great Depression. France responded with the Social Insurance Laws of 1928 and 1930 that provided benefits for retirement, maternity, illness, disability, and death.

In Central Europe, the Czech government between 1922 and 1925 passed a Social Insurance Law that was quite advanced for its time: it included public health services and a 40-hour week, although it was limited to trade union members who represented only one-third of the country's workers. Austria, which had emerged from World War I with an enormous social and economic crisis, faced a dire situation in Vienna. To assist the city's poor, Viennese government authorities created relief agencies, provided job retraining programs, and introduced social insurance for skilled industrial labor (see pp. 230–231).

Britain and Germany were leaders in welfare expenditures, followed by Austria, Ireland, and Scandinavia. Two other states created comprehensive welfare programs. In Fascist Italy, Mussolini constituted welfare agencies to deal with every aspect of social protection, while leaders in Russia vowed to take care of Soviet citizens from the cradle to the grave and created many welfare and health institutions to reach that goal.

Public health

Multiple forms of illness struck Europe at the end of World War I and in the years after. Tuberculosis, typhus, relapsing fever, cholera, malaria, dysentery, and typhoid fever touched millions of victims across Eastern, Southern, and Central Europe, threatening the security of some of the new nations. Continuing cross-border wars and civil wars in the East made the situation worse. A new round of typhus that started with Russian refugees fleeing the Russian Civil War in Ukraine threatened a world pandemic in 1920. The death toll from tuberculosis reached 400,000 in 1920 in the new countries of East Central Europe. In the West, a tuberculosis outbreak reached its peak in 1918, but remained a public health issue in the interwar years. Venereal disease, which had increased during the war, continued to be of concern as well. The legacy of the fighting took its toll on civilian health in other ways, too. Battlefield areas were dangerous and unfit for civilian life: shell holes, barbed wire, unexploded shells, and hand grenades caused many accidents, particularly in northeastern France where fighting had been fierce during the war. There were also considerable numbers of veterans who needed special care owing to war-related ill health, blindness, amputation, or shell-shock.

The health situation of civilians and veterans at the end of the Great War prompted many governments to create ministries of health as soon as the war was over. In Britain, a Ministry of Health, created in 1919, spearheaded important advances in public health and medicine over the next several years. Other countries quickly followed suit; they opened public clinics that provided such benefits as immunization programs and pre-natal and infant care, and they introduced public health policy laws. Various governments' efforts included public health education programs. The Bolsheviks conducted massive campaigns, traveling across the country to distribute millions of brochures. The British health ministry conducted a campaign against venereal disease in 1920, spending $25,000 on newspaper advertisements to explain how to obtain treatment. In 1921, the Scandinavian countries became leaders in the regulation of prostitution by providing universal, free, and confidential medical treatment to its practitioners.

The challenges of infectious diseases required a large-scale mobilization of resources that only international cooperation and information-sharing could achieve in that fight. The Red Cross transformed its war relief agencies into reconstruction work and sponsored health conferences that influenced European governments to adopt new policies. The League of Nations organized international conferences on public health. One of these was a European Health Conference on public health and epidemics held in Warsaw in March 1922. In addition, the League's Health Committee promoted public hygiene, and was helped by international medical committees, where countries could cooperate in finding cures for various illnesses.

Professional mobility

World War I blurred social class lines by placing men from all walks of life in battle together. As a result, new opportunities awaited workers to move up the social ladder in postwar Europe. Marriages between young men and women of different social classes became more common. The broadening of education opportunities also proved to be a great social equalizer, particularly in politics. Before 1914, birth, military service, or a university education, associated with social connections, insured young men access to high offices. Politicians were mostly recruited from the wealthy upper bourgeoisie, while the diplomatic corps remained the preserve of the aristocracy. The liberal professions were well represented among the representatives in parliamentary systems. After 1918, scientific and technical training began to share the stage with the traditional humanities education. France's *Ecole Polytechnique*, a prestigious military-engineering school founded in 1794, began to influence the creation of many polytechnical universities in the new countries of East Central Europe and the Soviet Union, where engineering degrees became common among university students. Almost all Soviet leaders trained in the 1930s graduated from agricultural or textile technological institutes.

The increased complexity of international politics brought a need for experts. From border settlements to reparations payments and electrification schemes, ambitious projects coordinated by the League of Nations required men with managerial skills and technical expertise. Modernity, synonymous with practicality, began to change the tone of political rhetoric along with the decision-making process. European countries strove to emulate American leadership and business acumen that was synonymous with modernization. These changes were gradual, but they reflected the age of technocrats selected on the basis of merit rather than connections or ancestry.

Women's rights

The evolving role of women in Europe, amplified during the Great War when females in large numbers contributed to the war effort in factories and on farms, continued in the interwar years. The issue of female suffrage, which had garnered considerable attention in Britain before the Great War, was still on the docket of governments across Europe in 1918. Neutral and northern countries were the first to act. Norway introduced female suffrage in 1913, and Denmark did so in 1915. Between 1917 and 1920, many European countries granted national voting rights to women, including Albania, Austria, the Baltic states, Czechoslovakia, Germany, Luxembourg, the Netherlands, Poland, Russia, and Sweden. In Britain, the government granted the right to vote to women aged 30 and over in late 1918; its decision was based on a fear that a lower minimum voting age would enable women to constitute a majority of the electorate due to the war-induced gender imbalance in favor of women. Younger British women were only enfranchised in 1928. Hungary, meanwhile, introduced in 1919 a limited form of female suffrage that involved passing an exacting literacy test. Belgian women obtained voting rights in municipal elections, and war widows in national elections; full female voting rights did not occur there until 1948. The governmental wave to enfranchise women in Europe ended in 1921, with France and virtually all southern European countries having failed to act.

As for access to public office, the record was mixed. The League of Nations tried to help the cause by mandating that the new countries give women the franchise and equal access to political appointments, although it lacked the power of enforcement. The Russian Constitution of 1918 guaranteed women equal rights as political candidates. British women, through the Sex Disqualification Act of 1919, also gained access to the country's civil service and the right to serve as lawyers and magistrates; it was the country's first equal opportunities legislation. The 1921 Yugoslav constitution gave women the right of appointment to public service, but not the right to vote or to be elected to office.

Men continued to dominate politics in most countries. Lingering traditional attitudes, social unrest, and economic uncertainty explain the lack of progress on women's political rights. Any progress made was largely halted in 1930. Czechoslovakia was the exception. Women there occupied numerous positions of high political office. Czechoslovak women were demographically strong, westernized, and led by an upper middle class that embraced social democracy. Having actively helped build the state in 1918, they enjoyed a significant share of power in the new regime. They also received support from Czechoslovakia's President Masaryk, whose American-born wife Charlotte was very progressive politically, as was his daughter Alice who assumed the role of first lady at her mother's death in 1923. Throughout the interwar years, the Czech governments' leftist majorities continued advancing women's causes. Elsewhere, the enlargement of the franchise in Europe saw the first women enter positions of administrative or political leadership, albeit in limited numbers.

In terms of legal rights, Western European women gained more ground than East Central European women after 1918. In Britain, they had equal access to divorce, with adultery having the same consequences for men and women, and they gained equal property rights in 1926. Such changes affected a small percentage of young and wealthy women. In Russia, the Bolsheviks decreed gender equality as one of their first measures in 1917. Women could buy land and work on it. The abolition of religious marriages made divorce easier, and the rate of Russian divorces rose to 26 times that of Britain. In several European countries, divorce became easier. Despite these measures, all European countries, including the Soviet Union, remained very conservative and frowned upon behavior that deviated from tradition.

Education greatly enhanced women's upward mobility in the interwar years. It also changed their appearance: professional women wore shortened skirts, sported short hairdos, used make-up, and enjoyed leisure. Called "garçonne" in France and "flapper" in

Britain, they were often perceived as transgressing gender lines, especially when they entered male professions, as British women did after 1918. French women gained equal access to secondary and higher education in 1919; one of the first women to earn a Ph.D. in philosophy was feminist writer Simone de Beauvoir. Estonia and Finland, where women constituted one third of the student body, offered favorable educational opportunities for women. Female medical doctors were limited to working in their own private clinics, because they were not deemed capable of hospital work. Marie Curie in France remained a role model for women entering the scientific professions. But there were limits. Even at the League of Nations, women's employment was overwhelmingly limited to clerical work.

Wartime changes in women's employment proved irreversible, but their progress slowed during the interwar years. In 1919, as war-related industries transitioned to peacetime work, women were returned to menial factory jobs or simply let go. Their wages dropped relative to those of men, and their percentage of the workforce declined, notably in the textile industry. Most women remained economically dependent; they had few skills, earned lower wages, and had no access to welfare. In the mid-1920s they suffered from high unemployment, especially in countries that adopted legislation barring women from traditionally male jobs and limited their education to vocational tracks, as was the case in Italy after 1923. As a result, many women sought employment in "female" jobs such as secretaries, typists, retail clerks, school teachers, nurses, or librarians, which kept them in supportive, care-taking jobs and represented a mere extension of their responsibilities at home. Despite Weimar Germany's progressive legislation for women, many still chose to become domestic servants, and women were encouraged to stay at home and raise children. Russian women did not fare better than women elsewhere in Europe. Most lost their jobs in 1921 following the introduction of the NEP, and half of them remained unemployed in the late 1920s, a rate that was partly the result of rural migration to the cities. Cost-conscious Russian employers preferred to employ men, in part to avoid the issue of pregnant workers. East Central European women entered the workforce in large numbers, but their rights were not always protected.

While women advanced their rights in many areas, society's norms and expectations were often at odds with the women's new freedoms, and patriarchal attitudes were slow to change, even in the Soviet Union where women were urged to return to their traditional roles as wives, mothers, and homemakers after 1922. In an attempt to increase fertility rates, states started providing special forms of support to mothers. In France, a powerful pronatalist current took hold shortly after World War I that had strong support from conservative politicians who controlled the Chamber of Deputies following the November 1919 elections. To counter a serious drop in the birthrate, the French government outlawed abortions and contraceptives in 1920. The French also launched an annual Mother's Day in 1920 and used the occasion to recognize mothers of large families: the government started awarding medals to mothers who had at least four children, with gold medals reserved for those with eight or more offspring. Italy encouraged families by giving loans to newly married couples, forbidding abortions, and punishing homosexuality.

In spite of widespread governmental campaigns, birth rates declined by 50 percent between 1890 and 1933, and birth control gained wider acceptance through newly opened women's clinics. Upper class women saw voluntary parenthood as an affirmation of their right to pursue creative endeavors; for working class women, birth control was a relief from health and financial hardships. Discussions of another taboo subject, female sexuality, were encouraged. British feminist Marie Stopes wrote a sex manual, *Married Love* (1918), and Dutch gynecologist Theodoor van de Velde's 1926 book *Ideal Marriage: Its Physiology and Technique* taught women the calendar-based method of birth control.

Feminists advocated the creation of institutional mechanisms to help women with children. Two women's visions stand out. Aleksandra Kollontai, born into an aristocratic Russian family and a supporter of both 1917 Russian revolutions, was one of the first feminists to advocate an integrated approach to motherhood. Her ground-breaking work *Communism and the Family* (1920) had enormous international influence. It advocated pre- and post-natal care, maternity leave, state-sponsored nurseries and kindergartens, protective labor laws for girls and women, and the abolition of rules that made pregnancy a cause for dismissal from one's job. As president of the Women's Section of the

Figure 4.4 Aleksandra Kollontai delivers a speech at the International Women's Congress in Moscow in October 1921.

Communist Party until 1922, Kollontai had an enormous, albeit fleeting, influence on early Soviet legislation. She convinced women all over Europe that it was possible for them to be mothers and professionals simultaneously. A decade later, Alva Myrdal, a leading member of the Swedish Parliament and wife of renowned sociologist Gunnar Myrdal, studied the relationship between low fertility rates and low standards of living. Her research led to the creation in 1937 of Swedish government loans to married couples and the introduction of prenatal care, free childbirth, a food relief program, and subsidized housing for large families. The government programs served 50 percent of Swedish mothers by 1940. Other Western European states emulated this model of state support for family care. In East Central Europe, progress was more uneven. Ukrainian and Yugoslav women in particular were still expected to fulfill their traditional household and child-rearing chores in addition to working outside the home.

Women's activism

During the First World War, Western European women's organizations suspended their work for equal rights, and turned their efforts towards peace: Rosika Schwimmer of Hungary and Millicent Garrett Fawcett of Britain were among those active at the 1915 Congress of the International Council of Women that addressed pacifist issues. French teacher Hélène Brion was prosecuted in 1918 for distributing peace leaflets. Feminist efforts resumed after 1918; feminist conventions across Europe, associations for women in the professions, and numerous newspapers and journals catered to women – from patriotic and professional to devotional and homemaking publications. The umbrella organization of a large network of women's groups was the International Council of Women (ICW). Created in 1888 in the United States, the ICW had branches in several Western and Northern European countries before the war and developed new ones in East Central Europe after 1918, in part because of the support of the League of Nations. Their progress reveals an important dynamic: better educated women were more receptive to improving their personal and professional conditions. This was particularly visible in Czechoslovakia, where Czech women were more progressive and more involved in women's causes than women in rural Slovak areas. In all East Central European countries, this pattern was repeated, as geography, religion, and ethnicity divided the women's movements. Overall, women gained more ground when they were able to organize.

Conclusion

In this decade of experimentation, women made great progress, even though the social climate's enduring conservatism changed little. Health also made great strides, if only to return the population to health after four years of malnutrition and epidemics. Social mobility took off. Among the newly formed countries of East Central Europe, Czechoslovakia distinguished itself for its progressive measures. Soviet Russia had perhaps the boldest reform agenda for women and social mobility, although the equality it preached was compromised by low standards of living and the disappearance of individual rights. Socially, Europe was a continent that was more multi-ethnic and more mobile than ever before. The challenges of mass, industrialized, and urbanized societies gave governments an incentive to work toward mass solutions in the areas of health, welfare, and housing.

Urban development

New urban geographies indicated broad socio-economic changes and changes in labor markets. Cities grew tremendously in the postwar years, with many architectural and urban planning models that testify to the vitality of urban life. At the same time, contrasts were sharp between old and new urban areas, and between comfortable residential areas and workers' quarters located in the vicinity of factories. Public spaces as stadiums, schools, and dispensaries were created. Mass transportation systems were also expanded or created to meet growing demands.

Urban renewal

By 1914, many of Europe's cities were in need of renewal. Heavily polluted and industrialized, cut off from the countryside, they were synonymous with cultural gloom and they caused frustrations among the peasantry. The outbreak of the Great War interrupted an international urban renewal movement that had begun in 1913 in the Netherlands. The war itself caused widespread destruction and severe housing shortages in both Western and Eastern Europe. After the war, there was an opportunity for major changes as governments became more involved, and relentless urban growth drove restoration and modernization programs. European cities embraced modernization with enthusiasm, and embarked on an unprecedented building boom. Large cities were more likely to feature modern amenities and architecture, while small towns were more likely to adopt local, conservative, even nostalgic styles, as was the case in East Prussia. Municipalities everywhere took a greater role in planning and funding private dwellings as well as public spaces, industrial infrastructures, office buildings, mines, factories, roads, and railroads. Street lighting, paved streets, sewers, utilities, and garbage collection insured the public's safety and comfort. Suburbs decluttered cities by means of garden cities, green belts, and apartment building complexes with integrated transportation systems.

In Britain, the government passed the Housing and Town Planning Act of 1919, which subsidized the construction of 170,000 inexpensive row houses for workers. Housing development in the mid-1920s showed the government's growing concern for providing low to moderate income housing. In 1924, the MacDonald Cabinet secured passage of a housing program – the Wheatley Housing Act – that provided rent controls and increased government subsidies for the construction of rental housing for low-paid workers. More than a half-million lodgings were constructed over the next several years.

In France, efforts to obtain passage of a major government-subsidized housing bill began in 1920, but these encountered government resistance, owing to the reconstruction program in northeastern France and the country's shaky financial condition in the early and mid-1920s. Only in 1928 did French legislators pass a major housing bill – the *loi Loucheur* – that provided for the construction of 200,000 low-cost dwellings for workers and 60,000 medium-priced rental units across the country to be completed by the end of 1933. The housing program was largely complete by January 1934.

Czechoslovakia's urban and architectural modernization accompanied the country's industrial and economic success and helped to strengthen a democratic and progressive middle class. Prague, already famous for its Black Madonna House, a department store built in 1912 in the cubist style, combined modern architecture with community planning, zoning, and historical protection to create a socially and politically vibrant urban environment. A central business and civic area of monumental proportions was girded with wide boulevards radiating out from central squares; garden-city suburbs surrounded the city center. Cafés, modern boulevards, and nightlife coexisted with industrial and commercial centers, department stores, leisure facilities, apartment blocks, and private houses. In Zlin, Moravia, the Bata Shoe Company built a standardized and rationalized industrial town around its headquarters. The company also developed a network of retail outlets, department stores, and schools across the country. In sharp contrast to these developments, East Central European cities generally lagged behind; often, their streets remained unpaved and unlit, with minimal public transportation and sanitation. The lack of modernization can be attributed in part to the lack of a vibrant middle class and to rigidly stratified relations between peasants and aristocratic landlords. Other problems included a lack of investment capital, poor infrastructure, insufficient schooling and health services, and low standards of living.

Two modernist styles adapted to the needs of mass construction in an industrialized world, albeit in very different ways. The Bauhaus reconceptualized space and used new materials such as steel, concrete, and plastic. The Bauhaus was an international Western European movement that included the German architect Walter Gropius, the Dutchman Ludwig Mies van der Rohe, and the Swiss-Frenchman Le Corbusier. Promoting rational efficiency, Gropius' box-like industrial buildings with their clean lines and glass walls became the prototype of postwar industrial plants. Van der Rohe favored extreme simplicity in structure and ornamentation to create open, flowing spaces, calling his buildings "skin and bones." Le Corbusier created the "domino house," which became a trademark of modernism with its large glass panels and concrete floors supported by minimal numbers of steel-reinforced columns. The Vienna-based secession style captured the age's anxiety and introduced visual instability through intricate curves; the most notable examples are Catalan architect Antoni Gaudi's Sagrada Familia (Holy Family) basilica in Barcelona, and Frenchman Hector Guimard's "noodle-style" Metro (subway) entrances in Paris.

The architecture of memory

The war transformed many public spaces in cities and villages and on battlefields. The killing of a generation of young men during the war left several long-lasting impacts on European peoples. Among the major antagonists in Europe, virtually every family went through mourning, be it the death of a family member or that of a friend, colleague, or schoolmate. Thus, the demand for the creation of memorials and rituals of remembrance was massive. One of them was the creation of a new form of artistic expression to enshrine the memorialization of the war dead and honor their sacrifices. After World War I, national and local governments as well as private groups across Europe put together memorials and rituals in the 1920s and 1930s to remember the enormity of the catastrophe that had taken place. The cult of memory turned into a universal phenomenon in the avalanche of activity that occurred after the conflict. There was a nationalization of mourning within a largely patriotic framework. And in contrast to the pre-1900 era, when commemorative statues primarily honored individual military commanders, Great War commemorations brought attention to the common soldier. All of these developments reflected the fact that in the twentieth century, war had come to have an impact on virtually everyone.

As a result, a great number of war memorials were constructed in the 1920s and 1930s. In France, 176,000 memorials were built during these years. Almost every British village contained a memorial as well, and memorials could be found in German, Austrian, and Italian churches and at village crossroads. Military cemeteries also emerged, dotting the landscape of northeastern France and Belgium. On the Allied side, they were set up with an individual headstone for each soldier; officers and enlisted men were buried randomly to demonstrate the egalitarian character of the fighting in the trenches. These monuments were artistic productions made for public viewing. They encouraged the shift from indoor to outdoor representation. French sculptor Antoine Bourdelle, a pioneer of expressionist and monumental sculpture, received several commissions for monuments and war memorials in the 1920s. He impacted the development of sculpture throughout Europe during the 1930s.

Numerous Western countries set up monuments to an Unknown Soldier, who symbolized all those soldiers whose remains were unidentified fighting for their country in the war. Many Allied countries established November 11 – Armistice Day – as a national holiday. On the other hand, the issue of commemorative events was problematic in Europe's former empires. The subject was largely neglected in Russia's public memorial culture during the Soviet era. Soviet leaders called World War I an imperialist war, and it was frequently referred to as the "forgotten war." In Germany, the Weimar governments, in spite of a succession of efforts, never created a national commemorative holiday for the German soldiers who died in World War I. During the 1920s, a commemorative day in the spring of the year gained widespread acceptance, but it resulted primarily from the efforts of a private charity known as the German War Graves Commission, not a government initiative.

Railroads

Modern cities were inseparable from the vital links of the railroad. Rail lines in Europe were already well developed by 1914 and expanded very little in most countries during the interwar years. Belgium had the best rail network, ahead of those in Germany and Britain. France's network lagged behind. Peripheral European countries had the least developed rail systems, as demonstrated in the weight of goods transported which was ten times lower than in the core European countries. During World War I, the increased use of railroads took its toll on both rolling stock and railway lines. After the war, railroads needed modernization, standardization, redirection towards new centers in East Central Europe, and internationalization to accommodate the new passenger and freight traffic. Uniform rail gauges were adopted, which was significant for the portions of Poland that had been a part of Russia, where the rail gauge was slightly wider. Rolling stock in the Baltic States was chaotic. As part of the American Relief Administration's work, massive amounts of rolling stock were sent to East Central Europe between 1918 and 1923.

Conclusion

Urban growth and railroad modernization count among the most positive developments of the postwar decade. This recovery, however, could not hide the regional differences between East Central and Western Europe that neither democracy nor capitalism could bridge. Historians have compared the challenges of urban development of Warsaw, for example, to those faced by post-colonial countries in 1945. Czechoslovakia, where a vibrant industry and middle class existed, was able to make greater progress than the Balkans which were burdened by large numbers of refugees and slower to adapt to the conveniences of modern living.

Overall conclusion

The dramatic disruptions of the Great War and the Great Depression delimited the economic and social developments of the 1920s. World War I revealed the ambivalence of modernization, deepened the divide between urban and rural areas, and sharpened the contrast between Western and East Central Europe. It set up the United States as a model of the new age.

During the 1920s, modernization progressed unevenly across Europe. Western Europe was overall more progressive than East Central Europe, and Northern Europe more progressive than Southern Europe. But social progress and economic modernization were not determined by ideology: democratic Sweden, Fascist Italy, and Bolshevik Russia embraced the future with equal zeal. Countries with opposite political systems shared common policy concerns such as land reform, unemployment insurance, pensions, or the woman's vote. The differences resided in the conditions attached to benefits and services. In authoritarian countries, the ideology limited citizens' rights to the fulfilment of their civic duties and excluded undesirable social elements; authoritarian states also favored collective solutions over those that served individual needs. Regardless of the ideology or political system, however, modernization efforts were hampered by runaway inflation, scarce resources, and porous borders. The old and the new coexisted in a fluctuating, uncertain world, and the Great Depression halted a decade of experimentation and precarious gains.

Note

1 Denis William Brogan, *The Development of Modern France, 1870–1939*, rev. edn (New York: Harper & Row, 1966), 2:599.

Suggestions for further reading

Aldcroft, Derek H. and Steven Morewood. *The European Economy Since 1914*. 5th edn. London: Routledge. 2013.

Atkin, Nicholas and Michael Biddiss. *Themes in Modern European History, 1890–1945*. London: Routledge. 2009.

Baron, Nick and Peter Gatrell. *Homelands: War, Population and Statehood in Eastern Europe and Russia, 1918–1924*. London: Anthem Press. 2004.

Berman, Sheri. *The Social Democratic Moment: Ideas and Politics in the Making of Interwar Europe*. Cambridge, MA: Harvard University Press. 1998.

Dutton, Paul V. *Origins of the French Welfare State: The Struggle for Social Reform in France, 1914–1947*. New York: Cambridge University Press. 2002.

Kuisel, Richard F. *Capitalism and the State in Modern France: Renovation and Economic Management in the Twentieth Century*. Cambridge: Cambridge University Press. 1981.

Lucassen, Leo. *The Immigrant Threat: The Integration of Old and New Migrants in Western Europe Since 1850*. Urbana, IL: Illinois University Press. 2005.

Newman, Michael. *Socialism: A Very Short Introduction*. New York: Oxford University Press. 2005.

Sejersted, Francis. *The Age of Social Democracy: Norway and Sweden in the Twentieth Century*. Princeton, NJ: Princeton University Press. 2011.

Tomka, Béla. *A Social History of Twentieth Century Europe*. London: Routledge. 2013.

Part 3

Dress rehearsals for war, 1929–1939

5 Revisionism and realignments

Introduction

Two seminal events opened the decade of the 1930s: the Great Depression, and the end of the Allied occupation of the defeated powers. Both events contributed to a power vacuum that left no European country untouched. On the surface, Europe continued to experience successes and setbacks in the areas of diplomacy, security, the formation of Europe, and colonial relations, while the failure of the international financial systems changed diplomatic relationships. Diplomatic leadership shifted from the Western European democracies to Europe's revisionist states that, in pursuit of nationalistic agendas, often with neocolonial ambitions, threatened the independence of other nations and regions. The increase in the number of these aggressive transnational interventions bode ill for institutions such as the League of Nations that worked to preserve peace. The new aggressiveness also threatened the security and international stability that lay at the heart of most European countries' foreign policies.

The end of the Versailles settlement, 1930–1935

European leaders undertook numerous initiatives during the 1930s to reduce the threat of another major war in Europe. The search for a permanent peace through disarmament and European integration continued despite the negative impact of the Great Depression and the aggressive foreign policies of Germany and Italy. Both Germany and Italy were revisionist powers determined to undo the perceived injustices of the Versailles settlement, and in the case of Hitler, there was the added ambition of carving out *Lebensraum*, or living space, for the German people beyond Germany's eastern frontiers. Western leaders, haunted by the horrific human losses and heavy financial costs of World War I, sought to rein in the increasingly bold initiatives of Hitler and Mussolini. Their diplomatic approach, marked by flabbiness and accommodation, only emboldened the emerging nationalist movements toward ever more perilous risk-taking. In the end, Europe slid into a world war for the second time in 25 years in 1939, when Nazi Germany invaded Poland. At the same time, Europe's colonial powers had to contend with depression-related economic issues, indigenous protests against unjust policies, and emerging Nationalist movements. For the Western European democracies, the 1930s represented a time of international aridness and irresoluteness.

First calls for revisionism

Soon after the Locarno Conference of October 1925, German, Hungarian, and Italian leaders took steps toward revising the Paris peace settlement. In 1926, Germany initiated talks with Belgium about purchasing the former German territories of Eupen and Malmedy that the Belgians had received in the Treaty of Versailles although the negotiations ultimately proved unsuccessful. In September 1927, Weimar President Hindenburg publicly denounced Article 231 of the Versailles treaty that established Germany's guilt for causing World War I. In Hungary, Prime Minister Count István Bethlen, hoping for the restoration of a large, powerful Hungary, found a protector state in 1927 when Hungary signed a friendship treaty with Italy, another revisionist country. In 1928, he asked Mussolini for help in creating a Central European bloc comprised of their two states as well as Austria and Romania to undercut the anti-Hungarian Little Entente that included Romania, Czechoslovakia, and Yugoslavia.

Italy's revisionism grew bolder as well. Mussolini secured a friendship treaty with Greece in 1928 to help isolate Yugoslavia, Italy's rival for influence in the world of the Adriatic Sea, and began shipping Italian arms to Hungary the same year, an action that caused much consternation, but no League of Nations economic sanctions. He also continued Italy's involvement in Albania until the Italians had virtual control over its economy by 1931. Unable to repay substantial Italian loans, Albania made one last attempt to get help from Greece and Yugoslavia in 1934, but Italian naval intimidation and a blockade reduced Albania to a glorified Italian colony. Shortly after Italy, along with France, refused to sign on to a new set of ratios for capital ships at the 1930 London Naval Conference, Mussolini made a rousing revisionist speech in which he announced the launch of a major buildup of Italian air and naval power in the Mediterranean Sea.

Germany assumed an aggressive revisionist course once Hitler took power in January 1933. Germany withdrew from the League of Nations in October of that year, and Hitler secretly began a military buildup. In July 1934, he tried to move into Austria, where Austrian Nazi Party members, with his backing, assassinated Chancellor Engelbert Dollfuss in a coup attempt, but he retreated when Mussolini ordered troops into the Brenner Pass along Italy's border with Austria as a countermove. This showdown between Hitler and Mussolini for diplomatic influence in Central Europe showed that Mussolini considered Austrian independence vital to Italian interests in the Danube basin. The abortive coup was a major German foreign policy setback.

Diplomatic efforts in the Danube basin, 1930–1931

The depression made the countries of the Danube basin especially vulnerable, and their responses to it and their neighbors varied. Turkey, for example, sealed off its borders with protective tariffs in 1929. In 1930, Romanian Prime Minister Iuliu Maniu proposed a Southeast European economic confederation that would eventually entail a defensive military alliance directed primarily at the Soviet Union. In that same year, Bulgaria, Turkey, and Greece settled their minority questions and the property claims of repatriated populations, and assured each other of their support for the status quo and naval parity in the eastern Mediterranean. The French endorsed this integrative approach, supported the Little Entente, and even offered loans to secure the partnership of Hungary, where revisionist voices were growing stronger. But Italy and Germany did much to undercut France's patient work during the 1930s.

Austria became a major focal point of European diplomacy in 1931, when the Germans and Austrians announced an Austro-German customs union project to combat the economic effects of the Depression. The proposal provoked strong opposition from France and Czechoslovakia. The French viewed the customs union as a poorly disguised first step toward *Anschluss* and a threat to the Versailles settlement. The Czechs saw the project as a danger to their economy and political independence. France used its financial leverage in Vienna to pressure the Austrians into withdrawing from the treaty in early September, two days before the Permanent Court of International Justice at The Hague vetoed it. The result was an embarrassing defeat for German diplomacy and a crushing blow to Austrian morale.

East Central Europe organizes, 1932–1934

As international tensions increased in the early 1930s, states in East Central Europe continued their diplomatic efforts to improve their national security. The Little Entente countries met in the Italian resort town of Stresa in February 1933, created a standing council and permanent secretariat to tighten their consultation mechanisms, and extended their alliance indefinitely. The Balkan Pact of February 1934 united Turkey, Greece, Romania, and Yugoslavia with guarantees of mutual security in the Balkans. The Baltic Countries of Latvia, Estonia, and Lithuania formed the Baltic Entente in 1934 to enhance their consultation procedures on foreign policy and defense issues. They also tried to expand their alliance to Finland and to form a Baltic–Scandinavian bloc against possible risks from Germany and the Soviet Union. Poland, unable to make progress on a "Third Europe" plan unifying East Central European countries from the Baltic Sea to the Balkans, strove to balance potential Soviet and German threats by signing nonaggression pacts with Russia in July 1932 and Germany in January 1934. French Foreign Minister Louis Barthou, concerned over Poland's friendship pact with Germany and determined to contain Hitler, spent much of 1934 vigorously pushing for an "Eastern Locarno" plan that would include military guarantees from the states of Western Europe; he traveled extensively in East Central Europe promoting mutual defense treaties between France, the Little Entente powers, and Russia as a part of the plan. Barthou's efforts collapsed in October 1934, when he, along with King Alexander I of Yugoslavia, was assassinated by a Croatian nationalist in the French city of Marseille. His death resulted in France becoming ever more dependent on Britain for leadership in foreign policy making.

The Soviet Union altered its foreign policy in the early 1930s by ending a period of isolationism and adopting a more conciliatory approach toward the West in reaction to the growing threat of Nazism. The key figure in the new Soviet attitude was Maxim Litvinov, a pro-Western, anti-Nazi Jew who served as commissar for foreign affairs from 1930 to 1939. Litvinov renewed a nonaggression treaty with Lithuania in 1931 and signed similar pacts with Finland, Latvia, Estonia, and Poland the following year. In 1933, the United States extended diplomatic recognition to the Soviet Union, the last major power to do so. More significantly, the Soviets started negotiations with Barthou in 1934 on a mutual assistance treaty that was finally signed in May 1935, although political divisions in France prevented the French from ratifying the agreement for another year. Two weeks after the signing of the Franco-Soviet Pact, the Soviets sealed an alliance with

Czechoslovakia that stipulated the treaty would take effect only if France gave military assistance to the victim of aggression first. It was also in 1934 that the Soviets, alarmed over Germany's withdrawal from the League of Nations, joined the League, where they championed collective security. It was then that they also ended their opposition to the Paris peace settlement. Finally, Stalin urged Communist parties in Western European countries to work with socialists and liberals in Popular Front election coalitions as a way of countering the rising tide of fascism in Europe. Popular Front governments were elected to power in both France and Spain in 1936.

The Allied debt crisis

In the late spring of 1931, Germany, facing a major banking disaster that had begun in neighboring Austria, found it virtually impossible to continue paying reparations. In the midst of this financial crisis, American President Herbert Hoover concluded that intergovernmental debt payments were unrealistic and in June proposed a one-year moratorium on war debts and reparations. After initial opposition from the French, the moratorium went into effect in July 1931, although it was too little and too late to blunt the deepening world economic crisis. Representatives of the creditor states of France, Belgium, Britain, and Italy, met with delegates from Germany in mid-1932 at the Lausanne Conference, where agreement was reached to cancel reparations claims against Germany except for one final payment of 3 billion *Reichsmarks* that was postponed for three years. The creditor countries also agreed that ratification of the Lausanne Protocol would be contingent on reaching a satisfactory settlement with the United States on their own wartime debts. The American government rejected the Allied war debt reduction plan in late 1932, and by mid-1933 all the Allies apart from Finland had defaulted on their wartime debts to the United States. Though the Lausanne Protocol was never ratified, the document basically marked the end of Allied efforts to demand reparations from the Germans. Germany resumed payments on its outstanding reparations debt only after World War II, making its final reparations payment of $94 millions on October 3, 2010, with the monies going to foreign investors.

Disarmament in disarray

The elusiveness of meaningful arms reduction became increasingly clear as the 1930s moved forward. The naval powers of Britain, France, Italy, Japan, and the United States had limited success at the London Naval Conference of 1930, where they extended provisions of the treaties signed at the Washington Conference of 1921–1922 to aircraft carriers, adopted stricter rules for submarine warfare, and agreed to a five-year extension of the moratorium on the building of capital ships. On the other hand, France and Italy refused to agree to a new set of ratios for capital ship tonnage that the Americans, British, and Japanese set among themselves at 10:10:7 respectively. A final attempt at naval disarmament was made at the Second London Naval Conference in 1935–1936, but Japan walked out when the British and Americans refused it parity for capital ships, and Italy left because of the League of Nations-imposed sanctions against it for waging war in Abyssinia. Though a naval treaty was signed, it was ineffective, since Japan, Germany, and Italy were not a part of it. Efforts at naval disarmament had reached a dead end.

The other major arms reduction effort came at the League-sponsored World Disarmament Conference in Geneva that drew representatives from 59 nations and met for two years beginning in 1932. The wide gap between divergent concepts of security made any breakthrough in the arms reduction talks almost impossible. Germany, already restricted militarily by the Treaty of Versailles, called on other European countries to disarm to Germany's level, and, should they not, claimed the right to rearm. France proved resistant to compromising its military superiority over Germany and insisted that dependable international security measures, such as a League-run international police force, precede any arms reduction. Britain proposed a reduction of European armies to half a million men each, with equality for France and Germany. The Russians called for an end to all weapons. When the negotiations bogged down, American President Franklin D. Roosevelt in 1933 recommended the elimination of all modern offensive weapons, although a major point of debate at the conference centered on what constituted offensive and defensive weapons. Hitler's accession to power and subsequent rearmament program dealt a major blow to the conference. Progress toward disarmament at the conference became virtually hopeless, since the countries still there dared not consider arms reduction when Germany was rearming. The conference ended in failure in June 1934. In contrast to the setbacks over disarmament, one hopeful sign for a safer world took place in June 1930, when Denmark, Finland, Iceland, Norway, and Sweden signed the Nordic Arbitration Treaty to resolve peacefully any disputes among them.

German rearmament and the Stresa Front

In March 1935, Hitler, aware that it was no longer possible to keep Germany's rearmament program secret, openly revealed Germany's rearmament plans. In the first of two successive Saturday surprises, he announced on March 9 the Nazi regime's intention to create an air force, which in fact already existed. The following Saturday, Hitler let it be known that Germany was reintroducing military conscription to increase the army to 550,000 men. Both decisions were violations of the Versailles treaty. Hitler's actions caused France, Italy, and Britain to meet in the Italian town of Stresa in April, where they promised to use "all possible means" against future unilateral treaty violations, pledged to cooperate and remain in close contact with each other to achieve that goal, and confirmed their support for Austria's independence. Britain and Italy also reaffirmed all their obligations as guarantors of the Locarno Pact (see p. 90).

The press used the term "Stresa Front" to characterize the strong stand the three powers demonstrated in their parting declaration, but it was not too long before the hollowness of the front became clear. The first blow came on June 18, 1935, when Britain and Germany announced the signing of an Anglo-German Naval Pact that gave the Germans the right to have a naval fleet equal to 35 percent the size of Britain's. Britain negotiated the treaty without consulting France and Italy. Moreover, the pact undercut the stand the three powers had taken at Stresa against Germany's unilateral violations of the military provisions in the Treaty of Versailles, since the naval agreement itself was a violation of those same clauses. The final blow to the Stresa Front was Mussolini's invasion of Abyssinia in October 1935, which provoked a much stronger negative reaction in the West, especially in Great Britain, than Mussolini had anticipated.

Figure 5.1 Leaders of France, Great Britain, and Italy – Pierre Laval, Benito Mussolini, Ramsay MacDonald, and Pierre-Etienne Flandin (left to right) – stand together on the last day of the Stresa Conference in April 1935.

The Second Italo-Abyssinian War

In late 1934, the East African Kingdom of Abyssinia had an armed skirmish with Italy at Walwal along the frontier dividing Italian Somaliland and Abyssinia, in which 30 Italian soldiers died. The episode created an excuse for Italy to attack the East African kingdom when ready. Mussolini's preparations included the signing of a Franco-Italian agreement in January 1935, wherein the French, in an effort to obtain Italian support against future German aggression (unsuccessfully as events bore out), made several concessions to Italy in Africa, including French acceptance of a virtually free Italian hand in Abyssinia. Following his show of unity with Britain and France at Stresa against German rearmament, Mussolini felt even more confident that his partners would not interfere with his Abyssinian venture. In October 1935, Italian forces invaded Abyssinia, launching the Second Italo-Abyssinian War. It was a brutal war where Mussolini, in addition to Italian forces, used colonial troops from Eritrea, Somaliland, and Libya to help defeat an African state. In response to public pressure, Britain took the lead in getting the League Assembly to vote in October for the imposition of economic sanctions on Italy; these went into effect on November 18. It was the first time that the League used this device against an aggressor state in application of Article 16 of the League Covenant. The League excluded oil from the list, in large part because Britain and France did not want to provoke the Italians, who needed that commodity to fuel their war machine in Abyssinia. Britain also refused to close the Suez Canal to Italian shipping, again out of fear of offending Italy.

French Foreign Minister Pierre Laval, trying to find a compromise to the war that would keep Italy in the Western camp, convinced his British counterpart, Samuel Hoare, to join in formulating a secret proposal that would allow Italy to annex some 60,000 square miles of Abyssinian land and create a special Italian economic zone in the southern part of the kingdom. But the Hoare–Laval Pact of December 1935 was leaked to the press before it could be made official. It caused such a public furor in Britain that Hoare was forced to step down on December 18, and Laval was removed the following month.

Mussolini responded by intensifying Italy's military effort, including the introduction of poison gas. The Abyssinian army, mostly ill-equipped and poorly trained, was no match for the technologically superior Italian forces that had impressive numbers of artillery pieces, warplanes, machine guns, and tanks. Italian soldiers captured the Abyssinian capital of Addis Ababa on May 5, 1936, to mark the end of the conflict, and shortly thereafter Mussolini merged Abyssinia with other colonial holdings to create the colony of Italian East Africa. The number of Italian soldiers killed in the conflict totaled about 10,000, while some 275,000 Abyssinian soldiers lost their lives. Military success in Abyssinia strengthened Mussolini's grip on power, but it was a Pyrrhic victory. The war as well as the reconstruction and colonial administration that ensued in East Africa placed a heavy financial burden on Italy. By August 1939, Italy's finances were further depleted as a result of its role in the Spanish Civil War and its 1939 invasion of Albania.

Mussolini's aggressive moves in the mid-1930s had important consequences internationally. Turkish fears about Italian intentions in the eastern Mediterranean, for example, prompted Turkey to call for an end of the demilitarization of the Dardanelles contained in the 1923 Treaty of Lausanne and to return them to Turkish military control; apart from Italy, all the Lausanne signatories plus the Soviet Union agreed to do that in the Montreux Convention of June 1936. Mussolini countered by publicly declaring Italy's friendship for Muslims around the world, and was hailed by Arabs as the protector of Islam. The impact of the Abyssinian crisis on the League of Nations was also significant, as the failure of League-imposed sanctions against Italy caused irreparable damage to the collective security system that the League had guaranteed. The biggest outcome was Italy's decision to distance itself from Britain and France, owing to their support of sanctions against Italy in the Abyssinian War. This opened the door to warmer relations between Italy and Germany.

Conclusion

Unreasonable and unrealistic expectations were placed on the League of Nations in the 1920s and 1930s. Carrying out an immense juridical and administrative consensus-building work, it repeatedly came up against power politics. It was law versus force, and force usually won. The League's power and prestige eroded in the 1930s, although it continued its efforts to prevent a return to a chessboard approach in international politics. By the early 1930s, the generation of postwar peacemakers had passed. Stresemann died in 1929, and Briand in 1932. Sir Arthur Salter, the distinguished lawyer who had worked tirelessly to promote peace and security in Europe, had returned to London. Jean Monnet, a wartime architect of Allied cooperation and an expert at stabilizing small nations' currencies, went back to managing his Bordeaux vineyards. Gone were the architects of European security. Gone were the era of civility and the rule of law. After 1931, European diplomacy became entangled in extremely complex issues that led to the fragmentation of collective security and international cooperation, and to the resurgence of bilateralism and aggressive national self-interest.

The twilight of the European idea

Experts today see the Great Depression that began in 1929 as the major turning point in the fate of the interwar European idea. European advocates found themselves overwhelmed by events: domestic and international political uncertainty grew, global financial markets destabilized, and economic nationalism intensified. Authoritarian visions of a coerced Europe replaced the fraternal, free association of countries that the Europeanists had envisaged and begun to build.

Late economic integration plans

In the spring of 1932, André Tardieu, then serving the dual role of French premier and foreign minister, introduced a plan to create a network of preferential tariffs among the Danubian states of Czechoslovakia, Yugoslavia, Romania, Austria, and Hungary, with the possibility of eventually lifting economic barriers completely. Since the industrial states of Czechoslovakia and Austria could not take in all of the farm surpluses of the three predominantly agrarian states in the scheme, the Tardieu Plan provided for outside powers to grant preferential treatment for those products without anything equivalent in return. The plan also contained an international loan from France, Italy, Britain, and Germany. Tardieu believed that his Danubian scheme would grant France financial security and increase its political and economic presence in the region. Czech President Edvard Beneš hailed it in the Czech Parliament as a move toward Briand's European union project. But Tardieu's plan never advanced very far. Britain, Germany, and Italy took negative positions toward it at a four-power conference that included France in April, and it became a dead letter in France after Tardieu's moderate conservatives lost the 1932 French national elections to a leftist coalition led by Edouard Herriot, who had other priorities.

In the meantime, the League of Nations continued to seek a freeze on customs duties among European nations and to support international ententes. This resulted in isolated and fragmentary, sometimes minor efforts that failed to recreate the momentum and the excitement of the 1920s. France, Austria, and Belgium half-heartedly discussed a customs union, for example. The "flexing" of the European will continued mostly in East Central Europe, where regional combinations tied military factors and political cooperation to economic issues.

At another level, Albert Thomas at the International Labor Organization in Geneva continued to push for the construction of a European transportation network as a way to alleviate high unemployment and for a European common market as the precursor to an economic entente with the United States. The Scandinavian countries also attempted economic union. The Oslo Group, created in 1930 between Denmark, Norway, the Netherlands, and Sweden to coordinate tariffs and promote trade, was characterized by weak economic interaction among them. In 1932, the Netherlands, Belgium, and Luxembourg signed the Ouchy agreement in Switzerland on mutual tariff reductions and the eventual creation of a customs union, but its implementation never occurred, owing to the refusal of Britain and the United States to waive special trading rights they enjoyed with the Belgians and Dutch. The French put pressure on Poland to revive a Polish–Czechoslovak union project, but border rivalries and disagreement about the role of the Soviet Union prevented success.

Finally, in 1936–1937, Milan Hodža, a Slovak who served as the prime minister of Czechoslovakia from 1935 to 1938, pushed a regional integration plan that included Czechoslovakia, Austria, Yugoslavia, Romania, and Hungary and rested on a customs union. Hodža's Danubian Plan foresaw the eventual creation of an agriculturally based federal governmental structure. A new middle class would emerge from a "real union" of countries, with an agrarian form of democracy at its foundation.

But the political climate was too polarized and troubled to produce a set of common values that would anchor the unity of purpose of European unification, and Hitler and Mussolini's successful inroads into the Balkans undermined Hodža's plan. Hodža himself was forced to resign as prime minister following his country's humiliation at the Munich Conference in 1938.

Demise of the European movement

One by one, the European movements and associations created in the 1920s declined or closed. The Pan-European Union of Germany and the German branch of the Committee of European Cooperation closed in 1933 because of Hitler's rise to power. The existence of colonies also forced Europe's colonial powers to include geographical regions outside the continent in their calculations, even if Europeans did not fully realize or discuss the implications of this situation. The Great Depression caused France, Great Britain, Belgium, the Netherlands, and Portugal to redirect their efforts toward bolstering economic ties with their colonies. If anything, the spirit of federalism and economic associations devolved to the colonies, which explains why there were renewed colonial development efforts in the 1930s.

Paradoxically, the League of Nations in the 1930s also became an obstacle to the internationalist principles that it promoted, because a united Europe within its jurisdiction required a certain abandonment of national sovereignty, which European governments were reluctant to do, especially those of East Central Europe. In July 1933, a League-sponsored international economic conference brought delegates from 66 countries to London to regulate tariffs, prevent economic nationalism, and stabilize currencies. The conference failed in part because the United States, having just abandoned the gold standard, was unwilling to support anything but bilateral financial and trade treaties.

The Soviet and Nazi visions for Europe

After 1935, the two most active countries in promoting European visions were the Soviet Union and Nazi Germany, and both waged crusades to annihilate the other's European vision. Using state Communist parties across Europe and the Comintern, party leaders in Moscow looked eventually to undermine "the global bourgeois order" and create a single worldwide Communist regime as a prelude to the complete dismantlement of the state and the emergence of a classless society. To keep his effort on track, Stalin also encouraged during the mid- and late 1930s the creation of leftist political coalitions or Popular Fronts in France and Spain that would stand up to the threat of fascism in Europe. After signing the Nazi–Soviet Nonaggression Pact in August 1939, the Soviet Union acted close to its borders by seizing large portions of East Central Europe. Disregarding his treaties with the Baltic states, Stalin annexed Estonia, Latvia, and Lithuania in 1940. This enabled him to establish political centralization, control populations, and subdue nationalist unrest. He grew increasingly suspicious of East Central European federation plans as the war progressed.

Hitler dreamed of a global empire dominated by the supposed racially superior German people and directed under a single leader from its capital city of "Germania," as Berlin was to be called. He would achieve world control through a series of wars, with each struggle serving as the stepping stone for the next. In his first move towards a new Europe, Hitler eliminated the residual self-government in Germany's historic provinces and established new centralized administrative districts directly accountable to Berlin, thus breaking centuries-old bonds of community. Hitler's "New Europe," in which his Aryan master race dominated non-German peoples, especially Slavic peoples, would subordinate foreign economies and labor forces to the German Reich's needs for security and well-being, create agricultural zones in the East, dismantle the industries of unreliable countries, and resettle ethnic Germans in leadership positions across Europe, beginning with East Central Europe and Russia. This was a quasi-colonial order based on coercion.

Conclusion

The dream of a united Europe did not die with the Great Depression, but it took a dramatic turn. Western European countries, having seemingly exhausted their energy for conceiving new ways to achieve European integration, and facing threats from totalitarian regimes, scrambled to secure alliances with East Central European countries that would safeguard their military and economic security. The two new visions for Europe were those of Hitler and Stalin; as they involved the military conquest of free countries, they were inseparable from military occupations and war, and thus were not begun until the late 1930s.

Colonial developments

Both the British and French faced important challenges in their colonies in the 1930s, owing to the effects of the Great Depression and growing resentment against European imperialism. These problems were compounded by the neocolonial pressures from Italy's Balkan, Libyan, and Abyssinian holdings and Germany's insistence on regaining its former African colonies. The Western powers had been under League of Nations scrutiny since 1919 because of their colonial mandates. Change occurred, but not always logically, since there was an ongoing tension between the lofty ideals of colonial development and national self-interest. The French chose to pursue a policy of assimilation, especially in their North African and Middle Eastern colonies, while the British favored indirect rule. The British and the French linked their economic recovery to the development of the colonies. Aware of the impending remaking of the world order, they also prepared their colonies to provide help in case of war. Often, however, repressive measures remained in place, especially in the area of labor. As a result, the wide moral and administrative authority that the colonial powers had enjoyed in the name of mentorship yielded diminishing returns as colonial peoples used the European discourse of liberal thought, education, and religion to shape a new national consciousness.

The Great Depression

The Great Depression of 1929 arrested the growth of the colonial economies. Its effects were felt well into the 1940s, with production, prices, and trade weakened. Some raw materials were in oversupply, especially where cheaper synthetic products were available. Single commodity economies that relied on raw cotton, rubber, and silk were hit particularly hard, and were unable to diversify fast enough to mitigate the loss of revenue. Taxes and charges increased, forcing entrepreneurs with new machinery to default on loan repayments. Making things worse, Britain's colonies were not allowed to devalue their currencies, so their citizens paid taxes in a high value currency to the British whose currency had undergone devaluation in 1931. Budgets were often earmarked to pay interest on capital loans that had financed infrastructure projects such as railroads. In the Belgian Congo, 40 percent of the budget was allocated to the colonial administration and police. Tax revenues fell, funds for social services suffered, and whatever was collected generally went for European settlers' needs.

The depression underlined the need for modernization, efficient administration, economic diversification, and public welfare – these were matters of national prestige as much as national and security interest. Drops in commodities prices and decreases in the demand for metals and rubber caused violent strike movements in the North Rhodesian copper-belt, other parts of Africa, and the Dutch East Indies. The colonial powers suddenly realized that they could no longer postpone reforms. Improved agricultural methods, increased welfare, political change, and modernization were now as desirable as quotas and tariff increases. Self-sufficiency was out and colonial aid was in.

Strengthening imperial ties

Imperial ties were strengthened by the same methods used in Europe to reverse the effects of the Depression: development budgets, preferential tariffs, integrated markets, and emigration towards the colonies to ease unemployment at home. The British Parliament passed the Colonial Development Act of 1929 that provided up to 1 million pounds sterling per year in funds for colonial capital projects, but it did not extend to social programs such as education. Another innovation was the creation of imperial-wide industrial units – such as the Dutch Shell Oil company – that represented a step toward a global economy. Overall in the 1930s, it was the colonies' taxes that paid for an important part of colonial economic expansion, and much of the development in fact benefited the European countries. Another measure taken by the European colonial powers was economic integration. In the summer of 1932, Britain, having abandoned free trade earlier in the year, met with its Dominions at an Imperial Economic Conference in Ottawa, Canada to work on a system of imperial preferences favoring Dominion agricultural products and British manufactured products. The wealthier parts of the empire in general benefited from these new dispositions, and, by 1938, 44 percent of British trade was conducted with her colonies. The poorest British African colonies of Central and East Africa (Kenya, Uganda, and Tanganyika) tried to counteract these measures by forming regional economic unions, to no avail. Only in 1940 did the Colonial Development and Welfare Act increase the colonial budget by setting aside up to 5 million pounds per year for five years for projects intended to assist any colony's development or its inhabitants' welfare, although these measures were most likely taken because of World War II.

Developing the colonies

In regard to France's overseas holdings, Albert Sarraut, twice the country's minister of colonies (1920–1924 and 1932–1933), saw his dream of systematically developing France's colonies move forward when the French in 1934–1935 allocated 5 billion francs in a vast 15-year plan aimed at standardizing business and economic transactions to improve effectiveness and productivity. A social welfare commission received 1 billion francs to improve hygiene and demographics. The ultimate goal was to create a business bubble to protect France and its colonies from international commercial fluctuations.

Nevertheless, the monies went mostly to the developed colonies and to self-serving projects. One example of the latter was a massive irrigation plan in the French African colony of Mali that was intended to help grow cotton for export, but by 1937 it had failed, because African farmers resisted growing cotton at the low prices then in place. Still, raw materials continued to flow towards the colonizing country and finished products towards the colonies. Development remained highly uneven until the late 1930s. Generally, France and other imperial states continued to treat their African and Asian colonies like immense plantations, profiting from their lands and products.

The imperial powers often gave high priority to transportation schemes. The triple age of railroads, air transport, and highways had arrived. New and improved railway systems crisscrossed Africa in the 1930s. The French opened a Moroccan–Tunisian Railway that united the French North African colonies economically, and in 1931 revived a project to unite North and West Africa by electric-powered trains. In East Africa, corridors were built from hinterlands to seaports, with borders at times adjusted to allow for the completion of rail line segments; the Belgians, for example, ceded 480 square miles of the Congo against 1 square mile of Portuguese land to complete a railway from the Congolese province of Katanga to the Indian Ocean port of Beira in Mozambique. The longest bridge in the world, at 12,064 feet, opened on the lower Zambezi River in 1935, to facilitate trade and transportation between the British protectorate of Nyasaland and Beira. Air transportation routes were built as well. The British opened a weekly airmail service in 1936 between Lagos in Nigeria and Khartoum in Sudan. Regular airmail service also started between Britain and Australia, and between the Belgian Congo city of Brazzaville and French Algerian city of Algiers. In 1936, the French launched a Toulouse to Dakar route. While trains were best for economic development, roads and air links were best for military strategy. One of the most impressive realizations was the Libyan coastal road that Italo Balbo, the Italian governor of Cyrenaica, built, extending 1,812 kilometers from Tripoli to Tunis. It was inaugurated in 1937. The most daring route was perhaps the British Takoradi air route in Africa that, begun on a modest scale in 1936, saw considerable expansion during World War II when it served as an Allied supply line.

The increase in colonial budgets is partly explained by the colonial powers' desire to provide white emigrants with comfortable living and working conditions, sound economic policies, and satisfactory schools. While colonies provided convenient outlets for alleviating unemployment at home, emigration to the colonies in the 1930s likewise became a matter of national and colonial security. Not only did it alleviate unemployment at home, but it also increased the ratio of white settlers needed to stem the rise of anti-colonial disturbances among the indigenous populations.

The International Colonial Exposition of 1931

A long time in the making, the International Colonial Exposition of 1931 in Paris was the culmination of a colonial epoch in which the ambivalence of European feelings towards their colonies was obvious. It displayed a pride in the white man's "civilizing" mission and colonial achievements. Grander in scale and broader in scope than a British Empire Exposition held in London's Wembley Park in 1924–1925, the Paris exposition, like that of London, presented a sanitized version of empire in which one found well-structured order and colorful variation.

Located on 500 acres of land on the eastern edge of Paris, the fabulous exposition had a global theme and featured the participation of a number of colonial powers. Consisting primarily of temporary buildings that took 18 months to construct, it offered visitors an "around the world [tour] in one day." The assemblage of exotic buildings, towers, a lake, lights, water fountains, and other attractions was a dazzling decor for the displays that several European countries organized. It presented a miniature colonial empire that employed 2,000 men, women, children, craftsmen, singers, camel leaders, and canoers. The Angkor Wat temple was the emblem of the whole exhibit: 70 meters wide, with five towers, it was covered in gold and emerald. Among the exposition's other attractions were a Bali dance ensemble, dioramas, one 40-meter-long fresco of Indochinese and Indian populations, and a funeral procession from Indochina with 90 chariots. Some 33 million people visited it during its eight months of operation, but only one permanent building housing a Museum of Colonies remained after it ended. Public outrage, especially women's protests, against treating colonial subjects and their cultures as curiosities, ended the age of colonial exhibits. The interest of Europeans in the colonial world did not diminish, however, as Europeans continued to show their fascination for non-European cultures in other ways.

The colonial city

Colonial cities continued to be an experiment in modernization in the 1930s. In 1931, an international Congress on Colonial Urbanism met in Paris in conjunction with the International Colonial Exposition and reaffirmed a commitment to modernism. Presided over by Marshal Hubert Lyautey, the general commissioner of the Colonial Exhibit, it studied the political dimension of spatial segregation. The French took the lead in architectural preservation by vowing to preserve traditional landmarks in the heart of colonial cities. But they still favored segregated cities and brought modernism in by designing satellite cities separated by green belts. This model was applied during the 1930s and early 1940s, as the French colonial authorities devised urban colonial policy. The new colonial city, however, remained first and foremost an expression of colonial power. The weight of this power was visible in New Delhi, India, where the new city, inaugurated in 1931, was foreign to the Indian style.

The idea of historic architectural preservation resulted in colonial hybrid styles. In the interwar years, such styles were quite visible in North Africa, the French Sudan, and Indochina, as the preservation of the local cultural heritage and pre-colonial buildings became an inspiration for European architects. In India, an Anglo-Indian style was born, that is, a Western style with Oriental motifs. From Morocco to Egypt, Muslim influences were felt in colonial buildings featuring "Moorish–Spanish" decorations. The French mixed Moorish, modern, and dirt architecture in Niger, French Sudan, and Upper Volta. In Indochina, Laotian, Cambodian, and Japanese shintoist styles were added to Western-style structures in the Vietnamese city of Hanoi, where the Museum of the French Far Eastern School was inaugurated in 1931.

Architectural preservation, however, was also used for political ends. One was the considerable growth of tourism after World War I, with travelers craving exoticism. This trend corresponded to a cultural revaluation of the colonized people which was in line with the new spirit and policies of the League of Nations. Even the new imperialism was benevolent: in Libya, Italian architects reached out to Muslims by building mosques and preserving ancient Muslim towns. There was, however, an ambiguity in this attitude. The colonial powers dictated the transformation of the central parts of cities into museums, which suggested that the local inhabitants had allowed their historical buildings to "degrade," and positioned the colonizers as "saviors" of the local cultural heritage. This policy often resulted in riots and demonstrations, as the new urban environment reflected the political and symbolic domination of the colonial authorities.

More radical architectural experiments moved forward as well – both for colonial and European cities. In 1923, Le Corbusier proposed in *Towards a New Architecture* a new urban style for Morocco. Built on the principles of unity, simplicity, and purity, this futuristic urban concept included a city business center made of vertical skyscrapers and a residential city featuring curves and horizontal lines. These two centers were to be joined by an elevated roadway. In the 1930s, this new style revolutionized the colonies as well as the metropole. Le Corbusier was the first to take the skyscraper to Africa, and the precursor of the modern freeway system. In 1934, he planned an entirely new city in Algeria called Nemours. In the 1940s, he put together a modernist residential block-housing design called the "radiant city" in Marseille, France, which, when completed in 1952, was a 12-story structure with 337 apartments.

Colonial discontent

The Dutch East Indies (Indonesia) was a microcosm of the difficulties that the colonial powers often experienced in this era. Demographic stagnation, uneven economic development, and structural inequalities existed despite the introduction of an "ethical policy," i.e., a policy of respect for the local populations and of commitment to their welfare that the Dutch began at the end of the nineteenth century. In 1918, this policy was renewed, and the Dutch provided subsidies to speed up rural development, education, and public health, in hopes of binding Indonesians more closely to the West. But revolutionary ideas had become popular during World War I, and ties existed between the Dutch Communist Party and Indonesian independence leaders who formed trade unions and their own Communist Party. The opposition was divided between the Chinese diaspora, the Sarekat Islam movement, and the Communists. The system remained exploitative and unequal. Persistent poverty and famine led to a significant Communist-led uprising in the winter of 1926–1927. The Great Depression ended Dutch subsidies, plunging the colony into dire poverty and unemployment, closing plantations, and deepening famine. People fled to the cities to work for small Chinese-owned enterprises, and started buying cheaper Japanese goods, while the Dutch authorities arrested and exiled opposition leaders.

In India, where radical nationalists in 1929 demanded that the British quickly give their country its basic independence, Mohandas Gandhi, in accordance with his practice of non-violent resistance, intervened in early 1930 by organizing a large-scale peaceful protest against Britain's tax on salt in that country. The tax law provided the British with a virtual monopoly on salt, a product that was essential to the welfare of the Indian people. In a dramatic demonstration of defiance to the law, Gandhi led a crowd of some 50,000 people to the sea where he produced his own salt. Other protests followed, with the British finally arresting Gandhi and thousands of his followers. Even with Gandhi in prison, the demonstrations against the tax continued until the British finally caved in by releasing Gandhi and undertaking negotiations with him regarding Indian self-rule.

The result was the Government of India Act of 1935 that, in abolishing the system of diarchy (see p. 104), considerably enhanced the Indians' participation in the country's governance. Although the act was never completely applied, it did provide a framework for the constitutions of both an independent India and Pakistan following World War II. The oppressive salt tax, meanwhile, continued until 1947 when it was finally abolished by the interim Indian government preparing the way for India's complete independence.

In Indochina, indigenous discontent was strongly demonstrated in February 1930 in the abortive Yen Bey coup. Seething over France's authoritarian rule and experiencing economic hardship, members of the nationalist Vietnam National Party (VNQDD) agreed to attack several French military garrisons with the goal of destroying French colonial power in their land. The plotters made their most forceful effort at the French post at Yen Bey near the Chinese frontier, but the uprising was brutally crushed and the VNQDD destroyed. The demise of the VNQDD opened the door for Ho Chi Minh's newly formed Communist Party of Vietnam (renamed the Indochinese Communist Party in October 1930) to generate major protests the same year. His followers in central Vietnam formed soviets (peasant councils), seized estates, conducted strikes, and engaged in anti-government marches that threw the French authorities off balance. The French slowly reasserted their control over the area in late 1930, and they broke up the Communist Party leadership. The French issued a death sentence *in absentia* against Ho, who was then in Hong Kong, for revolutionary activities, but he soon escaped to Moscow where he spent the next several years. The Vietnamese unrest in 1930 was the most severe that the French experienced in their colonies during the interwar years, but a certain calm then settled over the region for the rest of the 1930s.

Overall, the colonial powers misunderstood colonial nationalism. They set in motion repressive reactions that showed their unwillingness and inability to accept the deep social and political changes that were underway. The colonial powers likewise underestimated nationalism in the Muslim world (see pp. 104–105, 111–114).

Conclusion

By 1939, the imperial powers were overextended and hostage to their growing colonial budgets. For the British, Singapore – where construction on a system of defenses remained unfinished – and the Suez Canal were their Achilles' heels, since Britain's control over its empire in Africa and Asia depended heavily on them, and they were militarily vulnerable. Increasingly, colonial developments, such as reverse migration and calls for national independence, created social and political changes that tied the hands of European leaders and featured prominently in colonizing countries' domestic debates. The weight of the Great Depression caused a strengthening of the colonial bonds, but it also resulted in much friction. In that sense, the colonies became a part of the growing policies of economic and political nationalism of the 1930s. While the imperial states began a revaluation of colonial cultures and peoples and showed a new appreciation for their cultural heritage, there was little change in the economic exploitation that took place, and little doubt as to who was in charge.

The emergence of a German–Italian alliance, 1936–1938

The years 1936–1938 were pivotal in the lead-up to World War II, as Hitler vied with Mussolini for first place on the European scene. The boldness of his actions was calculated to test the reactions of France and Britain in particular, but also of the Soviet Union. While aggressively pursuing rearmament and revisionism, Hitler likewise sought to display Germany's military strength, as seen in his actions during the Spanish Civil War. During these two years, the death of the Versailles system was confirmed.

The occupation of the Rhineland

In 1936, the diplomatic initiative shifted from Italy to Germany when Hitler, in another Saturday surprise, ordered German troops into the demilitarized Rhineland on March 7. Hitler's action not only contravened the already broken Versailles treaty that Germany had been forced to sign, but it also violated the Locarno Pact that Germany had voluntarily initialed in 1925. International law was clearly on the side of France and the other signatory powers to the pact, should they decide to take military action, which Locarno entitled them to do in this circumstance. But France was in the hands of a caretaker government that, lacking any political cohesion, was deeply divided on how to react. The French military chiefs added to the government's hesitance by presenting it with an exaggerated view of the German army's strength and questioning any use of force in the crisis. The British made France's decision not to act militarily easier by their readiness to condone the German action. One leading British politician commented, "The Germans, after all, are only going into their own back garden."[1] The French took the issue to the League Council, which condemned Germany's illegal move, but nothing happened to Germany beyond that.

Figure 5.2 German soldiers march into the Rhineland on March 7, 1936, in violation of the Treaty of Versailles and the Locarno Pact.

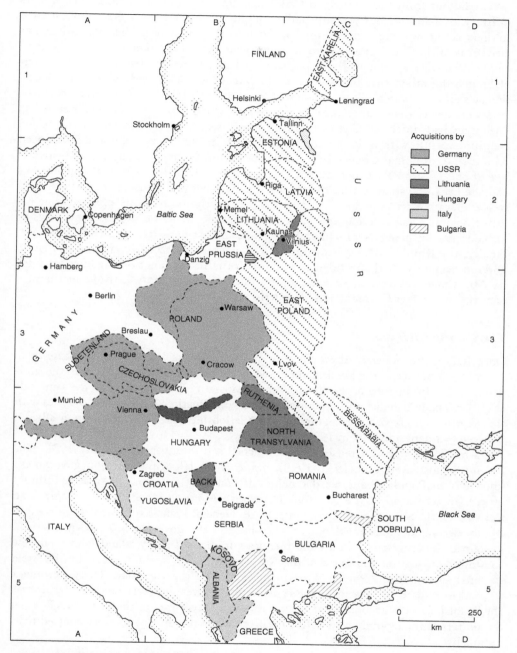

Map 5.1 Territorial changes in Europe, 1938–1941.

The fallout from the Rhineland Crisis was dramatic and decisive. France saw its military position seriously compromised along its border with Germany. French soldiers could no longer move unimpeded into the unguarded, heavily industrialized areas of the Ruhr, since German troops were now there. The change marked an end to France's superior military position in Europe and the beginning of a spirit of French defeatism that intensified in the late 1930s. The new reality also rattled France's alliance system. While the Little Entente reaffirmed its solidarity, its members were aware that France's military support, which was critical to their security, no longer had much value; the alliance folded as an entity in 1938. In the West, Belgium withdrew from its alliance with France in the fall of 1936 and announced its return to diplomatic neutrality shortly thereafter. Germany's unpunished thwarting of the Locarno Pact also caused the world's faith in international conventions and the League system to sink to new lows. In Germany, the success of Hitler's bold stroke elevated his popularity to new heights and reinforced his opinion that his intuition was a far better guide in decision making than the professional views of his conservative generals who had warned him against remilitarizing the Rhineland. Finally, the Rhineland coup ended a belated attempt by recently appointed British Foreign Secretary Anthony Eden to add oil to the list of sanctions against Italy for its Abyssinian aggression; France, hoping not to alienate Italy in light of the new security threat that Germany posed, scuttled it.

The Spanish Civil War

Once Italy had conquered Abyssinia, a reinvigorated Mussolini saw an opportunity to extend his influence in the Mediterranean, when civil war broke out in Spain in the summer of 1936. In supporting the Spanish rebels, Mussolini found himself on the same side as Hitler. The Italian dictator capitalized on this new situation to cultivate closer ties with the Nazi regime. It was the beginning of a relationship that culminated in an alliance between Germany and Italy in 1939.

As for Spain, political tensions there reached a breaking point in July 1936. The Second Spanish Republic (1931–1939), headed by a left-wing coalition government known as the Popular Front, faced a major crisis on July 17, when conservative military officers in command of the garrisons in Spanish Morocco rebelled and organized an uprising on the Spanish mainland. On July 18, General Francisco Franco, a right-wing, highly decorated professional officer who disliked the government's anti-militarism, explained the army revolt in a radio broadcast from the Canary Islands and then flew to Morocco to assume command of the Army of Africa. In Spain, General Emilio Mola declared an end to the Popular Front government on the same day. The government in Madrid refused to cave in to the conspirators' moves, however, and the result was the Spanish Civil War, one of the most devastating civil wars in the history of Europe. Supporters of the republic were called loyalists, while the insurgents were referred to as nationalists.

Franco, failing to receive support from either the Spanish navy or air force because of their ongoing loyalty to the republican government, looked abroad for assistance in transporting his forces across the Straits of Gibraltar. Soon German and Italian airplanes were ferrying troops to the northeast of the country, where the nationalist rebels had an important base. The quantity of German and Italian aid increased rapidly. Hitler dispatched the Condor Legion, a special air force unit, to provide air cover for the rebel forces, and Mussolini sent large contingents of Italian infantry as "volunteers" in the struggle against "international Communism." The conflict raised fears of a general war as it began to internationalize. In August 1936, the French and British proposed a policy of non-intervention in the war, and both countries pledged an embargo on military supplies to the republic as a way of getting other powers to adopt a non-intervention policy. On September 9, 1936, a Non-Intervention Committee first met in London to discuss ways of preventing foreign intervention in the Spanish conflict. Eventually, 27 nations, including Germany, Italy, and the Soviet Union, participated in the Non-Intervention Committee, but it proved ineffective in keeping foreign countries out of the conflagration. Stalin encouraged the formation of International Brigades from national European Communist parties; the brigades eventually recruited some 40,000 volunteers to fight for the republican cause. He also sent advisers, trucks, and military materiel to the loyalists. On the other side, Hitler and Mussolini recognized Franco's regime on November 18, 1936. The Italian government ultimately sent 75,000 troops to Spain. Hitler tested his new air force, trained Spanish soldiers, and sent other military resources. In April 1937, the German Condor Legion used saturation bombing – an intensive aerial bombardment intended to destroy everything in the target area – on the small town of Guernica in the Basque country, killing hundreds of civilians and provoking a world outcry. Eager to end the conflict, British Prime Minister Neville Chamberlain reached agreement with Mussolini in April 1938 to halt Italy's participation in the war, but Chamberlain's policy proved misplaced as Mussolini kept 40,000

Figure 5.3 The Spanish city of Guernica shows heavy damage following a German aerial saturation bombing attack on April 27, 1937, as a part of the Spanish Civil War.

men in Spain. The Germans' 10,000 airmen and armored soldiers also played a major role in the republicans' defeat. By late 1938, Franco had the upper hand. The republicans ended the fight on March 28, 1939, when Madrid fell to Franco's forces. In all, 700,000 men were killed in battle, 15,000 civilians killed in air raids, and 30,000 in mass trials and executions. Moreover, more than half a million Spaniards had fled the country.

The Spanish Civil War had broad consequences. It brought Mussolini and Hitler together, allowing a consolidation of Fascist ideology. Franco gained economic leverage over Hitler by giving Germany access to important iron and copper resources that helped in Germany's rearmament program. These resources had been reserved for Britain until Franco took them from the republicans in the summer of 1937. The Spanish republicans became increasingly dependent on Soviet aid; Stalin capitalized on this by bolstering the position of the Spanish Communist Party politically. Of the two competing Spanish governments that ran Spain until the spring of 1939, one republican and the other fascist, Franco's Falange emerged with the stronger ideology; the army and the Catholic Church buttressed its repressive, conservative power. In the larger scheme of European and world politics, the fact that Germany and Italy were on the same side in the Spanish war contributed in October 1936 to their two countries signing a general understanding that Mussolini referred to in a speech on November 1 as an "Axis." Indeed, the Rome–Berlin Axis represented a new alignment in European relations. The war-related cooperation between Germany and Italy also helped pave the way for their collaboration in Italy's invasion of Albania in April 1939 and their creation of a military alliance known as the Pact of Steel in May 1939.

The Anti-Comintern Pact

At the same time that Hitler established a new tone in his country's relations with Italy, he strengthened Germany's position in the Far East by signing an Anti-Comintern Treaty with Japan in November 1936. While the published part of the pact was directed against the Moscow-directed Comintern, it contained a secret protocol whereby the two nations agreed, should one of them be the target of an unprovoked Russian attack, to consult each other on how to safeguard their shared interests. Both parties also agreed not to sign political treaties with the Soviet Union that violated the spirit of the pact without mutual approval. Italy joined the pact in November 1937, and withdrew from the League of Nations shortly thereafter. The three signatories of the Anti-Comintern Pact would formally become known as the Axis powers after they signed a Tripartite Pact in September 1940 that established a defensive military alliance among them.

Conclusion

By 1938, leadership among Europe's revisionist powers had shifted to Germany. Italy had depleted its human and financial resources in the Second Italo-Abyssinian War and the Spanish Civil War. The internationalization of the Spanish conflict advanced the disintegration of the safeguard mechanisms that insured security in Europe, and it was another important event in which Hitler and Mussolini affirmed their leadership style through the use of force and their disregard of British and French requests for non-interference.

Prelude to war, 1938–1939

The last two years of peace saw a continuation of trends exhibited since 1936. Europe was living on borrowed time, as the Western powers with their ideal of peace through collective security proved unable to reclaim diplomatic leadership. The years 1938–1939 represented a travesty of open diplomacy and a disrespect for existing states; it was a diplomatic free for all in which the Western democracies went through the motions of procedure, but with little result. Increasingly, the dictators were in control of the situation.

Appeasement

When Neville Chamberlain replaced Stanley Baldwin as British prime minister in May 1937, he was determined to play a prominent role in the formulation of British foreign policy. Confident of his ability to achieve results through personal diplomacy with other heads of state, he took the lead in foreign negotiations and relegated his professional diplomats to a subordinate role. He repeatedly stated that the League of Nations was a broken experiment and that collective security was a failure. He was the chief proponent of the policy known as appeasement that, albeit pursued by his immediate predecessors, reached its climax during his tenure. Appeasement involved making timely concessions to a nation considered to have legitimate grievances based on past wrongs. Chamberlain had a deep abhorrence of Nazism, so he had no sympathy for Hitler's regime when he made agreements with the Germans based on appeasement. He was convinced that Hitler was a reasonable man who preferred peaceful means over war to achieving his goals, and that their two countries could reach compromise solutions through direct negotiations. Chamberlain, along with his closest advisors, believed that Germany had justifiable grievances directly related to the Versailles settlement. For the appeasers, these complaints appeared limited to the Nazis' insistence on incorporating the German-speaking areas of East Central Europe into Hitler's Reich. Accordingly, Chamberlain had cabinet member Lord Halifax inform Hitler during a meeting in Germany on November 19, 1937, that Britain was not averse to changes in that region – Danzig, Austria, and Czechoslovakia – so long as these were done peacefully. Hitler had to be encouraged by what he heard, since Britain was ready to tolerate territorial revisions in East Central Europe, but the changes he had in mind were much broader than those that Halifax mentioned.

On November 5, exactly two weeks before the Halifax conversation, Hitler had held a secret meeting with his foreign minister and top military commanders to discuss his general foreign policy plans. It is known as the Hossbach Conference owing to a highly secret memorandum that Colonel Friedrich Hossbach, Hitler's military adjutant, wrote about the event five days later. Hitler announced the need for *Lebensraum* for the German people in the East and his readiness to use war to accomplish this expansion. He insisted that the attack in the East take place by 1943–1945 at the latest. The first steps – the seizure of Austria and Czechoslovakia – would take place when political circumstances justified action. Shortly after his interview with Halifax, Hitler began preparations to strike against Austria.

Anschluss

The possibility of close links between Germany and Austria had happened twice in the early 1930s, first in 1931, with the proposed Austro-German customs union that France scuttled (see p. 165), and then in 1934, with the failed Nazi coup in Vienna that was a German foreign policy setback (see p. 164). The third effort came in early 1938. Angry over suppressive measures that the Austrian government had recently taken against the Austrian Nazi Party, Hitler met with Austrian Chancellor Kurt von Schuschnigg at Hitler's Bavarian mountain retreat of Berchtesgaden on February 12. Hitler browbeat the Austrian chancellor into agreeing to give the Austrian Nazis new freedoms, place several Nazis in key government posts, and align Austrian foreign policy with that of Germany. Once back in Vienna, Schuschnigg had second thoughts about his concessions and on March 9, with four days' notice, announced a plebiscite for Sunday, March 13, on Austria's independence. Furious over this action, Hitler immediately ordered military preparations for an invasion of Austria. He also called for a postponement of the plebiscite and Schuschnigg's resignation as chancellor. Schuschnigg canceled the vote and resigned on March 11, but by then, the German dictator was set on sending German troops into Austria, which took place on March 12. Hitler used as his justification a Berlin-dictated request from Arthur Seyss-Inquart, Austria's recently appointed Nazi minister of the interior, calling for German intervention in Austria to "preserve order." Austria officially became a German province on March 14, when the *Anschluss* was promulgated as law. Hitler triumphantly announced this fact to an enthusiastic crowd of some 200,000 people in Vienna the same day. An Austrian plebiscite held the following month returned a near unanimous vote in favor of *Anschluss*. Britain and France responded with diplomatic protests, but they did not even bother using the League of Nations Council this time round to denounce the action. When Hitler received a telephone call from his emissary in Rome that Mussolini would not interfere in Austria, the Nazi dictator gushingly responded:

> Then please tell Mussolini I shall never forget him for this! ... If he should ever need any help or be in any danger, he can be convinced that I shall stick to him whatever may happen, even if the whole world were against him.[2]

The Munich Conference

Hitler next moved against Czechoslovakia, where he had his sights set on the German-speaking region known as the Sudetenland, which had a common frontier with Germany and Austria in Czechoslovakia's north and west. The Sudetenland was vital to Czechoslovakia's defense, since the country had a formidable line of military fortifications there known as the "Czech Maginot Line." Its loss would mark the demise of Czechoslovakia as a credible player in the power politics of Europe.

The 3.25 million German inhabitants of the Sudeten province had only reluctantly accepted their place in the Czech Republic as a result of the 1919 Treaty of St. Germain. Provincial discontent against Czech authority grew considerably in the 1930s largely because of the Great Depression. Hitler decided to capitalize on that resentment when he told pro-Nazi Sudeten German Party leader Konrad Henlein in March 1938 to demand rights and privileges for the Sudetenland that the Czech government could never meet. At the same time Hitler ordered German military leaders to make plans for an invasion of Czechoslovakia. In line with Hitler's instructions, Henlein in April presented the

Czech government with a set of demands called the Karlsbad Program that would provide full autonomy to the Sudetenland. Little progress was made in the negotiations that followed between the Czech authorities and Henlein's Sudeten party.

The Western powers watched events unfold in Czechoslovakia with an increasing sense of urgency. France had a treaty obligation to defend Czechoslovakia, as did the Soviet Union once French military intervention had begun. But the French were reluctant to fulfill their pledge without a similar commitment from the British, and when that was not forthcoming, France let Britain assume the lead role in the affair, using appeasement as its guide. Since Chamberlain had no desire to go to war with Germany over Czechoslovakia, he put pressure on the Czech government during the summer to compromise with Henlein's group. His entreaties produced results in early September, when Czech officials agreed to implement almost all of the Karlsbad Program. In response, Hitler used a party congress in Nuremburg on September 12 to deliver a feisty speech in which he inveighed against Czechoslovakia for its oppression of the Sudeten Germans and promised them Germany's support. An armed revolt erupted in the Sudetenland immediately thereafter, forcing the Czech government to declare martial law. Henlein escaped to Germany amid rising indications that German military action appeared imminent.

Chamberlain, desperate to find a peaceful resolution of the crisis, took it upon himself to visit Hitler face-to-face to see what would satisfy the German leader short of war. At a September 15 meeting of the two men at Berchtesgaden, Chamberlain indicated his readiness to accept the cession of the Sudetenland to Germany. Then Britain, joined by France, forced Czech President Edvard Beneš to fall in line on an Anglo-French plan for separation by letting it be understood that his country would be left to fight Germany alone if he said no. Chamberlain confidently laid out the Anglo-French proposal to Hitler at a meeting in Bad Godesberg, Germany, on September 22, only to learn that Hitler, contending that the transfer process laid out at Berchtesgaden was too slow, now wanted an immediate German military occupation of the areas in question. At the same time, Hitler assured the British leader that the Sudetenland would be his last European territorial demand. A disheartened Chamberlain returned to London empty-handed. With war looming large, the Prime Minister, with French backing, petitioned Mussolini to propose a four-power conference of Britain, France, Germany, and Italy, which the Duce did. Hitler, who was ready to move militarily, grudgingly accepted Mussolini's proposal on September 28.

Hitler, Mussolini, Chamberlain, and French Premier Edouard Daladier met in Munich on September 29–30. The British and French leaders conceded the Sudetenland to Hitler on virtually all the terms he had demanded at Bad Godesberg. All parties promised to respect the sovereignty of the shrunken Czech state. After long hours of negotiations, the four leaders finally signed the agreement right before 2:00 a.m. on September 30, although they dated it September 29. Czechoslovakia, whose interests were at stake, was not allowed to participate in the negotiations, although the British and French intermittently briefed Czech officials sitting in an adjacent room on their progress. The Czech representatives took the completed document back to Prague for review. Knowing that a rejection of the agreement would mean facing Germany alone, the Czechoslovak government reluctantly submitted to its terms.

The Munich Conference was the high tide of Chamberlain's policy of appeasement, and he capped it off before leaving Munich on September 30 by getting Hitler to sign an Anglo-German declaration in which the two men agreed on "the desire of our two peoples never to go to war with one another again" and to take up issues of common concern by "the method of consultation."[3] The British leader received a triumphal welcome upon his return home, and he announced to a crowd gathered outside his official residence at 10 Downing Street: "I believe it is peace for our time."[4] Daladier also experienced an enthusiastic welcome after his plane landed at Le Bourget Airport in Paris, although, in contrast to Chamberlain, he was filled with misgivings and shame over what had happened in Munich.

In the end, the Munich Agreement failed to achieve the goals of the appeasers. The international guarantees of rump Czechoslovakia's sovereignty proved meaningless. Poland and Hungary quickly descended upon their weakened neighbor, with Poland grabbing the district of Teschen in early October and Hungary taking over a long slice of territory along Czechoslovakia's southern frontier in November. Hitler meanwhile directed his military chiefs on October 21, 1938, to prepare for the liquidation of the rest of Czechoslovakia, which occurred in March 1939. The exclusion of the Soviet Union from the discussions on the Sudetenland and the West's accommodation of Hitler on the matter gave pause to Stalin, who began to rethink his policies toward the West and Germany in the months thereafter. While the policy of appeasement preserved peace at a price in September 1938, war still came less than a year later.

The dismemberment of Czechoslovakia

Right after the Munich Agreement, on October 6, the rump state of Czechoslovakia was forced to grant autonomy to Slovakia, whose Slovak population had had a tense relationship with the Prague government since the country's founding in 1918. Jozef Tiso, a Slovak nationalist and Roman Catholic priest, became the prime minister of the Slovakian state, and the country officially adopted the hyphenated spelling of Czecho-Slovakia. In early 1939 Tiso, with German encouragement, tried to sever ties with the Prague regime, using a Slovak fascist militia for support. Deposed by the Czech government on the night of March 9–10, he flew to Berlin for help. Germany, using discontent in Slovakia as its excuse for action, sent troops into Czechoslovakia on March 15, established the Protectorate of Bohemia and Moravia in the west, and orchestrated the creation of an "independent" Slovak republic in the east. The Germans put Tiso in charge of Slovakia, which became the Third Reich's first satellite state. The British and French jumped on the domestic discord in Czechoslovakia to justify their refusal to take military action. French Foreign Minister Georges Bonnet, a leading advocate of appeasement, commented that "the renewed rift between the Czechs and Slovaks only shows that we nearly went to war last autumn to bolster up a state that was not viable."[5]

One week later, Hitler tore up another provision of the Versailles treaty, when he forced Lithuania to accept Germany's annexation of the German-populated Baltic port city of Memel. Hitler, who had secretly announced plans to annex Memel the preceding October, received an enthusiastic welcome from city residents on March 23, 1939. It turned out to be his last bloodless acquisition. Once again there was no opposition from the Western powers.

The Nazi liquidation of Czechoslovakia ended any illusion that Germany would limit its territorial acquisitions to German-speaking lands. The German occupation of Prague was undeniable proof that appeasement had dead-ended. Chamberlain, who initially reacted tepidly to Germany's invasion, did a complete about-face in a March 17 speech in Birmingham, when he stated that Hitler had broken promises and "taken the law into his own hands." Chamberlain asked: "Is this, in fact, a step in the direction of an attempt to dominate the world by force?" If so, he warned that Britain would respond "to the utmost of its power in resisting such a challenge if it ever were made."[6] Believing Poland to be Hitler's next victim, Britain and France on March 31 unilaterally guaranteed their full support for Poland's independence.

The Italian occupation of Albania

Tensions rose in the Balkans in April 1939, when Italy moved militarily against Albania. The Italian action caused little surprise, since Albania had already felt a strong Italian presence in its affairs for years. The invasion, for which the planning had begun shortly after Munich, involved 100,000 Italian troops and 600 planes that dropped bombs on several coastal towns. The Italians quickly defeated the troops of Albanian King Zog, who fled the country with his family. The Albanian Parliament then voted to unite with Italy and offered their crown to King Victor Emmanuel III. On April 15, 1939, Albania withdrew from the League of Nations. The Italian Empire in Europe was born.

The Danzig crisis

On October 24, 1938, German Foreign Minister Joachim von Ribbentrop, at a private three-hour lunch with the Polish ambassador in Berlin, stated that the Baltic port city of Danzig should revert back to Germany and that a highway and a double-tracked railroad enjoying extraterritorial rights should be built across the Polish Corridor. In return, Germany would guarantee Poland's frontiers and extend the time limit of the German–Polish friendship treaty. The reply of Polish Foreign Minister Józef Beck was negative, but the exchange of views did represent the start of a controversy over Danzig that developed into a major crisis in 1939. Danzig, a free city under the protection of the League of Nations with a German majority population, was a creation of the Treaty of Versailles. The Polish Corridor that surrounded the city and separated Germany's East Prussian province from the rest of the country so that Poland could have access to the sea also came from the Versailles settlement. In postwar Germany, these provisions were deeply resented and the focus of heated political debate led by German nationalists. After the Nazi Party gained control in 1933 of the Danzig Senate, the governing body of the city, the Poles saw the Senate increasingly restrict their statutory rights in Danzig and their minority rights in the Polish Corridor.

On March 24, 1939, Germany secretly made formal demands of Poland for the German annexation of the Free City of Danzig and the building of the road and rail links across the Polish Corridor. Beck kept the German demands secret since he did not want his country subjected to the kinds of Western pressures to compromise with the Reich that had led to the demise of Czechoslovakia. Even without this knowledge, the British and French saw Poland as Hitler's next victim and announced their guarantees of Poland's security on March 31. The German demands regarding Danzig and the Polish Corridor finally became public knowledge in early April.

Germany's occupation of Prague and Italy's annexation of Albania sparked other reactive moves by the Western democracies in the spring of 1939. The British in April introduced peacetime conscription for the first time in their history, and they launched a major rearmaments program. The French and British signed mutual assistance agreements with Greece and Romania on April 13. The Western powers also signed mutual aid declarations with Turkey, the British in May and the French in June, even though

Turkey had been a member of an Iraqi, Iranian, and Afghan Islamic Front against European imperialism since 1937. In May, the British secured open sea lanes to Africa and the Mediterranean through an agreement with the Portuguese, although Portugal was also on friendly terms with the fascist powers.

Hitler meanwhile took steps to firm up his own country's position in Europe in the spring of 1939. Under German influence, Hungary withdrew from the League of Nations in April, although it resisted the Nazis' pressure to sign the Anti-Comintern Pact until 1940. Fascist Spain signed the pact on April 7 and withdrew from the League, but refused to commit to war. On April 3, Hitler gave orders to his military High Command to begin preparations for an attack against Poland on September 1, 1939, and later that month he renounced Germany's 1934 friendship treaty with the Poles. The highlight of his spring moves was the Pact of Steel that Germany signed with Italy on May 22. A formal military alliance, the treaty committed both countries to close consultation on political and economic matters and mutual assistance in virtually any future war. Mussolini told Hitler that Italy would not be war-ready before 1942, but he signed the treaty anyhow, linking his fortunes ever more closely to Hitler's.

Soviet policy shift

On April 16, 1939, the Soviets, in an attempt to stop Hitler in East Central Europe, proposed that Britain and France join them in a tripartite treaty of mutual assistance that included a guarantee of assistance to East Central European states in case of aggression against them. But doubts existed in London and Paris about Russia's value as a partner, and there was as much fear among East Central European leaders of Stalin as of Hitler. The British and French began negotiations with the Soviet Union on the basis of the Russian proposal, but they did so with no great enthusiasm. Britain sent a low-level career officer to Moscow in June to lead a team of negotiators, a fact that offended the Soviets. In August, the British and French showed no sign of urgency as they transported their Anglo-French military missions to Russia for staff talks by slow boat instead of by plane. The military conversations quickly stalled over Poland's adamant refusal to allow Russian troops the right of passage across its territory to guarantee its western borders in case of war with Germany. The tripartite talks collapsed on August 17.

Meanwhile, Stalin showed a willingness, beginning in the spring of 1939, to deal with Germany. On March 10, 1939, in a speech to the Eighteenth Party Congress in Moscow, he was much harsher in his criticism of the Western Allies than of Germany. He accused the democratic powers of encouraging a Soviet–German conflict and warned that the Soviet Union would not "pull the chestnuts out of the fire for them."[7] The clearest indication of his new attitude came on May 3, 1939, when Stalin replaced Foreign Commissar Maxim Litvinov, who was Jewish, pro-Western, and pro-collective security, with Vyacheslav Molotov who was opposed to French and British imperialism. The change at the foreign ministry was not lost on the Germans, who applauded the decision. In July, the Russians initiated economic negotiations with Germany that culminated in a trade and credit treaty on August 19; the Soviets had insisted on making this agreement before moving to anything else.

By early August, Hitler was eager to reach a political deal with the Soviets, which led the Russians to conclude that an invasion of Poland was imminent. On August 14 Ribbentrop indicated in a telegram that he was ready to discuss with Molotov and Stalin the basis for "a final settlement of German–Russian relations." A flurry of diplomatic activity ensued, and on August 21, Germany publicly announced that Ribbentrop would shortly go to Moscow to conclude a nonaggression pact with the Russians.

The Molotov–Ribbentrop Pact

Ribbentrop led a German delegation that arrived in Moscow by plane on August 23, and signed the Nazi–Soviet Nonaggression Pact with Russian leaders the same evening. Also known as the Molotov–Ribbentrop Pact, the treaty assured both signatories of each other's complete neutrality should one of them be attacked by a third power. The pact also contained a secret protocol wherein Hitler and Stalin carved out spheres of influence between them in Eastern Europe. The secret protocol handed over Finland,

Figure 5.4 Soviet leader Joseph Stalin (left) and Nazi Foreign Minister Joachim von Ribbentrop shake hands following the signing of the Nazi–Soviet Nonaggression Pact in Moscow on August 23, 1939.

Estonia, Latvia, and Romania's Bessarabian province to the Soviets, while Lithuania was assigned to Germany; the two signatories divided Poland between them. In a modifying agreement signed on September 28, 1939, the Soviets gained Lithuania for their sphere in exchange for the cession to the Germans of some of their initially designated territory in central Poland. In addition to giving Stalin a buffer zone in case of a German attack, the secret protocol was the founding document of Soviet postwar domination in Eastern Europe. It basically reaffirmed the 1919 Curzon Line as Poland's eastern border. The secret protocol, which represented the fourth partition of Poland, was so politically embarrassing that the Soviets did not acknowledge its existence until the 1980s. What Stalin gained from Hitler – neutrality and the possibility of territorial expansion along Russia's western frontiers – appeared far more interesting to him in the summer of 1939 than the Western democracies' proposal of likely war against Germany in defense of Poland with no spoils. This fact made Stalin's decision in favor of Hitler easier to make. In the end, the deal was arguably the most cynical in the history of diplomacy.

Immediately following the August 23 signing, the Soviets and Germans began negotiations to boost their economic, military, and cultural cooperation. The nonaggression pact caused consternation in Europe and shattered any hope the French and the British had of winning Stalin over to their side; they blamed Poland for the failure of their negotiations. During the last week of August 1939, Hitler's demands for the reincorporation of Danzig into the Reich riveted the world's attention. Mussolini tried one last time to play mediator. The Germans and Italians met secretly in late August, but Mussolini was unsuccessful in getting a negotiated settlement. The last week also contained feverish appeals for peace from Roosevelt, Pope Pius XII, and other world leaders, but all were to no avail.

Undeclared war between Russia and Japan

At the same time Stalin was finalizing the terms of the Nazi–Soviet Nonaggression Pact with Germany, his military forces in the Far East were locked in a showdown battle with Japan. For years, tensions had simmered between Japanese and Soviet forces on the border of respective puppet states, namely, Russia's Mongolia and Japan's Manchukuo (Manchuria). A major undeclared war finally erupted in that region between Japan and Russia in the spring of 1939, and it climaxed in the Battle of Khalkhin-Gol (Nomonhan) that lasted from August 20 to August 30, 1939. The Japanese military defeat at Khalkhin-Gol was severe enough that Japan signed an armistice with the Soviets on September 15, which finally allowed Stalin to launch an attack against Poland two days later. Japan never again militarily challenged the Soviets during World War II. Indeed, the Japanese signed a neutrality pact with the Soviet Union on April 13, 1941, and held to it even after Japan's Axis partner Germany attacked the Soviet Union in June 1941.

Conclusion

In the last two years of peace, Hitler moved away from demanding revisions of what he called the "unfair" provisions of the Treaty of Versailles to expanding the Reich beyond its 1914 frontiers based on the principle of national self-determination to engaging in outright imperial conquest. Hitler fully exposed the Western European powers' weakness as he initiated one international crisis after another. The West's acquiescence only strengthened his ambitions and stiffened his resolve to take new risks, with war as his ultimate goal. Hitler discredited Chamberlain's policy of appeasement through Germany's actions against Austria, Czechoslovakia, and Poland. In the East, Stalin, looking at how best to protect the security of the Soviet Union, drifted toward Hitler in spite of profound ideological differences, and stunned the world by cynically signing the Nazi–Soviet Nonaggression Pact in August 1939. A German invasion of Poland came just days later.

Overall conclusion

The 1930s were diplomatically barren years for the Western European democracies whose leaders retreated from efforts aimed at European integration, failed to stop the internationally disruptive actions of Europe's major fascist dictatorships, and ultimately lost the support of the Soviet Union which pursued a policy of collective security for much of the decade. The European integration initiatives of the 1930s lacked widespread support, owing largely to the Great Depression. Meanwhile, the European powers' colonies, despite their growing importance, remained linked to their colonizers in a position of inferiority, as a periphery to the European core; a similar distribution of power and status could be seen in the relationship of Western Europe and its "periphery" of European powers in East Central Europe. In terms of the colonies, there was a definite technology transfer from the core to the periphery, destined both to strengthen the core and to provide it with a broad security belt against the increasingly global agendas of the Axis powers. In the end, the world order created in 1919 crumbled under the weight of the Axis powers whose aggressive designs were intended to transform not only Europe but the world, and whose actions were emboldened by the lack of reprisals from the international community. The final blows to the Versailles order came with Hitler's destructive moves against Czechoslovakia and Poland, both of which were creations of the postwar settlement. The Western leaders' weakness toward Hitler and ambivalence toward Stalin led to the latter's deep distrust of the West in 1939 and his willingness to reach an agreement with the German dictator. The result was the end of the Versailles dream of world peace.

Notes

1 William L. Shirer, *The Rise and Fall of the Third Reich: A History of Nazi Germany* (New York: Simon & Schuster, 1960), 293.
2 Joachim C. Fest, *Hitler* (New York: Vintage Books, 1975), 547–548.
3 Alfred Havighurst, *Twentieth-Century Britain*, 2nd edn (New York: Harper & Row, 1962), 273.
4 R. J. Q. Adams, *British Politics and Foreign Policy in the Age of Appeasement, 1935–1939* (Stanford, CA: Stanford University Press, 1993), 127.
5 Maurice Larkin, *France Since the Popular Front: Government and People, 1936–1996* (Oxford: Clarendon Press, 1997), 72.
6 Famous Speeches and Speech Topics, "Neville Chamberlain Speech – An Attempt to Dominate the World by Force," http://famous-speeches-and-speech-topics.info/famous-speeches/neville-chamberlain-speech-an-attempt-to-dominate-the-world-by-force.htm (accessed January 27, 2016).
7 Robert Conquest, *Stalin: Breaker of Nations* (New York: Viking, 1991), 220.

Suggestions for further reading

Callahan, Michael D. *A Sacred Trust: The League of Nations and Africa, 1929–1946*. Brighton, UK: Academic Press. 2004.

Chickering, Roger and Stig Förster. *The Shadows of Total War: Europe, East Asia, and the United States, 1919–1939*. New York: Cambridge University Press. 2003.

Cienciala, Anna M. *Poland and the Western Powers, 1938–1939*. London: Routledge. 1968.

Gatzke, Hans Wilhelm. *European Diplomacy Between Two Wars, 1919–1939*. Chicago, IL: Quadrangle Books. 1972.

Gooch, John. *Mussolini and His Generals: The Armed Forces and Fascist Foreign Policy, 1922–1940*. New York: Cambridge University Press. 2007.

Leane, Herbert S. *Hitler's Free City: A History of the Nazi Party in Danzig, 1923–1939*. Chicago, IL: University of Chicago Press. 1973.

Payne, Stanley G. *Civil War in Europe, 1905–1949*. New York: Cambridge University Press. 2011.

Ragsdale, Hugh. *The Soviets, the Munich Crisis, and the Coming of World War II*. New York: Cambridge University Press. 2004.

Wandycz, Piotr S. *The Twilight of French Eastern Alliances, 1926–1936: French-Czechoslovak-Polish Relations from Locarno to the Remilitarization of the Rhine*. Princeton, NJ: Princeton University Press. 1988.

Weinberg, Gerhard L. *Hitler's Foreign Policy, 1933–1939: The Road to World War II*. New York: Enigma Books. 2015.

6 Life as usual?

Introduction

The 1930s saw the limited optimism of the 1920s fade following the onset of the Great Depression and the subsequent collapse of the international financial order. As unemployment rose, misery followed, forcing governments to increase their proactive measures in the area of welfare. The priority of economic recovery became a dominant theme in politics and significantly altered political systems. Few democracies survived. The domestic scenes were further altered by the realities of continued tensions: persecutions in Germany, the Spanish Civil War, the continued plight of minorities in East Central Europe, and Stalin's ideological warfare against various groups of Soviet citizens continued to change demographic landscapes. These situations caused an almost continuous flow of refugees. In this decade of rising social tensions, social experiments became more timid, especially women's activism. As the economies of the authoritarian countries prepared to shift their industrial priorities to armaments production, the landscapes of cities changed: monumentalism took over architectural and urban design, while massive transportation projects prepared roads, railroad lines, and airports for war. In this decade of nationalistic "closing of the borders" climate and rhetoric, however, discrete transnational movements continued: international sports competitions, League of Nations conferences, and especially, involuntary migrations.

In measuring the extent of modernization in the 1930s, the following five factors will be examined: politics (democracy, human rights, liberal legislation, and political participation); demographic changes (refugees, resettlements, and migrations); economic progress (industrial modernization, agricultural reforms, and labor legislation); social policies (welfare, women's advancement, health, and consumerism); and urban development (urban planning and transportation).

Democracies challenged

Because of the Great Depression, the need to solve economic crises and alleviate social unrest increasingly dominated politics during the 1930s. This led to the polarization of politics and a series of vacillating governments that seemed paralyzed and reactive in their policies.

Uninspiring leadership in Great Britain

Britain in the 1930s experienced multiple domestic challenges, many stemming from the Great Depression. The country lacked inspirational leadership and creative ideas in a time of crisis. Governments appeared to react to events rather than take control of them.

Much of the decade was a time of drift and uncertainty. The Conservative Party was the dominant political force nationally for most of the 1930s, although the decade began with a coalition government that excluded it.

While the Labour Party emerged from the elections of May 1929 as the largest parliamentary party, it was still compelled, owing to its lack of an absolute majority, to form a coalition government with the Liberal Party. Labour Party leader Ramsay MacDonald returned as Britain's prime minister. When the Great Depression struck only four months into the government's term, Philip Snowden, the chancellor of the exchequer, quickly became the key man in the cabinet. Snowden lacked any formal economic training and believed that the government should adhere to the principles of thrift and integrity. His financial policy proved to be unbendingly orthodox. Identifying free trade with cheap food for workers, he was also a strong defender of that policy against the Tories' push for protectionism.

MacDonald and Snowden grappled with soaring unemployment as the depression deepened. When the Labour–Liberal government assumed office in June 1929, British unemployment stood at 1.2 million. By June 1930, it had risen to 1.6 million and by December of that year it stood at 2.5 million. The cabinet responded by expanding public works projects, providing unemployment assistance to ever more workers, and raising the income tax. But as the number of people who received unemployment benefits increased, tax monies diminished, with the result that the government faced a huge budget deficit in the summer of 1931. When a run on the pound sterling gained momentum in August, the government sought large loans in New York and Paris to firm up support for it. Hesitant foreign bankers insisted that the government cut unemployment benefits by 10 percent to obtain the needed money. MacDonald and Snowden accepted the benefit cuts to save the pound, but their decision caused a breakup of the Labour-dominated cabinet, since about half the government ministers refused to go along with them. In the end, their decision also failed to save the value of the pound.

When MacDonald informed King George V (r. 1910–1936) of the impending collapse of the Labour-led cabinet, the King met with the heads of the three major political parties, who agreed to form a coalition or National Government in which MacDonald would serve as prime minister and Conservative leader Stanley Baldwin as second in command. MacDonald's decision stunned Labour Party members, the bulk of whom abandoned him to form an angry government opposition. The National Government, created to assure the strength of the pound sterling, gained the credits it sought abroad. But currency speculation in the pound continued unabated, leading to Britain's abandonment of the gold standard on September 21, 1931. The dollar value of the pound soon dropped from $4.86 to $3.40 on currency exchange markets where it stabilized. The financial emergency had passed, but one of its victims was the Labour Party, which took years to regain its lost political strength.

Under pressure from the Conservative Party and eager to obtain legitimacy in the eyes of the electorate, the National Government announced a general election on October 27, 1931. The coalition partners proposed no specific program during the campaign. MacDonald went no further than to call on voters to give the new government "a doctor's mandate" to confront the crisis however it best saw fit. The election gave an overwhelming victory to the Conservatives, providing them with 472 seats out of the 615 seats available in the House of Commons. Their coalition partners obtained the second largest number at 81, while the opposition Labour Party's seats dropped to a mere 46. MacDonald remained prime minister, but he was nothing more than a figurehead. The driving forces in the cabinet were Baldwin and Neville Chamberlain of the Conservative Party.

Once the election was over, the Conservative-dominated National Government championed tariff reform to improve the British economy. Parliament in early 1932 passed the Import Duties Act that imposed a flat tariff rate of 10 percent on manufactured goods and agricultural products – the country's first peacetime tariffs since the 1840s. The government followed this up in the summer of 1932 by holding an Imperial Economic Conference in Ottawa, where it reached preferential trade agreements with the British Dominions. The political fallout in Britain from the preferential agreements was almost immediate: the Liberal ministers and Snowden, then serving as the Lord Privy Seal, resigned from the cabinet in protest against them.

As for the impact of the National Government's early economic measures, there was an initial boost to British trade when the devaluation of the pound made Britain's products cheaper on international markets. This advantage proved fleeting, as other countries, especially the United States in 1933, also abandoned the gold standard. The imperial preference agreements brought small gains to British trade, but in the end benefited the Dominions more than Britain. Overall, Britain's export trade improved slightly after 1932, though it remained well below pre-depression levels.

Baldwin replaced MacDonald as prime minister in June 1935, and remained in that post for two years. MacDonald had become increasingly ineffective as a leader, and even Baldwin commented on that fact in 1934: "He has reached the point where he is unable to make a decision about himself."[1] Baldwin continued the fiction of the National Government in the 1935 general election in which the Conservatives and their allies retained a solid parliamentary majority. In 1936, the prime minister faced a potential constitutional crisis when Edward VIII (r. 1936), who became king in January of that year, announced his intention to marry a twice-divorced American commoner named Wallis Warfield Simpson. The government disapproved of the marriage, as did the Anglican Church and most of the country. Baldwin told the King that he could either keep the crown or marry Simpson, but he could not have both. Constitutional tradition held that the King accept the Prime Minister's recommendation. Since Edward VIII did not wish to provoke a constitutional crisis, he abdicated in December 1936, went into exile, and married Simpson the following June. Edward was succeeded as king by his brother, George VI (r. 1936–1952). Although Baldwin's leadership was generally uninspiring, he demonstrated considerable skill in dealing with the abdication crisis and emerged from it with his prestige greatly enhanced. Baldwin left office in May 1937, still basking in the limelight of his recent political success.

Neville Chamberlain became Britain's new prime minister, a post he held until May 1940. He was the logical choice based on his abilities as a competent government administrator and his leadership position in the Conservative Party. He was industrious, methodical, and honest in his work, but he was also aloof in his relationships. He had few friends among his parliamentary colleagues. Although Chamberlain's previous government experience had been limited to domestic affairs, he concentrated on international matters as prime minister. He approached foreign policy with considerable self-confidence about his own ability to conduct diplomacy and with a certain disdain for the Foreign Office. Chamberlain's rude awakening about Hitler's intentions came when German soldiers occupied what remained of Czechoslovakia in March 1939. A dramatic shift in British foreign policy was the result.

By 1939, Britain had rebounded from the harshest effects of the depression. It had also survived the unimaginative leadership of its prime ministers. Britain's democratic political institutions remained firmly in place, with any opposition to the system coming largely from the small British Union of Fascists under Oswald Mosley and the tiny Communist Party of Great Britain.

France polarized

When Raymond Poincaré, who combined a long record of republicanism with conservative principles, stepped down as French premier in 1929, there was no conservative successor able to reassure an important segment of French voters that had deep suspicions regarding the authoritarian inclinations of the Right. Poincaré's immediate successor was the conservative André Tardieu, a brilliant but impatient and short-tempered politician who alienated many members of the Chamber of Deputies with his tactlessness. He served as premier on three separate occasions between 1929 and 1932, and even when not holding that office during those years, he dominated the government. He called for political reforms that would result in a workable two-party system and a strong, effective executive branch, but his political reforms went nowhere.

The years of Tardieu's ascendancy saw France slip from economic prosperity into depression. French governments, under conservative control, adopted deflationary policies to deal with the economic crisis. Their high tariffs and actions allowing small businesses to maintain high prices contributed to a drop in consumer demand. They also defended the value of the French franc while other countries were resorting to currency devaluations; this made French products less attractive on international markets. At the peak of the deflationary approach, Pierre Laval, the premier in the latter half of 1935 and early 1936, sharply cut government spending and the salaries of civil servants in an effort to balance the budget; he encouraged the private sector to follow his lead. He hoped to bring French prices down to world levels, but his policies instead slowed the economy even more.

In 1932, French voters expressed their frustration with conservative government policies by giving the left-leaning "Left Cartel" – an electoral alliance of the Radical and Socialist (SFIO) parties – a victory in the country's national elections. The Radical leader Edouard Herriot became French premier, but he proved no more capable of dealing effectively with the depression than his predecessors. He also faced a major political problem from the Socialists who, though agreeing to support the government, refused to participate in it directly as cabinet ministers; their stand hurt the Left, and it caused political instability and a gradual political shift towards the right. In the 20 months after Herriot assumed power, France had six different governments and no effective plan to combat the depression.

In the midst of the government's ineffectiveness in dealing with the crisis, extremist groups, particularly on the Far Right, tried to take advantage of the situation. One of these right-wing organizations was the Croix-de-Feu. Founded in 1927 as a veterans' movement, the Croix-de-Feu became a large conservative group known for its ultra-nationalism, anti-parliamentary themes, faintly fascist tendencies, and huge rallies. Another group, financially supported by Mussolini, was the Mouvement Franciste whose members wore their characteristic blue shirts during public outings and admired the ideas and regimes of Mussolini and Hitler. While the membership numbers in the right-wing organizations or leagues were generally not large, these groups had the potential of causing serious trouble if mobilized for a common action.

The spark that provoked a major right-wing outcry in early 1934 was a scandal involving a French embezzler named Alexandre Stavisky. He had a long history of illicit financial activities. He was first arrested in 1927, but his case had never gone to trial since he repeatedly succeeded in having the court date postponed through connections with well-placed individuals. In his last financial scheme, Stavisky worked through the municipal bank of Bayonne to sell large numbers of fraudulent bonds. By the time police sought his arrest in late December 1933, he had already gone into hiding, and when they finally cornered him in early January 1934, he apparently committed suicide. Rumors quickly spread that Stavisky had long received assistance and protection from high-ranking Radical Party politicians. Many on the Right openly questioned whether the police had not killed him on government orders to protect Radical Party officials from being compromised. The climax of the affair came on February 6, 1934, when an assortment of right-wing groups joined together in a huge demonstration against what they considered a corrupt system. The resulting protests were uncoordinated, with groups of demonstrators arriving at a meeting site near the Chamber of Deputies assembly building from several directions. In the ensuing violence the armed police repeatedly stopped them by using water hoses and bullets. By the time the bedlam ended well into the night, 15 people were dead and hundreds injured. The recently formed government of Radical Party leader Edouard Daladier resigned the next day, even though it still commanded a parliamentary majority. It was the first time in the history of the Third Republic that a government stepped down in response to turbulence on the streets. While people at the time believed that the goal of the demonstrators was to topple the regime, modern historians have largely debunked that idea by pointing out the divergence of interests of the groups involved and the general acceptance in France of the Gaston Doumergue government that succeeded Daladier's and that adhered to a moderate republican agenda.

Doumergue, a former president of the Republic, assembled a non-party national unity government that went from the Radicals on the left to representatives on the parliamentary right. Doumergue tried to correct perceived weaknesses in France's parliamentary system, focusing in particular on strengthening the power of the executive branch. He used radio addresses to go over the heads of the politicians and ask the people directly for their support of his constitutional reforms. Members of parliament attacked him for introducing an authoritarian method into French politics that violated the country's republican traditions and democratic spirit, and they found widespread support for their position. The Doumergue ministry resigned in the fall of 1934. The governments that followed were largely caretaker in nature, as political groups prepared for the 1936 elections.

The chief outcome from the events of February 6 was the galvanization of the Left into joint action to defend the republic against its enemies and establish a common social reform program for the 1936 elections. The Communists, under the influence of Moscow, gradually softened their longstanding hostility toward the SFIO, and by mid-1935 the two groups were closely aligned. Meanwhile, the Radical Party had begun collaborating with the other two leftist parties in what became known as the Popular Front. In January 1936, the Popular Front parties issued a common program that, while in no way threatening capitalism, included enough economic and social provisions to constitute a "new deal." In the May 1936 elections, the Popular Front parties won a sweeping victory. The SFIO, led by Léon Blum, emerged as the single largest party in the Chamber of Deputies, and the Communists gained an impressive 15 percent of the vote, making their party an important national political player for the first time. Breaking with the SFIO's previous policy of refusing to join governments following left-wing victories in national elections, the Socialists not only assented to join the cabinet, but Blum agreed to form it.

In the weeks between the Popular Front's electoral victory and Blum's takeover of the premiership, a wave of spontaneous worker strikes spread across the country. In greater Paris alone, close to 2 million workers were in control of industrial plants at the height of the strikes. The strikes resulted from longstanding labor grievances and the sense of empowerment that workers felt following the Popular Front's electoral victory. The strikers adopted a new strike technique: rather than staying away from their factories, workers occupied them to prevent plant owners from hiring replacements. Blum, worried over the direction the strikes might take, convened labor leaders and employers as soon as he took office in June and obtained the agreement of both sides to what were called the Matignon Accords. The arrangements provided workers with significant wage

Figure 6.1   French Premier Léon Blum makes a victory gesture at a Popular Front parade in Paris on July 14, 1936.

increases, the right to join labor unions without being fired, and collective bargaining rights. The broad gains these represented for labor brought the strikes to an end.

Blum's government quickly followed with legislative and ministerial actions to implement reforms. It enacted a 40-hour week and passed legislation that provided all workers with two-week paid vacations. In the area of the economy, Blum's ministry nationalized the French armaments industry and reformed the country's central bank, the Bank of France. It also created a Ministry of National Economy to coordinate and reinvigorate economic policy, although the well-entrenched Ministry of Finance and its political allies quickly reduced the new ministry to irrelevance.

In spite of its reform efforts, Blum's government failed to find ways to alleviate the country's ailing economy. To reassure conservatives, who were largely opposed to his measures, Blum initially refused to devalue the franc. This was despite the fact that French products had become increasingly uncompetitive in world markets after countries such as the United States and Great Britain had abandoned the gold standard in the early 1930s. The wage increases contained in the Matignon Accords enhanced the purchasing power of workers, but the implementation of the 40-hour week inhibited factories from manufacturing all the products that increased domestic demand required. This situation set off a round of inflation. There was also a significant flight of capital out of the country, and Blum imposed no currency controls to blunt it. These factors combined to force Blum to devalue the franc in September 1936, when France suspended its adherence to the gold standard. In the spring of 1937, Blum instituted a "pause" in his government's reform measures in an attempt to bolster confidence in the business community, but its main impact was to discourage supporters of the Popular Front; the Communists fretted about what they viewed as extreme moderation. There were also tensions within the coalition over how to handle the civil war in Spain: the Communists advocated the shipment of arms to the leftist republican government, while the Radicals, feeling that the Spanish regime was too left-wing, opposed military involvement. In the end, Blum adopted a policy of strict non-intervention in the Spanish conflict. Plagued by its economic failures and internal divisions, Blum's ministry fell in June 1937, when the Radical-controlled Senate rejected a request from the premier for decree powers to deal with financial matters. The Radical Party then took charge of the Popular Front government for several months and demonstrated irresoluteness domestically. The Popular Front itself effectively ended in the spring of 1938 when a second Blum government collapsed after less than a month in power.

Daladier replaced Blum as premier, and remained in that post until March 1940. He steered the country toward the center-right politically. It was the same pattern that had occurred following center-left victories in the elections of 1924 and 1932: the governments moved to the right after the election-supported left-wing ministries fell from power. Daladier began chipping away at the 40-hour week in August 1938 by granting exemptions to armaments manufacturers. The exemptions were widely extended to other industries, provoking a general strike at the end of November 1938. Daladier used the army and other forms of intimidation to shut down the strikers. Economic stimulus measures, combined with greater spending on weaponry and a healthier international economic climate, demonstrably increased France's industrial output in 1939, ending an eight-year economic downturn.

France on the eve of World War II was a deeply divided country. Many conservatives had become susceptible to authoritarianism. Embittered by the experience of the Popular Front, some even embraced the Far Right's slogan, "Better Hitler than Blum."

On the other extreme, many workers, disillusioned with failures of Blum's Popular Front government, turned to the Communists. Overall, there was a certain level of pessimism in the air as Frenchmen generally were disheartened by the duration of the economic slump, the parliamentary system's inefficiency, and increasing tensions internationally.

The Low Countries

The Great Depression took its toll on the Netherlands and Belgium as well. The Dutch and Belgian governments, facing an economic slowdown and soaring unemployment as the depression set in, adopted strict monetary policies and maintained their adherence to the gold standard. The governments cut spending and raised taxes to balance their budgets. This deflationary approach resulted in drops in the prices of consumer goods, cuts in workers' wages, and more unemployment. Signs of recovery did not appear until the latter 1930s, after both countries abandoned the gold standard.

As in many European countries, fascist movements enjoyed a certain level of popularity in the Netherlands and Belgium during the 1930s. In the Netherlands, a civil engineer named Anton Mussert joined with 11 other Dutchmen to create the Dutch National Socialist League in 1931. The League was anti-parliamentary, anti-Communist, authoritarian, and in favor of a national renewal; it took an openly anti-Semitic stance in 1936. The party garnered 300,000 votes or 8 percent of the total ballots cast in the 1935 elections for the country's upper parliamentary chamber (Provincial States), which made it the fifth largest party in the Netherlands. However, the parliamentary regime remained stable, and as the depression abated and concerns about Nazi Germany intensified, the movement's popularity diminished; it only managed to secure 4 percent of the vote in the parliamentary elections of 1937.

In Belgium, Léon Degrelle, a Walloon journalist, founded the Belgian fascist movement called Rex in 1930. The Rexists called for the end of democracy, the establishment of a corporatist authoritarian state, and a societal moral regeneration guided by Catholic teachings. Their anti-Marxist stand was captured in their slogan "Rex or Moscow." Originally working within the Belgian Catholic Party, the Rexists split from that group in 1935 to form their own political party. Capitalizing on depression-related discontent, the Rexists obtained 11.5 percent of the vote in the 1936 national elections and 21 seats in the Belgian Chamber of Representatives (lower house). Degrelle met Mussolini and Hitler that year, and both made financial contributions to his movement. Anti-Semitism was woven into the party's program. The Catholic Church condemned Rex in 1937, which resulted in a number of its members shifting their allegiance to more moderate Catholic parties. By the late 1930s, the movement was in decline, as demonstrated in the 1939 parliamentary elections, when it gained a mere 4 seats in the Chamber of Representatives. Nevertheless, the Rexist movement was illustrative of the deep dissatisfaction that existed toward parliamentary government in Western Europe during the 1930s.

Finland and Scandinavia

Across Finland and Scandinavia, general social and political stability emerged in the 1930s, when the main parties of the center-left and center-right joined in grand coalitions. In Finland, the mainstream political parties survived the threats of the 1920s that came from Communist-front parties and later from the Lapua Movement on the far right.

While right-wing extremism regrouped in the 1930s in a political party called the Patriotic Peoples Movement (IKL), the organization never had strong electoral support. Many Finnish leaders worked for national reconciliation in the 1930s, and one outcome was the formation in 1937 of a Red–Earth coalition government consisting of the leftist Social Democratic Party, the centrist Agrarian League, and the moderate National Progressive Party. The coalition benefited from the fact that the Finnish economy had pulled out of the depths of the depression and was experiencing industrial expansion and a strengthened agricultural sector. Moreover, most Finns by the late 1930s seemed to have put the bitterness of the 1918 civil war behind them and to have embraced the country's system of parliamentary democracy.

As for Sweden, a confluence of factors, including concerns about fascism, the Nazis' rise to power in Germany, and the Great Depression pushed Swedish politics toward compromise and cooperation in the 1930s. In 1931, Sweden abandoned the gold standard, a decision that made Swedish exports more competitive on international markets. Following the 1932 elections, a "Red–Green" coalition that the Social Democrats formed with the Farmers' Party finally established a stable majority in Sweden's parliament, and it lasted – with one brief interruption in 1936 – until the end of 1939. The key man in creating the coalition and holding it together was Per Albin Hansson, the leader of the Social Democrats, who served as prime minister almost continuously from 1932 to his death in 1946. To stimulate job growth, the government introduced a multitude of public works projects in which workers received market-rate wages. It launched numerous public housing projects to reduce shortages, and made housing loans available to large families. The government also improved unemployment benefits, guaranteed workers two weeks of paid vacation, implemented a form of national health insurance, and augmented old-age pensions. Income taxes were increased as one way of offsetting the costs involved. To protect farmers, the state provided price guarantees for key agricultural products, protection against grain imports, and improved access to agricultural loans. The authorities willingly accepted deficit spending, believing that the money spent to meet the country's economic emergency would be paid back once a recovery was achieved; Sweden's return to economic health was indeed rapid and its deficits were quickly erased. Sweden was the first country to recover fully from the depression, with unemployment dropping to a negligible level in 1937.

The depression struck Denmark in 1930, not long after the formation of a coalition government of the leftist Social Democratic Party and center-right Liberal Party. The government abandoned the gold standard in 1931, and economic recovery began shortly thereafter. The coalition partners concluded a grand bargain in 1933 in which the government provided subsidies to farmers to satisfy the wishes of the Liberal Party, and the Social Democrats gained the Liberals' support for expanded workers' rights and reforms that laid the foundations for a Danish welfare state. Unemployment dropped from a high of 10.9 percent of the total work force in 1932 to 7.4 percent by 1934 and to 6.7 percent in 1938.

In Norway, the socialist Labor Party dropped its revolutionary rhetoric in the early 1930s in favor of a reformist program. After winning its most parliamentary seats ever in the 1933 elections, albeit short of a majority, the Labor Party negotiated a "crisis accord" with the Farmers Party that resulted in a coalition government in 1935. This was quite a turn of events, as the Farmers Party had long been a bitter foe of any government concessions to the unemployed and to any form of agrarian trade unionism. According to the agreement, the Labor Party committed itself to making large financial expenditures for

Norway's distressed farmers. In return the Farmers Party agreed to support a legislative program that included public works projects to relieve unemployment and the beginning of an old-age pension system. The coalition remained in power until the Germans occupied Norway in 1940, whereupon the government fled to London.

Overall, democratic governments in Northern Europe steered clear of extremes, but they were also compelled to rely on coalitions to govern. The results were generally positive, as the governments in Finland and Scandinavia provided political stability and effective responses to the depression.

Turn to the Right in the new countries

In virtually all the East Central European countries created at the end of World War I, political polarization intensified in the 1930s, with right-wing authoritarian regimes becoming commonplace.

Austria, already handicapped during the 1920s by the losses of prewar provinces vital to its economic well-being and a heavy dependence on loans from the League of Nations to remain afloat fiscally, suffered two major economic setbacks in 1931. The first was the collapse of the country's largest bank, the Kreditanstalt in May, which triggered a worldwide financial panic. The second was the failure of Austria and Germany to gain international acceptance of a customs union they proposed in March – a devastating blow to any hopes that the Austrians had about their economy.

Politically, the country remained deeply divided in the early 1930s. Engelbert Dollfus, appointed chancellor of Austria in 1932, headed the anti-Marxist Christian Social Party that enjoyed the support of most Catholics outside of Vienna. The Austrian Parliament was essentially deadlocked, with neither the Christian Social Party nor the Social Democrats able to surpass 45 percent of the vote in national elections. Complicating the situation was the emergence of an Austrian Nazi Party that spread rapidly across the country. While the Austrian Nazis looked to Hitler for support, Dollfuss leaned on Mussolini. Dollfuss concluded that he could not govern within the country's constitutional system, so in early 1933 he suspended parliament and began to build an authoritarian, clerical-corporative state. One step involved the curtailment of the activities of political groups other than the Fatherland Front Party that Dollfuss had formed in May 1933 from a merger of the Christian Social Party and other right-wing groups. Another was the signing of a concordat with the Vatican that allowed the Catholic Church to exert considerable influence in public education. When the Social Democrats resisted his efforts in early 1934, Dollfuss used military force that included an artillery bombardment of a working class apartment complex in Vienna; the government's assault killed 193 civilians, although its own forces suffered 128 dead. Dollfuss outlawed the Social Democratic press and organizations in the aftermath of this event.

Dollfuss followed this up by promulgating a new Austrian constitution on May 1, in which he abolished the parliamentary system and replaced it with an authoritarian regime – often referred to as Austrofascism – that included a set of largely non-elective corporative councils. One threat to the regime was the Austrian Nazis who, after their party was banned in June 1933, went underground. They struck violently on July 25, 1934, when a group of them assassinated Dollfuss in his office and tried to set up a Nazi government. Mussolini immediately ordered Italian troops to the Brenner Pass along the Italo-Austrian frontier, and the Fatherland Front's paramilitary organization, the *Heimwehr*, restored order at home for Dollfuss' successor and fellow party member,

Kurt von Schuschnigg. Schuschnigg continued the authoritarian policies of Dollfuss at home and remained determined to keep Austria a separate state from Germany. But the nearly bankrupt Austria remained mired in economic depression, and the Austrian Nazi Party, supportive of *Anschluss* with Germany, gained in popularity. When Italy began to shift its foreign policy in favor of Hitler's Germany in 1936, Austria saw the key component in its efforts to protect itself from German domination slip away. The day of reckoning for Schuschnigg came in 1938. With the German state bearing down on Austria early that year, Schuschnigg, in an act of desperation, declared that a plebiscite on Austrian independence would be held on March 13. It never took place. Hitler sent German soldiers into Austria on March 12, where they received a generally jubilant welcome. Austrian independence ended with this German military action; Austria was annexed into Hitler's German Reich.

In Poland, Józef Piłsudski's quasi-dictatorship tightened its grip on power during the 1930s. When several parties of the Center and Left joined together in 1930 to demand Piłsudski's resignation, he responded by dissolving parliament and arresting a number of their leaders. He then tampered with the November 1930 parliamentary elections to assure himself of a submissive legislature. His government became increasingly dictatorial in the early 1930s, and in 1935 the country adopted a new constitution that created a presidential system of government. Piłsudski, having suffered from ill-health for several years, died shortly after the constitution was promulgated. His government was continued by his uncharismatic political associates, commonly referred to as "the colonels." They carried on a "dictatorship without a dictator," that included arresting political opponents and embracing anti-minority positions that Piłsudski had rejected. One of the leaders of the group was Colonel Józef Beck who served as foreign minister from 1932 to the outbreak of World War II.

Democracy also failed in Hungary and the Balkan states. The end result in all was the emergence of dictatorships. Democratic traditions were nonexistent in all of the countries, and none had a large middle-class base. Their economies rested heavily on agriculture, and that sector in each of them was marked by inefficiency and a lack of modern technology. Moreover, the increasing political atomization of East Central Europe under dictatorial governments, along with the general inability of these states to cooperate economically in any decisive way, made them more vulnerable to economic stress at home. The Great Depression also made them more willing to collaborate with Europe's fascist dictators abroad in the 1930s.

The economic misery that the Great Depression caused in Hungary emboldened the far-right-wing of the Party of National Unity to seek the ouster of conservative Prime Minister István Bethlen in 1932. It blamed him for the country's failure to obtain revisions in the Treaty of Trianon and bristled at his policy of Jewish toleration. As a result, Admiral Horthy, the Hungarian head of state, replaced Bethlen with Gyula Gömbös. Gömbös, who admired Mussolini, made the government more authoritarian but never realized his dream of creating a fascist state and becoming a Hungarian Duce. In 1934, Gömbös signed a trade pact with Germany that gave the Hungarians favorable prices for their wheat exports and stimulated the economy, but that also forced Hungary to purchase German industrial goods with the money earned. The treaty was instrumental in allowing Germany to secure a powerful grip on the Hungarian economy by 1938, and through it Hungary's fate became inextricably linked to that of Germany.

In January 1929, King Alexander I (r. 1921–1934) of Yugoslavia, using the previous summer's shooting of Croatian politicians in parliament as an excuse, launched a monarchical dictatorship in his country by suspending the constitution, proroguing parliament, and banning all political parties. He affirmed Serb political domination and dealt ruthlessly with opponents to his regime. He hoped to create a new kind of nationhood, but failed to obtain the backing he needed from the country's various ethnic groups, who remained wedded to their own identities. His assassination in Marseille, France, in 1934 by a Croat terrorist organization marked a turning point in Yugoslav foreign relations, as the new regency government thereafter drifted toward Mussolini and Hitler, and Yugoslavia became increasingly tied to Germany economically.

In Romania, Prince Carol, who had voluntarily renounced his claim to the throne in 1925 and gone abroad to live because of a marriage scandal, negotiated his return home in 1930. With government support, he immediately deposed his son as king and took the throne for himself. Carol II (r. 1930–1940) for several years played the center-right National Liberal Party and the mildly conservative National Peasants Party off against each other while he strengthened his own political position. The harshness of the depression and the emergence of a powerful fascist movement known as the Iron Guard added to the country's growing political crisis, as Romania averaged more than two governments a year. After the anti-Semitic Iron Guard obtained enough parliamentary representation in late 1937 elections to prevent the creation of a viable ministerial coalition, King Carol suspended the constitution and proclaimed a royal dictatorship. He instituted repressive measures against the Iron Guard, and when the group attempted to seize power in 1939, the King had hundreds of Iron Guard prisoners executed in revenge. His efforts, however, merely delayed a fascist takeover until 1940.

The grim realities of the depression brought social tensions back to the surface in Bulgaria following a 1931 national election that resulted in a moderate Popular Bloc government that included a reorganized Agrarian Party. A military-backed coup in 1934 set up a right-wing authoritarian regime that banned all political parties and introduced a corporatist economy modeled on that of Mussolini's Italy. King Boris III (r. 1918–1943), who saw his power eviscerated, deposed the military regime in 1935, and set up a government that he tightly controlled. Initially neutral in World War II, Bulgaria, with King Boris still dominant politically, joined the Axis forces in 1941, in part to regain territories it had lost at the end of World War I.

In Greece, a political shift to the right in the mid-1930s culminated in the dismantling of the Second Hellenic Republic in 1935 and the restoration of the monarchy under King George II (r. 1922–1924; 1935–1947). With the King's support, General Ioannis Metaxas set up a dictatorship in 1936 and adopted the fascist title of "leader." Indeed, Metaxas modeled much of his authoritarian system on that of Fascist Italy. He remained the dictator of Greece until his death in 1941.

During the 1930s in Albania, King Zog I (r. 1928–1939) continued to rule as a dictator. He dealt with numerous Italian attempts to dominate the country, and while he had some early success in resisting pressure from Italy, his country ultimately fell to its aggressive neighbor when Italy attacked Albania in the spring of 1939 and threw Zog out as ruler.

Conservative authoritarian regimes were also characteristic of the Baltic states during the 1930s. In Lithuania, President Antanas Smetona tightened his dictatorial grip over the country. He banned all political parties except his own Lithuanian Nationalist Union in the mid-1930s, and a new constitution that went into effect in 1938 widened his presidential powers. In Estonia, voters passed a referendum in 1933 that created a strong presidential system, but the election of an Estonian president did not take place.

In the midst of political violence during the presidential election campaign in early 1934, Konstantin Päts, Estonia's conservative prime minister, halted the campaign and began to rule by decree. In 1938, he introduced a new constitution, assumed the title of president, and consolidated his control over the country. In Latvia, where people also wanted a stronger executive branch, conservative Prime Minister Kārlis Ulmanis, claiming that a government takeover by right-wing extremists was imminent, staged a coup with the backing of key army officers in May 1934. In establishing authoritarian rule, he suspended parliament, banned all political parties, detained opposition political leaders, and imposed press censorship. Ulmanis's government exercised strict control over the agricultural and manufacturing sectors of the economy, nationalizing a number of industries along the way. The economic results of the government's heavy-handedness were positive, as the Latvians achieved a comfortable standard of living in the late 1930s, but their economic gains came with the loss of important freedoms.

Political stability in Czechoslovakia

In contrast to other countries in East Central Europe, Czechoslovakia's democratic institutions held up under the political and economic strains of the 1930s. The same five parties that had established a broad, durable coalition government in the early 1920s served as the foundation of all Czech governments between the 1929 parliamentary elections and the end of the First Czechoslovak Republic in October 1938. The two major issues that the coalition cabinets dealt with were the Depression and the country's minorities. During the winter of 1932–1933, one-third of the inhabitants in the province of Slovakia were without a steady income. The government did not react energetically until 1933, when it introduced a series of measures modestly reflective of Roosevelt's New Deal program in America to stimulate the economy. Recovery ensued, owing to the government's actions and to a general global recovery. An integral part of Czechoslovakia's economic improvement was a large increase in state spending on armaments because of the threat from Hitler's Germany.

The Czechoslovakian minorities problem intensified during the 1930s. Slovakian and Ruthenian autonomists pushed forward their demands for local self-rule with increasing determination in the late 1930s. Polish and Hungarian minorities did the same thing. Another trouble spot was the Sudetenland, where a large percentage of the people were ethnically German. Konrad Henlein, the head of the Nazi-influenced Sudeten German Party, led his party to a major success in the 1935 national elections as it emerged with the largest vote total nationally. While Henlein publicly spoke of Czech–German unity within the current political system, he privately maintained contact with Hitler, who provided Henlein's party with financial backing. In a meeting that Henlein had with Hitler in March 1938, the two men agreed that the Sudeten German Party would make demands on behalf of the German minority that were always greater than the Czechoslovakian government could meet. The Czech government conducted negotiations with the Sudeten German Party from April until September 1938, when Henlein ended them by fleeing to Germany. At that point the Sudeten crisis shifted to the international arena, where the outcome, decided at the Munich Conference of September 1938, was Germany's annexation of the Sudetenland. In early October 1938, a federalist Czecho-Slovak republic replaced the centralist First Czechoslovak Republic; the change represented a victory for the Slovak autonomists. The dismemberment of the interwar Czechoslovakian state continued in the ensuing weeks as the new Czecho-Slovak republic was forced to cede territory to Poland and Hungary. A climax came in March 1939, when Hitler ordered German troops into the Czech provinces and established the Protectorate of Moravia and Bohemia. Though the First Republic collapsed in 1938, it proved to be the longest-lasting and most effective democracy in interwar East Central Europe.

Conclusion

The gravity of the economic distress faced by European countries in the 1930s created challenges to the governments, dominated the elections, and dictated policy. It polarized politics by pitting the needs of the people against the imperatives of strong national economies. Maintaining social order became a priority for governments, forcing them to choose between an authoritarian and a socialist response to the crisis, creating see-sawed successions of governments. Across Europe, the impact of the Great Depression, greater urbanization, and modernization were the main causes of political polarization. The pull towards authoritarianism was greatest in East Central Europe where the minorities created potential unrest in an international climate that was becoming more uncertain. Democracy withstood the challenges of the depression in Western Europe, Scandinavia, and Czechoslovakia. One of the main developments of the decade was an increase in the power and responsibility of governments.

Two faces of totalitarianism

Two European countries experienced more dramatic changes than any other during the 1930s: Nazi Germany and the Soviet Union. In both, the rise of dictators – Adolf Hitler in Germany and Joseph Stalin in the Soviet Union – testified to the depth of the problems that the two countries faced. Both suffered defeat in World War I and were ostracized by the international community after the war. Both experienced revolutions immediately following World War I and subsequent fragile governments that failed to steer their countries satisfactorily through social, economic, and political change. Governments in both became paralyzed at the end of the 1920s, but for different reasons. When the Great Depression struck in Germany, the Weimar Republic wavered amidst political indecision on how to redress its finances and stem unemployment. By 1928, the Soviet Union, which later proved immune to the worst effects of the depression, confronted urgent economic choices due to the need to develop the industrial sector and to meet the needs of the bulk of its citizens. In these situations, the authoritarian cultures that Germany and Russia had experienced in their nineteenth-century monarchical systems provided fertile ground for drastic political solutions. It was therefore not surprising that extremist politicians, viewing themselves as the saviors of their countries, were able to take power. What they did was nothing short of full-fledged revolutions, complete with surveillance, terror, and agendas that contained plans for the social, economic, and cultural transformations of their states.

The rise of Adolf Hitler

Born in a small Austrian town in 1889, Adolf Hitler became a morose, aloof individual who never finished high school. In his late teens, he moved to Vienna where he hoped to pursue a career as an artist, but he was refused entrance to the architectural school at the

Academy of Fine Arts there. Once he had depleted a small inheritance from his family, he survived through odd jobs and the sale of postcards and posters that he painted, and developed a strident form of racism and anti-Semitism. In 1913 he moved to Munich, Germany, where he eked out an existence through the sale of watercolor paintings. By now a German nationalist, Hitler volunteered for the German army when war erupted in 1914. He served courageously on the military front, working as a runner between the front lines and the rear. Twice wounded, he attained the rank of corporal and received the prestigious Iron Cross First Class for bravery, an honor seldom granted to ordinary soldiers.

After the war, Hitler returned to Munich where he soon became a member of a fledgling right-wing political organization known as the German Workers' Party. Using his special oratorical skills, he caught people's attention as he railed against the Versailles treaty, the Weimar Republic, Communists, and Jews. On February 24, 1920, he announced a 25-point party program that was both nationalistic in its demands for an anti-immigration policy and a Greater Germany based on self-determination and socialistic in its calls for an expansion of old-age benefits, the right to a job, and profit sharing; it also contained a strong dose of anti-Semitism. He used the same occasion to change the party's name to National Socialist German Workers' Party (NSDAP), which became commonly known as the Nazi Party. Not long thereafter, he emerged as the party's absolute master. To provide him with protection, he set up a paramilitary organization – distinguished by the brown shirts that its members wore – known as the *Sturmabteilung* (Storm Troopers) or SA. The SA eventually expanded its role to include disrupting the political activities of other parties. Finally, the party purchased a newspaper called the *Völkischer Beobachter*; it formed a part of the party's official public look. In the chaotic months of 1923, the number of people who joined the party rose dramatically, reaching 20,000 members.

Hitler attempted a coup, known as the "Beer Hall Putsch," against the regional government in Munich on November 8–9, 1923. Hitler and members of the SA descended on a Munich beer hall where right-wing nationalists and Bavarian separatists were meeting. After firing a revolver shot into the ceiling, he jumped on a chair and screamed: "The national revolution has begun."[2] The next day, Hitler marched into the city with General Erich Ludendorff at his side. The marchers soon ran into a cordon of state police, which dispersed the crowds, killed 16 of the demonstrators, and sent Hitler fleeing the scene, only to be captured later. Ludendorff was arrested, tried, and acquitted. Hitler was found guilty of treason and received a five-year prison sentence, although he was released after just a few months of incarceration. While the Putsch failed owing to poor planning and miscalculations, the episode brought national attention to the Nazis for the first time. Hitler took full advantage of the trial to disseminate his ideas, scoring a propaganda victory.

While in prison, Hitler wrote his seminal work *Mein Kampf* in which he denounced the Treaty of Versailles, argued for a superior Aryan race that included the German people, spewed out hatred for the Communists, and denounced the Jews. It was also then that he decided his party would have to play by the electoral rules of the Weimar system to obtain power. During his imprisonment, he commented to a friend:

> When I resume work, it will be necessary to pursue a new policy. Instead of working to achieve power by an armed coup, we shall have to hold our noses and enter the Reichstag against the Catholic and Marxist deputies. If outvoting them takes longer than outshooting them, at least the result will be guaranteed by their own constitution. Any lawful process is slow … Sooner or later we shall have a majority – and after that, Germany.[3]

Freed from prison at the end of 1924, Hitler aggressively moved to rebuild his party. With a membership base of 27,000 in 1925, the party grew to 178,000 dues-paying members in 1929. At the electoral level, Hitler constructed a several-tiered organizational system that enabled his party to reach people in even the most distant parts of the land. He reconstituted the paramilitary wing of the party, the SA, with its membership attaining 70,000 in 1930. At that point, Ernst Röhm assumed control of the SA; he strengthened its effectiveness and increased its numbers to 400,000 by 1932. Hitler also resumed publication in 1925 of the newspaper *Völkischer Beobachter* that government officials had shut down after the Beer Hall Putsch. As the official mouthpiece of the Nazi party, its circulation rose to more than 120,000 in 1931. The revived Nazi Party's first electoral test came in the Reichstag elections of 1928, but the results the party obtained were unimpressive. The Nazis received a mere 2.8 percent of the popular vote and just 12 Reichstag seats out of a total of 491.

The Great Depression changed the Nazi party's fortunes and left the government scrambling for answers. The Grand Coalition government, in power since the 1928 elections, broke up in March 1930 because of a cabinet dispute over the country's unemployment insurance program. Heinrich Brüning, an authoritarian-minded member of the Catholic Center Party, became the new chancellor and kept that post until May 1932. Lacking a majority in the Reichstag, Brüning leaned on Hindenburg to govern by presidential emergency decree. Considered an expert on financial and economic matters, the chancellor pursued a deflationary policy to deal with the Depression. Brüning increased taxes, curtailed government spending, reduced salaries, cut unemployment insurance, and imposed high tariffs on foreign products. But his economic policies proved ineffective and the depression intensified. In 1931, all German banks were forced to close amidst a panic, and the number of unemployed citizens rose to 6 million in 1932. Fears of Communism among industrialists and landowners remained strong. Disorders broke out in many cities where the police and army confronted angry mobs.

These conditions favored a right-wing salvationist party, and for many Germans the Nazi Party seemed to be just that. The Nazis promised jobs for the unemployed, prosperity for ruined businessmen, a restoration of law and order, protection from Communism, a tearing up of the Versailles treaty, a powerful Germany, and harsh policies toward the Jews. In national elections held in September 1930, the Nazi Party's number of Reichstag representatives jumped to 107 (out of a total of 577 seats), as it garnered more than 18 percent of the national vote. Suddenly the Nazis had the second largest party in the Reichstag, exceeded only by the Social Democrats.

The Nazis had three national election opportunities in 1932 to obtain decisive political power. A presidential election in the spring pitted Hitler against the now 84-year-old Hindenburg. Although Hitler conducted a vigorous, modern-style campaign and Hindenburg did very little, the latter was re-elected in an April runoff with 53 percent of the vote to the Nazi leader's 36.8 percent. The outcome was a big disappointment to Hitler. Shortly after the election, Hindenburg appointed Franz von Papen to replace Brüning as chancellor. Papen, who had anti-democratic views and virtually no support in the Reichstag, quickly called for new parliamentary elections that he unrealistically hoped would give him a majority in the Reichstag. The election campaign, marred by numerous violent clashes between the Nazi SA and the Communists' paramilitary force, produced a major Nazi victory in the July 31 elections; they gained 37.3 percent of the vote and became the single largest party in the Reichstag with 230 representatives out of 608 total. The newly constituted Reichstag, set to pass a vote of no confidence, compelled Papen to dissolve it before that happened and to order new parliamentary elections for November. The elections kept the Nazi Party as the largest group in the Reichstag, but the Nazis received 2 million fewer votes than in July, their voting percentage dropped to 33.1 percent and their Reichstag representation fell to 196 out of 584 total seats. With the party also deeply in debt from the almost nonstop campaigning in 1932, Nazi leaders wondered if their moment for securing power in Germany had passed.

With the government deadlocked, Papen recommended using the president's decree power to set up an authoritarian regime that would eventually have a new constitution approved through a plebiscite or by a national assembly at its base. Kurt von Schleicher, the defense minister and a close political advisor to Hindenburg, warned that such a step would trigger a civil war. Alarmed at this news, Hindenburg dismissed Papen as chancellor and appointed Schleicher to the position at the beginning of December. An outraged Papen intrigued with Hitler and others against Schleicher, who was forced to resign as chancellor on January 28, 1933. Papen then played a decisive role in convincing Hindenburg to appoint Hitler as chancellor of a right-wing coalition government in which Papen would be vice-chancellor. Assured that the Nazis would be kept in line by their coalition partners, Hindenburg appointed Hitler chancellor of Germany on January 30, 1933.

Because he lacked a majority in the Reichstag, Hitler immediately announced a general election for March 5. The campaign was conducted in an atmosphere of fear and violence as the Nazis sent out members of the SA to disrupt opposition party rallies, harass leaders of other political parties, and vandalize trade union and left-wing party offices. The well-oiled Nazi propaganda machine used the radio to carry the voices of Nazi leaders to people throughout Germany, staged torchlight parades and mass rallies, and saturated the country with Nazi posters on billboards. A turning point in the campaign occurred a week before the election when, on February 27, the Reichstag building went up in flames. A mentally disabled Dutch Communist named Marinus van der Lubbe, acting on his own, was responsible for causing the blaze, but Hitler expanded the blame to include the Communists collectively. Indeed, the Nazis whipped up a "red scare" by contending that a Communist revolt was looming. He used the incident to obtain a presidential decree on February 28 that suspended individual civil rights and empowered the government to take whatever steps necessary to counter "Communist acts of violence."[4] The Nazis, who controlled the interior ministries of both the national and Prussian state governments, followed this up by shutting down opposition presses, preventing leftist political meetings, and making mass arrests. In spite of all their terror tactics and frenzied propaganda efforts, the Nazis came up short of a clear majority in the March elections, as they gained 43.9 percent of the total votes cast and 288 seats out of 647 seats in the Reichstag. Combined with the 8 percent vote total and 52 seats that the Nazi-allied right-wing German Nationalist Party received, however, Hitler now had a bare parliamentary majority to support his government.

The last key step in Hitler's quest for dictatorial powers over Germany was passage of an Enabling Act in the Reichstag. On March 23, 1933, he asked that body for a law that would free him from observing constitutional requirements and grant him complete legislative and budgetary authority for four years. A browbeaten Reichstag passed the bill overwhelmingly the same day, as storm troopers shouted outside the building "We want the Bill – or fire and murder."[5] Hitler was now the source of all laws, free from any parliamentary or constitutional control; the Reichstag had unconditionally surrendered its powers.

Gleichschaltung

The new government immediately began to consolidate its power through a policy known as *Gleichschaltung*, which meant the forcible coordination or taming of all independent institutions or organizations in the country. The regime in March and April of 1933 scrapped the longstanding rights of Germany's separate states and replaced their governments with Reich Commissioners who wielded wide powers and reported directly to Hitler. The process of stripping the states of their powers was completed in January 1934, when a law abolished the states' popular assemblies and centralized all authority in Hitler's government. In June 1933, the Nazi regime outlawed the Social Democratic Party, and shortly thereafter, other major parties agreed to disband. On July 14, 1933, a new law declared the NSDAP to be Germany's only legal political party; any attempts to form other political entities would result in prison sentences for those involved. To replace trade unions, the Nazis created a party-controlled Labor Front, whose purpose was to keep labor in a weakened position and subject to unceasing anti-Marxist indoctrination. The German civil service, judiciary, and universities were purged of undesirable elements under a law that Hitler declared on April 7, 1933. Opponents to the regime began to disappear after midnight visits from the regime's secret police, known as the Gestapo. Reinhard Heydrich, its director, created peoples' courts and opened the first permanent concentration camps for dissidents.

Hitler also took steps to undermine the influence of the church in Germany. Even though he signed a concordat with the Vatican in July 1933 guaranteeing Catholics in Germany religious freedom, Hitler quickly began to violate its provisions by attacking German Catholic church leaders and organizations. Hitler dealt with Protestantism by supporting the merger of the country's 28 regional Protestant church units into a single Protestant Reich Church that adhered to a doctrine compatible with Nazi principles. He also maneuvered to secure the church's leadership post for Ludwig Müller, a Protestant theologian and Nazi party member who became the Reich bishop in 1933. Many Protestant pastors rose in opposition to the state-endorsed church in 1934 to form a Confessing Church that Lutheran pastor and theologian Martin Niemöller founded and helped lead until his imprisonment in a Nazi concentration camp in 1938.

Gleichschaltung extended to the German media. The Reich Press Law of October 4, 1933, forced Jewish newspaper editors out of the profession, and required remaining editors to pass a Nazi citizenship test and demonstrate that their spouses were not Jews. The law placed newspaper editors under the control of the Joseph Goebbels' propaganda ministry, which imposed harsh censorship conditions upon their publications. The Nazi government early on established a monopoly over the radio medium that served as a propaganda weapon for the party. Goebbels, keenly aware of how important the radio was for mass communication, came up with the idea of making cheap radios readily available to all German citizens. In addition, Goebbels' ministry oversaw all areas of the German film industry.

Pageantry and grandiose displays of power were other propaganda tools that the Nazi Party used to impress and indoctrinate the German people. The party held rallies every September in Nuremberg, for example. Each rally had a theme that stressed the progress made by the German nation towards greatness. The 1935 theme was "the Rally of Freedom" that highlighted Germany's reintroduction of compulsory military service earlier that year – a clear denunciation of the Treaty of Versailles; the rally also served as a platform for the promulgation of the 1935 Nuremberg Laws against German Jews.

These rallies used symbols of the German Teutonic past to enhance the solemnity of the occasion, and were among the first mass displays of the power of ideology and propaganda. Hitler commissioned Leni Riefenstahl, a highly gifted movie director, to produce a documentary of the 1934 Nuremberg rally; her work, titled *Triumph of the Will*, is

Figure 6.2 Nazi paramilitary organizations take part in a mass ceremony at the Nazi Party's 1935 Nuremberg Rally that had the theme of "The Rally of Freedom."

generally considered one of the greatest propaganda films of all time. As in Italy and the Soviet Union, parades, loudspeakers, flags, and newsreels were used in Germany to bring the new ideology to people's every day attention and to create a sense of awe and pride.

Another important aspect of the Nazis' *Gleichschaltung* policy was the education of Germany's youth. The government dismissed Jewish teachers and faculty known to be hostile to Nazism. It introduced rewritten textbooks that taught blind obedience to the party, racism, antisemitism, national pride, and adoration of Hitler. A Nazi Teachers' League encompassed 97 percent of the country's teachers by 1937. Hitler considered the teaching profession to be one of the most politically reliable groups in the country. Beyond the schoolroom, the Nazis had a Hitler Youth organization for boys, whose main purposes were to integrate them into the party's national structure and to prepare them for military service. By late 1936, when the government banned all other youth groups, membership topped 5 million. For young women, the Nazis had a League of German Girls that used summer camps, sports activities, parades, holiday trips, and after-school meetings to indoctrinate them in National Socialist beliefs and train them for motherhood.

Hitler took another important step toward complete control over the country in June 1934, when he purged his own party of disgruntled members in what was called the Night of the Long Knives. Longtime members of the party's left wing were dismayed that Hitler had abandoned the socialist elements in the party program and adopted conservative policies that favored big business and old elites following passage of the Enabling Act in March 1933. Among the most outspoken in his criticism was SA Commander Röhm, a party radical who envisioned the replacement of the old army with a revolutionary force that he believed his SA of almost 4 million men represented. Military leaders, wary of Röhm's intentions, joined with conniving party members to spur Hitler into action. On June 30, Hitler carried out a purge that included the murders of Röhm, other discontented members of the party's old guard, former anti-Nazi political rivals, and many of Röhm's SA associates. It is estimated that more than 1,000 people were killed in the purge. So successful was Hitler in presenting his actions in a positive light that an ailing Hindenburg congratulated him for restoring order. As for the SA, Hitler did not disband it, but he significantly reduced its size and placed it under SS control.

To complete his drive toward absolute power in Germany, Hitler needed to subordinate the army to his will. He made a major move toward that end in August 1934. When Hindenburg died on August 2, Hitler immediately announced that he was combining the offices of President and Chancellor in his person and taking the title of Führer (leader) as the German head of state. At the same time, he became commander-in-chief of the armed forces, which enabled him to exact an oath of loyalty to his person from all officers and soldiers. The erosion of the army's independence was well on its way. Hitler completed the task in early 1938 when he dismissed two of the army's top generals and overhauled the military command structure. Hitler created a Supreme Command of the Armed Forces (OKW) over which he presided and to which all the armed forces were subordinated. Members of the army High Command now had to present their ideas to Hitler's own military staff for approval. Although members of the old General Staff were aghast, they nevertheless acquiesced. Hitler's control of Germany was now absolute. Within a few years, the Nazis had turned Germany into a massive, highly disciplined machine. Its internal foes had been liquidated or silenced. Its mesmerized masses, roaring their approval in giant demonstrations, were ready to follow the Führer wherever he might lead them. "Today Germany, tomorrow the world"[6] was a menacing Nazi slogan. The outbreak of World War II would only confirm the aggressive nature of the Nazi ideology.

Stalin's revolution

In Russia, Stalin spent the years after Lenin's death in 1924 consolidating his political power. By the late 1920s, he had defeated the party's left wing led by Trotsky who, following his expulsion from the party in 1927, went into exile; a Soviet agent murdered him in Mexico in 1940. Two other key leftist party leaders, Lev Kamenev and Grigory Zinoviev, also bore the brunt of Stalin's wrath. Like Trotsky, they were expelled from the party in 1927, but unlike him, they were readmitted the following year, after being forced to recant their views. All three had argued that socialism would prevail only when it had achieved victory through world revolution (see p. 136).

With the Left defeated, Stalin was more determined than ever to establish his personal rule firmly over the party and state, and lead a revolution from above. Starting a slow abandonment of Bukharin's gradualist economic approach in the fall of 1928, he shelved the New Economic Policy and embraced a centrally planned economy by introducing a Five-Year Plan that involved the collectivization of agriculture and rapid buildup of the Soviet Union's basic industries (see pp. 224–226). The first and second Five-Year Plans proved pivotal to Stalin's accrual of power, since they allowed him to tighten his control over the countryside and gain support among the Soviet Union's growing working class. In late 1929, Stalin openly denounced the Right, and Bukharin was stripped of his leadership posts in the Communist Party. Simultaneously, he ordered a dramatic change in the first Five-Year Plan from limited to all-out collectivization. Stalin had now outmaneuvered the leaders of both the party's Left and Right opposition in his drive for complete political control.

Stalin's actions of 1928–1929 marked the beginning of a second revolution characterized by violent transformations that exceeded the excesses of 1917. The revolution was deep and permanent, and created the bases and structure of Soviet society until 1991. It created a post-revolutionary dictatorship, a common sequel of many revolutions. In fact, it was almost a counterrevolution that used society's post-revolutionary fatigue to impose the dictatorship of the Communist Party and establish a brutal, centralized, militarized state that used the *nomenklatura*, i.e., a list of acceptable candidates to political office, to control local and regional party nominations and governmental appointments. There was no "dictatorship of the proletariat" as prophesied, but an absolute dictatorship of Stalin and the Communist Party that he dominated.

The Great Purge

Another phase in Stalin's amassing of power began in the mid-1930s, when he turned against the party elite in a ferocious reign of terror. The event that prepared the way for new violence was the December 1934 murder of Sergei Kirov, the flamboyant Leningrad party chief. Stalin more than likely ordered the murder of Kirov, although the factual evidence on Stalin's involvement remains inconclusive. Kirov had criticized Stalin in 1934 by advocating for a more flexible approach to the peasantry in the implementation of the dictator's Five-Year Plans and a suspension of the regime's wanton brutality. Kirov was also a rising star in the party and therefore a potentially troublesome political rival to Stalin.

Stalin used Kirov's murder as a pretext to launch his broad campaign of attacks against those who opposed him. He immediately issued a decree instituting accelerated procedures in the adjudication of cases involving political terrorism. While party leaders conducted an initial round of arrests, executions, and deportations in Leningrad, the Soviet secret police – the NKVD – laid the groundwork for the Great Purge that Stalin unleashed in 1936. High government officials, bank directors, and former Trotskyite supporters were charged with sabotage, conspiracy to assassinate Soviet leaders, and plotting with foreign governments. Most of the Old Bolshevik leaders – members of the party prior to the Russian revolution of 1917 – and those suspected of backing them were among the targeted. These included the former leftist opposition heads Kamenev and Zinoviev whom the government accused of plotting the murder of Kirov and conspiring against Stalin. The two men, subjected to behind-the-scenes psychological torture, caved in to the charges at their 1936 show trial and were duly executed. The turn of the rightist Old Bolshevik leader Bukharin came in 1938 in the last and most spectacular of the regime's show trials, the Trial of the Twenty-One. Bukharin was accused of outlandish crimes, of even plotting to kill Lenin in 1918 and after. The 21 defendants were found guilty on all counts, and Bukharin was among the 18 who were immediately executed.

Stalin expanded the purges to the Soviet officer corps in 1937. In May, Marshal Mikhail Tukhachevsky, a brilliant Red Army officer during the Russian Civil War who did much to modernize the Soviet army in the 1920s and 1930s, was among eight senior commanders arrested on charges of treason, found guilty in a closed-door trial, and immediately shot. This action marked the start of the military purge that resulted in the deaths of three of the army's five marshals, 14 of its 16 generals, and all eight of the navy's full admirals. In the end, more than half of all uniformed service officers were either imprisoned or killed in 1937–1938.

The purges were over by late 1938. As many as 8 million purge victims ended up in the hard labor camps of the Gulag (see pp. 228–229). Another million people were sent to prisons, and several hundred thousand were executed. All the Old Bolshevik leaders were gone as were many Stalinist party leaders. The purges had also spilled into the general population, where denunciations of ordinary citizens occurred, and the state compelled workers and peasants to admit to preposterous crimes. While the purges completed Stalin's drive to totalitarian control over the Soviet Union, they weakened the country economically and militarily. The elimination of a large number of engineers, for example, came at a time when their technical skills were desperately needed. Just when Hitler was conducting a massive military buildup in Germany, Stalin rendered the Soviet armed forces more vulnerable through his decimation of the officer corps.

The reasons why Stalin institutionalized terror may never be totally understood. The precedent of Lenin's mass execution of 10,000 people in retaliation for an assassination attempt on his life in 1918, Stalin's own belief in ruling by force, Communist ideology, and the dream of surpassing the United States' power all motivated Stalin to target his own citizens ruthlessly.

Stalin's Constitution of 1936

In late 1936, Stalin, claiming that the Five-Year Plans had reduced Soviet society to "two friendly classes, workers and peasants," obtained passage of the Stalin Constitution to reflect this new stage of socialism.[7] Individual civil rights and liberties were guaranteed, including freedom of speech, religion, assembly, press, and demonstrations, just as in Western constitutions. But these rights were protected only when they furthered the interests of the working people and strengthened the socialist system. This qualifier enabled the state to decide for itself whether or not an activity was legal. As a result, the state regularly trampled on its citizens' civil rights. Citizens also enjoyed guarantees of collective rights, such as the right to education, employment, and support in old age and illness.

Article 126 recognized the Communist Party and stated that the party "is the vanguard of the working people in their struggle to strengthen and develop the socialist system and is the leading core of all organizations of the working people, both public and state."[8] The document confirmed the primacy of the Communist Party in the Soviet Union; other parties were not permitted. Thus, while the constitution guaranteed unrestricted universal suffrage, elections were uncontested since ballots contained only one party-selected candidate for each office. The party was an elite group comprising just 4 percent of the country's people; it was an entity where the number of bureaucrats and intellectuals was greater than that of ordinary workers. Its massive bureaucracy, terrorized by the Great Purge, subserviently did the bidding of Stalin who had also developed a cult of personality that portrayed him as the all-knowing, almighty ruler of the Soviet Union. By the late 1930s Stalin's authority had reached unprecedented levels, and his centralized state was arguably the most powerful ever devised. Ironically, in getting there, the Soviet regime adopted practices similar to the fascist governments it so roundly denounced on a regular basis.

Conclusion

The totalitarian regimes of the 1930s in the Soviet Union and Germany introduced progress through mass controls backed by one-party states anchored in strong ideologies. Both Stalin and Hitler developed a sense of patriotic pride, and to achieve it, imposed totalitarianism through terror. Stalinism and Nazism also demonstrated a number of other similarities. For Stalin and Hitler, action was subordinate to ideology; ideology was to be tailored to the lowest intelligence level of the masses. Both regimes, through their constitutions, gave themselves a way to govern arbitrarily and to override the rule of democracy and political compromise. Emergency decrees in Germany, and a new constitution and penal code in the Soviet Union silenced dissent and imposed terror. Both regimes aimed to aggrandize the public realm at the expense of the private realm and to extinguish individual conscience. Sometimes they emulated each other or borrowed from Mussolini's Fascism. Moscow was seduced by the revolutionary, socialist tones of Italian Fascism and early Nazism that opposed bourgeois capitalist regimes. Hitler learned much about totalitarian control from Mussolini and the Bolsheviks. These aspects transcended the clear differences between both regimes, namely the fact that Nazism was an extreme-right ideology, while Communism, which was the official ideology of Stalinism, was on the extreme Left.

Demographic transitions

It is important to recognize that labor market issues and ethnic persecutions were present during the 1930s, creating constant migration and refugee problems. As these increased in the late 1930s, large-scale rescue operations were organized. By 1939, the demographic stability of European populations was compromised, and borders were porous. The resulting tensions among states was a significant factor prior to the outbreak of the Second World War – just as it had been a factor prior to the outbreak of World War I.

Labor migrations

The demographic trends at work in Europe put economic pressures on jobs and land in population-rich and population-deprived countries alike. In the 1920s, a combination of state controls on immigration – led by the United States with its Immigration Acts of 1921 and 1924 to limit migrants from Eastern and Southern Europe – and unsettled economic conditions in countries such as Germany, which had runaway inflation in 1923–1924, restricted the migration of European workers. An exception to this trend was France which adopted a liberal policy toward immigrants to compensate for a serious labor shortage that heavy manpower losses in World War I and a chronically low birthrate caused. French employers actively recruited Polish immigrants after the war. Polish miners went to work in the coal mines of northern France and the potash mines of Alsace, and they helped rebuild war-torn industries and towns; there were 287,000 Polish immigrant workers in France in 1931. There was also a large influx of Italian workers into France in the 1920s until Benito Mussolini energetically discouraged emigration late in the decade. Almost half a million Algerians, virtually all men, entered France during the 1920s, where they were often hired for military construction projects and the worst jobs in large companies. Their rate of repatriation was quite high, since their families often sent them only for brief stays; slightly more than 98,000 remained in 1931. There were some 1.4 million immigrant workers in France by 1931 and 2.7 million immigrants in all – the highest totals for both categories in Europe. Immigrants represented 6.6 percent of France's population at the time, and immigration comprised 75 percent of the country's population growth in the 1920s. France changed course on immigration in the 1930s, however, owing to the depression and a wave of xenophobia. The French government passed a quota law in 1932, introduced new alien worker regulations, and oversaw repatriation campaigns. As a result, the number of foreigners who left France in the years 1931–1936 far outstripped those who entered – 541,000 departed while 360,000 entered. Nevertheless, France still had a core immigrant population of 2.2 million people.

Another important phenomenon during the interwar years was rural migration. Civil wars and land redistribution schemes chased many East Central European peasants from their ancestral farms. In the West, numerous farmers left the countryside for the cities, swelling the ranks of new urban dwellers. An even more significant development in the Soviet Union was the explosive shift of people from the countryside to urban areas. Russian cities made a net gain of almost 12 million inhabitants between 1928 and 1932, the years of Stalin's first Five-Year Plan which emphasized the development of heavy industry. Large numbers of peasants moved to newly created industrial cities like Magnitogorsk in the southern Urals, and settled on the outskirts of established cities like Moscow, thus contributing to the ruralization of Soviet cities. Indeed, Moscow's 1939 population of 4.5 million – including its suburbs – contained some 2 million recently added peasants.

The plight of minorities

Ethnic tensions intensified in the 1930s. The unresolved issues of the 1920s were now compounded by the effects of the Great Depression that made jobs and resources scarce and caused European nations to shut out the outside world. Another turning point came in 1934 when Polish Foreign Minister Józef Beck renounced the Little Treaty of

Versailles that his country had signed with the League of Nations in 1919 guaranteeing the rights of all minorities in Poland (see pp. 36–37). Beck argued that Polish minorities in Germany and the Soviet Union had no protection, and that Germany used the treaty to interfere in the internal affairs of Poland. The Polish decision sounded the death knell for minority treaties in Europe, since other East Central European countries that had signed similar agreements with the League after the Great War no longer felt any compulsion to abide by their provisions. In fact, they had never liked the treaties, having ratified them only as a condition of Allied diplomatic recognition.

On the other hand, the Polish government's relations with its minorities generally improved under Marshal Piłsudski's leadership (1926–1935), although in 1930 the regime carried out a harsh pacification operation in its border regions of eastern Galicia following numerous acts of sabotage by Ukrainian nationalists living there. Poland's Ukrainian minority, comprising 15 percent of the country's population, experienced an upsurge in discrimination following Piłsudski's death in 1935: Polish military colonists were planted in Ukrainian-inhabited areas along the eastern frontier, the region's education system was increasingly Polonized, and large numbers of Orthodox churches were either destroyed or turned over to the Roman Catholic Church.

In Czechoslovakia, ethnic unrest escalated during the 1930s when unemployment soared in the heavily industrialized Sudetenland, which had a predominately German population. Frustrated over their economic condition and convinced of Czech government discrimination, a large majority of Sudetenland Germans threw their support behind the pro-Nazi Sudeten German Party whose leader, Konrad Henlein, demanded complete autonomy for the Sudetenland in April 1938.

In the Soviet Union during the 1930s, Stalin shifted from a nationalities policy that accepted ethno-federalism and ethnic diversity from the level of the Soviet republics to small villages, to one that curtailed ethnic autonomy and encouraged Russification. Stalin kept large ethnic regions geographically intact, but the regime accused ethnic minority leaders of promoting nationalism, and they became victims of the Great Purge. Stalin also deported members of ethnic minorities for military reasons, using them to "colonize" the remote borders of the Soviet Union. From 1935 to 1937, 130,000 Poles from Ukraine and Belorussia were deported to Kazakhstan, which contained 40 percent of all Soviet-purged minorities in the 1930s.

Polish, German, and Soviet anti-Semitism

Jews were one of the important minority groups in Europe during the interwar years, with a total continental population of about 9.5 million in 1933. The European country with the largest Jewish population in that year was Poland which had approximately 3 million. The Soviet Union, with more than 2.5 million Jews in its European area, had the second largest Jewish community on the continent. Germany's 525,000 Jews were the largest Jewish group in a Central European country; they represented 0.75 percent of Germany's total population. In Poland and Germany, where the Great Depression inflicted considerable economic pain on people's lives, anti-Semitic violence increased during the 1930s. Many citizens in these two countries, believing that Jews controlled their nation's banking and commerce systems, blamed them for precipitating the depression, profiting from defaulted farms, and damaging their national economic life.

Anti-Semitism worsened in Poland after the death of Piłsudski in 1935. At the governmental level, Foreign Minister Beck talked in 1937 about the need to reduce dramatically Poland's Jewish population and envisaged the emigration of 80,000 to 100,000 per year over the ensuing 30 years. He inquired about leasing a large area of land in Madagascar, but the French government, which controlled the island, rejected the idea. The Polish Catholic Church's chief cleric, meanwhile, arguing that Jews were opponents of Christianity and agents of immorality, defended boycotts of Jewish businesses, and many parish priests supported such actions at the local level. There were also a number of pogroms that took place in cities and towns across the country in 1935–1937.

The Nazi regime in Germany, where many Jews were members of the middle class and socially assimilated, first introduced important actions against the Jews in April 1933. New laws barred Jews from the country's civil service and limited how many Jewish students could enroll in schools and universities. On April 1, the government ordered a national boycott of Jewish stores and professionals, such as lawyers and physicians. The boycott failed to gain traction, however, as many Germans continued to shop at Jewish establishments; Hitler halted it after one day. Nevertheless, the boycott represented the beginning of a general Nazi campaign against the Jewish community as a whole. Other laws followed that slowly isolated the Jews from the country's general population.

A major turning point in the alienation of the Jews came with the 1935 Nuremberg Laws that deprived Jews of German citizenship and forbade Jews from marrying "Aryan" Germans or having extramarital relations with them. A supplementary decree of November 1935 defined a Jew as a person who had three or four grandparents who were of the Jewish religious faith regardless of whether that person viewed himself/herself as a Jew or not. With a definition of "Jews" in place, it became much easier to rob, bully, assault, expel, and one day murder them. Germany's legal and social forms of discrimination were extended to Austria following the *Anschluss* of March 1938, and were symbolized by the humiliation of prominent Viennese Jews forced to clean sidewalks in Vienna with nail brushes right after Hitler's forces took control.

Another decisive anti-Jewish episode took place in Hitler's Reich in the fall of 1938, after a teenage Polish-Jewish refugee in France named Herschel Grynszpan, enraged over the Nazis' expulsion of his parents from Germany, assassinated a German embassy official in Paris on November 7. Propaganda Minister Goebbels used the incident to unleash an anti-Jewish assault that the Nazis called *Kristallnacht*, or Night of Broken Glass. Led by Nazi militants, the pogrom took place on the night of November 9–10. Rioters across Germany and recently annexed Austria smashed the windows of thousands of Jewish-owned businesses, desecrated Jewish cemeteries, vandalized Jewish homes, burned numerous synagogues, and murdered close to 100 Jews. The Nazi authorities also arrested close to 30,000 Jewish men and sent them to concentration camps; it was the first time that Jews in Nazi Germany were imprisoned solely because of their ethnicity. Immediately blaming the Jews for the pogrom, the Nazi regime levied a heavy fine on the German Jewish community and forced the Jews alone to assume all the costs of damages done to their properties. The government followed with laws intended to take away the Jews' property and ability to earn a living. The Jews soon found themselves economically ghettoized and almost completely removed from German public life. *Kristallnacht* caused a surge in Jewish emigration from the Reich. When deciding to leave, Jews had to find a country willing to accept them, sell off their possessions for next to nothing, and pay exorbitant emigration fees to the German government. Over 77,000 Jews fled Germany and Austria in 1939.

In the Soviet Union, Stalin undertook discriminatory moves against Soviet Jews only starting in 1939, when he was seeking a diplomatic agreement with Hitler. In May, he replaced his Jewish foreign minister Maxim Litvinov with Vyacheslav Molotov who, at Stalin's behest, quickly purged the foreign ministry of all Jews. These actions became part of a larger trend to reduce the number of Jews in top positions of power in the state bureaucracy.

Refugees

If the emigrant situation of the 1920s reflected the impact of the Great War, the emigrants of the 1930s were largely the result of domestic repression, regime change, and war. From the mid-1930s, these trends accelerated and placed new strains on the resources of the League of Nations member states around the world. In the Saar, 7,000 residents migrated to France after a 1935 plebiscite returned the territory to Germany. That paled, however, in comparison with the stream of refugees who fled the Spanish Civil War and anti-Semitic persecution in Germany.

The Spanish Civil War was brutal. Blind hatred, senseless executions and counter-executions that decimated entire towns, civilian hostage-taking, and many more horrors from the first battles on caused large numbers of refugees to move into France. A first wave of 15,000 people streamed across the frontier in the fall of 1936. The Spanish flow into France in 1937 reached tens of thousands following a series of rebel offensives. French public opinion, anxious about the economic depression and increasingly xenophobic, was unenthusiastic about the arrival of so many Spanish republicans. The French government in 1937 adopted restrictive policies in dealing with the refugees, owing to their large numbers and the financial and logistical burdens that their presence placed on the French state and the towns obliged to accept them.

A climax to the Spanish refugee problem came in early 1939, when some 275,000 Spanish civilians and republican soldiers headed to France as the Republican war effort in Catalonia (northeastern Spain) unraveled. The French government initially refused the refugees entry, suggesting instead that a neutral zone be established along the French frontier to accommodate the displaced people. Since such an idea was unworkable, the French finally opened their borders to the refuge seekers and placed them in makeshift internment camps, where conditions were appallingly inadequate. One witness stated that at his arrival at the camp in Saint-Cyprien:

> There were no lodgings to house us, and we had to sleep on the sand ... There, those who were over the age of 55 died, because they were unable to bear the unhappiness, the ups and downs, the storms, the cold ... Each day we buried a number of them in the cemetery which was located facing the camp."[9]

Over the next several months the conditions at the camps slowly improved, due in part to the creation of new camps that had wooden buildings. By May 1940, a large percentage of Spanish Civil War refugees had returned to Spain (340,000 out of a wartime total of 465,000) by one means or another.

Rescue

Refugee work under the guidance of the League of Nations, begun in 1921 with the creation of the High Commission for Refugees, continued in the 1930s. The key development was the League's establishment in 1933, following Hitler's assumption of power in Germany, of a high commissioner for refugees coming from Germany, a post that remained in place until 1939. In creating the office, however, the League, fearful of offending the German delegation, limited the commissioner's power and resources. The financing of its efforts was almost completely dependent on private organizations and individuals. The commission's first leader was James McDonald, an American who had advocated for such a body for several months. McDonald experienced numerous frustrations while in office. One issue that the commission's supporters expected him to resolve was the transfer of Jewish property from Germany when Jews moved abroad, but the Germans contended that the issue was an internal affair and refused to negotiate with him. McDonald also encountered resistance, apathy, and indecision in the international community when seeking help in resettling German Jews. Nevertheless, he managed to oversee the resettlement of approximately 60,000 refugees, 27,000 of whom went to Palestine, before resigning in late 1935. The High Commission was reorganized twice thereafter, first in 1936 and again in 1938, and while it continued to provide legal, financial, and material assistance to Jews leaving Germany, the atmosphere in which it worked became more difficult as countries adopted increasingly discriminatory practices toward refugees.

One last prewar effort to find a workable solution to the Jewish emigration question occurred when Roosevelt, reacting to Germany's occupation of Austria in March 1938, called for an international conference to deal with the German/Austrian Jewish refugee problem. The conference, with delegates from 32 countries, met in the French spa town of Evian-les-bains in July 1938 to discuss ways to alleviate the plight of Jews facing Nazi persecution. Country after country gave excuses for not easing their restrictions on immigration. The U.S. representative announced that his country would maintain its current annual quotas for German and Austrian immigrants which to then had remained unfilled, although he added that the United States would move to fill the quotas completely in the future; filled quotas happened in 1939, although that was the only year it did. Britain cited high unemployment at home to justify its refusal to admit more refugees, and it made sure that Palestine, where it had recently tightened Jewish immigration, was not on the conference agenda. Poland and Romania, neither of which had official representation at Evian, took advantage of the conference to issue a demand that other countries open their borders to Polish and Romanian Jews, but the proposition never gained a hearing. The Evian conference did establish an Intergovernmental Committee on Refugees to facilitate the emigration of German/Austrian Jewish refugees, but the committee received little support from its member states and had virtually no success in securing the opening of borders to Jewish refugees. The international conference's failure to obtain more generous immigration policies for Jews among its participating countries – an exception being the Dominican Republic – led Hitler to conclude that the international community was largely indifferent to the plight of Europe's Jews and would not interfere with his anti-Semitic policies. His anti-Jewish policies heightened thereafter, as demonstrated by the *Kristallnacht* pogrom in Germany just four months later.

Efforts to save children received special attention. In 1936, the number of young Spanish refugees became so great that the French established a Committee to Aid the Children of Spain to provide over 5,000 foster homes and set up 20 "children's homes"; in 1937, the French accepted 37,000 Spanish children. With private organizations and the Quakers providing help as well, between 4,000 and 5,000 children were sent to Britain and the Soviet Union. An equal number of needy children remained in Spain, where Franco opened shelters for them. Appeals for the rescue of Jewish children began as early as 1933 and intensified during the last months of peace. The Netherlands took in a number of refugee children wandering in the woods on the German border. Britain stepped up for German and Austrian children, and began the *Kindertransport* program in October 1938 by which as many as 10,000 German Jewish children were brought into the care of British families. Even before the start of World War II, a significant exodus of children had begun.

Conclusion

Voluntary and involuntary migrations affected millions of individuals across Europe and created large displacements of individuals and communities. In the latter 1930s, however, involuntary migrations began to outnumber voluntary ones. This created a significant host fatigue by 1938, and a blurring of national borders. Human rights violations were on the rise, and European countries offered only limited help to support some semblance of normality of life for refugees in their countries.

Economic transformations

The Great Depression deeply transformed economic and labor policies in Europe. Economic recovery and prosperity depended heavily on industrial revival and modernization. This meant a restructuring of the national labor force and a greater involvement of the state in managing the economy.

The Great Depression

The Great Depression was an economic catastrophe unprecedented in size and scope. It began in the United States in October 1929, when prices on the New York stock exchange plummeted. Stock market prices had doubled between the start of 1928 and the early fall of 1929, with many stock purchasers doing so "on margin." This meant that buyers put very little money down for their stock purchases and borrowed the rest from their stockbrokers. When stock prices broke, many margin buyers, financially hard-pressed, began selling their stocks to pay off debts. In the ensuing panic, numerous speculators and investors were financially ruined in a matter of days or weeks. The crisis on the New York exchange proved extremely contagious; stock markets across the globe soon went into downward spirals, provoking a major drop in industrial production. Goods produced worldwide decreased by some 38 percent from 1929 to 1933, and unemployment rates reached historically unseen levels in many countries in the early 1930s. The Great Depression did not touch all countries equally or at the same time, and some recovered from the downturn more rapidly than others, but compared to previous crises, that which began in 1929 was particularly long and severe.

The crash quickly demonstrated just how closely tied the economic health of Europe was to that of the United States. During the 1920s, American financiers had lent large sums of money to European countries. With the onset of the depression, American lenders began calling in their short-term loans to meet debt obligations at home. An especially affected area was Central Europe where U.S. financiers rapidly withdrew their money. Finally, Austria's largest bank, the Kreditanstalt, went bankrupt in May 1931, triggering a financial panic in Central Europe. Germany saw a run on its banks, and several of them closed. The deteriorating situation forced the German government in July 1931 to declare a bank holiday and impose restrictive foreign exchange measures to prevent the flow of capital out of the country. Speculators and desperate bankers then turned their attention to London where the world's biggest open gold market still operated. They exchanged sizable amounts of pounds sterling for gold, causing a reduction in Britain's gold reserves to perilously low levels. The value of the pound quickly depreciated, forcing Britain to abandon the gold standard in September 1931. By the end of the year, the pound sterling was worth 30 percent less than when it was linked to gold. A number of European countries quickly followed Britain's lead in going off the gold standard; one notable exception was France, which remained wedded to gold until 1936.

Economic recovery

To alleviate the effects of the Great Depression, countries across the world steered toward economic nationalism in the early 1930s, i.e., toward greater government control over domestic economies and increased national self-sufficiency. Many nations raised their tariffs and imposed quotas – quantitative limits for imported goods – to keep out competing products from other nations. Even Great Britain, long a proponent of free trade, adopted protectionism in 1932 with its Import Duties Act. A number of governments at the outset of the depression also adopted deflationary policies, meaning that, as incomes and taxes fell, they reduced their spending and lived within their means. In the end, most countries shifted to inflationary measures to spur economic growth, such as large public works programs and prolonged unemployment benefits.

The depression bottomed out in Britain at the beginning of 1933, after which slow, steady economic growth occurred. Unemployment crested at slightly less than 3 million people, and then slowly dropped until January 1937, when it stood at 1.7 million, a figure that changed little until 1939. It was the domestic market that propelled the economy forward in the 1930s, with modest assistance from unimaginative and timorous government leaders. In the agricultural sector, the government introduced subsidies and import quotas for designated products, and established marketing boards to fix prices for certain commodities. To assist traditional industries, it granted a 50 percent tariff to steel producers, for example, and gave large subsidies to the shipbuilding industry. Officials also provided benign support to these same industries, when their members moved toward cartelization by agreeing to production quotas to keep up prices and amalgamations to eliminate inefficient firms. The single most important industry in Britain's revival was housing, where the country experienced a boom due mostly to private financing. The British auto industry also thrived and briefly became the second largest globally in the latter 1930s. Only in 1939, however, when Britain launched a large-scale rearmament effort, did the country's recovery become sustained. A combination of strong private initiative, modest government support, and an upward move in the business cycle had done the job.

The French appeared largely immune from the depression at the end of the 1920s. Their industry was well protected by high tariffs and their manufacturers exuded a new confidence in the aftermath of the recently stabilized franc. Many French leaders believed that their economy, which included a significant agrarian sector, contained the kind of balance between industry and agriculture to protect it from serious economic turbulence. But by 1931, France was in an economic downturn that, while never as harsh as in the most severely hit countries, lingered on until late 1938. Premier André Tardieu in 1931 introduced a "Plan for National Retooling" that was intended to modernize France's economic infrastructure but that ended up being much more of a counterweight to unemployment than a renovation tool. The more modernized segment of the economy generally fared worse during the 1930s than the static sector which often had protection through cartel arrangements or a monopoly. Government intervention, which was slow to occur and haphazardly applied, began in 1933 when various privately owned French airlines were compelled to join together in a single entity called Air France, with the state as a minority shareholder. Another state orchestrated merger involved the creation of a single French railway system from the country's five main private lines at the outset of 1938; known as the SNCF, it was a mixed company where the state held 51 percent ownership. Real economic recovery only started in 1939, after the government implemented a large rearmament program, stimulated investment in new factories, established increased production targets, and relaxed enforcement of the 40-hour week.

Spain, like other Western countries, was hit hard by the Great Depression. Its economy stagnated, exports fell, and unemployment rose. These difficulties were made dramatically worse by the Spanish Civil War, and when the conflict ended in 1939, Spain was a ravaged country. Its infrastructure was badly damaged and inflation skyrocketed. Entire blocks in cities were in ruins, factories destroyed, fields uncultivated, and large numbers of livestock dead. The war contributed significantly to the dramatically reduced productive capacities of both industry and agriculture that existed in 1939. Indeed, Spain was to remain in a state of harsh economic depression for another decade.

Sweden successfully attacked economic, social, and political problems in its response to the depression, not by resorting to compulsory measures or systemic change, but by building consensus among broad segments of the population – farmers, workers, and the business community. Key political parties joined together in broad-based coalition governments to introduce compromise measures that they defended as promoting the common good. These included: tax and debt relief for farmers who responded with increased production; the willingness of workers to limit strikes in order to obtain wage stabilization; and a tax increase on the wealthy in exchange for promises of social peace. The government also devalued the currency to boost exports and used public works programs to maintain consumer spending and bring economic modernization. As a result, Sweden, after experiencing initial hardship from the depression, saw its productivity rise considerably as the 1930s progressed.

Nazi economics

Nazi Germany emerged from the Great Depression with a speed that amazed the world. Unemployment dropped from 6 million in 1932 to below 1 million in 1936, winning Hitler solid popular support. In the early years, Hjalmar Schacht, who served as minister of economics from 1934 to 1937, used clever financial maneuvers to help fund Hitler's economic programs. To reduce unemployment, the Nazis launched extensive public works projects, such as the construction of German freeways, resorted to deficit spending, imposed price controls to prevent inflation, and introduced tax incentives for industry. But the most important component in Germany's rapid recovery was the government's aggressive rearmament program that Hitler announced publicly in early 1935. In just a few years, the Nazi revolution turned Germany into a huge, disciplined war machine.

In 1936, Hitler launched a Four-Year Plan whose goals were German autarky and preparedness for war. Hitler put the plan under the control of Air Force Chief Hermann Göring, who enjoyed broad powers in overseeing its implementation. The plan involved central planning, restricted foreign trade, production targets for key industries, raw material allocations, and the development of synthetic materials, an area where German chemical engineers had considerable expertise. Germany's munitions plants continued to engage in full-scale production as Hitler readied the country for war. Schacht meanwhile, in contrast to positions he had held earlier, called for an expansion of Germany's foreign trade and a reduction in armaments spending; he was forced to resign from his ministerial post in 1937. Among the big gainers from the Nazi economic miracle were large business concerns such as I.G. Farben Chemicals and the arms manufacturer Krupp. On the eve of World War II, Germany had full employment, the largest aluminum production in the world, and steel output that lagged only behind the United States. Private consumption continued to rise, along with armaments production. While Hitler might have called for individual sacrifice with the onset of hostilities, he refused to do so, lest he suffer a decline in his popularity.

The Soviet Five-Year Plans

In 1928, Stalin, in a major economic policy reversal, adopted the Left's program of rapid industrialization supported by a collectivization of agriculture. It came in the form of the country's first Five-Year Plan (1928–1933), which brought Lenin's New Economic Policy to an abrupt halt. Stalin wanted "socialism in one country" as quickly as possible, and for him a strong industrial base was the decisive factor in achieving it. The center-piece in the program was a rapid expansion of the Soviet Union's heavy industries by means of production quotas. Collectivization would put all agricultural resources in the hands of the state through the creation of large, state-run collective farms. The regime could then exploit the collectives by saddling them with painfully high grain output quotas for state purchase at artificially low prices, thereby allowing the government to secure the capital needed to finance industrial modernization. Stalin's economic plan, with its concomitant transformation of Russian society, represented a virtual revolution based on state centralized planning and control.

Agricultural production in 1927 had once again reached prewar levels, but many peasants were withholding grain from the market because of the government's refusal to raise prices. In addition, poor weather conditions in 1928 dramatically reduced the grain harvest that year. As a result, the state found it difficult to feed the cities and obtain financing for industrial projects. To help fill the void, the government resorted to grain requisitioning which met with resistance in rural areas.

Stalin's Five-Year Plan, officially approved by the party in April 1929, foresaw the collectivization of up to 20 percent of peasant households by 1933. The plan seemed to assure the primacy of private farming. Once Stalin had defeated his rightist colleagues, he threw caution to the wind and in late 1929 adopted a policy of immediate, full-scale forced collectivization. The number of peasant households collectivized skyrocketed from 15 percent in December 1929 to some 60 percent by the end of February 1930. Peasants resisted collectivization in massive numbers by slaughtering their livestock and refusing to turn over their harvests to the government. The regime responded with force and intimidation. In some instances, military units surrounded villages and bombarded them into surrender. There were large-scale deportations to forced-labor camps and thousands of executions. Chief among Stalin's targets were the well-to-do peasants – the kulaks – whose liquidation he sanctioned in late December 1929:

> Now we are able to carry on a determined offensive against the kulaks, eliminate them as a class ... Should kulaks be permitted to join collective farms? Of course not, for they are sworn enemies of the collective farm movement.[10]

Figure 6.3 Captured kulaks engage in hard labor in a Soviet gulag, i.e., a prison camp, in 1930. The kulak class, consisting of well-to-do peasants, was targeted for liquidation in Stalin's first Five-Year Plan.

The regime ultimately deported as many as 5 million kulak family members to work prison colonies and camps, and the kulaks as a class disappeared.

In March 1930, with Soviet agriculture facing disaster, Stalin, in an article titled "Dizzy with Success," temporarily suspended the collectivization program and blamed overly eager local officials for any excesses. Large numbers of peasants celebrated the decision and returned to their own farms. But once the 1930 harvest was in hand, the collectivization process resumed, triggering renewed violence between angry peasants and an overpowering government. By the end of Stalin's second Five-Year Plan (1933–1937), more than 90 percent of peasant households, representing 99 percent of the country's cultivable land, belonged to collectives. Economically, collectivization integrated the agricultural sector with the rest of the Soviet economy, but it did so at a heavy price: meat production, for example, only regained 1928 levels in the 1950s, and agriculture either stagnated or weakened in many regions during the latter 1930s. Politically, it was a victory for Stalin, for it established his totalitarian control over the Russian peasantry.

One of the most tragic events tied to Russia's agricultural collectivization was a huge man-made famine that struck the grain-producing regions of the Soviet Union in 1932–1933. The famine in Ukraine was especially severe; known as the *Holodomor*, it caused the deaths of 4 to 5 million Ukrainians, broke the Ukrainian peasantry as a political force, and decimated Ukrainian culture. Another 1.5 million people starved to death in Kazakhstan. The Soviet regime hid the event from foreigners and severely restricted domestic travel to the affected regions. When foreigners finally did ask questions, Russian officials denied that a famine had ever taken place. It was one of the most disturbing examples of the price Stalin was willing to pay to achieve the goals of his Five-Year Plans.

The centerpiece of Stalin's first two Five-Year Plans was the swift industrialization of the country, with a focus on heavy industry. It was also another way to consolidate his power on the road to totalitarianism. Stalin ordered significant increases in the production of coal, iron, steel, electricity, machine tools, and transport. The government sold surplus grain on international markets to fund equipment purchases and technical expertise from abroad. To jumpstart Russia's auto industry, for example, the government signed an agreement with the Ford Motor Company to obtain technical assistance in the construction of the Gorky Automobile Works in the city of Nizhny Novgorod; the plant produced its first 100,000 vehicles between 1932 and 1936. Showpieces of Russia's industrial modernization included Magnitogorsk which mushroomed from a small village to a burgeoning metallurgical city of 250,000 people, and the Dnieper Dam, which was Europe's largest hydroelectric power station until the 1950s. The plans resulted in some striking production increases in the targeted areas, so that by the end of the second Five-Year Plan in 1937, output in the Soviet Union's heavy industries had jumped anywhere from three to six times from 1928, depending on whether one used Soviet or Western statistics. The enormous rise in heavy industrial output between 1928 and 1941 far surpassed that of any other country in history for a similar length of time.

The Five-Year Plans had a significant impact on workers. Stalin undercut the trade unions, and workers lost considerable freedom. The government introduced repressive measures to curb absenteeism and worker turnover. Rural hostility toward collectivization triggered a flood of untrained peasants into cities to find work in factories. The regime countered the breakdown in labor discipline that resulted by introducing training programs to create a more skilled workforce. The programs contributed to an improvement in labor productivity as did the state's adoption of steeper wage differentials and a piecework system that paid workers, in Stalin's words, "according to their work, not need." The regime singled out a Donets basin coal miner named Alexei Stakhanov as a "hero of labor" for exceeding his one-day quota by 1400 percent in September 1935. Stakhanovism rapidly swept across other industries and added to increases in labor productivity. Workers contributed significantly to Russia's intensive industrialization between 1928 and 1941, but they also paid for it by enduring restrictions on job choices, workplace intimidation, reduced living standards, inadequate housing, and lower real wages.

The corporatist economies of Italy and Portugal

After 1926, Mussolini took firmer control of the Italian economy to achieve his goal of national greatness. He created a corporative state in which there would be harmony and cooperation between socialism and capitalism. Only in the 1930s did a final version emerge that divided the economy into 22 general areas with a corporation or assembly at the head of each. Representatives from Fascist-controlled labor organizations, business, and government met as corporation assemblies that jointly decided wages, industrial policies, prices, and working conditions. Overseeing the entire system was a National Council of Corporations tasked with the responsibility to plan autarky. The corporative system created a large layer of government bureaucracy that supervised inefficient, expensive, and generally unneeded organizations.

The Great Depression struck Italy hard, beginning in 1931. Unemployment jumped from 300,000 people in 1929 to over 1 million in 1932. As Mussolini increasingly subordinated domestic policy to foreign policy, he gave more attention to achieving autarky. This was a sensational and imprudent scheme that put strains on all areas of the economy and resulted in aggressive foreign policy ventures. One of his goals was to obtain Italian oil and gas independence by 1938. Domestic policies were expensive, ineffective, and unsound. The Battle for Wheat made Italy largely self-sufficient in that commodity by 1940, but it came at considerable cost to the government, and perpetuated agricultural inefficiencies.

Taking its cue from Italy, Portugal adopted a corporative system in the 1930s. This came after years of serious economic and financial disarray amidst political corruption and ineptitude. The mastermind of the Portuguese corporative state was Antonio de Oliveira Salazar, an economist who put the country's financial house in order in the late 1920s as finance minister in a dictatorial regime. By 1932, he had become the country's dictator, and he used his power to establish a "unitary, corporatist republic" in the Constitution of 1933. That document provided for a parliamentary body known as the Chamber of Corporations, whose members were appointed by a National Assembly. It was a consultative body that contained representatives from various corporative groups that the regime organized as a part of its Salazar-inspired corporatist state. Economically, Salazar adopted a conservative approach, with a strong emphasis on balanced budgets, a stable society, and slow, risk-free growth, or as he called it, "guided development." In a country where industrial output lagged far behind the agrarian sector when he became Portugal's dictator, Salazar did nothing to promote industrialization. As part of an inward-looking policy of economic autarky, the regime conducted a Wheat Campaign in the 1930s to achieve self-sufficiency in grain production, but finally had to abandon the program in 1937 because of soil erosion, the costs of using marginal lands, and inadequate transportation and storage facilities. Although Mussolini and Salazar wanted to present pictures of harmoniously operating economic systems, where different groups cooperated rather than bickered over industrial management-labor questions, their solutions were far from perfect.

Labor gains and losses

The 1930s dealt a setback to workers' rights. As the effects of the Great Depression set in across Europe, the general position of workers became less secure. Unemployment rates reached unprecedented levels in many countries and soared among union workers whose jobless rates were often double those of non-union laborers. Czechoslovakia was hard hit, especially in the rural Slovakian and industrial Sudetenland areas, showing that no economic sector in that country was immune from the crisis. In Scandinavia, high unemployment rates pitted Social Democrats against the agrarian and conservative parties, but in the end they were able to achieve a compromise. While labor strikes broke out in several countries, they were generally unsuccessful by the mid-1930s. France, which embraced large numbers of foreign workers after World War I, encouraged repatriation and introduced immigration restrictions with the onset of the depression. Other countries followed France's lead, adding to the unemployment burdens in the countries of return. This domino effect caused instability and forced governments to scramble for solutions.

A loss of labor freedom occurred in Germany, Italy, and the Soviet Union, where centralized economic planning and state distribution of investment and capital became the norm. In these countries, only one labor union was allowed, and it was state-sponsored, thus giving the state the power to control workers' protests. Mussolini's corporative state eliminated the harsh individualism of the liberal state and gave industrialists increased control over their factories and plants, including the labor force. The system was supposed to promote mutual understanding between management and labor, but in fact left little freedom to the workers. In Germany, labor unions were suppressed in January 1934, and industrialists gained more control over their workers. The ultimate decision-making power in both countries, however, rested with the state. A German work charter was passed in May 1934 that forbade workers to look for jobs elsewhere once they were employed. In October 1934, the Nazi trade union *Arbeitsfront* was created. It kept wages at a sustenance level and insured maximum worker productivity. In 1935, the Nazis introduced the "Work Book" without which a worker was considered delinquent. To alleviate unemployment further, the regime in 1935 introduced six months of compulsory labor service (*Arbeitsdienst*) for young men at age 18; the work included planting trees and digging ditches on farmlands. Similar practices had long been in place in the Soviet Union. Several right-wing governments in Europe besides Germany adopted the idea in the 1930s, albeit in a more moderate form.

In France, where the two major trade unions had been bitterly divided for years, the Popular Front that arose after the violent right-wing protests of February 1934 included a uniting of the Communists' CGTU union with the Socialists' larger CGT in March 1936. This newfound labor unity contributed to the electoral victory of the Popular Front in the 1936 elections and the rewards that came therefrom. The Socialist-led government oversaw the most comprehensive workers' rights gains of interwar Europe. As mentioned earlier, the government-brokered Matignon Accords brought significant benefits to French workers. Legislative and ministerial actions quickly complemented these gains, highlighted by the introduction of the 40-hour work week and two-week paid vacations for workers. Class tensions remained, however, and workers soon found themselves on the defensive as conservative forces struck back, attacking in particular the 40-hour week. Adding to labor's problems was the onset of divisions within the CGT between Communist and anti-Communist factions. Once the Popular Front officially ended in April 1938, the new premier, Edouard Daladier, started providing exemptions from the 40-hour week, first to the armaments industry, and then to other businesses after Paul Reynaud became finance minister on November 1, 1938. After workers launched wildcat strikes in protest, the CGT sponsored a one-day general strike on November 30. Daladier responded vigorously by requisitioning the country's public services and railways, and threatening punishment for government workers. The strike failed, and reprisals ensued. The CGT rapidly lost its influence in French national life, as a reinvigorated entrepreneurial class intensified its assault on the CGT and the Popular Front-enacted labor gains in the months prior to World War II.

Forced labor in totalitarian systems

The Bolsheviks began setting up camps of forced labor, also termed concentration camps, as early as 1918. They reached a new level of prison organization in 1923 with the establishment of their first major forced labor penal camp for criminals and political prisoners at Solovki, once the site of a Russian Orthodox monastery located on an archipelago in the White Sea. In the years immediately thereafter, Solovki served as the model for the growing system of prison labor camps that become known by the end of the decade as the Gulag, which stands for "Main Administration of Corrective Labor Camps and Labor Settlements." Stalin expanded the practice in the 1930s, using the prisoners as slave labor to exploit distant regions' resources, especially the Kolyma region of Siberia that was rich in uranium and other resources. Millions were processed through the Gulag administration and assigned to work on major public works projects and in industries such as timber and mining. Anyone suspected of unpatriotic activities could be awakened in the middle of the night, arrested, subjected to physical and mental tortures, interrogations, mock executions, summarily tried, and moved swiftly through the prison system to be dispersed wherever labor was needed. Kulaks, merchants, undesirables, and members of ethnic minorities were sent to the camps, along with common criminals, political prisoners, Red Army officers, and a majority of petty thieves who had acted out of desperation.

At the end of the 1930s, there were 53 main Gulag camp directorates and 423 labor colonies in the Soviet Union. Most of them were located in inhospitable regions, such as the Russian Arctic, where the cities of Norilsk, Vorkuta, and Magadan today bear their names. One camp, called Dmitlag and located some 40 miles north of Moscow, housed at its peak close to 200,000 prisoners who were assigned between 1932 and 1937 to build the 128 kilometer-long Moscow to Volga canal; 22,000 died in the process. One million forced laborers worked at the Kolyma camp complex in Russia's Far East between 1923 and 1955, exploiting the largest gold deposit in the world, and mining pewter, cobalt, tungsten, and uranium. Others built cities, factories, paper combines, roads, railroads, pipelines, and more forced-labor camps. Many prisoners in effect helped colonize Russia's Far East and procure resources needed to develop the Russian heartland. The economic and bureaucratic mobilization needed to carry out such a large resettlement of peoples required a greater effort than those that any other nation ever put in place. The Gulag helped provide free labor to develop the Soviet Union's industrial potential, but this achievement came at the cost of millions of lives.

Hitler also used criminalized Germans when he opened the first labor camp near Breslau (Wrocław) in 1933, away from prying eyes, to be followed shortly by the concentration camp of Dachau, where he sent political opponents, Jews, and criminals. By 1939, the Nazi government had established a network of free labor along Germany's eastern border.

Mortality rates were very high in the Soviet Gulag and Nazi concentration camps. Other similarities also existed: inhumane travel conditions in cattle cars, starvation and abuse in the camps, shabby housing, inadequate clothing, secrecy, mass executions, and mass graves. Both regimes committed similar crimes against their civilian populations in what could be called a terrible "mirror game."

Conclusion

The Great Depression provoked a variety of responses in Europe, although a common denominator was economic nationalism. Workers saw their freedom of action sharply curtailed or eliminated in Europe's most repressive regimes, and in countries where they did make gains, the advances sometimes proved fleeting. The totalitarian regimes of Russia and Germany, meanwhile, criminalized segments of their citizenry and then exploited them in the construction of ambitious, often monumental, modernization projects. Economic recovery left the Western democracies lacking visionary leadership and concerned about the future.

Social policies

In the economically depressed decade of the 1930s, social policies vacillated between conservatism and progressivism. States assumed increased responsibilities for securing the welfare of many of their citizens, showing progressivism. But in some instances, government largesse was intended to encourage an embracement of traditional values and gender roles. Women in particular saw their increasing independence and creativity of the postwar years questioned.

The welfare state

As unemployment rose with the start of the Great Depression, governments took steps to offset the suffering that the economic crisis caused. Some froze rents and food prices, for example. As infant mortality and child malnutrition rose and the health of mothers deteriorated, governments began to expand their social services. Health education and immunization campaigns were conducted. Prenatal and child care clinics and dispensaries became a staple of urban life. Other solutions included school lunch programs in Britain and the Netherlands, and a *Winterhilfe* (Winter Relief) service in Nazi Germany that distributed money, blankets, shoes, potatoes, milk, and sugar to the needy during the harsh winter months. These were palliatives, however, and the standards of living of most people decreased.

Vienna: a city with a social conscience

Vienna, once the bustling center of the Austro-Hungarian Empire and its 50 million people, emerged from World War I as the capital of the small, newly created state of Austria. Since its population of some 2 million constituted almost one-third of the country's population, Vienna was referred to as a "waterhead." It also became known as "Red Vienna" because of the city government's postwar leftist social agenda, which was intended to make the city a model of urban socialism.

The dominant political force in the governance of Vienna from 1919 to 1934 was the Social Democratic Party, which consistently received strong majorities from voters in city elections. This contrasted with the rest of the country which was politically much more conservative. Following a round of Austrian hyperinflation shortly after the war, the country's central government made the city a separate federal state, which gave it considerable power over tax policy. The Socialist-controlled Vienna municipal council used that authority in the 1920s to pay for generous social insurance benefits for workers and the construction of mass public housing projects. The new taxes that Viennese officials imposed fell heavily on the city's middle class and wealthy. Some cried that the municipal government was "soaking the rich." Between 1923 and 1934, the government built more than 60,000 apartment units for workers and kept the rents low. The large housing complexes included kindergartens, health clinics, theaters, lending libraries, and other amenities.

With the onset of the depression in 1929, the city government began to curtail its social programs because of shrinking tax revenues and pressure from the austerity-minded federal government. The cutbacks came when the number of people needing assistance was on the rise, the result of a sharp increase in unemployment and a decline in wages from a depressed labor market. The city council continued its housing construction program, but on a reduced scale. It also made large cuts in its welfare bugdet, redirected support payment funds from the elderly to other programs, and introduced payments in kind as substitutes for cash handouts in its aid policy. Large-scale unemployment among the city's young people prompted Viennese authorities to establish labor squads that carried out volunteer work in exchange for a hot meal. To deal with the increase in the number of homeless, the city's welfare department opened drop-in centers. The "Red Vienna" experiment sagged under the weight of the global economic crisis and the right-wing federal regime's restrictive financial policy. It collapsed in early 1934 when, following a brief civil war, the central government banned the Social Democratic Party and created a one-party system.

Backlash against women

In the 1930s, the position of women generally suffered legally, socially, and morally. Resistance to female emancipation surfaced in authoritarian regimes and democracies alike. Employment was an area where women were vulnerable in the early years of the depression. Their unemployment rates almost quadrupled between 1929 and 1932. As the depression deepened, they were hired in larger numbers because their salaries were on average only two-thirds the cost of men. Nevertheless, the overall number of women in the workforce continued to fall. Britain in 1931 decreed that employment was not a normal condition for women, denied women unemployment insurance, and kept them off unemployed rolls. Married women were still encouraged to fulfill their traditional role as housewives and mothers. Not only government officials, but people across large segments of Europe remained conservative, regardless of the nature of the regime or the state of modernization.

Mussolini in Italy and Hitler in Germany argued that a woman's role lay in marriage and motherhood. As a part of Mussolini's campaign for the Battle for Births, which was officially launched in 1927, the Italian dictator forbade contraceptives, increased the penalties for abortions, promoted marriage and large families through financial incentives, and outlawed divorce. In 1933, Mussolini restricted women employed in the public sector to 10 percent of the workforce. He applied quotas to women working in the private sector in the late 1930s, but with limited success. Ultimately, his "Battle for Births" failed, as the Italian birth rate dropped until 1936, and the Italian population never came close to his goal of 60 million by 1950; it stood at 47.5 million that year.

Hitler used many of the same ideas as Mussolini to encourage motherhood, such as financial benefits to promote marriage and large families, a ban on contraceptives, and tightened restrictions on abortions. In contrast to Fascist Italy, Nazi leaders took a different approach toward divorce due to their ideology of race: they supported divorces involving "racially incompatible" marriages and unhappy "racially pure" couples whose unions produced no "racially healthy" offspring. With regard to working women, Hitler viewed them with disdain and took steps to reduce dramatically their presence in the educational, medical, legal, and other professional fields. Hitler also prevented women from holding political office, so that there were none in the Reichstag, regional parliaments, or city councils during his rule; in the Weimar era, women had served at all three levels, with 42 women out of 475 members being elected to the Reichstag in the 1930 elections, for example.

In the Soviet Union, Stalin initially subscribed to Communist policies toward women that had been in place since the early days of Lenin's rule. Lenin's government had moved toward the emancipation of women by constitutionally granting them total equality with men. Women gained the same rights as their husbands in their marriages and easy access to free divorces and now-legalized abortions. Such steps militated against the traditional family as did the government's policy of assigning husbands and wives to different cities during Stalin's first Five-Year Plan. Negative fallout from the policies included a serious reduction in birthrates and a significant rise in juvenile delinquency. Stalin took a conservative turn in the early 1930s – primarily owing to economic considerations – by introducing measures that supported the traditional family. The regime reinvigorated the institution of marriage and emphasized that it was a life-long commitment. There was a resurgence of ceremonial weddings. Divorce became much more difficult to obtain and severe restrictions were placed on abortion. Stalin praised motherhood and provided tax breaks to women with large families. He also brought women into the workplace in large numbers, since he needed them to reach his goal of making the Soviet Union an industrial giant. Provided with new educational opportunities, women often learned skills that had previously been available only to men. The number of female industrial workers grew from 28.6 percent of the total workforce in 1928 to 42 percent in 1935. In 1936, females comprised 75 percent of the Soviet Union's new workers. While the overwhelming majority of women were relegated to low-paying jobs, the regime did attempt to facilitate the entry of females into managerial positions. In spite of their increasing role in the country's economic life, Soviet women continued to experience workplace harassment and discrimination as part of a male-dominated society. Even within the Communist Party, which ideologically endorsed the emancipation of women, men dominated the decision-making process. Many women also had to pull double duty as full-time workers and traditional homemakers.

In France, public support for the traditional family, female domesticity, and motherhood grew during the 1930s. In 1932, the government passed legislation requiring that all industrial and business employers offer family allocations to workers with at least two children. By 1935, a Chamber of Deputies pronatalist caucus, begun in 1911, counted more than half the deputies among its members. A climax to the conservative pronatalists' interwar efforts came in 1939 when the Daladier government issued a decree law establishing a Family Code (*Code de la Famille*). Consisting of 167 articles, the Code provided a one-time financial bonus to women who had their first infant during the first two years of marriage, reduced taxes on larger families, augmented the allowances for a family's third child and any thereafter, increased the penalties on abortions and pornography, and discouraged mothers from becoming wage-earners by granting stay-at-home allowances. At the same time, many on the Left argued for a woman's right to work and for equal pay with men for equal work. In a dramatic leftist show of support for women's rights, Blum innovatively named three women to his cabinet following the Popular Front's electoral victory in 1936. But his government did nothing to break down the barriers that kept female employees out of the upper levels of the civil service, nor did it take up the cause of women's suffrage since the Left feared that enfranchised women would largely vote for conservative candidates in elections.

Women's rights in Europe suffered other setbacks in the 1930s. Poland implemented laws against women in the workforce in 1935, and Hungary, Ireland, and Czechoslovakia followed suit in 1938. Limits were placed on the number of women in the civil service, and the male sector continued to be privileged at the expense of women. The only countries not to do so were the Benelux countries, Norway, and Denmark. Women's progress was seen by many as a sign of impending moral collapse: French fascist sympathizer Pierre Drieu la Rochelle stigmatized women thus. The Soviet Union repeatedly said that women in leadership positions were feisty and uncontrollable. Divorce was outlawed in 1940 in several countries and the women's movement suffered further setbacks in World War II.

Consumerism and lifestyles

From sewing machines, toasters, irons, radios, and phonographs to washing machines, technology had arrived to liberate women. Numerous consumer items were made more cheaply through mass production and influenced by industrial decor. Stuffed chairs, rugs, and heavy drapes were discarded in favor of streamlined, minimalist furniture; the first tubular chairs appeared, and the Bauhaus popularized the aesthetics of machine-made objects that were both functional and attractive. The modern kitchen resembled a laboratory, a hymn to the efficiency of housewives. New industries developed, including those for automobiles, home appliances, and office supplies. Health and medicine kept up as consumerism drove modernization even faster and farther. The new mass-produced culture seriously challenged more traditional lifestyles. Entertainment, vacations, sports, and home appliances encouraged a consumerist attitude; materialism increased as standards of living improved. This in turn created new industries in the areas of leisure, sports, and travel.

Conclusion

On the one hand, women made progress with the advent of state-sponsored welfare measures. On the other hand, conservative ideologies and prevailing attitudes limited their advance in the public sphere and the workplace. Women's social and professional mobility slowed down in the 1930s compared to the 1920s, and their activism declined as well.

Urban development

In the 1930s, urban planners continued designing the modern city for sizable numbers of people and for mass transportation. In order to make the modern city more vibrant, priority was given to big public spaces designed to accommodate urban culture. Large avenues and fields were designed for military parades, and broad avenues and parks for better air circulation. Stadiums, dispensaries, and schools were the temples of the new age. Cities added miles of paved streets, water lines, sewers, and numerous street lights. Not only was urban planning designed for mass living, but the architecture was designed to suit the spirit of national greatness that pervaded interwar culture. As centers of production and business, cities depended increasingly on modern communication and transportation with the outside world.

Urban monumentality

After the Great Depression, innovation in architecture was out and monumentality was in. In the 1930s, monumental architecture developed a more conservative approach and became a feature of urban planning, especially in Germany and the Soviet Union.

Modernist architecture took a step back, especially in Germany whose modernist architects, reviled by Hitler, took their style to Brazil, the United States, the Netherlands, Scandinavia, and Switzerland. Modernist architect and Berlin city planner Martin Wagner, who believed not only in beautifying cities but also in improving peoples' lives, was dismissed from his post in 1933. The new Nazi urban philosophy was to erase the past: Berlin, Nuremberg, and Munich were slated for reconstruction. With the help of Albert Speer, Hitler planned to rebuild Berlin on a gigantic scale. The city center would dwarf Paris and London and be as grandiose as those of ancient Egypt, Babylon, and Rome. Boulevards wider than a football field would be flanked by massive buildings. To prepare for the crown jewel of the city center, the People's Hall, Speer started clearing the area west of the Reichstag building. The People's Hall would accommodate 180,000 people and contain a dome reaching a height of 1050 feet. The outbreak of World War II put the project on hold before it could be realized, however.

In Russia, Stalin planned grandiose buildings as well. He is perhaps most remembered for a group of seven skyscrapers in Moscow known as the Seven Sisters comprised of hotels, apartments, government offices, the main building of the State University of Moscow, and the ubiquitous Palace of Culture. Construction on the first skyscraper began in 1941, but was quickly interrupted by Germany's invasion of the Soviet Union the same year. Only after World War II had ended did work on the Seven Sisters project resume and reach completion.

Unlike Stalin and Hitler, Mussolini planned historic continuity: his new cities copied the original layouts of the ancient Roman cities, with central squares containing columns, statues, or arches, and streets aligned with the cardinal points. Yet his style was just as monumental as that of the other two dictators. Monumental architecture was also meant to instill in people a sense of patriotic pride. The model was the Victor Emmanuel II Monument, which was built on a hill and visible to most of the city of Rome. Started in 1911, it was completed in 1925, and paid homage to the unification of Italy as well as to the sacrifices of Italian soldiers in World War I.

In Western Europe, architects in France pioneered the Art Deco style which exalted geometric shapes and exhibited a form of monumentality. In the area of urban planning, centralized planning systems characterized the 1930s. French and Belgian urban planners who had lived through World War I pushed for improved living conditions, such as better streets and sanitation, housing surrounded by open spaces, and modern utilities. Their goals included residential areas with clean air, designated industrial areas, and government buildings that reflected the majesty and accessibility of democracies.

Transportation

While railroads in Europe remained people's preferred mode of transportation for travel between cities in the interwar years, automobiles gained in popularity as an alternative. The production of automobiles became a vibrant industry in Europe after World War I, as manufacturers adopted American assembly line methods to offer affordable models to an expanding middle class. Frenchman André Citroën was the European ground-breaker in this regard when he began mass producing an automobile called the Model A in 1919. During the 1930s, car production reached 390,000 per year in Britain, 275,000 in Germany, and 182,000 in France. One result of large-scale automobile production was traffic congestion on Europe's roads. While European states were generally slow to modernize their road systems, Germany experienced a highway revolution under Hitler, in the form of a freeway system called the Autobahn. Rudolf Hess, Hitler's deputy party leader, said in 1934 that motorways represented a higher level of culture, and their technology symbolized the spirit of the age. Germany's highways did much to connect Germans with the far reaches of their country. Traffic codes and signs were standardized in Europe by 1925, and road safety campaigns emerged in some European countries in the 1930s.

Commercial air transport networks also developed. In the 1920s, most European nations had created airline companies, yet airline technology allowed only mostly mail routes. The most advanced state was Germany, where Lufthansa, created in 1926, was operating standard commercial air routes among 13 north German cities by 1930, and where the number of passengers carried grew from 2,000 to 250,000 people between 1919 and 1928. In the 1930s, air transport grew exponentially. After France in 1933 consolidated the operations of a number of small air carriers to create Air France, the new company became the main international airline in Europe. In the Soviet Union, Aeroflot was created in 1932 and quickly established commercial routes to the Pacific. During the decade, air safety increased, and air fares decreased significantly. In 1939, the industry's technology was ready for the soon to come military needs in air transportation.

Modern cities were vibrant, dynamic places of constant motion during the day. In Europe, many urban areas grew dramatically in the interwar years, especially those with populations exceeding 100,000. Virtually all of Europe's capital cities showed impressive population increases: Moscow, for example, nearly tripled in size to just over 4 million and Greater London shot up by 16 percent to more than 8.6 million. Commercial vans, automobiles, and motorcycles competed on paved roads with horse-drawn carriages and bicycles. By the mid-1930s, new publicly owned transportation networks that included metropolitan trains, subway systems, and motorbuses linked suburbia to city centers. Street and sidewalk regulations became a priority as traffic congestion and noise disturbed the peace. In Berlin, trams and motor vehicles increased one-hundred-fold during the interwar years.

Conclusion

The style and pace of life in European cities changed dramatically in the 1930s. Continued urban development introduced better living, yet was unable to ease the division between industrial and posh suburbs. Modernism continued to inspire architects and urban planners, although some of the new ideas did not gain recognition until after 1945. Architecture made powerful statements in totalitarian states, where the monumental style conveyed a feeling of strength and power to citizens and visitors alike; thus, architecture became a state propaganda tool. The introduction of automobiles and commercial airline travel quickened the pace of travel and improved long-distance travel. These transformations widened the gap between city and countryside, and created a two-tempo pace of development – slower in the countryside, faster in the cities.

Overall conclusion

The 1930s heightened the divide between the Western democracies and the totalitarian regimes. The Great Depression increased economic nationalism, exacerbated ideologies, and justified greater government intervention and outreach. While autarky and retrenchment prevailed in some corners, the number of international contacts continued to increase. European colonial powers became more involved in the development and trade of their colonies. Population migrations created a transnational dynamic that affected all European countries, and culminated in a refugee crisis during the last year of peace. Increased international travel enabled more Europeans to travel around the globe, changing economies, lifestyles, and cultures.

Politically, the Western democracies had trouble coping with the Great Depression owing to its scope, which was compounded by the end of the Versailles order. Both factors paved the way for the kind of political and economic overhaul seldom seen in history. Faced with this challenge, the Western democracies seemed frozen and suffered from uninspiring leadership, fragile financial situations, and a lack of innovative ideas. The undercurrent of political divisions often made government coalitions unavoidable, yet they were unstable by nature. Few democracies survived the decade, adding to the climate of political moroseness. In East Central Europe, authoritarianism was on the rise. The regimes of institutionalized terror in Nazi Germany and Stalinist Russia represent perhaps the darkest aspect of the decade. The reasons why Hitler and Stalin institutionalized terror against their own citizens may never be fully understood. Whether out of political revenge, economic need for cheap labor, or increased social unrest, the two dictators imposed untold suffering upon many of their own citizens.

While the West struggled from the effects of the Great Depression, the economies of Nazi Germany and the Soviet Union showed resiliency. Socially, the balance sheet was mixed: anti-Semitism and pacifism; labor rights improvement and human rights abuses; and xenophobia and humanitarian relief were all present in varying degrees. It was a decade of extremes and in many ways it was a bleak, barren period, an in-between time of anxious waiting.

Notes

1 Alfred Havighurst, *Twentieth-Century Britain*, 2nd edn (New York: Harper & Row, 1962), 242.
2 Joachim C. Fest, *Hitler* (New York: Vintage Books, 1975), 183.
3 Kurt G. W. Ludecke, *I Knew Hitler* (London: Jarrolds Publishers, 1938), 234–235.
4 Alan Bullock, *Hitler: A Study in Tyranny*, rev. edn (New York: Bantam Books, 1961), 222.
5 Ibid., 228.
6 David Welch, *The Third Reich: Politics and Propaganda* (London: Routledge, 1993), 88.
7 David MacKenzie and Michael W. Curran, *A History of Russia, the Soviet Union, and Beyond*, 6th edn (Belmont, CA: Wadsworth, 2002), 468.
8 Marxists Internet Archive, "Constitution (Fundamental Law) of the Union of Soviet Socialist Republics," www.marxists.org/reference/archive/stalin/works/1936/12/05.htm (accessed March 15, 2016).
9 Jean-François Berdah, "The Devil in France: The Tragedy of Spanish Republicans and French Policy after the Civil War (1936–1945)," in *CLIOHRES: Discrimination and Tolerance in Historical Perspective* (Pisa, Italy: Edizioni Plus, 2008), 311, https://hal.archives-ouvertes.fr/hal-00374318/document (accessed April 4, 2016).
10 MacKenzie and Curran, *A History of Russia*, 483.

Suggestions for further reading

Applebaum, Anne. *Gulag: A History*. New York: Doubleday. 2003.

Arendt, Hannah. *The Origins of Totalitarianism*. New York: Harcourt Brace Jovanovich. 1973.

Atkin, Nicholas and Michael Biddiss. *Themes in Modern European History, 1890–1945*. London: Routledge. 2009.

Ayçoberry, Pierre. *The Social History of the Third Reich, 1933–1945*. Trans. Janet Lloyd. New York: The New Press. 1999.

Burleigh, Michael. *Sacred Causes: The Clash of Religion and Politics, from the Great War to the War on Terror*. New York: Harper. 2007.

Clavin, Patricia. *The Great Depression in Europe, 1929–1939*. London: Palgrave. 2000.

Kershaw, Ian. *Hitler*. 2 vols. New York: W. W. Norton. 1999–2000.

Lampke, John R. and Mark Mazower. *Ideologies and National Identities: The Case of Twentieth-Century Southeastern Europe*. Budapest: Central European University Press. 2004.

Lucassen, Leo. *The Immigrant Threat: The Integration of Old and New Migrants in Western Europe Since 1850*. Urbana, IL: Illinois University Press. 2005.

Naimark, Norman M. *Stalin's Genocides*. Princeton, NJ: Princeton University Press. 2010.

Nord, Philip. *France's New Deal: From the Thirties to the Postwar Era*. Princeton, NJ: Princeton University Press. 2010.

Wasserstein, Bernard. *On the Eve: The Jews of Europe Before the Second World War*. New York: Simon & Schuster. 2012.

Part 4

World War II, 1939–1945

7 International dimensions of the war

Introduction

World War II proved to be much vaster in its global dimensions and carnage than the Great War of 1914–1918 that up until then had been the most destructive conflict in human history. Hitler's invasion of Poland in 1939 set off a series of events that soon touched much of Europe, starting with Britain and France's declarations of war against Germany in early September 1939. The Germans' successful military campaign in Western Europe in the spring of 1940 resulted in Britain being alone among the European states to face the Nazi war machine that summer. But the geographical dimensions of the war soon expanded, as Italy attacked British holdings in Africa in the fall of 1940, Germany invaded the Soviet Union in the summer of 1941, and Japan struck multiple sites in the Pacific and East Asia in late 1941, bringing the United States into the struggle as a belligerent. Hitler and Mussolini's declarations of war on the United States in December 1941 completed the process of arranging the major countries among the two sets of wartime adversaries, with the Axis powers of Germany, Italy, and Japan on one side and the Allied powers of Great Britain, the Soviet Union, and the United States on the other. Large-scale military campaigns took place on three continents, and new technology – climaxing in the atomic bomb – brought the destructive power of war to unprecedented heights on both the battlefield and the home front. Europe's colonies played an important part in the struggle both as battle zones and contributors of soldiers and raw materials. But the conflict also intensified colonial nationalist independence movements that dramatically altered colonial relationships by war's end. Diplomatically, the Grand Alliance of Britain, Russia, and the United States faced the challenging task of maintaining harmony in their wartime efforts despite mutual suspicions, differences in war aims, and incompatible political systems that divided totalitarian Russia from the democratic West. Finally, the Big Three would have to decide how to put a broken Europe back together again once the war was won.

Military operations

The Second World War bore resemblances to the First World War, including the major powers involved, key invasion paths, and the global nature of the fighting. But the resources the belligerents mobilized in World War II proved to be unprecedented in human warfare, with the Allies ultimately needing six years to defeat the Axis powers in the conflict.

The attack against Poland

On the morning of September 1, 1939, Hitler unleashed the fury of the German army – the Wehrmacht – on Poland to thrust Europe into World War II. The Germans' plan called for *Blitzkrieg* (lightning warfare): its operation rested upon a combination of air power, armored (tank) divisions, and motorized units moving rapidly and relentlessly forward, using surprise to overwhelm the enemy. One million German men were committed to the invasion, whereas Poland, which had delayed mobilization until August 31 to avoid giving the Germans an excuse to attack, had only 600,000 soldiers ready out of a potential force of more than 2 million. Moreover, the Poles had little in the way of modern mechanized forces, and their air power was vastly inferior to that of the Germans. Not surprisingly, the Germans tore through the main Polish defenses in the first days of the fighting and the German Luftwaffe (air force) quickly gained control of the skies. On September 1, the British and French warned the German government that they intended to fulfill their treaty commitments to assist the Poles unless the Germans ceased their campaign of aggression. Failing a reply, both countries declared war on Germany on September 3. Despite their guarantees of the spring of 1939 to protect Poland's borders, the French and the British did very little militarily to assist Poland.

Figure 7.1 Adolf Hitler looks through a binocular periscope to view the siege of Warsaw during a visit to the German front lines in Poland in late September 1939.

Germany's quick military successes, meanwhile, put increasing pressure on the Soviets to invade Poland from the east. The Soviet government, believing that the German offensive would advance more slowly into Poland than it actually did, accelerated its plans for military action against the Poles by launching an attack on September 17. The Soviet attack hastened, but did not cause, the collapse of Poland's organized military effort around Warsaw. It was the Germans who, through a combination of punishing aerial and artillery bombardments, forced the Warsaw garrison's surrender on September 27. All remaining pockets of formal resistance were crushed by early October. The war against Poland was over, and the costs were heavy. More than 100,000 Polish soldiers died, and another million fell into the hands of the Germans and Russians as prisoners. More than 200,000 troops fled abroad. By contrast, the German forces experienced some 40,000 casualties, while the Soviets had 2,600 dead and wounded.

The final partition of Poland was decided on September 28. The Russians gained just over half of Poland's land and approximately one-third of its population. The Germans gained two-thirds of the population along with the best agricultural land and the bulk of Poland's industrial centers. The final arrangement actually provided Germany with more Polish territory than agreed to in August, but the September 28 arrangement compensated the Russians for that change by granting to them a sphere of influence in Lithuania originally allotted to Germany. The Germans now began a brutal occupation of their newly established enclave. The Polish population under Russian control fared little better.

Phony war on the Western Front

The situation on the Western Front remained largely quiet. Outside of a few French probing actions and ineffective British bombing raids against German targets, the two Western democracies held to a defensive mentality. The French took refuge behind their Maginot Line, an elaborate network of defensive fortifications built in the interwar years along the Franco-German frontier, where they waited for a German offensive during the fall and winter of 1939–1940. No attack came, even though Hitler wanted to launch an offensive on several occasions; poor weather conditions and the Belgian capture of information related to German battle plans, caused postponements until May 1940. The Germans called this long lull the "sitting war," the British referred to it as the "phony war," and the French labeled it the "strange war."

The Russo-Finnish War

The main fighting in the winter of 1939–1940 took place between the Soviet Union and Finland. Known as the Russo-Finnish War, it began after Stalin demanded territorial changes in Russia's frontier with Finland, perhaps to improve the Soviets' military position against a future Nazi attack, and the Finns refused. The Russians threw 1.2 million men, 1,500 tanks, and 3,000 airplanes into the battle along a 600-mile front, mistakenly believing that they could quickly overpower the Finns. Against them stood 300,000 Finnish soldiers who were short on war materiel but long on tenacity, courage, and cleverness. The Soviet military leadership contained a number of frightened incompetents who had gained their posts after Stalin's purge of the army in the late 1930s. It was evident by early January 1940 that the Russian invasion had broken down, with thousands of their dead soldiers' frozen bodies scattered across roads and forests in the east-central part of Finland. The Soviets reorganized their forces under a new commander named Semyon Timoshenko. Timoshenko focused his attention on the Finns' key defensive barrier, the

Mannerheim Line, and spent January amassing a large army for a major offensive there. The Finns, outnumbered by a ratio of 50:1 and heavily outgunned, saw their positions quickly overwhelmed. The Finnish government requested an armistice on March 11 and hostilities ceased two days later. Stalin now imposed harsher terms than he had originally demanded. In all, the Finns were forced to cede about 10 percent of their territory to the Soviets, including the entire Karelian Peninsula. Because of the embarrassments the Soviets experienced in the war, they undertook major military reforms in the following months.

Denmark and Norway

The war in Finland brought all of Scandinavia into focus as a possible combat area. Hitler was interested in shoring up his northern flank as well as protecting his supply of iron ore from Sweden for Germany's armaments industry. Scandinavia was also on the minds of the Allies. The British and French considered sending a small military expedition to assist the Finns late in the war, but the neutral countries of Norway and Sweden would not allow such a force to traverse their territories, in part out of fear that such an action might provoke war with the Soviet Union. The Western democracies, at the urging of British First Lord of the Admiralty Winston Churchill, also developed plans to mine the coastline of Norway to prevent Swedish ore from reaching Germany. The British even considered an occupation of the northern Norwegian port of Narvik, which was a critical link in the ore shipments to Germany.

Just as the British mine-laying operation began, the Germans on April 9, 1940, launched an offensive against both Denmark and Norway. Using the element of surprise, which included the first wartime paratrooper operation in history, Germany overran Denmark in a matter of hours. Subduing Norway, on the other hand, took two months to complete. Germany committed most of its navy to the Norwegian operation, and it carried German soldiers to several disembarkation points along the Norwegian coast. The Norwegians were quite unprepared militarily for this multipronged assault, and the Germans quickly overran the south of the country. The British attempted to counter the German strikes with landings of their own in April, but they failed. For their part, the Germans experienced serious difficulties at Narvik. After German troops successfully landed in the port, British ships moved in, and sank several German warships and merchant vessels located there in mid-April. The British also landed troops near Narvik on April 14, but because of the timidity of their commander, they initially accomplished little. Finally, an Allied force of 24,000 soldiers drove the German occupiers out of Narvik in late May, only to retreat themselves in early June when the democracies abandoned Norway in light of events in France. Because Hitler feared an Allied assault on Norway, he eventually stationed as many as 500,000 soldiers there.

The fall of France

During the winter of 1939–1940, the Germans revised their strategy in the West. The new plan was based on a proposal devised by Erich von Manstein, one of Germany's most talented generals and strategists in World War II. Manstein's plan called for the main German thrust to take place through the Ardennes Forest in southern Belgium and Luxembourg, where the enemy would not expect armored units to pass because of the difficulty of the terrain. A convinced Hitler on February 18 ordered German commanders to transform the plan from a conception into a detailed operational order. On the

Allied side, both the French and the British faced challenges. France had an uninspiring supreme commander in 68-year-old Maurice Gamelin, a structurally flawed command system both within the French army and with the British Expeditionary Force (BEF) under Lord John Gort, and a demoralized army stuck in the damp fortifications of the Maginot Line. Moreover, the French kept their most effective and mobile forces ready to intervene on behalf of the Low Countries in the north, where the BEF was also located. If the Germans' main attack came farther south, the Allied forces in the north would risk being trapped. Gamelin added to this potential problem by putting his most important reserve unit, France's Seventh Army, in a position to race into the Netherlands on the far left flank. He also kept half of France's total available forces along the Maginot Line to the south. Should a battlefront crisis develop in the center, France would find itself without any serious reserve forces.

Early on the morning of May 10, the Germans, without a declaration of war, moved simultaneously against the Netherlands, Belgium, and Luxembourg. In the north, the German invaders included soldiers dressed in Dutch uniforms and several thousand paratroopers. While the German Luftwaffe dominated the skies over Holland, airborne troops seized key bridges and canals. Other German troops poured across the largely undefended Dutch border, and the Dutch army retreated away from the Allies rather than toward them, allowing themselves to be quickly encircled by the Germans. The Dutch government surrendered on May 15. In Belgium, the Germans met stiffer resistance than in Holland, because Belgium's army was larger and its defense system was more heavily fortified. Nevertheless, the Germans moved rapidly ahead. The French and British, believing that a recurrence of the Schlieffen Plan was unfolding, rushed troops northward to assist the Belgians. Their response was exactly what the Germans had hoped for, as it weakened their position in the Ardennes Forest to the south. Poor coordination between the Belgian troops and the incoming French and British forces soon forced the Allies to retreat into western Belgium. The deteriorating situation finally convinced the Belgian government to surrender unconditionally to the Germans on May 28.

The Germans' decisive push came through the Ardennes Forest in southern Belgium and Luxembourg. France's defense lines in that area were thin. French military leaders had concluded that the Ardennes region, with just two secondary roads available and lots of hills and thick forests to negotiate, was too difficult for Germany's armored units to traverse for it to be the central point of an offensive. The French High Command also calculated that should the Germans move through the Ardennes, they would need to bring up heavy artillery before crossing the Meuse River into France, and that task would take five to six days. Thus, the French reasoned that they had ample time to move in reinforcements to stop any German advance. The Germans only took two-and-one-half days to reach the Meuse, however, and they easily subdued the historic French fortress of Sedan on the river's east bank by the evening of May 12. Approximately 1,000 planes, not heavy artillery, provided powerful tactical support for German troops as they breached the Meuse on May 13. The Germans had bypassed the Maginot Line with their offensive, and their concentrated armored forces now moved rapidly toward the English Channel.

News of the German breakthrough had a dramatic effect on the Allies. At the French High Command headquarters outside of Paris on May 14, there was initial silence. One general commented: "The atmosphere was that of a family in which there has been a death."[1] On May 16, Paul Reynaud, who had succeeded Edouard Daladier as the French premier on March 21, told visiting Prime Minister Churchill that the situation was irretrievable. Gamelin admitted to the two leaders that there was no strategic reserve force available and that he was uncertain about the Germans' destination. On May 20, Reynaud replaced the discredited Gamelin with Maxime Weygand, a 73-year-old former French army commander-in-chief brought out of retirement when war erupted in 1939. Upon assuming command, Weygand discovered that he could not launch a counterattack quickly enough to stem the German tide. It behooved him to find another solution.

The most serious problem confronting the French and British was to determine what to do with their divided forces: one to the north and the other to the south of the driving German troops. As an armored force under the command of Heinz Guderian closed in on the Allied troops in the north, BEF Commander Gort on May 23 ordered his troops to fall back toward the English Channel. Seeing the hopelessness of the Allies' situation in the north, Churchill on May 26 ordered a British evacuation from the French coastal city of Dunkirk, where the soldiers were trapped. They were assisted in their evacuation by Hitler who on May 24 halted the advance of German land forces 15 miles from the port city to conserve his armor for use elsewhere. Instead, Hitler ordered the Luftwaffe to destroy the remaining Allied forces in and around Dunkirk, but it failed in its mission. By the time Hitler ordered a renewal of the land offensive on May 26, the British and French were dug in enough on the perimeter of the city to prevent the armored units from making much headway. That allowed the British to send in a large makeshift flotilla that included naval ships, yachts, motorboats, fishing vessels, ferries, and tugboats to rescue large numbers of soldiers during a nine-day effort that ended on June 4. All the while, the Luftwaffe engaged in strafing and bombing missions to thwart the Allied withdrawal. In the end, 338,000 Allied soldiers were evacuated. Of these, 224,000 were British, including the bulk of the remaining soldiers of the British Expeditionary Force. Churchill called the success of the operation a "miracle." In the eyes of many Frenchmen, however, Britain had acted selfishly in extracting its soldiers from Dunkirk, and had cared only about its own interests. The Franco-British alliance was strained.

In the south, Weygand hoped that his vitiated forces, by establishing a defensive position called the "Weygand Line," could keep the Germans at bay. But Weygand had just 62 divisions to go up against the 95 German divisions unleashed on June 5. The Germans quickly pierced the weak French defenses and drove into the heartland of France. The Germans were joined by the Italians when the surrender of the French appeared imminent. Mussolini, who had committed to the idea of war in the West as early as April, had underestimated the speed with which the Germans would achieve victory over the French and British. Belatedly, he declared war on the French on June 10, fearing that a failure to do so then would leave Italy out of the spoils once the war was over. The Italians launched their first assault on June 20, and were embarrassingly beaten back by outnumbered French troops.

With their forces rapidly disintegrating, French government officials engaged in emergency decision making. The government moved from Paris to Tours on June 10. Two days later it declared Paris an open city, which meant an official end to France's defense of the city on the understanding, under international law, that the Germans would not then militarily attack Paris as they moved in to occupy it. On June 14, the government installed itself in Bordeaux, and began to debate an armistice with Germany. Reynaud, who wanted to continue the war from France's empire in North Africa, resigned as premier on June 16, and his replacement, 84-year-old Marshal Pétain, called for an end to the fighting. The Germans dictated extremely harsh armistice terms to the French on June 21 in the same railroad carriage and at the exact same site in the Compiègne forest where a defeated Germany had signed an armistice with the Allies in November 1918. France agreed to the German terms late the following day. The Germans were to occupy three-fifths of the country, including northern and much of central France – with Paris at its heart – and all the Atlantic coastline. The French were to pay for Germany's occupation costs and limit their army to 100,000 men. The French would control the remainder of France as well as its colonies and fleet. Hitler insisted that France reach an agreement with Italy before the Franco-German armistice went into effect. The French and Italians quickly signed an armistice agreement allowing Italy an occupation zone up to 50 kilometers inside France along the Franco-Italian border. France's hostilities with Germany and Italy officially ceased at 12:25 a.m. on June 25. Hitler excitedly visited Paris on June 27. At one point he had contemplated the destruction of the city, but finally concluded that this was unnecessary, counting on time to turn it into a mere shadow of Berlin.

Germany's amazing success in subduing western continental Europe in 35 days was achieved at a cost of slightly more than 163,000 German casualties, including about 30,000 dead. The French, on the other hand, endured approximately 200,000 wounded and 123,000 dead. Close to 2 million more French soldiers were either missing or prisoners of war. The British military losses were in the tens of thousands. Having shown the world the effectiveness of *Blitzkrieg* through the swiftness and completeness of its triumph in France, the German war machine now had the appearance of an invincible force.

The Battle of Britain

Hitler still had to deal with Britain, however, since that country had not surrendered to the Germans. In the euphoric aftermath of Germany's victory over the French, Hitler was confident that the British would make peace. There was sentiment in late May among some British government officials for a negotiated peace with Germany. The feeling quickly evaporated as the success of the evacuation of Allied forces at Dunkirk became increasingly clear, and British leaders remained defiant and united behind Churchill. After the British rejected or ignored several German peace feelers transmitted through neutral third parties, Hitler on July 19 offered Britain peace if it would recognize Germany's dominion on the continent and return former German colonies it had obtained through the Treaty of Versailles. The British foreign secretary, Lord Halifax, categorically rejected the offer in a radio address three days later. Britain's refusal to consider peace on Germany's terms left Hitler with the option of moving toward a cross-Channel invasion to force a British surrender. Already on July 16, Hitler had ordered preparations for an invasion of Britain under the code name Operation Sea Lion. The Army High Command developed the initial draft of the plan that had August 15 as the launch date. After consulting with Navy Commander-in-Chief Erich Raeder, who was shocked at the unrealistically large size of the planned operation, army leaders drastically scaled down the operation and postponed the date of the assault until September 15.

For a cross-Channel invasion to succeed, the Germans knew that they had to control the skies over Britain first. Luftwaffe Commander-In-Chief Hermann Göring was confident that that could be achieved in approximately five weeks. The Luftwaffe committed more than 2,000 planes to the operation. But the German air force was largely built for tactical missions in support of the army, not for strategic tasks such as the ones assigned to it in the summer of 1940. Furthermore, the British had some important advantages. One of these was a fleet of 820 modern Hurricane and Spitfire fighter planes. They also had a radar system and a well-developed system of human airplane spotters, so that British fighter squadrons would not be caught on the ground when German planes arrived. A top-secret decoding device gave the British access to some of the German forces' most sensitive military information. Finally, British pilots had the advantage of fighting over British territory, so that if they safely bailed out of a downed plane, they could swiftly return to their bases to fight again.

The Germans unleashed the wrath of their air force on the British in August, beginning an air war that became known as the Battle of Britain. Major assaults on British airfields started in early August with the intention of destroying the Royal Air Force (RAF). A major attack against British radar stations occurred on August 12, but the damage was limited. It was on August 13 that the Germans first sent massive numbers of bombers to attack military targets in Britain. This represented the official start of their great air campaign. On August 24, the Germans intensified their efforts against British Fighter Command bases, and over the next several days, the Luftwaffe inflicted heavy losses on the RAF fighter units, actually reaching the point where British fighter losses outstripped the country's ability to produce replacement aircraft. By early September, it appeared as though Göring might be near his goal of driving the British out of the sky, although the Germans had experienced major losses, too.

It was then that the Germans shifted the focus of their bombing raids from military targets to British cities in a campaign called the Blitz that lasted until May 1941. It commenced with a bombing run over London on September 7. A major reason for the shift to cities resulted from Hitler's fury over retaliatory actions of the British against Germany after a group of German bombers mistakenly conducted a raid on London on August 24. Churchill responded by ordering the bombing of Berlin over the next several days. One dramatic moment in the Blitz came on September 15 in what the British now commemorate as the Battle of Britain Day: the Germans sent in two waves of planes to bomb London especially hard, but they inflicted little serious damage on the city and suffered heavy losses of their own. Nearly 250 British Spitfire and Hurricane fighter planes knocked some 60 German planes out of the sky that day; it was a turning point in the air war between the two sides. Two days later, Hitler postponed the date of the invasion, and, in early October, the German ground invasion of Britain was suspended indefinitely.

The Germans' bombing campaign went on for several more months after September 15. Daytime raids of London and other targets continued into October when the Germans, in an effort to reduce aircraft losses, shifted to nighttime bombings. German bombers continued to terrorize British cities until May 10, 1941, when the Blitz finally ended. At that point, the Luftwaffe's services were needed in the East for an impending invasion of the Soviet Union. The Battle of Britain officially lasted from July 10 to October 31, 1940. The British tenaciously withstood the powerful onslaught of the Luftwaffe, and emerged with a physical and psychological victory. During this period, the Luftwaffe lost 1882 airplanes, and British aircraft losses totaled 1265. While the British endured many months of heavy bombing thereafter, their Fighter Command in the Battle of Britain had thwarted any invasion hopes that the Germans had in 1940.

The Enigma machine

One of the key components in the British victory in the Battle of Britain was their ability to intercept German military messages sent from an encryption machine called Enigma, a highly sophisticated tool developed after World War I. Polish counterintelligence officials came upon one of the Enigma machines being shipped from Berlin to Warsaw in 1929, and they constructed an exact replica of it before allowing the original to be forwarded to the German legation in the Polish capital. Polish mathematicians broke the German cipher in 1932, but the Poles had to start afresh when the Germans adopted a new cipher at the end of 1938. On the eve of Germany's invasion of Poland, Polish code-breakers shared their information about the Enigma machine with stunned French and British cryptographers and gave them copies of the device. After Poland collapsed, a number of Polish cryptanalysts fled to the West and carried several Enigma devices with them. With Polish assistance, the British by April 1940 had broken several of the new German codes. The information that Britain's military intelligence obtained by such means was code named Ultra, and it enabled the British to use their air force more effectively during the Battle of Britain because of the information it provided about the direction, numbers, and times of impending bombing raids. It also informed the British about German aircraft losses and morale among the German forces. In regard to Operation Sea Lion, Ultra clearly demonstrated how confused and unprepared the Germans were in trying to organize a massive amphibious operation in the summer of 1940. Ultra was important to other Allied operations during the war as well. In the Battle of the Atlantic (see p. 255), for example, it was of great assistance to Allied convoys in avoiding German submarines.

The Ultra signals intelligence operators worked in total secrecy at an estate called Bletchley Park, not far from London. Because of the system's dependence on secrecy to succeed, the cryptanalysts were subject to the death penalty should they somehow compromise its operation. The Allies were so successful at keeping their Ultra activities hidden that the Germans never suspected that anyone had broken into their Enigma system and never changed either the cipher or the primary mode of transmission during the war. Indeed, the official secrecy of Ultra continued after the war, with its existence only being made public in 1974.

Italian offensives

Mussolini, after seeing the successes Hitler had achieved, launched some military ventures of his own without informing his ally in advance. It was his way of getting out from under the shadow of his highly successful partner in war. The focus of his attention was North Africa, East Africa, and Greece. The thrusts there were a part of his dream of creating a modern Roman Empire with the Mediterranean Sea at its center, an empire that also included the western shores of the Indian Ocean. While on paper Italy had a powerful military force to carry out the Duce's wishes, in reality the Italian army suffered from deficiencies in equipment, leadership, and training. What Mussolini ended up with was embarrassing failures in both Africa (see pp. 270–271) and Greece, even though his forces vastly outnumbered those of the Allies that they fought.

Against the advice of his military leaders, Mussolini unleashed an assault against Greece from Italian-occupied Albania on October 28, 1940. The Italian forces were ill-prepared and had little enthusiasm for the invasion. Moreover, the Greek army thwarted the Italian offensive shortly after it began, and Greek counterattacks soon threw the Italians back into Albania. At year's end the Greeks occupied close to one-fourth of Albania, but their offensive stalled in January 1941, and the conflict degenerated into a military stalemate. In mid-March, a major Italian counteroffensive failed.

The German Balkan campaign

Once Italy's campaign in Greece began unraveling, Hitler felt compelled to come to the aid of his Fascist ally, even though Germany had told the Italians during the summer of 1940 not to take military action against either Yugoslavia or Greece lest it disrupt the quiet that then prevailed in the region. As early as November 4, 1940, Hitler ordered the German High Command to create a plan for a German invasion of Greece, and he became fully committed to it as Mussolini's forces retreated into Albania. Hitler also feared British intervention in Greece, since a British presence there would threaten Germany's position in the Balkans. His fears were confirmed when Britain decided in late February 1941 to transfer 58,000 soldiers from North Africa, where the British had made impressive advances against the Italians, to Greece. Britain's decision not only halted its drive to take complete control of Libya, but also represented a military miscalculation in regard to Greece, since the number of British troops involved was substantially less than needed to stop a German offensive there.

Using diplomacy in the Balkans to strengthen his hand, Hitler scored an important victory on March 1 when Bulgaria, which shared a border with Greece, agreed to enter the Axis and let German troops move through its territory. Since Germany already had Hungary and Romania safely in the Axis camp, German troops could now move by land from Germany to Greece unimpeded. Hitler also succeeded in pressuring Yugoslavia to join the Axis on March 25, only to see that country's government overthrown two days later and the alliance renounced by the new Yugoslav leadership. Hitler's immediate reaction was to order an attack on Yugoslavia as well as Greece.

German forces launched their campaign in the Balkans on April 6. It began with a spectacular bombing assault on Belgrade: by the time it ended two days later, the Germans had destroyed the city center and killed approximately 4,000 people. At the same time, the Germans sent an army of 650,000 soldiers into Yugoslavia and the *Blitzkrieg* operation quickly overwhelmed the Yugoslav army before it had fully mobilized. Deep ethnic divisions in the Yugoslav kingdom among the Serbs, Croats, and Slovenes added to the plight of the defenders. A number of Croats refrained from participating in what they viewed as a Serbian war, and some Croat units shifted to the enemy as the invasion unfolded. The resistance of the Yugoslav army was so anemic that the German forces experienced only 151 deaths before Yugoslavia surrendered unconditionally on April 17.

The German invasion of Greece also began on April 6. German forces, moving through southern Yugoslavia from Bulgaria, crossed into Greece at two points, one to outflank the Greek army located along the Greek–Bulgarian border and the other to isolate the Greek forces fighting the Italians in southern Albania. The Greek defenders near Bulgaria surrendered on April 9, while the Greeks in Albania fought on for several more days, signing an armistice on April 23 with both Germany and Italy. Meanwhile, the Germans pushed the British troops in Greece southward to Athens, at which point the British began an evacuation of their forces. The evacuation, which lasted several days in late April, resulted in the withdrawal of 43,000 soldiers to Crete and Egypt. The Germans had overrun the Greek peninsula in well under a month and at a cost of only about 250 fatalities.

Germany followed its Balkan campaign with an assault in May on the Greek island of Crete, where approximately 35,000 British, New Zealand, and Greek troops were stationed. Launched on May 20, the German attack was the first large-scale primarily airborne operation in history and involved some 23,000 soldiers. The action may be viewed as the Germans' last step in securing their southern flank in East Central Europe before the German invasion of the Soviet Union. A key promoter of the undertaking was Luftwaffe Chief Göring who saw the airborne attack as a way of redeeming the reputation of the air force after its poor performance against the RAF in the Battle of Britain. The Germans assumed that they would dominate the skies during the operation and they did. More than 1,200 German aircraft participated in the campaign, while the Allies had no combat planes at all on Crete to challenge them. The Germans controlled the island by June 1. But the invasion of Crete was a costly venture for the Germans who suffered some 4,000 deaths and 2,500 wounded. The casualties were heavy enough that Hitler never again launched a major airborne attack in the Second World War. At this point, the Mediterranean theater of action faded into the background as most eyes turned to the main military event of 1941, the German invasion of the Soviet Union.

Operation Barbarossa

Hitler's plans for an attack on the Soviet Union began in late July 1940, when he ordered the German High Command to prepare for an offensive against that country within ten months. Hitler shored up relations with Finland and Romania so as to have both countries as allies during the invasion of the Soviet Union, and to assure Germany access to Romanian oil fields. Hitler approved the final plan on December 18, 1940. He gave the planned invasion the code name Operation Barbarossa. The Barbarossa plan divided Germany's forces into three major Army Groups: North, Center, and South. Army Group North would advance through the Baltic states toward Leningrad, Army Group Center through Smolensk on the way to Moscow, and Army Group South into Ukraine toward Kiev. The goal of the invaders was to crush the Soviet army quickly. To do that the Germans believed it imperative to destroy as much of the Red Army as possible near the Soviet Union's western borders, with the expectation that the entire Soviet structure would collapse shortly thereafter. The Germans optimistically anticipated that the campaign would last 8–10 weeks.

The campaign, originally scheduled to start on May 15, was delayed to June 22 because of Hitler's decision in late March to crush Yugoslavia first. In all probability the invasion could not have started until June in any case because of military hurdles and bad weather. The Germans found it more difficult than anticipated to put their military units in place in Poland for Barbarossa, and eastern Poland and western Russia experienced serious flooding as late as early June, rendering a German attack against the Russians before the third week of that month highly unlikely. The German attack commenced on June 22, 1941. At 3:00 a.m., Luftwaffe planes struck Soviet communications stations and air strips inside Soviet territory along a military front that stretched from Finland in the north to the Black Sea in the south. The planes succeeded in demolishing key Soviet communications networks and an estimated 1,200 Soviet aircraft on the first day. More than 3 million German soldiers and 500,000 troops from allied countries were a part of the ground force that began crossing the Soviet frontier at 3:30 a.m. It was the greatest assemblage of military forces for an invasion in the history of Europe.

The Nazi invasion initially moved forward with astonishing speed. By the end of the first week the number of Soviet planes lost stood at more than 4,000. Army Group North swiftly overran Lithuania and controlled much of Latvia by early July; the armored force spearheading the drive was just 80 miles from Leningrad (now St. Petersburg) by July 10. Army Group Center also scored some spectacular victories. By mid-July it had conducted two important encirclement battles and captured more than 600,000 Red Army soldiers and significant amounts of Russian armor; moreover, the center group had advanced 440 miles, captured Smolensk, and stood just 200 miles from Moscow. In the south, Germany encountered stronger resistance, since Stalin had put greater military resources there in anticipation of Hitler making Ukraine his primary invasion target because of the region's economic importance. But the Germans still quickly advanced through western Ukraine and by mid-July were not far from Kiev, the Soviet republic's capital city. Hitler was confident in July that victory was at hand.

The Germans' success was partly due to the fact that the invasion caught Stalin by surprise. Numerous sources, including Soviet agents and Western governments, had forewarned him of an impending German attack, but right up to the time of the invasion, he refused to accept what he was hearing, attributing the warnings to British ill-will. Instead, Stalin in the months leading up to the invasion tried to placate Hitler by scrupulously fulfilling the terms of Nazi–Soviet economic agreements reached in August 1939, February 1940, and January 1941. Stalin was convinced that Hitler would not wage war on two fronts, and the Nazi dictator was still locked in war with Great Britain. When Stalin learned of the invasion, he fell into a state of shock, and his condition bordered on a nervous breakdown. Indeed, he dropped out of sight for close to two weeks, only reemerging on July 3 to deliver a national radio address in which he uninspiringly called for all-out war against "Hitler's German-Fascist army." Stalin also reorganized the Soviet command structure to make it more effective, but he did so in a way to assure his continued dominance of Russia's war effort.

While the Soviets fought hard, the Germans continued their relentless advance during the remainder of the summer and into the fall. A segment of Army Group North completed the conquest of Estonia when it occupied Tallinn, the country's capital, on August 28. The major goal in the north, however, was the conquest of Leningrad. To facilitate Army Group North's task of getting there, Hitler ordered an armored unit from Army Group Center to join it in late August. The reinforced army group made significant gains in September and reached the outskirts of the old tsarist capital. But Army Group North was then stripped of all its armored forces as Hitler diverted them south to join in a final advance on Moscow. This decision virtually eliminated the possibility that a direct assault on Leningrad could succeed. The result was a siege that lasted three years before it failed.

While Hitler sent one armored unit north in late August, he shifted another commanded by General Guderian from Army Group Center to help Army Group South in a major battle unfolding near the Ukrainian capital of Kiev. The battle quickly ended after Guderian's armored unit and another linked east of the city to complete the envelopment of a massive Soviet force whose last remnants surrendered on September 26. The Germans took more than 650,000 captives in what turned out to be the biggest envelopment battle in military history. A euphoric Hitler then sent Guderian's armored force back to Army Group Center to prepare for a final push on Moscow.

On September 30, Army Group Center, whose advance eastward had been halted by the temporary diversions of its armored units to the armies in the north and south, launched a new offensive centered on Moscow. The Germans once again used envelopments to capture 650,000 Soviet soldiers in October. By October 13, German forces were just 60 miles from the Soviet capital. Panic swept across the city and many of its inhabitants fled eastward, but a calmer situation returned when it became clear that Stalin himself intended to remain in Moscow. Stalin also brought in General Georgi Zhukov to take charge of the city's defense. The battle-hardened commander, who had had success as a Soviet officer in the undeclared war between the Soviet Union and Japan in the late 1930s, immediately activated 250,000 Muscovites to construct anti-tank ditches on the outskirts of the city; he also brought in proven generals to shore up the threatened front and reinforced the approaches to the city with all the reserves that Stalin could find.

The Germans began experiencing serious problems as the month of October proceeded. Russia's heavy autumn rains turned the country's largely unpaved roads into impassable, muddy morasses. Wheeled transport moved forward only when pulled by tanks or other tracked vehicles. The Germans were also experiencing supply problems, as the railroads used to provide ammunition, food, and other items were unable to keep up with the demand. By the beginning of November, the Germans found it extremely difficult to move supplies. When winter weather emerged in early November, the Germans were caught largely unprepared, since they had invaded Russia on the assumption that the war would be over in a matter of weeks. Finally, while the Germans continued to capture or kill significant numbers of Soviet soldiers in the fall, the Russians kept coming up with replacements, some of which were battle-tested soldiers from the Far East, where the Soviets concluded that war with Japan was no longer a threat. German military leaders had a heated debate about their next step at a November 13 meeting. They decided that Army Group Center should make a final lunge for Moscow, since German forces were so close and the roads were hardening in the first winter frosts. The final offensive began on November 15, but ground to a halt at the beginning of December. Forward units had advanced to within 9 miles of the city's outskirts and 15 miles of the Kremlin.

In the midst of all this, the Soviets launched a counteroffensive on December 5. The Russians had brought in enough reinforcements to equal the numbers of soldiers in the Germans' Army Group Center. Zhukov's forces, catching the Germans by surprise, attacked both north and south of Moscow and drove them onto the defensive. The German generals argued in favor of retreating to a more secure line for the winter, but Hitler insisted that there be no withdrawal. As a result of Hitler's bullying and threats, his commanders took heart and demonstrated a new determination to hold firm against the Russian forces. The German lines stabilized and Zhukov's offensive came to a halt in March. Hitler's decision most likely saved Army Group Center from experiencing a rout at the hands of the Russians that winter. Another factor that helped them was Stalin's insistence in December that the Russians move to a general counteroffensive to destroy the entire German front. The decision diminished the Red Army's ability to secure a decisive victory in the center where its chances were greatest, since the troops Zhukov needed to achieve a rout were sent elsewhere. The Soviets proceeded to launch assaults in both the north and south of Russia in early 1942, but in neither instance did they decisively defeat the German forces they attacked.

The cost of the 1941 campaign was high for both sides. The Germans experienced some 918,000 casualties by the end of the year. The Germans also lost well over 2,700 tanks. As for the Russians, official figures indicated that they had more than 900,000 dead by the end of March 1942, and another 1.8 million men wounded or sick. In addition, the Germans captured over 3.3 million Soviet soldiers by December 1941. Russian equipment losses were massive as well. But Hitler's Operation Barbarossa had failed, since his military machine had not destroyed the Soviet army in 1941. The operation's goal ultimately proved beyond Germany's capacity to achieve it.

War against the United States

A new development in the war came in December 1941, when Hitler on December 11 declared war on the United States. It came on the heels of a surprise attack by Japan, another Axis power, on the American naval base at Pearl Harbor, Hawaii, on the morning of December 7. Hitler eagerly accepted the prospect of war with the United States, believing that the Japanese navy would be an effective weapon against the Americans, and he relished the thought of unleashing the German fleet to sink vessels at will in the North Atlantic. Hitler's decision represented the culmination of rising tensions between Germany and the United States dating to the outbreak of war in Europe in 1939. Mussolini also declared war on America on December 11.

The United States was neutral when the war began, but adopted a "cash and carry" policy on arms sales that benefited the Allies (see p. 280). The British took advantage of this to buy weaponry starting in 1939, but they were running out of cash reserves by the end of 1940. U.S. assistance to Britain intensified in March 1941, when the U.S. Congress passed the Lend-Lease Act, allowing President Franklin Roosevelt to lend, lease, sell, exchange, or transfer military equipment to any country whose defense was considered vital to the United States – in this case Great Britain. The Lend-Lease Act was extended to the Soviet Union in the fall of 1941. In July 1941, Roosevelt directed U.S. naval vessels and aircraft on patrol in the western Atlantic to inform the British of the whereabouts of any discovered German submarines. Finally, following a couple of serious incidents between German submarines and American warships, Roosevelt in October 1941 convinced the American Congress to allow U.S. merchantmen to arm and to carry their shipments to Allied ports. Roosevelt had now done about all he could to assist the Allied effort short of full-scale war with the Germans, which came with Hitler's December 11 announcement. After America's entry into the conflict, Roosevelt and Churchill quickly agreed on making the defeat of Germany their top goal.

The war at sea, 1939–1941

The key to any Nazi success on the high seas lay in Germany's submarines, called U-boats. When the war broke out in 1939, the Germans had slightly more than 50 submarines, of which a mere 22 were adequate for use in the Atlantic Ocean. It would take at a minimum another two years to construct a sizable U-boat force. In addition, Germany's surface fleet was hopelessly inferior to that of Great Britain. Taking advantage of that fact, Britain, along with France, instituted a blockade against Germany on September 3, 1939, but it lacked effectiveness since Germany was able to secure the bulk of its necessary raw materials by land from East Central Europe and the Soviet Union. By March 1940, German submarine attacks against the British had resulted in the sinking of 222 vessels totaling 886,000 tons. At that point the German threat to the British merchant fleet was still minor in nature. That fleet, the largest in the world, consisted of approximately 3,000 ocean-sailing ships and another 1,000 big coastal-water vessels; together, their total tonnage was 21 million tons. The British ships protected themselves on the high seas, as they did during World War I, with a convoy system.

After Italy entered the war in 1940, the British inflicted serious damage on the Italians' Mediterranean fleet in two major engagements. In November 1940, Britain carried out for the first time in history an all-airplane naval attack launched from an aircraft carrier, using torpedo-carrying Swordfish biplanes against the Italian fleet harbored at Taranto. The torpedo planes caused extensive damage to two battleships and blasted a third beyond repair. The following March, a British naval victory at Cape Matapan off the southern coast of Greece effectively rendered the Italian fleet inoperative.

It was in the Atlantic that the most critical fighting at sea took place, since that is where Britain's most frequently used trade lanes were located. Using their new bases in France, the German U-boat force, under the command of Admiral Karl Dönitz, created havoc for the British from June to November of 1940. The Germans destroyed more than 1.6 million tons of shipping with wolf-packs, i.e., groups of four to six U-boats locating Allied convoys and joining together on the surface at night to attack the vessels. In 1941, the German U-boats continued their devastation, sinking 324,550 tons of Allied shipping in May and almost as much in June, as the number of U-boats in operation reached 65. In fact, the Germans sank, particularly in the first six months of the year, far more British tonnage in 1941 than the British were capable of replacing. The British responded by rerouting a number of convoys, relying on information obtained through their partial decipherment of the German naval Enigma code system. British convoys also began receiving new assistance from the United States in the fall in the form of American escorts to a mid-Atlantic rendezvous point where British protection then took over. More relief came when the Germans decided in September to shift submarines from the Atlantic to the Mediterranean Sea. In regard to German surface ships, the British scored a major success on May 27, 1941, when Royal Navy ships sank the new, giant German battleship *Bismarck* in the Atlantic with a loss of over 2,000 crew members. The loss of the 50,000 ton behemoth had the effect of ending any significant role the Germans may have intended for its surface fleet in the Battle of the Atlantic.

The war in North Africa, 1942–1943

One theater that occupied the attention of both sets of belligerents in 1942 was North Africa. Hitler had moved troops under Erwin Rommel into Libya in the spring of 1941 to rescue an Italian army that the British had battered. A bold, brilliant risk-taker who had demonstrated heroism in World War I and distinguished himself as an armored division commander during Germany's invasion of France in 1940, Rommel quickly shifted the momentum in favor of the Axis side (see p. 271). Under considerable pressure from the British in late 1941, however, Rommel and his Axis forces abandoned a siege of the British-controlled Libyan port of Tobruk and fell back to the starting point of their offensive of the prior spring. In spite of Hitler's view of the fighting in North Africa as a sideshow to the war in the Soviet Union, Rommel was still able to undertake a major offensive in May 1942, using German and Italian troops. Though the British had greater numbers of soldiers, the Axis units moved ahead aggressively. On June 21, the Axis forces scored a spectacular victory by forcing the British to surrender at Tobruk after a week-long siege. In August, Churchill purged the command structure in the Middle East, which included North Africa. He assigned Bernard Montgomery to take charge of the British North African Army. Montgomery had fought in World War I, where he had become convinced of the importance of organization and caution when conducting military operations.

Montgomery postponed any fight with Rommel's Afrika Korps, which was deep inside Egypt and heading toward the Suez Canal, until the British had overwhelming superiority in men and equipment. The British finally attacked the German and Italian forces at El Alamein on October 23, 1942. Britain's advantage in numbers of soldiers was 230,000 to 80,000 for the Axis. In the area of tanks, the British enjoyed a numerically strong edge, 1,200 to 500. Even though the Axis inflicted important losses on the British – destroying four times as many British tanks as they themselves endured, for example – they were unable to rebuff the British onslaught, and by early November the remaining Axis soldiers had begun a 1,800 mile retreat to Tunisia. The Battle of El Alamein was the major turning point in the North African war, since it represented a shift in the momentum of the fighting in favor of the Allies.

As Rommel's forces retreated from Egypt, the Allies on November 8 landed troops in Vichy-held Morocco and Algeria as a part of a military offensive code-named Operation Torch. The goal of the operation was the capture of Tunisia. The November landings initially met armed resistance from Vichy French soldiers, but the fortuitous presence in Algeria of Admiral Jean François Darlan, the commander of the Vichy armed forces, allowed a political deal to be made. On November 10, U.S. General Dwight D. Eisenhower, the commander of Operation Torch, reached an agreement with Darlan in which Darlan ordered French troops to accept an immediate ceasefire and to join the side of the Allies in return for Allied recognition of the admiral as the head of government administration in French North Africa. Hitler's response to the Allied landings and Darlan's dealings was the dispatch of German troops into "unoccupied" France on November 11 to set up a permanent military occupation of the whole country. As for Darlan, he did not enjoy his new political ascendancy very long: a 20-year-old monarchist assassinated him on Christmas Eve. Allied leaders, whose arrangement with Darlan had already enraged Free French leader Charles de Gaulle, added fuel to the fire by naming General Henri Giraud as Darlan's replacement. De Gaulle refused to accept the decision, so the Allies launched an effort to bring Giraud and de Gaulle together, starting with a handshake between the two rivals at Casablanca, Morocco, in January 1943. Following complex negotiations, the two men agreed in June 1943 to serve as co-chairmen of a French Committee of National Liberation whose purpose was to free France from Nazi domination. Giraud proved to be politically inept, however, and de Gaulle emerged as the sole leader of the organization within a matter of months. For de Gaulle, the North African episode, coming at the hands of the Allies, was a bitter experience that he did not forget or forgive.

In North Africa, Hitler countered the Allies' November landings with a huge buildup of soldiers in Tunisia. Rommel's forces, retreating out of Libya, took up positions in Tunisia in late January 1943. Hitler also committed large amounts of equipment and hundreds of aircraft to the campaign. As a result of Hitler's actions, the fighting in North Africa, instead of ending in late 1942 as the Allies had initially hoped, lasted until mid-May 1943, when the last of the Axis defenders surrendered. In the end, Hitler's effort in Tunisia succeeded in delaying by at least several months any Allied invasion of France, but it also resulted in the diversion of resources that the Nazis urgently needed in the Soviet Union. In that sense, Operation Torch contributed important relief from the pressure that hard-pressed Soviet forces felt in the fall and winter of 1942–1943.

The Eastern Front, 1942–1943

Hitler's main focus in 1942 continued to be the Eastern Front, where the winter of 1941–1942 had been particularly harsh in Russia and the Balkans. When planning for the 1942 campaign season, Hitler gave considerable attention to economic targets. While the German offensive was designed to capture large numbers of Soviet soldiers through massive envelopments, the top priority was the seizure of economic resources, especially the capture of the Caucasus oilfields in the south of Russia, which would deprive the Soviets of a vital source of energy while providing a needed one for the Germans. Since the Germans lacked the military strength and provisions to launch a series of strikes along the full length of the Eastern Front simultaneously, they concentrated on the southern sector where Army Group South was situated. Stalin, who expected the Nazis' big push to be directed against Moscow and therefore kept the bulk of Soviet forces in that area, was caught by surprise.

The Germans launched their main offensive on June 28, 1942. Hitler divided Army Group South into two separate units, namely, Army Group A and Army Group B, for the campaign. Hitler claimed a great victory in July following the capture of 100,000 to 200,000 Soviet soldiers in three German encirclements. He then ordered the majority of the forces of Army Groups A and B to move south. Only the Sixth Army of Army Group B remained to move eastward toward Stalingrad. The Germans continued to push towards the oilfields of Grozny some 200 miles to the east, but supply line problems, rugged mountainous terrain, and front lines stretched to the limit brought their offensive to a halt just short of the goal, causing Hitler to relocate infantry and armored units to Stalingrad. He surmised that once Stalingrad had at least been neutralized, the effort to reach the oilfields of Grozny and then Baku, located even farther east, could restart. The German Sixth Army under the command of Friedrich Paulus had the responsibility of capturing Stalingrad, which initially received scant attention from German leaders.

The Sixth Army had the 20-mile long city with the mile-wide Volga River at the city's back completely isolated by early September. During the fall, the city took on a symbolic importance for Hitler, in part because of its name. But Stalin became just as driven to defend it. He refused to let citizens of Stalingrad leave, using them as a fighting incentive for the Soviet soldiers. To gain complete control of the city, the Germans brought in Romanian soldiers from the Caucasus to replace German soldiers on the northern and southern flanks, releasing the German troops for fighting in the city. The Romanian soldiers were poorly equipped and plagued by low morale. As for the German troops, they engaged in ferocious, bitter street battles against the Soviet defenders. Victories were measured by how many buildings one gained or lost in a single day. By October 18, the Soviets in some places were only about 300 yards from the Volga. As the battle continued, Hitler lost his military perspective, and seemed to obsess on gaining yards in Stalingrad rather than miles on other fronts. By early November, German forces controlled most of Stalingrad, and victory seemed assured.

The Soviets, meanwhile, had begun assembling large numbers of soldiers in September for a counteroffensive that they unleashed on November 19, 1942. The key planners of the Soviet operation were Generals Georgi Zhukov and Aleksandr Vasilevsky. The counteroffensive, launched west of Stalingrad and involving forces from the north and south moving toward each other in a double-pincer movement, surprised the Germans. Both Soviet forces quickly broke through Romanian-guarded sections of the German defense lines and closed the jaws of the pincers on November 23. The entire German Sixth Army was surrounded. All German military leaders in the Stalingrad sector favored withdrawal, but Hitler's response was negative, in part because he did not want to suffer the humiliation of abandoning the city he had recently promised in public speeches to retain. He instead sent a relief offensive toward the trapped Sixth Army and ordered the Luftwaffe to fly in needed supplies. The relief expedition stalled half-way to its goal 80 miles away, the Luftwaffe never came close to delivering all the supplies it promised, and Paulus' position became increasingly untenable as Soviet forces tightened the noose. Paulus asked for freedom of action in early January, but Hitler insisted that the Sixth Army "fight to the last man." On January 31, with his army's ammunition and food exhausted, Paulus capitulated and all remaining German resistance ended on February 2. Hitler railed against the German commander for his surrender, contending that he should have committed suicide instead. Hitler's distrust of his military leaders, present well before Stalingrad, deepened as a result of the German defeat.

The Battle of Stalingrad represented Russia's first true military victory against the Germans in the war. The Russians suffered heavy casualties, but the blow to the Germans was complete and obvious. Approximately 150,000 Germans trapped in the Stalingrad pocket died. The Russians also took 90,000 prisoners, including some 20 generals; only 6,000 of the captured men ever returned to Germany. The Battle of Stalingrad proved to be the turning point in the war on the Eastern Front. From this time on, the German war effort in the East was primarily a defensive struggle.

The war at sea, 1942–1943

The war at sea intensified in 1942, when the Germans ramped up their submarine campaign to destroy Allied shipping in the Atlantic. The number of U-boats in operation increased significantly during the year, reaching 100 by October. As many as 12 German submarines roamed along the east coast of the United States by then, sinking large numbers of merchant ships with little risk to themselves. U-boats sank close

Figure 7.2 A Soviet soldier waves a victory flag at the Battle of Stalingrad in early 1943.

to 500,000 tons of Allied shipping in the Atlantic in each of the months of February, March, and April, with Allied losses rising to 600,000 tons in May and over 700,000 tons in June. The Germans also switched the Enigma code used in their submarines in February. Before the new code could be unlocked, Allied shipping losses in the Atlantic reached a World War II record of 860,000 tons in November.

After a winter lull, U-boat attacks on Allied ships resumed, reaching almost half a million tons in March 1943. But then the Germans experienced a reversal of fortunes, owing largely to the efforts of British Admiral Sir Max Horton, who was in charge of Allied naval forces for the western approaches to Britain. Horton coordinated a highly effective antisubmarine campaign that came into its own in late March. He increased air support and developed warship support groups that assisted normal military convoy escort vessels by tracking down U-boats more freely and destroying them. In May, the Germans suffered U-boat losses representing 25 percent of the submarine fleet's operational strength. As a result, Admiral Dönitz on May 24 called off the Atlantic campaign. He tried to revive Germany's submarine campaign later in the year, but to little effect. In the end, the Allies decisively won the battle of the high seas.

The Eastern Front, 1943–1944

By March 1943, the Soviet Union had scored its dramatic victory at Stalingrad, established a narrow land corridor to Leningrad in the north to provide relief to its besieged inhabitants, and pushed the Germans largely out of the Caucasus, the Don basin, and eastern Ukraine in the south. The Russians also enjoyed a considerable edge over the Germans in military manpower, and they were benefiting from significant quantities of Lend-Lease materiel shipped from the United States and Great Britain. Despite these Soviet advantages, the Germans carried out a powerful counteroffensive in Ukraine in March and recaptured the eastern Ukrainian city of Kharkov that they had lost to the Russians one month earlier.

A three-month pause followed the March fighting as the two giants on the Eastern Front prepared for the 1943 campaign. Hitler's grand plan called for a large pincers movement against a Soviet salient in the area of the Ukrainian city of Kursk. The offensive, originally scheduled to start in April, was postponed in order to increase the number of tanks available for the operation. The German attack, unleashed on July 5, 1943, was halted after five days. At that point the Germans threw all their remaining armored forces into play. To counter this move, the Soviets also committed several hundred tanks to action, and the ensuing clash on July 12 became the largest tank battle of the Second World War. Once the day-long fight was over, the hulls of more than 700 destroyed tanks from both sides filled the battlefield. While the Soviets absorbed heavy losses that day, they stopped the German offensive. The Battle of Kursk demonstrated that the Germans no longer had the ability to undertake a sustainable major offensive against the Soviets. The initiative on the Eastern Front now weighed heavily in favor of the Soviet Union.

Indeed, the Russians began to launch several summer offensives. Even before the Battle of Kursk ended, the Russians drove the Germans out of their positions north of Kursk, retaking the Russian city of Orel in early August. To the south of Kursk the Russians recaptured Kharkov on August 22, following up with a powerful late-August offensive in the far south, where they pushed the Germans back nearly 200 miles in three weeks' time. By the beginning of October, the Russians had advanced along the entire 650-mile southern sector an average of 150 miles, which allowed them to recover valuable agricultural lands and industrial centers. In late September, they also liberated Smolensk after opening a major offensive on the central front in August. For the Soviets, the summer offensives, albeit costly, brought victory and an even greater sense of self-confidence.

The Soviets, known for commencing cold weather offensives, did just that during the winter of 1943–1944, launching an offensive around Leningrad in January 1944. The German Army North was unprepared, and the Russians broke the brutal 900-day German siege of Leningrad before the month was over. In the south, the Soviets began an operation in December to drive the Germans out of western Ukraine. At the beginning of February, Soviet forces reached Ukraine's prewar frontier with Poland. They then defied the wartime practice of waiting out the Russian springtime thaw by pushing forward in early March with a surprise "mud offensive" in Ukraine. Using new wide-tracked Russian T34 tanks and four-wheel-drive trucks from America, the Soviets achieved another spectacular victory. Indeed, Russian forces were in prewar Romania before the month was over. By early April, Ukraine was entirely free of German control.

Sicily and Italy, 1943–1944

In the Mediterranean theater of action in 1943, the Allies' next move, following their success in North Africa, was to attack the southern Italian island of Sicily. The Americans and British had agreed to that at the Casablanca Conference in January 1943. That decision was part of a British push for a Mediterranean strategy that involved striking at the Italian mainland and forcing Italy out of the war. The Americans accepted the British position on Italy only after Churchill gave a firm promise that Britain would support a cross-Channel invasion of France in the spring of 1944. The Sicilian campaign, launched on July 10, caught the Italian and German defenders unprepared, forcing many of the Axis soldiers to withdraw to the Italian mainland. By the time the Allies occupied the Sicilian city of Messina on August 17, 1943, the Axis had lost 164,000 soldiers, the bulk of them captured Italians. The Allied invasion of Sicily resulted in Mussolini's ouster from power and his arrest the next day. Marshal Pietro Badoglio, forming a new government, began negotiations with the Allies for Italy's unconditional surrender. His government signed a peace treaty on September 3, the same day that the British sent soldiers from Sicily to the Italian peninsula to start an Allied offensive there. As soon as Hitler received word of the Badoglio government's treaty with the Allies, he ordered German troops to occupy Rome and to disarm the Italian army. Faced with the possibility of German internment, most Italian soldiers deserted, so that German troops descending on the Italian capital encountered virtually no resistance. The Germans prepared for the possibility of an Allied advance up the peninsula by establishing a formidable defensive barrier, the Gustav Line, across central Italy from the Mediterranean to the Adriatic 80 miles south of Rome. Hitler also ordered Mussolini rescued from his imprisonment on September 12, 1943. At Hitler's insistence, Mussolini became the head of a puppet dictatorship in northern Italy called the Italian Social Republic.

The Allied offensive launched on mainland Italy in September encountered enormous challenges. The Germans demonstrated considerable tenacity in defending the southern approach to Rome. The rugged terrain of the Apennine Mountains, which ran down the spine of the Italian peninsula, created daunting obstacles: the Allies often had to use mules, for example, to carry supplies up steep, rock-riddled slopes, and when the mules could go no further, the soldiers had to finish the job. Mud added to the difficulties of the Allied advance as did torrential rains that transformed rivers into bloated, churning impediments. As autumn gave way to winter, a combination of snow, cold, and a lack of protection halted the Allied offensive in mid-January 1944, in front of the Gustav Line.

In an attempt to break the deadlock in Italy, the Allies in the latter part of January 1944 staged a surprise landing behind the German lines on the beaches near the town of Anzio, located a mere 33 miles south of Rome, and established a beachhead against no serious opposition. But rather than moving the Allied forces aggressively inland, the American commander decided to consolidate the position of his forces on the beaches first, thereby giving the Germans the opportunity to shift troops into the mountains around Anzio and subject the encircled Allies to a steady barrage of artillery fire. Only in May 1944 were the Allies, strengthened by reinforcements, able to break out of their Anzio beachhead.

It was also in January that the Allies decided to push through the Gustav Line by unleashing an attack against the German position at Monte Cassino, a site famous for its medieval abbey. The fighting at Monte Cassino was intense and brutal, and dragged on for several months. The stalemate finally ended in May when the Allies used an overwhelming advantage in manpower to force the Germans out of the area. The Germans withdrew to new defensive positions well to the north of Rome, declaring the Italian capital an open city, and on June 4, 1944, American troops moved in to take control of the Eternal City.

D-Day and after in the West, 1944

In the West, the Allies opened up a major second front against France in June 1944. It was the culmination of a long, bitter debate among the three major Allied powers. Stalin had wanted to see the creation of a significant cross-Channel invasion in 1942, and was frustrated and suspicious when that did not happen. Roosevelt and Churchill, meeting in Casablanca in January 1943, concurred that there could be no major cross-Channel invasion that year. At Roosevelt's insistence, they also agreed to require the "unconditional surrender" of the Axis powers of Germany, Italy, and Japan. This was partly done to reassure Stalin that the Western Allies were committed to fight the war to the end and would not make a separate peace with Germany. Debates about the timing of and commitment to a cross-Channel invasion continued throughout most of 1943 not just between the Soviet Union and its two Western Allies, but between the British and Americans as well. It was not until the Teheran Conference in November 1943 that Roosevelt, Churchill, and Stalin agreed on the essentials of a major cross-Channel invasion code-named Operation Overlord, that would take place in May 1944. The invasion of France would be the dominant focus of the Western Allies in 1944, pushing Italy into a subordinate position in overall Allied strategy. Stalin insisted that a commander-in-chief for the operation be named at once since he felt that without such a move, the invasion plan would never be implemented. Shortly after the conference, Roosevelt selected Eisenhower as the supreme commander of the cross-Channel operation. The choice of Eisenhower proved important to Allied cooperation as Operation Overlord moved forward, since he had a special ability to work well with leaders on both sides of the Atlantic.

The Allies committed enormous amounts of materiel with which to launch the invasion of France. By early June 1944, they had amassed 12,000 aircraft, 600 warships, and more than 4,000 landing craft and transports. Allied leaders had also assembled well over 2.8 million military personnel for the operation. They selected Normandy as the invasion site, in part because there was a major nearby port – Cherbourg – that could handle the influx of supplies once the Allies secured the area. The Allies also chose Normandy because they were aware through Ultra that the Germans expected the invasion to occur well to the northeast of Normandy. Not wanting to attack heavily defended Cherbourg at the outset, the Allies decided to drag two portable, concrete harbors, known as "Mulberries," across the Channel to serve as temporary unloading facilities at the landing site.

On the German side, Hitler had in 1942 expressed confidence in the Reich's ability to keep Anglo-American forces out of Western Europe. In September of that year, he had told a small group of top German officials that if Germany could keep the Allies from establishing a second front before mid-1943, the Reich would have all the time it needed to complete its Atlantic Wall, a supposedly impregnable shoreline defensive barrier stretching from the Pyrenees to Denmark. By November 1943, however, Hitler had revised his views. Believing that an Allied attack could come in the spring of 1944, if not sooner, he issued new instructions to strengthen the Western defenses, and appointed Rommel to supervise the effort. Rommel, shocked by the inadequacy of Germany's coastal fortifications, launched a crash program to improve them. But German military leaders mistakenly concluded that the main attack would come along the coast of the Pas-de-Calais region in northeastern France and not Normandy; consequently, their defense preparations were more vigorous at the former than the latter. Compounding Germany's problems in the West in the spring of 1944 were equipment shortages and troop deficiencies: there were only 300 fighter planes available, for example, and many of the soldiers were second-rate because the war in the East had taken away so many of the army's best fighters.

Worries and concerns among the Allies about the upcoming invasion persisted during the spring of 1944. In April, Churchill was still fretting about the cross-Channel attack that he feared might become another Dunkirk, end Britain's role in the war, and ruin his position as prime minister. Only in mid-May, when he saw the large role that Montgomery played at a final meeting to review the invasion plans, did Churchill harden in his support for the operation. Then bad weather forced Eisenhower to postpone the launch date until June 6, when Allied weather forecasters indicated that there would be a brief break in the dismal conditions. The Germans, without access to accurate weather reports, assumed that the poor weather would prevent an Allied attack until mid-June and perhaps even early July. They were completely surprised by the timing of the Allied attack.

The largest amphibious assault in the history of warfare began on the morning of June 6, 1944, when the Allies unleashed Operation Overlord. Known as D-Day, the Allied assault that day began early with the dropping of 23,000 Allied paratroopers inland to block the approaches to the coast and continued with the landing of 130,000 American, British, and Canadian troops on the coast of Normandy. After five days of fighting, the Allies had breached the German ring of defense, and after ten days of fighting, more than 500,000 Allied soldiers had made it onto the Normandy beaches. On June 26, the Allies forced the Germans to surrender at Cherbourg. The Allies now had a major port facility, although it took them close to three weeks to make it operable, owing to destruction by German demolition teams. Throughout June and July, the Germans considered the Normandy landing to be a diversion, and believed that the main thrust would come near the city of Calais. When they finally realized their error, it was too late to shift reinforcements to Normandy.

On July 25, the American forces in Normandy launched a breakout offensive in which they began a rapid drive eastward across France. With their entire position in Normandy threatened, the Germans, on orders from Hitler, attempted a counteroffensive rather than moving back to more defensible positions farther east. As Allied forces attacked from the north and south and the German position became untenable, Hitler ordered a withdrawal from what became known as the Falaise pocket. While 35,000 German soldiers escaped before the pocket closed on August 19, the Allies still killed 10,000 Germans and captured 50,000 more. The Allied victory in Normandy was complete.

Figure 7.3 The Allied forces carry forward Operation Overlord against Germany in Normandy, France, shortly after D-Day on June 6, 1944.

Other Allied successes in the West followed in the summer of 1944. Eisenhower granted a French armored division the privilege of carrying out the liberation of Paris, and on August 25 the Germans formally surrendered there. By mid-September, Allied forces had taken control of most of Belgium in the north and pushed into Lorraine in the east. In the south of France, notwithstanding bitter protests from Churchill who wanted to keep the Allies' focus in the Mediterranean on Italy, the Allies launched an enormously successful amphibious landing operation on August 15. Indeed, in the four weeks of the campaign, the Allies liberated much of southern and central France and dealt heavy blows to the German defenders. The Allies' pursuit of the enemy ended in mid-September, when they reached the Vosges Mountains in southern Alsace, where the remaining German soldiers had taken refuge.

Soviet offensives, 1944

As for the Eastern Front, the Soviets planned a massive summer offensive in 1944. They initiated a part of the plan on June 9 with a strike against the military positions of Finland, a co-belligerent with Germany since 1941. The Finnish government, desperate for German help, promised not to sign a separate peace with the Russians in return for German military aid. In spite of German assistance, the Finns, after experiencing heavy losses, signed an armistice with the Soviet Union in September. The peace terms were harsh, but at least Finland preserved its independence. The centerpiece of the Soviet offensive was Operation Bagration, which the Soviets unleashed against Germany's Army Group Center in Belorussia on June 22, 1944. It was one of the war's most sensational battles. The Soviets had some 1.7 million troops, more than 4,000 tanks and assault guns, and over 6,300 airplanes ready when the offensive began. The German strength in each of those categories was considerably less. The Soviets had used ruse and deception to convince the Germans that the main Soviet offensive would take place in Ukraine to the south, so that when the attack came, Wehrmacht leaders were surprised. The Soviets took control of the Belorussian capital of Minsk on July 3. By mid-July the Soviet offensive had moved forward some 200 miles along the central front, at which point they paused temporarily because they had outrun their supplies. When the offensive finally ended on August 19, the Soviets had driven the Germans out of Belorussia and eastern Poland. German losses were even greater than those suffered at Stalingrad: German Army Group Center basically disappeared.

The Warsaw Uprising, 1944

Soviet forces approached the outskirts of Warsaw during the summer offensive, but stopped their advance along the Vistula River, short of the city, at the end of July. As news of the Soviets' approach reached Warsaw and their artillery guns could be heard in the distance, the Polish underground took heart from the heavy blows that the Russians had inflicted on the Wehrmacht. Moreover, Soviet radio on July 29 encouraged the Poles in the capital to turn against the German occupiers. The leader of the underground Home Army on July 31 ordered that a Polish uprising begin the next day. On the very first day, the insurgents gained control over much of the city center. But they were poorly armed, and Hitler was determined to keep the city under Nazi control. He sent in units of the SS to help crush the rebellion. Weeks of intense fighting took place, with the Poles enduring vicious atrocities and heavy losses. As many as 10,000 insurgents and 200,000 civilians lost their lives in the uprising. The Polish rebels capitulated to the Nazis on October 2. In the aftermath, Hitler ordered that the city, already considerably damaged from the uprising and other war-related events, be completely destroyed. In an unprecedented move, the Germans removed Warsaw's remaining residents to other locations, including concentration camps and sites in Germany where they worked as slave laborers. The Germans then began a systematic destruction of what remained of the capital. By January 1945, approximately 85 percent of the buildings in Warsaw lay in ruins.

The apparent intention of the Polish Home Army in initiating the Warsaw Uprising when it did was to prevent the Russians from taking control of the city as conquerors. The Poles also expected that Soviet military pressure against the German troops around Warsaw would continue and facilitate their task of driving the Germans out of the city. The Soviets, however, had other plans. Operation Bagration had allowed the Soviets to advance considerable distances, but it ultimately cost them some 180,000 Russians dead or missing, and more than 590,000 wounded; many of these occurred before the Red Army approached the Polish capital. The Russians decided to remain in place outside Warsaw, rest and regroup, and let the Poles essentially fend for themselves. The fact that the Soviet army stayed on the outskirts of Warsaw without really assisting the Home Army throughout the Warsaw Uprising has stirred heated debate ever since. Were the Soviets justified militarily in their decision to stand pat or was the decision a cynical ploy by Stalin to weaken Polish opposition to his plans for a Soviet-dominated Poland? While some historians have argued in favor of military necessity, others have contended that the Germans did Stalin's work for him by gutting the Polish independence movement in Warsaw. For that reason, Stalin saw no need to order Soviet intervention to assist the Poles in fighting the Germans.

New German technology

As Allied military forces pressed in on Nazi-controlled Europe, Hitler looked to new weapons to tip the balance in his favor. One was the development of the V-1 and V-2 rockets. The V-1s were first fired on London in mid-June 1944, shortly after the D-Day invasion, and British locations were targeted for months thereafter. Most of the rockets were directed against sites in Belgium, however, with Antwerp bearing the brunt of most attacks. The V-2, which could travel at speeds in excess of 2,000 miles per hour, was also used primarily against targets in Belgium. Both types of rockets, because of the absence of precision-targeted guidance systems, had to be directed against large cities in order to cause any serious damage, and ultimately their numbers were insufficient to influence the outcome of the war. The Germans were also in the forefront in the development of jet aircraft, but their first jet planes only became operational late in the spring of 1944. By that time the Allies dominated the skies, and the small number of German jets in combat had no impact on the outcome of the air war. In the end, Hitler never did find a new weapon that Germany could produce in sufficient numbers and employ effectively enough to redress the deteriorating position of his forces in both Western and Eastern Europe.

The Western Front, September 1944–January 1945

As September 1944 arrived on the Western Front, Eisenhower insisted that the Allies pursue a broad-front approach, calling on his generals to move their forces forward at a roughly equal pace. Montgomery, who opposed that strategy, proposed to Eisenhower, on September 10, a single thrust offensive against the Germans in the Netherlands. Montgomery believed that the Allies could reach northern Germany, with airborne units securing vital Dutch river bridges and ground forces racing across the Netherlands to the eastern Dutch city of Arnhem, where they would create a bridgehead on the Rhine River. From there the Allies could outflank the northernmost section of Germany's border fortifications – the Westwall or Siegfried Line – and proceed to capture the Reich's industrial Ruhr region. His plan was code-named Operation Market Garden. With Eisenhower's approval, massive paratrooper drops were made on September 17, followed by ground forces that succeeded in relieving the airborne units at all bridges except one. The British paratroopers assigned to take the key bridge in faraway Arnhem encountered such stiff German resistance that they abandoned the bridge after nine days. With that defeat, Operation Market Garden was at an end. The failure of this operation blunted Allied progress in the Netherlands and shattered any hopes of crossing the Rhine in 1944.

The Allies' frustrations grew in the late fall as supply shortages and stiffening German resistance stalled their advance. It was in these circumstances that the Germans, in what became known as the Battle of the Bulge, staged one final show of strength in December, when they launched a surprise offensive in the area of the Ardennes. Their goal was to reach Antwerp and cut off Montgomery's forces from the rest of the Allied armies. Low overcast skies, which kept the Allies' air power grounded, allowed the Germans to advance during the first days, creating a bulge in the Allied lines in Belgium. The return of clear skies on December 23 allowed the Allies to unleash a fierce aerial bombardment on German troops

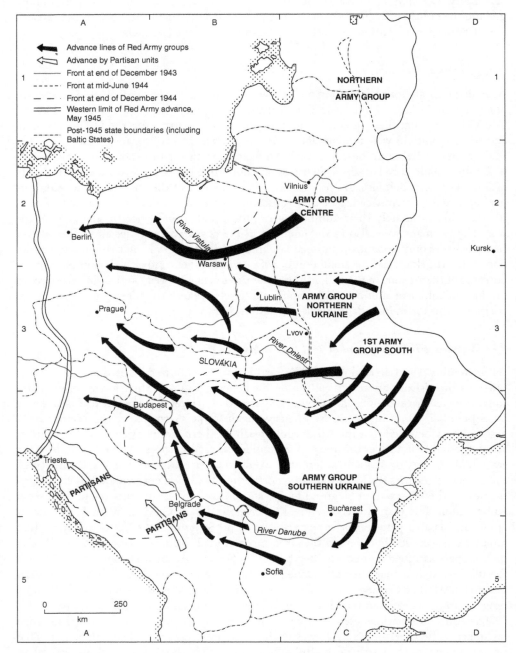

Map 7.1 The advance of the Red Army in World War II, 1943–1945.

and supply points, and that, combined with a lack of fuel, forced the German offensive to a halt on Christmas Day. The Allies launched attacks in late December both north and south of a narrow but deep salient that the Germans had created, and by mid-January the Allies had eliminated the bulge and achieved victory. Hitler had thrown his last reserves into the battle, and now had little left to stop the Allies on the Western and Eastern fronts. It was a defeat from which the Germans never recovered.

The last months, 1945

Eisenhower's next step was to order a broad-front Allied offensive to the Rhine, establish bridgeheads, and then envelop the Ruhr region. The thrust began in early February 1945, and over the next few weeks the Allies, in extremely bitter fighting, pushed the German defenders to the east side of the river. On March 7, American soldiers came upon an intact railroad bridge on the Rhine at Remagen. It was the only one along the entire length of the waterway that the Germans had not yet demolished, although German demolition experts were there when the Americans arrived. The Americans stormed the bridge and established a bridgehead on the river's east bank. Thousands of Allied soldiers poured across the bridge in the days that followed. By the end of March, the Allies had set up several more bridgeheads and were now poised to move into Germany's heartland. In April, one of the major encirclements of all time occurred in the Ruhr, when American forces captured 300,000 German soldiers, effectively ending large-scale German resistance on the Western Front. Along other sectors of the front, Allied soldiers also moved rapidly forward. In north Germany, forces under Montgomery crossed the Elbe River in April and took control of the Baltic port city of Lübeck on May 2. In the south, General George Patton's army drove into Bavaria and Czechoslovakia, but stopped short of Prague. Under pressure from the Soviets, Eisenhower had given the order not to advance on the Czech capital.

In Italy, the Allies, after suspending an offensive in the northern part of the country at the end of 1944 because of winter weather, embarked on a new push against the Axis in early April 1945. As the position of the Axis soldiers crumbled around him, Mussolini attempted to flee to Switzerland, but partisans captured him and his mistress short of the border on April 27. The partisans, after shooting them to death the following day, suspended their bodies upside down in a square near the main train station in the Italian city of Milan. In the meantime, the German commander in Italy signed an unconditional surrender document and fighting on the Italian front officially ended on May 2.

On the Eastern Front, a four-month lull that began in September 1944 ended on January 12, 1945, when the Soviets embarked on a broad-front offensive, with the conquest of Berlin as one of its key goals. The Red Army assembled 1.5 million soldiers to face off against less than 600,000 German troops. On January 17, Soviet forces under Zhukov occupied Warsaw, and three days later another army led by Commander Ivan Konev moved into the highly important German industrial area of Silesia. By early February, Zhukov had troops at the Oder River, slightly more than 30 miles from the outskirts of Berlin, although major supply problems and a German counterattack stopped his army's advance at that point. Konev soon had his forces lined up on the Oder as well. Further south, Soviet soldiers reached the approaches to Vienna on April 4, and after several days of street fighting, they had the city under their complete control. Zhukov and Konev regrouped their respective forces in March in preparation for a final assault on Berlin. The two army groups initiated their attacks on April 16 – in Zhukov's case, with one of the greatest artillery assaults in military history – and had Berlin encircled by

April 25. On that same day, elements of the U.S. army and the Red Army met at several locations on the Elbe south of the German capital. The Eastern and Western fronts had linked together in another sign of the imminent fall of Hitler's Third Reich.

On April 26, the Russians began to push into Berlin itself. The Soviet forces waged street by street combat, and though suffering heavy casualties, they drove toward the Reich's government buildings, where Hitler, protected in a bunker more than 50 feet underground, continued to exercise power in Germany. Hitler committed suicide on April 30, which was the same day that Soviet soldiers marked their triumph in Berlin by planting a Soviet victory banner on the dome of the gutted Reichstag building. The German commander of the Berlin garrison surrendered unconditionally to the Soviets on May 2. This act ended all German resistance in the city. The Battle of Berlin was a complete victory for the Russians.

With the collapse of Hitler's thousand-year Reich at the end of 12 years, it was left to his successors to make peace with the Allies. In his final testament, which he dictated on April 29, Hitler had designated Admiral Dönitz to succeed him. Thus, it was under Dönitz's brief leadership that the Germans surrendered unconditionally to the Allies, first in Reims, France, on May 7, and then, at the insistence of Stalin, in a ceremony repeated in Berlin on May 8. The long nightmare in Europe had finally ended. In Britain, more than 1 million people took to the streets to celebrate the Allies' victory over Hitler. May 8, 1945 became known as V-E Day: Victory in Europe Day.

With the defeat of the Axis in Europe, the Allies now focused their military efforts on the Pacific, where war between the West – led by the United States – and Japan had raged since December 1941. The United States had taken the strategic initiative away from the Japanese in mid-1942, when they launched an "island hopping" campaign to push the Japanese back to their homeland. By the spring of 1945, American forces had reached Okinawa, where they defeated the Japanese in a bitter 82-day battle. This put them a mere 340 miles away from the Japanese mainland. In addition, the Americans had begun regular bombing raids on Japan itself in June 1944, using long range B-29 Superfortress aircraft. In one especially destructive raid over Tokyo in March 1945, 334 B-29s loaded only with incendiary bombs participated in a bomb drop that caused a huge firestorm in the largely wood-built city, destroyed 267,000 buildings, and killed close to 90,000 people. Similar raids took place in other Japanese cities in the months that followed. In spite of the tremendous destruction that the bombings caused and Japan's continued loss to the Allies of strategically vital islands closer and closer to its homeland, there was no indication that the Japanese were prepared to surrender. Consequently, the Americans pressed ahead with plans for an invasion of Japan itself that they believed would cause massive American casualties.

By the summer of 1945, the Americans were also in the final stages of developing a new weapon that had a destructive capacity far beyond anything then in existence. The weapon was the atomic bomb, whose development early in the war involved British and American scientists studying the problem separately. The original motivation of the American and British promoters of the bomb project was a belief that the Germans were actively pursuing a bomb of incredible power and that if they succeeded, they would use it in the war. Once the United States entered the war in late 1941, work on the bomb project quickly evolved into an American-led, top secret program known as the Manhattan Project that eventually employed over 130,000 people. News of a successful atomic test explosion on July 15 in a desert near Los Alamos, New Mexico, reached Harry Truman, the United States president since Roosevelt's death on April 12, just prior to a conference of Allied leaders in Potsdam, Germany. Truman told Stalin of the weapon's existence at the conference, and in the Potsdam Declaration issued on July 26, 1945, the Allies demanded that the Japanese surrender unconditionally or face "prompt and utter destruction." When Japan refused to cave in, a single American B-29 Superfortress flew over the Japanese city of Hiroshima on August 6, 1945, and dropped a single atomic bomb that caused the deaths of some 80,000 people. Two days later, the Soviet Union declared war on Japan and began pouring soldiers into Manchuria. The United States followed on August 9 by dropping an atomic bomb on the city of Nagasaki, killing 35,000 people. The world had already seen heavy bombings of cities and their inhabitants become a common practice in World War II, but the use of a single bomb on Hiroshima and then on Nagasaki to cause their destruction took the horror and devastation of war to a level that was without equal in human history. In the aftermath of the atomic bombs, the Japanese offered to end hostilities. The formal signing ceremony for Japan's unconditional surrender took place on September 2 on the U.S. battleship *Missouri*. The nightmare of the Second World War was at last over.

Casualties

World War II caused more deaths than any other conflict in history. Over 60 million people died in the war worldwide. In Europe, it is estimated that at least 40 million people were killed, a majority of whom were civilians. This shows how dramatically the lines dividing the military and civilian sides of a conflict had dissipated from World War I to World War II. Russia suffered the most deaths, somewhere above 25 million; no more than one-third of these were military. Poland was the hardest hit of the war-devastated countries in percentage of population lost: approximately 20 percent of its population – about 6 million people – died, of whom 3 million were Jews killed in the Holocaust. In each of Britain and France, the military and civilian dead from the war totaled more than 400,000. United States military losses stood at almost 300,000 dead. On the Axis side, German military deaths stood at close to 5 million, with an additional 1 million civilians dead. Italy suffered 400,000 military and civilian deaths. The war took the cheapening of human life, a process that began in the First World War, to a new low. Finally, technological innovations in military weaponry caused uncertainty and pessimism about what another major war might bring. The development of rockets, jet aircraft, and atomic bombs, first introduced during the war, had the potential – especially when coordinated – of carrying the destructive power of war to unimaginable, apocalyptic heights. One of the great challenges facing world leaders after the war was to find ways to prevent the use and proliferation of the most formidable of these technological advances, namely, atomic weaponry.

Conclusion

Violence in the form of war was a major component of European history in the period from 1914 to 1945. Indeed, unprecedented bloodshed occurred in the world wars that dominated the era. Both wars became total wars in which all of the military and domestic resources available to the belligerent states were mobilized to achieve victory. The industrial age in which the wars took place provided the technology that allowed the production of new and evermore deadly weapons that, along with mass armies, contributed to the deaths of tens of millions of people on the military and home fronts. When World War I ended, it was the deadliest war in European history, but its numbers of dead were dwarfed by World War II which was by far the largest and most horrific war in the history of mankind. Adding to the gruesomeness of World War II was the fact that far more civilians died in it than military personnel. In 1945, much of Europe lay in ruins, with many of its major cities nothing but heaps of rubble. One European leader commented that the continent could not afford a third major war, because there would then be no European civilization left. Thus, postwar European officials were ready to move in new directions to work out their problems and to render a major war on the continent virtually unthinkable.

The colonies in the war

Reluctant involvement

The lands of the British Empire were not ready or eager to go to war in 1939. The British Dominions contained considerable anti-war sentiment in the 1930s, as demonstrated in 1937 when Canada at an Imperial Conference told British Foreign Secretary Anthony Eden that Britain should solve its disputes with Germany and Italy peacefully. By August 1939, however, loyalty to the empire prevailed, albeit reluctantly. Four of the independent British Dominions (Australia, Canada, New Zealand, and South Africa) concluded that Britain's demise would bring about their own ruin; while free to choose their own path regarding war as laid out in the provisions of the 1931 Statute of Westminster, they nevertheless entered the war on Britain's side against Germany in September 1939. Ireland was the exception in that group; it remained neutral. Britain's September 3, 1939, declaration of war against Germany automatically committed the rest of its empire to the struggle, including the Dominion of Newfoundland, then under a temporary Crown-appointed government. France's declaration of war on Germany on September 3, 1939, bound its colonial empire to the conflict as well. The French situation became more complicated in the summer of 1940, when the autocratic Vichy regime replaced the Third Republic as the country's government. While the areas of Indochina, North Africa, and West Africa pledged their loyalty to Vichy, the pleas of Free French leader de Gaulle to support his cause on the side of the Allies quickly led to support from the bulk of French Equatorial Africa in the south and New Caledonia in the Pacific. The two sides then fought over the French Empire, starting with a naval venture that de Gaulle headed against the Vichy-controlled port city of Dakar in French West Africa in September 1940. It consisted of a joint Anglo-French expedition that de Gaulle hoped would impress the French West African Federation enough that French officials there would decide to embrace his cause. He encountered unexpectedly strong resistance in the battle for Dakar, however, and was forced to withdraw in failure. It was merely the first act in a struggle between the two sides that continued for some time thereafter.

Africa

De Gaulle's setback at Dakar came on the heels of other important events that affected fighting in the colonial world. One was Italy's declaration of war on France and Britain on June 10, 1940. Mussolini had dreams of a large colonial empire that included expansion of his Abyssinian–Eritrean empire in East Africa and a *Mare Nostrum* – an Italian dominated Mediterranean Sea basin that would incorporate French holdings in North Africa as well as in officially independent Egypt, where Britain had a strong influence. Mussolini used the term *Mare Nostrum*, the Roman name for the Mediterranean, as a rallying cry for Italian expansion. Italy's commitment to war brought into play the powerful Italian Mediterranean naval fleet. Churchill, following France's surrender to Germany, feared that should the French fleet fall into the hands of the Germans, the combined German–Italian navies would secure superiority over Britain. Consequently, the British on July 3, 1940, seized a French naval squadron in the Egyptian port of Alexandria, and destroyed an important part of the

French fleet at the Algerian base of Mers-El-Kebir, with well over 1,000 French sailors killed in the incident. The Vichy government broke diplomatic relations with Great Britain over the Algerian episode, and support among exiles for de Gaulle temporarily dropped. De Gaulle was dismayed over the British action, but grimly accepted it.

In Africa, Mussolini had a considerable advantage over the British in numbers of troops. The Italian forces in Libya vastly outnumbered the British troops in neighboring Egypt, and there were about 300,000 Italian-commanded soldiers in Italian East Africa (Abyssinia, Eritrea, and Italian Somaliland) as opposed to 16,000 British soldiers scattered across British Somaliland, Kenya, and Sudan. Italian forces initially overran British Somaliland in East Africa during the summer of 1940 and pushed 50 miles into Egypt from Libya in the fall, with the Suez Canal in their sights. But Archibald Wavell, the popular commander of British troops in Egypt and East Africa, then launched attacks of his own. In an offensive that began in February 1941, the outnumbered British drove the poorly equipped Italian forces out of British Somaliland and almost all of Italian East Africa by late May. The British success allowed Abyssinian Emperor Haile Selassie to reenter Addis Ababa on May 5, 1941, after a five-year exile. It was the first time that a nation under Axis control had been freed. In Egypt, Wavell's troops went on the attack in December 1940, and by the time the offensive ended in February 1941, the British had thrust the Italians from Egypt and taken complete control of the eastern Libyan province of Cyrenaica.

When the gravity of Italy's situation in North Africa became apparent, Hitler dispatched a small German force to Libya to retrieve the situation for the Axis powers. The leader of the troops was Erwin Rommel, who soon earned the nickname the "Desert Fox" for his tactical surprises. Known for his impatience, Rommel ordered attacks against the British before his complete force was in place. His troops pushed the British eastward to the Egyptian border, but they outran their supply lines toward the end of the year and were forced to retreat. A deadlock in the desert war had emerged. As mentioned earlier (see pp. 255–256), the fighting in North Africa continued until May 1943, when Allied armies under Eisenhower in the west and Montgomery in the east squeezed the Axis forces completely out of North Africa by way of Tunisia. The North African campaign had pulled the Allies toward a Mediterranean strategy where the next step was an assault on the Italian island of Sicily in the summer of 1943. As for Mussolini, his African wars had ended in disaster. He had lost the greater part of the Italian army and his reputation, and Italy was now dependent on Hitler.

De Gaulle's Free French movement made important headway in Africa in 1942 and beyond. The islands of Madagascar and Réunion in the Indian Ocean declared for the Free French in November 1942, and French Somaliland in East Africa did so shortly thereafter. De Gaulle also came out on top in a struggle for French leadership that emerged following the Allied invasion of Vichy-held Morocco and Algeria in late 1942. At the Casablanca Conference in January 1943, Allied leaders forced him to share control of French colonial troops in North Africa with General Henri Giraud. Then, after several months of negotiations that grew out of the conference, de Gaulle was compelled to share leadership responsibility with Giraud of a Committee of National Liberation set up in Algiers in June 1943 to serve as the provisional government of Algeria and all French colonies supportive of the Free French. But De Gaulle engaged in some deft political maneuvering thereafter, so that by the time the committee moved its headquarters to London in July 1944, he had gained complete ascendancy over the committee.

With an Allied military victory seemingly certain, de Gaulle in late January 1944 convened a conference of colonial administrators from all the French African colonies in the city of Brazzaville, then the capital of French Equatorial Africa. The purposes of the conference were to decide the future governmental structure of the colonies and the postwar relationship of France with its colonial empire. The attendees looked at internal reforms, a system of local and regional representative assemblies to assist in the govern-ance of each of the territories, and an expanded franchise. But the conference, in line with de Gaulle's belief that French greatness depended on its colonial empire, issued a state-ment about France's colonial mission that adhered to a longstanding policy:

> the goals of the task of civilization accomplished by France in her colonies rules out any idea of autonomy, any possibility of evolution outside the French bloc of empire; the eventual creation, even in the distant future, of self-government for the colonies is to be set aside.[2]

Iraq, Syria, and Lebanon

Iraq, Syria, and Lebanon became hotbeds of fighting in 1941. In Iraq, a pro-Axis coup in early April brought Iraqi nationalist Rashid Ali al-Gaylani to power; vehemently anti-Brit-ish, Rashid Ali hoped that a German victory would usher in better days for his country. The British, still exercising influence in the kingdom, responded quickly by invoking a defense treaty that they had signed with Iraq in 1930 and using Indian troops to smash the pro-German regime in May 1941. A British occupation of Iraq that lasted until 1947 ensued.

In the French mandate of Syria and Lebanon, Vichy elements headed by High Commissioner of the Levant Henri Dentz held complete authority at the outset of 1941. The military danger that this situation posed to the British was demonstrated in the spring when the regime sent weapons to Rashid Ali in Iraq and allowed German warplanes access to Syrian airfields on their way to Iraq. Troops from Britain, Free France, Australia, and India attacked the Vichy-controlled Syrian–Lebanese mandate on June 8. In bitter combat, the Allied forces, reinforced by British troops from Egypt, overran the Syrian capital of Damascus on June 21. Dentz then combined his remaining forces in defense of the Lebanese city of Beirut which fell on July 10. The two sides signed an armistice on July 14, 1941, allowing de Gaulle's Free France to take over control of the Syrian–Lebanese mandate. De Gaulle gave the post of high commissioner of the Levant to General Georges Catroux who recognized the independence of Syria and Lebanon in November 1941. The French officially agreed to the two countries' change of status to independence in 1946, and all remaining French troops withdrew from the two states the same year. The Allied success in Syria closed any hope the Axis may have had in establishing a base of operations on Syrian territory. The end of the fighting in the Levant also allowed the British to return soldiers to Egypt for the war against Rommel.

French Indochina

While French Indochina was a part of Japanese military strategy during World War II, the colony was never subjected to intensive fighting. With the collapse of France in June 1940, the Japanese quickly took advantage of the situation to begin a pro-cess of establishing an effective indirect control over the colonial administration of the region. The Vichy regime installed Admiral Jean Decoux as the governor-general in Indochina on July 20, 1940. Unshakeable in his support for Vichy, Decoux proved a capable administrator who, in an effort to improve relations with the indigenous popula-tion, hired Vietnamese as civil servants, using the same pay scale as for Frenchmen. But in September 1940, he was forced to sign a treaty with the Japanese that allowed them to take control of several Indochinese airfields, to use colonial railroads for the transport of their troops to the military front in China, and to allow the stationing of 30,000 Japanese soldiers in the Tonkin region in the north of the colony. In 1941, following threats of a Japanese invasion, Decoux began to mobilize the colony's natural resources and workforce for the Japanese war effort. Japan allowed the French to exercise sovereign authority in the region, but the Japanese became the colony's virtual masters. The Japanese finally took over direct control of the colony in March 1945, and maintained their occupation until they surrendered in August 1945.

When French forces returned to Indochina in 1945, they found the colony in near chaos, as the Japanese left behind a power vacuum. While the British, who occupied the southern part of the area at war's end, turned over control of that region to France after a few weeks, the French found Ho Chi Minh's Viet Minh, a Vietnamese nationalist organization dominated by Communists, exercising authority in northern Indochina. Admiral Georges Thierry d'Argenlieu, the French high commissioner in Indochina, reasserted France's colonial authority and backed a separate puppet republic in the south. D'Argenlieu and other key French officials naively believed that Ho's nationalist movement was weak and could easily be disposed of militarily. Negotiations that the French had been conducting with Ho Chi Minh in Fontainebleau, France, about Vietnam's future status collapsed in September 1946, and the First Indochina War between France and the Viet Minh erupted before year's end. The war only ended after the Communist Viet Minh inflicted a heavy military defeat on French forces at the Battle of Dien Bien Phu in the spring of 1954. A peace agreement was achieved at a nine-power conference in Geneva that same summer. According to the settlement, Vietnam was divided at the seventeenth parallel: the Viet Minh received total control north of that line while the territory to the south of that point remained tied to France, though it was promised independence. An all-Vietnamese referendum was to occur within two years to decide on the reunification of the country. But the referendum never happened, and American influence replaced that of France in Vietnam in the ensuing years.

India

It was Britain that unilaterally declared war on Nazi Germany for India in early September 1939. Mohandas Gandhi, Jawaharlal Nehru, and other leaders of the country's most powerful political force, the Indian National Congress or Congress Party, deeply resented the British action since they, though appalled at Germany's military moves, thought there was insufficient justification for India to enter the conflict. They were also angry over the British failure to consult with them before the decision for war was made. The Congress leaders serving as government ministers resigned their posts in protest against the British decision.

Japan added a new theater to World War II when, in December 1941, it launched attacks against U.S. interests in the Pacific, including the American naval base of Pearl Harbor in Hawaii (December 7), and against Britain's Pacific empire. The Japanese overran British-controlled Hong Kong in December 1941, and in another assault, raced down the British colony of Malaya in December–January. They climaxed their military success in the Malayan campaign by capturing the island fortress of Singapore on February 15, 1942. The loss at Singapore was the single-most devastating military defeat in British history, and it caused irreparable damage to Britain's prestige in Asia. In another major offensive launched from recently occupied Thailand, Japan moved into the British territory of Burma in late January 1942, and by mid-May, the last of the Allied defenders in Burma had retreated into India. With the conquest of Burma, Japan had reached India's eastern frontier. The Japanese claimed that they were liberating people from European rule as part of a plan called the

"Greater East Asia Co-Prosperity Sphere," but in fact it was nothing more than a façade for Japan's ruthless exploitation of the conquered territories.

In the midst of Britain's demonstrated military weakness, Churchill was ready to make concessions to Indian nationalism. In March 1942, he sent Stafford Cripps, the leader of the House of Commons, to India to negotiate with Indian leaders. When Cripps held out the prospect of independence for India following the war in return for Indian support for the war against Japan, Gandhi likened the offer to "a post-dated cheque on a failing bank."[3] Indian Congress negotiators insisted on immediate self-government as the price of their support for the war and their return to the government. The lack of a British response caused Gandhi in August 1942 to organize a civil disobedience movement called "Quit India" that demanded Britain's withdrawal from the subcontinent at once. British officials reacted by imprisoning Gandhi and all leading members of the Congress Party. The arrests triggered protests across the country and calls for strikes. There were acts of violence, including bomb explosions, the burning of buildings, and electricity stoppages. The British resorted to mass arrests, heavy fines, and public floggings. The British were fortunate in that the vast majority of Indian military units continued their allegiance to the Crown, so that government authority remained intact.

By early 1944, the possibility of any revolt in India had dissipated. The wartime military strength of the Allies was much greater by then, and there was widespread knowledge in India that the Japanese were brutal conquerors intent on oppressing rather than freeing colonized peoples under European rule. When the Japanese launched an invasion of India in March 1944, a British–Indian force roundly defeated them in the ensuing months at the battles of Imphal and Kohima, two Indian towns near the frontier with Burma. The combat at Kohima was so fierce that the battle there has been described as the Stalingrad of the East. The two battles cost Japan 53,000 dead and missing soldiers, while the British side suffered 16,500 casualties. The Imphal–Kohima campaign ended any Japanese invasion threat of India, and the British forces went from there to drive out the Japanese from neighboring Burma by mid-1945.

When Gandhi was released from prison in May 1944, he resumed his political effort for an independent India, but one that was united. In regard to unity, he faced an enormous problem in the form of India's powerful Muslim League headed by Muhammad Ali Jinnah, a British-educated lawyer who feared a Hindu-dominated India in any united-state formula. In March 1940, Jinnah had called on the British to separate India into autonomous Hindu and Muslim national states. Gandhi argued that Jinnah's view represented a victory of hate over love. Gandhi appealed to Jinnah to join him in presenting a united front to the British, but to no avail.

After the Labour Party gained control of the British government in 1945, Prime Minister Clement Attlee quickly moved to fulfill a longstanding party pledge of self-determination for India. A decisive step was the appointment of Lord Mountbatten, a successful Allied commander in Southeast Asia in the war's final months, as viceroy in March 1947. Mountbatten contended that a partition of India into two separate independent states, one Hindu and the other Muslim, was the only viable political solution for the subcontinent. Both Indian parties accepted the Mountbatten Plan, and Britain officially granted independence to the states of Hindu India and Muslim Pakistan at the stroke of midnight on August 14, 1947. The partition was anything but smooth as there were mass migrations, killings by both sides, and other forms of violence. Gandhi himself was assassinated by a Hindu fanatic in January 1948.

The Dutch East Indies

The Dutch government-in-exile in London declared war on Japan on December 8, 1941. The Japanese in turn launched a strike against the Dutch East Indies, beginning with a successful attack on the British-controlled section of the oil-rich island of Borneo in mid-December, and then grabbing key points on the Dutch-administered side of the island not long thereafter. The Japanese expanded their East Indies campaign to other islands in early 1942 with attacks on Celebes, Sumatra, and Java. Dutch troops, fighting alongside other Allied soldiers, were unable to withstand the Japanese assaults, and they surrendered to Japan on March 8, 1942. The indigenous population initially viewed the arrival of the Japanese quite favorably, as the Japanese once again presented themselves as liberators of the people from European rule. Indeed, Indonesian nationalist leader Achmed Sukarno embraced Japan's success and served as that country's principal adviser during the wartime occupation. He assisted Japan in recruiting forced laborers and securing raw materials and food, but he also used the Japanese to spread his nationalist ideas to the Indonesian masses and later in the war to obtain weapons and training for his followers. On August 17, 1945, two days after the Japanese announced their surrender in the war, Sukarno declared Indonesia an independent state.

The Dutch tried to reestablish their prewar position in the East Indies, both through the use of force and political maneuvering. A first round of fighting took place right after the war, highlighted by the Battle of Surabaya in November 1945 between Indonesian nationalists and British troops charged with reestablishing Allied control in the region. Though the British won, the battle demonstrated that Sukarno's republic was capable of serious resistance and enjoyed popular support. The Dutch signed an agreement with Sukarno's government in late 1946 for the creation of 15 additional republics across the East Indies as components of a United States of Indonesia of which Sukarno's state representing the islands of Java and Sumatra would be but one part; it was a Dutch way of diluting his political power. Disagreements over the treaty quickly developed, however, and war resumed. The Dutch finally gave way in late 1949, and turned over complete sovereignty of virtually all of Indonesia to Sukarno's republic.

Military recruitment

As in World War I, Europe's colonies provided large numbers of soldiers to participate in the Second World War. In the British Empire, India, for example, supplied and equipped 2.5 million men who were used in every service. About 1 million African men – and some women – were in uniform at one point or another, representing the biggest commitment of manpower to a single conflict in the continent's history. In their African colonies, the British at first encouraged voluntary enlistments, but when Italy entered the war in 1940, they introduced conscription. By May 1945, 400,000 British African soldiers were engaged in the conflict, although more than that had been in and out of the service during the struggle. Italy, meanwhile, claimed to have recruited 250,000 men, mainly from its new East African empire, but many of them proved unreliable both as combatants and laborers. Colonial soldiers were also important to France. They were a component in the French army in the spring of 1940 when Germany invaded Western Europe. De Gaulle's Free French movement, recruiting initially in the colonies of French Equatorial Africa and Cameroon, signed up some 17,000 soldiers between 1940 and 1943. Since there were already 10,000 soldiers – 2,000 of whom were Europeans – in place in 1940, the total contribution from these areas during this timeframe reached 27,000 soldiers. When one considers that the total in the Free French army numbered between 54,000 and 73,330 in July 1943, the size of the African contingent was significant. Large numbers of French African soldiers fought for the Free French forces in Italy and then in France between 1943 and 1945.

Colonial soldiers fought on every war front. Indians and South Africans were sent to North Africa, while West and East Africans traveled to as far away a place as Burma. More specifically, the 4th Indian Division fought in North Africa, Syria, Palestine, Cyprus, Italy, and Greece. The 5th Indian Division participated in Sudan, Libya, Iraq, Burma, Malaya, and Java. African soldiers fought against the Germans in France at the Aisne River and on the Somme in May 1940, and many ended up in German prisoner-of-war camps thereafter. African soldiers also fought against each other either on the side of the Vichy regime or the Free French in Lebanon and Syria. In August 1944, approximately 120,000 French colonial soldiers took part in an Allied landing on the southern coast of France.

Economic considerations

The colonies of European countries also served as vital sources for war supplies, including rubber, cloth, timber, minerals, and food. When Japan's conquests in the Far East in late 1941 and early 1942 deprived the Allies of key sources of rubber, the Allies partially compensated for that in Africa where rubber production tripled from 1941 to 1944–1945, with the British colony of Nigeria serving as a major producer. The number of acres devoted to rubber production in the Belgian Congo, whose governor-general remained committed to the Allies following Germany's occupation of Belgium in May 1940, jumped from 17,000 in 1938 to 136,000 in 1948. Even after the sharp wartime boost in Africa, however, the continent's rubber production remained well below the annual output of the British colony of Ceylon that, while subject to Japanese raids, remained the primary wartime supplier of rubber to the Allies, producing 98,000 tons in 1943. India, ranked second among Allied rubber suppliers, provided 17,000 tons that same year. Rubber was a critical war material, since an array of combat-related vehicles needed it for their large tires. Additionally, a single American battleship contained at least 75 tons of rubber in its structure, a tank close to a ton, and a Boeing B-17 "Flying Fortress" bomber almost half a ton, although some of the rubber content in them was synthetic or recycled. India's major industrial contribution to the war was the production of cotton textiles, supplying some 1.2 billion yards of cloth per year for war use. By the end of the conflict, India had manufactured a total of 4 million cotton supply-dropping parachutes and some 400 million cotton apparel items. India's Tata Iron and Steel Company produced landing craft, engine parts for airplanes, and large quantities of munitions. Overall, India was producing as many war supplies by 1943 as the combined totals of South Africa, Australia, and New Zealand. The Allies' colonies also proved to be key suppliers of forest products that were needed for bridge, rail, and road construction, mining operations, and the fueling of trains and ships. The British colony of Tanganyika, for example, provided some 300,000 railroad ties per year in both 1941 and 1942.

Regarding minerals, the Allies turned to Africa for an important part of their wartime needs. During the high tide of the conflict, Africa accounted for 50 percent of the world's gold supply. Indeed, gold mining in French Equatorial Africa skyrocketed during the war, with Free French leaders capitalizing on its production to strengthen their financial autonomy and secure a certain level of freedom from the United States and Great Britain. All the uranium that the U.S. used in the conflict came from the Belgian

Congo, including that involved in the creation of the atomic bomb. When the Japanese seized Malaya in January 1942, they deprived Britain and America of their major source of tin. To compensate, the British launched a massive effort to increase production in northern Nigeria, recruiting some 100,000 men over a four-month period in 1942 to work in the Nigerian mines. Meanwhile, wartime exports for copper and tin from the Belgian Congo to the United States jumped by 1,000 percent.

Food was a major concern of all belligerents, and it played a vital role in the life of the Allies' colonies. One success story in the production and distribution of food was the British-operated Middle East Supply Center. It was an agency of Britain's Middle East Command based in Cairo, Egypt, and it worked as an economic coordinator for the general supply needs of an immense area that extended from Turkey in the north through Syria, Lebanon, Palestine, and Iraq to Iran in the east, to the Island of Malta in the west, and to Somalia, Sudan, and Abyssinia in the south. Four British colonies and four League of Nations mandates were among the territories for which it provided economic oversight. Its responsibilities included control over the region's collectively pooled foodstuffs and their allocation based on need. The agency's plan prevented a major food disaster in the Middle East by keeping the region's food supplies largely stable during the struggle. As a part of the effort, the British pressured Egypt, technically independent but still under British influence, to grow less cotton and more wheat, maize, and rice; as a result, Egypt provided the Allies with large quantities of these products. In fact, Egypt supplied the food rations for Montgomery's British-led forces from the Battle of El Alamein in 1942 to the end of the North African campaign in Tunis in 1943.

On the other hand, the British colonial government in India demonstrated complacency toward India's wartime food supplies, an attitude that contributed to the Bengal Famine of 1943–1944. After Japan's occupation of Burma in early 1942 cost India 15 percent of its rice supply, the province of Bengal, which bordered Burma, was especially hard hit by the food loss. Only belatedly did the government realize the seriousness of the crisis, and even then, it hesitated to act decisively. Approximately 3 million people died from the famine.

Strategic importance

Operating militarily on a global scale, the Allies used Europe's colonies as important components in their wartime strategy. This was especially true after Italy entered the war in June 1940 as an Axis power, making the Mediterranean a much more dangerous area for Allied shipping. The Germans rendered the Mediterranean shipping lanes virtually impassable when, in January 1941, they began repeatedly to bomb and mine the Suez Canal. The Allies turned to a safer but much longer and more wasteful sea route between Europe and ports in the Indian Ocean and beyond by sailing around the Cape of Good Hope off the southern tip of Africa. The port city of Freetown, which was the capital of Britain's West African colony of Sierra Leone, was central to the new strategy; it served as a major convoy station for several years and at times had as many as 200 ships moored in its broad, well-shielded harbor. Elsewhere, 10,000 African workers built the secret Takoradi air route, known as the Trans-African Air Ferry Route, in 1940-1941. It commenced in the city of Takoradi in Britain's West African colony of the Gold Coast and ended in the important East African supply center of Khartoum, Sudan. In Takoradi, workers transformed the city's small airport into a large Royal Air Force base that became a key assembly point for aircraft sent to fight the Axis forces in North Africa. By early 1942, the United States was regularly sending American planes to Takoradi via South America for flights eastward. The first heavy bombers that the U.S. sent to American General Douglas MacArthur in the Pacific traveled via the Takoradi air route.

Conclusion

The events of World War II intensified the desire for independence across the colonial world, as demonstrated by the actions of nationalist movements in places like India, French Indochina, and the Dutch East Indies. These campaigns ultimately prevailed after the war, but not without difficult, and sometimes long, transitions. On another front, the globalization of World War II made Europe's colonies an integral part of the conflict. As the war progressed, the Allied powers developed a heavy dependence on colonial support in the areas of military recruitment, war supplies, and strategy. The colonies strengthened a fragile Gaullist movement whose wartime nerve center began in Africa, and they propped up the British war effort against the Axis powers on three continents. In the case of the Belgian Congo, it became a vital source of income for Belgium's government-in-exile in London and an indispensable supplier of critical raw materials for the Allied cause. Ultimately, the Allies' colonies, through their myriad contributions, proved vital to the war's outcome.

Diplomatic initiatives

The diplomatic activities of the belligerents between 1939 and 1945 also bear resemblance to those of the First World War in that alliance reversals changed the course of the war, and that for the Allies, the country to defeat was, once again, Germany. The unfinished business of the Versailles settlement was also exposed, as the Curzon Line remained an important consideration throughout the war. Perhaps the most important difference was the fact that Britain, the United States, and the Soviet Union dominated war-time diplomacy, rallying several governments-in-exile in their camp.

Expanding alliances

After World War II began on September 1, 1939, the lineup that emerged in the first days among the European nations was Nazi Germany on one side and Britain, France, and Poland on the other. The Soviet Union temporarily joined the conflict in mid-September by attacking Poland from the east but the Soviets ended their hostilities there following Poland's surrender in early October. The Soviets launched another unprovoked assault against Finland in November 1939 to start the Russo-Finnish War that ended in March 1940. The Soviets then returned to the sidelines until June 1941.

While Hitler gained Italy's support in the war when the latter declared war on France in June 1940, he also looked elsewhere for allies in his push to achieve a quick victory. One of Hitler's goals in the summer of 1940 was to gain Spain's entry into the war. Spanish dictator Franco initially took a cautious approach to the war, and kept his nation neutral. In June 1940, Franco showed some interest in joining the war on Germany's side, but he had dreams of gaining Gibraltar from Britain and large areas of France's colonial empire in Northwest Africa and French West Africa in return for Spain's services. He also wanted economic and military aid. Hitler, albeit ready to support Spain's quest for Gibraltar, was disinclined to offer French colonial territories to the Spanish, lest he offend Vichy France. At Germany's invitation, formal negotiations between the two sides regarding Spain's entry into the war started in August 1940 and culminated in a meeting between Hitler and Franco at Hendaye on October 23. At that meeting, Franco, who was now less interested in joining the Axis partly because of Germany's failed air campaign against Britain, held firm to his demands for empire and German supplies as the price for his country's war commitment. He also remained adamant in his refusal to accept a German request for naval bases in Spanish-held territories. The discussion ended with no agreement. Hitler later told Mussolini that he would prefer to have three or four teeth pulled than to go through another meeting of that sort with Franco. Spain remained neutral for the duration of the war.

Hitler also wanted the participation of Vichy France in the war against Britain. He discussed the idea with French Chief of State Pétain at Montoire, France, on the day after his meeting with Franco. Pétain was non-committal and vague in their meeting, although he affirmed the policy of French collaboration with Germany. Both Pétain and his premier, Pierre Laval, hinted that the degree of France's future commitment to Germany would depend on the Reich's generosity toward the French in a final peace settlement, but Hitler offered them no specifics. Hitler returned to Germany disappointed at the disinclination of the French to enter the war opposite the British.

On the other hand, the Axis powers of Germany and Italy signed a Tripartite Pact with Japan in September 1940. By its terms, Germany and Italy agreed to respect Japan's leadership in a new Asian order, and Japan committed to respect Germany and Italy's interests in Europe. The three countries also agreed on cooperation should any of them be attacked by a country not yet involved in the war in Europe or the Sino–Japanese War in Asia. That provision was an attempt to deter the United States from entering the war. Hungary, Romania, and Slovakia formally joined the Tripartite alliance in November 1940, and Bulgaria and Croatia followed suit in 1941. Finland, the victim of Soviet aggression in the Winter War of 1939–1940, joined Germany in Operation Barbarossa in June 1941, but despite repeated German appeals, it refused to sign the Tripartite Pact, arguing that its aims in the war were distinct from those of Nazi Germany.

With regard to German–Soviet relations after the signing of the Ribbentrop–Molotov Pact in August 1939, the two powers maintained an uneasy alliance in which diplomatic tensions escalated during 1940. At the same time, however, economic ties grew in a remarkable fashion and remained strong right up to Germany's invasion of Russia in June 1941. Germany benefited from a generous supply of raw materials and foodstuffs that helped offset the effects of a British naval blockade against the Reich, and the Soviets received important quantities of German equipment and machinery. By mid-1940, Russia was Germany's main supplier of raw materials. One major source of friction in their relations in 1940 was Finland, where Germany permitted secret arms sales to begin in August and soon thereafter obtained permission to use Finland as a transit point for German troops going to Norway. Both actions were violations of German–Soviet agreements placing Finland in Russia's sphere of influence. In September, the Germans belatedly invited the Soviets to join the Tripartite Pact, and indicated that the topic could be discussed at talks between the two countries in Berlin in November. Meanwhile, the Germans were secretly moving forward with plans for an invasion of the Soviet Union.

At the Berlin conference, the two sides covered a wide range of issues. Soviet Foreign Commissar Molotov indicated Russia's intention to annex Finland, though the Germans made it clear that they would not tolerate such a move. Molotov accepted in principle Soviet participation in the Tripartite alliance, although a set of counter-proposals for Russian adherence that the Soviets sent to Germany a fortnight later was never answered. While the Germans encouraged the Russians to direct their strategic efforts toward the Persian Gulf and Indian Ocean, Molotov countered by pointing to Russia's interests in the eastern Mediterranean and the Baltic. At the last meeting, which ended up in Ribbentrop's air-raid shelter owing to a British nighttime bombing raid, the German foreign minister talked about how much Russia would gain from the division of Britain's empire and insisted that Britain's defeat was imminent. Molotov replied, "If that is so, then why are we in this shelter and whose are those bombs which are falling?"[4] One month later (December 18), Hitler issued a top secret directive to his military chiefs for the invasion of Russia in the spring of 1941 under the code name of Operation Barbarossa.

In the last months before the German invasion of the Soviet Union, trade between the two countries boomed. The Germans made the Soviet Union a privileged trading partner. They did this in part to assure the Reich of needed raw materials from Russia right up to the day of the German attack, and in part to deceive the Kremlin about their war plans against the Soviets. On the Russian side, Stalin, aware of rumors about a possible German assault, dramatically increased Russian deliveries to Germany in an attempt to appease Hitler economically and blunt any German threat to his country. Stalin's belief that Hitler would not attack a country from which he derived such great economic and strategic benefits was shown to be a mistake when Germany unleashed Operation Barbarossa on June 22, 1941.

By June 1941, Germany had created Fortress Europe out of Germany, Austria, Czechoslovakia, the western half of Poland, Norway, Denmark, occupied France, Greece, Yugoslavia, and the three Benelux countries. Most European countries had been annexed, incorporated, partitioned, or conquered by Germany, Italy, or the Soviet Union. National boundaries were erased, administrative jurisdictions redrawn, international trade redirected, international finance reorganized, and millions of people forcibly resettled. Germany's invasion of the Soviet Union would now change the scope of the war in ways that no one could have imagined beforehand.

Allied cooperation prior to December 1941

Great Britain was the lone European power still at war with Nazi Germany in the summer of 1940. Churchill, though unwavering in his determination to fight on, had little faith that the British could win by themselves. Hoping that at some point the United States would enter the war on Britain's side, he turned to the Americans for whatever aid he could obtain while waiting. America was a neutral country and therefore limited in what it could do to help the British. Roosevelt, while sympathetic to the British cause, had to move cautiously owing to a strong American isolationist movement. The U.S. had already provided some assistance beginning in November 1939 with its "cash and carry" program that allowed the British to purchase American war materiel if they paid for it in cash and transported them in their own ships from U.S. shores (see p. 254). More American help came in September 1940, when the U.S. agreed to turn over 50 mothballed destroyers to the British in return for 99-year leases on naval and air bases in the British West Indies. The most important immediate outcome of this action was symbolic, signaling the beginning of a closer partnership between the two nations. Following his reelection as president in 1940, Roosevelt felt comfortable in offering Britain greater assistance. He said that the United States must serve as "the arsenal of democracy" in a December 1940 speech, and in March 1941, the U.S. Congress, over fierce isolationist opposition, passed the Lend–Lease Act that allowed the president to lend or lease military equipment to Britain and other nations viewed as indirectly protecting American interests by fighting aggression. When Nazi Germany attacked the Soviet Union in June 1941, both Churchill and Roosevelt promised military aid to Stalin. The British quickly forged a program for the delivery of weapons and other materials to the Russians, and the provisions of the Lend–Lease Act were extended to the Soviet Union in November 1941.

In August 1941, Roosevelt and Churchill secretly met on a British battleship off the coast of Newfoundland to formulate the Atlantic Charter, a document that represented their two countries' goals for the postwar world. The eight aims included: the right of all peoples to determine their own government; the lowering of trade barriers; freedom of the seas; the refusal of their two nations to seek territorial aggrandizement; no postwar territorial adjustments without first consulting the people affected; the disarmament of aggressor states followed by a global reduction in arms; the promotion of economic progress to improve global living standards; and a world in which the peoples of all nations could live in freedom from fear and want. The agreement contained more than a dash of the idealism that Woodrow Wilson had espoused at the end of World War I. The Atlantic Charter was also important for the message it sent about the growing bond between the United States and Britain. Once the United States entered the war, it joined the Soviet Union, Great Britain, and 23 other nations in signing the Declaration of the United Nations that pledged the signatories to common action against the Tripartite Pact members and to the principles of the Atlantic Charter. A broad Allied consensus concerning the postwar order was thus established immediately after the war expanded.

The Grand Alliance

The presence of the United States added a new dimension to Allied wartime cooperation. Britain had already extended a helping hand to the Soviet Union beginning in June 1941, by providing the Russians with limited amounts of military supplies, including tanks. Right after the United States entered the war, Churchill went to Washington D.C. to discuss strategy and military organization with Roosevelt. In a series of meetings that lasted from December 22 to January 14, the two men agreed on a "Europe First" strategy, which meant that their countries' top priority would be the defeat of Germany, lest the Germans achieve victory and knock Great Britain or the Soviet Union out of the war. The war against Japan would be more defensive in nature, limited primarily to thwarting Japanese expansionism. With the assistance of their staffs, they also agreed on a joint military command structure and the pooling of shipping tonnage and raw materials. On the other hand, the Soviets' high command never developed close cooperation with the top military planners of the Western powers.

Allied tensions

One of the main issues of controversy among the Big Three – Churchill, Roosevelt, and Stalin – was Stalin's demand for a second front, which for him meant an invasion of France across the English Channel. A second front in Western Europe would provide him with desperately needed relief against Hitler in the East, as Hitler would be forced to divert military forces to France. Roosevelt promised during talks in Washington with Soviet Foreign Commissar Molotov in May 1942 that a second front in France would take place that year. British leaders, who had earlier agreed in principle to the 1942 cross-Channel assault, concluded by mid-year that it was not possible. They argued instead for an Allied offensive in French Northwest Africa in 1942, which Churchill told Roosevelt was "the true second front of 1942."[5] Roosevelt, who firmly believed that a major military action had to occur against Germany in 1942 to divert American attention from the war against Japan, acceded to the British point of view in spite of protests from the U.S. Joint Chiefs of Staff. It was left to Churchill to convey the decision to Stalin, who viewed the fulfillment of the promised second front in France as his top priority in dealing with his Western partners. Churchill said that breaking the news to Stalin, at the Moscow Conference of August 1942, "was like carrying a large lump of ice to the North Pole."[6]

He tried to soften the blow by telling the Soviet dictator that the British and Americans "were preparing for a very great operation [against the French coast] in 1943."[7] Stalin reacted angrily, accusing the Allies' of breaking their word regarding a second front in 1942. He refused to go to an Allied conference in Casablanca, Morocco, in January 1943, but pressed the British and Americans at the end of 1942 to fulfill Churchill's August promise of a 1943 invasion.

At the Casablanca Conference, American and British officials, including Roosevelt and Churchill, discussed several issues dealing with strategy and priorities. Strategically, the two countries agreed, once hostilities in North Africa had successfully concluded, to begin an invasion of Sicily in 1943, with the intention of forcing Italy out of the war. The decision represented a victory for Churchill's Mediterranean strategy that the Americans, uneasy about further operations in the Mediterranean, saw as self-serving, since it was a way to protect British access to Middle East oil and to India. The decision also effectively postponed a major cross-Channel offensive against France until at least 1944. As a way of reassuring Stalin of their nations' determination to stay in the war to the end, Roosevelt and Churchill publicly announced their policy of demanding the unconditional surrender of Germany.

The second front issue continued to cause considerable discord in the Grand Alliance in 1943. While Churchill's military advisors knew after Casablanca that the planned attack against Italy that year would postpone an invasion of France until 1944, Churchill appeared to think otherwise: he wrote Stalin in February 1943 that preparations were pushing ahead for a cross-Channel invasion later that year. When Stalin learned in June from his Western partners that an invasion of France would not occur before May 1944, he recalled the Soviet ambassadors to Washington and London in protest. The new postponement deepened Stalin's sense of betrayal by the West on the issue.

There were other complications in Allied relations. One was the Polish question. The Soviet Union had diplomatically recognized Poland's government-in-exile after Germany's invasion of Russia in June 1941, but relations between them had been cool from the start. In April 1943 came the disclosure of the 1940 Katyn murders of thousands of Polish army officers and members of the Polish intelligentsia. When Władysław Sikorski's exiled Polish government questioned the Soviet account blaming the Germans and called for an international inquiry, Stalin in late April severed relations with it. Eager to placate Stalin, the British and U.S. governments muted the Polish cries for action, meekly accepted the Soviet version of events, and raised no protest against Stalin's break with Sikorski's government. Their first priority was to keep Stalin in the Grand Alliance at a time when they still feared that the Soviet Union might make a separate peace with Germany. Another issue that centered on Poland was postwar boundaries. Stalin had already indicated to the Sikorski government in the summer of 1941 that the Soviet Union intended to keep the Polish lands it had gained from its pact with Germany in 1939 – lands that almost completely corresponded to the frontier established by the Curzon Line of December 1919. The London Poles by contrast had insisted on regaining their lost territory in the east, while the British and Americans had refused to make a firm commitment in favor of either side. The question of postwar borders was still unsettled in the fall of 1943.

U.S. Secretary of State Cordell Hull, British Foreign Secretary Anthony Eden, and Soviet Foreign Commissar Molotov met in Moscow from October 18 to November 1, 1943, to discuss the postwar world and prepare the way for an upcoming summit conference of their three countries' leaders in Teheran, Iran. They reaffirmed an Allied demand for Germany's unconditional surrender and agreed to work together in a new postwar international assembly. They also agreed to a tripartite occupation of Germany and the creation of a European Advisory Commission in London to draw up occupation plans. When Eden also sought specific accords regarding the political futures of the countries in Eastern and Central Europe, his two colleagues refused to go along, leaving that issue in limbo.

Summit conferences at Teheran and Yalta

The Teheran conference of November 28–29, 1943, was the high point of Allied wartime cooperation. It was the first conference at which Churchill, Stalin, and Roosevelt met face to face. Stalin was incessant in his demand for a second front, and he joined Roosevelt in convincing Churchill, who argued for his Mediterranean strategy, to accept the establishment of a second front in France in May 1944. To insure that the invasion, codenamed Operation Overlord, would actually take place, Stalin insisted that a commander-in-chief be quickly appointed, noting that without someone in charge "nothing will come of these operations."[8] Roosevelt, promising that this would be done shortly, gave the responsibility to Eisenhower during his trip back to Washington.

Though future military operations were the principal topic at the Teheran Conference, the three leaders also dealt with postwar political questions. Stalin pressed his case for keeping the Soviet Union's frontier with Poland based on the Curzon Line. Churchill, informally accepting Stalin's Russian border changes with Poland, used three matches during a private conversation with him to demonstrate how Poland's territorial losses in the east could be offset with German territory in the west. Roosevelt unofficially endorsed Stalin and Churchill's ideas of shifting Poland's borders westward, but he insisted that his views be kept private since, as he explained to Stalin, he did not want to lose the votes of several million Polish-Americans in the 1944 presidential election. There was also lively discussion about dividing postwar Germany into several small independent states, but no decision was made. In the end, the three men postponed any concrete territorial settlements in Europe until a later date.

In the months after the Teheran Conference, Stalin's forces moved into Poland and the Balkans. By early August 1944, they had reached the outskirts of Warsaw, and Stalin had recognized the Soviet-sponsored pro-Communist Lublin Committee as the provisional government of Poland. After Romania surrendered to the Soviets in late August, the door was open to large swaths of the Balkans, and the Russians quickly took advantage of that. Soviet troops took control of Sofia, the capital of Bulgaria, on October 18. Russian soldiers teamed with Josip Broz Tito's partisans to capture the Yugoslav capital of Belgrade on October 20, and Red Army forces were at the gates of Budapest in Hungary by early November. The Soviet advance through the Balkans forced the Germans to abandon Greece, and British troops moved in to help fill the vacuum, occupying Athens on October 13.

It was in these circumstances that in October 1944, Churchill, in an attempt to counter the Soviets, proposed an old-fashioned political deal to Stalin in Moscow to create British and Soviet spheres of interest in the Balkans. He offered – and Stalin accepted – a percentage formula that included a 90 percent Soviet dominance in Romania and Bulgaria, a 90 percent British influence in Greece, and a 50–50 Anglo–Soviet split in the affairs of Yugoslavia and Hungary. Roosevelt, who wanted to leave specific political and territorial settlements until the war's end, condemned Churchill's proposal as immoral. Nevertheless, Churchill immediately used the agreement to justify sending British troops into Greece to fill a vacuum created by retreating German soldiers. When Communists in Greece started a revolt in December 1944, Stalin did nothing to assist them. On the other hand, the agreement was also an indication that the West would likely not pose any serious resistance to Soviet control in Eastern Europe, though that was not the impression the prime minister had meant to convey.

Figure 7.4 The Big Three –Winston Churchill, Franklin Roosevelt, and Joseph Stalin
(seated, left to right) – meet at Yalta in February 1945.

When Stalin, Roosevelt, and Churchill held their second summit conference at Yalta in the Crimea in February 1945, the war was in its final stages. The Soviet army was just 40 miles from Berlin, and the Western Allied forces had largely rebounded from the shock of Germany's desperate winter offensive in the Ardennes, though they were still over 250 miles away from Berlin. The Big Three, meeting from February 4 to 11 and accompanied by large delegations, dealt with several pressing issues, including Germany, reparations, Poland, the United Nations organization, and the war against Japan.

The Big Three agreed on the denazification and demilitarization of Germany. They also ratified with adjustments the work of the European Advisory Commission dividing Germany into zones of occupation, with the Soviets gaining control of eastern Germany, the British the northwestern sector, and the U.S. the southwestern section. Berlin, located deep inside the Russians' east German zone, was similarly split. At Churchill's behest, Roosevelt and Stalin agreed to allot an occupation zone to France, although it was created from parts of the American and British zones only, since Stalin refused to give up any of the Soviet zone for the purpose. The inclusion of France was based on the assumption that the United States' military presence in Germany would be short term, and that France could take over the American occupation zone when U.S. troops left. Stalin, with the support of Roosevelt, suggested that Germany pay $20 billion in reparations in kind, half of which would go to Russia, but Churchill objected, and the issue remained unresolved.

Poland was the most discussed issue at the conference, with negotiations centering on the country's postwar borders and the makeup of its government. Poland held enormous symbolic significance for the British, since they had entered World War II over Poland and saw the Polish state as their key hope for stopping the spread of Soviet domination in Eastern Europe. The Americans viewed Poland as a test of Soviet postwar cooperation. The three heads of state reaffirmed Russia's claim to the Curzon line as its western border with Poland, and all agreed that Poland would gain extensive land in the west from Germany but without establishing precisely how far west. The U.S. and Britain wanted a new interim government representative of all political parties and one pledged to hold early free elections. Stalin, determined to keep the Warsaw-based Lublin regime in place, compromised on its composition only to the point of accepting a "reorganization" of the Lublin government to include non-Communist representatives, i.e., London Poles. But this Soviet concession proved meaningless, as the Russians undermined it after the conference. The Russians also failed to live up to their promise of early free elections in Poland, even though Stalin said that they could take place in as little as a month's time; indeed, none ever took place in the more than four decades of Soviet domination over Poland that followed. The Big Three underscored the importance of early free elections in Poland and other countries freed from Axis control in a Declaration of Liberated Europe that they signed at the conclusion of the Yalta meetings.

A top priority for Roosevelt at the conference was firming up support from the Soviet Union for a future United Nations. After Stalin demanded that the Soviet Union receive 16 votes in the organization's General Assembly – one for each Soviet republic – the U.S. countered by offering the Soviets three votes, and the Russian leader accepted the deal. The three heads of state also reached agreement on the veto power that each of them would have as permanent members of the U.N.'s Security Council, the body charged with maintaining international peace and security. In addition, they agreed to accept France and China as permanent Security Council members enjoying the same veto power as the Big Three. Securing Russian membership in the United Nations was one of Roosevelt's main goals at the conference, and he got it.

Roosevelt achieved another one of his major conference objectives when Stalin agreed to enter the war against Japan within three months after the conclusion of hostilities against Germany. American military leaders were eager to obtain Soviet intervention since they estimated that an invasion of the Japanese home islands would entail American casualties of up to 1 million men. To gain Russian adherence, Roosevelt promised Stalin the southern half of Sakhalin Island and the Kurile Islands from Japan, and American assistance in obtaining special rights in Manchuria from China.

The actions of the Western Allies at the conference, especially Roosevelt, became the source of unending controversy for long thereafter, with accusations of appeasement repeatedly thrown at them in their dealings with Stalin. In the end, however, they gave up nothing they already held in early 1945, and they operated from a position of weakness in dealing with Stalin on Poland.

Between war and peace

With Soviet troops spread across Eastern Europe in 1945, Stalin steadily increased Russia's influence in the region between the Yalta Conference of February and the Potsdam Conference in July of that year. In Romania, for instance, he forced the creation in March of a Communist-controlled government that gave only two ministerial posts to "bourgeois" parties, and in April the Communist-led government in Poland signed a 20-year security pact with the Soviets. In Czechoslovakia, the Communists received posts in a National Front coalition formed in April, and when Stalin demanded that the Czechs hand over the province of Ruthenia, they did so in June. Stalin also strengthened his authority over the recently reincorporated Soviet Baltic republics of Latvia, Lithuania, and Estonia. The United States, meanwhile, enjoyed a preponderant position among the Western democracies, but it wanted to reduce its military and financial role in Europe quickly and usher in free elections and liberal democracies across the continent. Stalin's aims increasingly appeared at cross-purposes with those goals. President Truman adopted a sterner tone toward the Soviets than his predecessor, bluntly telling Molotov during a meeting in Washington in late April that the Soviets needed to fulfill their Yalta commitment regarding free elections in Poland. When Molotov complained about Truman's brusque tone, the president responded: "Carry out your agreements and you won't get talked to like that again."[9] Yet East–West cooperation continued: one example came on June 26, 1945, when the United States, the Soviet Union, Great Britain, and a number of other countries joined together in San Francisco, California, to sign the United Nations Charter that pledged its signatories to resolve international disputes peacefully and encourage international cooperation.

Conclusion

In 1945, the situation of Europe was similar to that of 1919: politically and economically devastated, divided, and altered, a mass graveyard with human beings struggling to find their way home. The enormity of the continent's devastation rendered imperative a massive territorial, political, and economic reorganization. This explains the frequency of diplomatic meetings after December 1941. While these conferences were initially held to plan war strategies and coordinate Allied efforts, about midway through the conflict they began to focus on the organization of the postwar order in Europe and in the world. With Stalin's unwavering insistence on the Curzon Line and his designs on Eastern Europe, the boundaries of the new Europe were uncertain.

The peace conferences and the future of Europe

Again, a comparison imposes itself between the Versailles settlement and the treaties that ended World War II. In both instances, the peace negotiators had to deal with issues such as a new world order, the status of European colonies, the survival of democracy, massive demographic dislocations, and the need for economic recovery. If the the Versailles settlement had failed to usher in the peace to end all wars, would the post-1945 peace negotiators be able to bring about a stable new European and world order?

Peace with Germany and other defeated nations

The last summit conference of the three principal Allies took place from July 17 to August 2, 1945, in the Berlin suburb of Potsdam; France was not present. Truman, Stalin, and Churchill attended, although in mid-conference Clement Attlee replaced Churchill after Attlee's Labour Party won the British national elections in July. Stalin's new order in Eastern Europe was accepted, with the Allies demanding only that the Soviets honor the Declaration of Liberated Europe.

Germany was the primary focus of the conference. The three powers reaffirmed the denazification and disarmament of the country. They also agreed on trials for Nazi war criminals, a decision that led to the International Military Tribunal in Nuremberg from November 1945 to October 1946, where 22 leading Nazis were tried for war crimes. Concerning reparations, the Allies, at Truman's behest, agreed that the Russians would obtain most of their reparations from their own occupation zone, and the restricted amount that they could now obtain from the other occupying powers' zones would be offset with deliveries of agricultural produce and raw materials from the Soviet area to the other zones. The Allies specified the tasks of a recently implemented Four-Power Allied Control Council (the three wartime partners plus France) that served as the governing agency overseeing the four zones of occupation in Germany. The Allied leaders' insistence on the principle of unanimity in the council's decisions, however, resulted in each zone's occupation administration basically deciding for itself what to do since unanimity proved virtually impossible to achieve in the council's deliberations. Thus, while the three wartime parties expressed their opposition to the dismemberment of Germany and pledged themselves to treat Germany as a single unit, dismemberment is what occurred in fact.

With regard to borders, Stalin insisted that the new Polish–German frontier be the Oder–Neisse Line that included the Oder River and western Neisse River (Lusatian Neisse River). He had already passed the administration of the lands to the Polish government by the time the three leaders met. The Western Allies argued in favor of the eastern Neisse River (Glatzer Neisse River) for the German–Polish border, since Stalin's proposition would necessitate the expulsion of too many Germans. Churchill also argued that by giving the Poles administrative control of the lands east of the Oder–Neisse Line prior to a final peace treaty, they would in effect be making Poland a fifth occupying power in Germany, and he was opposed to that. But Stalin contended that those areas were now Polish, and the U.S. and British leaders finally accepted Stalin's position on the issue subject to a final peace settlement. On August 17, 1945, the Poles signed a border treaty with the Soviet Union, ceding to the Russians the region east of the Curzon Line with small modifications. As for Germany's province of East Prussia, the three leaders confirmed Russia's control over the northern half with its valuable warm water port of Königsberg (renamed Kaliningrad) and Poland's takeover of the territory's southern section. The Allies also accepted the expulsion of all Germans from Czechoslovakia and the new lands that Poland acquired in the west; the displacements had actually begun earlier in 1945 and they continued through 1946 (see pp. 316–317).

Truman achieved one of his goals early in the conference, when Stalin confirmed that Russia would declare war on Japan in August 1945. The president was eager for Soviet participation, even after having received word on his way to Potsdam of the successful detonation of an atomic bomb at Los Alamos, New Mexico. Indeed, the Soviet Union's entry into the war two days after the dropping of an atomic bomb on Hiroshima on August 6 played a crucial role in bringing the war to an end. The Soviet decision deprived the Japanese of the one great power that could have served as a mediator in any negotiated peace and the Soviet army's rapid advance through northern China deprived the Japanese of their one remaining important military asset – its army in Manchuria. The Japanese announced their surrender on August 15 (see p. 269).

The Potsdam Conference left many questions unanswered, so before adjourning, the three Allies agreed to the formation of a Council of Foreign Ministers to work on peace terms, determine final boundaries, and decide other policies for postwar Europe. Composed initially of the foreign ministers of the United States, the Soviet Union, and Great Britain, the foreign ministers met in London in September and in Moscow in December 1945. Amidst much wrangling, the three powers agreed in Moscow to prepare draft peace treaties for several minor Axis states in Europe. In 1946, the council admitted France to its ranks, and continued its peace treaty work at conferences in Paris and New York. The Allies signed final treaties in Paris on February 10, 1947, with Italy, Romania, Bulgaria, Hungary, and Finland. All of the defeated powers lost lands, saw their military forces reduced, and had various reparation amounts assessed to them. While successful in drafting peace agreements for these countries, the four powers found themselves at odds on other questions. One was the Soviet refusal to fulfill a commitment it made at the Yalta Conference to hold free elections in Poland and other Eastern European countries. Russian intransigence led the United States to believe that the Soviets were reverting to their former goal of world revolution and planning to expand Communist control across Europe. There were also bitter disagreements over the terms of a final peace treaty for Germany, so that the 1940s ended with no peace treaty at all and with Europe divided between a Soviet-dominated Communist East and an American-backed democratic West.

New international organizations

One of the goals of the Allies, first articulated at the Moscow meetings of the Big Three's foreign ministers in 1943, was to establish a new international organization to replace the discredited League of Nations. Representatives from the United States, Great Britain, the Soviet Union, and China met at Dumbarton Oaks in Washington D.C. in November 1944 to lay out the framework for a postwar United Nations (UN). A climax to the process came in the spring of 1945, when an international conference convened in San Francisco to complete the drawing up of the United Nations Charter, the international body's foundational document; 50 nations signed the document on June 26, 1945. The UN, headquartered in New York, had as its goals the maintenance of international peace and security, the encouragement of friendly relations among nations, and the promotion of improved standards of living and human rights. Contrary to the League of Nations, the United Nations had the ability to use peacekeeping forces in global trouble spots. The League of Nations held its last session on April 18, 1946, at which it voted to transfer its assets to the UN.

In the area of international finance, the United States, backed by liberal European economists, took the lead in developing a postwar system intended to avoid the high tariff barriers and currency manipulation that contributed to the international economic anguish of the 1930s. Representatives from 44 nations, including the Soviet Union, met in Bretton Woods, New Hampshire, in July 1944, to focus on the postwar monetary order. They established two permanent financial institutions and a new international fixed currency exchange system pegged to the U.S. dollar and gold. One of the new bodies was the International Bank for Reconstruction and Development (World Bank), set up to provide long-term capital for the rebuilding of war-ravaged countries and the growth of underdeveloped nations. The other was the International Monetary Fund (IMF), tasked with giving short-term financial assistance to countries that had temporary balance of payments problems within the currency exchange rate system. While the Soviet Union, along with all other conference participants, signed the Bretton Woods Final Agreement at the conclusion of the July meetings, the Soviets never ratified it. The Russian-controlled Communist states in Eastern Europe did not participate in the World Bank or IMF either. As for loan recipients, France was the first country to obtain financial assistance from both the World Bank and the IMF, doing so in 1947. Though it failed to realize all of the hopes of its founders, the Bretton Woods system nonetheless contributed significantly to the remarkable postwar economic expansion that occurred.

Conclusion

Unlike the Paris Peace Conference of 1919, the peace negotiations of the latter 1940s yielded no treaty with Germany. On the other hand, peace settlements with other European Axis powers were concluded in early 1947, and the newly formed United Nations organization quickly launched initiatives to promote peace around the world. Germany was caught in a legal vacuum masked by the supposedly temporary conditions of the Allies' military occupation. These short-term measures eventually became frozen in the Cold War that paralyzed Europe and delayed its return to normalcy for the next 40 years. As in 1919, Eastern Europe remained secondary concerns to Western Europeans, and the members of this "other Europe" would have to await the end of the Cold War before gaining acceptance as equal partners.

Overall conclusion

Violence in the form of war was a major component of European history in the period from 1914 to 1945. Indeed, unprecedented bloodshed occurred in the world wars that dominated the era. Both wars became total wars in which all of the resources available to the belligerent states militarily and domestically were mobilized to achieve victory. The industrial age in which the wars took place provided the technology needed for the new and evermore deadly weapons that, along with mass armies, contributed to the deaths of tens of millions of people, both on the military and home fronts. When World War I ended, it was the deadliest war in European history, but its numbers of dead were dwarfed by World War II which was by far the largest and most horrific war in the history of mankind. Adding to the gruesomeness of World War II was the fact that far more civilians died in it than did military personnel. Financially, World War II had cost over $1 trillion in 1945 U.S. dollars, which would amount to almost $13 trillion in today's money; the United States bore one-third of the war's financial cost. In 1945, much of Europe lay in ruins, with many of its major cities nothing but heaps of rubble. One European leader commented that the continent could not afford a third major war, because there would then be no European civilization left. Thus, many postwar European officials were ready to move in new directions to render a major war on the continent inconceivable.

As the war expanded from Europe to Africa and Asia, Europe's colonies became major points of interest for both sides, owing to their strategic value and their importance as sources of manpower and raw materials. Major military operations took place on both continents, with one result being altered relationships between Europe's colonial powers and their colonies. By 1945, nationalist movements in many colonies were strong enough to challenge their colonizers' authority and ultimately gain independence for their countries, although in some instances only after prolonged struggles.

Finally, World War II confirmed the Soviet Union and the United States as the world's two superpowers, but the two countries, though wartime allies, emerged from the conflict increasingly as rivals holding competing worldviews. Rifts in their partnership started appearing at the wartime conferences involving the Big Three and the disagreements became serious enough that the two sides could not reach a final agreement on postwar Germany. The war also left behind a power vacuum in Europe owing to Germany's destruction and a considerably weakened Britain and France. The Soviet Union, emerging from the war as Europe's dominant military power, seemed poised to fill the void. It was then that the United States stepped forward as the decisive counterbalance to the Soviet Union in Europe. The U.S. decided to maintain its military presence in Western Europe and to provide the continent with massive economic assistance in the form of the Marshall Plan that went into effect in 1948. By the end of the decade, Europe found itself locked in a Cold War that had the United States and its North Atlantic Treaty Organization (NATO) allies of Western Europe and Canada on one side, and the Soviet Union and its Communist satellite states of Eastern Europe on the other.

Notes

1 Julian Jackson, *The Fall of France: The Nazi Invasion of 1940* (New York: Oxford University Press, 2003), 47.
2 Raymond F. Betts, *Uncertain Dimensions: Western Overseas Empires in the Twentieth Century* (Minneapolis, MN: University of Minnesota Press, 1985), 190.
3 Arthur Herman, *Gandhi and Churchill: The Epic Rivalry That Destroyed an Empire and Forged Our Age* (New York: Bantam Books, 2008), 489.
4 John Keegan, *The Second World War* (New York: Penguin Books, 1989), 135.
5 Mark A. Stoler, *Allies in War: Britain and America against the Axis Powers, 1940–1945* (London: Hodder Arnold, 2007), 68.
6 Winston Churchill, *Memoirs of the Second World War* (Boston, MA: Houghton Mifflin, 1959), 619.
7 Ibid., 620.
8 Joseph Balkoski, "Who Will Command This Operation?: Ike Takes on Overlord," January 20, 2014, in *The Liberation Trilogy: The Epic Story of the Liberation of Europe in World War II*, http://liberationtrilogy.com/the-road-to-d-day/who-will-command-this-operation/ (accessed May 10, 2016).
9 Stoler, *Allies in War*, 206.

Suggestions for further reading

Byfield, Judith A., Carolyn A. Brown, Timothy Parsons and Ahmad Alawad Sikainga, eds. *Africa and World War II*. New York: Cambridge University Press. 2015.
Citino, Robert M. *The Wehrmacht Retreats: Fighting a Lost War, 1943*. Lawrence, KS: University Press of Kansas. 2012.
Ferguson, Niall. *The War of the World: Twentieth Century Conflict and the Descent of the West*. New York: Penguin Books. 2006.
Gilbert, Martin. *Churchill: A Life*. New York: Henry Holt and Company. 1991.
Glantz, David M. and Jonathan M. House. *Stalingrad*. Lawrence, KS: University Press of Kansas. 2017.
Jennings, Eric T. *Free French Africa in World War II: The African Resistance*. New York: Cambridge University Press. 2015.
Keegan, John. *The Second World War*. New York: Penguin Books. 2005.
Khan, Yasmin. *India at War: The Subcontinent and the Second World War*. New York: Oxford University Press. 2015.
Müller, Rolf-Dieter and Gerd R. Ueberschär. *Hitler's War in the East: A Critical Assessment*. 3rd edn. New York: Berghahn Books. 2009.
Stoler, Mark A. *Allies in War: Britain and America against the Axis Powers, 1940–1945*. London: Hodder Arnold. 2007.
Weinberg, Gerhard L. *A World at Arms: A Global History of World War II*. 2nd edn. New York: Cambridge University Press. 2005.

8   The home fronts, 1939–1945

Introduction

When Europe became engulfed in war following Germany's invasion of Poland on September 1, 1939, there were no throngs of people in the streets of capital cities to celebrate the event. Even in Berlin, the public mood was subdued following the invasion announcement. Hitler, planning to make a speech about the matter from his balcony, found the crowd outside so small that he went back inside without delivering it to save himself from embarrassment. In a generally grim frame of mind, the belligerent and neutral states of Europe responded apathetically to meet the challenges that the conflict imposed upon them. But in virtually all instances, wartime politics reflected a shift away from politics as usual – suspended elections, governments-in-exile, and occupying forces were the norm. The peoples' political activities, deprived of normal participatory outlets, frequently moved to resistance.

As the Soviet Union became fully involved in the war effort against Hitler in 1941 and as Hitler's control over his "Fortress Europe" climaxed in 1942–1943, the magnitude of the changes imposed on defeated countries became obvious: the exploitation of occupied nations' economic and human resources, the erasure of prewar national borders, vast population relocations, and widespread destruction were changing the demographic and geographic makeup of Europe. The Nazis pursued their goal of exterminating European Jews and Slavs relentlessly, committing untold crimes in the name of racial purity. Hitler's grandiose plan of mass murder and social engineering led to the Jewish Holocaust, an unprecedented example of an "industry of death." Global war spared nothing and no one in the belligerents' efforts to win a war whose contest was not only for Europe, but for control of a new postwar world order.

Wartime economies

Although military readiness had increased in the 1930s, many countries were not prepared when war broke out on September 1, 1939. Centralized military production controls were already in place in Italy, Germany, and the Soviet Union in the late 1930s, and one can assume that they were in many ways better prepared than others. After the Nazi attack on Poland, the speed of industrial mobilization increased, but it varied greatly from country to country, depending on financial resources, industrial organization levels, and labor markets. Overall, one can observe similar trends: combatant countries went quickly from unemployment to labor shortages and began competing for workers, as the labor-intensive demands of wartime economies employed all available manpower. An increase in women's employment had been present before 1939, and it accelerated. The rapidity with which European countries fell during the first year of the war enabled the occupying powers to avail themselves of the industrial, human, and military resources of the defeated countries they occupied, transforming their economies drastically. Virtually all sectors of the combatant countries' economies were mobilized and retooled for war.

Economic mobilization in Germany

When World War II began, Hitler wanted to make sure that its effects were kept to a minimum on the home front. Hermann Göring's four-year economic plan, established in 1936, was extended and, while the government imposed rationing in late August 1939, it did everything it could to maintain rations at a high level. In this regard, the Nazis' plundering of much of Europe helped keep Germany's ration levels higher than any other belligerent state in Europe until late in the conflict. In the area of resources, both human and material, the Nazis refrained from total mobilization in the early stages of the struggle, lest such a commitment adversely affect the morale of the people. Even though millions of men were called into military service, the Nazis continued to grant generous numbers of deferments for work in industry and the government bureaucracy until early 1942, when German setbacks in the East forced a shift in policy. The production of consumer goods also remained at a high level until 1942. The Nazi war economy was a mixed economy, somewhere between Western capitalism and the Soviet command economy.

In February 1942, Albert Speer, who had served as Hitler's chief architect, became minister of armaments following the death of his predecessor in a plane crash. A brilliant organizer, Speer set out to augment German war production, but he faced major challenges. Obtaining the cooperation of other government ministries was difficult. As Hitler focused more and more attention on the battlefront, government departments responsible for domestic affairs found themselves with ever greater autonomy. Labor was not managed well, as many workers remained employed in nonessential industries. In armaments plants, they were often used inefficiently, and many war-related factories had only a single shift. Hitler kept munitions production at well below full capacity. Not long after his appointment, Speer visited a Berlin munitions factory at night, only to discover that the plant had closed for the day.

To increase war output quickly, Speer decided to put large numbers of women to work in the armaments plants. Over the objections of Göring, his nominal superior, Speer persuaded Hitler to allow him not only to use large numbers of them in munitions factories, but also to bring into Germany as many as 500,000 women from Eastern Europe to work in German homes. Speer significantly upped the number of slave laborers and foreign workers in German plants. In the area of organization, Speer created "industrial self-responsibility," i.e., standardization in the fabrication of war materiel, single item production in individual factories, and technical information sharing. At the same time, Speer began replacing civil servants with technical experts in government bureaucracies. In addition, he established special oversight committees for the allocation of raw materials, the management of Germany's arms production, and the development of new weaponry. Toward the end of the summer of 1942, when German forces were zeroing in on Stalingrad and oil fields in the Caucasus, Speer feared that Hitler might order a slowdown in munitions production, as he had done in the summer of 1941 in the belief that Germany was on the verge of victory over the Soviet Union. Speer used all of his powers of persuasion to convince the Führer to keep the higher production levels in place. German industries were also encouraged to relocate in the East near concentration camps. In 1943, Speer received an endorsement from Propaganda Minister Joseph Goebbels who proclaimed "total war" in order to save Germany and Europe from Bolshevism, resulting in an even higher level of economic and industrial mobilization. Indeed, by 1943, Speer had managed to achieve a threefold increase in armaments output, especially in aircraft and armor production. The peak in German munitions production coincided with the Allied invasion of Normandy in mid-1944.

Forced labor in the Reich

With the mobilization of large numbers of German men into the armed forces, labor shortages forced the German authorities to overrule racial considerations in their organization of a home-front labor force. Three hundred thousand Polish prisoners of war were rushed into the Reich in September 1939 to help with the harvest. Later that fall, Food and Agriculture Minister Walter Darré requested 1.5 to 2 million workers, while the Nazis created 115 labor offices on Polish territory and made labor participation compulsory for all Polish men between 18 and 60. Poland became a long-term reservoir of manpower for the Reich: by mid-1944, over a million Polish adults, women, and teenagers had been sent to the Reich from the German zone of occupation in Poland – the General Government.

The massive deployment phase of forced labor began in the fall of 1941, as Germany realized that it could not win the war quickly and that the military front's needs required a sustained and prolonged war effort. In early 1942, the Nazis began recruiting prisoners of war (POWs) from all the occupied countries and extended the policy gradually to civilian populations, which in time formed the majority of the labor force. The Nazis worked according to their preferred racial hierarchy, hiring first Germanic, Nordic, Anglo-Saxon, and Romance peoples, then Slavic peoples, and finally Jews, Gypsies, and non-whites. Soviet and East Central European citizens provided large numbers of workers. By late 1942, there were 2.8 million Eastern European workers and Soviet POWs working in Germany, including children as young as 14. By the end of 1944, Germany had some 8 million foreign civilians at work within its frontiers.

The network of German labor camps and sub-camps across Europe needed to house the slave workers eventually numbered 42,500. By 1945, 15 million forced laborers had passed through their gates. Discipline was harsh and hunger reigned. Many of the camps grew over time and added extermination facilities. The town of Auschwitz is a good example of the camps' organization, for it was home to two labor camps and a large number of sub-camps that attracted some of the main war manufacturing industries such as I. G. Farben, Siemens, and Krupp. Auschwitz I, housed in a former Polish army barracks, became a minor labor camp in 1940. A second labor camp was established in the nearby town of Monowice in 1942 to provide free labor for an I. G. Farben plant producing synthetic rubber. Prisoners working at the Buna Werke, as the factory was called, were housed in temporary barracks across the street. Two Holocaust survivors, Elie Wiesel and Primo Levi, spoke of the hard labor, hunger, disease, and mistreatment that were their daily lot. To survive the starvation rations and harsh treatment at the camps, prisoners had to "organize" the distribution of food and shoes as well as the provision of medical care. Labor camp prisoners could be sent to death camps at any time if their physical condition worsened or they broke camp rules.

Military production in the Soviet Union

The Soviet Union's economy was put to the test following Germany's invasion in June 1941. In the early months of fighting, the Soviets saw their coal fields and steel-making facilities diminish by half, but they still managed to move 2,500 key manufacturing plants to points east of the Volga River and the Ural Mountains, reaching into the Soviet Central Asian republics and Siberia. The hardships were immense, but the results were equally impressive: the Soviet GNP fell by more than 50 percent in the fall of 1941 but recovered to prewar levels in 1942. Priority was given to the production of armaments, especially those that helped the Soviet armed forces dig in against the Germans and begin pushing them back. The Soviets rationalized and streamlined the production of their highly successful T-34 tank, whose technology was heavily based on the ideas of American engineer J. Walter Christie. They also rationalized the production of their vital Ilyushin Il-2 ground-attack aircraft. In 1943 and 1944, the Soviet Union outstripped the Germans in tank production by 6,000 and aircraft manufacture by 10,000. In areas where Soviet production lagged, such as truck fabrication, the Lend-Lease program filled the gap. To offset the void left by the Soviets' large losses of manpower early in the war, the government pressed women, elderly people, and teenagers into war manufacture and had them work long hours under harsh conditions. Ten million civilians moved east of the Urals and often worked in the open, living in harsh settings where there were no houses, fuel, electricity, or supplies. All holidays were abolished. In spite of the numerous hardships Soviet citizens faced at home, they remained committed to the war effort largely out of a deep sense of patriotism that the regime underscored in its propaganda by portraying the war in nationalistic rather than ideological terms.

Forced labor in the Soviet Union

The Soviet government also used forcibly relocated populations and prisoners of war as free labor. In the spring of 1940, they began deporting Poles and refugees from an area of eastern Poland stretching from Vilna to Lvov, sending over 2 million of them to Siberia and Kazakhstan to do farm and forestry work. The prisoners' journey was arduous. With hardly any food or medical assistance, many died from exposure. The surviving prisoners were sent to 350 large new labor camps and 4,000 new sub-camps where living conditions were primitive. After the Nazi invasion of the Soviet Union, Stalin sought to use some of the deported Polish men to fight alongside the Red Army. An amnesty decree freed more than 70,000 Poles who in July 1941 formed a military unit under the leadership of Polish General Władysław Anders, a hero of the September 1939 campaign who was then languishing in a Moscow prison. The Anders Army eventually requested a transfer to Iran where it was placed under Anglo-American control. Meanwhile, another 40,000 Polish deportees were molded into a Polish army under Soviet command in 1943. Overall, less than 300,000 Polish deportees survived the war.

Military preparedness in Britain

When the war broke out, the British navy was the country's only military branch that was combat-ready, and the British government under Neville Chamberlain moved unevenly with wartime preparations. The government immediately used the navy to impose a naval blockade against Germany. Chamberlain also set up a small war cabinet and created ministries for economic warfare, shipping, information, food, and home security. In late September, the government introduced gasoline rationing and a wartime budget involving an important rise in income taxes. Nevertheless, government spending increased little more than the rate of inflation during the winter of 1939–1940, and Chamberlain was not eager to modify the British economy in any dramatic way. Some 1 million people were still unemployed in the spring of 1940, and women were still largely at home. In late June, the country had a mere 160 tanks available for combat.

Following Churchill's accession to power in May 1940 and the sense of political unity that emerged as the country stood alone in Europe that summer in defiance of Germany, Britain's economic mobilization accelerated. Churchill brought Labour Party leaders into his government, including Ernest Bevin – a matter-of-fact trade union head – who was assigned to oversee all labor-related matters. As labor minister, Bevin was eminently successful in mobilizing Britain's wartime labor force. Along the way, he obtained important wage increases and better workplace conditions for

Figure 8.1 British Prime Minister Winston Churchill watches a female riveter do her job in the assembly of a Spitfire fighter plane at an aircraft factory in Birmingham, England, on September 28, 1941.

workers. In its mobilization of the economy, the government achieved impressive results. The amount of land under cultivation rose from 12 million acres to 18 million. Aircraft production increased from less than 3,000 airplanes in 1938 to more than 26,000 in 1943. The economy added 3 million jobs during the war, with the result that only 75,000 were unemployed in 1945. But the British were ultimately limited in what they could do owing to the small size of their population (47 million) relative to other major combatants and their limited financial resources. The country relied to an important degree on the largesse of the United States in the form of Lend-Lease and loans to stay afloat in 1940–1941, and that dependence continued thereafter. The British endured many hardships and sacrifices without ever wavering in their belief that Hitler must be defeated militarily.

Conclusion

In all combatant countries, patriotism, hyped by propaganda, kept workers at their work stations and induced them to accept unprecedented sacrifices. In the Axis-occupied countries, workers used sabotage and other forms of resistance against their occupiers, and managed as well as they could to serve the needs of the civilian populations by maintaining whatever economic normality could be achieved. After 1941, the Allies pooled their resources in an effort that American financial and logistical contributions dominated. This created integrated commercial structures and increased world trade to an even greater degree than had happened during the Great War. In this integrated global world, the Allies' colonies played a significant role. As for Germany, it revolutionized the economies of Europe by breaking national barriers, reorganizing markets and labor pools, and engineering the largest migrations and displacements of populations in modern times. These developments together were of such great magnitude that they made a return to prewar normalcy impossible.

The primacy of war over politics

As the war expanded across Europe, a variety of changes – often dramatic – took place in the world of politics. The mildest political adjustments involved the suspension of elections, the growing political power of the military, the reprioritization of political decisions, and the creation of governments of national unity. In their most drastic form, political disruptions resulted in the disappearance of governments, the imprisonment or killing of prewar politicians, and the destruction of political structures. Nazi-occupied countries were split between collaborators and resisters, the latter often escaping to London to form governments-in-exile. The polarization of politics was inevitable.

Great Britain

In Great Britain, Chamberlain remained in power even though, as he told parliament on September 3, 1939, all he had sought during his public career "has crashed into ruins."[1] When asked to join Chamberlain's National Government, the Liberals and Labourites refused. Chamberlain did reshuffle his government by bringing in Churchill, an old political rival, to serve as first lord of the admiralty and a member of his war cabinet. Overall, Chamberlain's record as a wartime prime minister was lackluster. Though he quickly introduced higher taxes, civilian defense efforts, and large-scale conscription, Chamberlain seemed undisturbed by the slow expansion of armaments production, did little to obtain the active support of Britain's non-Conservative parties, and ignored suggestions for the creation of a Ministry of Economic Planning. His uninspiring leadership was reflected in a momentary downturn in the country's morale during the winter of 1939–1940. When British operations in Norway floundered in the spring of 1940, parliamentary anger against Chamberlain reached a boiling point during a May 7–8 debate on the conduct of the war, with Conservative backbenchers in the forefront of the attacks. Chamberlain resigned.

Churchill took over the prime minister's office on May 10. As a Conservative member of the House of Commons, he had spent the 1930s in a "political wilderness" – out of a cabinet post from 1929 to 1939 and shunned by the party establishment for first opposing its policies toward India and later toward Germany. Imperturbable, self-confident, and determined, Churchill welded together a truly national government that included leaders from the Labour and Liberal parties. At its center was a five-man war cabinet in which Churchill, as defense minister, oversaw the execution of the war. In his initial speech to the House of Commons after taking office, Churchill said that he had "nothing to offer but blood, toil, tears, and sweat," but added that "victory at all costs" was the goal.[2] During the summer and fall of 1940, when the country was alone in Europe in the war against Nazi Germany and its cities were under heavy bombing attacks, Churchill did much to maintain British morale through inspirational speeches and acts of defiance toward Germany.

In joining together in Churchill's National Coalition, the major parties agreed that there would be no national elections for the duration of the conflict, so that the country could focus on the war without the disruptions of political campaigns. Even though there was sincere wartime bipartisanship, certain developments indicated that the spirit of political cooperation would not outlast the conflict. The chief among these was the publication in 1942 of the Beveridge Report, the outcome of a government-spon-sored committee led by Sir William Beveridge. The report called for a comprehensive social insurance structure including pensions to housewives and the guarantee of a minimum level of existence, a government-sponsored system of universal health care, and a guarantee of full employment after the war. Receiving enthusiastic approval from the public, the document presented the framework for a postwar welfare state. While the Labour Party's ministerial members voted for a government-sponsored par-liamentary resolution that shelved the report, virtually all rank-and-file Labour MPs, clearly committed to social reform, defied their party leaders and voted against the government's stand. In the end, the report set the tone for the domestic political agenda during the remainder of the conflict, as social reform issues overshadowed all others, though no major reforms were passed. The National Coalition dissolved shortly after the cessation of European hostilities in May 1945, when the Labour Party refused an offer from Churchill to continue the coalition until the military defeat of Japan.

Vichy France

The initial war months created new policy debates and weighed on public morale in France. In contrast to World War I, France's political parties failed to join together in a "sacred union." When the French Communist Party (PCF), acting on orders from Moscow following the Nazi–Soviet Nonaggression Pact, withdrew its backing for the war effort, Premier Edouard Daladier in September 1939 declared the party illegal, causing Communist Party leader Maurice Thorez to seek refuge in the Soviet Union. Following the collapse of Poland, Daladier, albeit pessimistic about the chances of victory, resisted attempts from leading politicians to withdraw from the war and make peace with Hitler. Support for the war among the civilian population declined during the winter of 1939–1940, as some Frenchmen concluded that no German invasion was imminent. Other Frenchmen became dismayed because of squabbles between French and British leaders over war plans and renewed political discord at home. The end of the Russo-Finnish War in March 1940 precipitated the downfall of the Daladier government, since the Premier had advocated Allied military support for the Finns, but failed to achieve it before Finland's collapse. His political rivals, seeking someone more dynamic, turned to Paul Reynaud who became the new premier by a parliamentary majority of one. Quarrels with Daladier, whom Reynaud was forced to accept as his defense minister, led to another cabinet crisis on May 9, but since Hitler launched his major offensive in the West the next day, Reynaud remained in power on an emergency basis. As the French military situation rapidly deteriorated, a demoralized cabinet abandoned Reynaud on June 15 by voting to seek armistice terms from the Germans. Marshall Philippe Pétain replaced Reynaud the next day and signed an armistice with Germany on June 22. On July 10, the French Parliament ended the Third Republic, when it voted to give Pétain the power to write a new constitution.

Germany divided France into an occupied zone that included the northern and western areas, with Paris situated deep inside it, and a "free zone" that encompassed the southeastern part of the country with the resort town of Vichy as its capital. Adopting the title of French chief of state, Pétain brought into his government a number of anti-republican traditionalists who were committed to an anti-democratic, authoritarian system. They moved to impose a "National Revolution" on the country that involved the expulsion of foreigners and a return to the soil. The regime used the motto "work, family, country" in place of the republican "liberty, equality, fraternity" on its coins and elsewhere. The Vichy government sought the support of the Catholic Church by abolishing divorce and Masonic lodges. Economically, it introduced corporatist ideas that included the issuance of a Labor Charter banning free trade unions and strikes, and the creation of government-organized steering committees for each sector of manufacturing. Propagandists in the Vichy regime also worked hard to develop a cult around the person of Pétain.

One of the major issues facing the Vichy government centered on collaboration with the Germans. One of the chief advocates of collaboration was Pierre Laval, Pétain's first premier. Laval, a three-time Third Republic premier whom *Time* magazine had named its "Man of the Year" in 1931, sought ways to cooperate with the Germans in the belief that a cooperative policy would provide France its salvation. The Germans had little interest in pursuing close collaboration with the French in 1940, however, and Laval failed to obtain anything of importance in the way of concessions. His failure caused Pétain to dismiss him from office late in the year. But his successors also fell short of achieving real collaboration with Germany, and thus Laval, with the strong support of Germany's ambassador to Vichy, returned triumphantly to power in 1942. He remained as premier after the Germans occupied the Vichy-controlled "free zone" in November 1942, and continued in that role right up to the fall of the Vichy regime in France in August 1944. He pursued collaboration with Germany on several fronts, including a system by which Germany was to release one French prisoner of war for every three volunteer laborers France sent to German war factories. France eventually provided Germany's war plants with several hundred thousand laborers, most of them conscripted, since the number of volunteers turned out to be miniscule. Laval later claimed that his collaborationist policies, which involved dilatory tactics and efforts to retain some French autonomy, mitigated the most brutal effects of the Nazi occupation on France. Following the Allied liberation of Paris in August 1944, the Germans transported Vichy leaders to Sigmaringen, Germany, where they unsuccessfully tried to set up a French government-in-exile.

The Free French movement

An alternative to the collaborationist Vichy regime was the Free French movement that a junior French general named Charles de Gaulle established in London following France's defeat in June 1940. De Gaulle insisted that France had lost a battle – not the war – and that the French should continue the conflict from abroad. With the support of Churchill, de Gaulle used his small movement to create the trappings of a government-in-exile. One early setback was the decision of the United States to disregard de Gaulle by establishing and maintaining full diplomatic relations with the Vichy government. As the war progressed, de Gaulle proved unafraid to cross both Churchill and Roosevelt when he felt it necessary, and he outwitted several rivals on his way to achieving leadership over the French resistance forces, both at home and abroad. Just before the Allies launched their D-Day invasion in Normandy on June 6, 1944, a French Committee of National Liberation, that de Gaulle headed, proclaimed itself the provisional government of France to counter an attempt by the Communists, an important component of France's internal resistance movement, to take power once the Germans were gone. For political reasons, he insisted that the Allies make a modification in their advance across France to allow for the liberation of Paris before French resistance forces could set up a government independent of his. Eisenhower, the Allied supreme commander, reluctantly accommodated de Gaulle. French soldiers were in the forefront of the Allied forces that liberated the city on August 25, and de Gaulle, as president of the provisional government, marched triumphantly down the Champs-Elysées the following day. Nevertheless, the Allies did not extend official recognition to him as France's interim president until October. By then, he had solidified his power at home and was looking ahead to France's transition from war to peace.

Governments-in-exile in Britain

As one country after another in Europe fell victim to Nazi-led Germany early in the war, their heads of state, including kings, queens, and presidents, often left for Britain where they established governments-in-exile. In some instances these governments exercised a limited control over their armed forces which cooperated with the British in the war against the Axis powers. They also maintained contacts with resistance organizations in their countries and worked closely with Allied intelligence agencies by relaying information from underground groups back home. Countries with Allied-recognized governments-in-exile in Britain included Belgium, Czechoslovakia, the Netherlands, Norway, Poland, Yugoslavia, and Greece.

King Haakon VII of Norway (r. 1905–1957) and Queen Wilhelmina of the Netherlands (r. 1890–1948) were among the monarchs who headed governments-in-exile. King Haakon became a symbol of Norwegian unity in the face of the German occupation, and Norwegians used the king's monogram H7, which they sketched on fences, homes, roads, and in the snow, as a symbol of their defiance toward the Nazi occupiers. One of the key actions of the king's government in London was to take control of a large portion of the country's merchant fleet, which was of considerable size, and put it to work for the Allies. Dutch Queen Wilhelmina, as the titular head of her country's government-in-exile, encouraged her people to resist the Nazis in late-night radio messages transmitted from Britain, denouncing Hitler as "the arch-enemy of mankind" in one of them. She also opposed Dirk Jan de Geer, the initial prime minister of the Dutch government in London, when he expressed his desire to sign a peace settlement with the Germans. Working through another minister, Wilhelmina succeeded in obtaining de Geer's ouster from office in September 1940.

Poland's government-in-exile was particularly active during the war. First set up in Paris with the full diplomatic support of the Western Allies, the Polish government shifted to London when France collapsed in 1940. The key leader in the government hierarchy was General Władysław Sikorski, who served as prime minister until his death in mid-1943. In July 1941, Poland and the Soviet Union signed a treaty reestablishing diplomatic relations that had been severed in 1939 when the Soviets participated with Germany in the dismemberment of the Polish state. The creation of the Anders Army from amnestied Polish prisoners seemed to cement the alliance, but the Polish soldiers never saw battle on the Eastern Front and were evacuated in the spring of 1942. They ended up fighting in Italy as an independent unit in the British army. Tensions in the relationship between the Polish government-in-exile and the Soviets escalated rapidly in the spring of 1943, following the retreating German soldiers' discovery of a mass grave containing the bodies of thousands of Polish officers in the Katyn Forest near Smolensk in Russia. When Sikorski called for an independent investigation into the matter, Stalin severed diplomatic relations with the Poles in London. The British and Americans, meanwhile, showed frustration with the Polish government-in-exile over its inflexible position on Poland's postwar frontiers.

The London-based Polish government played an important role in the war, exercising considerable influence inside Poland through its connections with the large Polish underground resistance movement known as the Home Army. It also controlled the bulk of Poland's navy which, while not large numerically, had managed to escape to Britain; Polish ships participated in many successful operations at sea during the war. Large numbers of Polish soldiers and pilots, also loyal to the government-in-exile, made noteworthy contributions to Allied efforts in France in 1940, the air war over Britain in 1940, North Africa, bombing runs over Germany, the campaign in France and Belgium in 1944, and elsewhere. In the end, the London-based Poles not only lost on the issue of postwar borders, but also on the legitimacy of their government. Stalin oversaw the creation of a Communist regime in Poland that contained a smattering of representation from opposition parties. France, Britain, and the United States abandoned their recognition of the Polish government-in-exile in the summer of 1945.

The neutral states

Several European states that adhered to a policy of neutrality at the outset of World War II were successful in maintaining that position internationally for the duration of the conflict. These countries included Sweden, Switzerland, Spain, Portugal, Ireland, and Vatican City. Neutrality, however, was a relative term. The Swiss tolerated the use of their secretive banking system by the Nazis. The Swedes provided the Germans with iron ore until 1942. Spain played a delicate game to avoid being drawn into the Axis camp in the conflict. Ireland worked with Britain – an unusual step in light of their longstanding history of distrust and conflict – to devise a plan for joint action in Ireland should Germany invade the Irish republic. The Vatican remained largely silent on the issue of the Holocaust. Political life went on as usual, however. While some of the states continued with their democratic systems, Spain and Portugal remained under the authoritarian regimes of Francisco Franco and Antonio Salazar, respectively. Norway, a neutral country with a democracy at the outset of the war, began to prepare for the possibility of war during the winter of 1939–1940, but it was unable to stop the Nazi invasion of the spring of 1940, after which a collaborationist authoritarian government took control under the leadership of Vidkun Quisling, a prewar Nazi sympathizer.

The Nazi regime

There were shifts in the structure of the Nazi state during the war, but its operating principles remained largely the same as in the prewar years. Lacking any clearly defined organizational unity, the regime consisted of a number of overlapping administrative jurisdictions in which various departments and individuals competed with each other to gain more power and Hitler's favor. Early in the war, a key Nazi functionary was Deputy Führer Rudolf Hess who oversaw party operations and had veto power over civil service appointments. After Hess flew to England in May 1941 on a self-appointed peace mission that ended with the British arresting him, Martin Bormann replaced him and quickly emerged as an especially powerful force within the party bureaucracy. Completely devoted to the Führer, Bormann became the person through whom people passed to gain access to Hitler. As the war progressed, Hitler handed over increased responsibilities to the Reich's *Gauleiters* (governors) who were the party's highest-ranking administrative chiefs at the regional level. Hitler did so because he viewed them as the only party leaders who were completely trustworthy. For example, Fritz Sauckel, the *Gauleiter* of Saxony, in 1942 was given the task of securing foreign workers to replace Germans called to arms in ever great numbers to meet increasing arms production demands. By the end of the war, Sauckel had brought some 5 million foreign workers into Germany where they were used as forced or slave laborers. The sheer management of this new organization consumed considerable human, material, and financial resources. In 1943, Hitler assigned Goebbels, the *Gauleiter* of Berlin and Germany's propaganda minister, the responsibility of directing the entire civilian side of Germany's war effort; with his new title of plenipotentiary for the total war effort, Goebbels' power reached its peak.

An entity that gained considerable prominence during the war was the Nazi party's elite guard – the SS or *Schutzstaffel* – under the leadership of Heinrich Himmler. Soon after the war began, the state security service (SD) – an internal spy agency – and the state police (Gestapo) were merged into a single unit called the Reich Security Main Office under the general supervision of the SS. The SS, which became a force of 900,000 men functioning as part of a state within a state, practiced a campaign of terror at home, implemented Nazi racial policies across German-occupied Eastern Europe, supervised Germany's concentration camp system, and planned and directed the Final Solution that called for the extermination of Europe's Jews. Himmler emerged as arguably the second most powerful leader in Nazi Germany as the war progressed.

On the other hand, there was also a German opposition to Hitler, but it was splintered and weak. The one serious attempt to overthrow Hitler was led by a group of conservative military officers in a plot codenamed Operation Valkyrie. Colonel Claus von Stauffenberg, the key conspirator, set off a bomb at Hitler's Eastern Front military headquarters of Rastenburg in East Prussia (the Wolf's Lair) on July 20, 1944, while the Führer was present. When Hitler survived the assassination attempt, the coup quickly unraveled. Stauffenberg and other leading plotters were arrested the same evening in Berlin and shot. Mass arrests and executions ensued in the months thereafter as part of an ever-tightening regime of terror.

With the Allies advancing into Germany in late 1944, Hitler gave the order to destroy all of Germany's industrial potential, an order that Albert Speer quietly disobeyed. On April 30, 1945, with bombs raining upon Berlin and the Russian army advancing on the Reich Chancellery, Hitler, along with his new bride Eva Braun, committed suicide in his underground bunker. He was preceded in death at the same site by Goebbels and his family. The German High Command signed Germany's surrender on May 7–8, and Nazi Germany ceased to exist.

The Soviet regime

Between September 1939 and June 1941, Stalin cast his lot with Hitler and cooperated with Germany on the partition of Poland, the population transfers that resulted therefrom, and treaty-related commercial exchanges, mostly of food for munitions. Stalin still trusted Hitler in the spring of 1941, counting on continued fighting between the British and the Germans to exhaust the German army and either spare the Soviet Union from invasion or blunt an attack. He chose to disregard reports sent by Richard Sorge, a Soviet spymaster working for the Red Army in Tokyo, about an impending German assault. After Germany invaded the Soviet Union in June 1941, Stalin temporarily dropped out of sight. When he reemerged, he delivered a radio speech in which he called on the Soviet people to engage in a national resistance to the "cruel and implacable" enemy. He implored them to adopt a scorched earth policy to deprive the advancing Germans of food and factories, and guerrilla warfare to create havoc in German-occupied lands. Governmentally, he set up a five-member war cabinet over which he presided; it remained in place until Japan's official surrender to the Allies in early September 1945.

Playing down Communist ideology, the government portrayed the war as a patriotic struggle and used terms such as "the Great Patriotic War" and "Fatherland War" to describe it. In the fall of 1941, Stalin decided to remain in Moscow rather than flee to the east, and his decision helped stem a panic among the Muscovites who saw government officials moving to a new headquarters in the city of Kuibyshev on the banks of the Volga. To assure the world that the regime was no longer intent on world revolution, Soviet leaders highlighted Slavic solidarity when celebrating the Bolshevik revolution's twenty-fifth anniversary in November 1942. In 1944, a new Soviet national anthem replaced the

Russian version of the political left-wing's "International." Stalin recognized the wartime loyalty of the Orthodox Church, long the target of Communist persecution, by reestablishing the patriarchate under state protection in 1943; the newly elected patriarch declared Stalin to be "the divinely anointed." Stalin's goal in these actions was to forge a unity among the Soviet citizenry and to thwart German efforts at creating disloyalty. His long-term domestic goals did not change, however, as was evident in Stalin's policies once the war had ended.

At the same time, Stalin used his ideological links with Communist parties across Europe to pursue the creation of a new Communist-dominated European order. After the German invasion of June 1941, the Soviets stressed unity with foreign Communist parties in fighting the Nazis. Despite these efforts, divergences soon emerged. Yugoslav Communist resistance leader Josip Broz Tito assembled a large partisan army that proved decisive in the liberation of Yugoslavia in 1944–1945 and that allowed him later to practice a brand of Communism independent of Moscow as Yugoslavia's postwar dictator.

In East Central Europe, Communist leaders, whom Stalin controlled, began in 1944 to play an active role in establishing provisional governments of national unity in Poland, Bulgaria, Romania, Hungary, and Czechoslovakia as the Red Army liberated them late in the war. In the case of Poland, Stalin had already begun preparing the way for a puppet Communist regime before the war. During the Soviet Great Purge of the 1930s, he had executed the Polish Communist leadership on suspicion of collaborating with the "colonels' regime," dissolved the Polish Communist Party on grounds of supporting the Trotskyite faction, and spared only low-level members such as Bolesław Bierut who would serve as the head of Poland's quasi-parliamentary State National Council from 1944 to 1947. During the war, Stalin turned his attention to the Polish Home Army which, though it assisted the Soviets in battling against Germany, was pledged to the Polish government-in-exile in London. Not long after the pro-Communist Lublin Committee set up a provisional government with Soviet backing in mid-1944, Stalin began a campaign of persecution against the Home Army that included the arrest of large numbers of its soldiers, many of whom ended up in Soviet labor camps or prisons. A climax to Stalin's crackdown came in mid-1945 when 16 underground leaders, both civilian officials and Home Army commanders, were put on trial in Moscow on trumped-up charges and imprisoned. Stalin's brutality against the Poles was an extreme example of his paranoia, but other Eastern European countries also began the postwar era under a cloud of political terror owing to Soviet interference.

Italy

Once Mussolini was certain of a German military victory in France, he declared war on France and Britain on June 10, 1940, with Italy gaining a small zone of occupation in southeastern France when hostilities against the French ended two weeks later. Mussolini saw this action as a logical development in the revolution he had started a war of ideology against capitalism. Yet Italy soon experienced military setbacks in Greece and Libya that gave some Italians pause regarding Mussolini's regime. A temporary reprieve for Italy came in 1941, when the Germans turned military events in favor of the Axis forces in the Balkans and North Africa through their military intervention in both places. Mussolini felt confident enough in mid-1941 that, to Hitler's dismay, he sent 200,000 soldiers to participate in Germany's offensive against Russia. In the latter part of 1942, however, Axis reversals in North Africa, an increasingly unpopular war in Russia, and shortages of foodstuffs and basic commodities created widespread pessimism among the Italian people about the war's outcome. But it was only after the Allies invaded Sicily and bombed Rome in mid-1943 that Mussolini faced a serious challenge to his dictatorship. The Fascist Grand Council met for several hours on July 24 and passed a vote of no confidence against him. The next day King Victor Emmanuel III, anxious to protect his crown, removed Mussolini as prime minister, ordered his arrest, and appointed Marshal Pietro Badoglio as head of state. The King continued to pledge his country's support for Hitler while Badoglio simultaneously conducted secret talks with the Allies for an armistice that was finally signed on September 3, 1943, though not announced until September 9. Hitler, suspicious of the new Italian government's intentions from the start, used the time between Mussolini's fall and the announcement of the armistice to strengthen considerably Germany's military position in Italy. When the Italian surrender was publicly announced, the King and Badoglio fled Rome and reestablished the government's headquarters in southeastern Italy. The Italian army, left without orders, saw the bulk of its soldiers desert their units.

German troops immediately rushed troops into Rome and down the Italian peninsula as far south as Naples, putting the country under a German occupation. In a bold rescue operation, German commandos freed Mussolini from his captors on September 12, and Hitler set him up as head of a puppet Fascist government in northern Italy called the Italian Social Republic. On October 13, Badoglio, representing the Kingdom of Italy, declared war on Germany and sought the support of leftist partisans in the fight to liberate the country. In addition to the Allies fighting the Axis in Italy, the country became locked in a civil war between Fascist forces loyal to Mussolini and an Italian resistance movement that had a strong Communist component. In June 1944, Badoglio gave way as head of the government to Ivanoe Bonomi, a moderate socialist and veteran of anti-Fascist politics who formed a broad coalition to oversee the transition from war to peace. Bonomi's government laid the groundwork for Italy's postwar economic, administrative, and social welfare systems. In late April 1945, Italian partisans captured Mussolini and executed him by machine gun fire.

Hungary

Hungary played a dangerous game and had a rocky ride during the war years, politically and territorially. Hungary benefited at first by annexing, with Hitler's approval, approximately one-fourth of the territory of Slovakia shortly after the Munich Conference in 1938. In April 1941, the Hungarians let German soldiers pass through their country to invade neighboring Yugoslavia and then sent in troops of their own to carry out their claim to a portion of the defeated Yugoslav state. Hungary committed itself militarily to the Axis powers in late June 1941 when, under pressure from Hitler, it declared war on the Soviet Union. By early 1942, Miklós Horthy, the country's head of state, was ready to distance his regime from Hitler's Germany; consequently, he replaced his pro-Nazi prime minister with the more moderate Miklós Kállay, who stopped the government's cooperation with the Nazis on a number of fronts, including the seizure of Hungarian Jews. When Kállay, with Horthy's backing, reached out to the Western Allies about the possibility of peace in early 1944, Hitler responded by sending German troops into Hungary, placing Horthy under house arrest, and overseeing the creation of a pro-Nazi government. The compliant government worked closely with Adolf Eichmann, a high-ranking Nazi official who coordinated the deportation of nearly half a million Hungarian

Jews in the summer of 1944 to the death camp at Auschwitz-Birkenau. After Horthy tried to make peace with the advancing Soviets in October 1944, the Germans forced his abdication and sent him to Bavaria where he lived in comfortable captivity until war's end. The Nazis installed the fascist Arrow Cross Party in power. Heading what it called a Government of National Unity, the Arrow Cross Party launched a vicious reign of terror against the Jews of Budapest, triggering Swedish diplomat Raoul Wallenberg's successful efforts to save thousands of them. Budapest fell to the Soviets at the end of 1944, and by April 1945 the country was under Soviet occupation. Hungary signed peace treaties in 1946 that returned its territory to the borders that the Treaty of Trianon had established in 1920.

Conclusion

Democracy, which had collapsed in many countries of Europe between the wars, experienced a new set of challenges between 1939 and 1945. In belligerent countries where it functioned, such as Great Britain, normal political operations were quickly suspended for the duration of hostilities. Several of them, such as Norway and Belgium, were displaced when Hitler's armies overran their countries, only to reemerge as governments-in-exile in Britain. Other governments-in-exile, such as Poland and Greece, represented countries whose authoritarian systems had collapsed under the weight of Hitler's forces; they promoted democracy, but they lacked the legitimacy that democratic governments would normally possess, and over time they lost touch with core constituencies. The divisions between them and home-based resistance groups that had a strong Communist presence heightened political tensions and polarizations that were already evident in the interwar years; the differences also threatened the postwar unity that government-in-exile leaders sought based on nationalist aspirations and the renewal of their countries. The fate of democracy in Europe ultimately rested primarily in the hands of its chief defenders, Great Britain and the United States which, through their victory in the war, were able to preserve it as an option for the European postwar world.

Demographic chaos and human tragedies

World War II destroyed the demographic recovery that had taken place during the interwar years. The war affected demographic patterns in three major ways. Firstly, people who became homeless either fled as refugees or hungered and died in bombed-out cities and villages. Secondly, Europe became a human checkerboard when tens of millions of people were sent away from their homes. Vast population relocations took place in western Russia and Eastern Europe at the hands of Germany and the Soviet Union, and ethnic groups were forcibly resettled from their ancestral lands. Undesirable groups and minorities were persecuted, and the Nazis targeted the Jewish population of Europe for extermination. Thirdly, normal work patterns ceased when millions of men went to war. A scarcity of labor led to the forcible relocation of manpower in occupied countries, first in Poland following the Nazi and Soviet attacks of September 1939, then in Western European countries in 1940. The war against civilians was a war within the war. It tore the social and ethnic fabric of Europe apart and destroyed the history of countless communities and cultures.

Prewar exodus and Nazi invasion

As war approached, lands near national borders became increasingly risky for civilian populations. Expecting a German attack, several countries made plans to relocate their border populations. For example, the Netherlands in the fall of 1939 planned to evacuate 440,000 of its citizens from border areas but executed the plan too late. When the Netherlands surrendered on May 14, 1940, the fourth day of the Nazi invasion, thousands of evacuees were caught by the Germans. France relocated more than 250,000 Strasbourg residents to the center of the country. The French also interned nationals of Axis countries, Eastern European and Spanish refugees, and anyone suspected of Communist sympathies in 46 detention camps. Numbering nearly 250,000 in 1940, the internees lived in conditions worse than those found at the Nazi concentration camp of Dachau near Munich, Germany.

On September 1, 1939, when the Germans attacked Poland, millions of Polish civilians fled eastwards. Bombed and strafed by German airplanes, between 150,000 and 200,000 refugees died during the September campaign, while 1 to 2 million Jews and Poles fled to the cities of Lvov and Wilno which were now in the Soviet sector. Himmler's *Einsatzgruppen*, special mobile SS death squads, conducted sweeping operations behind the front lines and killed 60,000 Polish civilians during the first three months of the war. The *Einsatzgruppen* targeted priests, lawyers, government officials, teachers, Polish aristocrats, Jews, and ethnic Russians. Two months into the Polish campaign, SS Security Chief Reinhard Heydrich boasted that 97 percent of Poland's upper classes had disappeared.

During the first two years of the war, each time a front opened – Poland in September 1939, Belgium, the Netherlands, and France in May 1940, and the Soviet Union in June 1941 – refugees fled Hitler's invading armies. German dive-bombers attacked long lines of evacuees who jammed the roads below. Food, fuel, transportation, and hotels were in short supply.

Nazi-controlled Poland

Nazi officials, as the first step towards building their racially pure empire, put in place in 1939 and 1940 a massive bureaucratic apparatus to relocate Polish populations. To achieve their goal, the Nazis redrew the map of Poland. The central part of the country, consisting of Warsaw, Radom, Cracow, Lublin, and Galicia, was consolidated into a German-occupied administrative region known as the General Government where senior Nazi party official Hans Frank served as governor general. The Nazis annexed western Poland, the Polish Corridor, Danzig, and Upper Silesia. They selected Poles of "good racial extraction" for resettlement in the German Reich, and sent "suitable" children under the ages of 8 or 10 to be raised in the Reich. They also emptied the newly annexed territories of Poles and Jews, who were relocated into the General Government. With between 850,000 and 920,000 Poles and Jews deported during the winter of 1939–1940, detention centers proved insufficient. In regard to the Jews, the Nazis did all that they could to isolate them and make them as contemptible as possible in the eyes of non-Jews. As a temporary solution, they herded Jews from across German-occupied Poland into Jewish-designated urban ghettos that were sealed off from the rest of the community. The largest ghettoes were located in the cities of Warsaw and Lodz. The Jews lived in overcrowded, unsanitary conditions, where

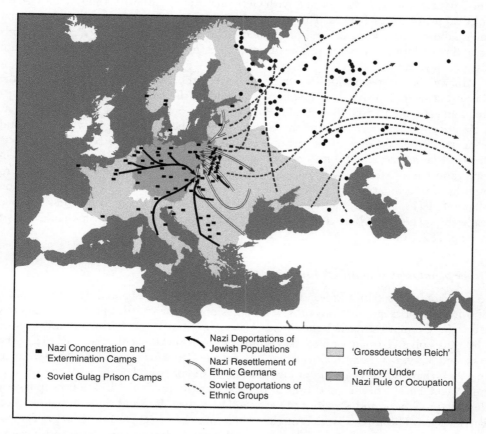

Map 8.1 Population resettlements in World War II. © Jefferson S. Rogers.

many died of starvation, disease, shootings, and beatings. Meanwhile, Austrian and Czech Jews were brought to eastern Poland and Galicia; often they were dumped in a wilderness or left to suffer at the hands of the locals. By December 1940, the General Government had gained close to a million people. To relieve overcrowding, Frank, with the agreement of German economy chief Hermann Göring, stopped the deportations and, in June 1940, attempted to revive a plan to deport Jews to Madagascar – a plan that ultimately did not materialize. While the Nazis found themselves in a holding pattern from 1939 to 1941 on how to deal with the Jews permanently, more than 500,000 Polish Jews died in ghettoes and labor camps.

Soviet-controlled Poland

After the Soviets took control of eastern Poland in the fall of 1939, they implemented a deportation process that led to the relocation of 1.5 million people, mostly Poles, from the newly acquired Polish lands to Central Asia and Siberia between 1939 and 1941.

The Russians also shared arrest lists with German military authorities and cooperated on political prisoners' exchanges. This allowed both invading powers to get rid of potential spies, saboteurs, resisters, and traitors. Like the Nazis, the Soviets targeted political leaders and the educated classes, and contributed to destroying the Polish people's ability to resist occupation.

Among the most notorious attempts to destroy the Poles' ability to resist was the Katyn Massacre. During their invasion of Poland in the fall of 1939, the Soviets captured an estimated 250,000–450,000 Polish soldiers. Some of them were released, but a majority of them were sent to the Gulag. Those who were born in western Poland were transferred to Germany as part of a prisoner exchange with the Nazis. The Soviets detained more than 20,000 military officers and members of Poland's intelligentsia in four camps near Moscow and eastern Ukraine. After the prisoners were subjected to months of interrogation and indoctrination during the winter of 1939–1940, Stalin on March 4, 1940, ordered their execution, which effectively decimated Poland's national leadership. They were buried in mass graves in the Katyn Forest near Smolensk, Russia (see pp. 282, 300).

Other population relocations involving the Soviet Union

In addition to resettling Poles early in the war, the Soviets engaged in the uprooting of other minority populations on several occasions as the conflict progressed. Shortly after the Germans attacked the Soviet Union in June 1941, Stalin forcibly moved 400,000 Volga Germans and 80,000 ethnic Germans in the Leningrad area to Central Asia and Siberia. When the Soviets recaptured the Caucasus region from the Germans in 1943, they took revenge on groups that had had cordial relations with the occupying Nazis. Local Chechen and Ingush populations totaling over 500,000 people were deported to Siberia and Kazakhstan between December 1943 and the summer of 1944. Russians and Ukrainians were brought to colonize the Chechen–Ingush region where they renamed streets, destroyed mosques and graveyards, purged atlases and dictionaries, and burned nearly all central Caucasian literary and historical texts. In May 1944, Stalin ordered the deportation of the entire Crimean Tatar population, close to 240,000 people, from Crimea to Central Asia as a collective punishment for the collaboration of a small percentage of their number with the Nazis in the war; thousands of deportees perished in sealed box cars during the train journey to Uzbekistan and other far-off destinations.

Stalin returned to the question of Polish resettlement in September 1944, when Soviet Ukrainian officials signed a repatriation agreement with the pro-Communist Polish provisional government (Lublin Committee) that provided for population "exchanges" of Poles and Ukrainians who were suddenly on the wrong side of the new Soviet–Polish border that Stalin claimed along the Curzon Line. Between 1944 and 1946 some 1.1 million Poles were resettled to the new Poland in the west, while a half million Ukrainians were transported to locations east of the Curzon Line.

Population relocations in the Balkans

Population relocations took place in the Balkans as well after the Germans overran Yugoslavia and Greece in the spring of 1941. This practice included large people exchanges among several countries. Romania and Hungary, for example, exchanged

Transylvanians and other minorities, with Romania losing 3.5 million non-Romanians while gaining 1.5 million ethnic Romanians. Romania and the Soviet Union swapped close to 1 million people at their northern border. In the south, Romania sent over 250,000 Muslims, Serbs, and Bulgarians to Bulgaria for 100,000 Romanians. The refugees experienced countless miseries and lost all of their belongings. In a macabre game of home trades, Hungarian Transylvanians settled in the dwellings vacated by 270,000 Romanian Germans who were sent to the Reich, while over 450,000 Romanians expelled from Yugoslavia settled in the homes of deported Hungarian Transylvanians. The large-scale movement of human populations and the swelling ranks of refugees that accompanied them taxed the resources of every Balkan country.

Axis powers' killings on the Eastern Front

When Hitler's armies attacked the Soviet Union on June 22, 1941, they conducted a war of annihilation. Hitler's goals were the destruction of the Soviet Union, the use of its land for German colonization, mass murder, and the enslavement of millions. There was to be no mercy for Jews, Communists, Gypsies (Sinta), resisters, and Soviet prisoners of war.

German *Einsatzgruppen* followed the invading forces, with the purpose of murdering Jews and political enemies behind the front lines. The special killing units and their accomplices – special German police units called Order Police and non-German auxiliaries – focused primarily on the slaughter of Jews, but they also killed thousands of local officials, wiping out the Communist leadership of entire cities. Other targets in 1941, though dealt with in a less systematic fashion, included Gypsies and mental hospital inmates. Even in the spring of 1943, with the Wehrmacht in retreat, the Germans used an *Einsatzgruppe*, first in Ukraine to protect their pullback by murdering civilians where there were reports of resistance and then in Belorussia to burn villages and confiscate cattle as preparatory steps for their retreat. Romania, an active military partner of the Germans in the 1941 offensive, also cooperated with the *Einsatzgruppen* in the murder of large numbers of Jews and Gypsies during the war. It is estimated that the mobile killing units ultimately murdered close to 2 million people, of which about 1.3 million were Jews and 250,000 were Gypsies.

German and Soviet prisoners of war

In their war of annihilation against the Soviet Union, the Germans treated Soviet prisoners of war with shocking brutality, viewing them as part of the Nazi-claimed "subhuman" Slavic race of people. Since the Soviets had also not signed the Geneva Convention of 1929 regarding the treatment of POWs, the Germans felt no obligation to abide by its terms in dealing with the Russians. Soviet soldiers surrendered to the invaders on an unprecedented scale in 1941, so that the Germans had captured 3 million Soviet troops by the close of the year. As many as 200,000 prisoners died during the journey to POW camps, victims of death marches or barbaric train transports. At the camps, which were essentially open fields ringed by barbed wire, the Wehrmacht applied a policy of intentional starvation and exposure to the elements. By February 1942, 2 million Soviet prisoners were dead from mass shootings, inhumane conditions during transit, starvation, exposure, or disease. This meant that on average some 10,000 Soviet prisoners of war died every day during the war's first seven months. As the war continued the death rates diminished, in part because the Germans decided to use Soviet POWs as forced laborers; indeed, there were over 1 million captured Russian soldiers working in Germany in 1945. Overall, the Germans captured 5.7 million Red Army soldiers, of whom 3.3 million died. This made them the largest group of non-Jews killed during the war.

The Soviets captured close to 3 million German soldiers during the Soviet–German War. The total number of Germans seized in the war's initial months was small, but by early 1942, following a Russian counterattack near Moscow, there were 120,000 Germans in Russian prison camps. A major Soviet gain in German POWs came shortly into 1943, when the remaining 90,000 soldiers in General Paulus's Sixth Army surrendered at Stalingrad. The Soviets captured the bulk of their German prisoners of war during their large offensives in the last year of the conflict. At the beginning of 1945, the Russians held approximately 600,000 German POWs and that number reached 2 million in April 1945. It is estimated that approximately 1 million Germans died as prisoners of the Soviets between 1941 and 1950.

Limited resources and Russia's freedom from the Geneva Convention of 1929 condemned German prisoners to an abysmal fate. Captured troops were shipped to Gulag camps in quasi-death marches or overcrowded railroad box cars. Those who made it to the camps were enrolled in work squads, lived in run-down shacks, and were undernourished – circumstances that mirrored the conditions of Nazi concentration camp victims. Soviet treatment of German POWs improved in the final year of the war owing in part to the Russians' need for forced laborers. Many Germans remained in captivity after the war to help rebuild the war-torn Soviet Union. The Soviets released some German prisoners in the months after the war, and then opened the prison gates to a large number of Germans POWs in 1947, most likely because of a postwar famine that created grave difficulties for the Soviet leadership. The last German prisoners were released in the 1950s.

Building a greater Reich, 1942–1943

Obtaining *Lebensraum* for the German people was Hitler's most radical social engineering project. It involved cleansing large historically Slavic territories of their populations – as many as 51 million would be pushed east of the Urals – and bringing in ethnic Germans settlers. To prepare for this project, the Nazis during the 1930s established and maintained files about the German diaspora to identify racially desirable settlers. The first phase occurred in Poland in 1939–1940. The second phase was launched after December 1941, when 50–60 million Eastern Slavs were under German control. Himmler was put in charge of executing the plan. The first step was to remove the local populations. Then German colonists from Nordic and Baltic countries and Aryanized Russians of German origin would be brought in. As warrior-farmers, they would build a belt of rural colonies separating the Slavs from the Aryanized center of Europe. Eventually, the Nazis would import agricultural slave labor and public-service workers, and establish military outposts and industries to create a balanced, self-sufficient economy.

The first colony was opened in the summer of 1942 at Hegenwald, 80 kilometers west of Kiev. When the land vacated by the local Ukrainians was put up for sale, the SS grabbed it so greedily that they had to be stopped. The Danish, Norwegian, and Dutch settlers whom Himmler had hoped to recruit never materialized, although some ethnic Germans from nearby areas relocated there. A second, more ambitious colony opened in November 1942, in the Lublin–Zamosc area, some 100 miles southeast of Warsaw. Himmler hoped to transfer 100,000 ethnic Germans to the settlement and, in anticipation of its success, he renamed Lublin "Himmlerstadt." District SS and Police leader Odilo Globocnik prepared the area with ruthless brutality. Between November 1942 and March 1943, he expelled approximately 110,000 Poles and Jews from 300 villages to make room for German peasant families from Transnistria, hoping to move in 60,000 settlers by the end of 1943. Half of the expellees were sent to concentration camps and half to serve as forced laborers in Germany. The brutality of Globocnik's ethnic cleansing convinced many Poles that a "final solution of the Polish problem" was in process. They put up a fierce resistance that eventually derailed Himmler's settlement, but they were unable to prevent the forcible relocation of 5,000 "suitable" Polish children to the Reich or the murder of the area's Jewish prisoners held at the nearby death camps of Belzec, Sobibor, and Majdanek. The utopia of a Greater Reich quickly ended in disaster. In the fall of 1943, the remaining German settlers fled as the Red Army advanced against the retreating Wehrmacht.

The euthanasia program

The first program of mass murder under the Nazis started in the spring of 1939, when the regime implemented a secret program that aimed at the elimination of handicapped individuals as a part of the party's eugenics-based racial policies. Labeled the "Euthanasia Program," its first target was children with physical or mental disabilities. Children chosen for death were transported to designated clinics where medical staffs used lethal drug injections or starvation to kill them. Hitler expanded the program in the fall of 1939 to include institutionalized adults suffering from mental illnesses and physical handicaps that suddenly designated them as unsuitable for living. The secret killing program had the codename "T-4," which was an abbreviation for the address of its headquarters at Tiergartenstrasse 4 in Berlin. By early 1940, the T-4 planners had set up six gassing centers to kill their victims. By August 1941, the T-4 program had claimed the lives of 70,000 to 90,000 Germans. Because of the scale of the euthanasia program and the large number of people associated with it, secrecy was difficult to maintain. Consequently, it was an open secret by the summer of 1941. On August 3, 1941, Catholic Bishop Clemens August von Galen delivered a sermon in which he protested against the euthanasia program by calling it murder. He then had copies of the sermon distributed across the country. Nazi officials, though livid, dared not take action against the popular Catholic clergyman. Hitler responded two weeks later by officially suspending the program, though it continued, but with greater secrecy. The executioners reverted to old and more concealed killing methods such as starvation, drug overdoses, and lethal injections. When the war ended, the T-4 and other euthanasia programs had killed some 200,000 people across Germany. These silent deaths made the idea of mass murder more acceptable and pioneered the technology of gassing.

The Holocaust

The term Holocaust denotes the genocide of millions of European Jewish men, women, and children at the hands of the Nazi regime during World War II. When Germany invaded the Soviet Union in June 1941, the Nazis shifted their policy toward Jews from forced displacement, incarceration, and some killing to systematic mass murder.

Germany's *Einsatzgruppen*, closely following the German forces into Russia, played a key role in implementing the plan. Once an *Einsatzgruppe* entered a town or city, its members brought the Jews together, marched them to the town or city's outskirts where they either shot them or gassed them in mobile gas vans. From the small village of Jedwabne – near the city of Bialystok in northeastern Poland – where hundreds of Jews were massacred in July, to the killing field near Kiev, at the ravine of Babi Yar, where the Germans murdered 33,000 Ukrainian Jews in two days in September 1941, the blood-bath went on throughout the summer. By the end of the year, approximately 1 million Jews had been murdered on the Eastern Front.

At the same time that Himmler and Heydrich, the key overseers for the Jewish Question, coordinated the murderous activities of the *Einsatzgruppen* against the Jews during Germany's 1941 offensive against the Soviet Union, they pondered the fate of the Jewish people in territories that the Germans already occupied elsewhere. Some guidance came on July 31, 1941, when Göring signed a memorandum to Heydrich in which the phrase "final solution of the Jewish question" was used for the first time in official communications; the expression was a euphemism for the liquidation of Europe's Jews. The document confirmed the leadership role that Heydrich would play in organizing the Final Solution. As for the ways to kill Jews, Himmler and Heydrich concluded by the fall of 1941 that mass shootings and gas vans were slow and inefficient. They looked for other killing tools, and they found one in the lethal pesticide Zyklon B. In September 1941, the Germans in charge at the Auschwitz concentration camp, near Krakow, Poland, had experimented with Zyklon B on humans and successfully used it to gas 600 Soviet prisoners there. By early 1942, Zyklon B, which was both quick and efficient in its results, became the Nazis' favored execution method at Auschwitz/Birkenau in their Jewish extermination campaign. The road to systematic genocide was now wide open.

On January 20, 1942, Heydrich convened the heads of several Nazi ministries and departments in a beautiful villa located on the shores of Lake Wannsee in a posh Berlin suburb. In the midst of lavish food and drink, the high-ranking Nazi officials in attendance at the Wannsee Conference agreed to the liquidation of the Jewish people. The representative for the territory of the General Government asked that his region be the first to carry out the Final Solution, a request that was realized in the ensuing months. Adolf Eichmann, an SS colonel who was the deportation expert at the Reich Main Security Office, was put in charge of supervising the transportation system for the Final Solution that Himmler's SS would administer. While the Wannsee Conference did not forward a comprehensive plan for the extermination of Europe's Jews, it was a decisive step on the road to a sweeping program, which rapidly materialized in the spring and summer of 1942, for their systematic destruction.

Six death camps were instrumental in carrying out the Final Solution. All of them were located in places that had been a part of interwar Poland. The SS launched the first extermination camp in December 1941 – before the Wannsee Conference – at Chelmo, a small town in an area of western Poland annexed to the German Reich in 1939. The Nazis murdered some 145,000 people – mostly Jews – at the camp from its opening through December 1942, when the camp was closed except for a brief re-activation in 1944. The killing centers at Belzec, Sobibor, and Treblinka were part of Operation Reinhard, the codename for the complete liquidation of Jews in the territory of the General Government. They started their operations in the spring and summer of 1942. All three were situated in secluded, wooded areas that hid the horrific crimes committed there. Some 600,000 Jews were killed at Belzec before it closed in the spring of 1943. At Sobibor, which shut down in the fall of 1943, not long after a prisoner uprising, the Germans and their abettors slaughtered 250,000 Jews. Treblinka, the last of the three Operation Reinhard killing centers to become operational, was the site of almost 1 million Jewish murders prior to its closure in late 1943. A fifth death camp was at Majdanek, situated 1 mile outside the city of Lublin in eastern Poland. By the time Soviet forces liberated the camp in the summer of 1944, 125,000 Jews and 75,000 gentiles had lost their lives there.

The last death camp to start up was Auschwitz. The camp actually consisted of three forced labor camps, one of which – Auschwitz/Birkenau (Auschwitz II) – doubled as the killing center. Jewish exterminations began there in the spring of 1942. The completion a year later of four massive gas chambers greatly enhanced the camp's killing capacity. Birkenau reached its peak activity in mid-1944, when in the space of just a few weeks, 438,000 Hungarian Jews were transported there and camp officials gassed, at least, 327,000 of them. More than 1 million Jews died at Auschwitz-Birkenau, along with large numbers of Gypsies, Poles, and Soviet war prisoners. In contrast to the other five death factories, where the overwhelming majority of the Jewish victims had resided within Poland's interwar frontiers, Auschwitz/Birkenau acted as the primary killing center for Europe's Jews living outside of Poland. With the Russians approaching the extermination facility in late 1944, Himmler ordered an end to the gassings and the destruction of the camp. By the time the Soviets liberated Auschwitz on January 27, 1945, just a few thousand prisoners remained, since the Germans had evacuated the vast majority of them westward shortly before. Though the Germans had demolished most of the buildings, those that still stood contained ample evidence to prove that mass murder had taken place.

The Auschwitz complex combined the Nazi goals of killing Jews and promoting German economic activity. The Nazis used labor from the initial Auschwitz concentration camp (Auschwitz I) to build the nearby labor camp/death camp of Auschwitz-Birkenau. When the German chemical conglomerate I. G. Farben selected the Auschwitz area for the construction of a synthetic rubber plant, a third camp (Auschwitz III) was opened in the nearby town of Monowitz in 1942 to provide virtually free labor for the plant's construction. Tens of thousands of camp prisoners died in its construction.

Multiple state agencies concerned with transport, resources, and labor supply, to mention only a few, collaborated in the mass killing of Jews and turned the Final Solution into a profitable economic enterprise. The policy was executed to insure maximum profit from slave labor, maximum killings at minimum cost, and added income from the recycled belongings of the dead. The prisoners had to pay a fare for their travel in cattle cars to the death camps. Upon arrival, the camp authorities confiscated their suitcases and valuables. All these belongings were processed by specially created units, with their valuables sorted and sent to Germany: glasses, clothing, shoes, watches, kitchenware, suitcases, jewelry, currency, human hair, and gold teeth. Between July 1943 and August 1944, the Nazis shipped 32,000 railway freight cars of confiscated goods to Germany.

There were Jewish acts of resistance to Nazi cruelties. One major event was the Warsaw Ghetto revolt in the spring of 1943. The ghetto, created in 1940, had once contained well over 400,000 Jews, but by early 1943 that number had dropped by 80 percent, largely due to the murder of many of its residents at Treblinka in 1942. The Germans made an attempt to shut down the ghetto in January 1943, but ran into an unanticipated organized resistance, forcing them to withdraw after four days and rethink their plans. The Germans returned in April 1943 with a force of 2,000 heavily armed men and overpowered the poorly armed resistance effort after several weeks of fighting. The Germans liquidated the ghetto and burned it to the ground. They shot many of the remaining Jews at once and shipped the others to concentration camps and death factories. The uprising in Warsaw was the largest single act of Jewish resistance in German-controlled Europe during the war and symbolically the most powerful. Other Jewish acts of defiance included revolts at the ghetto of Bialystok (Poland) in September 1943, the death camps of Treblinka and Sobibor, in August 1943 for the former and in October 1943 for the latter, and the killing center of Auschwitz-Birkenau in October 1944.

Official and individual responses to the Holocaust

To round up Jews in Western Europe, the Nazis relied on their own resources in occupied countries as well as on the assistance of collaborationist governments and sympathetic local authorities. One example was France. In German-occupied France, roundups of foreign Jews for deportation to concentration camps began in the spring of 1941. Once the Final Solution went into full operation in the spring of 1942, the German occupiers transported 42,000 Jews to Auschwitz/Birkenau by the end of that year. Among them were some 11,000 mostly foreign Jews that officials in Vichy-controlled France turned over to the Nazis, in an attempt to protect their French Jewish national community from deportation. Once the Nazis occupied all of France in late 1942, they also included many French Jews in their deportation sweeps, although Vichy leaders, led by

Figure 8.2 German forces round up Jewish civilians for deportation during the Warsaw Ghetto Uprising in the spring of 1943.

Pierre Laval, used bureaucratic complications to hinder Germany's efforts, especially in regard to Jewish French citizens. While a large percentage of Jews residing in France in 1939 were alive at war's end, more than 75,000 Jews were deported from France to death camps during the Vichy years, and only about 2,000 of them survived. In the Netherlands, where the German occupiers firmly controlled the civil administration and had the support of Dutch collaborators, the percentage of Jews who perished during the war was far greater than in France. Between 1942 and 1944, the Nazis transferred some 107,000 Jews from the Netherlands to camps in the East, most to Auschwitz-Birkenau and Sobibor, where over 100,000 of them were murdered. On the other hand, 25,000–30,000 Dutch Jews lived in hiding during the war, often with the aid of the Dutch resistance, and most of them survived the ordeal.

As for the American and British governments, their main focus was on winning the war. Both Roosevelt and Churchill believed that this was the best way to save Jewish lives. Once the U.S. State Department had confirmation in November 1942 that the Nazis were pursuing a policy of extermination against Europe's Jews, the United States, the Soviet Union, Great Britain, and several other Allied nations issued a declaration the following month in which they condemned Germany's actions against the Jews and warned of retribution for the perpetrators. A 1943 conference of U.S. and British representatives in Bermuda focusing on Jewish refugees yielded no new initiatives. Under pressure from several government officials, Roosevelt finally issued an executive order in January 1944 establishing a War Refugee Board. The board aided in the rescue of as many as 200,000 Jews by the time the war ended. When the question of bombing Auschwitz to disrupt Nazi mass killings there came up in 1944, Churchill supported it, but the idea got nowhere, owing to opposition from both British and American government officials who argued that the risks were too great. In the end, Roosevelt might have done more to rescue Jews had there not been active currents of anti-Semitism and xenophobia in the U.S. Congress and among the general public.

Pope Pius XII (r. 1939–1958), adhering to a strict policy of neutrality, refrained from openly condemning German atrocities against the Jews, even though he was aware of them by the end of 1941. In his Christmas address of 1942, he only went as far as speaking sympathetically for "the hundreds of thousands of persons who, without any fault on their part, sometimes only because of their nationality or race, have been consigned to death or a slow decline."[3] He refused specifically to mention the Jews as the victims or the Nazis as the perpetrators in his address largely out of fear of German retaliation against the Church. On the other hand, the Pope privately helped secure shelter for thousands of Jews in Rome after German forces occupied northern and central Italy in the fall of 1943. In 1944, he called on Hungarian leader Horthy to stop Jewish deportations from Hungary, and his efforts, along with those of other world leaders, led to Horthy's decision to suspend them – albeit temporarily as it turned out – in July of that year. Historians are divided over Pius XII's role regarding the Holocaust, although it is generally felt that the Pope's efforts were insufficient.

Ordinary citizens also had a number of options to choose from: they could be perpetrators, bystanders, or rescuers. The majority of people were bystanders who did nothing out of fear or indifference. Others tormented the Jews through pogroms, extortion, and denunciation. But many also took great risks to help the Jews, and in so doing, they not only defied the Nazi authorities, but often challenged the policies of their own countries. Rescue methods varied. German businessman Oskar Schindler, for example, saved over 1,000 Jewish workers' lives by employing them first at his enamelware factory in

Krakow, Poland, and then at an armaments factory he set up in the Sudeten town of Brünnlitz in October 1944. In another instance, American journalist Varian Fry, working out of an office in Marseille, France, starting in August 1940, assisted in the escape from France of more than 2,000 anti-Nazi and Jewish refugees who risked extradition to Germany, owing to Article 19 in the Franco-German armistice of June 1940. The Vichy regime expelled him in September 1941.

Members of various countries' diplomatic corps also took bold risks to protect Jews from the Nazis. Japanese Consul Chiune Sugihara, posted in Lithuania in 1939–1940, issued more than 2,100 Japanese transit visas without his government's approval to Jewish refugees in the summer of 1940. In Denmark, Georg Ferdinand Duckwitz, an attaché at the German embassy in Copenhagen, secretly warned the Danish underground in late September 1943 of an imminent Nazi roundup of all Danish Jews for deportation. The Danes, with nationwide support, reacted swiftly by carrying out a clandestine operation that transported 95 percent of Denmark's Jews – some 7,200 people – to neutral Sweden before the German arrests began. Finally, Raoul Wallenberg, a Swedish diplomat in Hungary, used a number of unusual diplomatic methods, symbolized by Swedish protective passes issued to thousands of Jews, to help protect Budapest's 200,000 Jews from deportation in the latter half of 1944.

European Catholics and Protestants at the local level were ready to risk their lives to protect Jews from certain death. In France, the nuns of Notre-Dame-de-Sion in Paris found shelter for 450 Jewish children in private homes. French Protestants became very active in saving Jewish lives. The 3,000 people in the French Protestant community of Le Chambon hid a total of 5,000 Jews during the war. Reformed Protestant pastors placed several thousand Jewish children in hiding and saved many lives by issuing baptism certificates. These and countless other acts of bravery across Europe have largely remained anonymous and unacknowledged, due to the need for secrecy and the absence of documentation.

Expulsion of the Germans

One dramatic, albeit little known, event that emerged from the war was the flight and expulsion of massive numbers of ethnic Germans from lands in Eastern and Central Europe to the shrunken territory of postwar Germany. It was the single largest forced migration of a people in modern times. The forced resettlement, initiated during the conflict, continued for several years after the end of the fighting in 1945, ultimately affecting 12 to 14 million ethnic Germans. The Soviet Union, Poland, Czechoslovakia, Hungary, Yugoslavia, and other countries participated in varying degrees in the uprooting of Germans. The flight and evacuation of ethnic Germans in Eastern Europe began in the summer of 1944 as the Soviet army pushed westward. In East Prussia, a large majority of the Germans had escaped to the West by war's end, although many lost their lives in transit; the Soviets expelled virtually all who remained in the years immediately thereafter. In the spring of 1945, authorities in Poland and Czechoslovakia, with Moscow's backing, launched brutal ethnic cleansing operations, known as the "Wild Expulsions," that lasted until August 1945. The Czechs forced the exit of 700,000–800,000 Sudeten Germans during that time, while the Poles, focusing on new western lands taken from Germany – the "recovered territories" – pushed out several hundred thousand Germans.

When Allied leaders, at the end of the Potsdam Conference of July–August 1945, issued a call for the expulsion of Germans from Poland, Czechoslovakia, and Hungary

Figure 8.3 Sudeten Germans board railroad boxcars in Liberec, Czechoslovakia, for deportation to Germany in 1946.

in "an orderly and humane manner," the forcible resettlement of Germans was already firmly in place. The Czechs, making their deportation conditions more humane following Potsdam, removed another 2 million Sudeten Germans between January and October 1946, when the expulsions officially ended. The Poles, on the other hand, worked after Potsdam to create inhospitable conditions for the Germans in Poland in order to encourage "voluntary" departures; in the latter half of 1945, some 600,000 Germans reached Germany from Poland by train, after having endured appalling hardships en route. Ultimately, 7 million Germans left Poland's "recovered territories" between 1945 and 1947 either as refugees or deportees. While Czechoslovakia and Poland steadfastly pursued German deportations, Hungary found itself forced to move against its German population after the Allies, due to Soviet pressure, endorsed in the Potsdam Agreement of August 1945 the expulsion of Germans from Hungary. Hungarian deportations of ethnic Germans began in January 1946, moved forward haphazardly amid considerable controversy, and finally ended in mid-1948, after Hungary, with the Communists leading the way, had expelled 180,000 ethnic Germans. In Yugoslavia, the vast majority of its 500,000 ethnic German inhabitants escaped with the retreating German forces, experienced deportation, or went to labor camps where close to 50,000 of them died. Romania and the Netherlands also deported ethnic Germans in the latter 1940s.

Conclusion

During World War II, widespread death occurred not only on the military front but also behind the battle lines. Some 11 million noncombatants were intentionally killed by the Nazi regime. Poland lost 3 million of its non-Jewish citizens in the camps, more than any other nationality. Europe's Jewish population suffered grievously. Six million Jews died: 3 million of them were Polish and 2 million Russian. Poland lost 90 percent of its prewar Jewish population; the Netherlands, 94 percent; Germany, 88 percent; Hungary, 75 percent; Romania, 34 percent; Russia, 28 percent; and France and Italy, 22 percent. All over Europe, Russians, Gypsies, Jehovah's Witnesses, homosexuals, political dissidents, mentally and physically handicapped individuals, and minorities were decimated. Whether in death camps, in ghettos, at the front, in the cities, or in the countryside, the killing went on all over Europe. Accompanying the killings were two massive exoduses, deportations, and relocations, first in 1939–1941 and then again in 1944–1947. The demographic chaos that the war unleashed eclipsed every other aspect of life during the war. It affected millions of people and left virtually no European country untouched.

The lives of the people

There were many European home fronts at one point or another during World War II, although a number of them disappeared when Germany overran and occupied much of the continent. Populations that formed home fronts experienced a high level of uncertainty and suffering in their daily lives. Since victory depended not only on military success, but also on destroying the enemy's human and economic potential, both sides to the conflict waged war against civilians. Cities, factories, and railroads were the targets of bombings, and women, youth, the elderly, and prisoners of war were drafted into the workforce. Rationing affected virtually everyone, and daily terror and deprivations were the norm.

The misery of war

The military fronts created widespread destruction of villages and cities. The eastern zone of Poland, which was first occupied by the Soviets in September 1939, then invaded in June 1941 by the Nazis, suffered doubly. In the fall of 1941, Soviet territories experienced considerable adversity as well. In its retreat, the Red Army practiced a scorched earth policy, exposing a bombed out, destitute, starving, and vulnerable civilian population composed mostly of women, children, and the elderly to the risk of death. The situation became desperate when German armies moved in to plunder, eat much of the remaining food, and burn crops and villages. With the arrival of winter, famine caused the same hardships for German soldiers as for the local Russian populations.

The Balkan populations during Axis occupations of their countries were little better off than the Jewish populations in ghettos and concentration camps. Greece was placed under the triple occupation of Italian, German, and Bulgarian troops in the summer of 1941, and soon was on the brink of starvation. Its trade was disrupted first by a British blockade, then by German requisitions of fuel, industries, goods, and foodstuffs. The extremely cold winter of 1941–1942 added to the civilian population's misery. The Germans in Greece and the Bulgarians in Thessaly and Macedonia plundered the homes in which they were housed, and conducted a ruthless policy of exploitation. Western European-occupied nations saw bicycles and radios confiscated, and foodstuffs requisitioned and rationed.

Martyred cities

For the first time in history, large-scale strategic bombing campaigns were used against cities to cripple the enemy's nerve centers, destroy industries and transportation, and demoralize civilian populations. During the German campaign against Poland in September 1939, Warsaw and other Polish cities suffered grievous bombings at the hands of the German Luftwaffe. The Germans followed their bombing of Rotterdam in May 1940, the first major air attack on the Western Front, with regular air raids on British industrial cities during the Battle of Britain (July 10–October 31, 1940). East London's urban and industrial areas and even Buckingham Palace, the royal residence, were hit. Between September 1940 and May 1941, German airplanes dropped 74,000 tons of bombs on Britain and killed 51,000 people. During the last year of the war, the Germans used V-1 and V-2 rockets on the Western Front against London, Antwerp, and Liège.

On the Allied side, British air raids against Germany began in 1940, followed by large-scale Anglo-American strategic bombings of German and Italian cities from 1942 to 1945. Allied bombing campaigns in northern Italy caused 62,000 casualties. In July 1943, 1.5 million incendiary bombs were dropped on Hamburg. In 1944–1945, Berlin, Cologne, Munich, and major industrial centers in the Ruhr were also heavily bombed. One of the most controversial Allied bombing attacks took place against the city of Dresden on February 13–15, 1945. Although Dresden had no major industrial complex and had escaped Allied air attacks until then, the Allies heaped destruction on the city over a 37-hour timeframe with massive bombing raids that included large numbers of incendiaries. The February "terror bombing" of Dresden took the lives of about 35,000 people, and came to symbolize the Allies' strategic bombing campaign against Germany, an effort intended to force an early surrender of that country. The Allies' terror bombing campaign stirred debate during the war and still continues to do so, with critics using such terms as "war crimes" and "Holocaust" to describe the Allied actions. Overall, the Allies dropped 2 million bombs on Germany, killed 650,000 German civilians, injured 900,000 more, and destroyed millions of homes.

Three Soviet cities experienced especially intense misery because of prolonged battles. Beginning in September 1941, Leningrad endured a three-and-a-half year German siege, during which it suffered daily artillery bombardments and regular heavy aerial bombing attacks. It lost 1.2 million civilians, more than any other wartime city. Many residents starved or froze to death, since food was scarce and supplies of coal and oil to heat buildings quickly disappeared. Often there were no coffins to bury the dead, and corpses lay in the streets until carts could take them away. Russian forces lifted the siege in January 1944. The Soviet Black Sea port of Odessa endured a 73-day siege that Romania, a member of the Axis powers, waged – with assistance from the German army – from August to October 1941. After extremely bitter fighting, the Soviets evacuated 350,000 soldiers and civilians from the city prior to its surrender on October 16. Several days later, the Romanians murdered as many as 39,000 Jews either by shooting or burning them. They herded the remaining Jews into ghettos set up on the city's periphery. Stalingrad was the site of fierce fighting between the Germans and Soviets, in which the German air force used incendiary bombs to destroy the bulk of the city's wooden structures, and savage street-by-street combat in the fall and winter of 1942–1943 reduced the city's remaining buildings to rubble, but the Russians finally won. In 1945, Stalin named all three places Hero Cities of the Soviet Union.

Daily hardships

Arbitrariness and insecurity ruled daily life across German-occupied Europe. Even in the countries of Western Europe where the terms of the Nazi occupation were less severe, no one was safe. Arrests, deportation, and resettlement separated families and put mothers and children at risk. Employment opportunities declined as factories faltered or ground to a halt. Lower consumer demand upset trade. Forced labor departures to Germany disrupted factory production and agricultural work. Ukraine suffered a dramatic decline in grain output, Norway in fishing activities, and France in wine-making. Villages were ravaged by the invading armies, and agricultural potential destroyed. Between 1939 and 1941, Warsaw, which was a major industrial town, saw its manufactured goods production fall to one-third of its prewar capacity. Health services were deficient, schools closed, mail deliveries irregular, and housing shortages widespread.

Germany began to feel the pinch when Speer, the minister of armaments, slashed consumer goods production by 12 percent in 1942 while asking workers to put in 16-hour days to increase armaments output. All who worked less than 48 hours a week had to register for war work, and the military draft age was lowered to 16-year-olds. Nazi leaders, however, were exempt from these hardships. Hitler employed work crews totaling 28,000 people to maintain his various residences. More concrete was poured on his bunker at Bad Charlottenbrunn in 1944 than was allocated for the construction of air-raid shelters for Berlin's entire civilian population. Nazi oligarchs continued to refurbish castles, build party forums, and remodel Nazi administrative buildings. While average Germans sacrificed greatly, many Nazi leaders placed themselves above the rigors of total war and lived in luxury with big houses or palaces, hunting lodges, servants, and lavish food and drink.

On the Allied side, British civilians' lives changed little during the first months of the war. Movie theaters were briefly closed and then reopened. There were more casualties from motor accidents during blackouts than from combat. The greatest change was the evacuation of children from major cities to the countryside and the relocation of 2.5 million people by the end of September 1939. Not unlike occupied Europe, people experienced multiple relocations during the war.

In the Soviet Union, a great patriotic surge occurred in 1941 as the Russian people rose to defend their country. Membership in the Communist Party tripled from 2 to 6 million. The Order of Victory, a military medal, was now presented for civilian service. For the first time since the tsars, civilian ranks, uniforms, titles, and insignia reappeared. At the same time, the suffering of the lower classes increased tremendously. Food and consumer goods rationing reached extreme levels, making lives difficult. In the summer of 1941, hundreds of thousands of Russian factory workers were hastily relocated beyond the Urals. Once again, families were separated, as children went to orphanages when the government mobilized their parents for war work. The elites, however, continued just as before the war to enjoy preferential treatment. Certain stores, for example, remained closed to all but the elite.

Food and famine

As diets and standards of living declined throughout Europe, malnutrition and disease appeared. Food rationing was adopted everywhere, as early as January 1940 in Britain. The loss of considerable Soviet territory to the Germans in 1941 and 1942 caused a dramatic drop in Russian agricultural output and consumer goods production. The Soviets quickly resorted to the rationing of basic food items, in which even the most privileged workers in armaments plants received only meager amounts. In German-occupied countries, civilians often did not eat much better than concentration camp inmates. In Greece, for example, the average daily food intake in 1941 went from 800 to 600 calories, compared to 600–700 calories for Jews in forced labor camps. In East Central European countries left bereft in the wake of the German invasion, many citizens relied on public assistance for food, clothing, and blankets. By mid-1941, Warsaw soup kitchens were serving 162-calorie meals. In the Netherlands, people were reduced to eating tulip bulbs, sugar beets, and stray dogs and cats during the country's Hunger Winter of 1944–1945. France introduced rationing in September 1940, and the rations became increasingly meager as the war progressed. Food production dropped dramatically during the war from the 1930s, and much of what the French produced was shipped to Germany. The severe deprivations that Europeans experienced not only caused an immediate rise in health problems but also compromised the physical well-being of large numbers of Europeans in the long term.

Epidemics

Epidemics and disease accompanied the war. Typhus struck the German army when it invaded the Soviet Union in 1941, although the Soviets succeeded in keeping it at bay. The Eastern Front also suffered from a variety of other ills, dysentery being the chief among them. Conditions worsened as the war dragged on. Severe typhus epidemics ravaged North Africa, the Near East, and Iran in 1942–1943. Diseases such as diphtheria, typhoid fever, scarlet fever, and influenza increased in multiple countries, as did malaria, syphilis, and tuberculosis. In Northern and Western Europe, including Spain and Portugal, tuberculosis cases doubled or tripled during the conflagration. Malaria reached epidemic proportions in 1943–1944 in Greece, and several Balkan states as well as western Ukraine suffered typhus epidemics in early 1945. In numerous countries, healthy individuals succumbed to tuberculosis and infectious skin diseases due to weakened immune systems combined with time spent in overcrowded, unsanitary conditions. The release of concentration camp inmates in 1945 brought new threats of disease. In May 1945, the European health outlook in many ways looked quite bleak, owing to limited medical personnel available to serve overwhelming numbers of displaced and homeless persons and the weakened physical health of many European people. On the other hand, significant medical advances occurred during the war. These included: the mass production of penicillin to combat infections in war wounds; vast improvements in the science of blood transfusions; and the introduction of DDT to control typhus and malaria, both of which were transmitted by insects.

Young people

Millions of small children and youth experienced a multitude of tragedies during the war. In countries across Europe, they were often separated from their families, obliged to live with strangers, forced into hiding, imprisoned in concentration camps, trapped in ghettos, and killed in horrific circumstances. Fear, loneliness, and loss of identity were common among them.

Jewish children suffered more than any other group of young people. One-and-a-half million Jewish children were killed during the Holocaust. Many of them died at the Nazis' killing centers or as victims of German mobile killing squads. Those who survived were frequently placed with foster families or hidden by locals. They secured new names, adopted new accents, and learned new identities.

Youth in the Soviet Union and Eastern Europe also endured extreme hardships. The siege of Leningrad caused tens of thousands of children to starve or freeze to death. The Battle of Stalingrad of 1942–1943 left 120,000 children in the city orphaned. Nazi and Soviet population transfers and relocations often separated children from their families or orphaned them. Russian officials sent hundreds of Polish children to Russian orphanages to be raised as Soviet citizens. Russian children were separated from their parents when hundreds of thousands of Soviet workers were transferred to relocated industrial plants beyond the Urals. A number of abandoned youth joined street gangs that terrorized local populations. Thousands of East European young people were taken for use as forced laborers. Many died at the labor camps or as casualties of bombing raids. Local resistance movements recruited youth, who faced execution when caught for underground activities.

The wartime experiences of German youth were generally not as harsh as their counterparts in Russia, although recruitment of volunteers for military service who were 16 and 17 years old began in 1943. In the final stages of the war, members of the Hitler Youth became part of a last line of defense, as they manned anti-aircraft guns and joined a newly formed Home Guard (*Volkssturm*), a people's army consisting of boys as young as 12 years of age and men as old as 60. Though poorly trained, the conscripted children were among the most ardent defenders of Berlin in 1945.

The Nazi racial program affected multitudes of children. Ironically, in their attempt to create a "pure race," the Nazis ended up blending populations. Nazi officials often separated ethnic German youth from their families, as was the case of 18,000 boys and girls who were brought to Germany from the Baltic states, Belorussia, and Ukraine. In Axis-occupied countries, non-German children deemed fit to become "healthy, Aryan children" were also taken away from their parents and placed with German families. Between the vicissitudes of war, the traumas of separation, relocation, and death, and the Nazi racial program, children had anything but normal experiences, the effects of which included emotional scars and a legacy of shame.

Women

Women were used in the conflict according to each country's ongoing wartime situation. When the war caused labor shortages, women often volunteered to move outside the home and into the workforce. But there was also resistance to abandoning the cult of domesticity in several countries. Longstanding traditions and interwar legislation discouraged married women from leaving the home. It took the war to pare down gender barriers.

German women for much of the conflict did not play as significant a role in warrelated activities as women did in other countries. In fact, the Nazis had no plans for taking women out of the home when the struggle began. To fill the eventual labor shortages that occurred, the government initially imported millions of forced laborers from occupied countries and encouraged German industries to relocate in the East, near concentration camps that provided free labor. In January 1943, the regime finally made a major attempt to put 3 million new women into the workplace when it introduced labor conscription for females aged 17–45, though the Nazis exempted mothers who had a child under 6 years old or two children below 14. In the end, the Nazis only found an additional 900,000 women from the call-up. By 1945, there were also over 500,000 German women serving as uniformed auxiliaries in the country's armed services, although, outside of manning anti-aircraft guns, they performed noncombat duties only.

In Britain, the government knew as early as 1940 that the need for women in the war effort would go beyond volunteers. But it delayed drafting women into the workforce until December 1941, when parliament, in the National Service Act No. 2, made single women between the ages of 20 and 30 subject to call-ups for work in war-related industries, civil defense, and the country's auxiliary forces. Women comprised a third of the country's factory workers by the end of 1943, contributing to the assembly of airplanes, ships, artillery shells, tanks, and guns. Close to a half a million women served in Britain's auxiliary services at their wartime peak, while more than 80,000 females at one point worked in the Women's Land Army doing hard agricultural work such as ploughing, picking potatoes, and baling hay.

Soviet women also played a vital role in the war, both on the home and military fronts. They performed much of the agricultural work, primarily done manually, because tractors, horses, and other equipment were requisitioned for the battlefront. The proportion of women in factories remained as high as in the 1930s, with women often working double shifts to increase production and free up more men for combat service. An estimated 800,000 women were a part of the Soviet armed forces, serving primarily in medical, auxiliary, and clerical capacities. Even when placed in auxiliary roles, they often operated in quasi-combat conditions. Soviet women also fought as soldiers, disguising themselves as men and serving in the infantry. In 1942, there were 8,500 females in the army and navy, and their numbers grew to form three women's battalions by the end of the war. Two thousand of those doing frontline service were snipers, while others participated as machine-gunners or tank crew members. The Soviet Union was the first country to allow female pilots in combat, starting in October 1941. Yet at the end of the war, Soviet women did not get much recognition, with Stalin not even allowing female combatants to march in Moscow's victory parade in June 1945. Pronatalist policies quickly reemerged, and public opinion demanded that women return to their traditional roles as faithful wives and doting mothers.

Collaborationists

In several countries, the German occupation was an opportunity for extreme right-wing groups to support the new social order and to show their admiration for Nazism. Among them were many intellectuals. Moved by opportunism, anti-Semitism, anti-Communism, or a distorted sense of nationalism, they bought into the Nazi vision of a renewed ethos of national values, racial purity, and a corporative society. Rightist leaders Henri de Man in Belgium and Marcel Déat in France collaborated with the Nazi authorities during the war. But collaboration was often forced upon local populations. The Nazis created "volunteer" military units in the occupied countries of Albania, Belgium, Denmark, Estonia, Greece,

Yugoslavia, Latvia, Lithuania, Ukraine, and Russia. The extent to which these forces participated in violence against the Jews and fought the local resistance is still the subject of intense debate today, although some facts are irrefutable. Ukrainian forces participated in the destruction of the Warsaw Ghetto in 1943. Belorussian members of a collaborationist Home Defense Corps formed the bulk of the Thirtieth Waffen Grenadier Division of the SS created in 1944 under German leadership; it was transferred to southeastern France where it performed poorly in combat against French resistance fighters. General Andrei Vlasov, a Soviet hero in the defense of Moscow in 1941, defected to the Germans after his capture in 1942. Hoping to topple Stalin, he gathered anti-Communist Soviet prisoners of war and White émigré Russian volunteers. This group, known as the Vlasov Army, fought alongside retreating German forces in 1944 before changing sides to help the Red Army liberate Prague in February 1945.

As for governments, collaboration with the German occupier varied from country to country. While France's Vichy government possessed a certain level of autonomy, its leaders at times were ready to collaborate beyond what the Germans viewed as necessary. In Norway, the puppet government of Vidkun Quisling cooperated with the Nazis in deporting Jews, ordered the executions of Norwegian resistance movement members, and encouraged Norwegians to volunteer for the German war effort. The Croatian fascist state under Ante Pavelić had mixed motives. His party militia, the Ustase – a terrorist organization – committed countless atrocities against Orthodox Serbs, Jews, and Gypsies in Pavelić's drive to make his state as purely Croatian as possible. Though he came to power as a puppet of the Axis powers, Pavelić saw his wartime Croatia as the realization of his longstanding goal of a Croatian state independent of Yugoslavia. On the other hand, Poland could claim insignificant collaboration with the Germans. Regardless of their avowed or hidden aims, collaborators were generally distrusted by the Nazis, who denied them full powers.

Resistance movements

Local resistance groups in most German-occupied countries enjoyed logistical and intelligence support from leaders abroad. The governments-in-exile in London supported underground home armies, while officials in Moscow, where many Communist leaders had taken refuge, supported Communist resistance groups. Yet, as adhesion to the Communist parties surged, churches were likewise full, especially in East Central Europe and Italy, where religion had a strong presence before the war. As the two main institutions left standing, the Catholic Church and the Communist parties were in a position to provide structure, international contacts, ethical direction, funds, and organizational skills to resistance groups. They attracted broader social groups: conservative parties and nationalists rallied around the Catholic Church, while socialists, leftist sympathizers, trade unions, and railway workers, joined the Communists. The resistance drew adherents from all walks of life and from all social classes. It also attracted many young people. Boy and girl scouts who had received paramilitary training during the interwar years, fought side by side with orphaned and homeless teenagers seduced by the romantic and heroic aspect of conspiracy in the name of a higher cause. There were Jewish and Zionist resistance fighters, Polish partisans, French *maquisards* (rural guerrilla resistance fighters), and Ukrainian, Greek, Italian, Dutch, and Czech resistance organizations. In Germany, the German White Rose group, manned by young people, distributed resistance leaflets, while the *Abwehr*, the military intelligence unit, harbored resisters as well.

Resistance actions were heroic and secretive. Everyday acts involving industrial sabotage, the distribution of resistance leaflets, and intelligence work were as vital to the underground effort as the more spectacular acts of terrorism and mass armed resistance. Because of the need for secrecy, many resisters' activities went unrecorded, especially those of young women who worked in intelligence and whose activities were invisible extensions of their everyday life – running errands, acting as liaisons, transporting unlawful arms and supplies, doing secretarial work, serving as decoders, and providing shelter. Among the more daring feats were: the assassination of SS leader Reinhard Heydrich by Czech resistance activists in 1942; the actions between 1942 and 1944 of the Jewish Bielski partisan group that saved approximately 1,200 Jews in the forests of western Belorussia while fighting the Nazis and their collaborators; the smuggling of maps of Auschwitz and V-2 rocket plans out of Poland in 1944 by the Polish resistance; and the Polish Home Army's Warsaw Uprising in 1944.

German retribution was quick and brutal. Arrests, torture, executions, terror, and even the destruction of entire towns were used to break down resistance networks. In June 1942, the Germans liquidated the Czech village of Lidice as a reprisal for the assassination of Heydrich several days earlier. As retribution for the Germans' belief that villagers in the French town of Oradour-sur-Glane were aiding the resistance, a Waffen SS battalion on June 10, 1944, massacred 642 of its citizens – most of the town's inhabitants – and then destroyed the town. On the same day in Distomo, Greece, following a Greek partisans' attack on an SS division several miles away, the SS troops killed 214 of the town's citizens and burned down the village.

Relief operations

As in World War I, state and private institutions organized wartime relief efforts. Owing to the large extent of Nazi control over Europe and the vast numbers of refugees, international humanitarian aid was often difficult to disperse. After Axis-occupied Greece experienced a massive famine in the winter of 1941–1942, for example, the British had to be pressured into lifting a naval blockade there in February 1942 to allow the entry of food shipments under the direction of the International Committee of the Red Cross (ICRC). The Germans, meanwhile, refused to give the ICRC access to any of its concentration camps.

The United States played a leading role in providing wartime relief assistance, with a number of private charities emerging to help early in the struggle. Faced with the magnitude of the private relief operations, Roosevelt organized what eventually became known as the War Relief Control Board (WRCB) to consolidate their number and coordinate their work. The government's preferred private relief agency to work with was the American Red Cross (ARC). During the war, the ARC prepared more than 27 million parcels, mostly food, that it shipped to the International Red Cross for distribution to some 1.4 million Allied war prisoners in Europe. At its peak in 1945, the ARC had a paid staff of 39,000 people and 7.5 million volunteers.

In preparation for the end of World War II, a 44-nation conference meeting in Washington D.C. in December 1943, created the United Nations Relief and Rehabilitation Administration (UNRRA). Initially a relief agency of the Allies with considerable funding from the United States, it became an integral part of the United Nations organization in 1945, where it remained until its operations ceased in 1947. It supervised a multitude of displaced persons camps in Germany, Austria, and Italy, where it assisted in the repatriation of millions of refugees. It also distributed relief supplies to war-ravaged countries.

Plans for urban reconstruction

The massive destruction of European metropolitan areas opened up the opportunity to heal urban blight and design technologically modern cities. Urban reconstruction involved town planners, authorities, politicians, private citizens, property owners, architects, and workers, many of whom belonged to the generation that had rebuilt European cities after 1919. It was a complex task requiring large budgets and complicated logistics that included rubble clearing, building materials, and labor allocations. Historic facades were often preserved and used to dress up apartment buildings furnished with modern amenities. Where destruction was total, conservative aesthetics and regional styles were preferred. Two patterns dominated, however. The prewar metropolitan model of a great industrial city with crowded working class tenements was seen as a dead social form of human organization. French architect Le Corbusier and German planners alike planned to reestablish the contact between man and nature and favored smaller cities that integrated natural landscapes. The other pattern was that of the faithful reconstitution of historic districts and structures. Thus, Polish planners, architects, and students rescued eighteenth-century Italian painter Canaletto's views of Warsaw's Old Town and used them to sketch detailed drawings of the historic cityscape. The fourteenth-century Italian abbey of Monte Cassino, which was almost completely destroyed during a huge Allied bombing attack in February 1944, also underwent faithful historic reconstruction after the war.

The end of the war and early postwar chaos

As the Red Army rolled into East Central Europe, an immense number of people took flight, overpowering transportation networks and the countryside. Fear of Communism, rumors of ethnic persecution and soldiers' mistreatment of civilians triggered an exodus westwards. Indeed, Red Army soldiers behaved barbarically in East Prussia, Silesia, and Berlin by terrorizing, plundering, raping, imprisoning, and expelling individuals. Citizens of the Axis powers fled alongside camp survivors, forced laborers, released POWs, and hundreds of thousands of political refugees. The retreating German army evacuated a number of ethnic Germans from the Greater Reich areas, but the majority of them returned to Germany on their own. One million Hungarian soldiers and civilians also fled to Germany.

By the end of the war, much of Europe was shattered, economic chaos was common, and food was scarce. Millions of displaced individuals yearned to return home, but not all of them could do so. Refugees, evacuees, and liberated prisoners from as far away as Asia roamed through Europe. In many cases, they had nowhere to go since their properties had been confiscated and their cultural heritage destroyed. Many Jewish survivors of concentration and death camps were chased away when they returned home to claim their property. A postwar demonstration of hostility toward the Jews in Poland was the Kielce Pogrom of July 1946, when local Polish authorities and civilians attacked a group of Jews, killing 42 and wounding 40 others. In the lawlessness of the immediate postwar months, retaliation by local authorities, arbitrary justice, arrests, imprisonments, and forced labor were daily occurrences. The malnourished populations of Greece and Norway faced extreme postwar hardships, while the residents of Warsaw, Stalingrad, Berlin, and many other European cities faced the daunting task of reconstructing their cities.

FINLAND

Leningrad

ESTONIA

SOVIET
UNION

Riga
LATVIA

DENMARK
Copenhagen

BALTIC
SEA

Memel
LITHUANIA
Vina

Minsk

Kiel

Danzig EAST
PRUSSIA
Connect by Poland

Stettin

US
Bremen   Betlin ◉

BRITISH

SOVIET

Poznan

Warsaw

POLAND

Breslau

Lvov

HOLLAND

FRENCH

US

Prague

Cracow

Nuremberg
(Trials 1945–46)

CZECHOSLOVAKIA

FRENCH

US
SOVIET

Vienna ◉

FRANCE

AUSTRIA
FRENCH   *BRITISH*

Budapest

SWITZERLAND

HUNGARY

Cluj

Trieste

British and US
occupation
1945–1955

ITALY
Monarchy
abolished after
Plebiscite June
1946

ADRIATIC SEA

YUGOSLAVIA
Monarchy abolished 1945

Belgrade

ROMANIA
Monarchy abolished 1947

Bucharest

BULGARIA
Monarchy abolished 1946

Sofia

ALBANIA
Monarchy abolished 1946

Communist activity 1946–1949

GREECE

TURKEY

Map 8.2 Europe's borders in 1945.

To accommodate the flood of refugees, the Allies opened 113 Displaced Persons (DP) camps in Germany. Reserved for non-German refugees, they soon hosted an estimated 5.8 million DPs whose temporary camp shelters were barely better than those of the Nazi concentration camps. Close to 1 million refugees were still waiting for repatriation or emigration papers in 1947.

Conclusion

The war was a grim affair for occupied populations and a great test of character. The options of perpetrator, bystander, or victim lay in front of everyone, and affected every choice: whether or not to hide a Jewish child, whether or not to do business with the occupier, whether or not to hoard or share food. These choices divided social groups, communities, and families. This situation was aggravated by ubiquitous scarcity. Even in neutral countries and Britain, which was not occupied, food was rationed. Work and employment patterns, education and medical care, nutrition and culture, were all disturbed. The health of the population declined, particularly in the Soviet Union and Poland, where living conditions were harshest. Surviving was an act of courage, a significant accomplishment. Amidst these difficulties, life went on, and plans for the postwar era began. The architects' plans for postwar urban reconstruction testified to human resilience in the midst of tragedy, as did every act of resistance against the occupying powers.

Overall conclusion

World War II proved to be an extremely brutal affair behind the military front lines in Europe, directly touching the lives of civilians on an unprecedented scale. In the end, approximately 23 million European civilians, including Holocaust victims, lost their lives. Not only did Europe become a killing field and a graveyard for soldiers and civilians alike, but its human environment was massively changed. Among the living in 1945 were large numbers of uprooted people: death camp survivors, refugees and displaced persons, and repatriated and transferred populations. The tragedy of war changed the demographics of Europe in unprecedented ways, even if Western Europe suffered comparatively less than East Central Europe and the Soviet Union. These realities helped shape the postwar leaders' commitment to human rights and human dignity. Nazi Germany created "sub-humans" and systematically planned their elimination or enslavement. Hitler's leadership led to the Nazis' murder of 6 million Jews. One could argue that the human tragedy of the war eclipsed other wartime developments, and even shaped some of them. Politically, Europe experienced deep divisions between domestically based governments that were often collaborationist and governments-in-exile dedicated to the liberation of their countries from foreign interference. In the area of politics, as in people's personal lives, ethical choices were made. The economic side of the war proved critical to its outcome. Nazi Germany could never have sustained a war of long duration without the resources of the occupied countries, which it ruthlessly exploited. In the end, the Axis powers could not match the productive capacities of the Allies, especially those of the United States, without which Britain and the Soviet Union could not have sustained their war efforts. Overall, World War II followed many of the same patterns as World War I. American participation, colonial contributions, and massive human and environmental destruction were present in both conflicts. These factors did much to drive Europe from its position as the center of the world.

Notes

1 http://hansard.millbanksystems.com/commons/1939/sep/03/prime-ministers-announcement# S5CV0351P0_19390903_HOC_32 (accessed July 18, 2016).
2 Christopher Catherwood, *Winston Churchill: The Flawed Genius of World War II* (New York: Berkley Caliber, 2009), 56.
3 Michael Phayer, *Pius XII, the Holocaust, and the Cold War* (Bloomington, IN: University of Indiana Press, 2008), 53.

Suggestions for further reading

Bergen, Doris. *War and Genocide: A Concise History of the Holocaust.* 2nd edn. New York: Rowman & Littlefield. 2009.

Collingham, Lizzie. *The Taste of War: World War II and the Battle for Food.* New York: Penguin Books. 2013.

Douglas, R. M. *Orderly and Humane: The Expulsion of the Germans after the Second World War.* New Haven, CT: Yale University Press. 2012.

Friedrich, Thomas. *Hitler's Berlin: Abused City.* New Haven, CT: Yale University Press. 2012.

Nicholas, Lynn H. *Cruel World: The Children of Europe in the Nazi Web.* New York: Vintage Books. 2006.

Paul, Allen. *Katyn: Stalin's Massacre and the Triumph of Truth.* DeKalb, IL: Northern Illinois University Press. 2010.

Phayer, Michael. *The Catholic Church and the Holocaust, 1930–1965.* Bloomington, IN: Indiana University Press. 2000.

Snyder, Timothy. *Bloodlands: Europe between Hitler and Stalin.* New York: Basic Books. 2012.

Stafford, David. *Endgame, 1945: The Missing Final Chapter of World War II.* New York: Back Bay Books. 2009.

Zahra, Tara. *The Lost Children: Reconstructing Europe's Families after World War II.* Cambridge, MA: Harvard University Press. 2011.

Part 5

European civilization in the crucible, 1914–1945

9 Culture in turmoil, 1914–1945

Introduction

Major innovations took place in Europe's intellectual and artistic life between 1890 and 1914. Psychology, sociology, painting, education, and religion all searched for new values, paradigms, and canons, challenging fundamental certainties that had existed for centuries prior. These innovations reflected a questioning of the tempestuous artistic currents of the nineteenth century, as well as the unease created by the indomitable quest of European nation-states for power. By the turn of the century, European world dominance was revealing not just glorious progress and power, but also the disappearing veneer of Western civilization. One of the events that shook up Europeans was the brutality of the Anglo-Boer War (1899–1902) between Great Britain and the Dutch-descended Afrikaners in South Africa; the British resorted to a scorched earth policy and concentration camps to force the Afrikaners into submission. Another was the Russo-Japanese War of 1904–1905 in which a non-European society, i.e., the Japanese, came out victorious over one of Europe's Great Powers.

Reason, dogma, and rationalism were under attack. A sense of urgency and pessimism impressed itself upon the artistic and intellectual world. Different artists and philosophers began to probe the hidden, yet real nature of humans and the universe, delving into uncomfortable, unstructured, and uncharted realms. Expressionism in art, as seen in the works of French painter Paul Gauguin after he moved to Polynesia, or in Norwegian painter Edvard Munch's tortured painting *The Scream* (1893), introduced numerous new venues to depict a world increasingly adrift. German philosopher Friedrich Nietzsche proclaimed "God is dead," and spoke of a coming European nihilism that would define the next few centuries. In Russia, Ivan Karamazov, a protagonist in Fyodor Dostoyevsky's novel *The Brothers Karamazov* (1880), spoke of Europe as a "graveyard." Pioneering sociologists, such as Emile Durkheim and Max Weber, were fundamentally preoccupied with the modern world taking shape. Durkheim, much like Nietzsche, spoke of the "death of the gods" – underscoring modernity's erasure of past traditions and institutions, including religion – and worried that their absence left Europe in a state of "anomie," i.e., a void-like condition in which there was a breakdown of values and standards. Weber wrote about the increasing rationalization of modern society and its dehumanizing and destabilizing effects.

Temporarily halted by World War I, these trends and lines of thought re-emerged in 1918 as self-questioning in the West increased, leading many historians to call the interwar years the "age of anxiety." A deep sense of dislocation characterized the interwar years. Exiled by war, revolution, or political persecution, artists and intellectuals flocked to continental Western Europe. American musicians brought jazz to Europe, while European anthropologists and artists embraced primitive art and culture from Latin America to Oceania and Africa, thereby introducing new ways to think, live, paint, and sculpt. In the midst of international cultural encounters, artists and intellectuals began to reflect on European identity and on the place of European culture in the world.

In addition to these developments, new technologies of mass communication and universal education shaped the production, distribution, outreach, and purpose of culture. This was true in democracies and totalitarian regimes alike, and people were able to influence what culture they wanted to consume. This move towards mass communication was tied to the emergence of mass society, and it dramatically transformed the way Western societies informed themselves and thought about the world. Artists and intellectuals also confronted a different and more serious question, however, one that was tied to the existing political situation. While the ability to be seen and heard was growing, the turbulent and worrying political and social contexts in Europe made it difficult for artists and intellectuals to be neutral. For many this led to an ethical problem: was one to become socially engaged and use art or philosophy to defend certain values, or escape into art for art's sake? Was art possible without a future Europe? The intellectuals' engagement in conceiving a future united Europe reflected their sense that this was both the only hope for European culture and the only way out of the abyss of totalitarianism and war. These choices, combined with the pessimistic and worried feelings that characterized the age, deeply marked the artistic and intellectual production of the first half of the twentieth century.

The political tumult that dominated the years 1914–1945 is a theme that permeates this entire chapter, because of the intimate relationship between art and reality. The chapter first addresses the cultural and religious tumult created by World War I and the coming of modernity in the 1920s, and the response of artists, writers, intellectuals, theologians, and church leaders to the rise of authoritarian regimes. Secondly, the chapter examines the reaction of political and cultural authorities to mass culture, and their use of the new technologies of mass communication in the 1930s. Two trends were visible: the use of mass communication by politicians for propaganda purposes in the fascist and totalitarian states of Europe; and the use of mass communication by business for consumerist purposes. It addresses the roles of cultural propaganda, mass education, and consumerism.

Cultural dissonance

From art to literature, science, and religion, the first half of the twentieth century was full of rupture and attempts to make sense of a rapidly changing world. World War I had a profound effect on the European collective conscience and touched cultural production in many ways. Cynicism and contestation replaced faith in reason and progress. This was seen particularly in the modernist movement. Although prewar modernist experiments in art and architecture were not totally interrupted, the war sharpened cultural forms and gave them a sense of urgency and a renewed purpose. New international communities of artists and intellectuals sprang up after the war, particularly in Paris and Berlin, and art was endowed with the power to destroy and rebuild, a mission that Europeans who had experienced the tremendous destruction of the Great War eagerly embraced. The 1920s were a period of rebuilding, but also of opposites and extremes oscillating between optimism and despair, pacifism and militarism, old and new aesthetic canons, and realism and surrealism. Scientific developments, both in the hard and the social sciences, challenged the way Europeans thought of the world and themselves. World War II also brought challenges to artists and intellectuals, forcing many into a moral conflict of whether to fight or to flee.

Postwar cultural centers

The uprooting of European intellectuals that took place immediately after World War I created an international intellectual movement. Paris and Berlin quickly emerged as magnets for artistic and intellectual life with their modern, daring atmospheres. Paris attracted gifted artists from all over Europe, notably Russian ballet dancers and choreographers, and artists from Austria, Hungary, Italy, Poland, and Spain. Many artists gathered around the *École de Paris*, a loosely defined network of French and international artists whose leaders were painters Pablo Picasso and Henri Matisse. Paris also attracted numerous British and American writers such as James Joyce, Gertrude Stein, and Ernest Hemingway. Berlin became the matrix of transformations that affected all of life, from fashion to revolution, from sexual behavior to the arts. In this tormented world, cabaret and theater were obvious matrixes, as seen in the 1972 movie *Cabaret* – set in Berlin in 1931 – and the plays of German playwright Bertolt Brecht. In Britain, now more receptive to continental influences, Cambridge became a preeminent center of European physics and philosophy, and the Bloomsbury Group – an informal association of intellectuals, writers, and artists – made French painting, Russian ballet, and Viennese psychoanalysis fashionable.

Western European culture was profoundly influenced by developments in East Central Europe and Russia. The euphoria of independence in Poland and Czechoslovakia produced great optimism, and culture was an intricate part of building the new states, bringing political and aesthetic concerns closely together. Polish cybernetics, philosophy, and mathematics were famous in Western European circles. Prague became the capital of modernistic architecture, especially with its cubist houses. One Russian artist who revolutionized the world of performance was ballet impresario Sergei Diaghilev whose *Ballets Russes* company based in Paris performed between 1909 and 1929 throughout Europe. Diaghilev secured the collaboration of an international coterie of avant-garde choreographers, composers, designers, and dancers, and the financial backing of Polish pianist and patron of the arts Misia Sert. The group inspired whimsical pieces that encouraged the interaction of art forms and radically broke from traditional ballet. In 1913, Diaghilev caused a firestorm at the premiere of his ballet *The Rite of Spring* in Paris, when his dancers violated the rules of classical ballet – an art form that to then had been resistant to avant-garde ideas – and did so to the accompaniment of a jarring, dissonant musical score. The shocked fashionable set in attendance screamed in protest while the avant-garde attendees cheered the performance.

Art in search of modernism

In the world of the visual arts, the break with traditional canons was dramatically demonstrated by a group of artists known as Dadaists. Dadaism started in 1916 as a protest against the absurdity of the mass killings of World War I. The purpose of Dadaism was to show the meaninglessness of all established moral and aesthetic values, and to return to a simpler, purer world of childhood, using the French word "dada" ("horsie") as a moniker. Dada rejected reason and preached anti-art and non-sense; exhibiting the subconscious on stage, it stressed that art is about the artist as much as it is about the world. Bizarre titles for art works such as *Sitting Buddha, Ask for Your Doctor* (1919), and antics and cacophony on stage became typical. During a 1920 event, one participant read incomprehensible poems, another simultaneously read an article from the day's newspapers, and loud bells and buzzers drowned out both readers' voices. At a performance in the spring of 1920, the audience left the theater during intermission and came back to pelt the actors with local produce, creating the first "happening." The artists were elated. One commented: "For the first time in the history of the world, people threw at us not only eggs, salads, and pennies, but beefsteaks as well . . . The audience were extremely Dadaist."[1] The French artist Marcel Duchamp did one of the most famous works of Dada when he took a print of the Mona Lisa, added a moustache and goatee, and called it *LHOOQ* (1920), an off-color pun in French.

Fading after 1922, Dada had nevertheless created a new freedom that a school of artists known as surrealists were able to exploit. Their message was that there was a greater reality beyond the world of physical appearances, namely, the world of the subconscious and dreams. It was a universe that the Spanish surrealist painter Salvador Dali captured in *The Persistence of Memory* (1931) with his melting watches, and in his sexually explicit landscapes.

The international trends in painting produced a renewal of cubism. Pablo Picasso and Georges Braque had initiated the movement before the Great War in Paris. Cubism's early iconic masterpiece was Picasso's *Les Demoiselles d'Avignon* (1907) that, in its depiction of five female nudes, shattered the human form and then pieced it back together in distorted patterns and fragmented geometric shapes. The work broke with the nearly

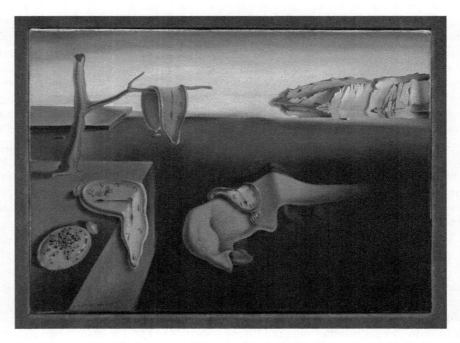

Figure 9.1 The painting *The Persistence of Memory*, done in 1931, is one of surrealist artist Salvador Dali's most recognizable works.

400-year-old Renaissance system of a single-point perspective by introducing multiple viewpoints. In the central figures, for example, Picasso presented profile views of the noses and frontal looks of the remainder of their faces. Cubism's push toward abstraction influenced many artists in the early decades of the twentieth century, including Paul Klee and Piet Mondrian. Marc Chagall, a Russian–French artist raised in a devoutly Jewish family, blended cubist forms and Jewish folklore. Cubism was a precursor to the avant-garde, geometrically based art movements of futurism in Italy and constructivism in Russia, both of which extolled the dynamism of the modern era. Picasso later used cubist techniques to dedicate his mural *Guernica* (1937) to the memory of the civilian victims of an indiscriminate German–Italian aerial bombing of the Spanish town of Guernica during the Spanish Civil War.

Other creative artists introduced new ideas in the search for modernism in the early twentieth century. Wassily Kandinsky, an expressionist painter, turned entirely away from nature in his art and painted one of the first totally abstract works in art history in 1910 as an untitled watercolor. The Italian artist Giorgio di Chirico captured the sense of alienation present in cities in his barren, desolate urban landscapes. Amedeo Modigliani, a Jewish Italian painter, epitomized linear profiles and fluid body lines in his paintings, and he shocked his contemporaries with his frank, uninhibited portrayals of female nudes.

The search for modernism also became inseparable from the discovery in the early 1900s of primitive art. The new aesthetic that emerged coincided with the apex of African and Oceanian colonialism. Newly discovered art objects from those regions were labeled as primitive, but perceived as both pristine and modern. These artefacts were popularized by a colonial commerce that placed a number of them in the hands of Parisian artists, collectors, dealers, and critics, and many artists visited ethnographic museums to learn more about primitivism. Artists associated with the *École de Paris* were early enthusiasts of the new aesthetic that became known as "Black Art." Picasso demonstrated his interest in the aesthetic in *Les Demoiselles d'Avignon* by portraying the faces of two of his female figures in the form of wood-carved African masks. The canon of the new aesthetic moved across national borders, and its appeal was strong enough that a special exhibit was devoted to it at the Paris Colonial Exhibition in 1931.

Music

Music also underwent a transformation in the early twentieth century, as composers, just like painters, were drawn to the subjective emotional powers of expressionism. Igor Stravinsky composed the innovative ballet *The Rite of Spring* that had its raucous premiere in Paris in 1913. The ballet contained harsh realism, violence, and intense energy, and the music was jarring, dissonant, and rhythmically provocative. Shortly after its controversial opening, the ballet was hailed as a revolutionary masterpiece. It is one of the first examples of musical modernism. In addition, Stravinsky was one of the first major foreign composers to incorporate American jazz into his music, which he first did in small bits during the interwar years.

Austrian composer Arnold Schönberg also played a decisive role in the birth of modern music. In 1908, he moved away from the traditional harmonies of classical music that were based on a central tone or key by introducing atonality (literally, without tonality) to the musical world in his String Quartet No. 2, op. 10. In 1912, he used atonality in *Pierrot Lunaire*, op. 21, an expressionist musical piece that contained poetry highlighting the emotional struggles of the work's main character. *Pierrot Lunaire* (1912) was the most famous work from the expressionist phase (1908–1921) of Schönberg's career. He went on to complete his musical revolution in the interwar years with his invention of the 12-tone musical scale. In his system, he established a row of 12 different tones that he used as the building blocks of his work and that he could combine in multiple ways. Indeed, it has been said that the system put some 500 million combinations at the composer's disposal. Schönberg revealed his new system in its complete form for the first time in 1923 in his *Five Piano Pieces* (op. 23).

Literature and the war

World War I had a powerful impact on writers both during and after the event. The poetry of British soldier Wilfred Owen, killed one week before the armistice of November 11, 1918, at the age of 25, not only documented the horrors of war, but became a symbol of a lost generation. The French novelist Romain Rolland, a life-long pacifist, wrote an anti-war pamphlet entitled *Above the Battle* in 1915; he was awarded the Nobel Prize for Literature that same year in part for that piece. Jaroslav Hasek, a decorated Austro-Hungarian war veteran, reacted after the war by writing the multi-volume novel *The Good Soldier Schweik* (1921–1923) in which he pointed out the absurdity of war generally and the ridiculousness of Austrian military discipline more particularly. One of the most graphic depictions of the nightmare that soldiers experienced in the trenches came in German war veteran and novelist/essayist Ernst Jünger's memoir *Storm of Steel* in 1924. German writer Erich Maria Remarque, who also served in World War I, published *All Quiet on the Western Front* in 1929. In the novel he pointed to the sacrifice of an entire generation, leaving his readers with a haunting vision of the main character's senseless death just as the carnage was about to end in late 1918. In 1935, Polish poet/novelist and 1929 Nobel Literature Prize nominee Józef Wittlin published *The Salt of the Earth*, which turned out to be the first and only tome of a projected three-volume work called *Tale of a Patient Infantryman*. It depicted the contrast between the idyllic summer of 1914 in the Hutsul province of Galicia and the upended world that resulted when the general mobilization order came from the Austro-Hungarian government. American writer Ernest Hemingway, who served in Italy as a volunteer ambulance driver, used his war experiences to write his anti-war novel *A Farewell to Arms* (1929). In addition, several literary-gifted veterans had written their memoirs by the end of the 1920s, which left no doubt about the influence of war.

Literature exploring the self

The aesthetic freedoms visible in the plastic arts with expressionism were mirrored in the literary world, in which the artist now was allowed to be true to himself and to escape from the outside world. Fascinated with the self's unlimited possibilities, writers moved to an exploration of the inner world, away from external realities. While this attitude was more passive than existentialism, it nonetheless carried the same feeling of meaninglessness and hopelessness. These thoughts bear witness to the profound civilizational disruptions that World War I caused in the human soul. Austrian writer Robert Musil captured the mood in his novel about the cultural collapse of the Austro-Hungarian monarchy. Started in 1921, *The Man without Qualities*, a three-part novel of 1,770 pages, is considered a masterpiece of the modernist novel, even though death prevented Musil from finishing the third volume. French writer Marcel Proust's deep inner monologues depicted countless mood nuances and obsessions and epitomized the neurotic character of the age. His lifework, begun in 1909, ended up being a seven volume, 3,400-page novel entitled *Remembrance of Things Past*. Czech novelist Franz Kafka, in his novel *The Trial* (1925), reflected on a broken world, anticipated totalitarian dehumanization, and depicted the modern bureaucracy's encroaching power.

In Ireland, novelist James Joyce went one step further with his stream-of-consciousness narratives, playing with language to show a disarticulated world. Using scraps of recollection and fragments of foreign languages, he wrote in a hermetic style that took the novel almost to its dissolution point. In his novel *Ulysses* (1922), he depicted 24 hours in the lives of three Dubliners, stressing the importance of place in a world adrift. The erotic nature of the work caused it to be banned in Britain.

British writer Virginia Woolf presented conflicted individuals through whom she tried to depict an accurate rendering of the functioning of the conscious mind. In her highly praised novel *Mrs. Dalloway* (1925), she used internal monologues and random images, thoughts, emotions, and memories corseted by a plot that took place in a decisive single day. It was an example of stream-of-consciousness storytelling, and it also touched on such issues as homosexuality and mental illness. In her novel *Orlando* (1928), she depicted an eternally youthful character gliding through several centuries as man/woman. On the other hand, Woolf returned to real world concerns to affirm womanhood and advocate for a strong female identity in her essay *A Room of One's Own* (1929).

For some, historical or exotic topics provided a venue for attempting to stabilize society. This genre was favored by German writers Thomas Mann who returned to the Germanic past, and Hermann Hesse, who discussed Indian mysticism. Italian businessman and writer Italo Svevo was a groundbreaker in the development of the psychological novel; his most famous work was *Zeno's Conscience* (1923), which consisted of a fictional patient's memoirs prepared for his psychiatrist.

Drama brought about a sense of unease and the absurd. Norwegian playwright Henrik Ibsen's prewar plays were well-suited to the dark, introspective mood of the postwar years and were performed regularly on Western European stages. Italian dramatist Luigi Pirandello's *Six Characters in Search of an Author* (1921) portrayed a haunting descent into despair, when the main character confronts different versions of the truth and cannot reach a conclusion.

Poetry freed itself from the conventions of rhythm and rhyme. Free verse was well suited to the playful ramblings of Dadaist and surrealist poets such as T. S. Eliot in Britain and W. B. Yeats in Ireland. But poetry showed a wide range of genres. Paul Valéry of France and Rainer Maria Rilke, a Bohemian–Austrian poet and novelist, wrote melancholic philosophical poetry. Federico García Lorca was a popular poet of the Spanish-speaking world and one of the most powerful dramatists in the modern theater. His *Book of Poems* (1921) made him famous for his spontaneous and refined language, startling imagery, and original metaphors. Concerned principally with the rural and Roma people of Spain, Lorca's works portrayed elemental human passions and emphasized the interplay of dreams and reality.

New views of Europe

The postwar world started with a shortage of dynamism, optimism, and vision. Pessimism about the future of Western civilization was evident in 1918. Intellectuals and poets spoke of the end of European world dominance. German historian and philosopher Oswald

Spengler gave expression to this in his 1918 work *The Decline of the West*, which discussed the rise and decline of civilizations. In 1919, French poet Paul Valéry, looking at the rise and fall of great ancient civilizations, commented on the end of European predominance, "We, the civilizations, we now know that we are mortal . . . Is Europe becoming what it really is, that is, a small cape of the Asian continent?"[2] Many people saw the war as responsible for the ruin of Western civilization.

Intellectuals felt compelled to effect a renaissance of European values, and several writers called for an aesthetic and moral renewal. They argued in favor of cultural diversity and affirmed the importance of the cultural sphere. They debated the notion of humanism, and often criticized the cult of science and progress that had prevailed during the nineteenth century. One main concern that German writer Thomas Mann expressed was an important contradiction inherent to humanism, namely, that its tolerance made it powerless to stop fanaticism. For most thinkers, however, Europe's rebirth would be European-wide in scope. The 1920s were thus a fecund decade for advancing the discussion about the future of a united Europe. German writer Ernst Jünger called for a democratic federation of states organized along the lines of economics, technology, and trade, with cultural diversity as an integral feature. Artists and intellectuals participated in the many meetings, associations, congresses, resolutions, and institutes that various pro-European movements sponsored. But the failure of the Briand plan for a more tightly organized Europe and Hitler's rise to power threw them into a tailspin of discouragement. In a powerful rebuke to such developments, Spanish philosopher José Ortega y Gasset, a noted critic of modern civilization, denounced nationalism and urged a revival of Europe. He claimed in his highly influential work *The Revolt of the Masses* (1930) that this new beginning was imperative to save civilization. Ortega in a prescient way warned against the power of the masses, their irrationalism, and their impact on the rise of totalitarianism. In Gasset's eyes, Europe was the only salvation, a soul supplement for the masses. More importantly, during the Great Depression, he stressed the importance of building a solid economic foundation for Europe.

Pacifist and leftist writers addressed the issue of nationalism as a threat to peace and raised the specter of mass violence and social exclusion. French philosopher Julien Benda echoed such sentiments in his 1927 essay *The Betrayal of the Intellectuals*, in which he addressed the crisis of Western liberalism and accused Europeans of worshipping nationalism and racism at the expense of political and spiritual unity. In 1933, he recommended the creation of a European-wide educational system to promote European ideals, among which cultural diversity would occupy an important place. The pacifist French writer Romain Rolland tried to establish relationships with Soviet writers and corresponded regularly with Indian independence leader Mohandas Gandhi. Swiss diplomat Carl J. Burckhardt and Christian philosopher Jacques Maritain advocated a free association of European peoples and nations based on Western Christianity.

Science: the relativity revolution

Already before World War I, scientists had made advances in electricity that questioned Isaac Newton's laws, revealed the atom to be a miniature solar system, invented X-ray technology, and discovered radioactivity. They no longer saw time and space as universal and immutable, but rather as defined by relativity, as Albert Einstein explained in a paper published in 1916. From Einstein to Max Planck and Niels Bohr, physicists now explained matter through energy, waves, and primal space. Quantum mechanics revolutionized the way in which scientists viewed the world. The discovery of the mass spectroscope in 1919 enabled scientists to identify isotopes, which would lead to the atom's fission – minute basic matter bombardments. These developments in physics had practical applications that led to large-scale financing of research and development institutes and laboratories in several European countries, including Germany and the Soviet Union. Eventually, these discoveries gave birth to the nuclear age in 1945, and fundamentally altered the way many people perceived religion, reality, and truth.

Interpreting society: the social sciences

Immediately before, during, and after World War I there were important developments in the social sciences that had considerable impact on the interwar years. These shifts often reflected the political realities of the time or were part of larger movements that challenged certain previous taboos, such as those dealing with sexuality or religion.

The First World War accentuated developments that had emphasized subjectivity, unconscious mental processes, and self-criticism, and questioned existing knowledge about society. According to Sigmund Freud, the inner, unconscious universe of thoughts and emotions was driven by repressed desires and sexual urges. In 1918, Freud was at the height of his career, and saw psychoanalysis – a technique intended to bring people's unconscious thoughts and feelings to the surface – become an international movement. Swiss psychiatrist Carl Jung, a colleague of Freud until 1913 when the two split, founded a school of psychotherapy called analytical psychology. Like Freud, he explored the unconscious part of the mind, but he deviated strikingly from Freud in developing a theory of the unconscious that included a controversial personality layer he referred to as the collective unconscious. This was a level of unconscious that one shares with other human beings based on innate memories – primordial images or archetypes – etched into one's mind from man's evolutionary past.

Sociologists too were caught in the crossfire of history. Emile Durkheim, the father of modern sociology, laid out a framework for studying society that remained highly influential during the interwar years. His methodology, which involved the study of "social facts," i.e., objects of social life that compel individuals to act in a certain way, led him to study a diverse array of social phenomena such as religion, morality, suicide, the division of labor, and language. His argument that religion was a man-made product of social forces proved particularly controversial. Following Durkheim's death in 1917, several of his followers, including the Frenchmen Marcel Mauss and Céléstin Bouglé, carried his ideas forward. Max Weber, another prominent and pioneering sociologist, wrote about the issues of the time, including the hyper-rational logic inherent to capitalism, the nature of state power, and the problem of political legitimacy.

Sociology was also influenced by the founding in 1923 of the first center for Marxist studies: the Institute for Social Research, in Frankfurt-am-Main, Germany. Known as the Frankfurt School, the institute had a lasting influence on the development of social theory until well after 1945. Theodor W. Adorno, György Lukács, and Herbert Marcuse were the best-known representatives of this school. They sought to undermine traditional Western society by analyzing and criticizing economic, social, and cultural structures and beliefs from a Marxist and Freudian perspective. An important element was the school's new theory of aesthetics that denied the existence of a universal, absolute canon of beauty. As precursors to postmodernism, the Frankfurt School theorists recognized that one individual cannot perceive or comprehend the totality of experience.

Anthropology moved in a new direction through the work of Polish-born Bronisław Malinowski who was a founder of social anthropology. He did extensive research among the primitive societies in the western Pacific and deeply influenced anthropology in the English-speaking world. He propounded the theory of "generalized exchange," i.e., the existence of a common good benefiting all in the presence of non-reciprocal gifts. Malinowski stressed the irrational and the unconscious elements in interwar social thought and saw in them a reflection of the disoriented world the Great War had left behind.

A major interwar development in the discipline of history was the emergence of the Annales School of social history in France. Marc Bloch and Lucien Febvre founded the Annales School that revolutionized the theory and practice of history by rejecting events – and leaders-driven history in favor of *la longue durée*, i.e., the long-term importance of steadily evolving historical structures. It was history slowly moving over an extended period of time. They borrowed from geography and economics to explain historical mechanisms, and analyzed under-studied subjects such as the rural world and economic exchanges.

Writers and intellectuals: persecutions and protests

The interwar years provided writers and intellectuals with many opportunities to denounce the shortcomings and flaws of their times, and many did that by promoting the ideals of social justice. In the 1920s and 1930s, left-leaning writers and intellectuals championed freedom and equality, which they saw as important values in a new, modern world. The French surrealist poets André Breton and Paul Éluard considered their artistic revolution as a rejection of the prewar bourgeois capitalist world that had led to the war. Their concern for social justice was echoed in many corners. German playwright Bertolt Brecht, a champion of the underdog, depicted painful social and ethical dissonances in his musically complemented plays *The 3-Penny Opera* (1928) and *Rise and Fall of the City of Mahagonny* (1930). Teaming up with German music composer Kurt Weill, he staged avant-garde productions full of bitter social satire. It was their way of resisting institutional oppression in Germany and conducting an artistic revolution of their own.

The spread of fascism in Europe in the 1930s had the effect of cooling the cultural and intellectual effusion that had taken place across the continent. Authoritarian systems, with the Nazi regime in the lead, were stridently anti-modern, and they threatened many of the artists and writers who had risen to prominence in the 1920s. Nationalist forces in Spain executed poet Federico García Lorca at the beginning of the Spanish Civil War. In Germany, the Nazis, with the enthusiastic support of thousands of pro-Nazi students, sponsored public book burnings of Jewish and left-wing intellectual writers in May 1933. Many artists, scholars, thinkers, and scientists, now targets of the regime, chose exile. One of the most famous scientists to leave Germany for political reasons was Einstein, who emigrated to America in 1933. In 1935, Germany's Frankfurt School, with its many German Jewish intellectuals, relocated to Columbia University in New York. There they continued to produce Marxist thought in the heart of a capitalist, liberal democracy. France provided protection for a number of artists and intellectuals until the war years, when many fled to the United States; those who moved to America included Russian/French artist Marc Chagall, Polish writer Józef Wittlin, and German philosopher Hannah Arendt.

Intellectuals who remained in Europe faced difficult choices. The German-Jewish philosopher and social critic, Walter Benjamin, for example, committed suicide in 1940 when he tried to escape invading Nazi forces by crossing the border into Spain. Victor Frankl, an Austrian Jewish psychologist, was sent to Auschwitz and Dachau during the war. Miraculously he survived and wrote movingly about his ordeal in *Man's Search for Meaning* (1946). The French-Jewish sociologist Marcel Mauss remained in Paris and suffered the indignities of the occupying Nazis, including the loss of academic posts and the destruction of his personal library, although he, like Frankl, survived the war.

A number of Western European writers joined the resistance during World War II. French-Jewish medieval and economic historian Marc Bloch joined the French underground in late 1942 and became one of its leaders. Arrested by the Vichy authorities in March 1944, a German firing squad executed him ten days after D-Day. French novelist and art theorist André Malraux served as a soldier in a tank unit in 1939–1940. Though the Germans captured him, he soon escaped and eventually participated in the French resistance until stopped by the German Gestapo in 1944. He served as the minister of information in Charles de Gaulle's French provisional government in 1945–1946. Italian writer Ignazio Silone, famous for his novel *Fontamara* (1933) which deals with the Spanish Civil War, became the leader of a clandestine socialist organization that, working from Switzerland, supported German resistance groups during the war.

Two important writers who wrote works in which they denounced totalitarianism during World War II were Arthur Koestler and George Orwell. Koestler, a Hungarian-born Jewish author and journalist who became a British citizen in the late 1940s, joined the Communist Party in 1931, but in the wake of Stalin's excesses, left it in 1938. He won international acclaim in 1940 for his novel *Darkness at Noon*, in which he disavowed totalitarianism. Orwell, a British novelist, expressed his opposition to totalitarianism in his book *Animal Farm* (1945). Both of these works deeply influenced the postwar era.

The looting of art in World War II

There was little chance of resistance when Hitler's regime started appropriating art collections during World War II. The Nazis practiced the theft of art works from Jewish collectors, art owners, and museums in all the European countries they occupied. Beginning with the confiscation of German Jews' art works and continuing with the looting of occupied countries' museums and private collections, the Germans acquired an impressive set of masterpieces. The art works experienced various fates. Hitler gave some as gifts to his subordinates. The Führer also created his own collection of artwork and furnishings worth millions of dollars at the time. Poland lost over 500,000 of its works of art. Some 200,000 religious and cultural Jewish artifacts confiscated by the Nazis were warehoused in Prague, awaiting the opening of a "museum to an extinct race." Much non-Jewish confiscated art was destined for an art museum that Hitler planned for his native city of Linz, which he intended to make the Reich's capital of culture. The legacy of the Nazi thefts still affects the art world today. Many owners fought for decades in courts to try to recapture their works, one of the most famous being Gustav Klimt's *Woman in Gold*, which sold at auction for $135 million in 2006. Nazi art looting changed the art collections, galleries, and museums in France, the Netherlands, Italy, Austria, Hungary, and Poland.

Conclusion

The war and postwar years saw important experimentation in all art forms. In the 1920s, traditional art was displaced by artistic experiments that were confronted daily with political developments, ideology, and social change. Methods, artistic canons, delivery, message, medium, and audiences were rapidly changing. Never in the history of the arts did so much change happen so quickly. In the midst of this effervescent climate, artists were divided: while some favored artistic anarchy, which was a form of violence, others – especially intellectuals – endeavored to stem the tide of violence by embracing the mission to rebuild Europe and to establish a new canon of European values. Engagement became a large part of the European intellectual scene between 1914 and 1945.

Religious shifts

In the late nineteenth and early twentieth centuries, religion faced increasing scrutiny and skepticism as well as institutional and political challenges, including the rise of atheistic Communism. Religion in some quarters became more engaged, more liberal, and more probing as theologians and religious leaders sought new groundings for faith. As time went on, the intellectual challenges remained, but the turbulent politics, especially in the 1930s, forced difficult decisions. This time period saw restrictions imposed in many authoritarian states, but also agreements between church and state in several of them. In addition, religious diversity increased as a result of war displacements and postwar migrations, forcing a reappraisal of believers' and church leaders' attitudes.

Religion in crisis

By 1914, scientific and secular trends and the growing social unease of the late Victorian period had created a culture of skepticism that challenged Europe's religious faiths. One expression of doubt could be found in what would later be called existentialism, although there were marked differences in the ideas of the authors listed in this movement. Some existentialists were Christian and their doubt led them to God. Danish philosopher Søren Kierkegaard emphasized the importance of a subjective relationship with God based on beliefs "by virtue of the absurd." Faith required the reconciliation of paradoxes that ran counter to reason, such as the coexistence of an infinite, all-powerful God and his seemingly finite human form in the person of Christ. Fyodor Dostoyevsky grappled with the idea of nihilism and a world in which there was no God or morality, and famously said, "If god does not exist everything is permitted." This idea was acted out in Dostoyevsky's *Crime and Punishment* (1866) by the character Rodion Raskolnikov who murdered a woman for no purpose whatsoever during a break-in. He even left behind all of the woman's valuables to add to the senselessness of the crime. Dostoyevsky rejected the nihilistic path, however, as in the end Raskolnikov found redemption in God's salvation. Many, if not most, existentialists did not believe in God, and many, especially Friedrich Nietzsche, were highly critical of religion. But they also dealt with humanity's precarious place in a universe that seemed without purpose. Martin Heidegger and Jean-Paul Sartre wrote at length about existential angst and coming to grips with human finitude, or death, while Nietzsche and Albert Camus sought to affirm life despite its absurdities and purposelessness.

In 1914, the situation of the established religions and their spiritual and institutional authority in Europe varied across the map. If there were few denominations in Western Europe and Russia due to the fact that national governments had traditionally controlled official religion, the religious map was much more diverse in East Central Europe, where minorities were intertwined. Protestants, Roman Catholics, Orthodox Christians, Muslims, Jews, and other smaller sects had coexisted there for centuries. In France, where a law established the separation of church and state in 1905, there existed a strong anticlerical movement that adversely affected the Roman Catholic Church. German Protestants were challenged to abandon their comfortable middle class, nationalist, conservative approach to religion. Judaism, divided between Reform and Orthodox strands, had become politicized in the late nineteenth century by the advent of Zionism, a movement to reestablish a Jewish homeland in Palestine.

Once war came, the Christian churches found themselves in the uncomfortable position of having clergy and parishioners across Europe supporting one or the other side in the conflict, and the various combatants were convinced of the justness of their cause. The Vatican had to walk a delicate line, since Roman Catholicism was the dominant faith in lands of both sets of belligerents. Pope Benedict XV (r. 1914–1922) devoted considerable time in 1916 and 1917 to trying to mediate an end to World War I. Neither side accepted his initiatives, believing them to be biased in favor of the other. Meanwhile, the death and destruction of the war caused many people to question or lose their faith. Once the war was over, Benedict XV spoke out against the League of Nations as a secular organization that lacked a Christian foundation, but he also rejected nationalism and called for European unification in a papal encyclical in 1920.

Between faith and social engagement

In the interwar years, Catholic and Protestant theologians alike felt the need to revitalize organized religion and faith. Swiss-born Protestant Reformed theologian Karl Barth sought to return Christianity to a faith founded on revelation and emphasized man's inability to achieve salvation without the grace of God. Barth feared that the contemporary liberal religious movement's emphasis on reason as the force that would save humankind would undermine the cohesion of the church by allowing man to create whatever kind of religion he felt necessary. Barth opposed all forms of tyranny, and served as a leading voice among German pastors opposed to Hitler. Another approach was that of liberal German Lutheran theologian Rudolf Bultmann, who attempted to rediscover the original forms of the Scriptures buried in layers of traditional interpretation, in order to make them relevant to modern-day situations. Theologians across Europe felt the urgency to oppose the dehumanizing forces of industrial society. French thinkers Gabriel Marcel, Emmanuel Mounier, Henri Bergson, and Jacques Maritain were part of a Catholic intellectual revival that attempted to give new relevance to the Catholic faith in an age of materialism.

In 1931, the Catholic Church reiterated its concern for economic and social justice when Pope Pius XI (r. 1922–1939) updated the church's position on the nature of modern industrial society in the Encyclical *Quadragesimo Anno*. This document, which criticized the heartlessness and exploitative nature of the capitalist system, endorsed the corrective role of the state and took a position halfway between individualism and collectivism, liberalism and socialism. It advocated harmony between social classes through profit-sharing and corporative self-governing bodies within each branch of the economy.

But it fell short of endorsing socialism. It served as a blueprint for Catholic churches, which began to support the welfare state and assume welfare initiatives of their own. The renewed commitment to a strong Christian social conscience grew out of the sufferings that people witnessed during the Great Depression and a new concern for workers who had turned from religion to political ideologies for guidance.

The Catholic Church in Italy and Germany

Pope Pius XI had a lasting impact on Italian Catholicism. Referring to Mussolini as "the man sent by Providence," he signed the Lateran Pact with the Italian government in 1929, ending decades of strife between the two entities. The papal enclave of Vatican City became the smallest independent state in the world in return for renouncing the Papal States lost during Italy's unification process in the nineteenth century. Catholicism was made the state religion of Italy, religious teaching restored in all the country's schools, and canon law concerning marriage accepted, in exchange for the clergy refraining from political activities. The Lateran Pact enhanced Mussolini's prestige internationally just when democratic countries were starting to view fascism frightfully. The Vatican was also pleased when Mussolini berated the participation of women in sports, restricted Protestant publications, and outlawed cursing in public. The Pope's generally sympathetic response to the Italian Fascist regime was reflective of the positive response of many European Catholics toward the development of fascist organizations and authoritarian governments during the 1920s. Relations between the papacy and Mussolini cooled dramatically in the 1930s, however, as Mussolini increased the power of the state at the expense of the church. In 1931, the Pope protested vehemently when Mussolini closed down Catholic youth organizations to allow Fascist youth groups to obtain a dominant position among the country's young people. The Pope also denounced in the early 1930s what he called "the pagan worship of the state" in Italy.

On April 26, 1933, Pius XI also signed a Concordat with Nazi Germany, which protected the autonomy of the Catholic Church and assured it of a tax return in exchange for the Vatican's recognition of the legitimacy of Hitler's regime and refrainment from engaging in politics. Aware of the Nazis' staunch anti-Communism, the Pope hoped that the agreement would allow him to use the German government to thwart Communism across Europe and secure the position of Roman Catholicism in Germany. For Hitler, it was a clever move on the part of his new government which had been tarnished by its first wave of persecution against the Jews earlier in the month, and he found the agreement quite useful in gaining support domestically and internationally. Papal relations with Germany deteriorated quickly, as five days after signing the Concordat the Nazi government banned Catholic youth associations to make room for the Hitler Youth organizations.

The Nazi regime's repeated violations of the Concordat in the years thereafter and its false accusations against a group of priests and nuns who ended up on trial triggered the German bishops into action. They asked Pope Pius XI to call the Nazis out, which he did in March 1937 in the encyclical *With Burning Sorrow*. The pope condemned Nazi violations of the Concordat and the regime's "idolatrous" worship of race and state. The encyclical was secretly distributed to churches across Germany and read by clergymen to parishioners on Palm Sunday. An infuriated Hitler ordered all copies of the document seized and anyone caught circulating it apprehended.

The regime also heightened its anti-Catholic propaganda. By early 1939, the bishops were looking for an accommodation with Hitler, and toward that end, they invited the newly installed Pope Pius XII to send the Führer a hopeful message for improved relations between the Vatican and Germany. The new pope, also eager for a lessening of tensions, invited the German ambassador at the Vatican for a private audience to express "his warmest wish for peace between Church and State."[3] Once war came in September 1939, an undeclared truce set in between Hitler and the German episcopate. Hitler did not want to create distractions for Christians when the country was at war, so he restrained the anti-Catholic sentiments of some of his top lieutenants, and the bishops, not wanting to look unpatriotic, supported Hitler's attack against Catholic Poland. Nevertheless, animosity between the two groups remained throughout the war.

The German Protestant Church

Hitler also took steps to gain control over the main Protestant Church body in Germany. Known as the German Evangelical Church (Lutheran and Reformed congregations), it was a federation of 28 regionally organized churches, with each emphasizing different doctrines, and it had the nominal support of about two-thirds of the country's population. In 1933, the Evangelical Church was deeply torn by theological and ideological disputes. Hitler decided to take advantage of a broad desire within the Church to end the divisions and create a revitalized, unified institution. In his mind, a unified national church would facilitate his ability to control it. He threw his support behind Ludwig Müller for the Church's top position of Reich bishop. Müller headed a conservative wing of the Church called German Christians, who embraced many of the ideological ideas of Nazism, including German nationalism, Aryanism, and anti-Semitism. In elections in the summer of 1933, Müller's German Christians gained control of the Church's administration, and he was elected Reich bishop in September. The German Christians' fanaticism – its radical wing wanted to get rid of the Old Testament and repudiate the New Testament's Pauline letters owing to their Jewish authorship – proved detrimental to Hitler's interests, so he distanced himself from them in the fall of 1933.

Clerical opposition quickly emerged to the German Christians' attempts to accommodate the Evangelical Church to Nazi doctrines. In the fall of 1933, Martin Niemöller, a well-known Lutheran theologian and pastor, founded a dissenting Pastors' Emergency League that led to the founding in 1934 of the Confessing Church within the broader Evangelical Church. The Confessing Church, with the support of approximately 25 percent of the Evangelical Church's clergy, rejected the subjection of the Church to state control and any racially based interpretation of Christianity. Niemöller preached against state interference in church affairs, and Gestapo officials (Nazi secret police) arrested him in 1937. He ended up as a prisoner at the concentration camps of Sachsenhausen and Dachau from 1938 to 1945. Another prominent member of the Confessing Church was Dietrich Bonhoeffer, a Lutheran theologian and pastor who opposed the Nazi regime from its earliest days. He oversaw an illegal Confessing Church seminary at Finkenwalde, Germany, to train theology students from 1935 to 1937, when the Gestapo closed it. In 1938, Bonhoeffer became associated with the German resistance, and his anti-Nazi activities landed him in prison in 1943. He was executed at the Nazi concentration camp at Flossenbürg in April 1945. Meanwhile, the Confessing Church, weakened by Nazi intimidation and internal strife, was increasingly forced underground in the latter 1930s. The situation of the Confessing Church was further handicapped in 1939, when, with the outbreak of war, a number of its clergy and laity were called up for military service. The Confessing Church continued to function during World War II, but was subject to frequent Nazi harassment. It discontinued operations in 1948 following a reorganization of the German Evangelical Church.

Religion in the Soviet Union

More than anywhere else in Europe, religion suffered greatly during the interwar years in the Soviet Union, which the Bolsheviks made the continent's first officially atheist state. The Russian Orthodox Church was a major target of persecution because of the beliefs it taught and because of its former association with the rich and powerful. The government tried and killed many clerics. Churches were turned into granaries, beer halls, dance halls, and breweries. Priceless treasures of Russian-East Slavic culture were destroyed. Soviet agents also encouraged schism in the church, and in 1922, some reform-minded clergy, with the sympathy of the Soviet authorities, set up the Renovated Church to compete with the traditional patriarchal authority for control of the Orthodox Church. The Renovated Church found little following among the people, who remained loyal to the old patriarchal administration, but the schism further weakened the Orthodox Church.

Persecution against the Church intensified after Stalin took power. Between 1927 and 1940 the number of Orthodox churches dropped from some 29,600 to less than 500. The state persecuted people for attending church and arrested clergymen and religiously involved lay members in massive numbers. During Stalin's Great Purge of 1936–1938, more than 100,000 Russian Orthodox clergy were executed. At the end of the 1930s, Stalin softened his approach to the Church and granted the clergy full civil rights. Although membership in the Orthodox Church diminished substantially during the regime's interwar persecutions, those who remained in the Church developed a much deeper faith. Stalin completed his reconciliation with the Orthodox Church in 1943 when, as an act of gratitude to the Orthodox hierarchy for its loyalty in the war against Hitler, he restored the patriarchate with state oversight. The Church's newly elected patriarch declared Stalin to be "the divinely appointed."

Conclusion

Religion in Europe experienced developments similar to those in other areas of culture and life. Early in the century, Christianity confronted important intellectual and theological questions. Later, it was challenged by political events that forced Roman Catholic and Protestant denominations to become more engaged socially and internationally, and Orthodox denominations to deal with official state censorship. While the Catholic Church in Italy was largely immune from political persecution, it achieved this position only by signing a treaty with Mussolini. In Nazi Germany, meanwhile, Protestant and Catholic religious leaders alike were forced to choose between collaboration with the new regime or resistance. In the Soviet Union, religion was banned and openly persecuted, and churches used for granaries or other secular purposes in the interwar years, but the Orthodox Church experienced a rehabilitation during the Second World War.

Mass communication and propaganda

One of the most important developments in mass communication in the first part of the twentieth century involved government propaganda. Propaganda efforts were facilitated by advances in print and transportation, but also by radio and film. The result was the creation of powerful propaganda campaigns involving posters, short films, pamphlets, and other artistic endeavors in the service of a government agenda. During World Wars I and II, these activities concentrated on the war effort. But propaganda activities also became major peacetime components in European dictatorships, such as the Soviet Union and Nazi Germany. In these instances, the governments carefully monitored artistic endeavors that often had clear political messages.

Propaganda during World War I

The expansive wartime propaganda campaigns that took place among all the belligerents between 1914 and 1918 did much to advance the popularity of mass communication. Governments on both sides set up propaganda offices to oversee official efforts in that area, and propaganda quickly became a powerful government weapon at home and abroad. Military high commands controlled information moving to and from the battlefront. Propaganda's aims changed during the war, as did its media support and forms of delivery. The war increased the use of patriotic messages and slogans tied to art forms and the dissemination of propaganda among the general population. Slogans and brochures were edifying and simple, the art dramatic and emotional, and the musical lyrics inspirational.

When a military stalemate and massive deaths occurred during the fall of 1914, the belligerents devoted considerable energy towards keeping up morale. Governments published army newsletters aimed at uplifting soldiers' spirits and controlled the news through press censorship. Newspapers published stories minimizing the most anguishing aspects of the war in order to inspire confidence in victory. Controls were imposed on mail sent to and from the front. In France, for example, the French High Command set up a postal control system for such mail in January 1915; at the height of its operations, postal control agents, using French military units as regular sounding boards, opened some 180,000 letters per week out of the 5 to 7 million that exchanged hands, in an attempt to stop the most pessimistic from getting through. Film was also widely used to make carefully edited war news available to the masses. Newsreels showed leaders and royalty visiting the wounded and recounted tales of courage and heroic feats by the soldiers. Symbolic gestures were also used, such as the Russians' decision right after the war started to change the name of their capital from St. Petersburg to Petrograd, because the original name sounded too German.

Artists and intellectuals actively participated in the war propaganda campaigns. Shortly after the struggle began, a nascent British War Propaganda Bureau secretly enlisted 53 prominent British authors, including Arthur Conan Doyle, Rudyard Kipling, and H. G. Wells to append their names to a widely published manifesto called the "Authors' Declaration." The document, first presented to the public in September 1914, declared that Germany's invasion of Belgium was a barbaric crime and that "Great Britain could not without dishonor have refused to take part in the present war."[4] The Germans followed in October 1914 by publishing their own manifesto, popularly known as the

"Manifest of the 93," in which 93 distinguished scholars and artists defended Germany's actions at the outset of the war. In France, sociologist Emile Durkheim wrote propaganda pamphlets in which he disparaged not just Germany's militarism but its culture as well.

Posters were the most noticeable propaganda tool, proving to be powerful vehicles for conveying government messages to the public. One important theme in Allied posters focused on recruiting men into military service. In the case of the British, the Parliamentary Recruiting Committee, formed in August 1914, had issued well over 22 million recruitment publications, including more than 5.7 million posters, by September 1915. To remind people of the importance of conserving food, the British in 1917 distributed a poster that portrayed a mother slicing bread in a kitchen with her daughter – as a British ship confronts a German submarine in the seascape background – and that contained the words "Don't waste bread! Save two slices every day and defeat the 'U' boat."[5] Another frequent Allied poster theme involved appeals to buy war bonds. One French poster that showed a soldier in a trench read, "Standing in the trench illuminated by dawn, the soldier dreams of victory and home. So that he may secure the former and return to the latter, subscribe to the 3rd National Defense Loan."[6] Posters on both sides also depicted the enemy as evil, barbaric, and villainous.

The Bolshevik break with the past

In the search for a working class aesthetic in Soviet Russia, some Bolshevik leaders supported a radical leftist experiment in the form of an Association of Proletarian Cultural and Education Organizations (*Proletkult*) that focused on the cultural education of workers. Aleksandr Bogdanov founded the *Proletkult* in 1917 and shortly thereafter gained the support of Anatoly Lunacharsky, the first Soviet commissar of education. *Proletkult* aimed at creating a "pure" proletarian culture, and to achieve that, it established workers' universities and palaces of culture, and it even held a workers' writers conference in 1918. But the association's aggressiveness caused friction with Lunacharsky's commissariat, and Lenin concluded that it was a haven for avant-garde bourgeois intellectuals. Lenin ordered the *Proletkult* absorbed into the education commissariat in 1920. In contrast to those who sought a radical change of culture stood a group of Russian writers, known as the Serapion Brotherhood, who wished to preserve artistic freedom and intellectual integrity. Trotsky labeled them fellow travelers and "bourgeois specialists." Other literary groups and organizations also formed, and intense debates took place between them all. In the midst of this confusion, the Bolsheviks finally settled for a relaxed policy of cultural transition that remained in place during the New Economic Policy years (1921–1928). The All-Union Conference of Proletarian Writers, created in 1925, lent support to this policy by calling for cultural pluralism and diversity. Nevertheless, the result was uncertainty and equivocation in the area of the arts in Russia, as there were no clear-cut boundaries for what was culturally permissible, and the regime's dictatorial tendencies regarding culture remained intact.

Some Russian writers who had supported the Bolshevik revolution became disillusioned with the regime when it failed to deliver on its promises. Poet Aleksandr Blok, the principal representative of Russia's symbolist movement which involved the subjective portrayal of emotions or ideas, initially embraced the revolution. But he became distraught over the Bolsheviks' cultural policies and use of violence, and quit writing poetry in 1918, three years before his death. Vladimir Mayakovsky was another notable poet who welcomed the November revolution. He joined the Bolshevik Party shortly thereafter and set out to create a proletarian culture freed of bourgeois influences, but by the late 1920s he believed that a heartless bureaucratic regime had emerged. Subjected to severe attacks from within and without the government for criticizing weaknesses in Soviet society, he committed suicide in 1930.

The first major Russian novelist to question the dictatorial predilections of the regime was Yevgeny Zamyatin. A Bolshevik party member as a youth, he abandoned it prior to the 1917 revolution. It was in his masterpiece *We*, a dystopian novel completed in 1920, that Zamyatin questioned the society that was emerging in Russia under Communism by describing a future society where an all-powerful "Benefactor" controlled every area of one's life. Although it was the first literary piece banned by the Soviet censorship board, it still circulated in Russia for decades before its formal publication there in 1989. Zamyatin managed to smuggle the manuscript to the West, and an English translation appeared in 1924. Mercilessly harassed for his writings, he emigrated to France in 1931.

At the end of the 1920s, Stalin started tightening the party's controls over the arts, a policy turn that was symbolized by the dismissal of Lunacharsky as the education commissar in 1929. Socialist realism became the new aesthetic, which basically meant representing socialism in a glorious light. The goal was to re-educate the masses in the ideology of socialism. Writers had to idealize their heroes and portray them as Communists or, on the rare occasions when they were not party members, as individuals whose positive qualities could be attributed to the Communist system. In 1932, Stalin established a single, party-controlled writers' organization called the Union of Soviet Writers to replace all other literary groups; all writers had to be members. The new writers' union adopted the new aesthetic at its inaugural meeting in 1934. Conformity in literature became the order of the day, and as a result, few quality literary pieces appeared in the 1930s, either as novels or poetry.

Filmmaking under Lenin and Stalin

Lenin, who was particularly fond of film, once said, "Of all the arts, for us cinema is the most important."[7] The Bolsheviks used films as a propaganda tool and pioneered the use of traveling motion picture shows to win adherents to the regime. The aesthetic appeal of the movies masked their political, manipulative message, and the masses were easily impressed.

Regardless of the propaganda connection, Soviet filmmaking achieved remarkable artistic qualities in the interwar years. Dziga Vertov, a pioneer of the documentary film, created a classic with his 1929 on-camera reporting movie, *Man with a Movie Camera*. But it was Sergei Eisenstein who was the uncontested master film producer in the interwar years. His 1925 silent movie *Battleship Potemkin* was shown in the Soviet Union and abroad, where the violence of its images shocked viewers. Written as a revolutionary propaganda film, it depicts the fate of the battleship sailors' revolt in 1905. In it, Eisenstein combined theatrical techniques such as caricature and contrast with documentary montage, which was a novel technique at the time. His unique metaphorical imagery style and revolutionary themes won him the authorities' approval. From 1928 to 1933, however, his travels to the West, notably to Hollywood and Mexico, ended up in disappointment and earned him Stalin's displeasure. He struggled upon his return to the Soviet Union, had several movie projects cancelled, and was assigned to teach film. He re-emerged as a filmmaking force in 1938, when he directed the film classic *Alexander Nevsky*, for which the well-known composer Sergei Prokofiev wrote the musical score. Set in the thirteenth century, the movie extols the victory of Alexander, Prince of Novgorod, over the Swedes and the Teutonic Knights. Growing tensions between Russia and Germany made the choice of this historical character ideal for Stalin to use as propaganda in preparing every Russian man, woman, and child to face war with optimism. *Alexander Nevsky* ushered in the last phase of Eisenstein's career, a phase that was stylistic, elegant, and simple. Eisenstein crafted the cinematic battle epic genre that is still emulated in movies today. After the premiere of the film, Stalin proclaimed Eisenstein "a good Bolshevik after all" and awarded him the Order of Lenin.[8]

Propaganda and Soviet life

Through its double role as propagandist and principal ideological educator, the Communist Party had a direct influence on Soviet life. A central Institute of Marxism–Leninism in Moscow with branches all over the country was tasked with preparing propaganda publications on historical or current political events. Its instructors gave public lectures and refresher courses, and supervised the press. In addition to this continuous political indoctrination, short campaigns were conducted to promote specific issues. The party secured the regime ideologically and politically. Its goal to move Soviet society towards an advanced stage of socialism was embodied in the 1936 constitution and in Stalin's newly published interpretation of Soviet history, the *Short Course* (1938). Both documents gave a complete picture of the organization of a one-party totalitarian state, and not only served as a blueprint for all ideological indoctrination, but informed the educational system as well.

Art and propaganda in Nazi Germany

Culture became an instrument of social engineering in Germany. State-sponsored activities benefiting body and soul were aimed at creating a healthy citizenry. Leni Riefenstahl's propaganda movie *Triumph of the Will* (1935), which documented the 1934 Nazi party rally in Nuremburg, portrayed Germany as a restored powerful nation with Hitler as its guiding light. She introduced new techniques, such as aerial filming and moving cameras, that contributed to making the production one of the greatest propaganda films ever. She followed this by filming the Berlin Olympic Games in 1936. Entitled *Olympia*, the documentary pioneered sports filming techniques and represented a paean to the new age of showcasing the ideal human body in heroic settings. In art, the crisp Aryan body, male and female, was sculpted and painted nude. It was idealized and idolized alike. Nazi artists, like Soviet social realists, used the power of art to help shape Germans into new citizens. Complementing these trends was the new Germanic cult based on the grandeur of the Teutonic past and the grandiosity of Wagnerian music.

Hitler created the concept of the "average man" – a patriotic, anti-Jewish, politically iconoclastic individual who hated modern art, despised intellectuals, and believed in severe punishment for criminals – and he used the "masses" to isolate and weaken the educated elites. Hitler himself was fond of popular culture. He was an admirer of German writer Karl May who authored trite adventure stories, and he enjoyed Wagnerian operas, sentimental operettas, and military march music. The "modernism" of his popular culture preached a return to the ideals of purity and simplicity of pre-industrial society – while retaining all the perks of modern technology.

Figure 9.2 Leni Riefenstahl (center, wearing a white dress) directs the Nazi propaganda film
Triumph of the Will (1935) that featured the party's 1934 Nuremberg Rally.

Non-propagandistic German art in the 1930s was pleasant to look at and non-
challenging. It borrowed from the nineteenth-century Romantic tradition of landscape painting that exalted nature, idealized an idyllic past, and created a longing for
the simplicity of rural life. Artists openly used art as a symbol of enlightenment and
made it a central tool for character improvement. Themes included the perfect German
family (preferably farmers), the happy German worker, and the heroic soldier.

Underneath these idyllic representations lay a darker side. As soon as he took power,
Hitler ordered a general redistricting of Germany's regions, which severed old friend-
ships and loyalties and made room for the new Nazi order. Book burnings in the
spring of 1933 symbolized the coming of a new culture that promoted anti-Semitism,
Germanic and Nordic virtues, and faith in the state. The media were closely controlled
as well. Editors were to be ideologically and racially "pure." A law made on October 4,
1933, forbade the publication of information that was misleading, offensive, or destructive toward the German state. At the urging of Propaganda Minister Goebbels, most
German newspapers were purged of their Jewish editors after 1933. The news became
uniform and began using the regime's newspeak. Criticism of the regime was punishable
by publication suspension and imprisonment. Public displays of criticism such as boo-
ing and hissing became gestures of treason. Radio and cinema were also placed under the
authority of the propaganda ministry. The mechanisms of government control did much
to create a culture in Nazi Germany based on conformity and fear.

Propaganda and engagement, 1939–1945

World War II subjected culture to a state of abnormality on a grander scale than World War I. Demographic disruptions represented by war casualties, involuntary deportations, and persecutions caused a break between wartime culture and prewar culture. Because of the widespread destruction of cultural institutions, paradigms shifted and priorities changed. No coherent trends emerged during the six years of war, as circumstances differed too widely from country to country to allow any. From the official art and propaganda of Italy, Germany, and the Soviet Union, to the underground art and publications of resisters in occupied countries, culture found itself subjected to adverse conditions. Shortages of supplies, censorship, and punishment of any production or utterance provoking dissent put cultural production in a straitjacket.

The Soviet Union highlighted past and present heroes to promote patriotism during the war. On the occasion of the forty-first anniversary of the Bolshevik revolution in November 1941, Stalin praised heroic figures from Russia's past, such as Alexander Nevsky (thirteenth-century Grand Prince of Vladimir), Dimitri Donskoy (fourteenth-century Grand Prince of Vladimir), Alexander Suvorov (eighteenth-century generalissimo), and Mikhail Kutuzov (early nineteenth-century field marshal). He created new heroes, such as Zoya Kosmodemyanskaya, a partisan who was portrayed as a Soviet Joan of Arc following her hanging by the Nazis in November 1941.

Stalin, eager for domestic unity and cooperation in Russia's struggle for survival, relaxed the party's censorship controls and allowed writers greater freedom to reveal their talents. While some of the writing was pure propaganda intended to boost people's spirits, there were also instances of works that rose to the level of literature. An example of the latter was war correspondent Konstantin Simonov's short novel *Days and Nights* that provided a vivid account of the Battle of Stalingrad. Composer Dmitri Shostakovich began work on his Seventh Symphony in 1939–1940, and when he finished it in December 1941, he dedicated it to the city of Leningrad which was then under German siege. His symphony became a symbol of Soviet resistance. Sergei Prokofiev, struck by the parallels between Napoleon and Hitler's invasions of Russia, began work on the patriotic-themed opera *War and Peace* in 1942, although its first public performance did not occur until 1946.

Nazi wartime propaganda, under the control of Goebbels, initially displayed themes of German invincibility, and the designs for world domination were a part of the daily news. Russian troops were depicted as sub-human creatures and murderers. After the German defeat at Stalingrad in early 1943, however, it became more difficult to talk about how well the war was progressing. Goebbels blamed the German generals' lack of commitment to the cause of Nazism for the failure at Stalingrad. Following the assassination attempt on Hitler in July 1944, Goebbels pressed the German people in a Berlin speech to support "total war." His reasoning behind the speech was that if Germany should lose the war, the German nation should be obliterated in the process. The Nazis also intensified the use of terror and fear as deterrents to opposition. The security forces apprehended dissidents for immediate execution. Terror reigned until the very last days of the war amid surreal news of future German victories against the British–American invaders.

Conclusion

The spread of authoritarian and totalitarian regimes across Europe in the 1930s had a cooling effect on the cultural and scientific transformations of the 1920s. Artistic and intellectual propaganda began in the Soviet Union in 1917 and continued throughout the 1930s. Once fascist and totalitarian regimes took control of cultural production, most of it became official art and propaganda and used mass communication methods to influence art production and reception. It forced artists to conform to the values of the regime they lived under. This use of cultural propaganda aimed at creating new values and, as a consequence, culture became a tool of social engineering experiments conducted in autocratic regimes.

Mass media and culture

New technologies, including mass printing techniques, the invention of movies and radio, and advances in transportation and advertising, also led to the growth of popular or mass culture in many domains, including the media, movies, literature, and fashion. These developments exposed Europeans to a wider variety of cultural influences, especially from the United States, and had a homogenizing effect on public opinion, as more and more people were getting their news from the same sources. The new forms of communication also introduced the question of high versus low culture, a distinction that still remains with us today.

The media

The hunger for news and entertainment continued in the 1920s. Newspaper circulations increased significantly after 1920. By 1930 there were five newspapers in Britain with a circulation of over 1 million. The radio, which had started as a military tool during World War I, became widely popular with the public. By 1929, one in four households in Britain and one in six households in Germany owned one. The British Broadcasting Corporation, which served as a model for broadcasting in other countries, began in 1922 as a private company, and became a public corporation in 1927. While theoretically accountable to parliament, it enjoyed virtually complete independence in its operations, which rapidly spread across the British Isles. There was considerable collective listening to the radio. In the West, it happened in bars and clubs, while in the Soviet Union and East Central European countries, loudspeakers were installed on street corners. The new forms of communication went beyond entertainment, as news reporting spread from newspapers to the radio and newsreels in movie theaters.

Mass entertainment

Culture became a marketable product and sparked new industries that started catering to "markets" of consumers with free leisure time who needed to be entertained. The new mass entertainment events clashed with the more traditional, high culture forms of entertainment. The new spectator arts provided education, but also promoted sensationalism and exoticism. The public's appetite for thrills and adventure grew tremendously. The discovery in 1922 of Egyptian King Tut's tomb by a British archaeologist triggered a craze in Western popular culture for all things tied to ancient Egypt. Thousands watched Charles Lindbergh's solo flight from New York to Paris in 1927. People went to boxing and soccer matches, spent their holidays and weekends in popular spots, and in general were bombarded with media advertisements for new entertainment to fill their leisure time. Culture was consumed and digested faster and faster. New popular songs appeared every few weeks, and athletes multiplied as fast as their new records, which began to be recorded for posterity. Cabaret, a modern musical and dance genre that began in France in the early 1880s, thrived in Germany, especially Berlin, during the latter 1920s. It reflected the relaxed social mores of the Weimar era when compared to the strict regulations of social activities in place under the earlier German Empire. The new taste for exoticism and sensationalism fostered a new kind of literature: comic books flourished and detective stories became very popular.

American influences

New technologies provided a welcome relief from the tragedy of the Great War. Increased leisure time helped open the way to diversions and positive outlooks on life. These factors were important in the creation of a new culture of entertainment and mass consumption. The United States, whose economic power many Europeans feared and admired, had a powerful cultural influence on Europe during the 1920s, owing in part to the presence in Europe of many American imported, mass-produced items, including airplanes, automobiles, movies, radios, and phonographs. Another important American import was jazz that, after its introduction in Paris in 1917 by an all-Black military band, spawned a culture of fox-trot and ragtime. Dance clubs and revues entertained the public with shows that featured casts of all-black performers during what became known as "the crazy years." American jazz singers Josephine Baker and Florence Mills dazzled European crowds in the 1920s with their stage shows. Jazz music inspired Belgian guitarist Django Reinhardt to join French violinist Stéphane Grappelli in forming one of the world's first all-string jazz groups in 1934. The new American culture was lively, modern, and popular, but it provoked strong reactions from detractors who argued that it appealed to the lowest common denominators of taste and mass consciousness.

Filmmaking in the West

Movies created an international language, even though styles were still very much tied to their cultural contexts. German cinema was expressionist, French cinema avant-garde, Soviet cinema patriotic, and Spanish cinema surrealist. German cinema produced important films such as Austrian/German Fritz Lang's *Metropolis* (1927), a critique of the decaying modern industrial city. French filmmaker René Clair advocated freedom from the industrial world in his 1931 movie *Freedom for Us*. Women were represented in the profession, and made innovative contributions; French avant-garde film director Germaine Dulac, for example, directed the first surrealist film called *The Seashell and the Clergyman* (1928). Painting influenced sets, as seen in Spanish film director Luis Bunuel's short French film *An Andalusian Dog* (1929), for which he collaborated with surrealist painter Salvador Dali. Film also bridged Europe and America. Silent movie star Charlie Chaplin was a British actor and film director who made most of his best-known movies in Hollywood. He used pathos and slapstick comedy to show man's alienation in the modern, industrial world.

The movie industry that developed in Hollywood was very popular in Europe. Yet film exports from America were in some ways re-imports into Europe, since at least two of Hollywood's most famous early producers came from East Central Europe. They were Samuel Goldwyn of Goldwyn Pictures and Adolph Zukor of Paramount Pictures. Movies exemplified the alliance between technology, creativity, and business: they were manufactured on the model of an assembly line, with elaborate organizations that included producers, directors, actors, carpenters, painters, photographers, electricians, special effects experts, and, after 1928, sound technicians. With the help of dazzling techniques and large movie screens, films captured the public's imagination. Film was the quintessential modernist art form, offering fluidity and perspective, both spatial and temporal. It captured speed and, more than any other art form, reconciled high and low culture.

"High" versus "low" culture

An intense debate took shape after 1918. Would popular culture elevate the masses or debase taste? High culture was found in museums, symphony halls, serious novels, and sophisticated publications, and it focused on an ensemble of cultural items that a culture looked upon with the highest regard, primarily in the arts. Its appeal was limited mostly to the upper echelons of society. Low culture emphasized mass production and the interests of the consumer. The possibility that it would produce half-educated individuals with non-discriminating, easily manipulated tastes created many fears. Popular culture had long existed in the form of folklore, popular songs, and festivals in traditional peasant societies, and was a part of the urban, mass entertainment of nineteenth-century industrializing societies. Popular culture was not only entertaining, but it taught values and wisdom, and fostered a sense of belonging. It also provided a stepping stone for the appreciation of finer things, and therefore enabled transformation, even social climbing. If at first it was associated with "shop-girl" values, this began to disappear as old and new media developed sophisticated artistic voices of their own. Thus the new technologies gave it almost unlimited opportunities. Also, it occupied the increasing leisure of workers in large urban centers. Entire new industries were born, in which the consumers of culture were divided from its producers. These developments not only affected commercial relationships, but brought profound changes to the lives of artists.

Body, fashion, and gender

In the interwar years, the search for a new culture affected everyday life, including one's body image. The male body tended to be muscular and fit, trim and tanned, healthy and heroic. The new heroes were athletes and soldiers who projected an image of strength and health. The new body image was most pronounced in totalitarian regimes, particularly in the Soviet Union where physical prowess was publicly displayed during anniversary parades, and in Nazi Germany, where the new body image was epitomized in Riefenstahl's propaganda film *Triumph of the Will*. In France, the sculptures of Antoine Bourdelle also announced the new male body, and emphasized its glory in his monumental sculptures.

While the female body image generally remained subordinated to the ideals of femininity and beauty, a new feminine body emerged in the 1920s that was boyish and youthful. This caused French writer Victor Margueritte to introduce a feminine form for the French word "boy" (garçon) with the word "garçonne" (flapper) and to devote a book to the new lifestyles of young women. Not only was the new feminine body active and publicly conspicuous, but it was also slender and fit. To preserve its youthful appearance, women used cosmetics, hair products, clothes, and even fitness training. Fashionable appearance was no longer reserved for the rich; with the advent of mass consumerism, beauty was within the reach of most people's budgets. Domesticity was out, glamour was in, as seen in the appearance of film stars such as Swedish actress Greta Garbo and German-American movie star Marlene Dietrich.

To this modern, active body belonged a modern wardrobe. Men's fashions changed little, except for simplifying and streamlining the cut of their vestments to make them more comfortable and give them a more youthful, slender look. The jazz age, the "Roaring Twenties," and the emphasis on sports all gave a new edge to men's fashions. At work, men wore suits and ties, and they still were not generally seen in public spaces without hats. Women's fashions, however, were dramatically revolutionized when a young

Figure 9.3 French fashion designer Coco Chanel models some of her company's clothing and costume jewelry in 1928.

French seamstress named Coco Chanel crafted an entirely new style in 1914 after luxury fabrics disappeared from stores. Using knit materials and other common fabrics, shortening hem lines, and streamlining the cuts, she produced cheap, practical, yet elegant wear, suited for women whose role was shifting from the hearth to the factory. Her style became the rage first in France, then across Europe, during the 1920s. Its symbol became the little black dress, which was a long-lasting, versatile garment that every woman, regardless of social class, wanted in her wardrobe. Short haircuts complemented the new streamlined clothing that was designed for urban, active, emancipated, and often single young women. In the 1920s, as prosperity returned, luxury fashions once again became available, but Coco Chanel's "garçonne" line remained.

Both male and female body images underwent a transformation not just in their appearance, but in their significance. No longer solely confined to the aesthetic realm, appearance acquired a social and moral value. The powerful male body was meant to compensate for the horrendous losses men had suffered during World War I and to emphasize the spirit of devotion, sacrifice, and courage. It was meant to instill confidence in the rebuilding of Europe and in the future. The new female body was meant to exude a sense of energy, willpower, and control. A slim and fit female body meant social success and the ability to "keep your man." On the other hand, body neglect meant low morals such as laziness and a lack of devotion to the common good. In a sense, acquiring a new body was a social obligation. This bit of mass social engineering was entirely an urban phenomenon, as fashion, beauty aids, and stadiums were mostly available in large cities. Such was the power of this new trend that it became a value standard to gauge social progress. Europe, overall, remained divided between "more modern" cities that throbbed with the latest fashions, and backward rural areas where one could only glance at fashion and fitness magazines and dream. In countries with low standards of living, the body image, fashions, and gender roles changed considerably less. Yet, while many body images competed, it is safe to say that the new body image across Europe became an experiment in social democratization. It contributed to the blurring of social classes by making it more difficult to recognize people's social class by their clothing.

Mass education and well-being

Education underwent significant democratization both in content and form, thus challenging traditional liberal arts curriculums. It broke social class barriers, serving as a gateway to professional and social advancement. If the number of children in primary schools remained relatively steady across Europe in the 1920s, the number of students in secondary schools doubled or increased significantly. Middle and high schools received state-mandated, uniform programs. Beyond that, significant differences emerged between France, Germany, and Britain on the one hand, where school systems were already established and did not undergo much change, and the periphery of Europe on the other. In the newly independent countries, new programs were built. Often, revolution and civil war brought about important school and curricular reforms, as in Russia after 1917 and in Spain after 1931. In most countries, religious schools coexisted with secular schools, which often brought conflict about the secularization of the curriculums and other pedagogical methods. Totalitarianism brought about important changes in curriculums and educational philosophies. In the Soviet Union after 1917 and Nazi Germany after 1933, new ideologies became a part of the curriculums. Russian and German national histories were rewritten to glorify the new regimes and emphasize civics; physical fitness was stressed over intellectual pursuits. For Hitler in particular, building bodies was more important than building minds, educating men more important than educating women, and universal education unnecessary.

Higher education underwent the greatest change. The number of university students tripled between 1920 and 1939 in Scandinavia and Eastern European countries; the increase was half as fast in Western European states, due to the fact that they already had larger numbers of university students to start with. The interwar years confirmed the supremacy of scientific degrees, especially in engineering, over traditional liberal arts studies. Europe experienced a tremendous growth in its educational programs and facilities to keep up with the new industrial age in which technological skills were vital. Several polytechnic institutes were created in the Soviet Union and the newly independent countries of East Central Europe. Soviet universities in 1917 adopted an open admissions policy, abolished examinations, and transformed "bourgeois" lectures into "laboratories" for political discussion groups. In 1922, however, the Bolshevik government restored examinations and streamlined the country's universities.

Another significant development was the creation of adult literacy programs in East Central Europe and the Soviet Union. While average adult illiteracy rates during 1914–1945 were 40 percent, there was a significant difference between Western Europe, where 70 percent of the people were literate, and Eastern Europe, where the illiteracy rates could be as high as 80–90 percent, as in some Balkans countries. The Bolsheviks mounted the largest adult literacy campaigns of the era, creating Rabfaks, or special schools for adult workers with little or no education. Opened in February 1919 and attached to universities, they required proof of social origin and loyalty to the Soviet regime. After Stalin's massive literacy campaign of 1931–1932, they were phased out and the last one closed in 1941. One Rabfak graduate was future Soviet leader Nikita Khrushchev. The results were impressive. By 1941, 85 percent of all Soviet citizens were literate, most of them male workers. Women and peasants lagged far behind.

Youth programs

Grooming young people to be productive citizens was a high-agenda item in the interwar years. After World War I, every European country resumed or created youth programs, from religious education to civic organizations. Scouting in particular was widely adopted by Catholic, Protestant, and Jewish congregations alike. The European organizations were modeled on principles established by scouting's British founder Robert Baden-Powell, whose book, *Scouting for Boys* (1908), sold millions of copies and was the fourth best-selling book of the twentieth century. Scouting focused on outdoor and survival skills; the uniform was meant to hide social standing distinctions. Baden-Powell drew his inspiration from his experiences in the Anglo-Boer War and his knowledge of Native American scouting and woodcraft skills. His philosophy emphasized a return to nature and the observance of a code of honor.

In Germany, Hitler used an organization known as the Hitler Youth as his chief vehicle in training the country's young people in Nazi ideology. His goal was to make loyal citizens out of them, and to stem the formation of opposition movements. Hitler entrusted the Hitler Youth organization to Baldur von Schirach, a fanatical follower of the Führer, in June 1933. Schirach expanded the organization to include almost all German youth from ages 10 to 18. By 1936, the Nazis had banned all other youth groups, and enrollment in the Hitler Youth became obligatory in 1939. The Hitler Youth's experiences focused on outdoor activities, sports, and ideology, and they resulted in a mixing of all social classes. Girls, who at age 14 entered the Hitler Youth's League of German Girls, were trained for future roles as housewives and mothers. At age 18, male members of the Hitler Youth were required to join the Reich Labor Service (*Reichsarbeitsdienst*) for six months of work in public works projects.

In the Soviet Union, young people participated in socio-political organizations until age 28. Children up to age 10 were grouped into an organization called the Little Octobrists that, in addition to teaching them nursery rhymes and games, incorporated a political agenda into their programs. The Leninist Young Pioneers for children 10 to 14 was created in 1922–1924. It emphasized good citizenship, proper personal and public manners, and reverence for Soviet leaders; it provided some military drills as well. Graduating from this training, the youth went into the Communist Youth League – the Komsomol after 1926 – for young people aged 14 to 28. It had a national, hierarchical organization modeled on that of the Communist Party. Once Stalin was firmly in power in the late 1920s, Komsomol membership grew dramatically, molding the lives of millions of young people in the 1930s. In 1941, more than 10 million youth were enrolled in it. The Komsomol developed cadres for the Communist Party; failure to join resulted in social ostracism and less attractive jobs.

Leisure, sports, and recreation

While the upper classes had long enjoyed leisure activities, members of the working class entered that world in many countries during the interwar years. Especially in the 1930s, governments began to take a new look at leisure time, conceiving it as a multifaceted benefit designed to provide emotional satisfaction, educational value, and improved physical health. Several countries, such as Belgium, France, and Germany, created government bureaus for leisure and recreation to deal with this growing field.

Governments and municipalities highlighted the advantages of leisure pursuits to workers as an antidote to their crowded urban living quarters. Shorter work weeks and paid vacations also gave workers the chance to engage in more physical activities. Fitness, youth, and beauty were the symbols of bodily modernity just as innovative architecture, artistic experimentation, and technology were the symbols of social and cultural modernity. Physical conditioning was an integral part of civic education programs in schools and youth organizations. Women's opportunities for athletic training and competition, however, were practically nonexistent, as almost all the attention was focused on men's sports, where professional athletes enjoyed newfound fame. The interest in sports also resulted in the construction of large stadiums. For example, the Great Strahov Stadium in Prague, which opened in 1926, seated some 220,000 people and was home to large-scale synchronized gymnastics displays.

Another hallmark of the new age was the emphasis on the Olympic Games which resumed in 1920 after a wartime disruption. Germany, invited to the postwar Summer Games for the first time in 1928, won 31 gold medals that year, and hosted the 1936 Summer Olympic Games in Berlin. For the 1936 event, Germany built a sports complex that consisted of four stadiums, the largest of which could hold 110,000 spectators. Controversy surrounded the run-up to the Games, since Hitler, in pursuit of his Aryans-only policy, intended to exclude Jews from the German team. Threats of a boycott forced him to back down, and in a token gesture, he added a part-Jewish female athlete to Germany's squad. Hitler also agreed, albeit reluctantly, to allow foreign Jews to compete. The breathtaking displays of pageantry that accompanied the Games awed foreign visitors, and Germany captured 89 medals, the most of any country.

Postwar travel and tourism increased considerably. Rail travel peaked out in the 1930s, and the bus industry enjoyed a remarkable expansion, as mass transportation changed people's travel habits. Annual vacations, though generally limited to one week per year, promoted mass tourism. Leaders in the British labor movement founded the Workers' Travel Association in 1921 to arrange vacations for workers. A British Youth Hostels Association was founded in 1929 to assist the travel of young people who had limited financial means, and by 1939 its membership had reached 80,000. Camping associations were founded, and working class families started going to the seaside, the mountains, and other trendy vacation spots. The presence of 10 million bicycles in Britain by the end of the 1930s provided urban dwellers with a new means to gain access to the countryside. International travel in Europe during the 1920s crested in 1928 and 1929, and after a slowdown due to the Great Depression, it reached new records in the late 1930s.

Focused on social engineering, the Nazis put together comprehensive, large-scale programs aimed at creating the "new" German. They took advantage of the opportunities that leisure time afforded by regulating it through a state-run Strength through Joy (*Kraft durch Freude*) leisure organization affiliated with the German Labor Front, the country's official labor union. Strength through Joy became the largest travel agency in the world during the 1930s. Workers were obliged to pay into the organization, but the benefits were substantial: workers who had never been on vacation before could now afford to stay at resorts where they skied, swam, and relaxed. Factory workers were even offered Adriatic cruises that allowed them to observe the sea for the first time in their lives. A spectacular project associated with the Strength through Joy organization was the seaside resort of Prora on the Baltic island of Rugen. Construction began in 1936 but was still unfinished by the outbreak of war in 1939, when the project was put on hold. The waterfront complex, 2.8 miles long and six stories high, was intended to accommodate 20,000 vacationers in 10,000 compact rooms. In fact, Hitler had planned to make the resort "the grandest and most impressive ever."[9]

Conclusion

The 1920s and 1930s saw education used to better societies and further the cause of modernization, especially in the scientific and engineering fields, adult literacy, and youth civics. Great strides were made in educating the general population as well as expanding the opportunities for people to participate in recreational activities, but education often served a general social engineering purpose. As high and low culture began to merge, a new consumer culture appeared. "Lowbrow" influences began to win accolades in "highbrow" spheres as they created new forms of art and new artistic competencies. The coming of large-scale, popular culture by the end of the 1920s was helped in no small way by consumerism, American culture, and modern conveniences. Mass taste democratized the cultural field into the 1930s just as efficiently, one could argue, as the Bolsheviks and Mussolini. Sports, leisure, and vacations were also transformed by technology and politics, helping promote civic-mindedness, good health, and happiness.

Overall conclusion

The First World War's destruction and displacement of artists and their works, unparalleled in human history, affected all of Europe. The relativity revolution threw established scientific, philosophical, and ethical values into disarray. A new version of the battle between traditionalism and modernism caused artists to experiment with an unprecedented range of techniques, philosophies, and technologies, and then to see their art challenged by political demands for artistic conformity and cultural engineering. With the advent of mass society, the modes of artistic and intellectual production and distribution changed considerably, and influenced the rise of "low" culture alongside "high," elite culture. If mental habits changed radically during the first half of the twentieth century, appearances changed just as dramatically in several areas, including fashion and urban design. These in turn brought about a change in ways of life, entertainment, and leisure. These developments were more pronounced in urban areas than in rural areas. In general, the effervescence of the 1920s gave way to a more restrained pace in the 1930s, as the Great Depression and the rise of authoritarianism tilted creativity towards cultural engineering.

After Auschwitz, European culture was at point zero, polarized, broken, and having experienced such a traumatic moment that words and images seemed inadequate, even scandalous, to describe reality. European cultural institutions needed to be built anew. From the ashes of the war, there sprang new hope. Yet the past was not completely cast aside. Postwar culture would in large part see the fulfillment of interwar hopes for new beginnings.

Notes

1 Calvin Tomkins, *The World of Marcel Duchamp* (New York: Time Incorporated, 1966), 61–62.
2 Paul Valéry, *La Crise de l'esprit,1919* (Paris: Robert Laffont, 2000), 4, 9, http://classiques.uqac.ca/classiques/Valery_paul/crise_de_lesprit/valery_esprit.pdf (accessed November 16, 2016).
3 Gerhard Besier, *The Holy See and Hitler's Germany*. Trans. W. R. Ward (London: Palgrave Macmillan, 2007), 191.
4 OpenCulture.com, "H. G. Wells, Arthur Conan Doyle and Other British Authors Sign Manifesto Backing England's Role in WWI," printed in *New York Times*, October 18, 1914, p. 5, www.openculture.com/2014/10/british-authors-sign-manifesto-backing-englands-role-in-wwi.html (accessed April 28, 2016).
5 Imperial War Museum, World War I Poster: "Don't Waste Bread," www.iwm.org.uk/collections/item/object/31468 (accessed May 1, 2016).
6 World War 1 Propaganda Posters, "French World War I Propaganda Posters," www.ww1propaganda.com/world-war-1-posters/french-ww1-propaganda-posters (accessed May 1, 2016).
7 Richard Taylor, "Red Stars, Positive Heroes and Personality Cults," in *Stalinism and Soviet Cinema*, edited by Derek Spring and Richard Taylor (London: Routledge, 1993), 73.
8 John Aberth, *A Knight at the Movies: Medieval History on Film* (London: Routledge, 2003), 118.
9 Peter Monteath, "Swastikas by the Seaside," *History Today* 50, no. 5 (May 2000): 32.

Suggestions for further reading

Cook, Nicholas and Anthony Pople, eds. *The Cambridge History of Twentieth-Century Music*. Cambridge: Cambridge University Press. 2004.

Eksteins, Modris. *Rites of Spring: The Great War and the Birth of the Modern Age.* Boston, MA: Houghton Mifflin. 1989.

Englund, Magnus and Chrystina Schmidt. *Scandinavian Modern.* London: Ryland Peters & Small. 2014.

Fussell, Paul. *The Great War and Modern Memory.* New edn. New York: Oxford University Press. 2013.

Galenson, David W. *Conceptual Revolutions in Twentieth-Century Art.* New York: Cambridge University Press. 2009.

Gay, Peter. *Weimar Culture: The Outsider as Insider.* New York: Harper and Row. 1970.

O'Shaughnessy, Nicholas. *Selling Hitler: Propaganda and The Nazi Brand.* London: Hurst & Company. 2016.

Vaughan, Hal. *Sleeping with the Enemy: Coco Chanel's Secret War.* New York: Vintage Books. 2012.

Watson, Peter. *The Modern Mind: An Intellectual History of the 20th Century.* New York: Harper. 2001.

Williams, Trevor I. *A Short History of Twentieth-Century Technology.* London: Oxford University Press. 1982.

10 Whither Europe?

The legacy of the era of 1914–1945 was the effort to focus on a common core of cultural and humanistic values, with the goal of creating a new, united Europe after World War II. The dream of an integrated, free Europe, which had been shelved during most of the 1930s, revived after the outbreak of World War II, as Hitler's vision for a future Europe – a Fortress Europe dominated by Germany – became a tangible threat to democratic values. In the climate of crisis that the war created, intellectual debates gave way to political action. Building on more than 20 years of theory and discussion of European projects, groups of resisters, clergymen, workers, academics, and politicians gave their support to and actively campaigned for European federation projects during the entire six years of the conflict. What makes their proposals unique is the strong link between theory and political action.

Britain emerged as the center of renewed pro-Europeanist activities. Several British associations favored schemes that had ties to pacifism and included the League of Nations as a major player. The Federal Union in particular, founded in 1938, advocated a Franco-British Union. Its abundant literature on subjects such as federal institutions, trade liberalization, people's migration, exchange rates, and the role of European colonies contributed to popularize the European idea. The Federal Union linked forces with other federalist groups and in 1941 became a rallying point for continental European militants-in-exile. It was an intellectual powerhouse that enjoyed the support of British politicians Sir William Beveridge and Harold Wilson, Austrian economist Friedrich von Hayek, and Spanish exiled diplomat Salvador de Madariaga, all of whom would play key roles in postwar Europe. Most importantly, it began to argue for the inclusion of Germany with Britain and France as the nucleus of a new Europe to cure "inflamed nationalism." These British projects remained focused on Western Europe until later in the war, when they considered the inclusion of the Soviet Union and the United States. At the same time that Britain served as a wartime center for exiled pro-European movements, Count Richard Coudenhove-Kalergi, the interwar advocate of an integrated continental Europe centered in the former Austro-Hungarian lands, continued to push his ideas for a united Europe in both the United States and Europe.

The efforts of these associations were reflected in Allied diplomatic negotiations during the war. The first evidence of this was the Franco-British Union project, championed by King George VI and Churchill, which the British Parliament actively pursued until the fall of France in June 1940. For all its merit, the initial Franco-British union project lent itself to the division of Europe into a western industrialized region and a divided eastern agricultural area. To remedy this, George VI in 1940 issued the London Resolution calling for a united agrarian bloc comprised of Poland, Hungary, Romania, Yugoslavia, Bulgaria, and Czechoslovakia. This proposal rallied the approval of exiled

Hungarian leader Milan Hodža, who in 1942 specified several sweeping reforms such as land redistribution, a balanced agriculture, and the development of agro-alimentary industries.

Charles de Gaulle also favored the Franco-British project upon his arrival in London in June 1940, as did Frenchman Jean Monnet, who also continued to push his World War I model of integration based on Anglo-French cooperation. After the Franco-British project failed, de Gaulle in the summer of 1943, rallying the French Committee of National Liberation (CFLN) and the French National Resistance Council, unveiled his vision of a modernized France in a pacified Europe. Based on the condemnation of nationalism but staunchly supportive of national sovereignty, his project foresaw an economically integrated nucleus composed of France, the Benelux countries, Switzerland, and Italy. De Gaulle planned some form of association with the Soviet Union in the future and, following the liberation of France in the summer of 1944, he agreed eventually to include Germany in his group of cooperating states. His vision was based on the definition of a new European unit from Britain to the Urals. Monnet endorsed the CFLN's position that there would be no peace in Europe without a federation, which for him meant a single economic entity.

Another wartime project came from Władysław Sikorski, the prime minister of Poland's government-in-exile in London. His scheme consisted of a bloc of Slavic states from the Baltic to the Black Sea and across to the Adriatic Sea. Sikorski conceived a federation between Poland and Czechoslovakia as the starting point for his plan, which the Polish and Czechoslovak governments-in-exile confirmed in a joint declaration in November 1940. The Polish–Czechoslovak federation project followed Aristide Briand's lead from 1929: it used both the functionalist and the federalist approaches to integration by advocating an economic sector by sector approach to integration and by including a number of supra-national institutions regulated by checks and balances with national governments. Although constitutional acts drafted by both governments in 1941 and 1942 appeared successful and even inspired Greeks and Yugoslavs to work toward a Balkan Union, the Sikorski–Beneš agreement, as it came to be known, was doomed. Stalin was suspicious of any form of union of East Central European nations that did not include the Soviet Union. Under pressure from Stalin, Edvard Beneš reversed himself and prepared a Czech–Soviet alliance, and the British, fearful that Stalin might agree to a separate peace with Hitler, signed a military agreement with the Soviets in May 1942. From that point on, Stalin opposed any federal entity that interfered with his goal of securing the Curzon line as the eastern border of Poland and acquiring a Soviet zone of influence in Eastern Europe. Sikorski's plan was never realized.

Churchill, meanwhile, came up with alternative plans to his original Western European scheme. In March 1943, he spoke of a United States of Europe in general terms, and two months later, he talked at a luncheon meeting with Roosevelt and a group of American leaders about the creation of a World Council composed of Soviet, American, and British representatives, with separate regional units for Europe, the Far East, and South America. But his luncheon remarks were unofficial and vague, and Churchill put his pro-European designs on hold thereafter.

There were new efforts to create an integrated Europe as the war reached its latter stages. One proposal came from Europe's resistance movements. On May 20, 1944, leaders from several national resistance movements secretly met at an International Conference of Resistance Fighters in Geneva to adopt a "Manifesto of the European Resistance."

The document called for a federal European Union that contained political, judicial, and military organizations to maintain peace, freedom, and the national independence of its members. There would be no national armies, and the supranational government would be accountable to the people of Europe, not to its member states. The manifesto even held open the door for German membership, and it endorsed the application of universal values such as democracy and human rights. Finally, the declaration insisted that the peace that followed the war "must be based on justice and progress and not upon vengeance and reaction."[1] Resistance leaders championed their federalist program in the ensuing months, but Allied leaders had other plans for postwar Europe, so in the end, the resistance movements' proposal went nowhere. The League of Nations also formed a Committee of Study of the European Union in the last months of the war. This proposal espoused the spirit of the 1929 Briand proposal, and like the resisters' Geneva manifesto, it accepted the inclusion of Germany in the new Europe and a curb on national sovereignty. But it too remained a dead letter.

There were also political leaders who, often coming from national borderlands and representing quite diverse backgrounds, were ready to move Europe toward some kind of union: they included France's Robert Schuman, Germany's Konrad Adenauer, Italy's Alcide de Gasperi, and Belgium's Paul-Henri Spaak. These proponents for an integrated Europe were pragmatists committed to a new humanism and determined to avoid extreme political ideologies. They proposed a fundamental rethinking of society, with a new balance between socialism and individualism. They advocated reconciliation, the preservation of diversity, the sharing of cultural ties, and political and economic interdependence. They also wanted the integration of Europe to include a system of collective security that would allow flexibility in designing a system of defense based on diplomacy and military alliances. How the integration of Europe would unfold became theirs to determine in the postwar years.

The crucible of World War II provoked an unprecedented level of civilizational and political soul-searching out of which emerged a common set of values and a firm resolve to alter the nation-state. The European projects of World War II built on the legacy of European ideas going back to the years of World War I. While the wartime proposals were not new, they fulfilled two purposes. First, they kept the discussion about Europeanism alive. Second, the men and women who conceived European federal plans actively pursued them, thereby allying theory and practice. Mixing idealism and pragmatism, their proposals had depth, attracted broad support for an integrative system fortified by moral considerations, and charted a clear path toward unity in the postwar era. Too long ignored by historians, movements to unite Europe between 1914 and 1945 can be considered a "dress rehearsal" that deepened visions, sorted out structural and organizational issues, and built a legal framework. They helped limit the territorial and cultural fragmentation that resulted from two world wars. This maturation process was crucial to the success of the post-1945 policies regarding the unification of Europe. Indeed, postwar Europe probably would not have been as successful without these wartime activities, even if strategic Allied political considerations superseded them. Europeanism emerged as a dominant ideology from the ashes of the war, with the potential of healing the fissures of the first half of the century. It did not diminish the ideological polarization of Europe, but it did provide a new perspective on ideologies, and championed a new humanism in which freedom and democracy were predicated on high moral ground.

Note

1 CVCE.EU by UNI.lu, "Draft declaration of the European resistance movements (20 May 1944)," www.cvce.eu/en/obj/draft_declaration_of_the_european-resistance_movements_20_may_1944-en-d68ca0ad-c24b-4906-8235-96b82814133a.html (accessed June 6, 2016).

Suggestions for further reading

Fransen, Frederic. *The Supranational Politics of Jean Monnet: Ideas and Origins of the European Community.* Westport, CT: Praeger. 2001.
Urwin, Derek W. *The Community of Europe: A History of European Integration Since 1945.* 3rd edn. Harlow, UK: Longman. 2009.

Index

Note: References to figures are in *italics*, while references to maps are in **bold**.